# DEATH NOTE

## Black Edition
## IV

Story by Tsugumi Ohba     Art by Takeshi Obata

# Original Graphic Novel Edition
## Volume 7

# Original Graphic Novel Edition
## Volume 8

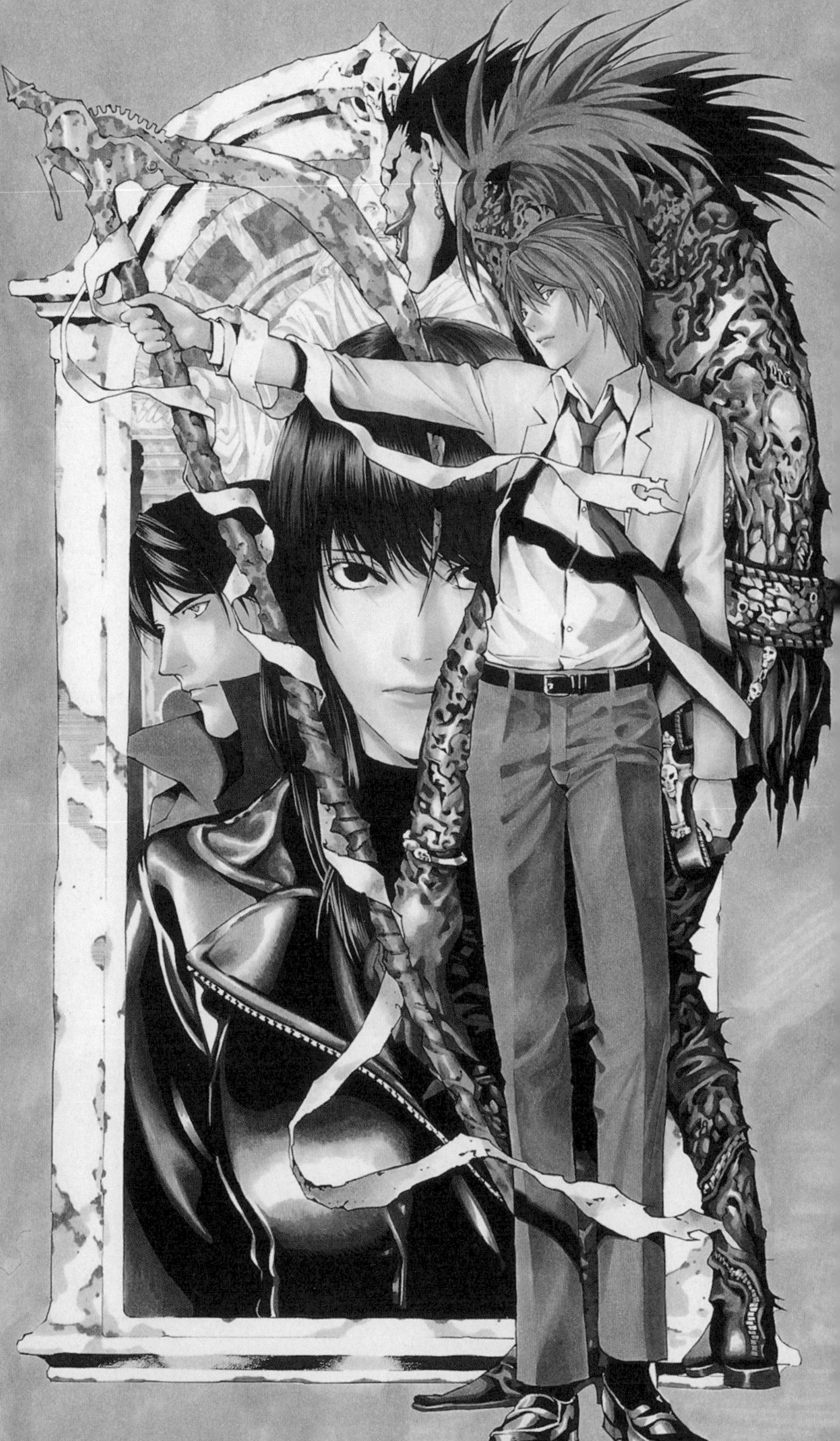

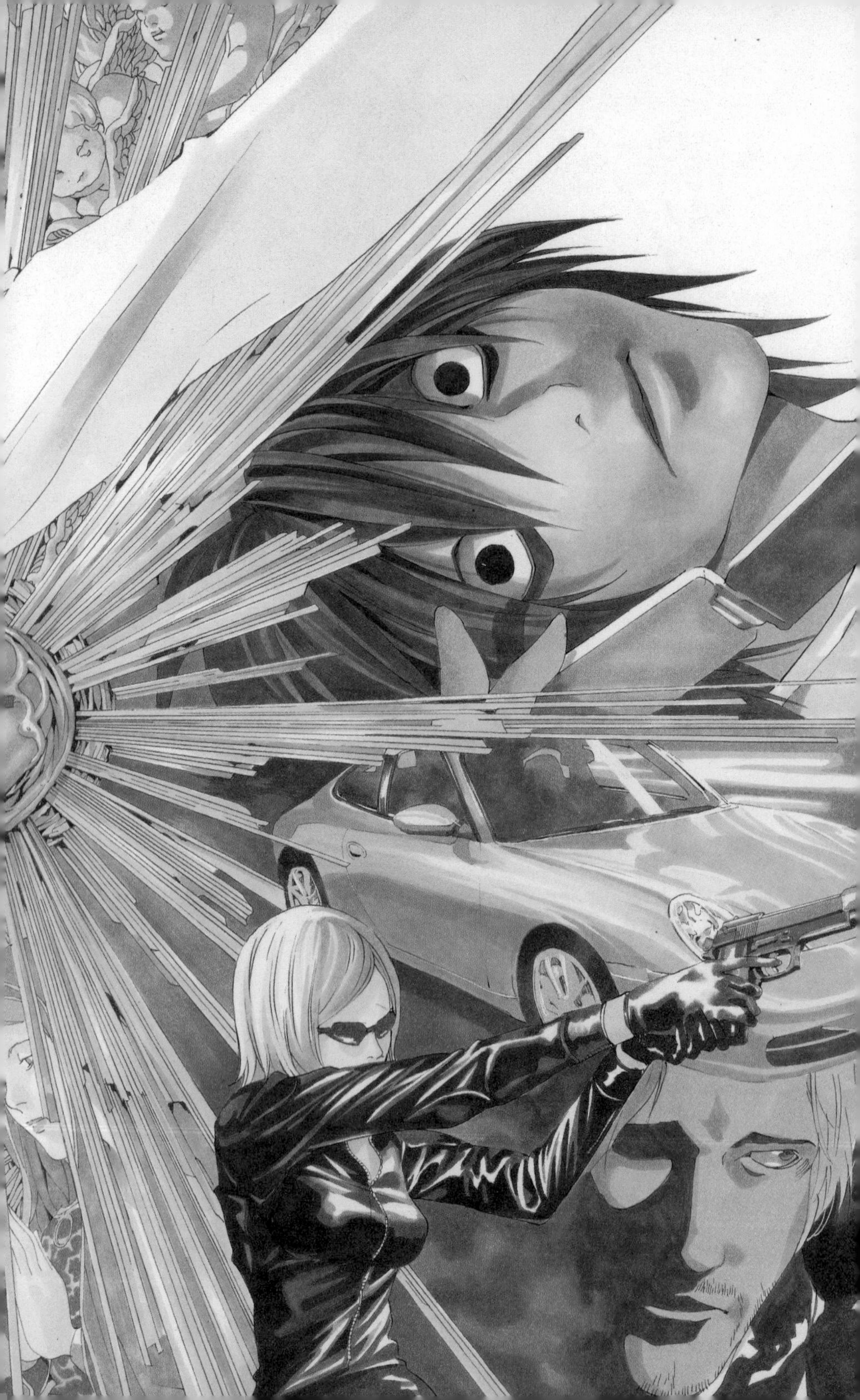

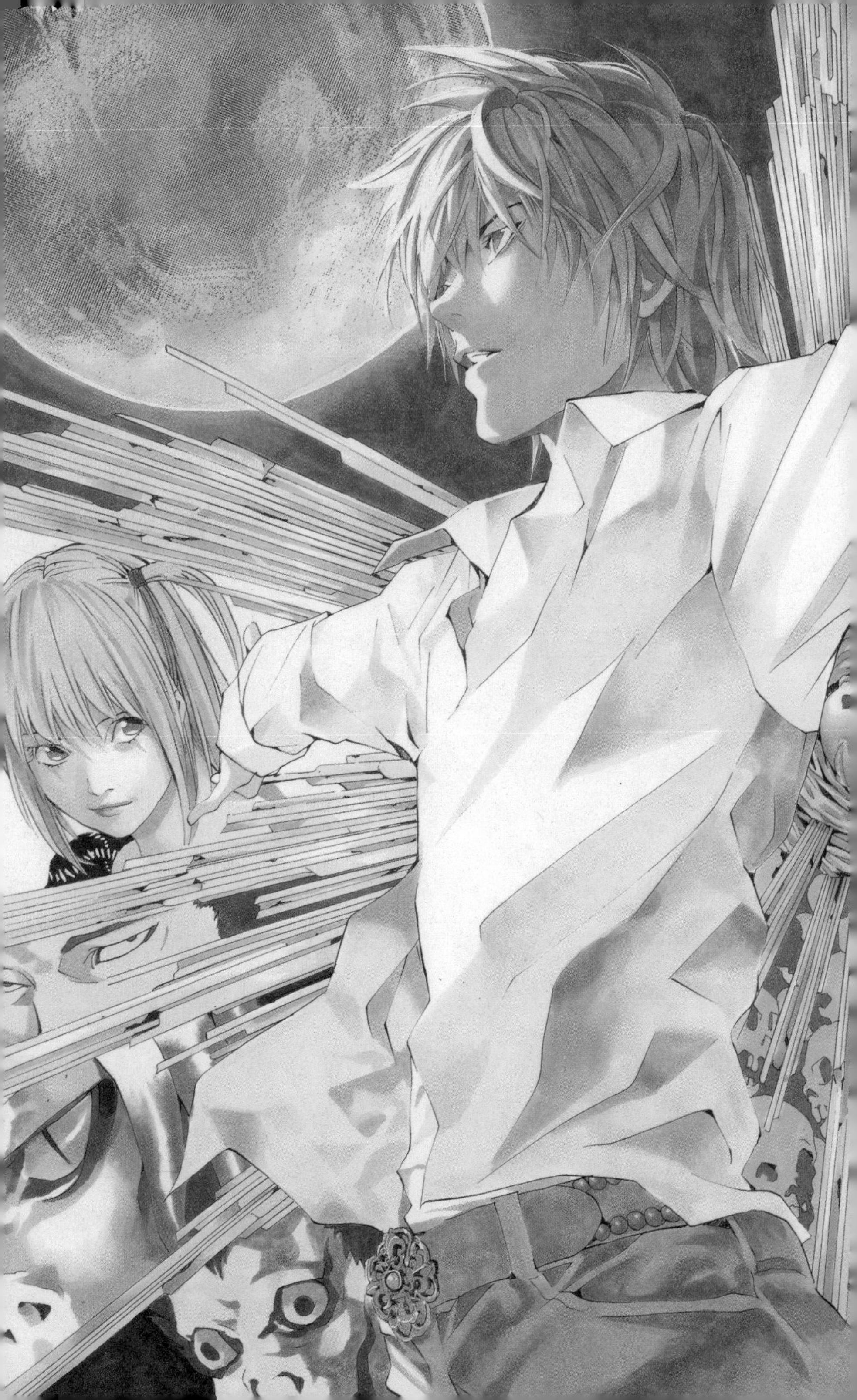

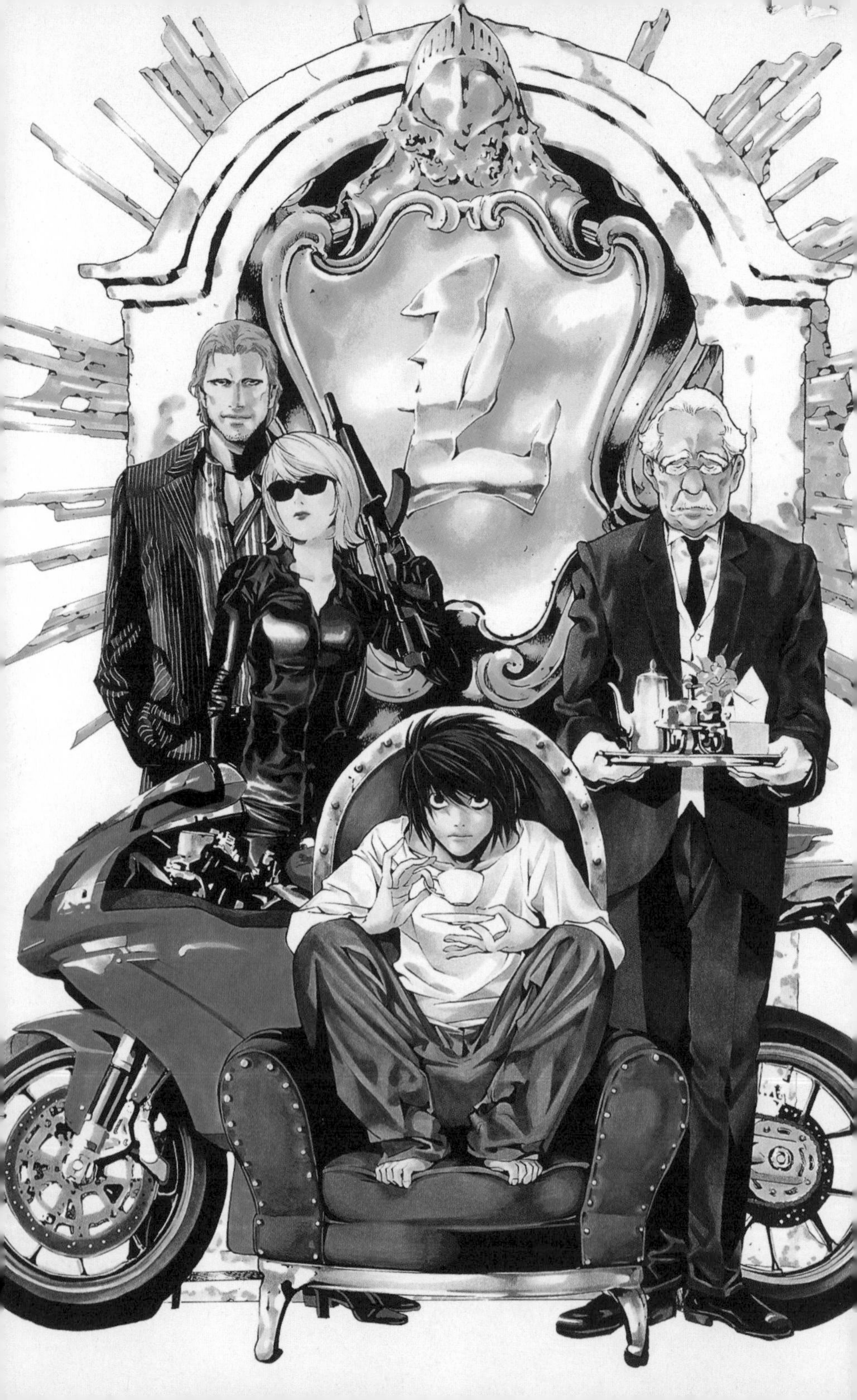

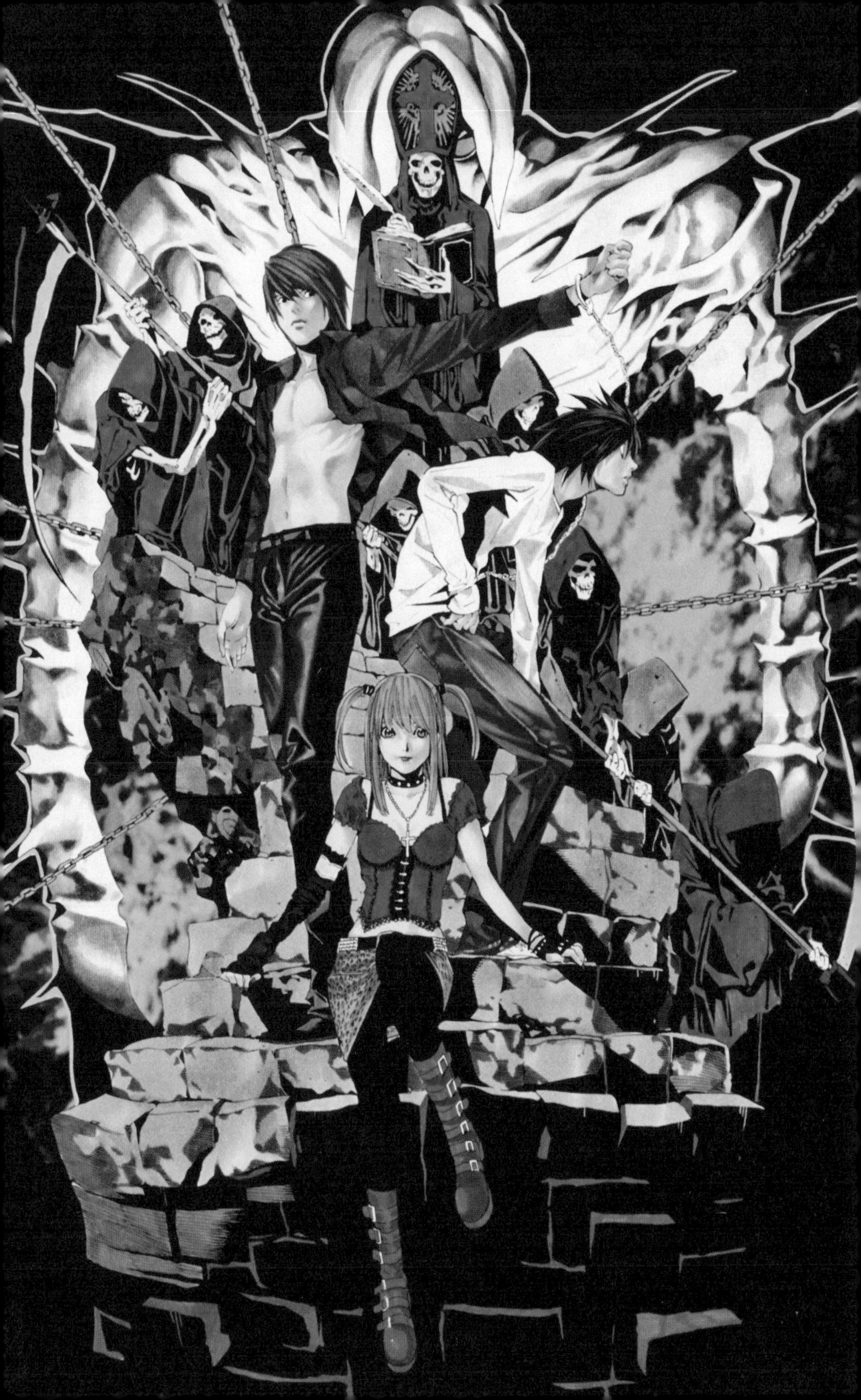

# chapter 53 Scream

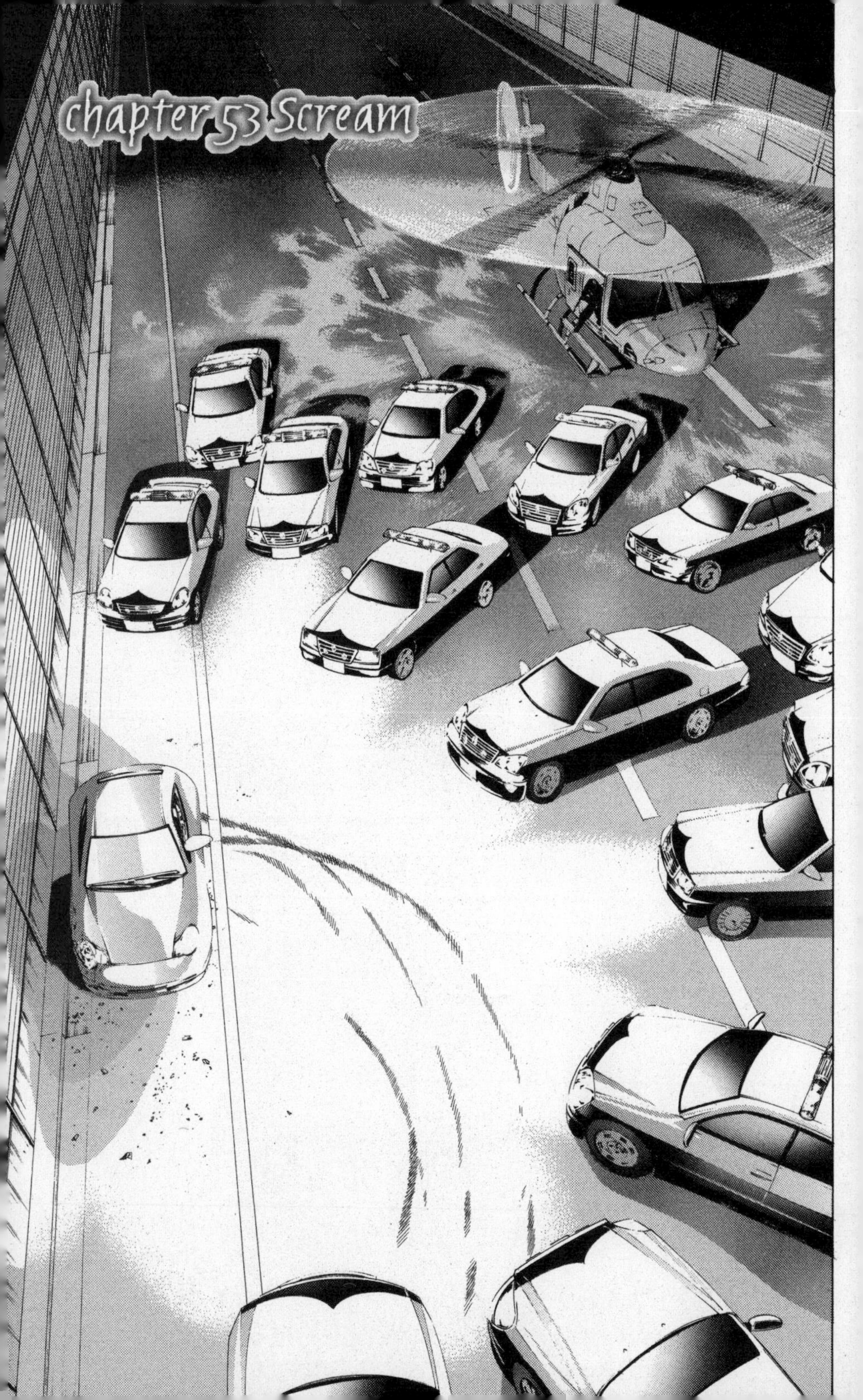

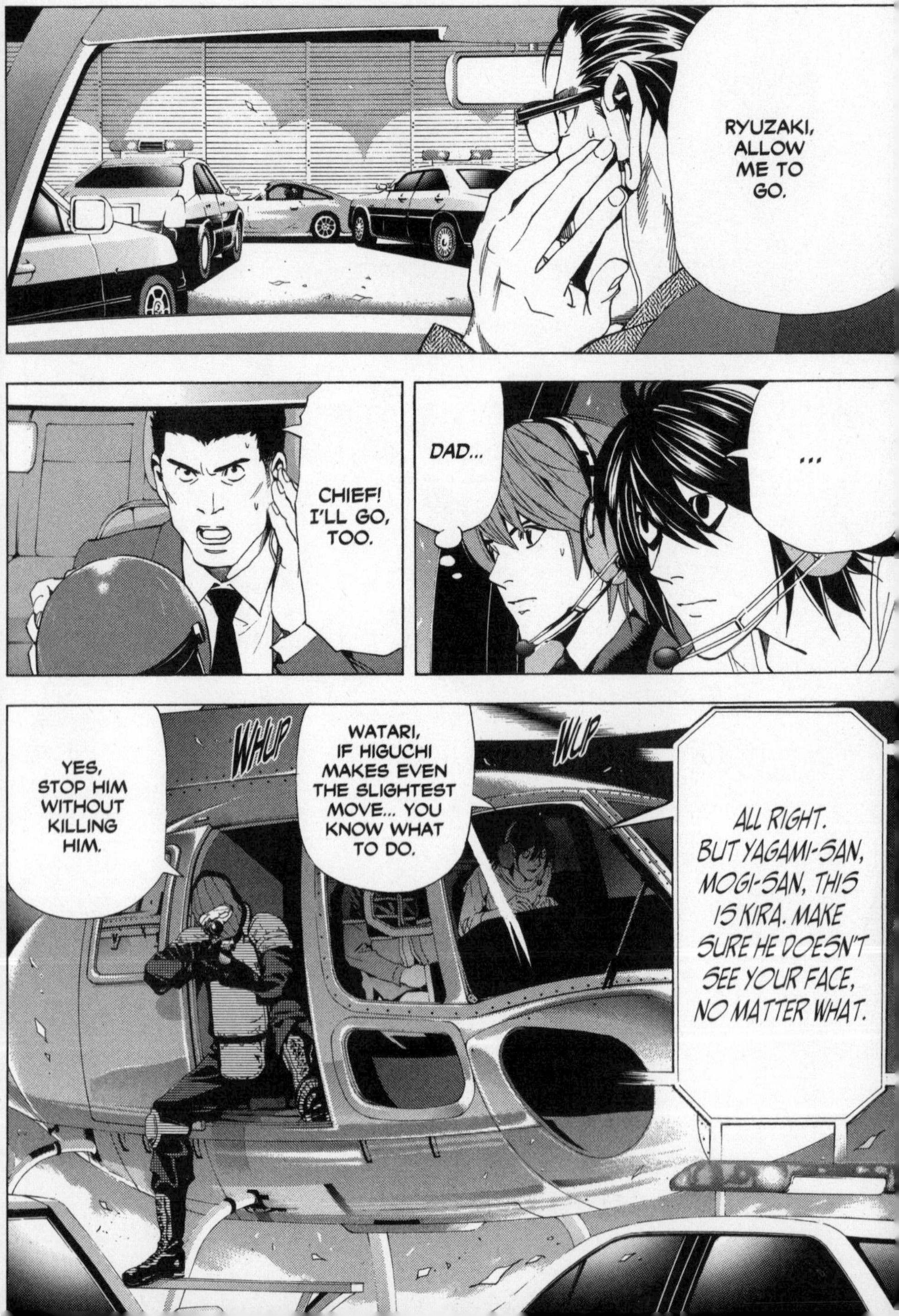
RYUZAKI, ALLOW ME TO GO.
...
DAD...
CHIEF! I'LL GO, TOO.
ALL RIGHT. BUT YAGAMI-SAN, MOGI-SAN, THIS IS KIRA. MAKE SURE HE DOESN'T SEE YOUR FACE, NO MATTER WHAT.
WUP
WATARI, IF HIGUCHI MAKES EVEN THE SLIGHTEST MOVE... YOU KNOW WHAT TO DO.
WHUP
YES, STOP HIM WITHOUT KILLING HIM.

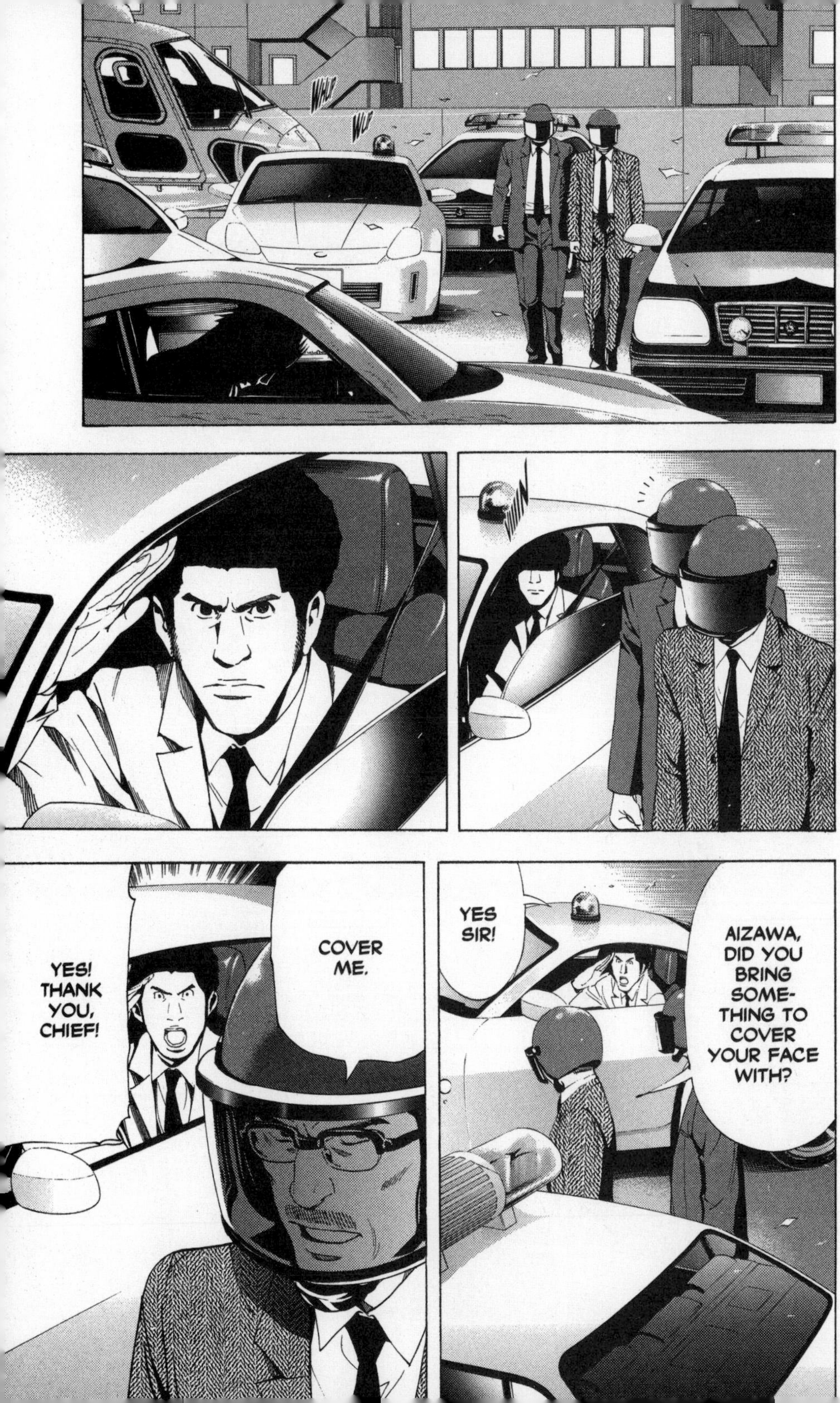
AIZAWA, DID YOU BRING SOME-THING TO COVER YOUR FACE WITH?
YES SIR!
COVER ME.
YES! THANK YOU, CHIEF!

...

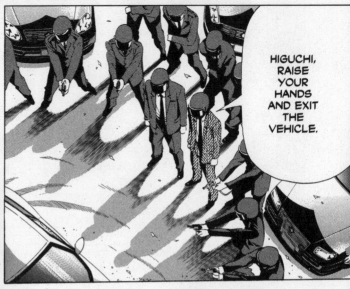

HIGUCHI, RAISE YOUR HANDS AND EXIT THE VEHICLE.

CLACK

clink

KEEP YOUR BACK TO US.

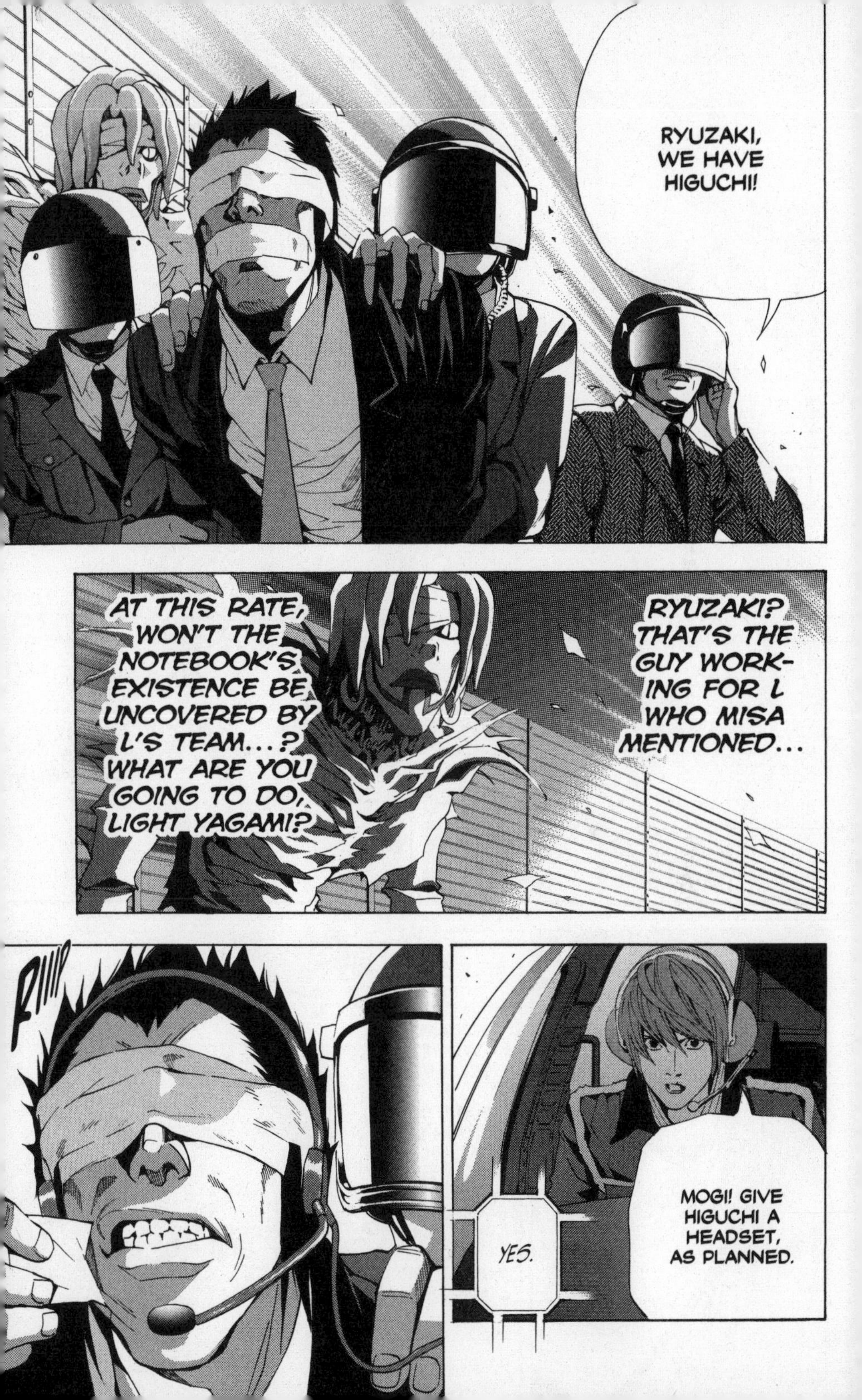
RYUZAKI, WE HAVE HIGUCHI!
RYUZAKI? THAT'S THE GUY WORK-ING FOR L WHO MISA MENTIONED...
AT THIS RATE, WON'T THE NOTEBOOK'S EXISTENCE BE UNCOVERED BY L'S TEAM...? WHAT ARE YOU GOING TO DO, LIGHT YAGAMI?
MOGI! GIVE HIGUCHI A HEADSET, AS PLANNED.
YES.
PIIIP

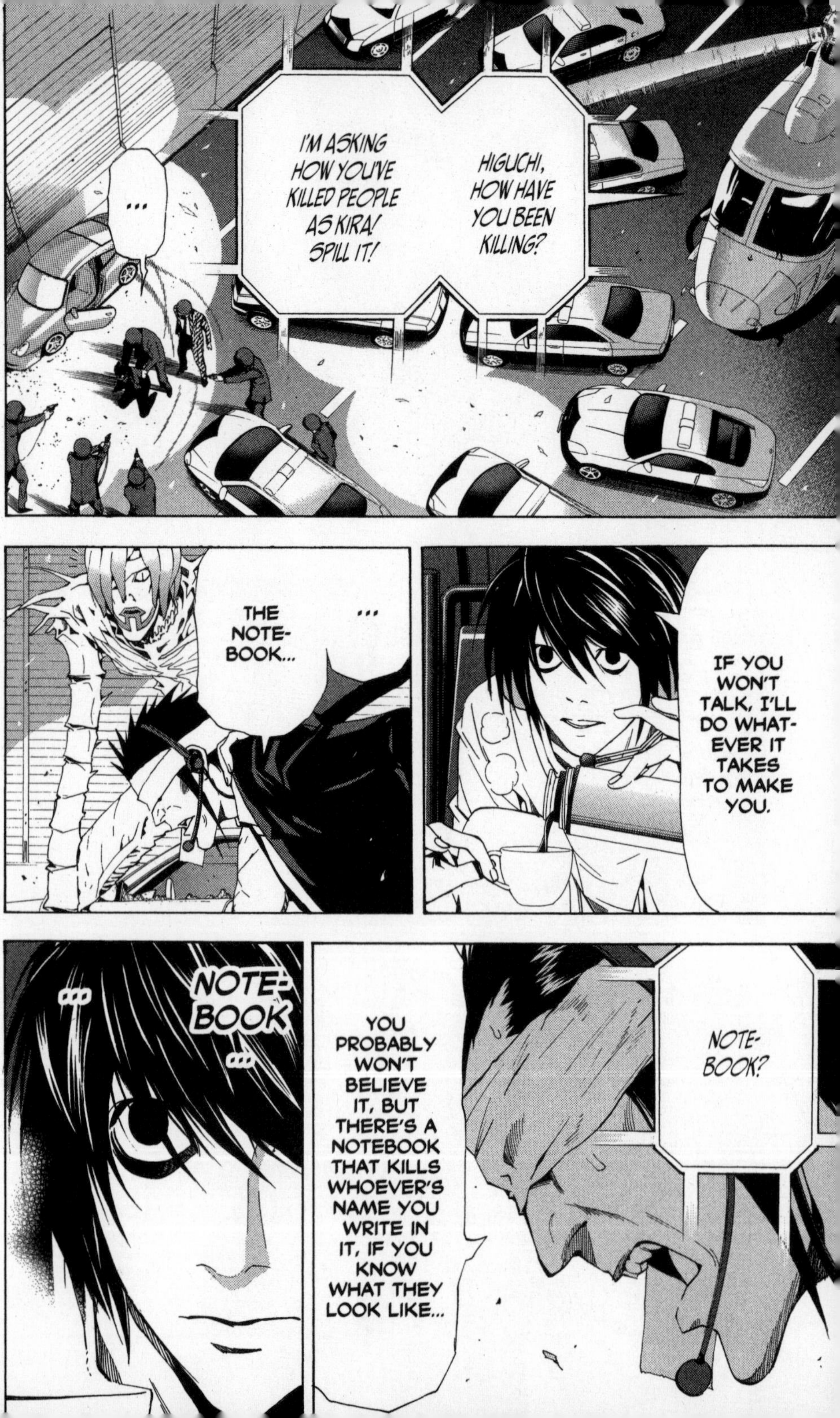
HIGUCHI, HOW HAVE YOU BEEN KILLING?
I'M ASKING HOW YOU'VE KILLED PEOPLE AS KIRA! SPILL IT!
...
IF YOU WON'T TALK, I'LL DO WHATEVER IT TAKES TO MAKE YOU.
...
THE NOTEBOOK...
NOTEBOOK?
YOU PROBABLY WON'T BELIEVE IT, BUT THERE'S A NOTEBOOK THAT KILLS WHOEVER'S NAME YOU WRITE IN IT, IF YOU KNOW WHAT THEY LOOK LIKE...
...
NOTEBOOK
...

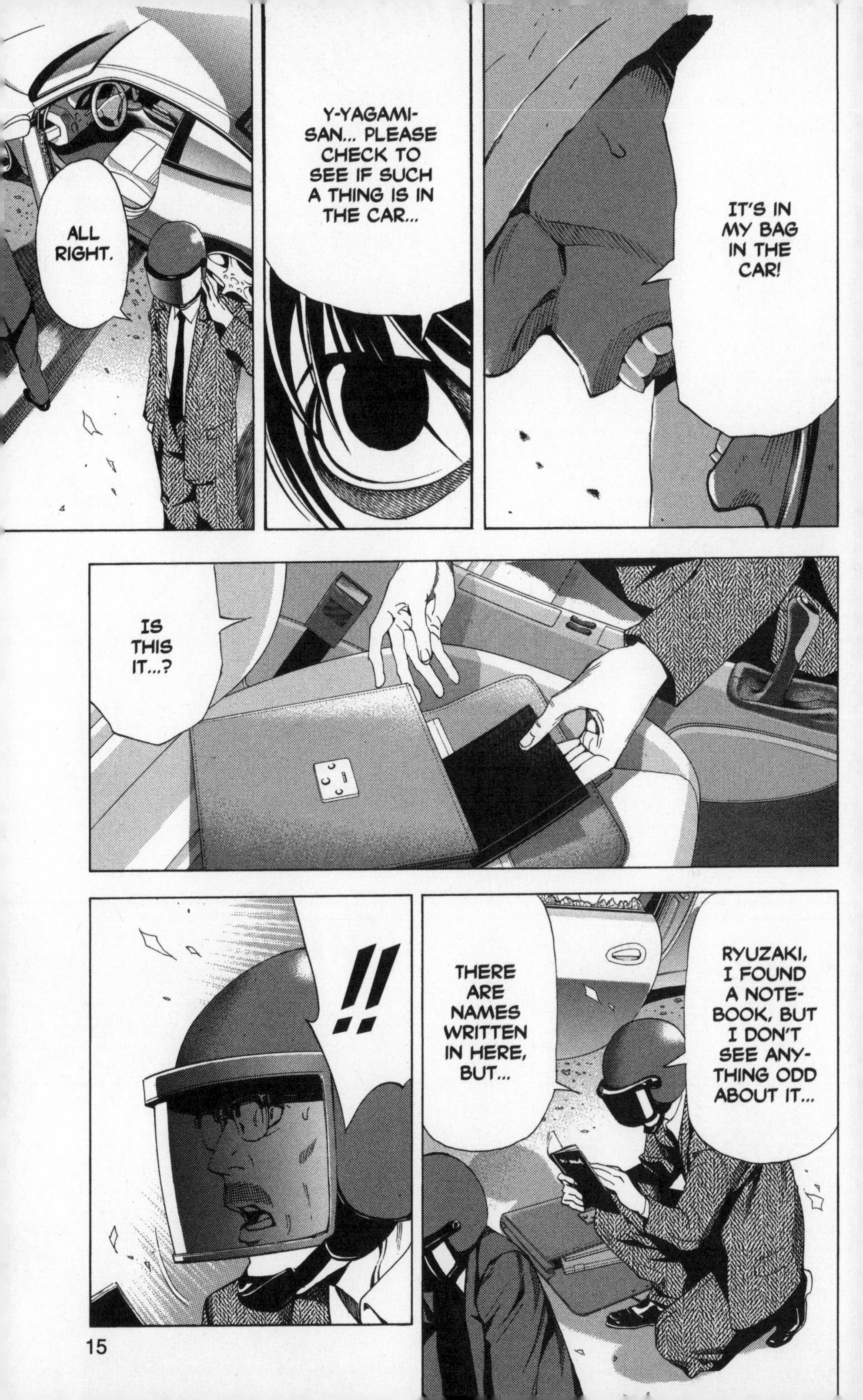
IT'S IN MY BAG IN THE CAR!
Y-YAGAMI-SAN... PLEASE CHECK TO SEE IF SUCH A THING IS IN THE CAR...
ALL RIGHT.
IS THIS IT...?
RYUZAKI, I FOUND A NOTE-BOOK, BUT I DON'T SEE ANY-THING ODD ABOUT IT...
THERE ARE NAMES WRITTEN IN HERE, BUT...
!!

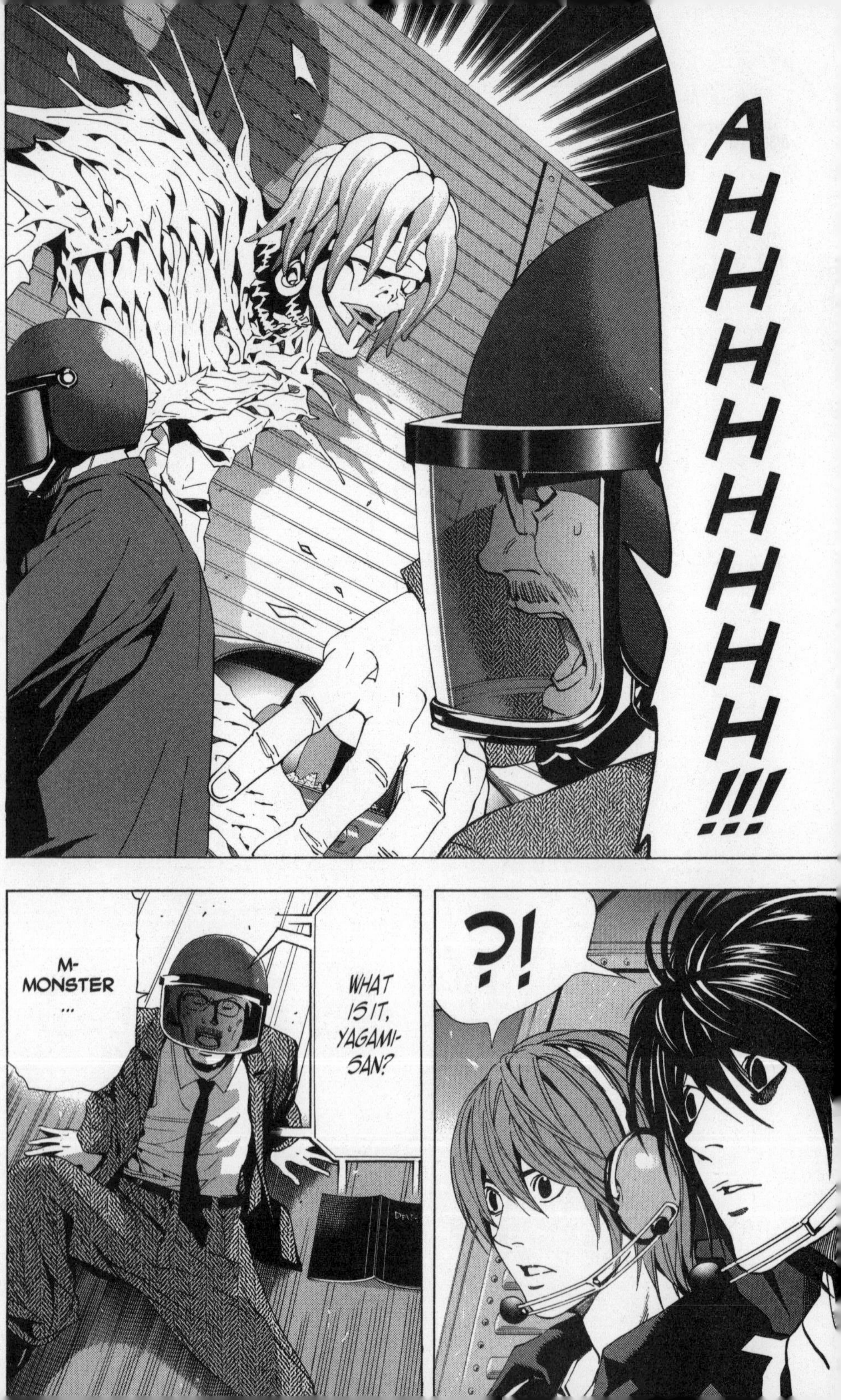
AHHHHHHHH!!!
?!
WHAT IS IT, YAGAMI-SAN?
M-MONSTER ...

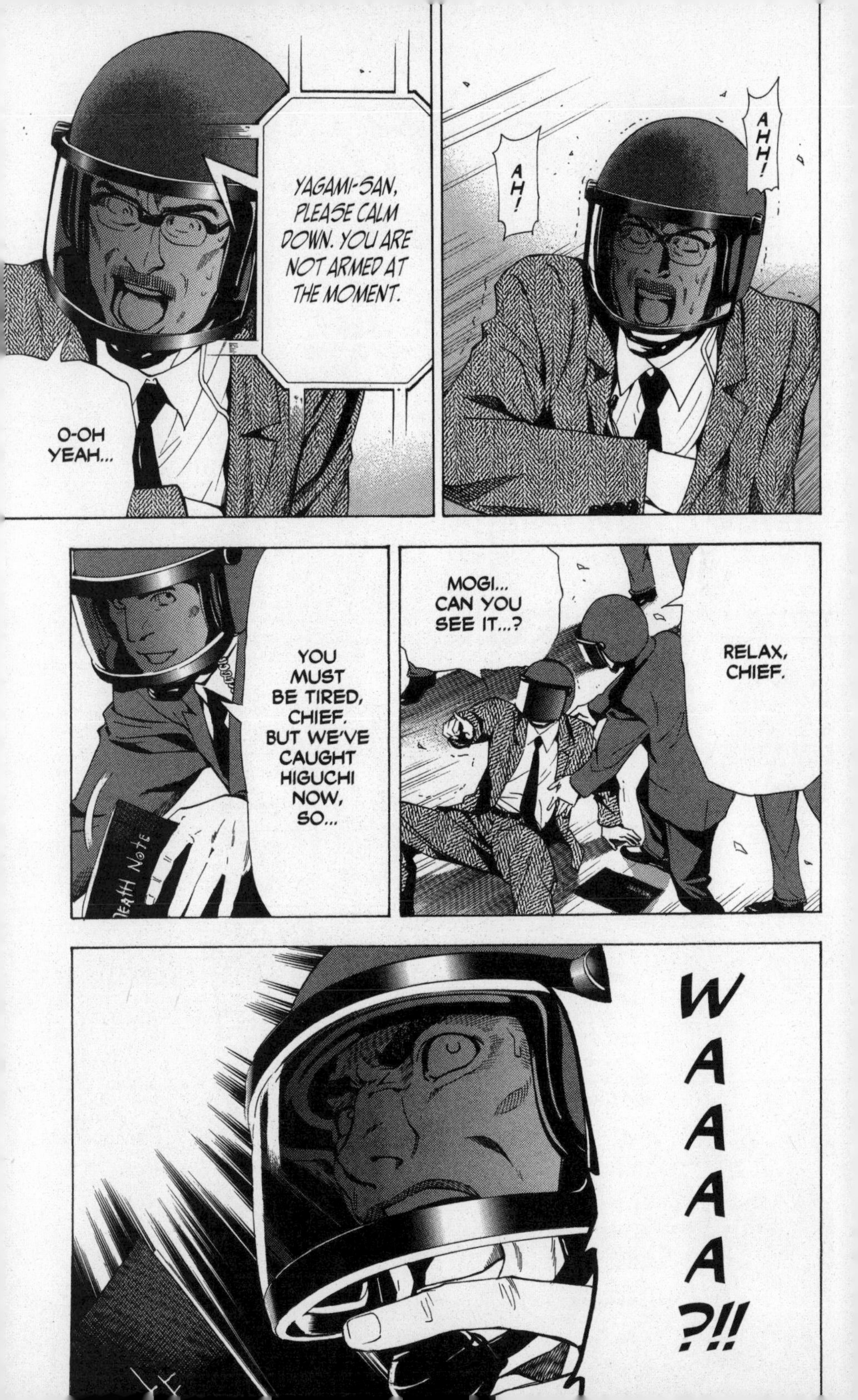
AHH!
AH!
YAGAMI-SAN, PLEASE CALM DOWN. YOU ARE NOT ARMED AT THE MOMENT.
O-OH YEAH...
MOGI... CAN YOU SEE IT...?
RELAX, CHIEF.
YOU MUST BE TIRED, CHIEF. BUT WE'VE CAUGHT HIGUCHI NOW, SO...
DEATH NOTE
WAAAAA?!!

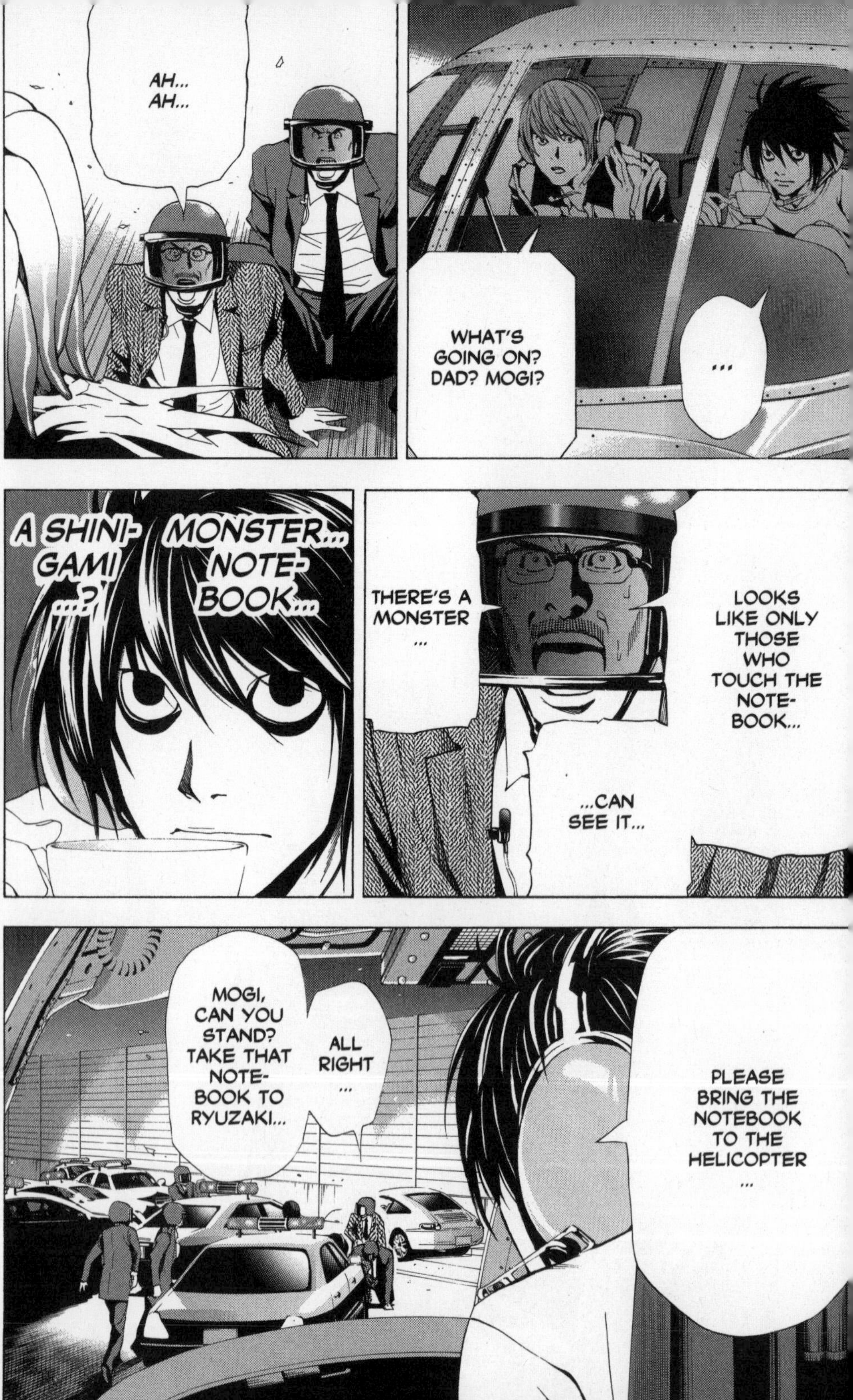
WHAT'S GOING ON? DAD? MOGI?
...
AH... AH...
THERE'S A MONSTER ...
LOOKS LIKE ONLY THOSE WHO TOUCH THE NOTE-BOOK...
...CAN SEE IT...
MONSTER... NOTE-BOOK...
A SHINI-GAMI ...?
PLEASE BRING THE NOTEBOOK TO THE HELICOPTER ...
MOGI, CAN YOU STAND? TAKE THAT NOTE-BOOK TO RYUZAKI...
ALL RIGHT ...

READ THIS WAY

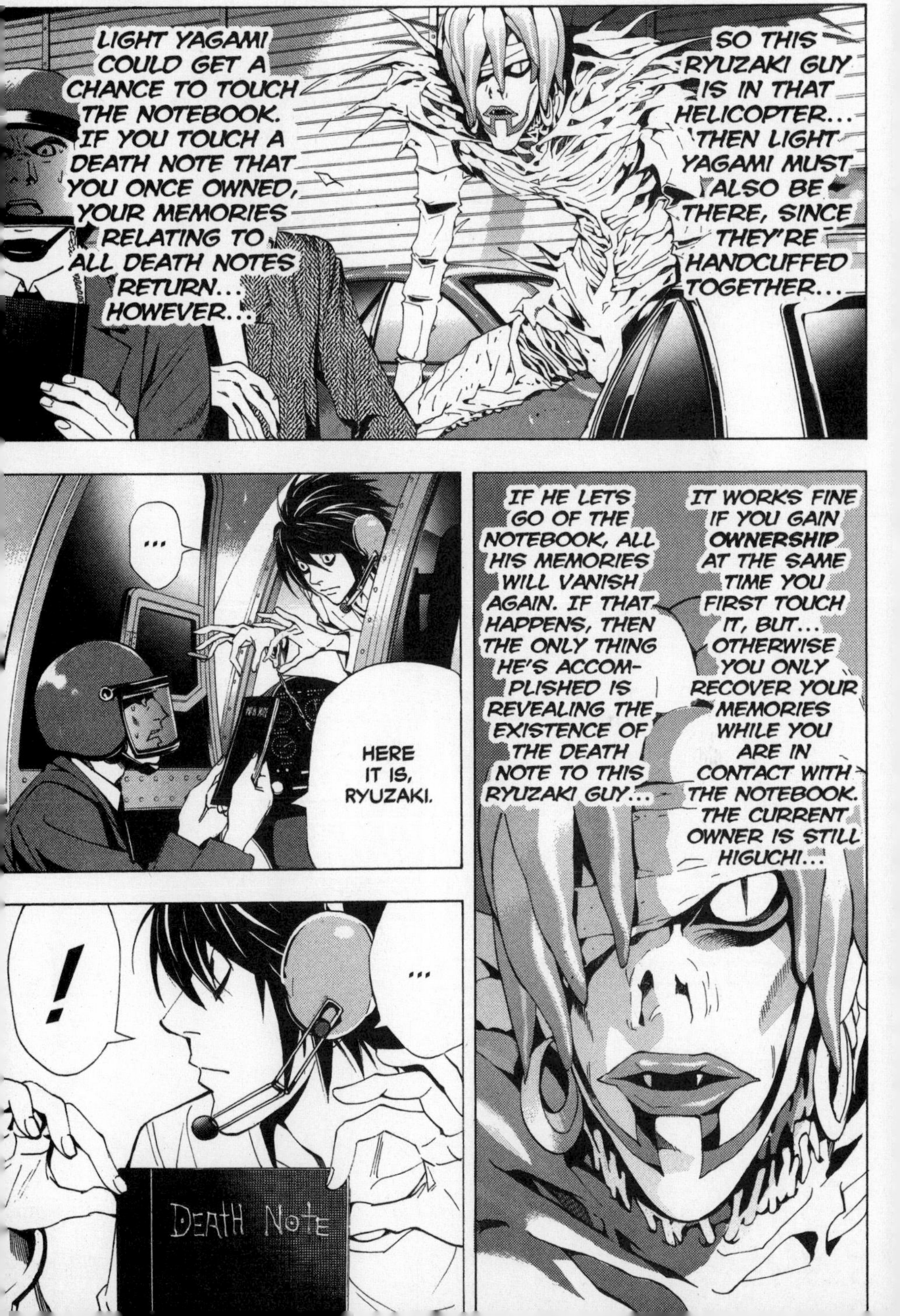
SO THIS RYUZAKI GUY IS IN THAT HELICOPTER... THEN LIGHT YAGAMI MUST ALSO BE THERE, SINCE THEY'RE HANDCUFFED TOGETHER...
LIGHT YAGAMI COULD GET A CHANCE TO TOUCH THE NOTEBOOK. IF YOU TOUCH A DEATH NOTE THAT YOU ONCE OWNED, YOUR MEMORIES RELATING TO ALL DEATH NOTES RETURN... HOWEVER...
IT WORKS FINE IF YOU GAIN OWNERSHIP AT THE SAME TIME YOU FIRST TOUCH IT, BUT... OTHERWISE YOU ONLY RECOVER YOUR MEMORIES WHILE YOU ARE IN CONTACT WITH THE NOTEBOOK. THE CURRENT OWNER IS STILL HIGUCHI...
IF HE LETS GO OF THE NOTEBOOK, ALL HIS MEMORIES WILL VANISH AGAIN. IF THAT HAPPENS, THEN THE ONLY THING HE'S ACCOMPLISHED IS REVEALING THE EXISTENCE OF THE DEATH NOTE TO THIS RYUZAKI GUY...
HERE IT IS, RYUZAKI.
...
...
!
DEATH NOTE

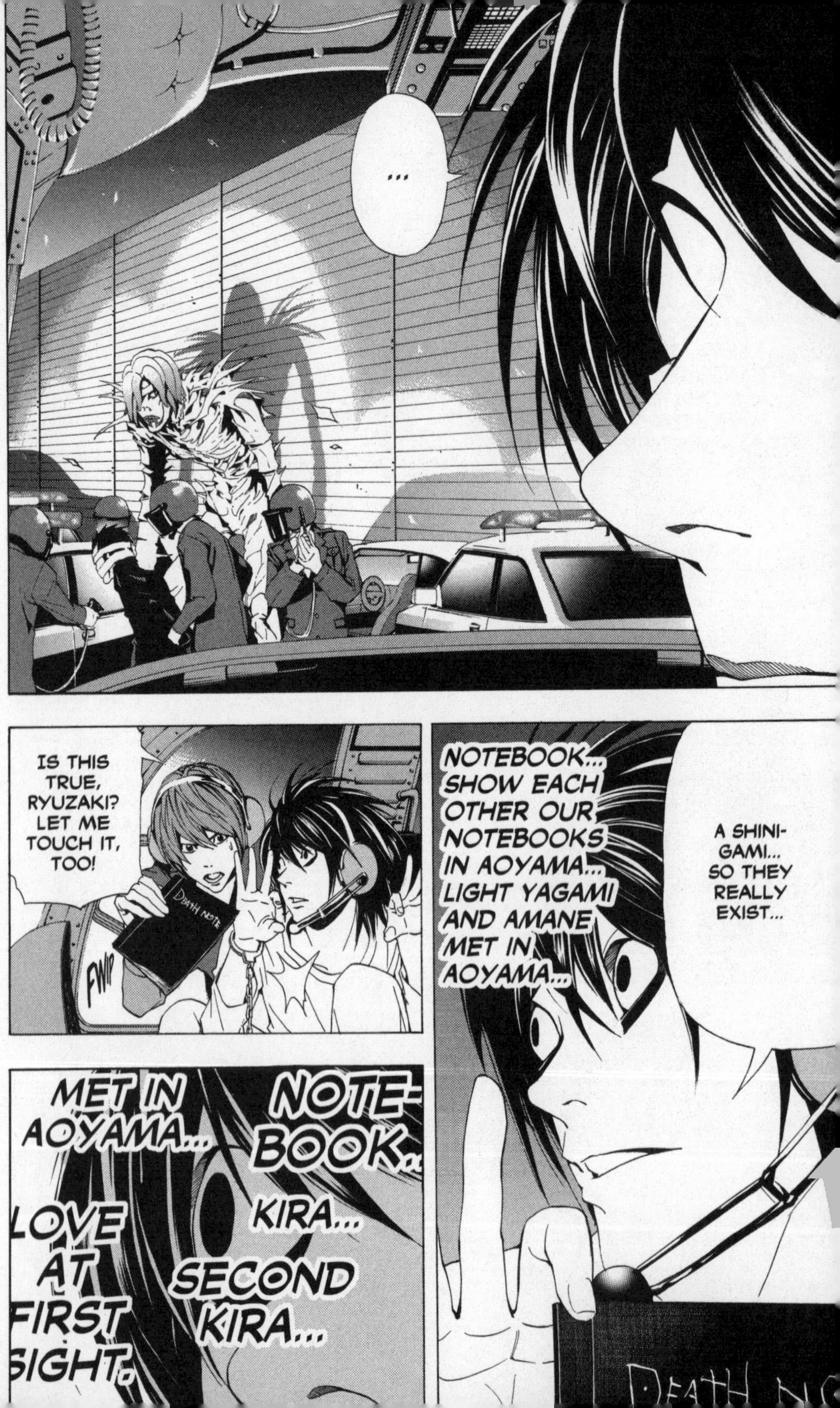
...
A SHINI-GAMI... SO THEY REALLY EXIST...
NOTEBOOK... SHOW EACH OTHER OUR NOTEBOOKS IN AOYAMA... LIGHT YAGAMI AND AMANE MET IN AOYAMA...
IS THIS TRUE, RYUZAKI? LET ME TOUCH IT, TOO!
FWIP
NOTE-BOOK..
MET IN AOYAMA..
KIRA...
SECOND KIRA...
LOVE AT FIRST SIGHT.

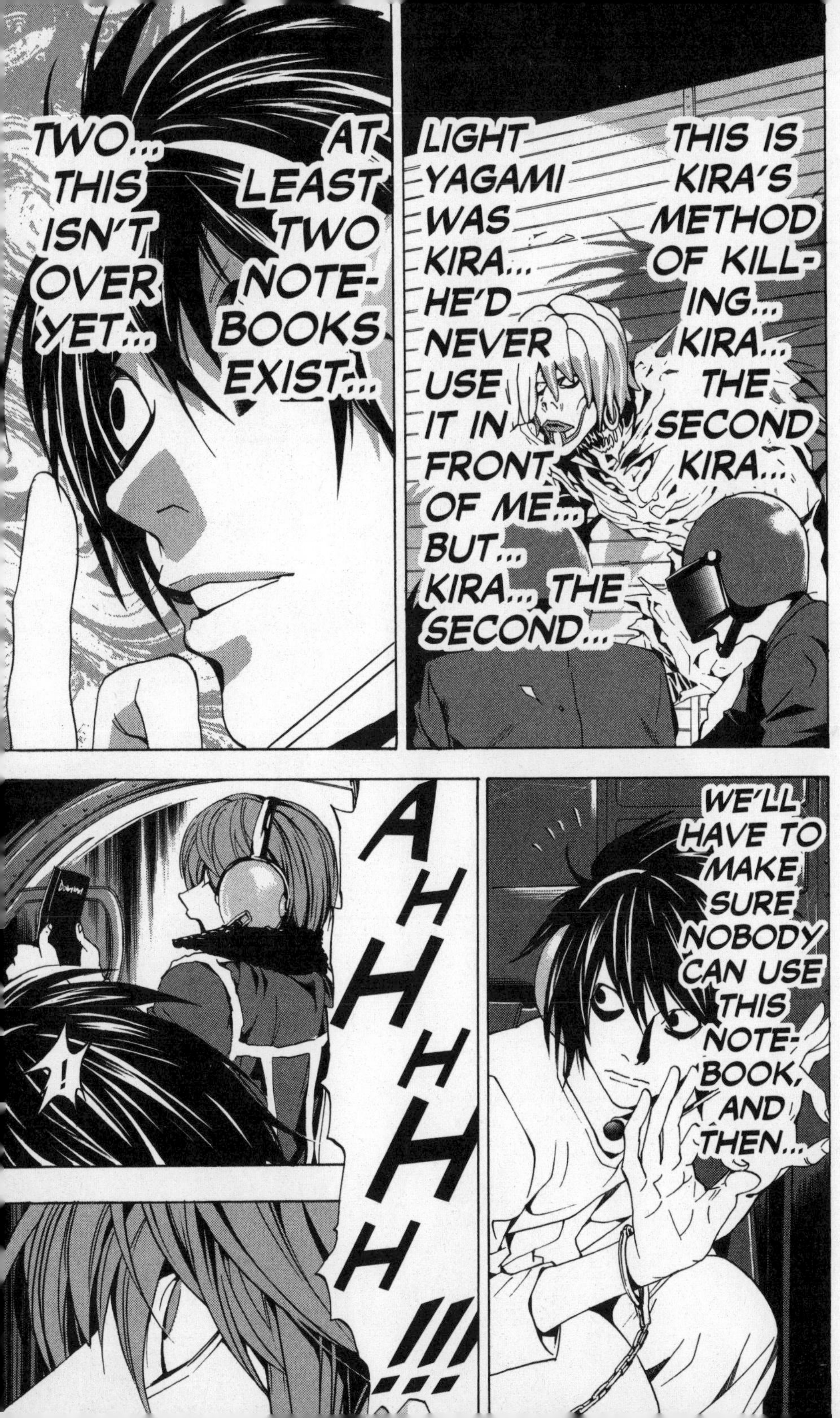
THIS IS KIRA'S METHOD OF KILL-ING... KIRA... THE SECOND KIRA...
LIGHT YAGAMI WAS KIRA... HE'D NEVER USE IT IN FRONT OF ME... BUT... KIRA... THE SECOND...
AT LEAST TWO NOTE-BOOKS EXIST...
TWO... THIS ISN'T OVER YET...
WE'LL HAVE TO MAKE SURE NOBODY CAN USE THIS NOTE-BOOK, AND THEN...
!
AHHHHH!!!

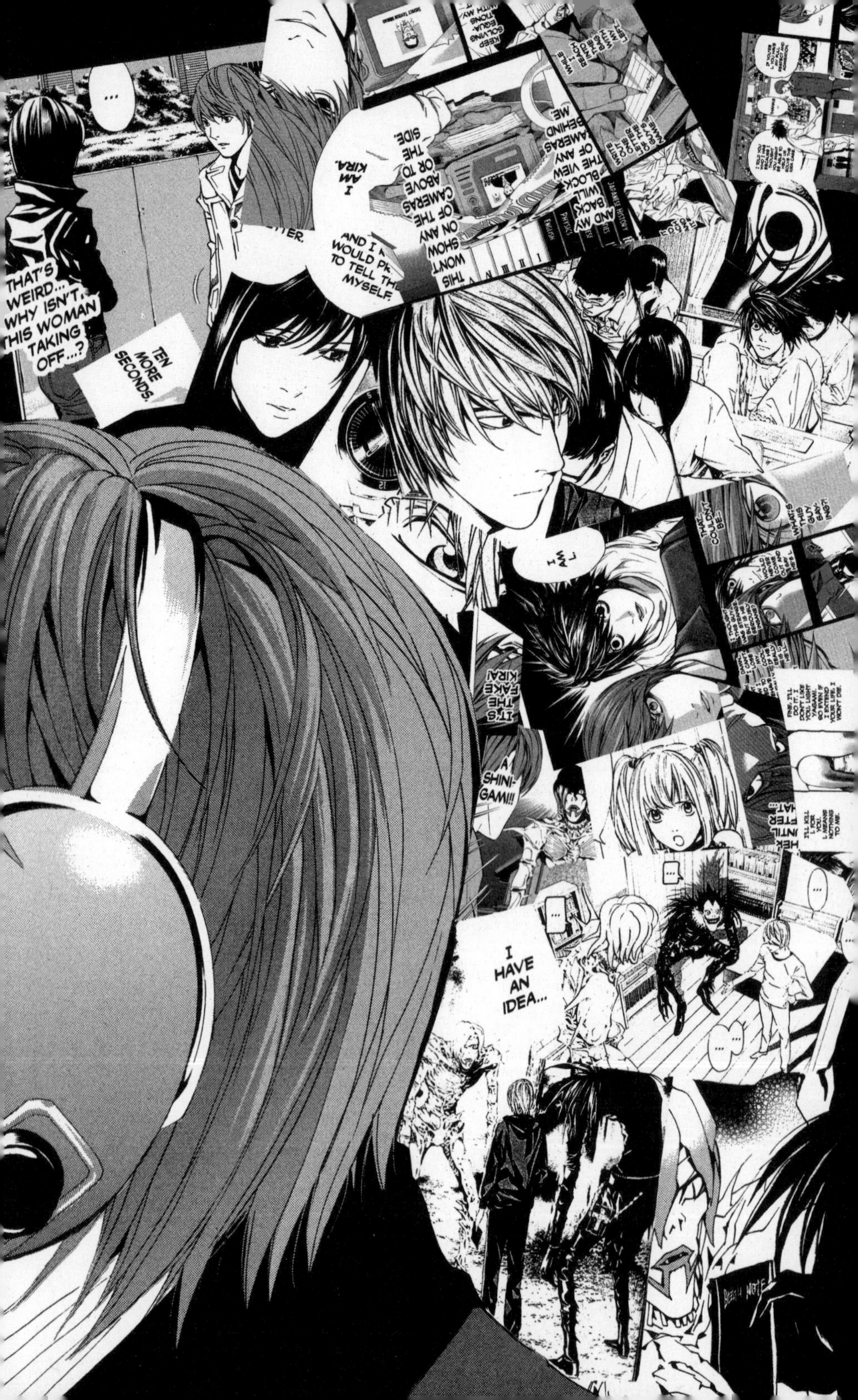

AND MY BACK WILL BLOCK THE VIEW OF ANY CAMERAS BEHIND ME.
THIS WON'T SHOW ON ANY CAMERAS ABOVE OR TO THE SIDE.
I AM KIRA.
...
THAT'S WEIRD... WHY ISN'T THIS WOMAN TAKING OFF...?
TEN MORE SECONDS.
WHAT'S THIS GUY SAYING!?
THAT COULDN'T BE...
I AM L
IT'S THE FAKE KIRA!
A SHINIGAMI!!!
...
...
I HAVE AN IDEA...
...

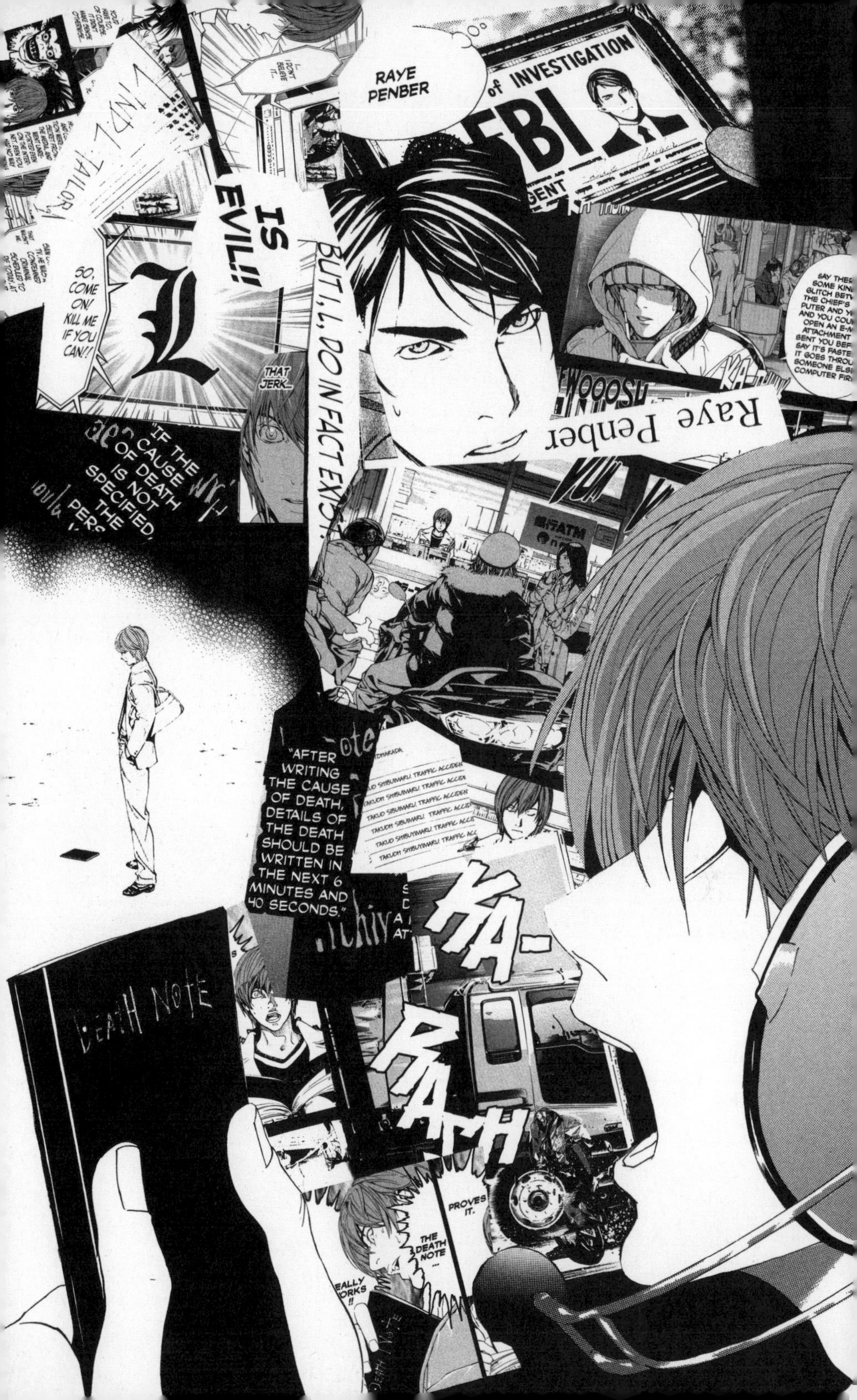

of INVESTIGATION
FBI
RAYE PENBER
I DON'T BELIEVE IT...
IS EVIL!!
SO, COME ON! KILL ME IF YOU CAN!!
BUT I, L, DO IN FACT EXIST.
Raye Penber
THAT JERK...
"IF THE CAUSE OF DEATH IS NOT SPECIFIED,
"AFTER WRITING THE CAUSE OF DEATH, DETAILS OF THE DEATH SHOULD BE WRITTEN IN THE NEXT 6 MINUTES AND 40 SECONDS."
TAKUO SHIBUIMARU, TRAFFIC ACCIDENT
KA-RASH
PROVES IT.
THE DEATH NOTE...
DEATH NOTE

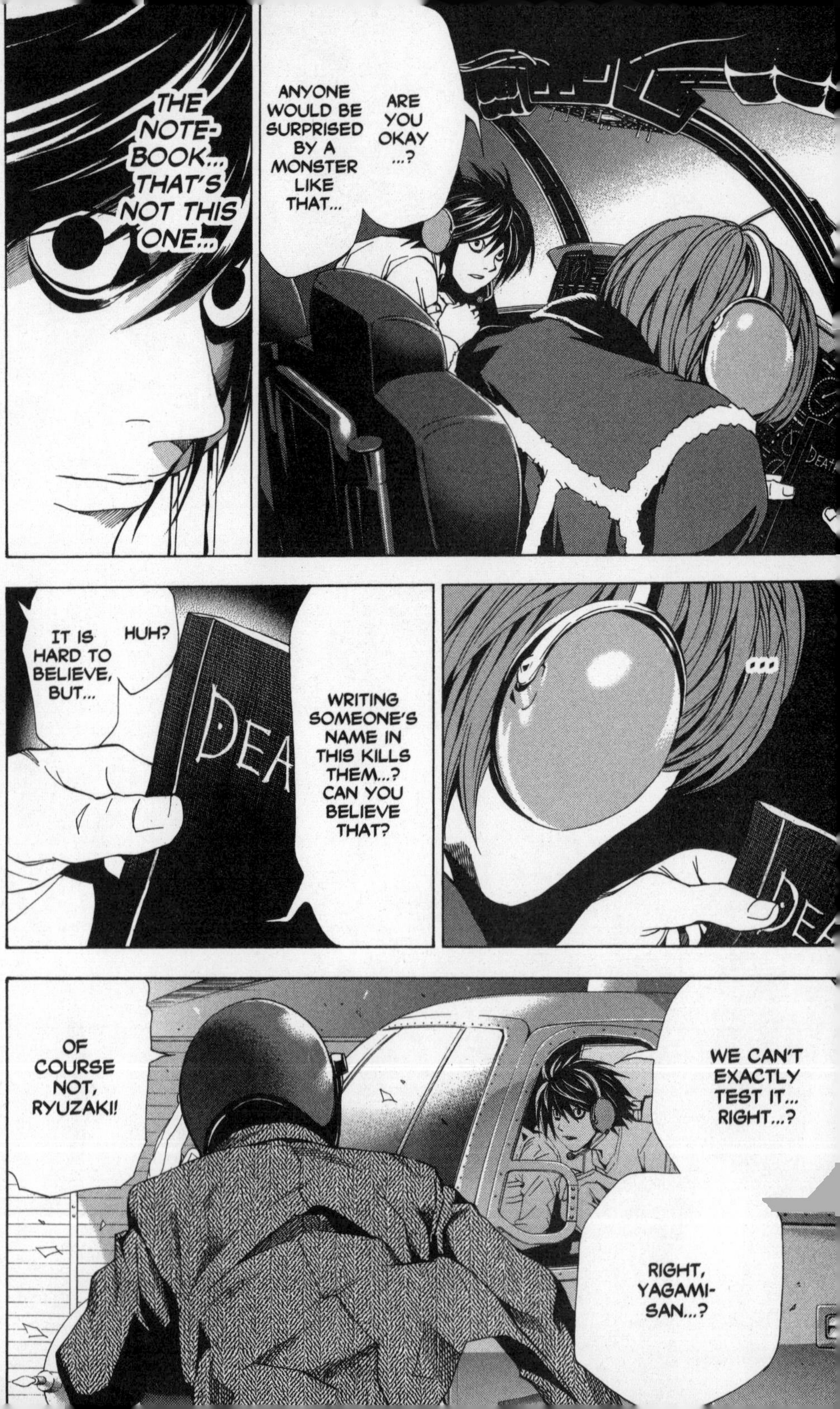
ARE YOU OKAY ...?
ANYONE WOULD BE SURPRISED BY A MONSTER LIKE THAT...
THE NOTE-BOOK... THAT'S NOT THIS ONE...
...
WRITING SOMEONE'S NAME IN THIS KILLS THEM...? CAN YOU BELIEVE THAT?
HUH?
IT IS HARD TO BELIEVE, BUT...
WE CAN'T EXACTLY TEST IT... RIGHT...?
RIGHT, YAGAMI-SAN...?
OF COURSE NOT, RYUZAKI!

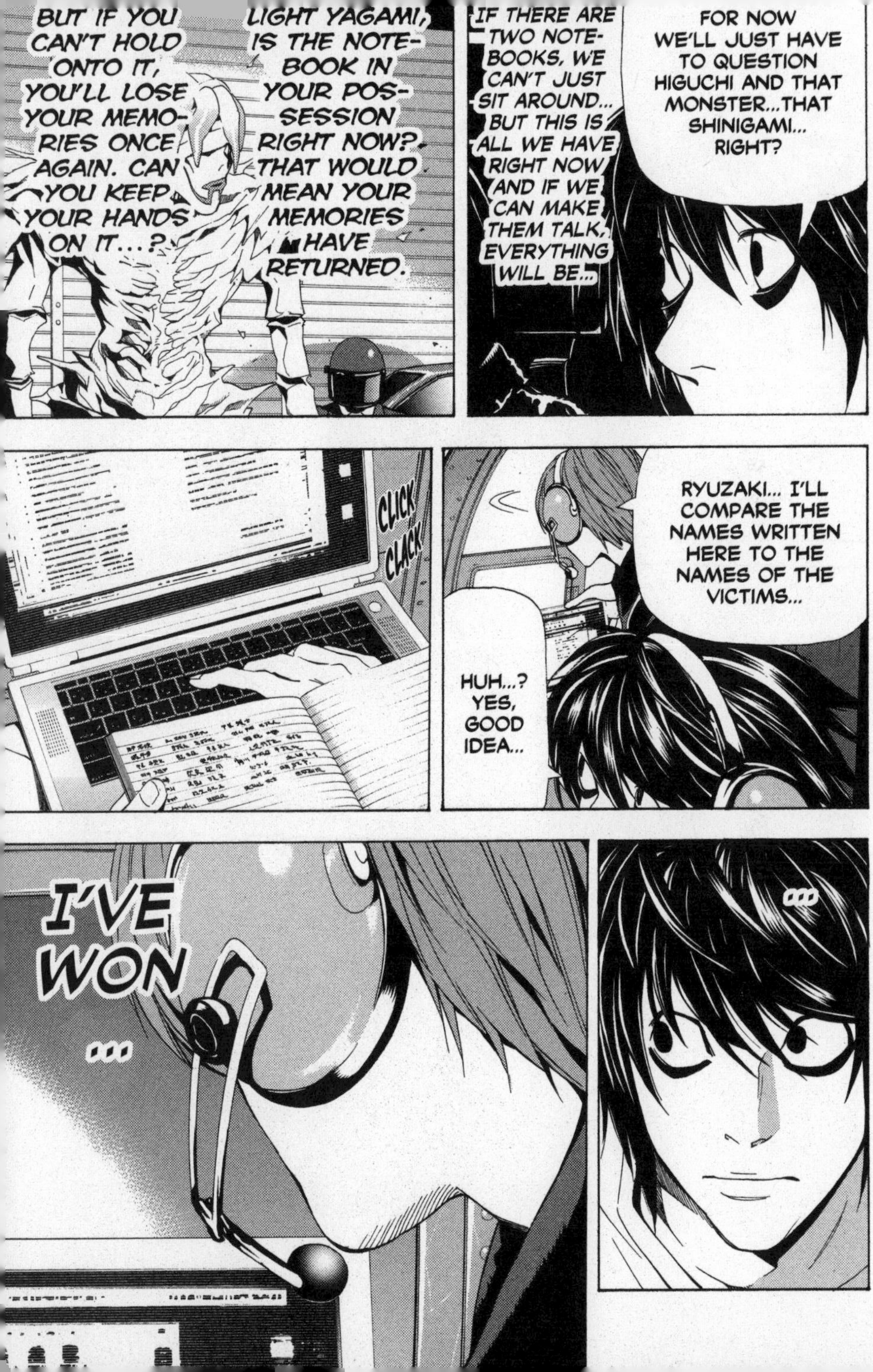
FOR NOW WE'LL JUST HAVE TO QUESTION HIGUCHI AND THAT MONSTER...THAT SHINIGAMI... RIGHT?
IF THERE ARE TWO NOTE-BOOKS, WE CAN'T JUST SIT AROUND... BUT THIS IS ALL WE HAVE RIGHT NOW AND IF WE CAN MAKE THEM TALK, EVERYTHING WILL BE...
LIGHT YAGAMI, IS THE NOTE-BOOK IN YOUR POS-SESSION RIGHT NOW? THAT WOULD MEAN YOUR MEMORIES HAVE RETURNED.
BUT IF YOU CAN'T HOLD ONTO IT, YOU'LL LOSE YOUR MEMO-RIES ONCE AGAIN. CAN YOU KEEP YOUR HANDS ON IT...?
RYUZAKI... I'LL COMPARE THE NAMES WRITTEN HERE TO THE NAMES OF THE VICTIMS...
HUH...? YES, GOOD IDEA...
CLICK CLACK
...
I'VE WON ...

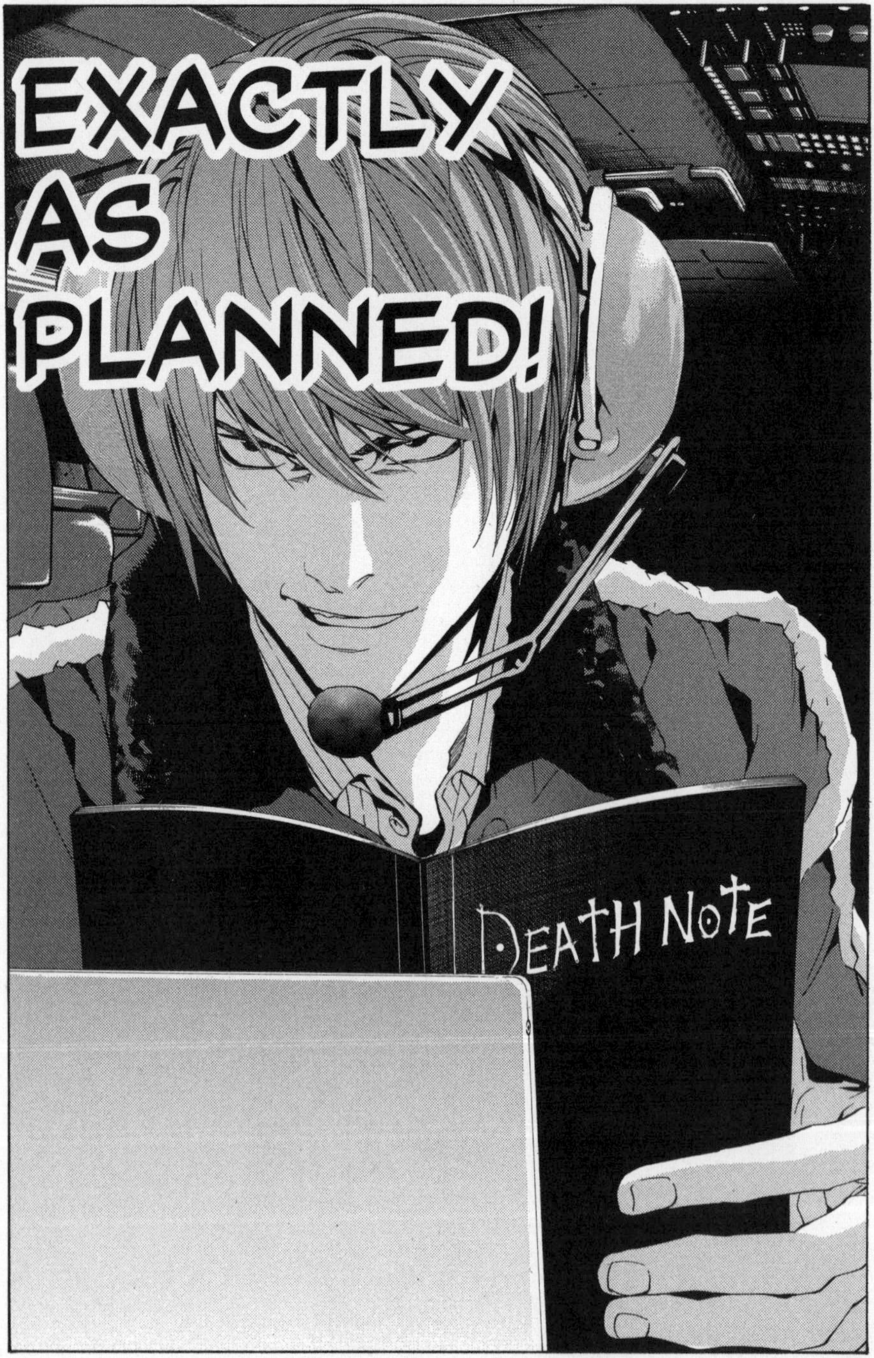
EXACTLY AS PLANNED!
DEATH NOTE

READ THIS WAY

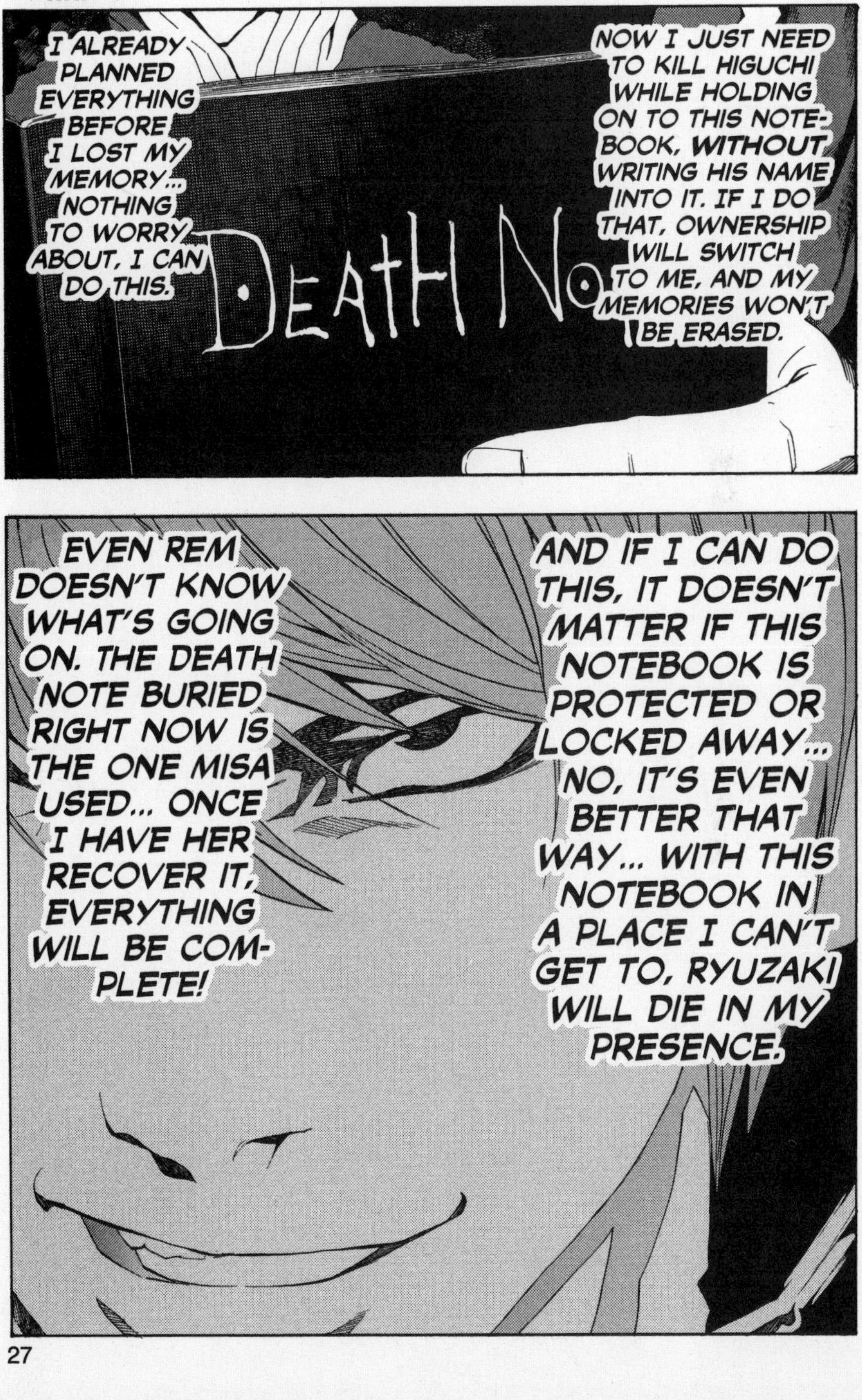

NOW I JUST NEED TO KILL HIGUCHI WHILE HOLDING ON TO THIS NOTE-BOOK, **WITHOUT** WRITING HIS NAME INTO IT. IF I DO THAT, OWNERSHIP WILL SWITCH TO ME, AND MY MEMORIES WON'T BE ERASED.
I ALREADY PLANNED EVERYTHING BEFORE I LOST MY MEMORY... NOTHING TO WORRY ABOUT, I CAN DO THIS.
DEATH NO
AND IF I CAN DO THIS, IT DOESN'T MATTER IF THIS NOTEBOOK IS PROTECTED OR LOCKED AWAY... NO, IT'S EVEN BETTER THAT WAY... WITH THIS NOTEBOOK IN A PLACE I CAN'T GET TO, RYUZAKI WILL DIE IN MY PRESENCE.
EVEN REM DOESN'T KNOW WHAT'S GOING ON. THE DEATH NOTE BURIED RIGHT NOW IS THE ONE MISA USED... ONCE I HAVE HER RECOVER IT, EVERYTHING WILL BE COM-PLETE!

# DEATH NOTE
## How to use it
## XXX VII

○ When regaining ownership of the DEATH NOTE, the memories associated with the DEATH NOTE will also return.
In cases where you were involved with other DEATH NOTES as well, memories of all the DEATH NOTEs involved will return.

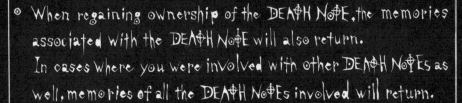

所有権をなくしたノートの所有権を再び得れば、
そのノートに関する記憶が戻る。
万が一、他にも関わったノートがあれば、
関わった全てのノートに関する記憶が戻る。

○ Even without obtaining ownership, memories will return just by touching the DEATH NOTE.

また、所有権を得なくとも、ノートに触れていれば、
触れている間のみ記憶は戻る。

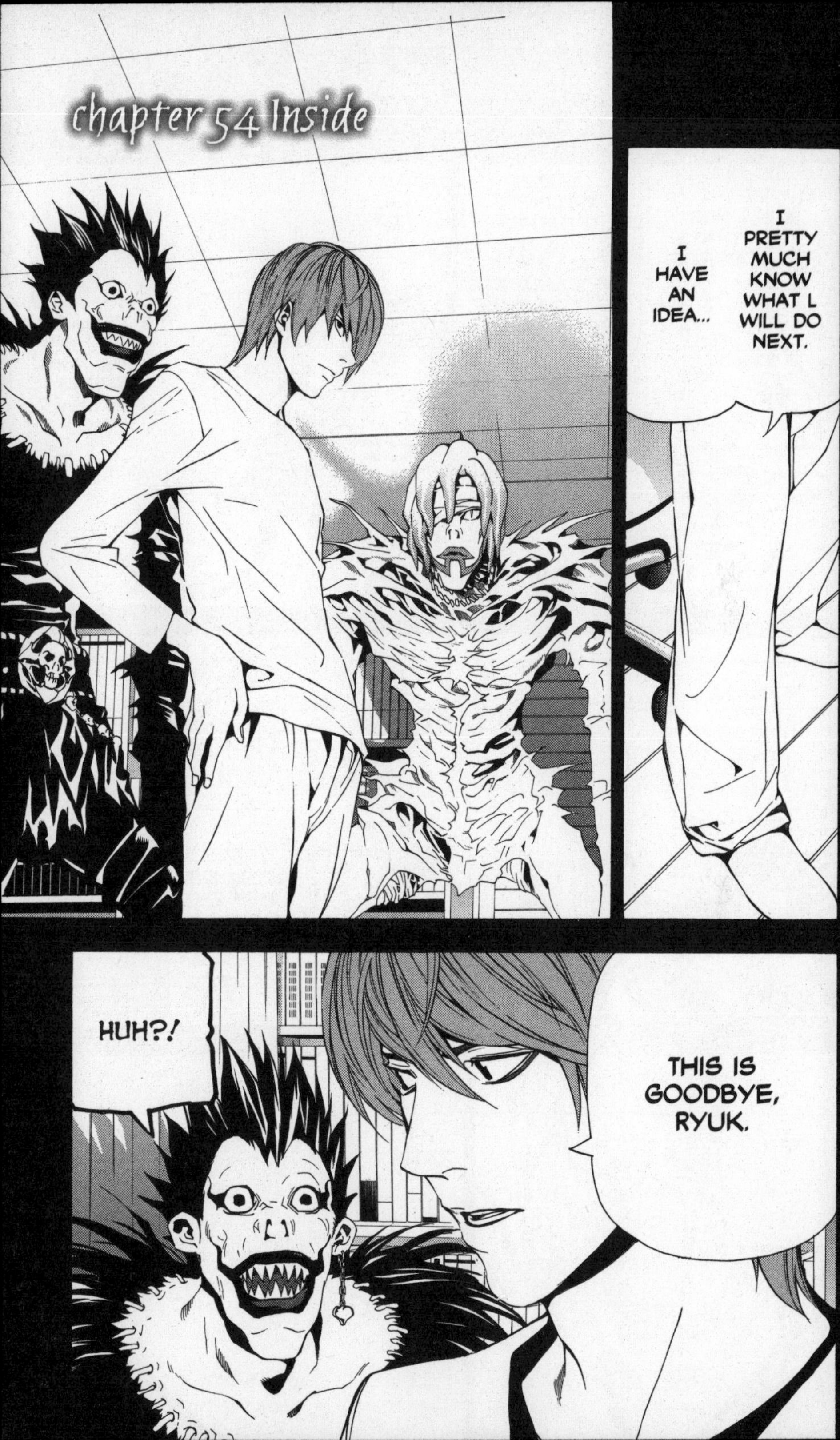
I PRETTY MUCH KNOW WHAT L WILL DO NEXT.
I HAVE AN IDEA...
chapter 54 Inside
THIS IS GOODBYE, RYUK.
HUH?!

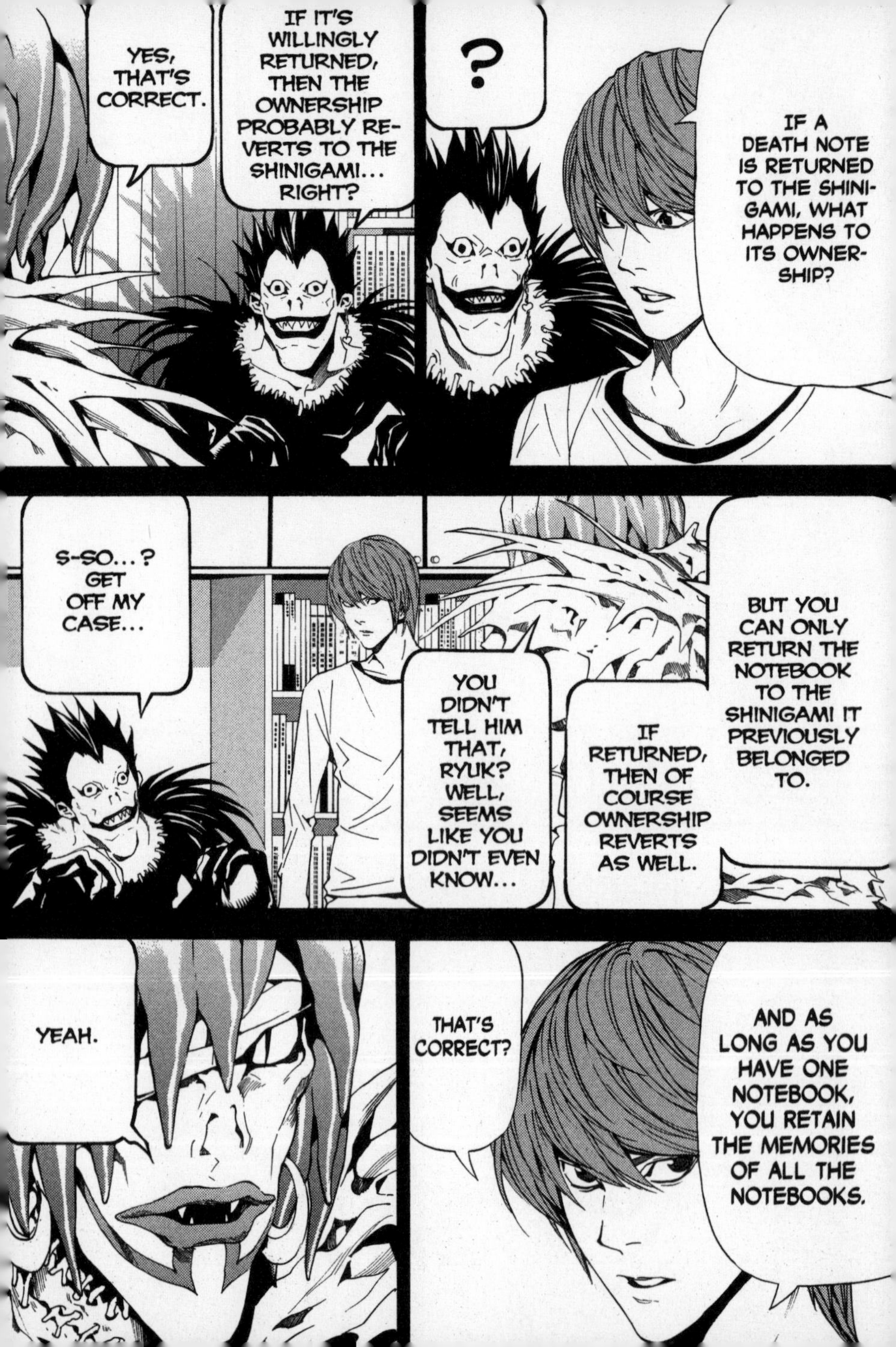
IF A DEATH NOTE IS RETURNED TO THE SHINIGAMI, WHAT HAPPENS TO ITS OWNERSHIP?
?
IF IT'S WILLINGLY RETURNED, THEN THE OWNERSHIP PROBABLY REVERTS TO THE SHINIGAMI... RIGHT?
YES, THAT'S CORRECT.
BUT YOU CAN ONLY RETURN THE NOTEBOOK TO THE SHINIGAMI IT PREVIOUSLY BELONGED TO.
IF RETURNED, THEN OF COURSE OWNERSHIP REVERTS AS WELL.
YOU DIDN'T TELL HIM THAT, RYUK? WELL, SEEMS LIKE YOU DIDN'T EVEN KNOW...
S-SO...? GET OFF MY CASE...
AND AS LONG AS YOU HAVE ONE NOTEBOOK, YOU RETAIN THE MEMORIES OF ALL THE NOTEBOOKS.
THAT'S CORRECT?
YEAH.

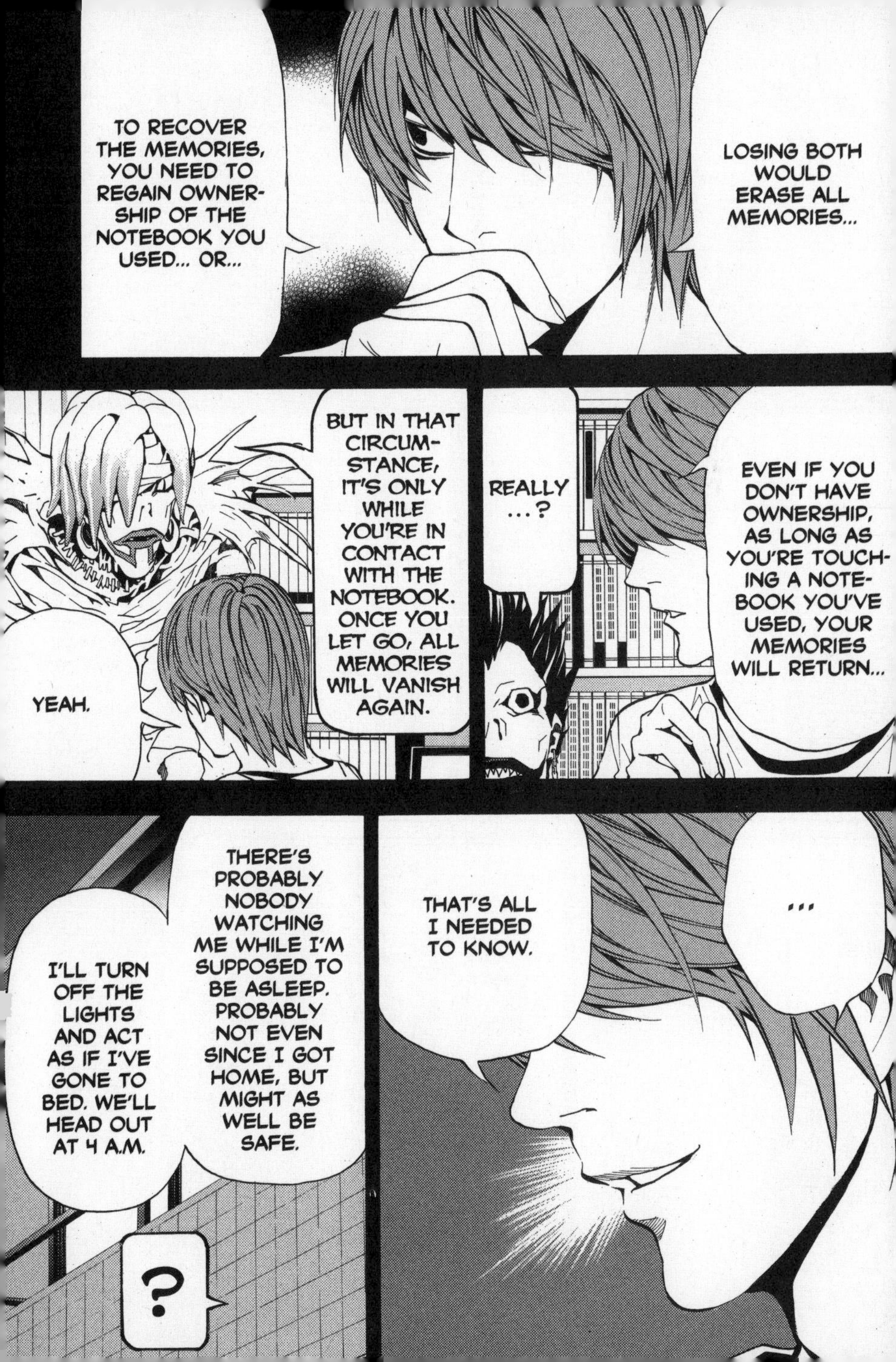
LOSING BOTH WOULD ERASE ALL MEMORIES...
TO RECOVER THE MEMORIES, YOU NEED TO REGAIN OWNERSHIP OF THE NOTEBOOK YOU USED... OR...
EVEN IF YOU DON'T HAVE OWNERSHIP, AS LONG AS YOU'RE TOUCHING A NOTEBOOK YOU'VE USED, YOUR MEMORIES WILL RETURN...
REALLY ...?
BUT IN THAT CIRCUMSTANCE, IT'S ONLY WHILE YOU'RE IN CONTACT WITH THE NOTEBOOK. ONCE YOU LET GO, ALL MEMORIES WILL VANISH AGAIN.
YEAH.
...
THAT'S ALL I NEEDED TO KNOW.
THERE'S PROBABLY NOBODY WATCHING ME WHILE I'M SUPPOSED TO BE ASLEEP. PROBABLY NOT EVEN SINCE I GOT HOME, BUT MIGHT AS WELL BE SAFE.
I'LL TURN OFF THE LIGHTS AND ACT AS IF I'VE GONE TO BED. WE'LL HEAD OUT AT 4 A.M.
?

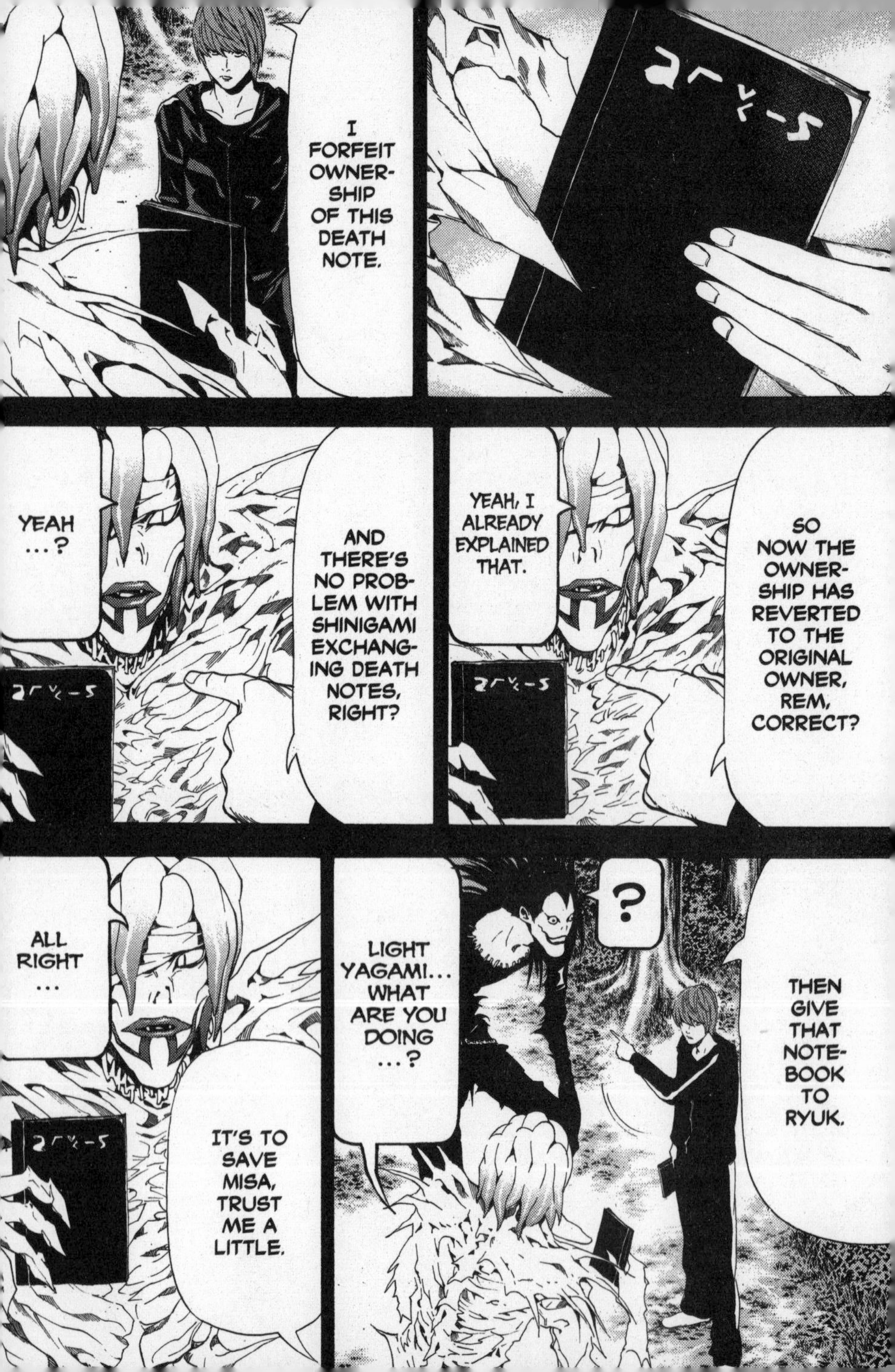
I FORFEIT OWNERSHIP OF THIS DEATH NOTE.
SO NOW THE OWNERSHIP HAS REVERTED TO THE ORIGINAL OWNER, REM, CORRECT?
YEAH, I ALREADY EXPLAINED THAT.
AND THERE'S NO PROBLEM WITH SHINIGAMI EXCHANGING DEATH NOTES, RIGHT?
YEAH ...?
THEN GIVE THAT NOTEBOOK TO RYUK.
?
LIGHT YAGAMI... WHAT ARE YOU DOING ...?
IT'S TO SAVE MISA, TRUST ME A LITTLE.
ALL RIGHT ...

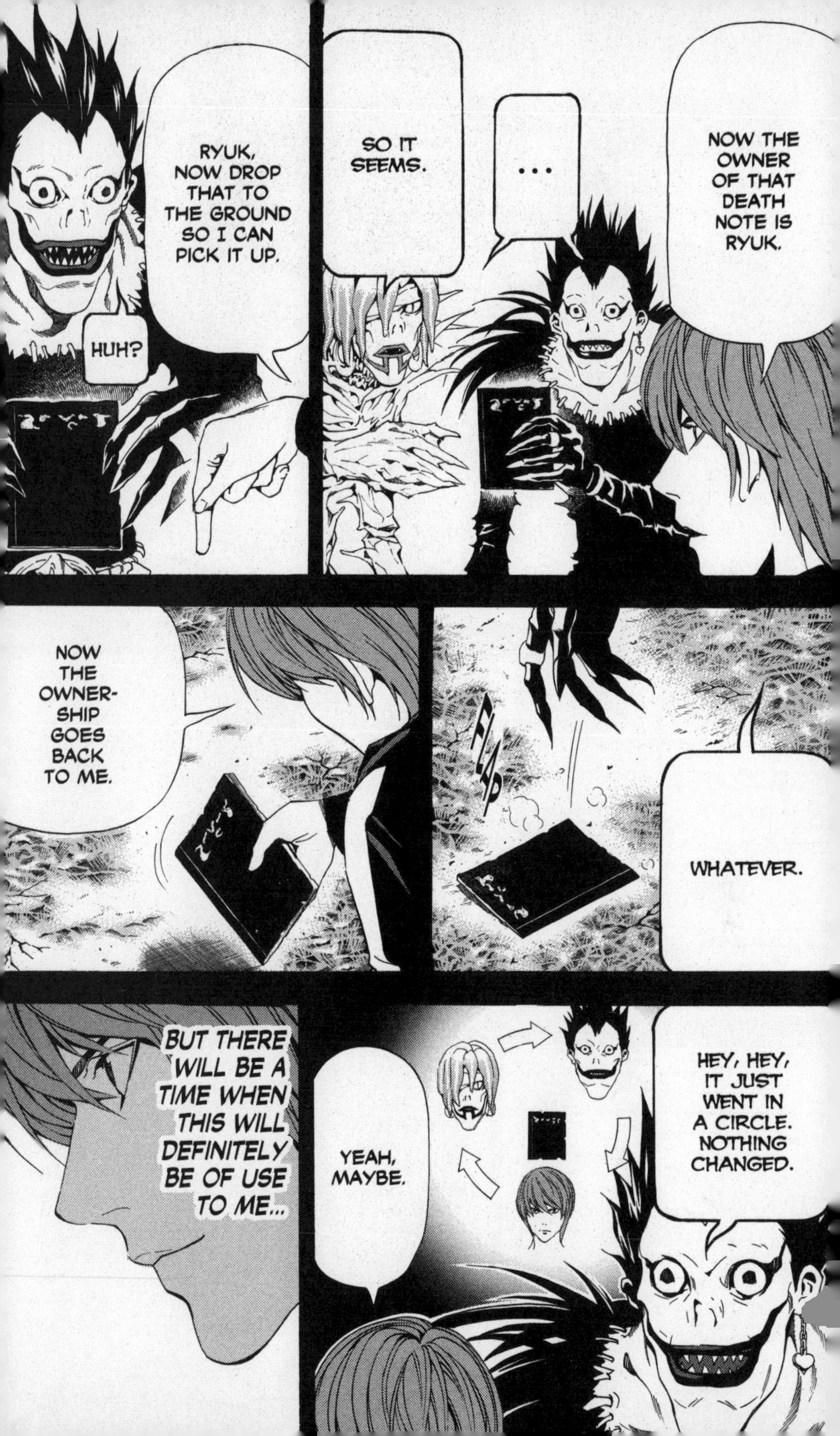
NOW THE OWNER OF THAT DEATH NOTE IS RYUK.
...
SO IT SEEMS.
RYUK, NOW DROP THAT TO THE GROUND SO I CAN PICK IT UP.
HUH?
WHATEVER.
FLAP
NOW THE OWNERSHIP GOES BACK TO ME.
HEY, HEY, IT JUST WENT IN A CIRCLE. NOTHING CHANGED.
YEAH, MAYBE.
BUT THERE WILL BE A TIME WHEN THIS WILL DEFINITELY BE OF USE TO ME...

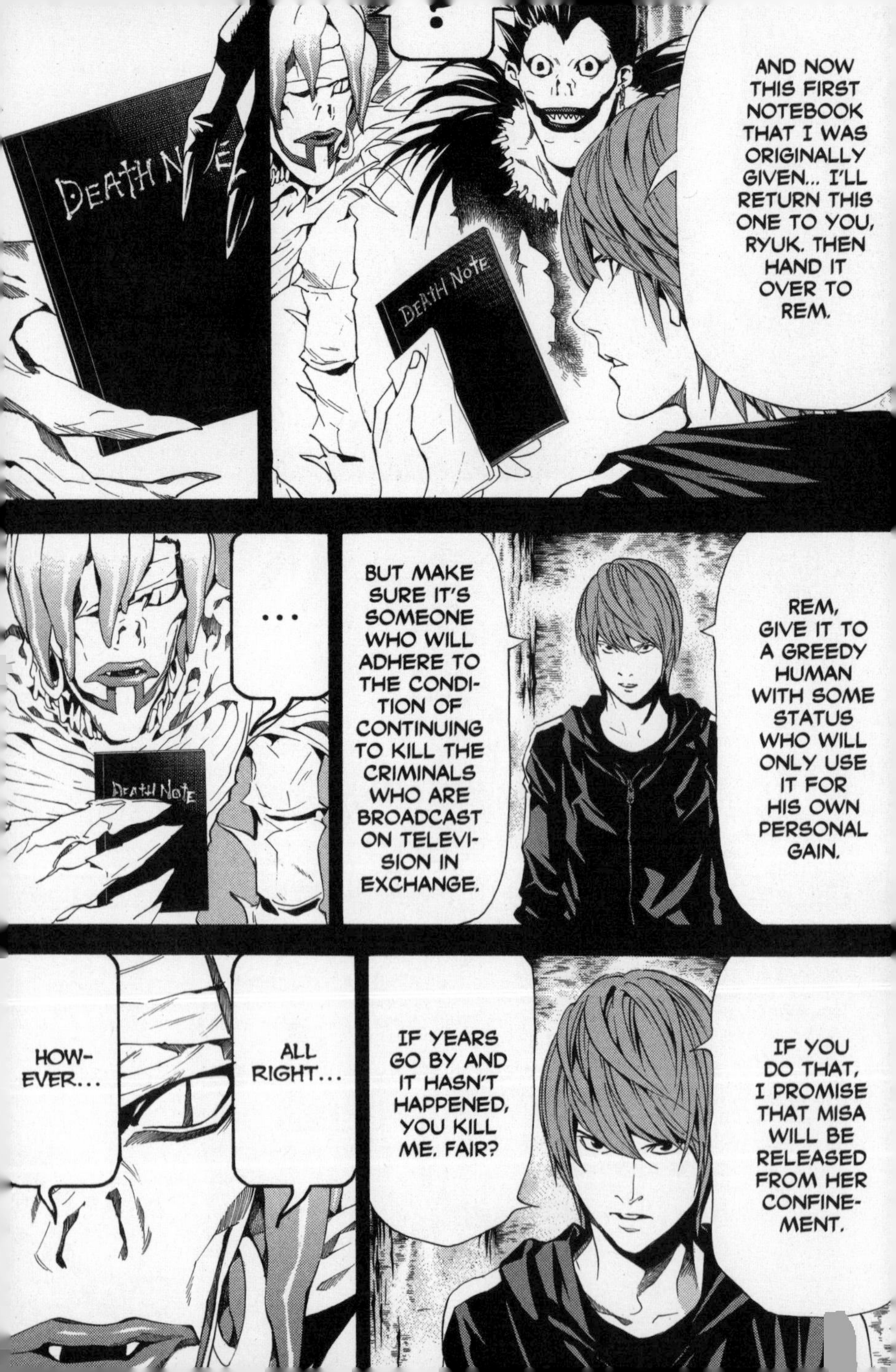
AND NOW THIS FIRST NOTEBOOK THAT I WAS ORIGINALLY GIVEN... I'LL RETURN THIS ONE TO YOU, RYUK. THEN HAND IT OVER TO REM.
DEATH NOTE
DEATH NOTE
REM, GIVE IT TO A GREEDY HUMAN WITH SOME STATUS WHO WILL ONLY USE IT FOR HIS OWN PERSONAL GAIN.
BUT MAKE SURE IT'S SOMEONE WHO WILL ADHERE TO THE CONDITION OF CONTINUING TO KILL THE CRIMINALS WHO ARE BROADCAST ON TELEVISION IN EXCHANGE.
...
DEATH NOTE
IF YOU DO THAT, I PROMISE THAT MISA WILL BE RELEASED FROM HER CONFINEMENT.
IF YEARS GO BY AND IT HASN'T HAPPENED, YOU KILL ME. FAIR?
ALL RIGHT...
HOW-EVER...

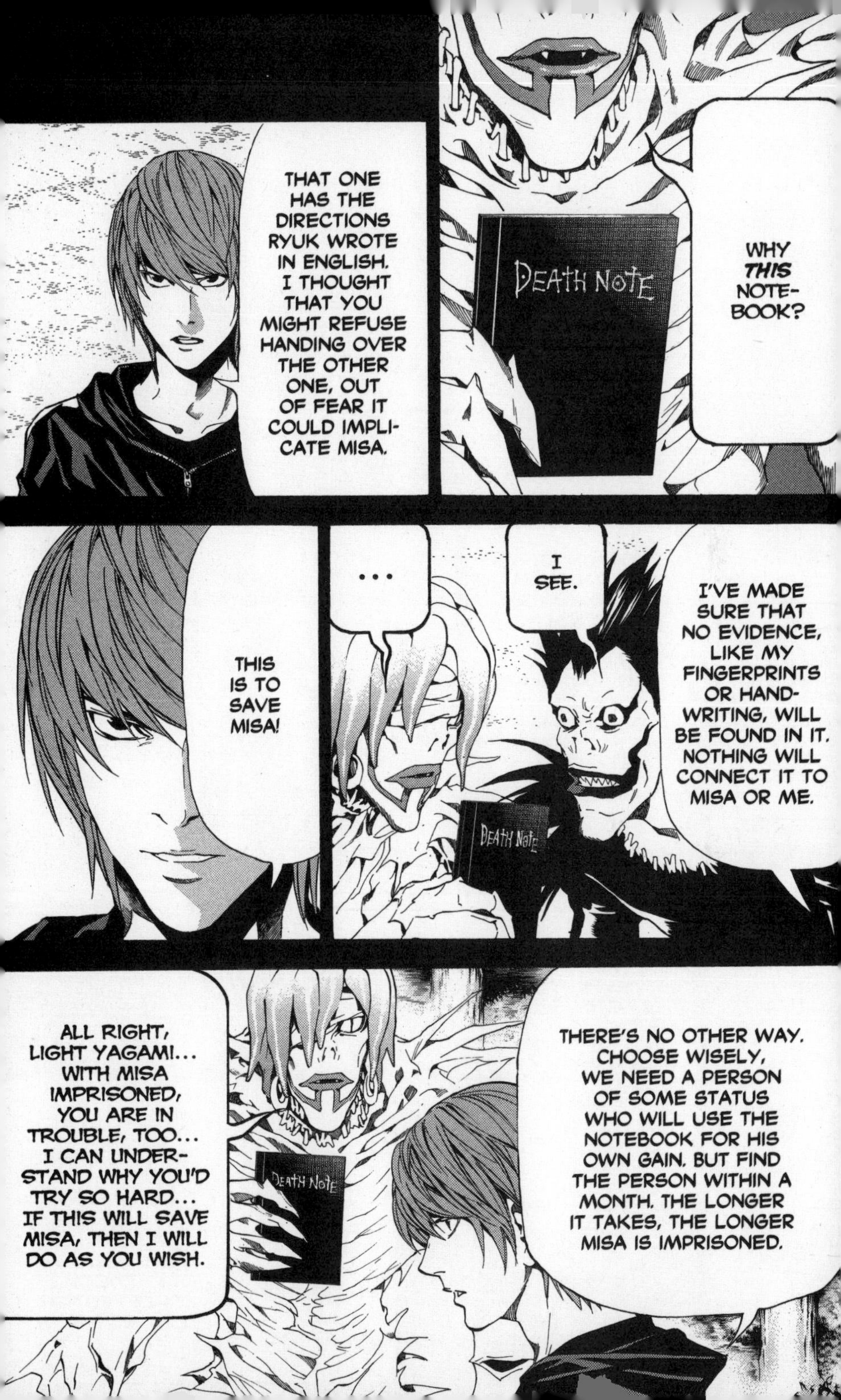
WHY *THIS* NOTE-BOOK?
THAT ONE HAS THE DIRECTIONS RYUK WROTE IN ENGLISH. I THOUGHT THAT YOU MIGHT REFUSE HANDING OVER THE OTHER ONE, OUT OF FEAR IT COULD IMPLI-CATE MISA.
I'VE MADE SURE THAT NO EVIDENCE, LIKE MY FINGERPRINTS OR HAND-WRITING, WILL BE FOUND IN IT. NOTHING WILL CONNECT IT TO MISA OR ME.
I SEE.
...
THIS IS TO SAVE MISA!
THERE'S NO OTHER WAY. CHOOSE WISELY, WE NEED A PERSON OF SOME STATUS WHO WILL USE THE NOTEBOOK FOR HIS OWN GAIN. BUT FIND THE PERSON WITHIN A MONTH. THE LONGER IT TAKES, THE LONGER MISA IS IMPRISONED.
ALL RIGHT, LIGHT YAGAMI... WITH MISA IMPRISONED, YOU ARE IN TROUBLE, TOO... I CAN UNDER-STAND WHY YOU'D TRY SO HARD... IF THIS WILL SAVE MISA, THEN I WILL DO AS YOU WISH.

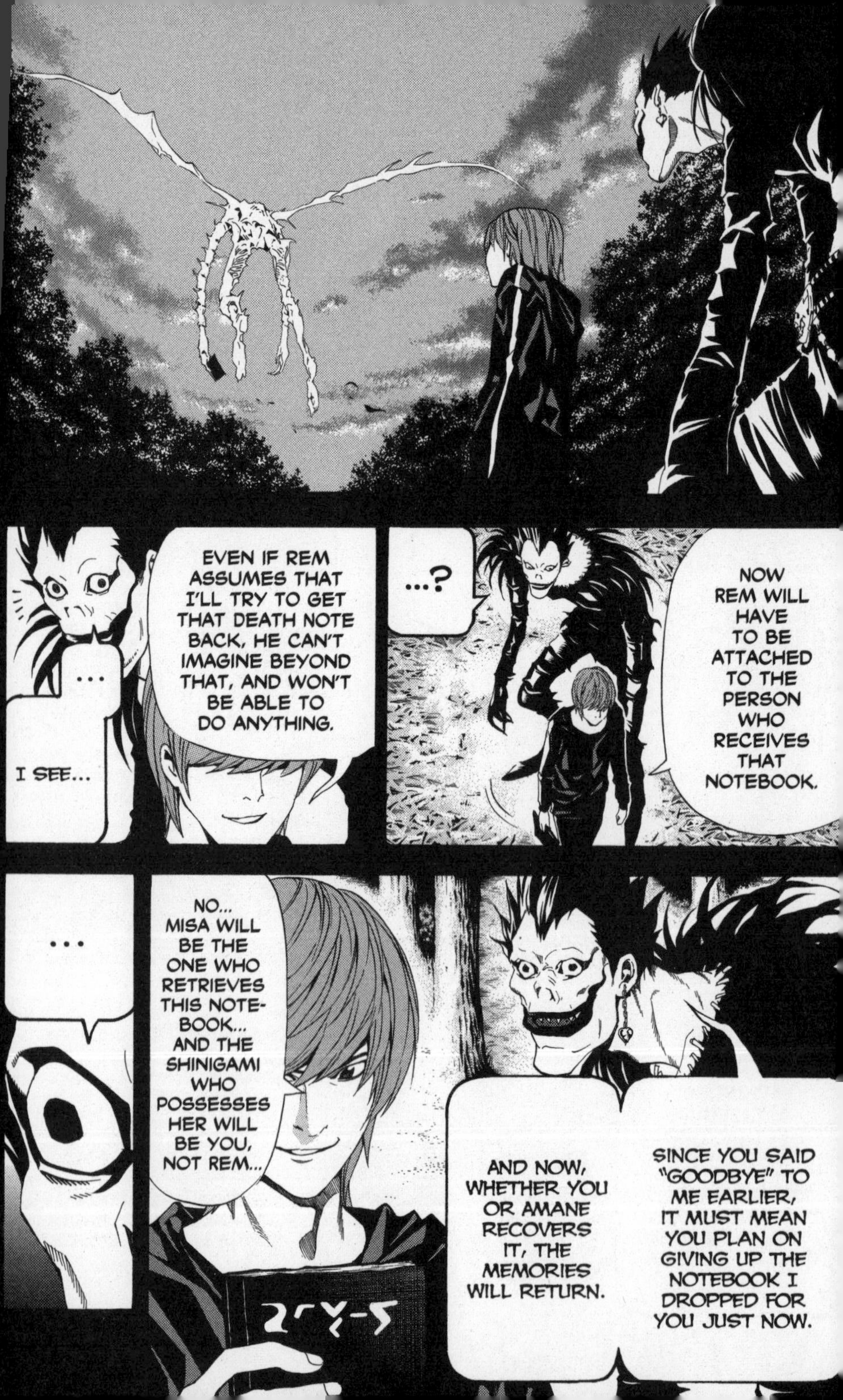
NOW REM WILL HAVE TO BE ATTACHED TO THE PERSON WHO RECEIVES THAT NOTEBOOK.
...?
EVEN IF REM ASSUMES THAT I'LL TRY TO GET THAT DEATH NOTE BACK, HE CAN'T IMAGINE BEYOND THAT, AND WON'T BE ABLE TO DO ANYTHING.
...
I SEE...
SINCE YOU SAID "GOODBYE" TO ME EARLIER, IT MUST MEAN YOU PLAN ON GIVING UP THE NOTEBOOK I DROPPED FOR YOU JUST NOW.
AND NOW, WHETHER YOU OR AMANE RECOVERS IT, THE MEMORIES WILL RETURN.
NO... MISA WILL BE THE ONE WHO RETRIEVES THIS NOTE-BOOK... AND THE SHINIGAMI WHO POSSESSES HER WILL BE YOU, NOT REM...
...

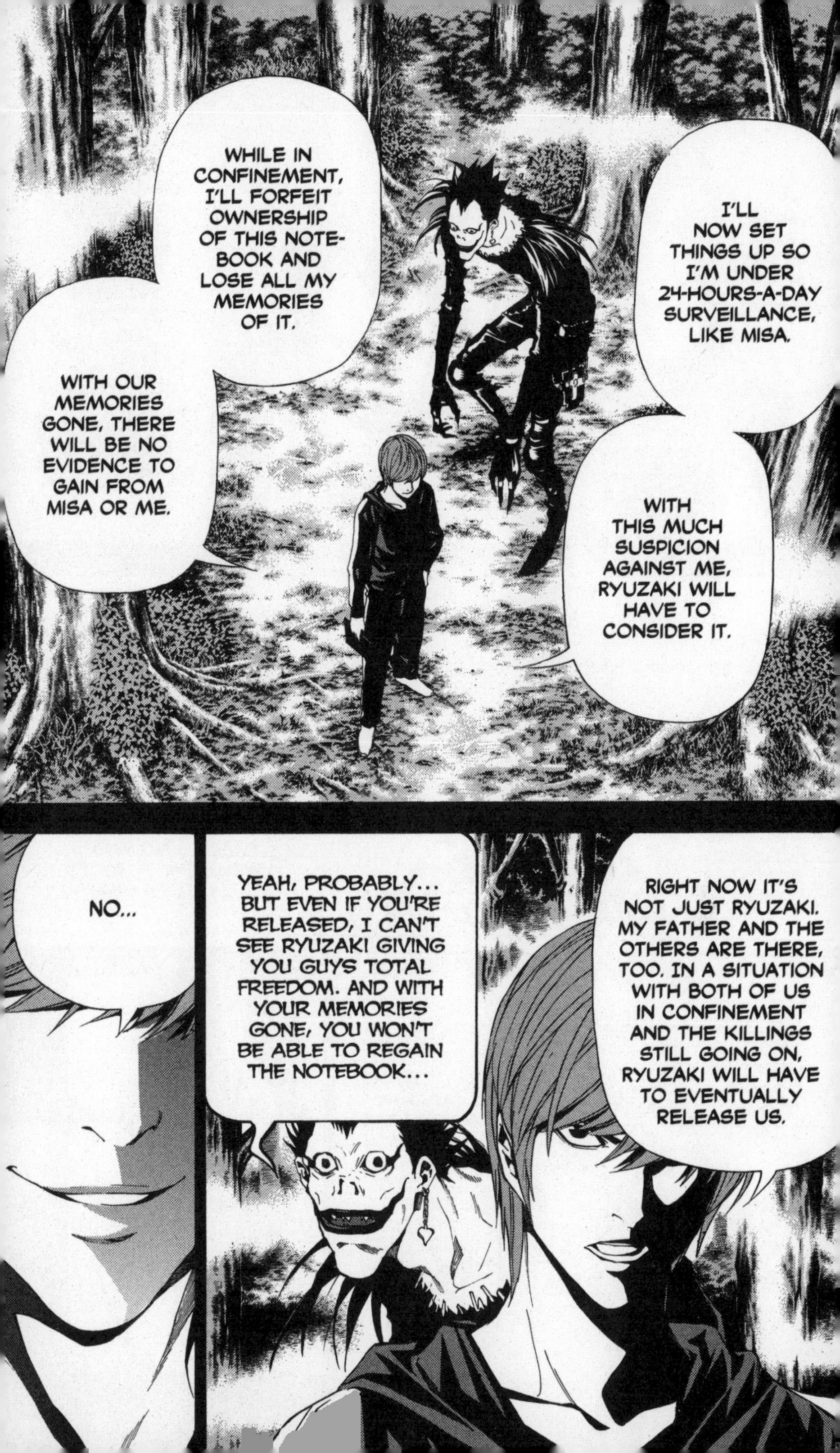
I'LL NOW SET THINGS UP SO I'M UNDER 24-HOURS-A-DAY SURVEILLANCE, LIKE MISA.
WHILE IN CONFINEMENT, I'LL FORFEIT OWNERSHIP OF THIS NOTE-BOOK AND LOSE ALL MY MEMORIES OF IT.
WITH THIS MUCH SUSPICION AGAINST ME, RYUZAKI WILL HAVE TO CONSIDER IT.
WITH OUR MEMORIES GONE, THERE WILL BE NO EVIDENCE TO GAIN FROM MISA OR ME.
RIGHT NOW IT'S NOT JUST RYUZAKI. MY FATHER AND THE OTHERS ARE THERE, TOO. IN A SITUATION WITH BOTH OF US IN CONFINEMENT AND THE KILLINGS STILL GOING ON, RYUZAKI WILL HAVE TO EVENTUALLY RELEASE US.
YEAH, PROBABLY... BUT EVEN IF YOU'RE RELEASED, I CAN'T SEE RYUZAKI GIVING YOU GUYS TOTAL FREEDOM. AND WITH YOUR MEMORIES GONE, YOU WON'T BE ABLE TO REGAIN THE NOTEBOOK...
NO...

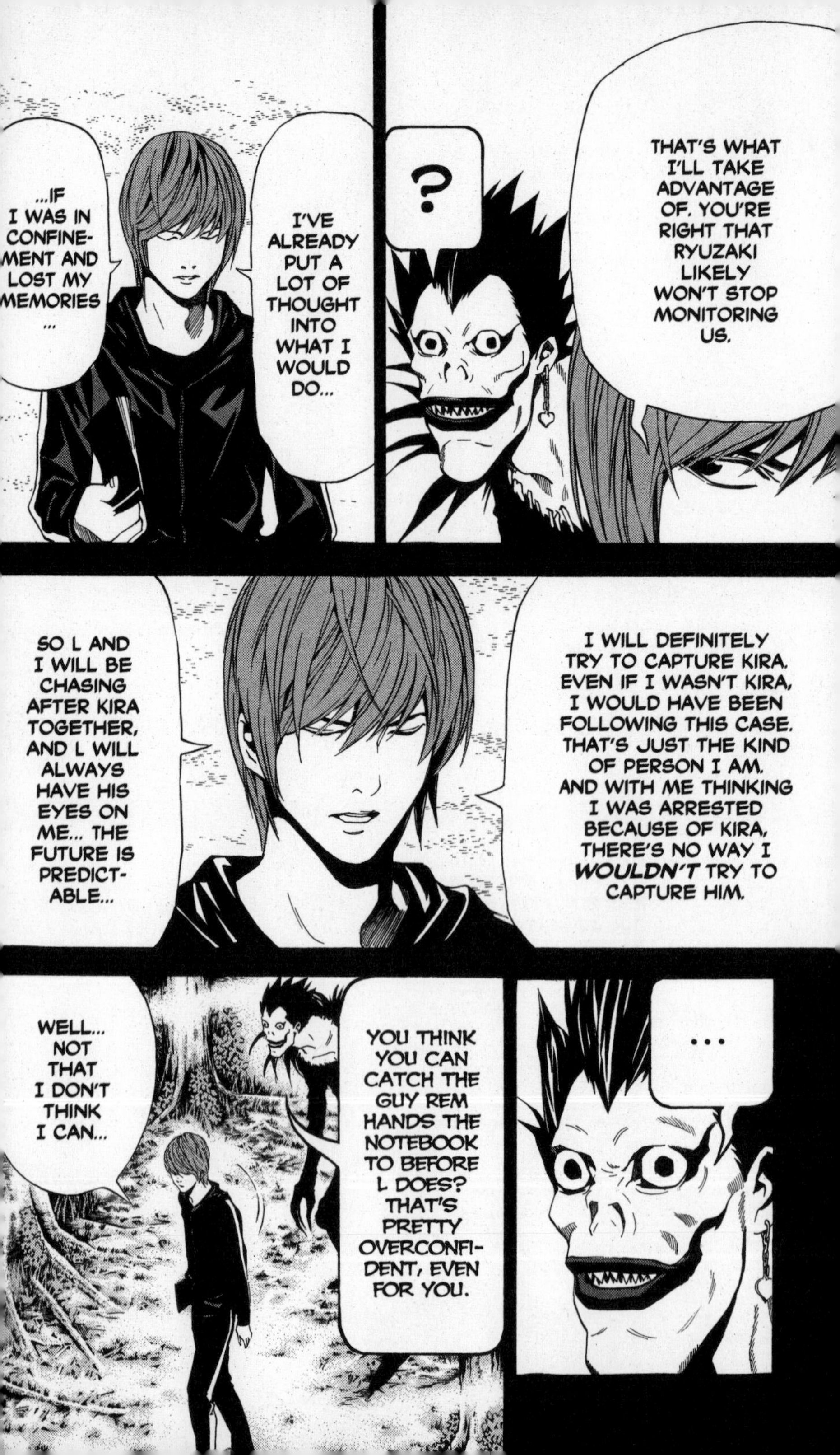
THAT'S WHAT I'LL TAKE ADVANTAGE OF. YOU'RE RIGHT THAT RYUZAKI LIKELY WON'T STOP MONITORING US.
?
I'VE ALREADY PUT A LOT OF THOUGHT INTO WHAT I WOULD DO...
...IF I WAS IN CONFINE-MENT AND LOST MY MEMORIES ...
I WILL DEFINITELY TRY TO CAPTURE KIRA. EVEN IF I WASN'T KIRA, I WOULD HAVE BEEN FOLLOWING THIS CASE. THAT'S JUST THE KIND OF PERSON I AM. AND WITH ME THINKING I WAS ARRESTED BECAUSE OF KIRA, THERE'S NO WAY I ***WOULDN'T*** TRY TO CAPTURE HIM.
SO L AND I WILL BE CHASING AFTER KIRA TOGETHER, AND L WILL ALWAYS HAVE HIS EYES ON ME... THE FUTURE IS PREDICT-ABLE...
...
YOU THINK YOU CAN CATCH THE GUY REM HANDS THE NOTEBOOK TO BEFORE L DOES? THAT'S PRETTY OVERCONFI-DENT, EVEN FOR YOU.
WELL... NOT THAT I DON'T THINK I CAN...

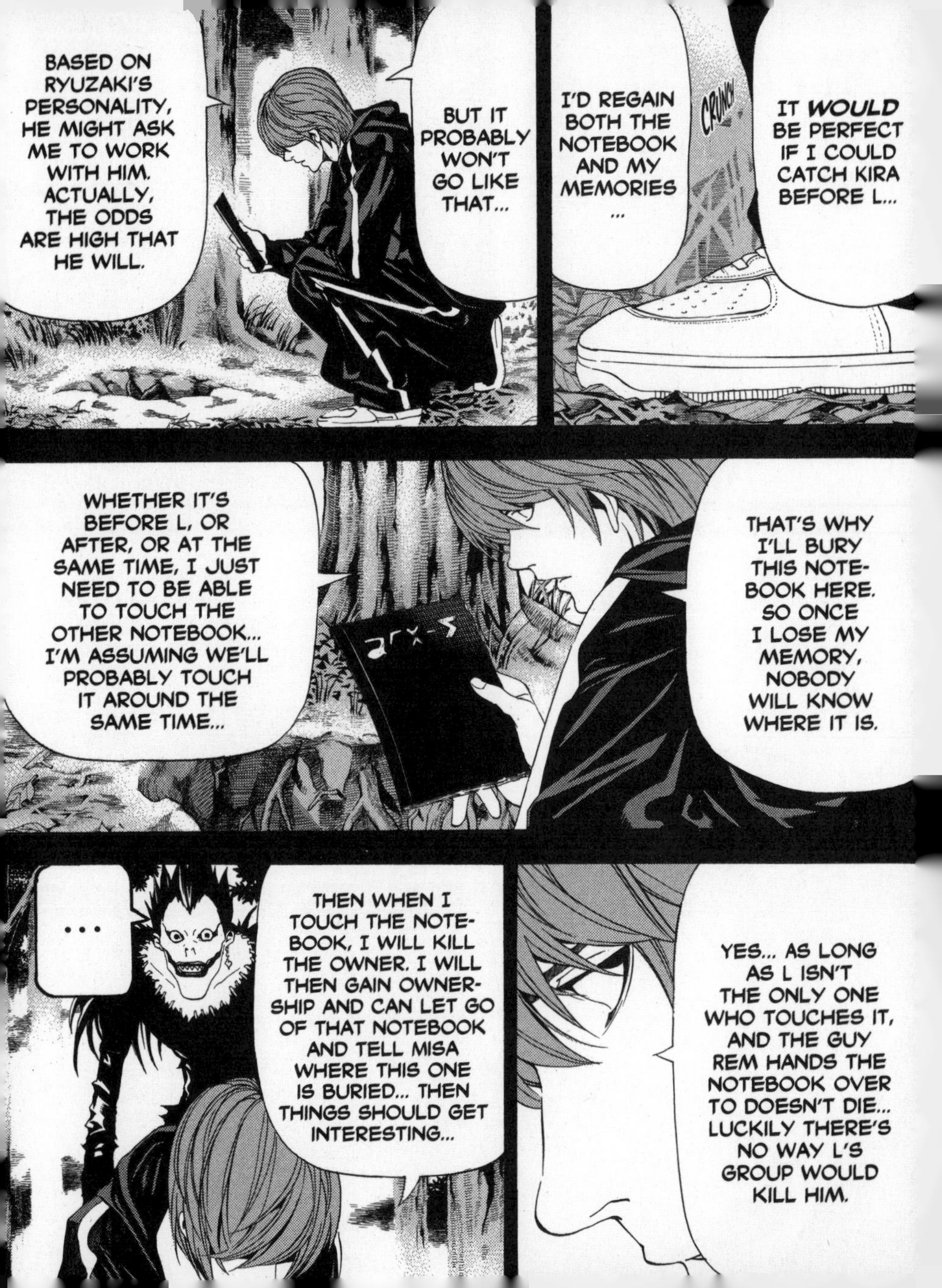
IT *WOULD* BE PERFECT IF I COULD CATCH KIRA BEFORE L...
CRUNCH
I'D REGAIN BOTH THE NOTEBOOK AND MY MEMORIES ...
BUT IT PROBABLY WON'T GO LIKE THAT...
BASED ON RYUZAKI'S PERSONALITY, HE MIGHT ASK ME TO WORK WITH HIM. ACTUALLY, THE ODDS ARE HIGH THAT HE WILL.
THAT'S WHY I'LL BURY THIS NOTEBOOK HERE. SO ONCE I LOSE MY MEMORY, NOBODY WILL KNOW WHERE IT IS.
WHETHER IT'S BEFORE L, OR AFTER, OR AT THE SAME TIME, I JUST NEED TO BE ABLE TO TOUCH THE OTHER NOTEBOOK... I'M ASSUMING WE'LL PROBABLY TOUCH IT AROUND THE SAME TIME...
YES... AS LONG AS L ISN'T THE ONLY ONE WHO TOUCHES IT, AND THE GUY REM HANDS THE NOTEBOOK OVER TO DOESN'T DIE... LUCKILY THERE'S NO WAY L'S GROUP WOULD KILL HIM.
THEN WHEN I TOUCH THE NOTEBOOK, I WILL KILL THE OWNER. I WILL THEN GAIN OWNERSHIP AND CAN LET GO OF THAT NOTEBOOK AND TELL MISA WHERE THIS ONE IS BURIED... THEN THINGS SHOULD GET INTERESTING...
...

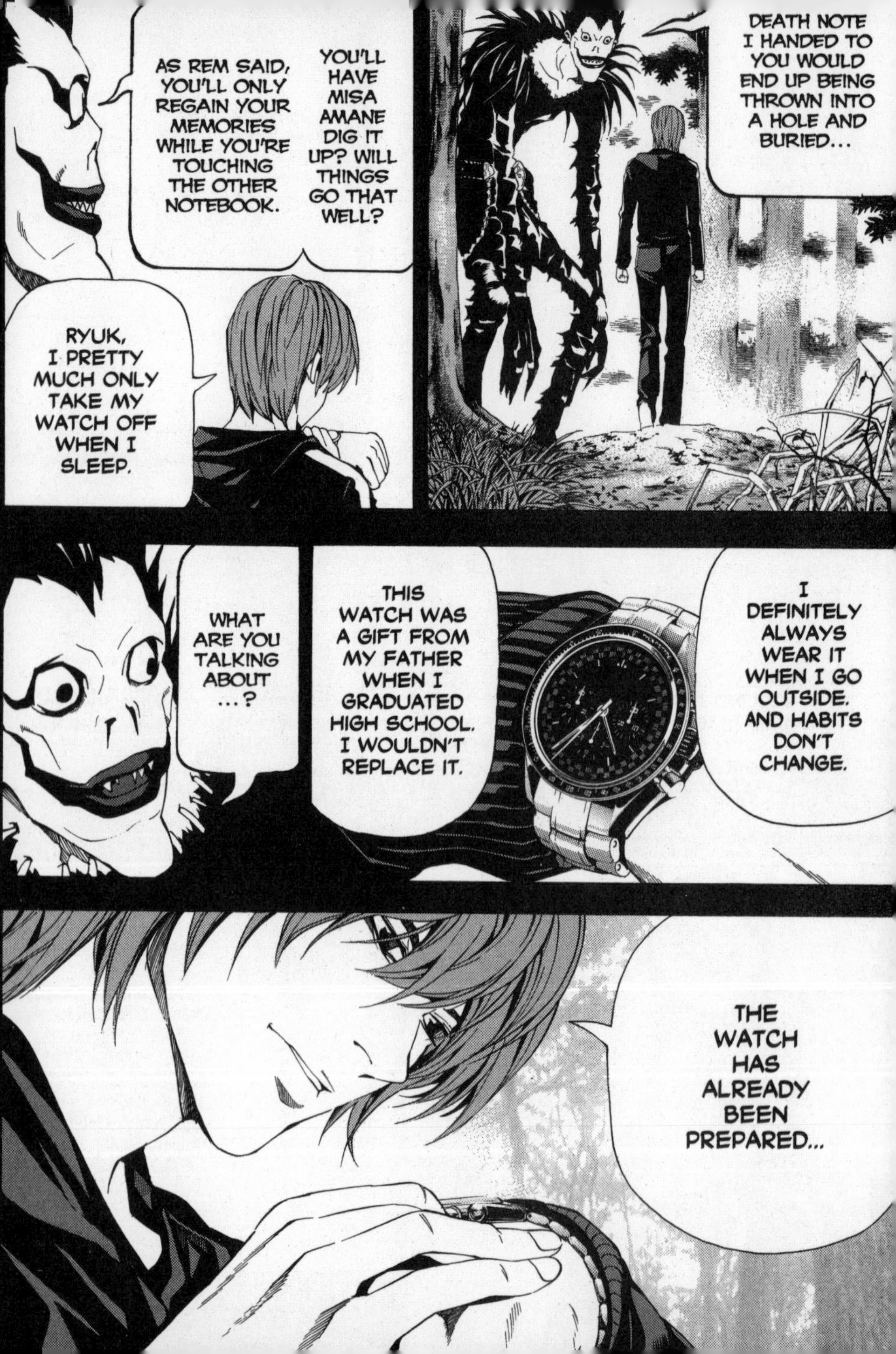
DEATH NOTE I HANDED TO YOU WOULD END UP BEING THROWN INTO A HOLE AND BURIED...
YOU'LL HAVE MISA AMANE DIG IT UP? WILL THINGS GO THAT WELL?
AS REM SAID, YOU'LL ONLY REGAIN YOUR MEMORIES WHILE YOU'RE TOUCHING THE OTHER NOTEBOOK.
RYUK, I PRETTY MUCH ONLY TAKE MY WATCH OFF WHEN I SLEEP.
I DEFINITELY ALWAYS WEAR IT WHEN I GO OUTSIDE. AND HABITS DON'T CHANGE.
THIS WATCH WAS A GIFT FROM MY FATHER WHEN I GRADUATED HIGH SCHOOL. I WOULDN'T REPLACE IT.
WHAT ARE YOU TALKING ABOUT ...?
THE WATCH HAS ALREADY BEEN PREPARED...

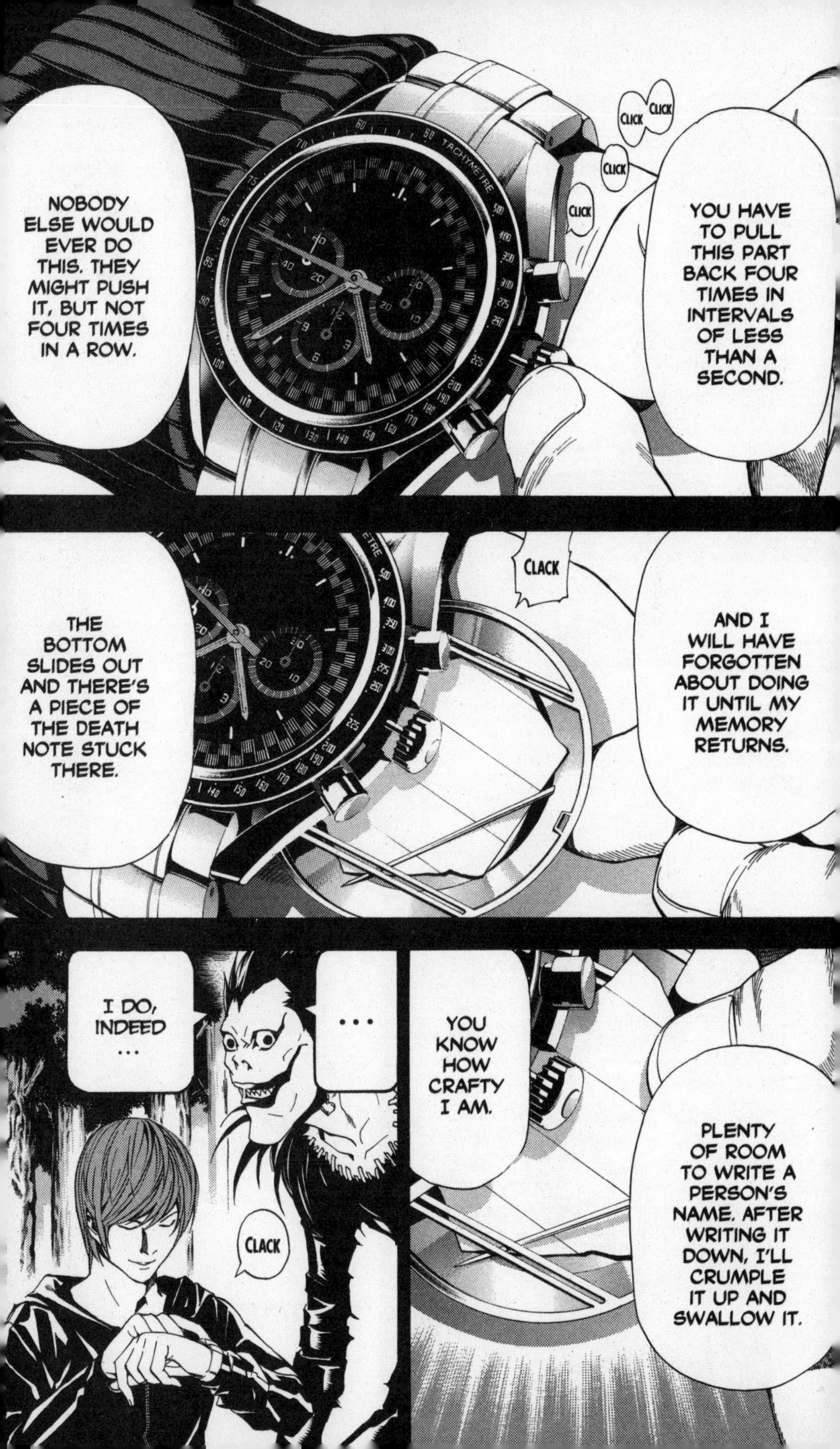
CLICK
CLICK
CLICK
CLICK
YOU HAVE TO PULL THIS PART BACK FOUR TIMES IN INTERVALS OF LESS THAN A SECOND.
NOBODY ELSE WOULD EVER DO THIS. THEY MIGHT PUSH IT, BUT NOT FOUR TIMES IN A ROW.
CLACK
AND I WILL HAVE FORGOTTEN ABOUT DOING IT UNTIL MY MEMORY RETURNS.
THE BOTTOM SLIDES OUT AND THERE'S A PIECE OF THE DEATH NOTE STUCK THERE.
PLENTY OF ROOM TO WRITE A PERSON'S NAME. AFTER WRITING IT DOWN, I'LL CRUMPLE IT UP AND SWALLOW IT.
YOU KNOW HOW CRAFTY I AM.
...
I DO, INDEED ...
CLACK

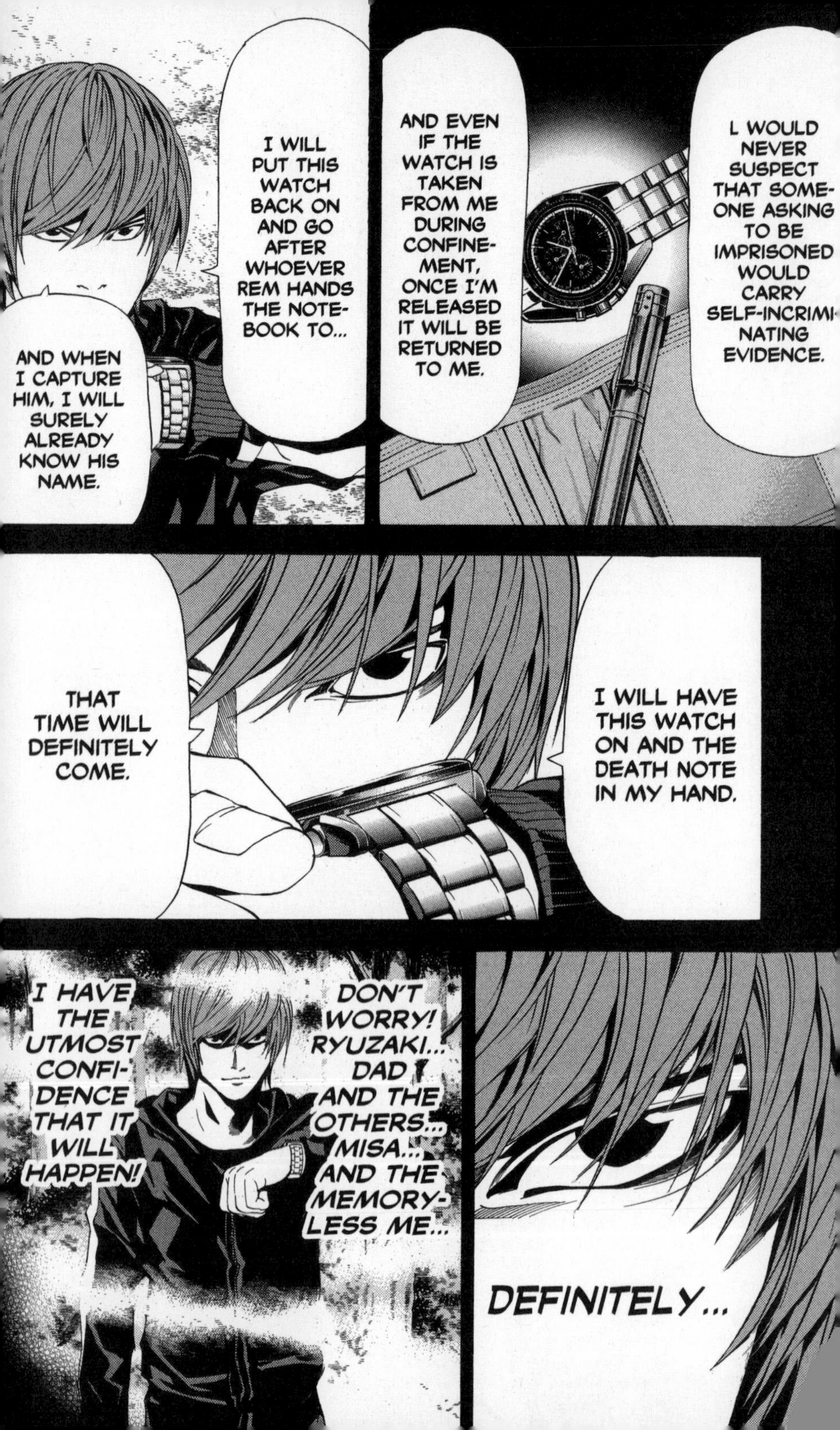
L WOULD NEVER SUSPECT THAT SOMEONE ASKING TO BE IMPRISONED WOULD CARRY SELF-INCRIMINATING EVIDENCE.
AND EVEN IF THE WATCH IS TAKEN FROM ME DURING CONFINEMENT, ONCE I'M RELEASED IT WILL BE RETURNED TO ME.
I WILL PUT THIS WATCH BACK ON AND GO AFTER WHOEVER REM HANDS THE NOTEBOOK TO...
AND WHEN I CAPTURE HIM, I WILL SURELY ALREADY KNOW HIS NAME.
I WILL HAVE THIS WATCH ON AND THE DEATH NOTE IN MY HAND.
THAT TIME WILL DEFINITELY COME.
DEFINITELY...
DON'T WORRY! RYUZAKI... DAD AND THE OTHERS... MISA... AND THE MEMORYLESS ME...
I HAVE THE UTMOST CONFIDENCE THAT IT WILL HAPPEN!

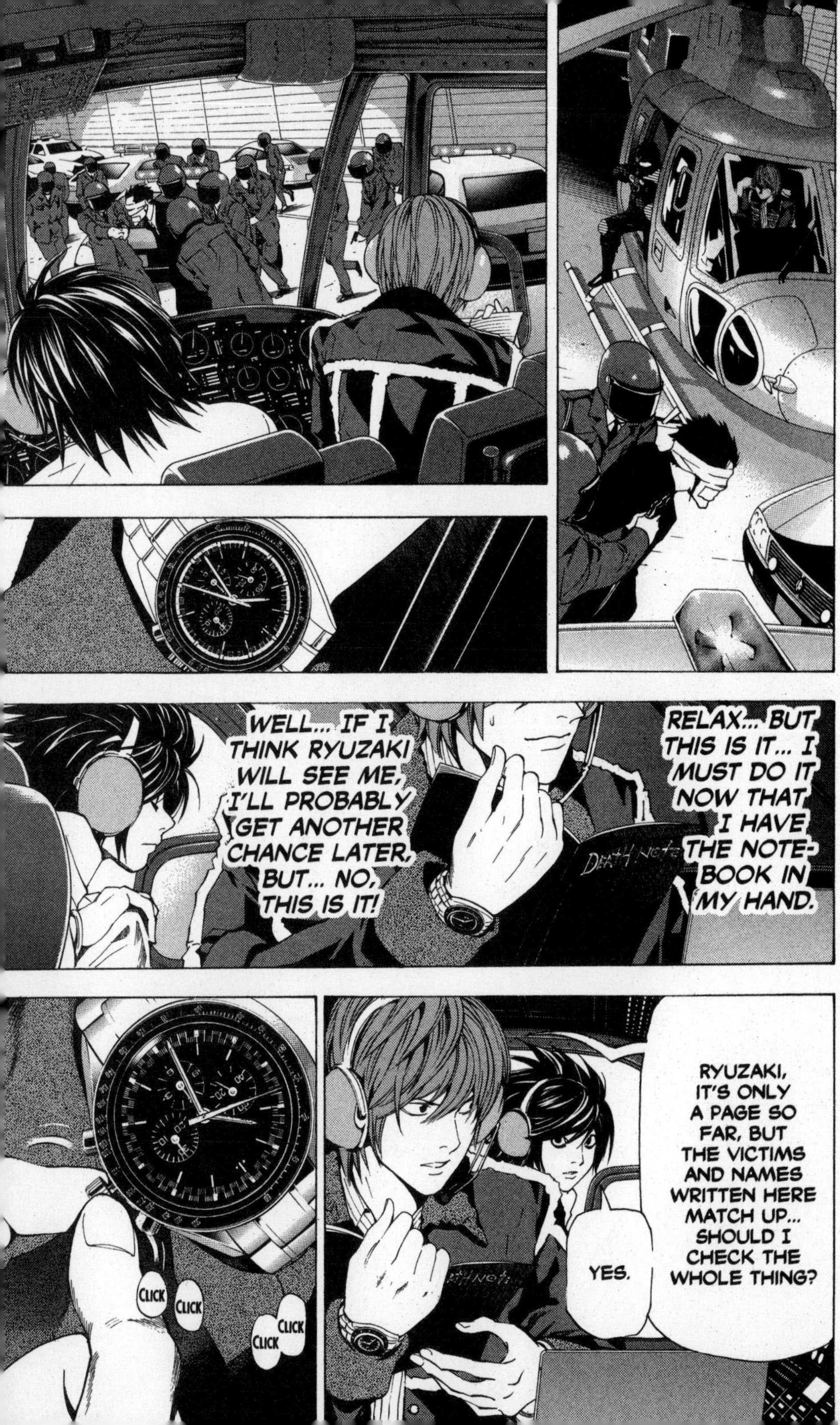
RELAX... BUT THIS IS IT... I MUST DO IT NOW THAT I HAVE THE NOTE-BOOK IN MY HAND.
WELL... IF I THINK RYUZAKI WILL SEE ME, I'LL PROBABLY GET ANOTHER CHANCE LATER, BUT... NO, THIS IS IT!
DEATH NOTE
RYUZAKI, IT'S ONLY A PAGE SO FAR, BUT THE VICTIMS AND NAMES WRITTEN HERE MATCH UP... SHOULD I CHECK THE WHOLE THING?
YES.
CLICK
CLICK
CLICK
CLICK

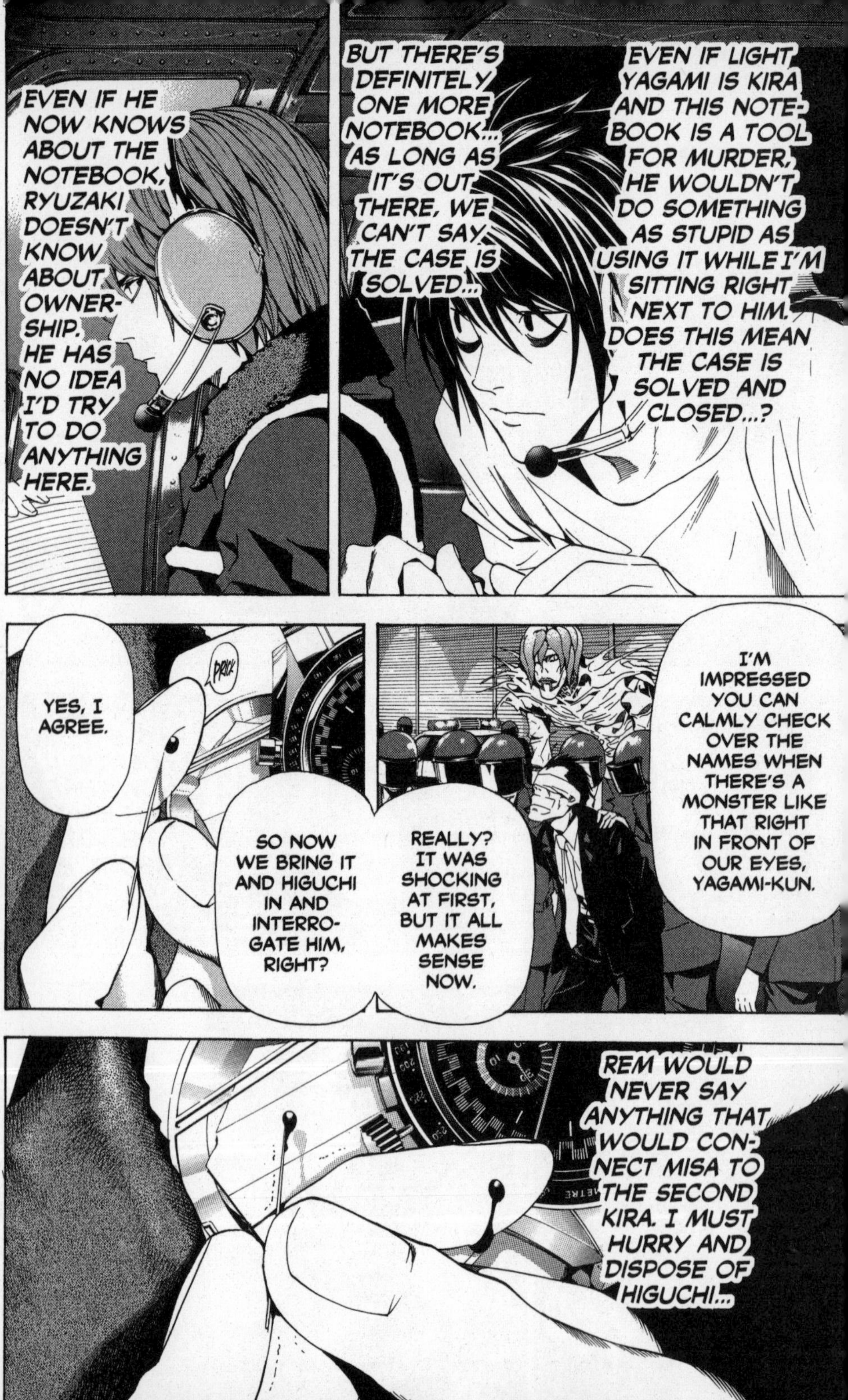

EVEN IF LIGHT YAGAMI IS KIRA AND THIS NOTEBOOK IS A TOOL FOR MURDER, HE WOULDN'T DO SOMETHING AS STUPID AS USING IT WHILE I'M SITTING RIGHT NEXT TO HIM. DOES THIS MEAN THE CASE IS SOLVED AND CLOSED...?
BUT THERE'S DEFINITELY ONE MORE NOTEBOOK... AS LONG AS IT'S OUT THERE, WE CAN'T SAY THE CASE IS SOLVED...
EVEN IF HE NOW KNOWS ABOUT THE NOTEBOOK, RYUZAKI DOESN'T KNOW ABOUT OWNERSHIP. HE HAS NO IDEA I'D TRY TO DO ANYTHING HERE.
I'M IMPRESSED YOU CAN CALMLY CHECK OVER THE NAMES WHEN THERE'S A MONSTER LIKE THAT RIGHT IN FRONT OF OUR EYES, YAGAMI-KUN.
REALLY? IT WAS SHOCKING AT FIRST, BUT IT ALL MAKES SENSE NOW.
SO NOW WE BRING IT AND HIGUCHI IN AND INTERROGATE HIM, RIGHT?
PRICK
YES, I AGREE.
REM WOULD NEVER SAY ANYTHING THAT WOULD CONNECT MISA TO THE SECOND KIRA. I MUST HURRY AND DISPOSE OF HIGUCHI...

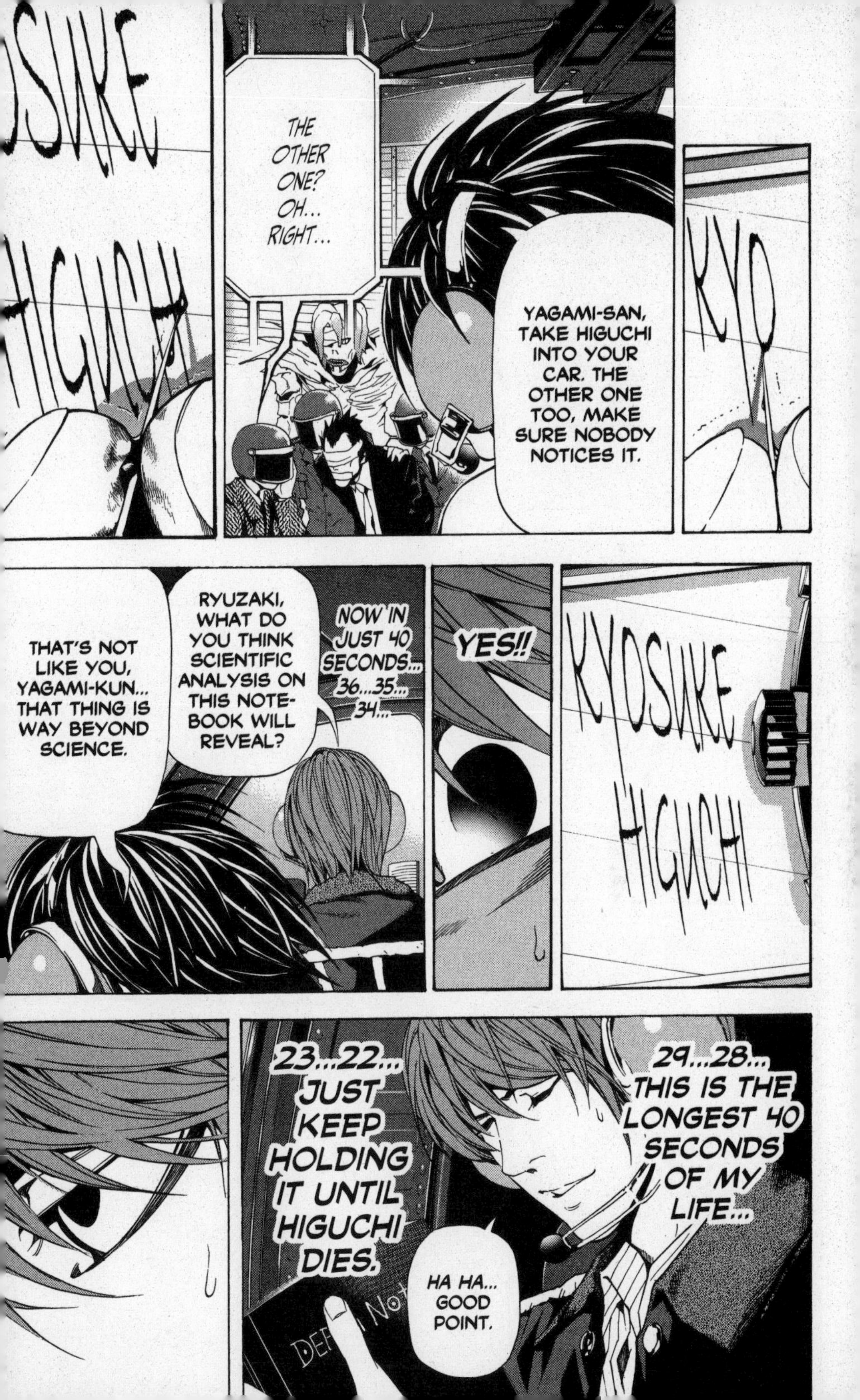
KYO
YAGAMI-SAN, TAKE HIGUCHI INTO YOUR CAR. THE OTHER ONE TOO, MAKE SURE NOBODY NOTICES IT.
THE OTHER ONE? OH... RIGHT...
OSUKE
HIGUCHI
KYOSUKE HIGUCHI
YES!!
NOW IN JUST 40 SECONDS... 36...35... 34...
RYUZAKI, WHAT DO YOU THINK SCIENTIFIC ANALYSIS ON THIS NOTE-BOOK WILL REVEAL?
THAT'S NOT LIKE YOU, YAGAMI-KUN... THAT THING IS WAY BEYOND SCIENCE.
29...28... THIS IS THE LONGEST 40 SECONDS OF MY LIFE...
23...22... JUST KEEP HOLDING IT UNTIL HIGUCHI DIES.
HA HA... GOOD POINT.

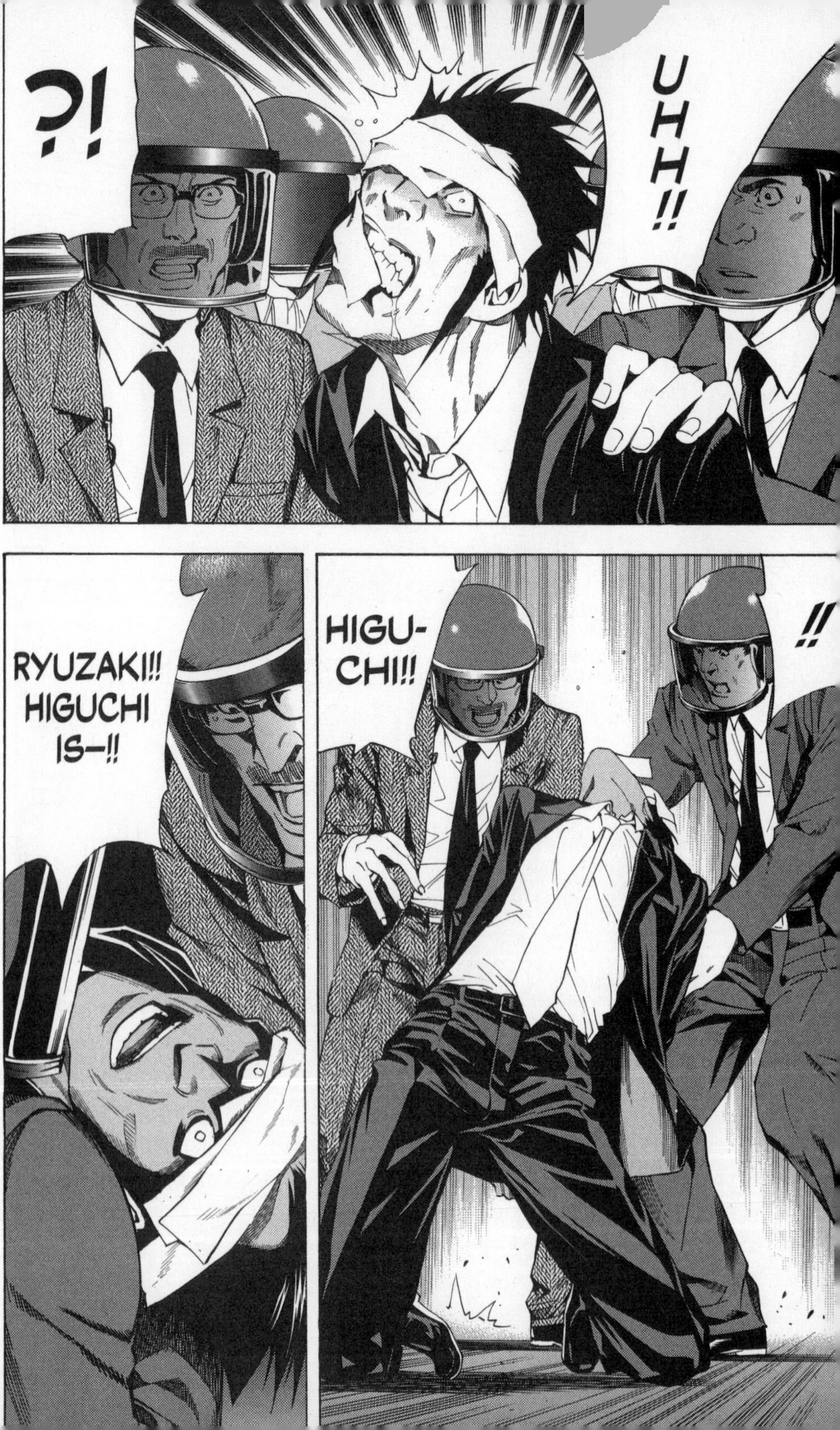
UHH!!
?!
!!
HIGU-CHI!!
RYUZAKI!! HIGUCHI IS–!!

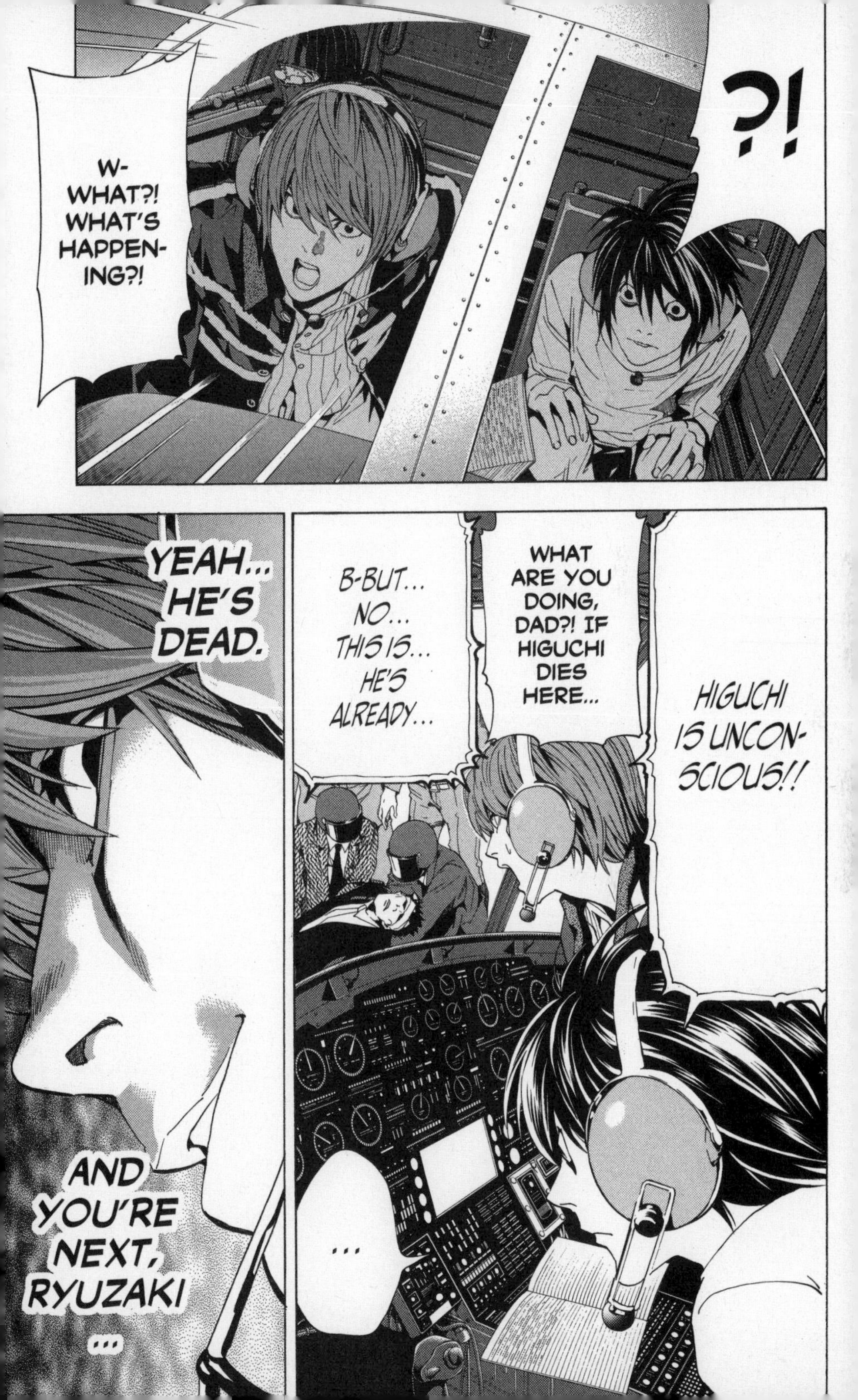
?!
W-WHAT?! WHAT'S HAPPENING?!
HIGUCHI IS UNCONSCIOUS!!
WHAT ARE YOU DOING, DAD?! IF HIGUCHI DIES HERE...
B-BUT... NO... THIS IS... HE'S ALREADY...
...
YEAH... HE'S DEAD.
AND YOU'RE NEXT, RYUZAKI ...

# DEATH NOTE
## How to use it
## XXXVIII

○ You will lose memory of the DEATH NOTE when losing its ownership . But you can regain this memory by either obtaining the ownership once again or by touching the DEATH NOTE. This can be done up to 6 times per DEATH NOTE.

デスノートの所有権をなくした事で、そのノートに関する記憶がなくなり、
再び所有権を得る事か触れる事で記憶が戻るのは、一冊のノートで6回まで。

○ If the 6 times are exceeded, the person's memory of the DEATH NOTE will not return and they will have to use it with out any previous memory of it.

よって、触れたり所有権を得る事で6回記憶を戻し、
さらに同じノートを手にした場合、それを使うならば、
記憶は戻らない状態で新たに使用する事になる。

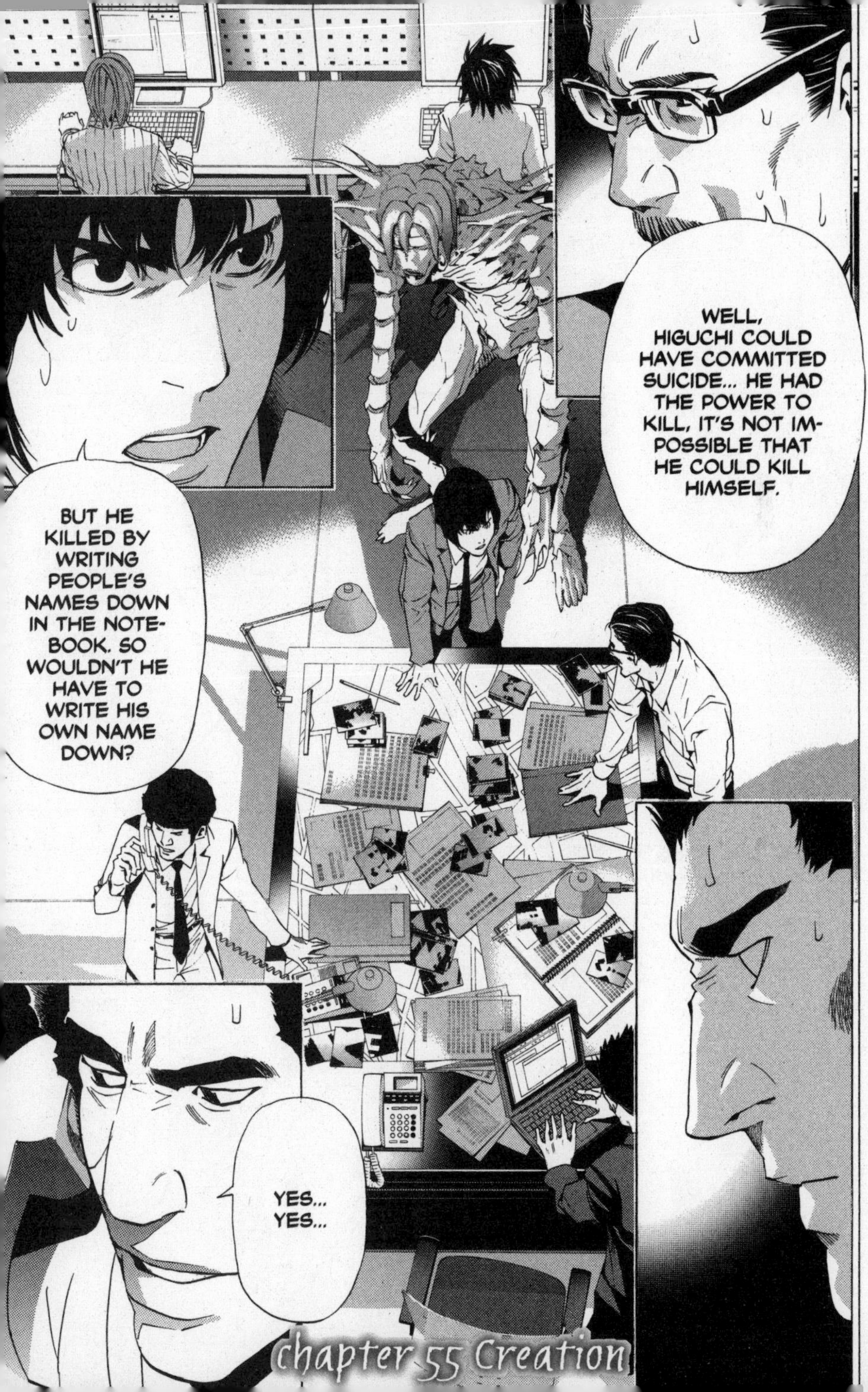
WELL, HIGUCHI COULD HAVE COMMITTED SUICIDE... HE HAD THE POWER TO KILL, IT'S NOT IMPOSSIBLE THAT HE COULD KILL HIMSELF.
BUT HE KILLED BY WRITING PEOPLE'S NAMES DOWN IN THE NOTEBOOK. SO WOULDN'T HE HAVE TO WRITE HIS OWN NAME DOWN?
YES... YES...
chapter 55 Creation

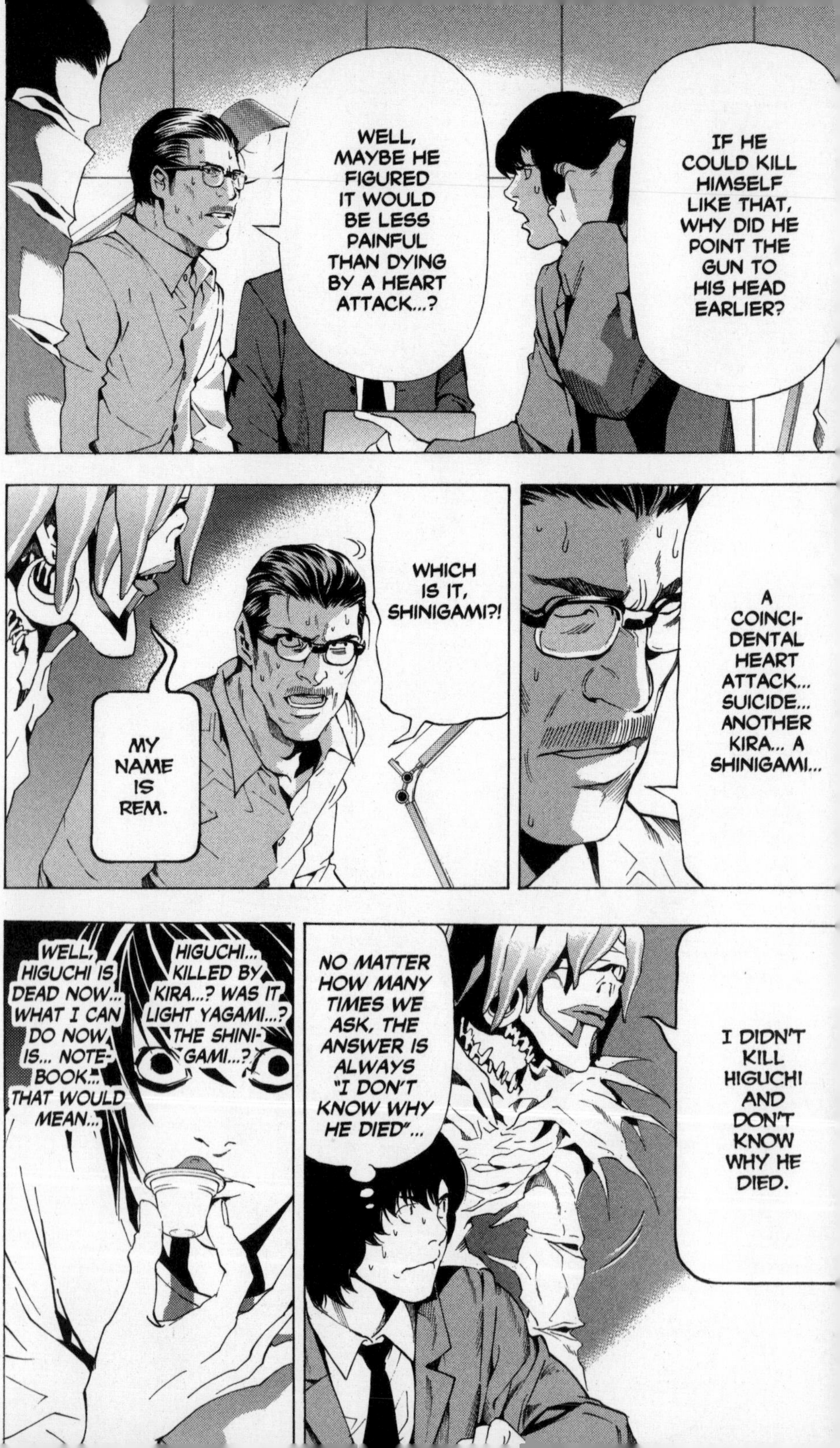
IF HE COULD KILL HIMSELF LIKE THAT, WHY DID HE POINT THE GUN TO HIS HEAD EARLIER?
WELL, MAYBE HE FIGURED IT WOULD BE LESS PAINFUL THAN DYING BY A HEART ATTACK...?
A COINCIDENTAL HEART ATTACK... SUICIDE... ANOTHER KIRA... A SHINIGAMI...
WHICH IS IT, SHINIGAMI?!
MY NAME IS REM.
I DIDN'T KILL HIGUCHI AND DON'T KNOW WHY HE DIED.
NO MATTER HOW MANY TIMES WE ASK, THE ANSWER IS ALWAYS "I DON'T KNOW WHY HE DIED"...
HIGUCHI... KILLED BY KIRA...? WAS IT LIGHT YAGAMI...? THE SHINIGAMI...?
WELL, HIGUCHI IS DEAD NOW... WHAT I CAN DO NOW IS... NOTEBOOK... THAT WOULD MEAN...

READ THIS WAY

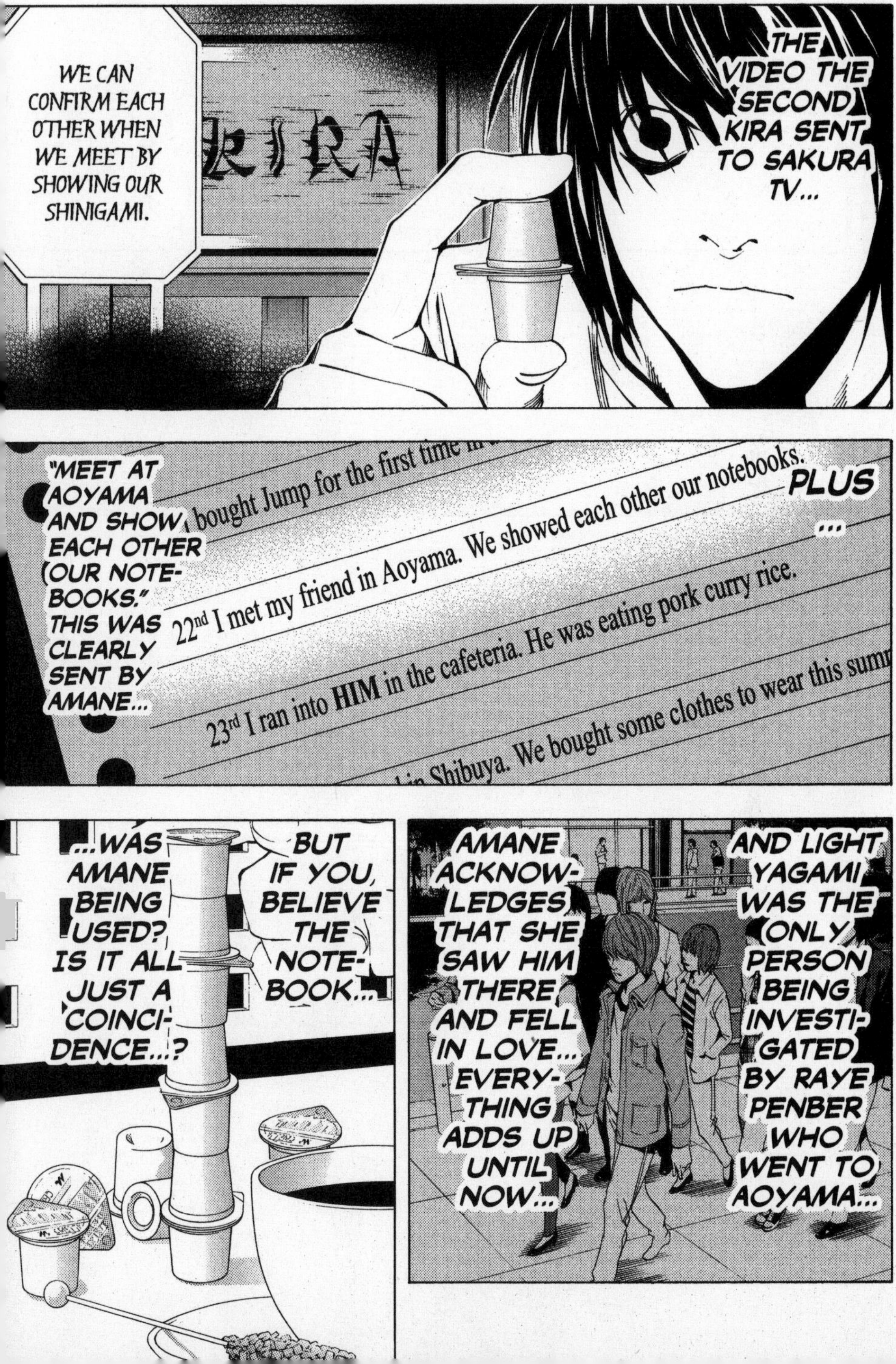
THE VIDEO THE SECOND KIRA SENT TO SAKURA TV...
WE CAN CONFIRM EACH OTHER WHEN WE MEET BY SHOWING OUR SHINIGAMI.
KIRA
PLUS...
"MEET AT AOYAMA AND SHOW EACH OTHER OUR NOTEBOOKS." THIS WAS CLEARLY SENT BY AMANE...
bought Jump for the first time
22nd I met my friend in Aoyama. We showed each other our notebooks.
23rd I ran into HIM in the cafeteria. He was eating pork curry rice.
in Shibuya. We bought some clothes to wear this
AND LIGHT YAGAMI WAS THE ONLY PERSON BEING INVESTIGATED BY RAYE PENBER WHO WENT TO AOYAMA...
AMANE ACKNOWLEDGES THAT SHE SAW HIM THERE AND FELL IN LOVE... EVERYTHING ADDS UP UNTIL NOW...
BUT IF YOU BELIEVE THE NOTEBOOK...
...WAS AMANE BEING USED? IS IT ALL JUST A COINCIDENCE...?

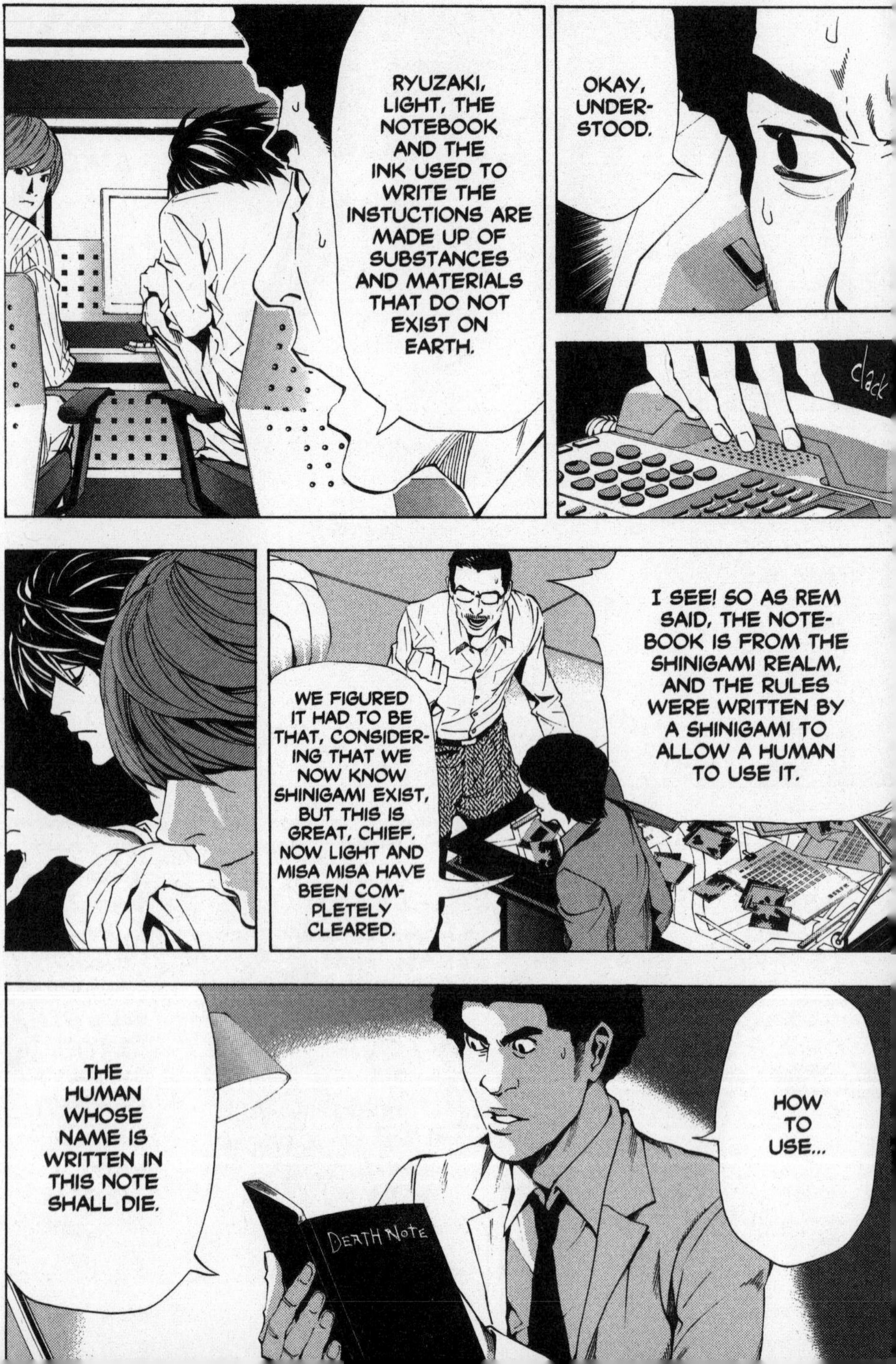
OKAY, UNDER-STOOD.
clack
RYUZAKI, LIGHT, THE NOTEBOOK AND THE INK USED TO WRITE THE INSTUCTIONS ARE MADE UP OF SUBSTANCES AND MATERIALS THAT DO NOT EXIST ON EARTH.
I SEE! SO AS REM SAID, THE NOTE-BOOK IS FROM THE SHINIGAMI REALM, AND THE RULES WERE WRITTEN BY A SHINIGAMI TO ALLOW A HUMAN TO USE IT.
WE FIGURED IT HAD TO BE THAT, CONSIDER-ING THAT WE NOW KNOW SHINIGAMI EXIST, BUT THIS IS GREAT, CHIEF. NOW LIGHT AND MISA MISA HAVE BEEN COM-PLETELY CLEARED.
HOW TO USE...
THE HUMAN WHOSE NAME IS WRITTEN IN THIS NOTE SHALL DIE.
DEATH NOTE

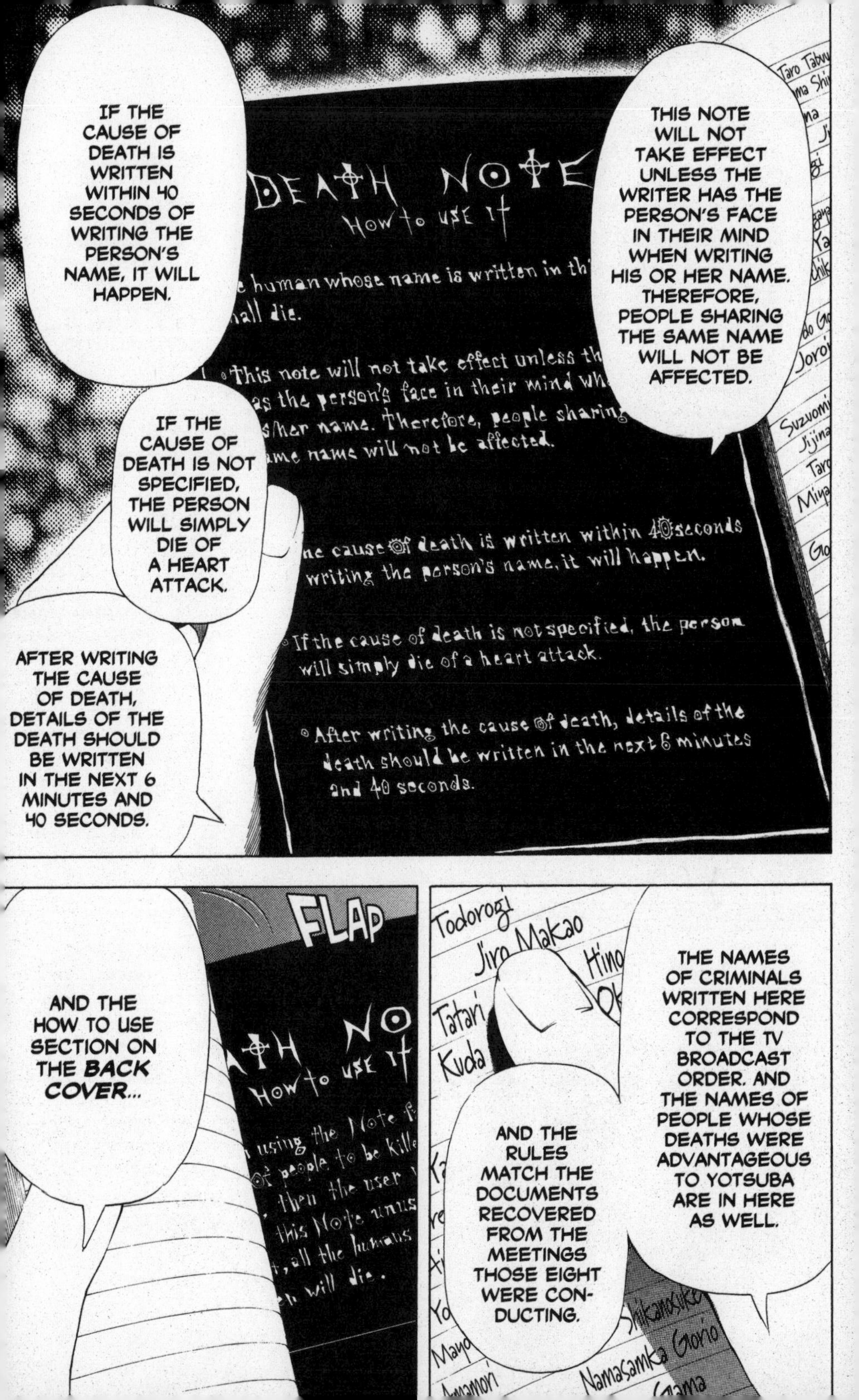
THIS NOTE WILL NOT TAKE EFFECT UNLESS THE WRITER HAS THE PERSON'S FACE IN THEIR MIND WHEN WRITING HIS OR HER NAME. THEREFORE, PEOPLE SHARING THE SAME NAME WILL NOT BE AFFECTED.
IF THE CAUSE OF DEATH IS WRITTEN WITHIN 40 SECONDS OF WRITING THE PERSON'S NAME, IT WILL HAPPEN.
DEATH NOTE
How to use it
• This note will not take effect unless th
as the person's face in their mind wh
s/her name. Therefore, people sharing
ame name will not be affected.
ne cause of death is written within 40 seconds
writing the person's name, it will happen.
• If the cause of death is not specified, the person will simply die of a heart attack.
• After writing the cause of death, details of the death should be written in the next 6 minutes and 40 seconds.
Suzuomi
Jijina
IF THE CAUSE OF DEATH IS NOT SPECIFIED, THE PERSON WILL SIMPLY DIE OF A HEART ATTACK.
AFTER WRITING THE CAUSE OF DEATH, DETAILS OF THE DEATH SHOULD BE WRITTEN IN THE NEXT 6 MINUTES AND 40 SECONDS.
Todorogi
Jiro Makao
Tatari
Kuda
Shikanosuke
Namasamka Gorio
THE NAMES OF CRIMINALS WRITTEN HERE CORRESPOND TO THE TV BROADCAST ORDER. AND THE NAMES OF PEOPLE WHOSE DEATHS WERE ADVANTAGEOUS TO YOTSUBA ARE IN HERE AS WELL.
AND THE RULES MATCH THE DOCUMENTS RECOVERED FROM THE MEETINGS THOSE EIGHT WERE CON-DUCTING.
FLAP
How to use it
AND THE HOW TO USE SECTION ON THE *BACK COVER*...

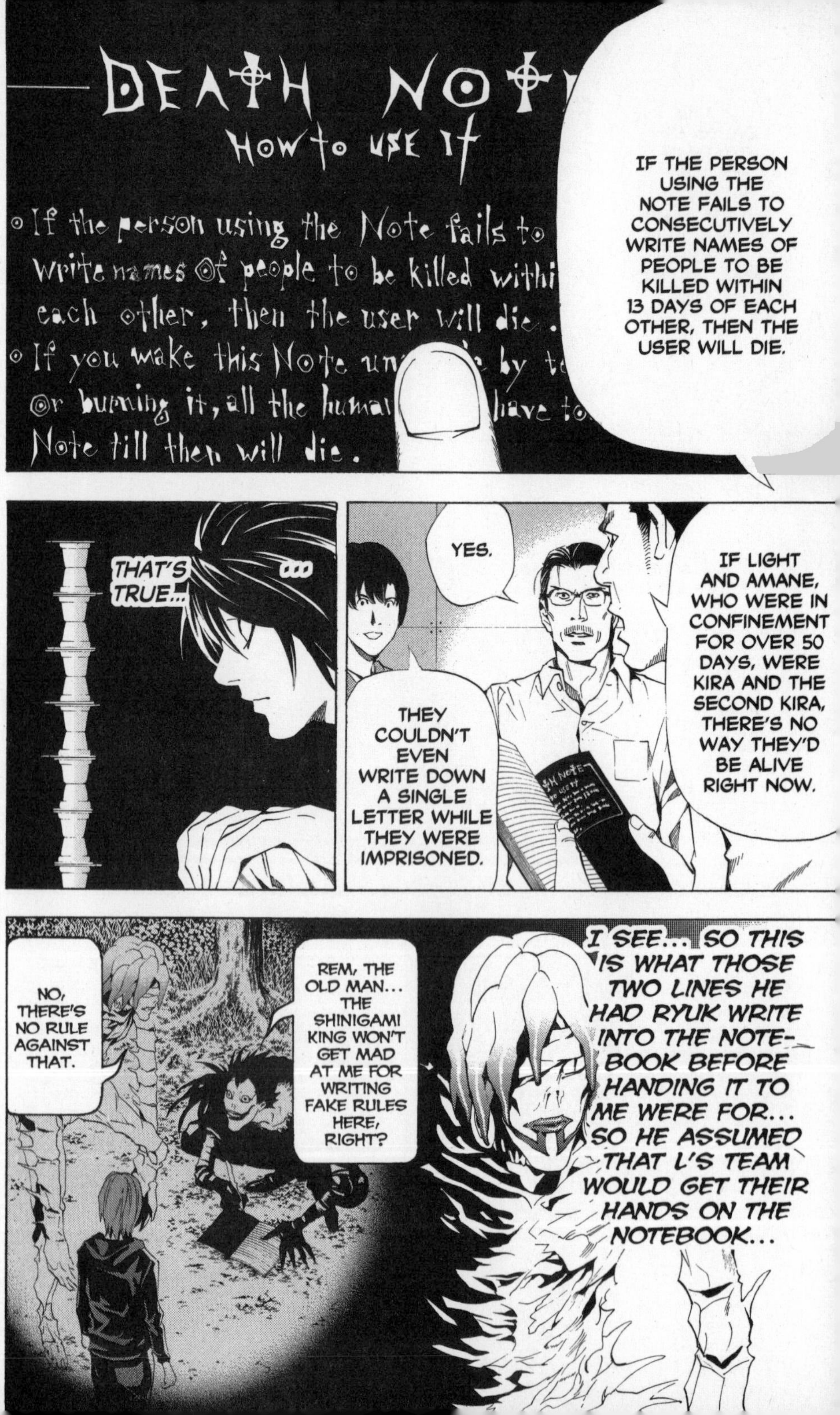
IF THE PERSON USING THE NOTE FAILS TO CONSECUTIVELY WRITE NAMES OF PEOPLE TO BE KILLED WITHIN 13 DAYS OF EACH OTHER, THEN THE USER WILL DIE.
DEATH NOT
How to use it
If the person using the Note fails to
write names of people to be killed withi
each other, then the user will die.
If you make this Note un
or burning it, all the huma
Note till then will die.
IF LIGHT AND AMANE, WHO WERE IN CONFINEMENT FOR OVER 50 DAYS, WERE KIRA AND THE SECOND KIRA, THERE'S NO WAY THEY'D BE ALIVE RIGHT NOW.
YES.
THEY COULDN'T EVEN WRITE DOWN A SINGLE LETTER WHILE THEY WERE IMPRISONED.
...
THAT'S TRUE...
I SEE... SO THIS IS WHAT THOSE TWO LINES HE HAD RYUK WRITE INTO THE NOTE-BOOK BEFORE HANDING IT TO ME WERE FOR... SO HE ASSUMED THAT L'S TEAM WOULD GET THEIR HANDS ON THE NOTEBOOK...
REM, THE OLD MAN... THE SHINIGAMI KING WON'T GET MAD AT ME FOR WRITING FAKE RULES HERE, RIGHT?
NO, THERE'S NO RULE AGAINST THAT.

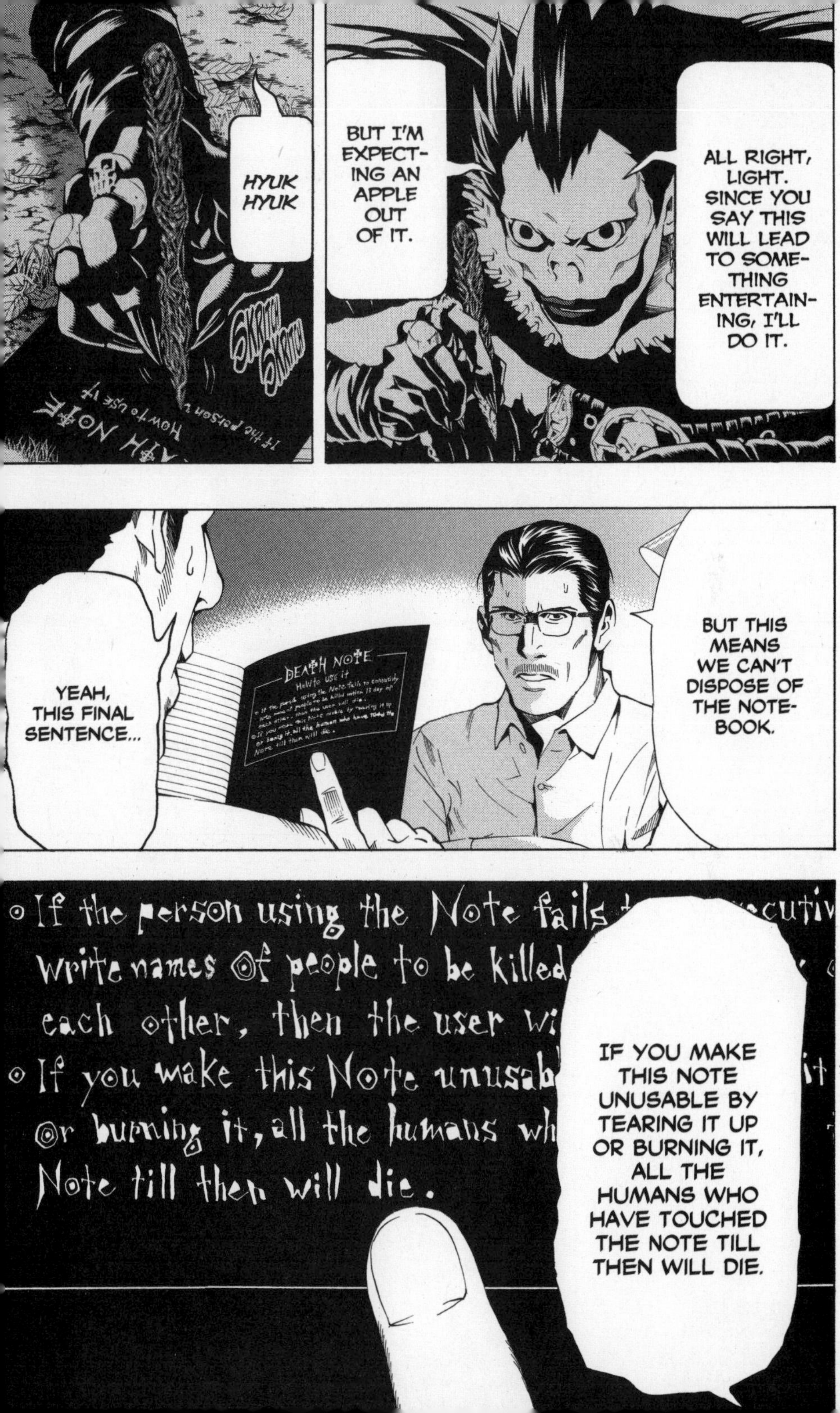
ALL RIGHT, LIGHT. SINCE YOU SAY THIS WILL LEAD TO SOMETHING ENTERTAINING, I'LL DO IT.
BUT I'M EXPECTING AN APPLE OUT OF IT.
HYUK HYUK
SKRITCH SKRITCH
BUT THIS MEANS WE CAN'T DISPOSE OF THE NOTEBOOK.
YEAH, THIS FINAL SENTENCE...
DEATH NOTE
IF YOU MAKE THIS NOTE UNUSABLE BY TEARING IT UP OR BURNING IT, ALL THE HUMANS WHO HAVE TOUCHED THE NOTE TILL THEN WILL DIE.
If the person using the Note fails
write names of people to be killed
each other, then the user wi
If you make this Note unusab
or burning it, all the humans wh
Note till then will die.

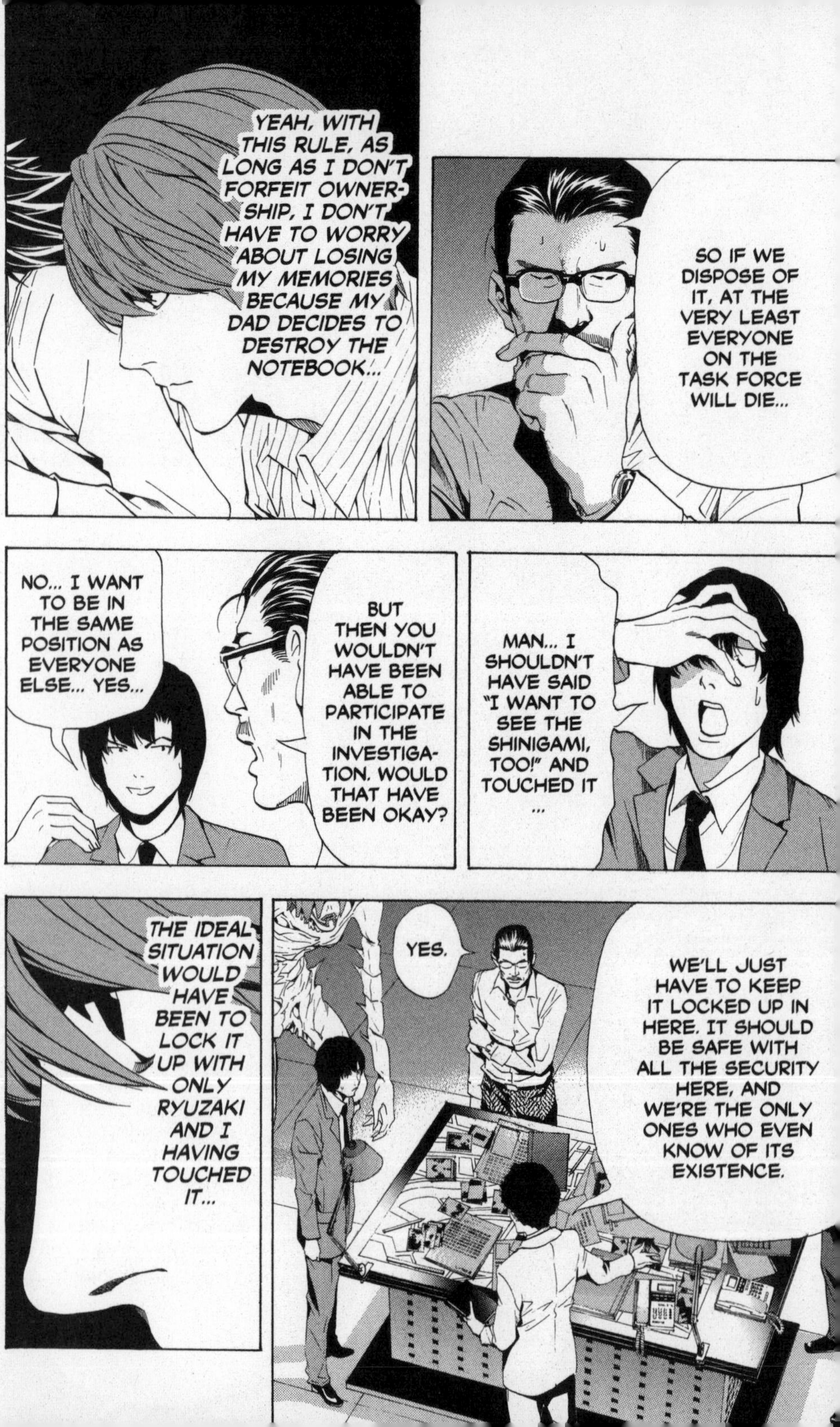
SO IF WE DISPOSE OF IT, AT THE VERY LEAST EVERYONE ON THE TASK FORCE WILL DIE...
YEAH, WITH THIS RULE, AS LONG AS I DON'T FORFEIT OWNERSHIP, I DON'T HAVE TO WORRY ABOUT LOSING MY MEMORIES BECAUSE MY DAD DECIDES TO DESTROY THE NOTEBOOK...
MAN... I SHOULDN'T HAVE SAID "I WANT TO SEE THE SHINIGAMI, TOO!" AND TOUCHED IT ...
BUT THEN YOU WOULDN'T HAVE BEEN ABLE TO PARTICIPATE IN THE INVESTIGATION. WOULD THAT HAVE BEEN OKAY?
NO... I WANT TO BE IN THE SAME POSITION AS EVERYONE ELSE... YES...
WE'LL JUST HAVE TO KEEP IT LOCKED UP IN HERE. IT SHOULD BE SAFE WITH ALL THE SECURITY HERE, AND WE'RE THE ONLY ONES WHO EVEN KNOW OF ITS EXISTENCE.
YES.
THE IDEAL SITUATION WOULD HAVE BEEN TO LOCK IT UP WITH ONLY RYUZAKI AND I HAVING TOUCHED IT...

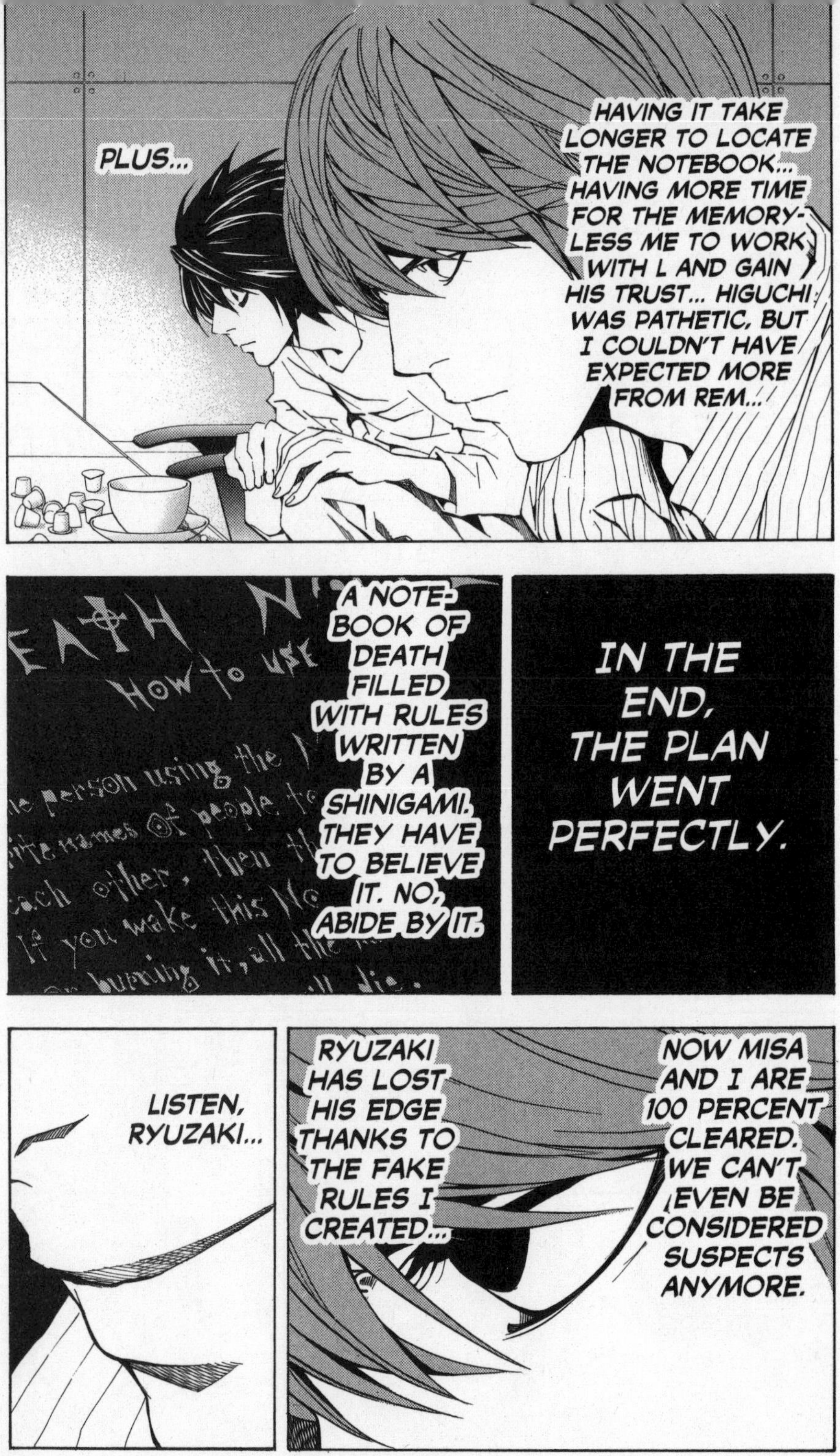
HAVING IT TAKE LONGER TO LOCATE THE NOTEBOOK... HAVING MORE TIME FOR THE MEMORY-LESS ME TO WORK WITH L AND GAIN HIS TRUST... HIGUCHI WAS PATHETIC, BUT I COULDN'T HAVE EXPECTED MORE FROM REM...
PLUS...
IN THE END, THE PLAN WENT PERFECTLY.
A NOTE-BOOK OF DEATH FILLED WITH RULES WRITTEN BY A SHINIGAMI. THEY HAVE TO BELIEVE IT. NO, ABIDE BY IT.
How to use
NOW MISA AND I ARE 100 PERCENT CLEARED. WE CAN'T EVEN BE CONSIDERED SUSPECTS ANYMORE.
RYUZAKI HAS LOST HIS EDGE THANKS TO THE FAKE RULES I CREATED...
LISTEN, RYUZAKI...

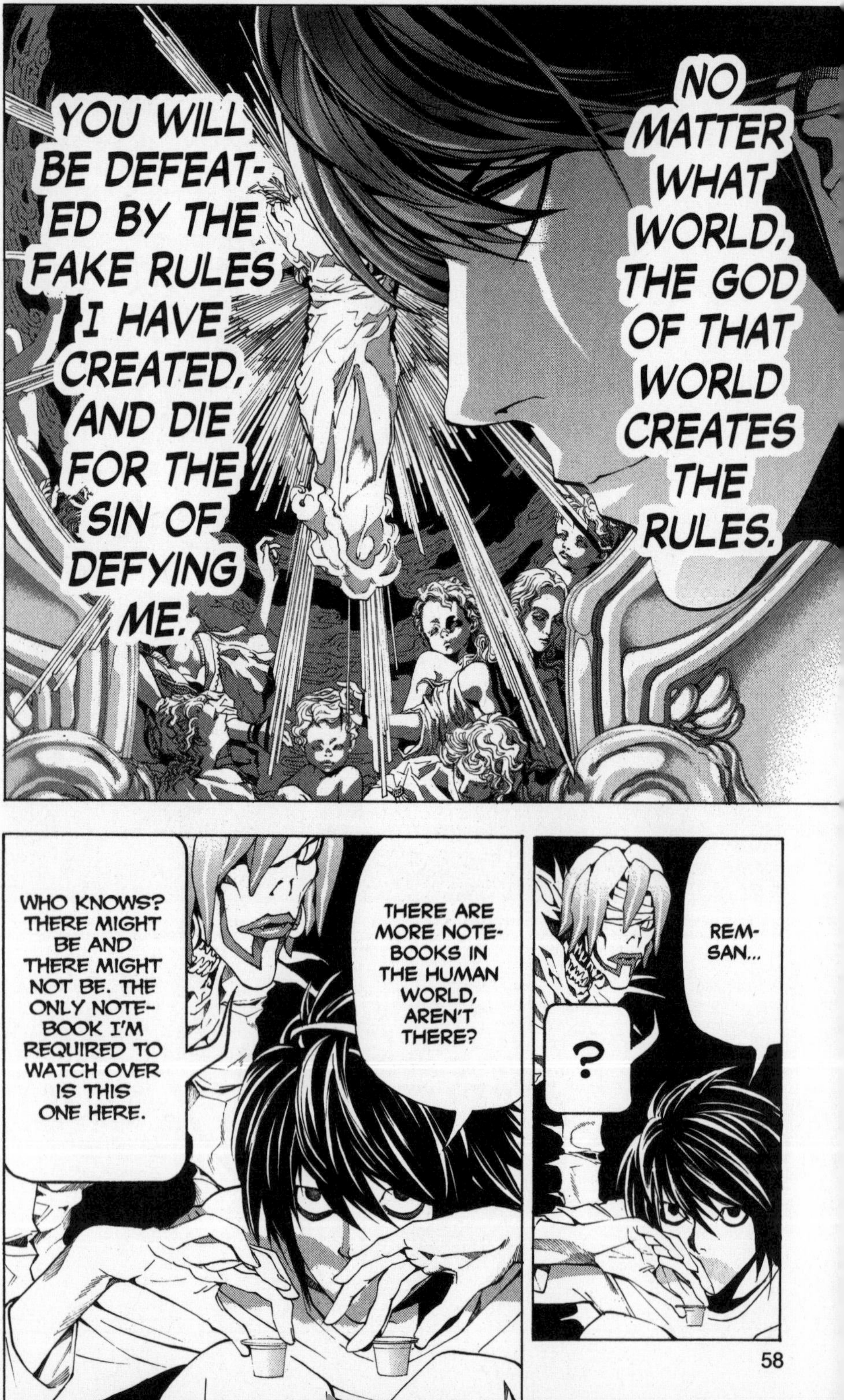
NO MATTER WHAT WORLD, THE GOD OF THAT WORLD CREATES THE RULES.
YOU WILL BE DEFEAT-ED BY THE FAKE RULES I HAVE CREATED, AND DIE FOR THE SIN OF DEFYING ME.
REM-SAN...
?
THERE ARE MORE NOTE-BOOKS IN THE HUMAN WORLD, AREN'T THERE?
WHO KNOWS? THERE MIGHT BE AND THERE MIGHT NOT BE. THE ONLY NOTE-BOOK I'M REQUIRED TO WATCH OVER IS THIS ONE HERE.

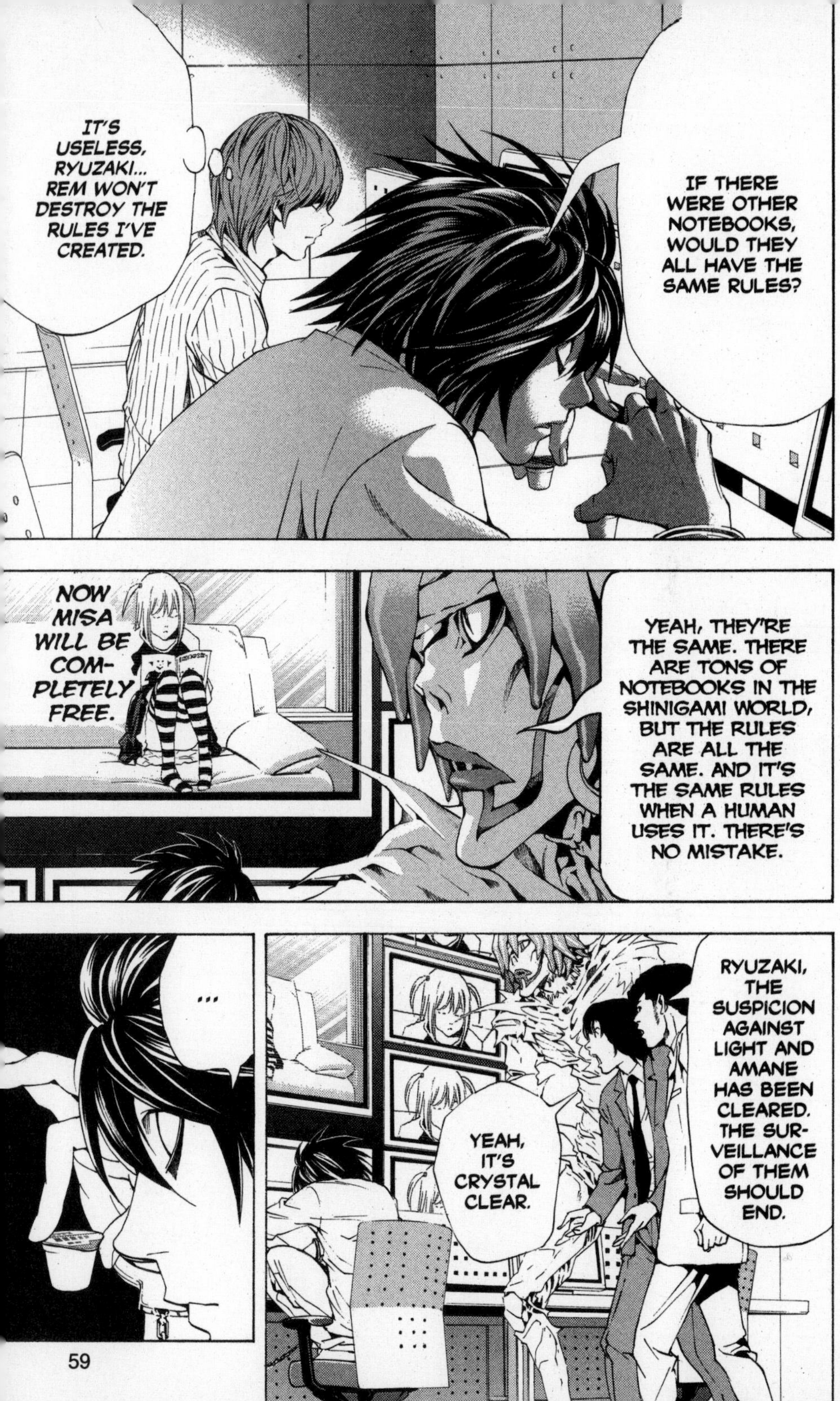
IF THERE WERE OTHER NOTEBOOKS, WOULD THEY ALL HAVE THE SAME RULES?
IT'S USELESS, RYUZAKI... REM WON'T DESTROY THE RULES I'VE CREATED.
YEAH, THEY'RE THE SAME. THERE ARE TONS OF NOTEBOOKS IN THE SHINIGAMI WORLD, BUT THE RULES ARE ALL THE SAME. AND IT'S THE SAME RULES WHEN A HUMAN USES IT. THERE'S NO MISTAKE.
NOW MISA WILL BE COM-PLETELY FREE.
RYUZAKI, THE SUSPICION AGAINST LIGHT AND AMANE HAS BEEN CLEARED. THE SUR-VEILLANCE OF THEM SHOULD END.
YEAH, IT'S CRYSTAL CLEAR.
...

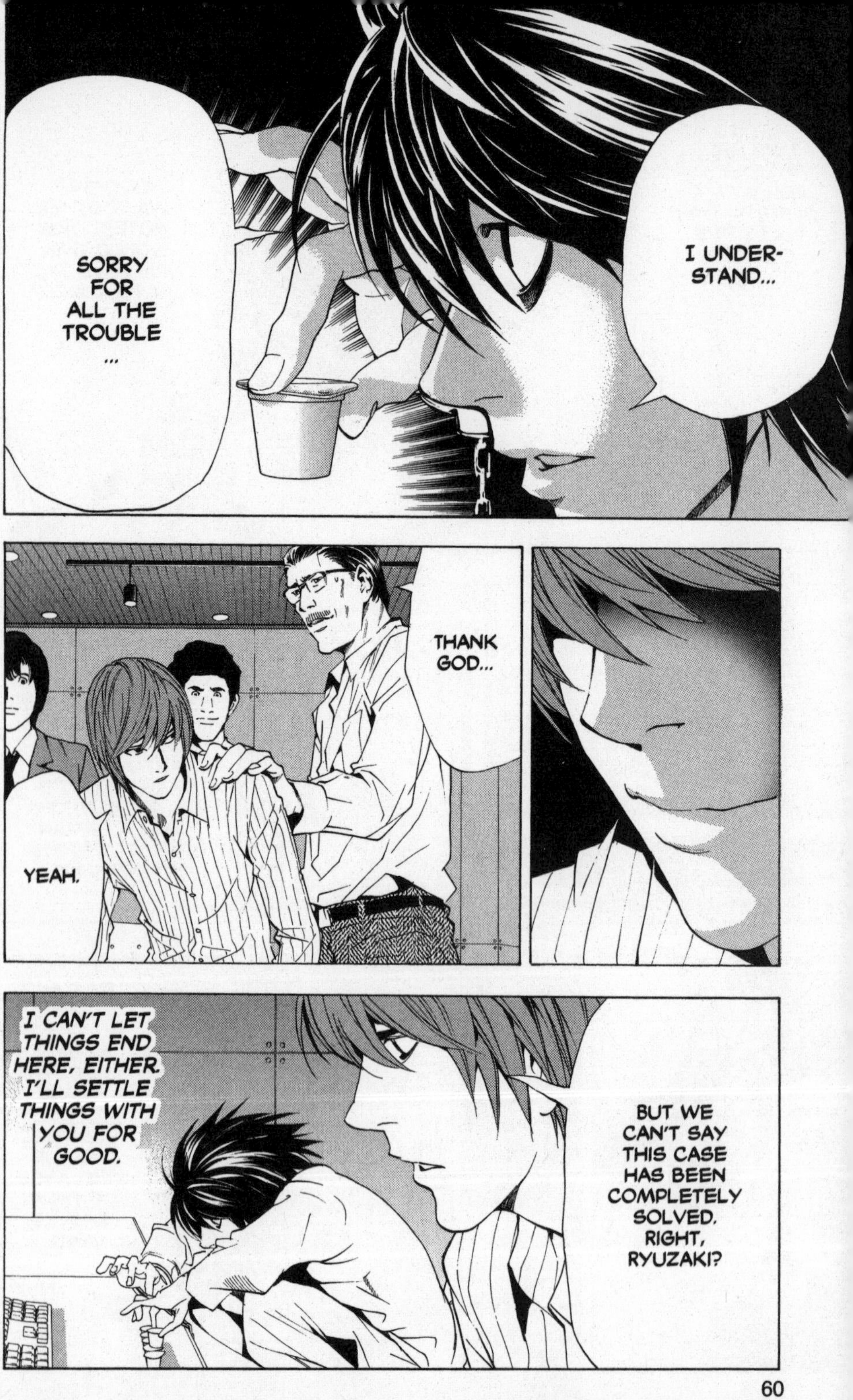
I UNDER-STAND...
SORRY FOR ALL THE TROUBLE ...
THANK GOD...
YEAH.
BUT WE CAN'T SAY THIS CASE HAS BEEN COMPLETELY SOLVED. RIGHT, RYUZAKI?
I CAN'T LET THINGS END HERE, EITHER. I'LL SETTLE THINGS WITH YOU FOR GOOD.

READ THIS WAY

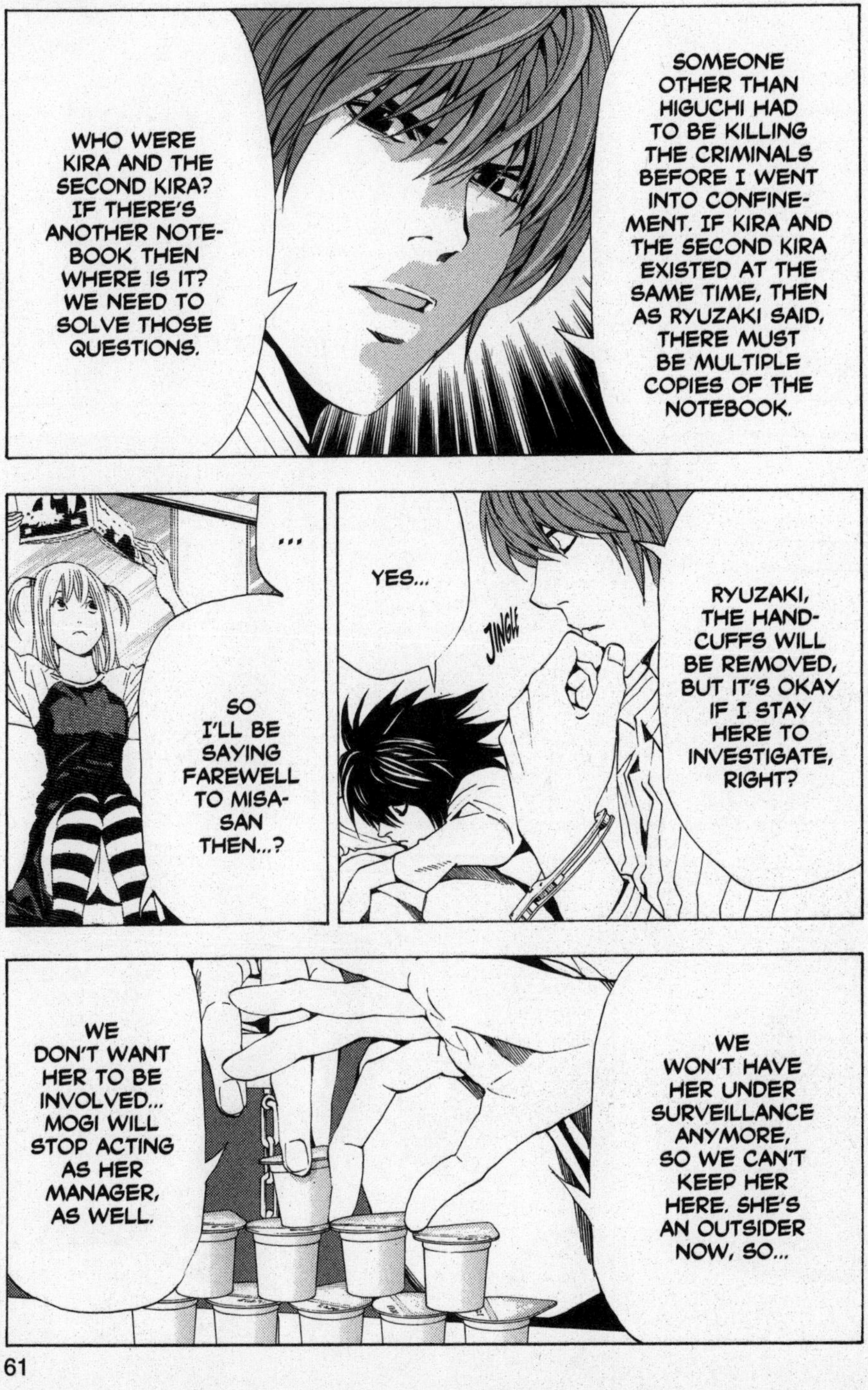

SOMEONE OTHER THAN HIGUCHI HAD TO BE KILLING THE CRIMINALS BEFORE I WENT INTO CONFINEMENT. IF KIRA AND THE SECOND KIRA EXISTED AT THE SAME TIME, THEN AS RYUZAKI SAID, THERE MUST BE MULTIPLE COPIES OF THE NOTEBOOK.
WHO WERE KIRA AND THE SECOND KIRA? IF THERE'S ANOTHER NOTEBOOK THEN WHERE IS IT? WE NEED TO SOLVE THOSE QUESTIONS.
RYUZAKI, THE HANDCUFFS WILL BE REMOVED, BUT IT'S OKAY IF I STAY HERE TO INVESTIGATE, RIGHT?
YES...
JINGLE
...
SO I'LL BE SAYING FAREWELL TO MISA-SAN THEN...?
WE WON'T HAVE HER UNDER SURVEILLANCE ANYMORE, SO WE CAN'T KEEP HER HERE. SHE'S AN OUTSIDER NOW, SO...
WE DON'T WANT HER TO BE INVOLVED... MOGI WILL STOP ACTING AS HER MANAGER, AS WELL.

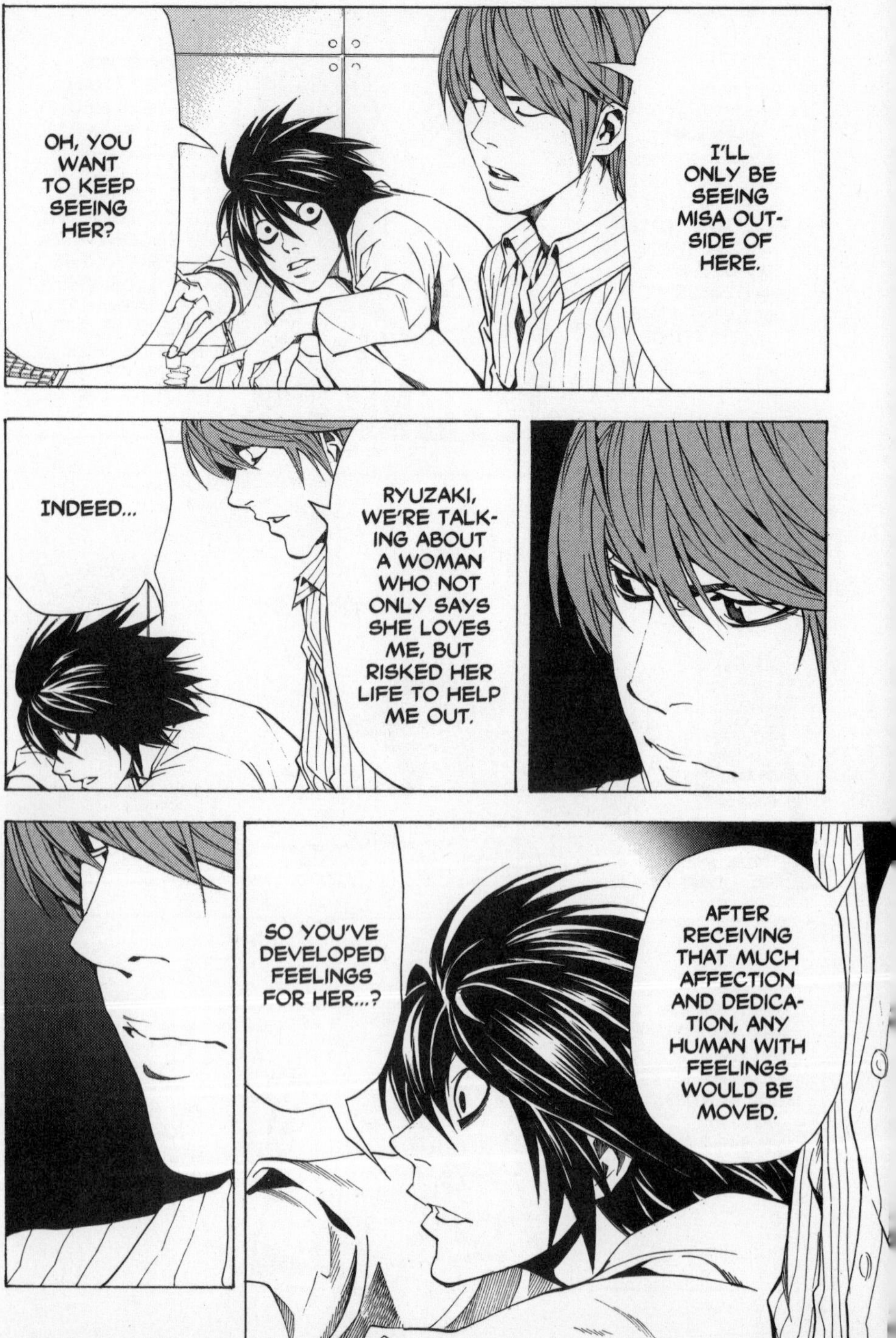
I'LL ONLY BE SEEING MISA OUT-SIDE OF HERE.
OH, YOU WANT TO KEEP SEEING HER?
RYUZAKI, WE'RE TALK-ING ABOUT A WOMAN WHO NOT ONLY SAYS SHE LOVES ME, BUT RISKED HER LIFE TO HELP ME OUT.
INDEED...
AFTER RECEIVING THAT MUCH AFFECTION AND DEDICA-TION, ANY HUMAN WITH FEELINGS WOULD BE MOVED.
SO YOU'VE DEVELOPED FEELINGS FOR HER...?

READ THIS WAY

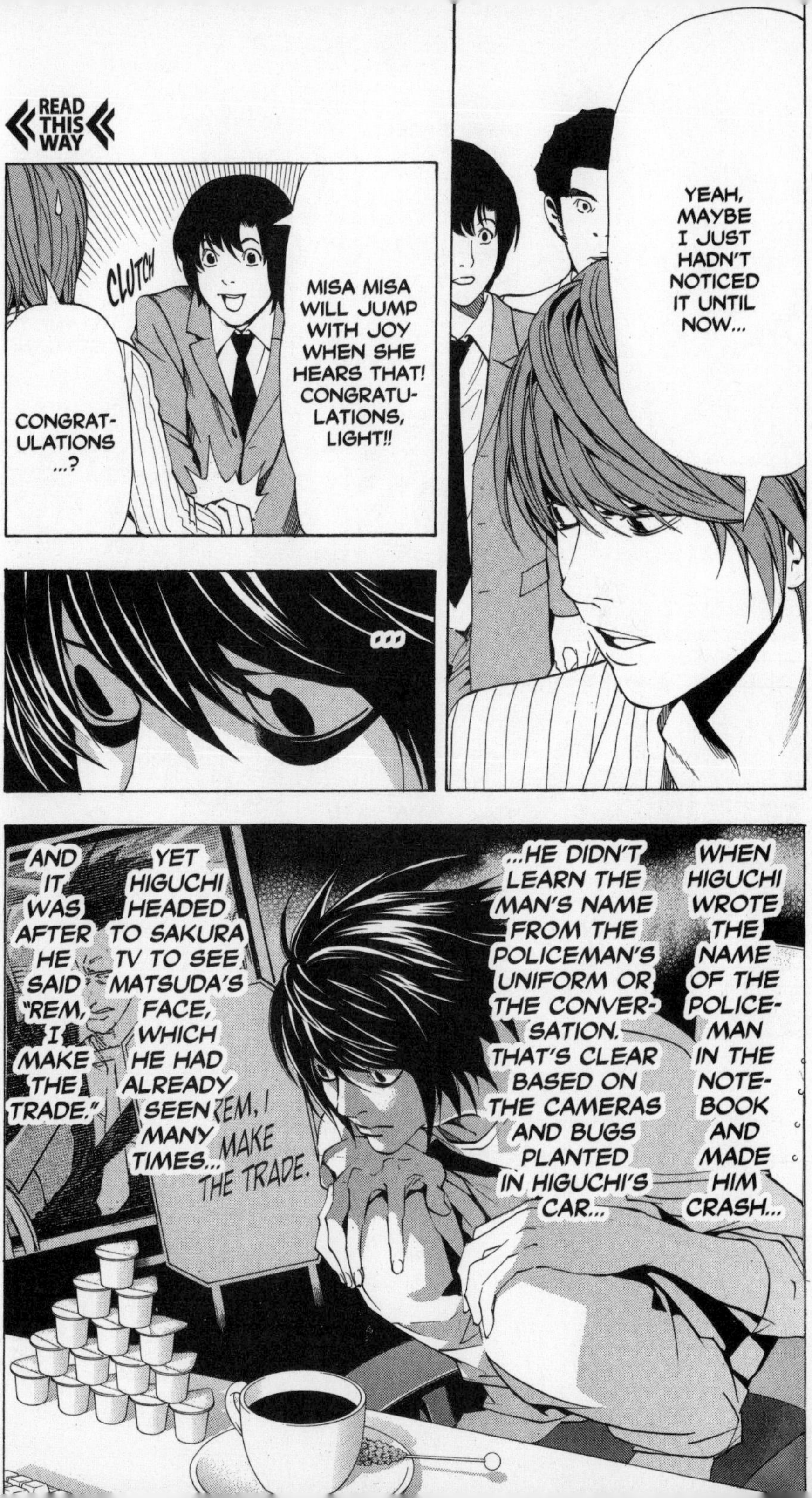
YEAH, MAYBE I JUST HADN'T NOTICED IT UNTIL NOW...
MISA MISA WILL JUMP WITH JOY WHEN SHE HEARS THAT! CONGRATULATIONS, LIGHT!!
CLUTCH
CONGRATULATIONS ...?
...
WHEN HIGUCHI WROTE THE NAME OF THE POLICEMAN IN THE NOTEBOOK AND MADE HIM CRASH...
...HE DIDN'T LEARN THE MAN'S NAME FROM THE POLICEMAN'S UNIFORM OR THE CONVERSATION. THAT'S CLEAR BASED ON THE CAMERAS AND BUGS PLANTED IN HIGUCHI'S CAR...
YET HIGUCHI HEADED TO SAKURA TV TO SEE MATSUDA'S FACE, WHICH HE HAD ALREADY SEEN MANY TIMES...
AND IT WAS AFTER HE SAID "REM, I MAKE THE TRADE."
REM, I MAKE THE TRADE.

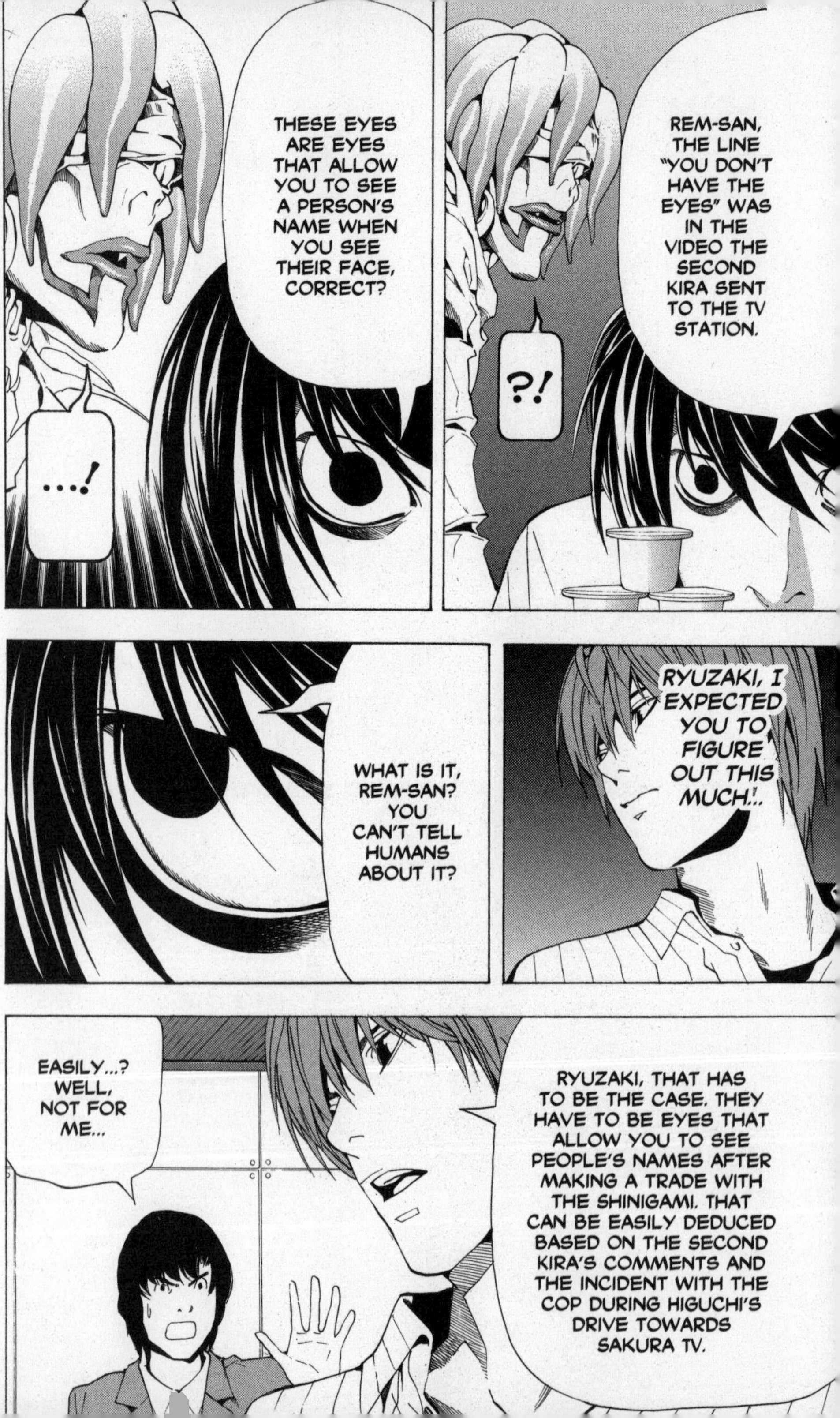
REM-SAN, THE LINE "YOU DON'T HAVE THE EYES" WAS IN THE VIDEO THE SECOND KIRA SENT TO THE TV STATION.
?!
THESE EYES ARE EYES THAT ALLOW YOU TO SEE A PERSON'S NAME WHEN YOU SEE THEIR FACE, CORRECT?
...!
RYUZAKI, I EXPECTED YOU TO FIGURE OUT THIS MUCH...
WHAT IS IT, REM-SAN? YOU CAN'T TELL HUMANS ABOUT IT?
RYUZAKI, THAT HAS TO BE THE CASE. THEY HAVE TO BE EYES THAT ALLOW YOU TO SEE PEOPLE'S NAMES AFTER MAKING A TRADE WITH THE SHINIGAMI. THAT CAN BE EASILY DEDUCED BASED ON THE SECOND KIRA'S COMMENTS AND THE INCIDENT WITH THE COP DURING HIGUCHI'S DRIVE TOWARDS SAKURA TV.
EASILY...? WELL, NOT FOR ME...

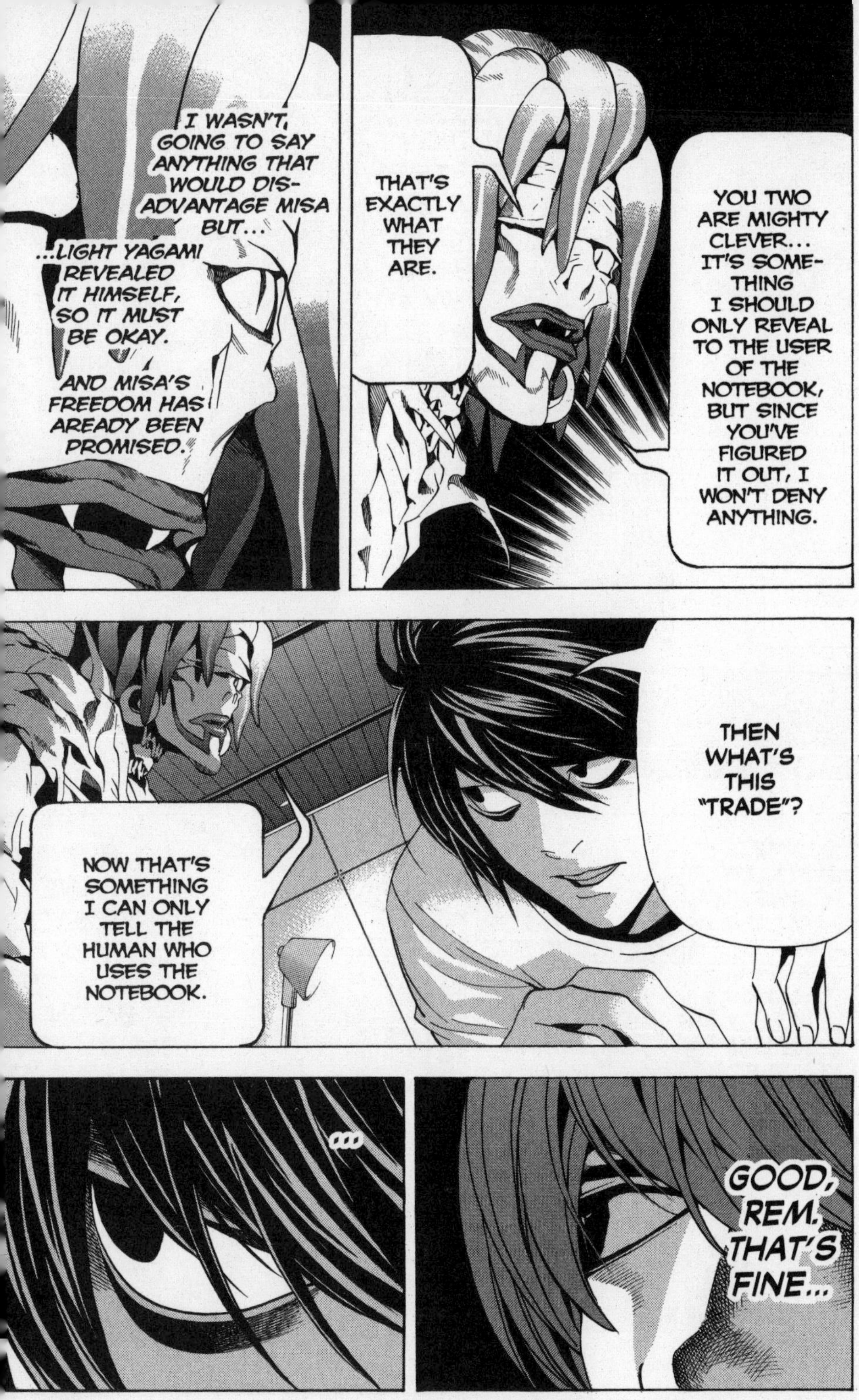
THAT'S EXACTLY WHAT THEY ARE.
YOU TWO ARE MIGHTY CLEVER... IT'S SOMETHING I SHOULD ONLY REVEAL TO THE USER OF THE NOTEBOOK, BUT SINCE YOU'VE FIGURED IT OUT, I WON'T DENY ANYTHING.
I WASN'T GOING TO SAY ANYTHING THAT WOULD DISADVANTAGE MISA BUT...
...LIGHT YAGAMI REVEALED IT HIMSELF, SO IT MUST BE OKAY.
AND MISA'S FREEDOM HAS AREADY BEEN PROMISED.
THEN WHAT'S THIS "TRADE"?
NOW THAT'S SOMETHING I CAN ONLY TELL THE HUMAN WHO USES THE NOTEBOOK.
GOOD, REM. THAT'S FINE...
...

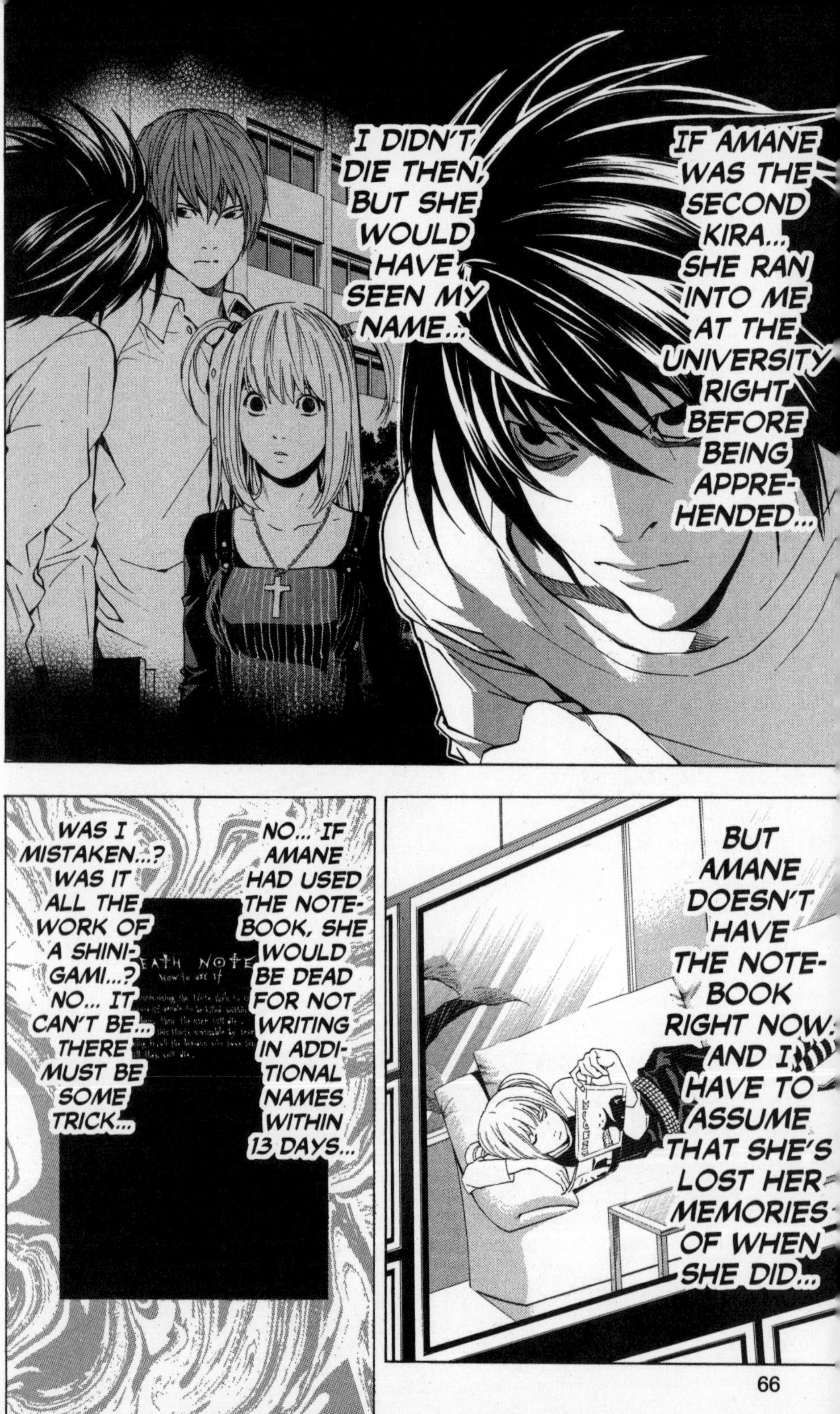
IF AMANE WAS THE SECOND KIRA... SHE RAN INTO ME AT THE UNIVERSITY RIGHT BEFORE BEING APPRE-HENDED...
I DIDN'T DIE THEN, BUT SHE WOULD HAVE SEEN MY NAME...
BUT AMANE DOESN'T HAVE THE NOTE-BOOK RIGHT NOW. AND I HAVE TO ASSUME THAT SHE'S LOST HER MEMORIES OF WHEN SHE DID...
NO... IF AMANE HAD USED THE NOTE-BOOK, SHE WOULD BE DEAD FOR NOT WRITING IN ADDI-TIONAL NAMES WITHIN 13 DAYS...
WAS I MISTAKEN...? WAS IT ALL THE WORK OF A SHINI-GAMI...? NO... IT CAN'T BE... THERE MUST BE SOME TRICK...

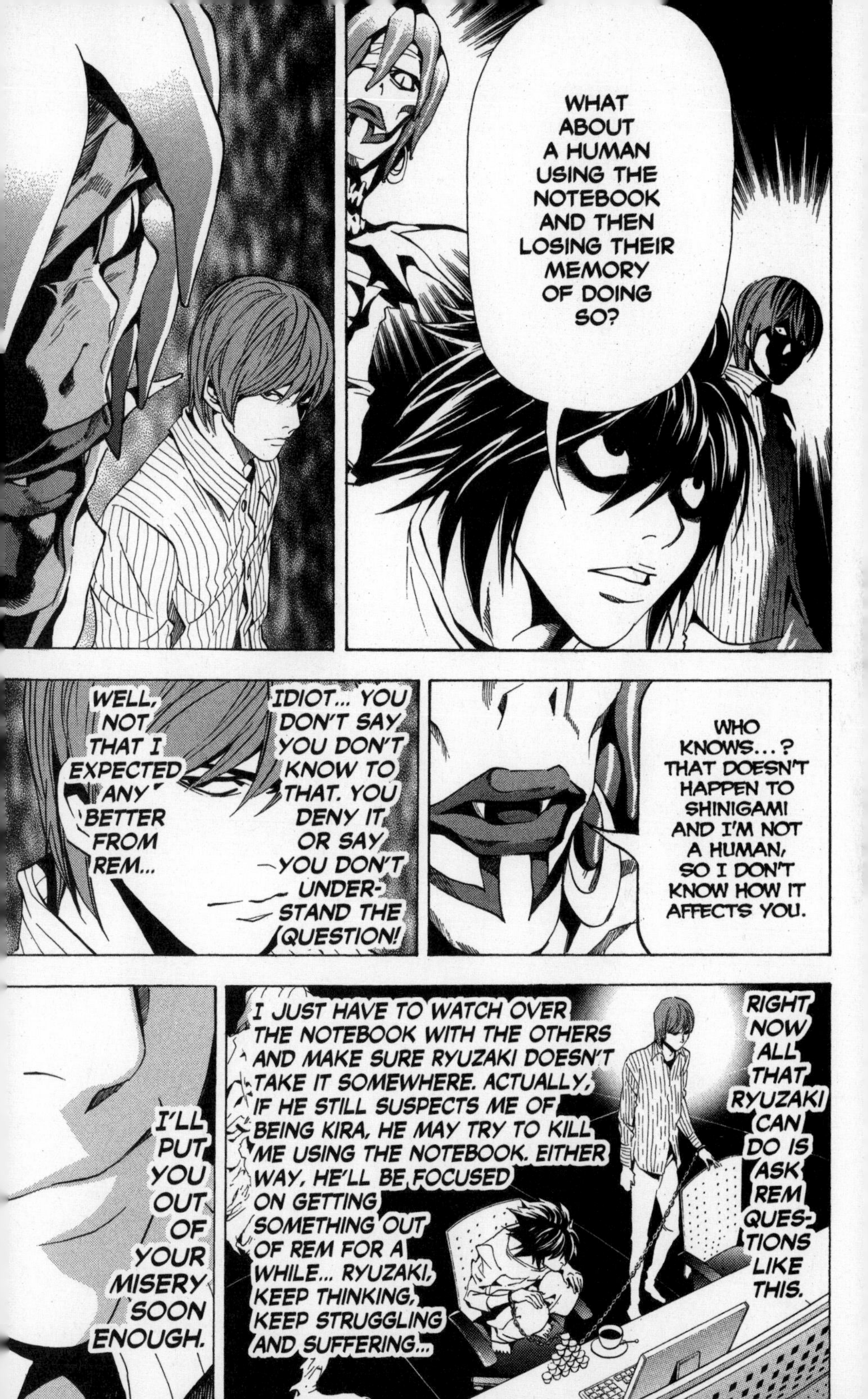
WHAT ABOUT A HUMAN USING THE NOTEBOOK AND THEN LOSING THEIR MEMORY OF DOING SO?
WHO KNOWS...? THAT DOESN'T HAPPEN TO SHINIGAMI AND I'M NOT A HUMAN, SO I DON'T KNOW HOW IT AFFECTS YOU.
IDIOT... YOU DON'T SAY YOU DON'T KNOW TO THAT. YOU DENY IT OR SAY YOU DON'T UNDERSTAND THE QUESTION!
WELL, NOT THAT I EXPECTED ANY BETTER FROM REM...
RIGHT NOW ALL THAT RYUZAKI CAN DO IS ASK REM QUESTIONS LIKE THIS.
I JUST HAVE TO WATCH OVER THE NOTEBOOK WITH THE OTHERS AND MAKE SURE RYUZAKI DOESN'T TAKE IT SOMEWHERE. ACTUALLY, IF HE STILL SUSPECTS ME OF BEING KIRA, HE MAY TRY TO KILL ME USING THE NOTEBOOK. EITHER WAY, HE'LL BE FOCUSED ON GETTING SOMETHING OUT OF REM FOR A WHILE... RYUZAKI, KEEP THINKING, KEEP STRUGGLING AND SUFFERING...
I'LL PUT YOU OUT OF YOUR MISERY SOON ENOUGH.

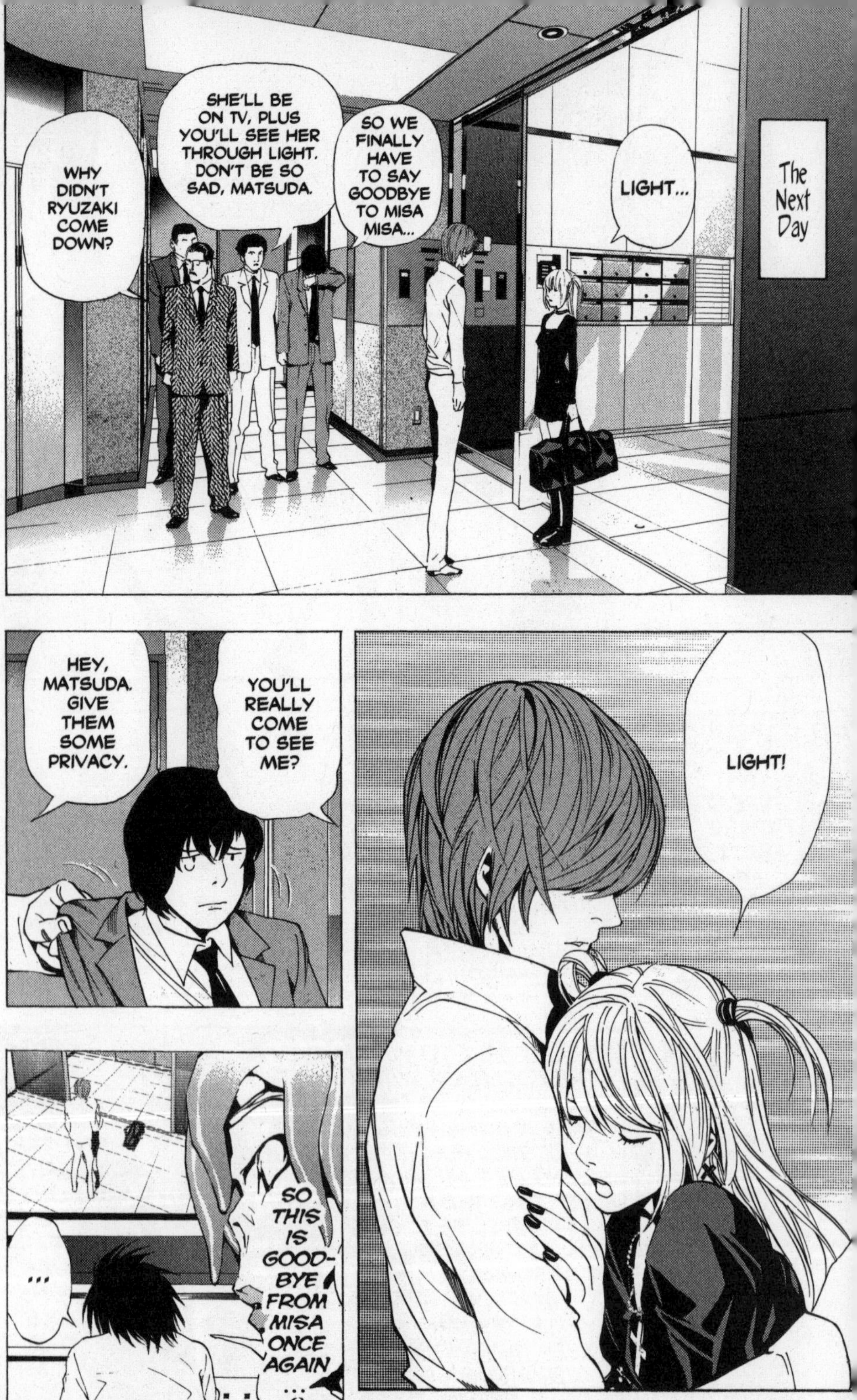
The Next Day
LIGHT...
SO WE FINALLY HAVE TO SAY GOODBYE TO MISA MISA...
SHE'LL BE ON TV, PLUS YOU'LL SEE HER THROUGH LIGHT. DON'T BE SO SAD, MATSUDA.
WHY DIDN'T RYUZAKI COME DOWN?
LIGHT!
YOU'LL REALLY COME TO SEE ME?
HEY, MATSUDA. GIVE THEM SOME PRIVACY.
SO THIS IS GOOD-BYE FROM MISA ONCE AGAIN
...
...

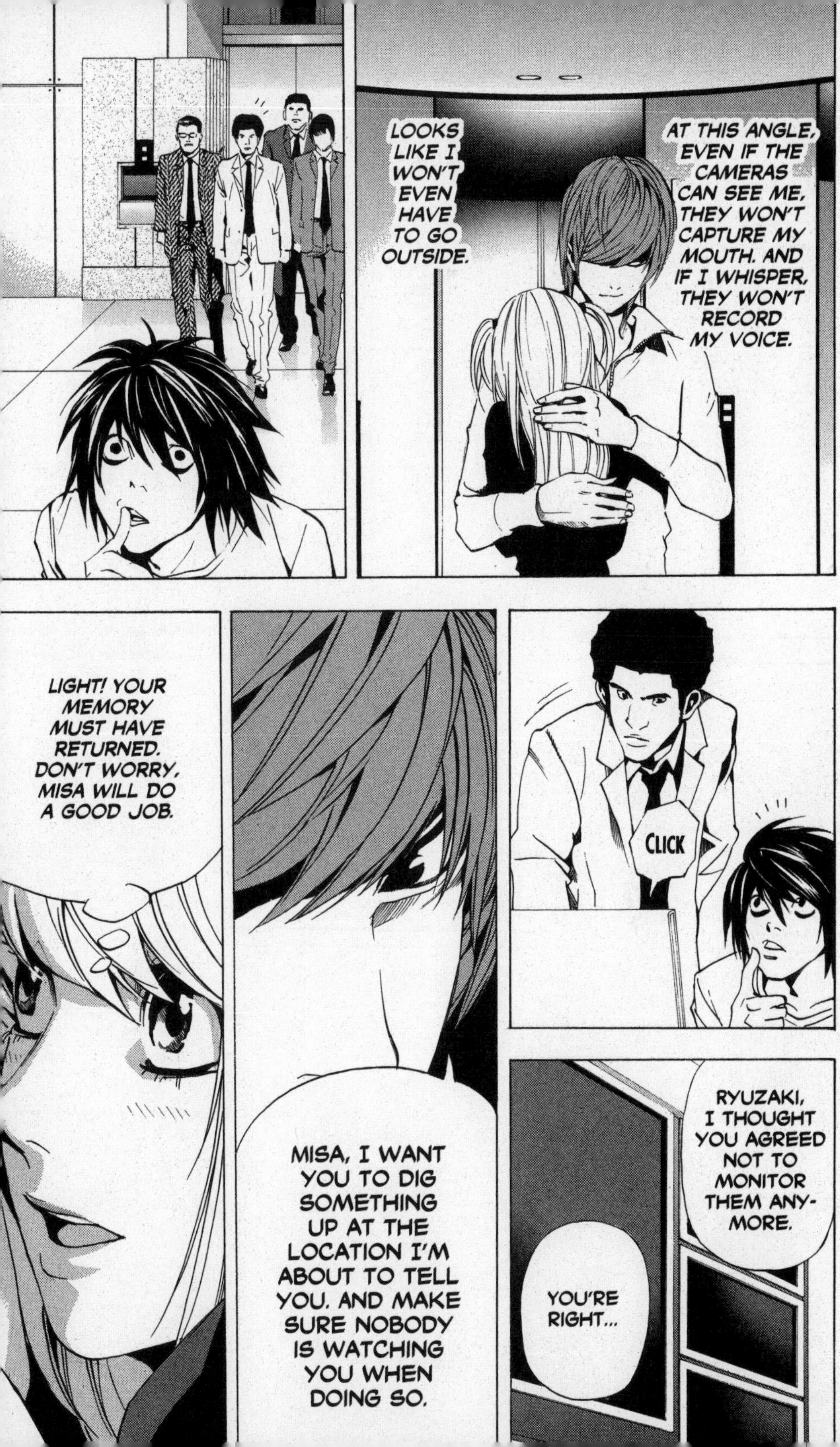
AT THIS ANGLE, EVEN IF THE CAMERAS CAN SEE ME, THEY WON'T CAPTURE MY MOUTH. AND IF I WHISPER, THEY WON'T RECORD MY VOICE.
LOOKS LIKE I WON'T EVEN HAVE TO GO OUTSIDE.
CLICK
RYUZAKI, I THOUGHT YOU AGREED NOT TO MONITOR THEM ANY-MORE.
YOU'RE RIGHT...
MISA, I WANT YOU TO DIG SOMETHING UP AT THE LOCATION I'M ABOUT TO TELL YOU. AND MAKE SURE NOBODY IS WATCHING YOU WHEN DOING SO.
LIGHT! YOUR MEMORY MUST HAVE RETURNED. DON'T WORRY, MISA WILL DO A GOOD JOB.

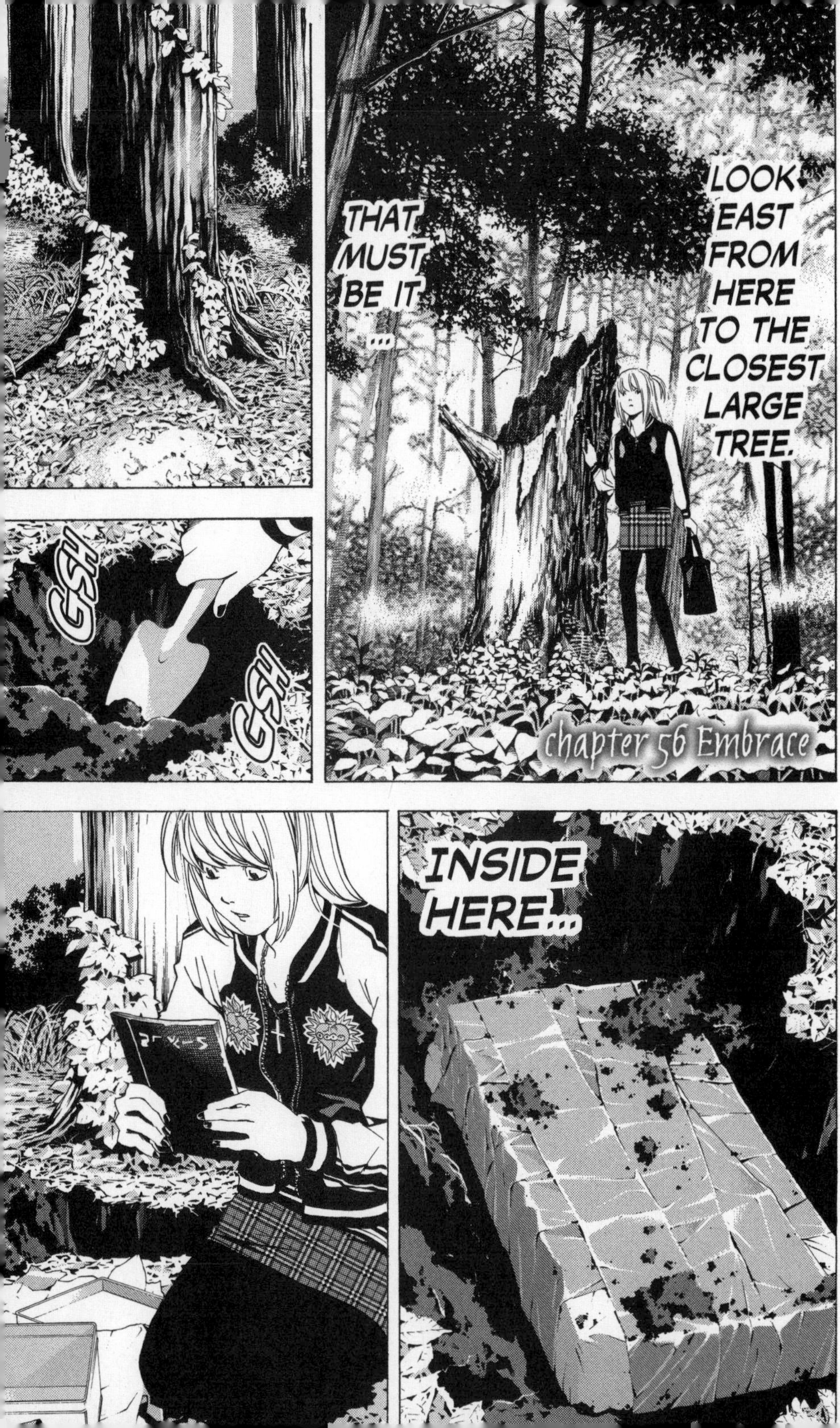
LOOK EAST FROM HERE TO THE CLOSEST LARGE TREE.
THAT MUST BE IT ...
chapter 56 Embrace
GSH
GSH
INSIDE HERE...

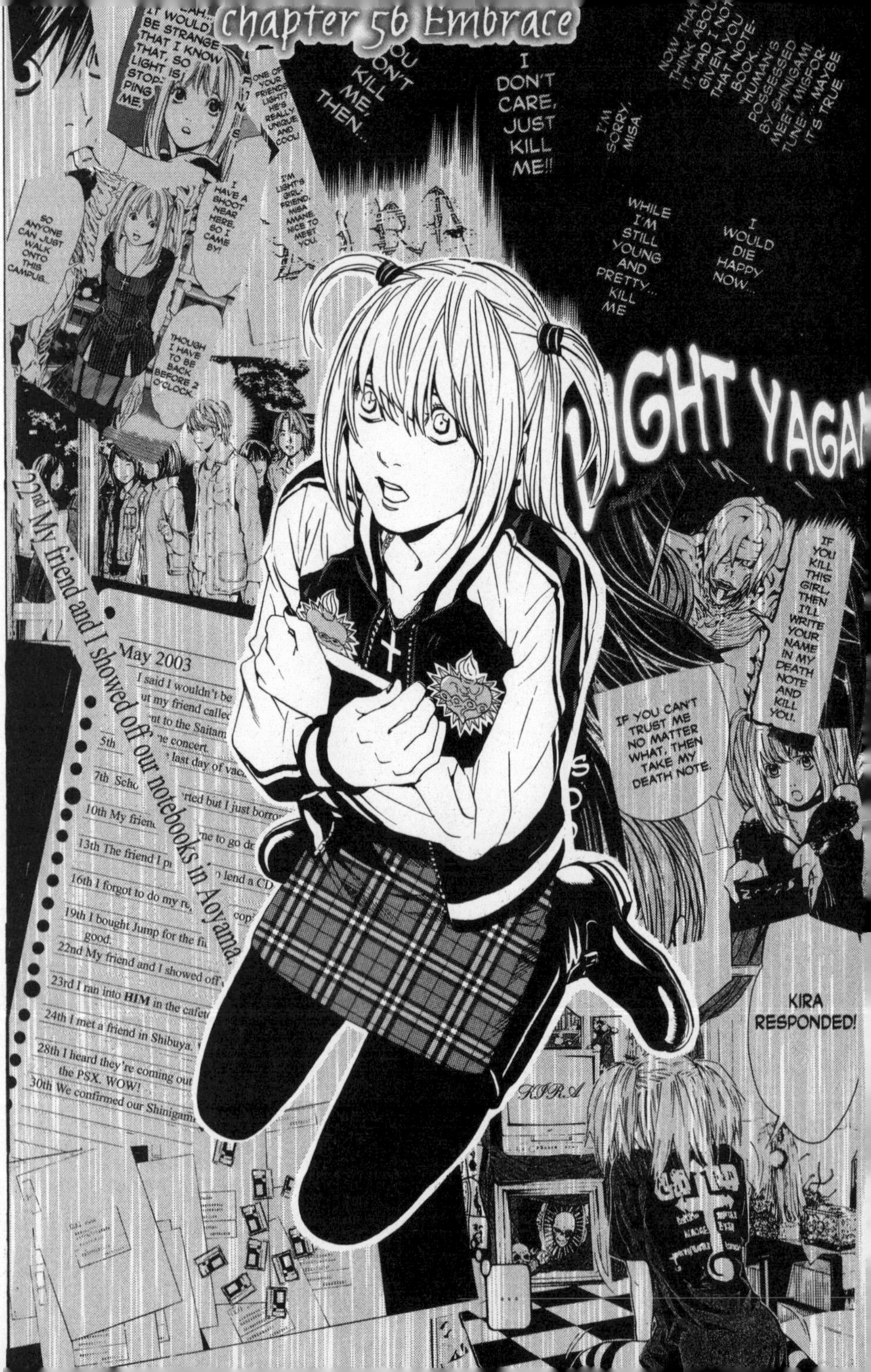
chapter 56 Embrace
NOW THAT I THINK ABOUT IT, HAD I NOT GIVEN YOU THAT NOTEBOOK. "HUMAN'S POSSESSED BY SHINIGAMI MEET MISFORTUNE"... MAYBE IT'S TRUE
I'M SORRY, MISA
I DON'T CARE, JUST KILL ME!!
YOU DON'T KILL ME, THEN...
I WOULD DIE HAPPY NOW...
WHILE I'M STILL YOUNG AND PRETTY... KILL ME
ONE OF YOUR FRIENDS, LIGHT? HE'S REALLY UNIQUE AND COOL!
YEAH! IT WOULD BE STRANGE THAT I KNOW THAT, SO LIGHT IS STOPPING ME.
I'M LIGHT'S GIRLFRIEND, MISA AMANE. NICE TO MEET YOU.
I HAVE A SHOOT NEAR HERE, SO I CAME BY!
SO ANYONE CAN JUST WALK ONTO THIS CAMPUS...
THOUGH I HAVE TO BE BACK BEFORE 2 O'CLOCK.
LIGHT YAGAMI
IF YOU KILL THIS GIRL, THEN I'LL WRITE YOUR NAME IN MY DEATH NOTE AND KILL YOU.
IF YOU CAN'T TRUST ME NO MATTER WHAT, THEN TAKE MY DEATH NOTE.
KIRA RESPONDED!
KIRA
22nd My friend and I showed off our notebooks in Aoyama.
May 2003
I said I wouldn't be
ut my friend callec
ut to the Saitam
ne concert.
5th
last day of vac
7th Scho
rted but I just borro
10th My frien
me to go d
13th The friend I p
lend a CD
16th I forgot to do my r
19th I bought Jump for the fi
good.
22nd My friend and I showed off
23rd I ran into HIM in the cafet
24th I met a friend in Shibuya.
28th I heard they're coming out
the PSX. WOW!
30th We confirmed our Shinigam

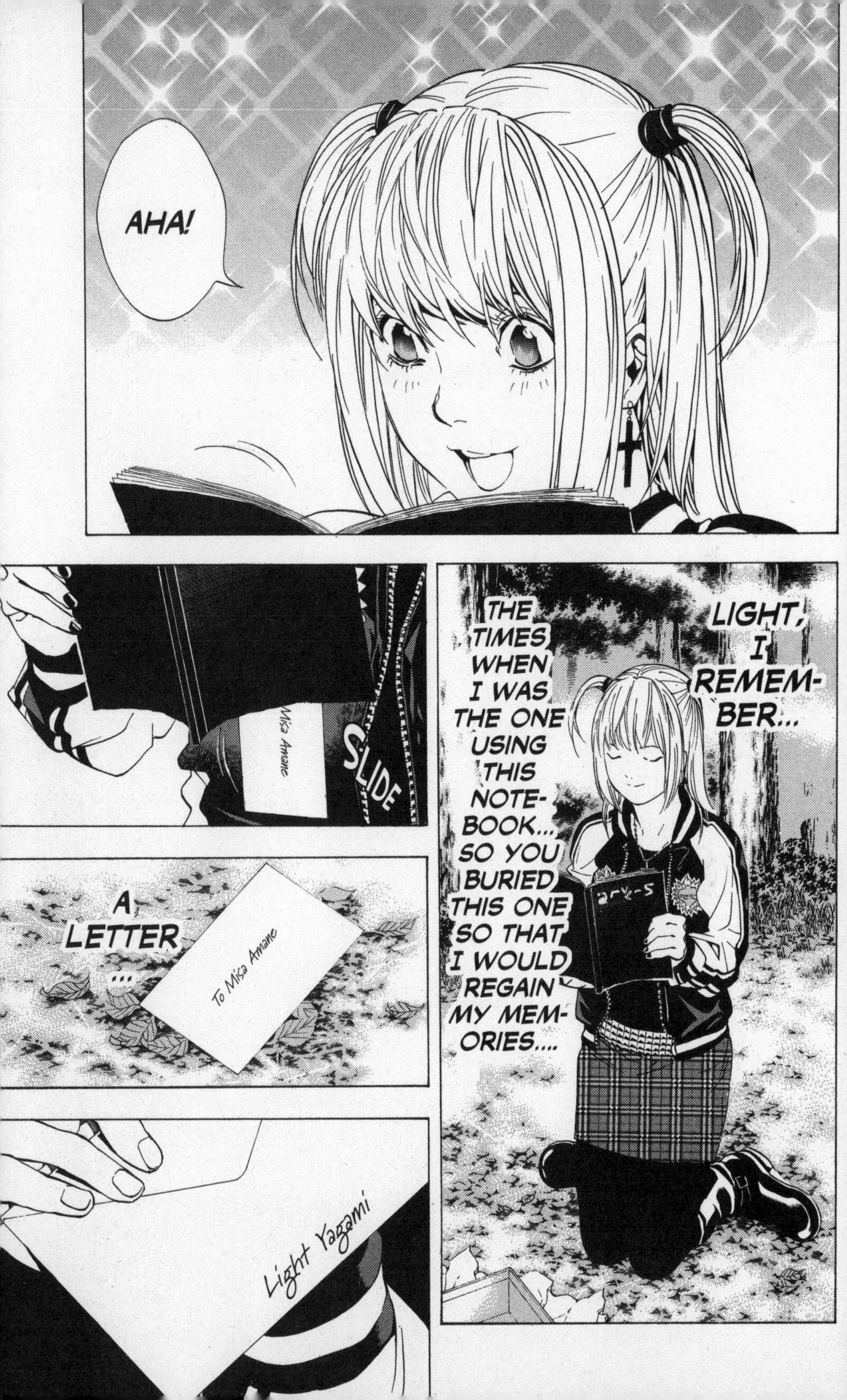
AHA!
LIGHT, I REMEMBER...
THE TIMES WHEN I WAS THE ONE USING THIS NOTEBOOK... SO YOU BURIED THIS ONE SO THAT I WOULD REGAIN MY MEMORIES....
Misa Amane
SLIDE
A LETTER ...
To Misa Amane
Light Yagami

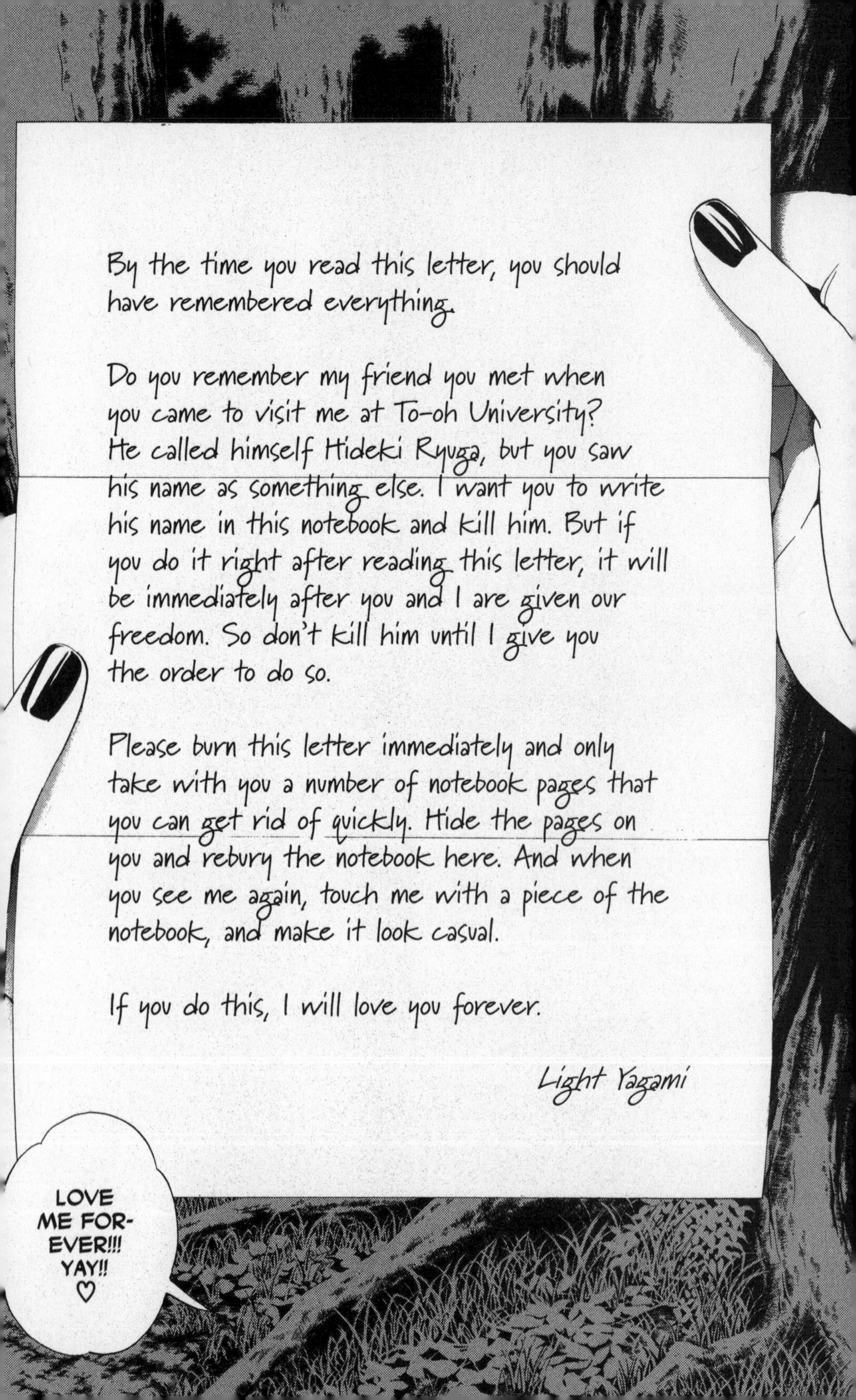
By the time you read this letter, you should have remembered everything.
Do you remember my friend you met when you came to visit me at To-oh University? He called himself Hideki Ryuga, but you saw his name as something else. I want you to write his name in this notebook and kill him. But if you do it right after reading this letter, it will be immediately after you and I are given our freedom. So don't kill him until I give you the order to do so.
Please burn this letter immediately and only take with you a number of notebook pages that you can get rid of quickly. Hide the pages on you and rebury the notebook here. And when you see me again, touch me with a piece of the notebook, and make it look casual.
If you do this, I will love you forever.
Light Yagami
LOVE ME FOR-EVER!!! YAY!! ♡

READ THIS WAY

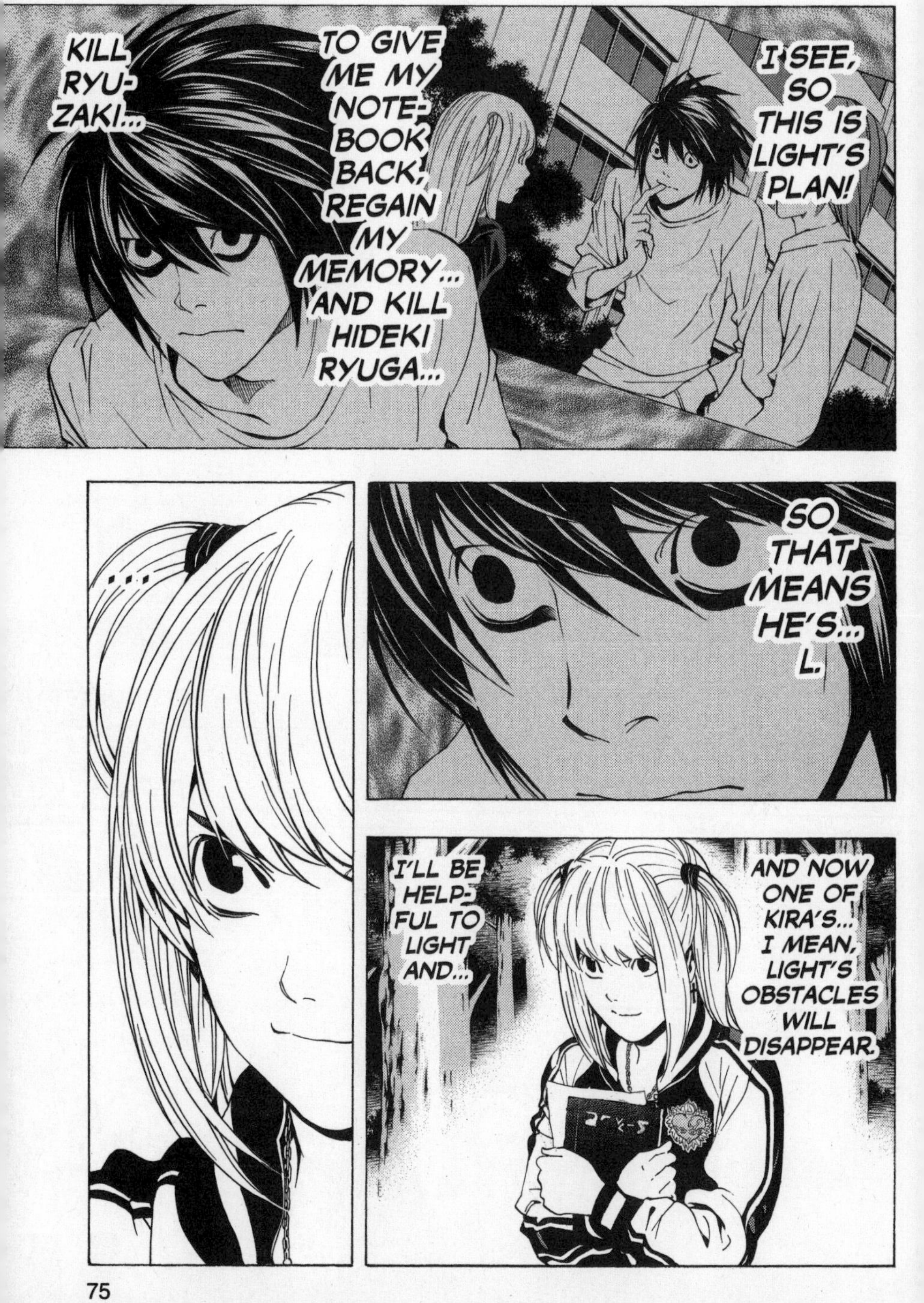
I SEE, SO THIS IS LIGHT'S PLAN!
TO GIVE ME MY NOTE-BOOK BACK, REGAIN MY MEMORY... AND KILL HIDEKI RYUGA...
KILL RYU-ZAKI...
SO THAT MEANS HE'S... L.
AND NOW ONE OF KIRA'S... I MEAN, LIGHT'S OBSTACLES WILL DISAPPEAR.
I'LL BE HELP-FUL TO LIGHT AND...
...

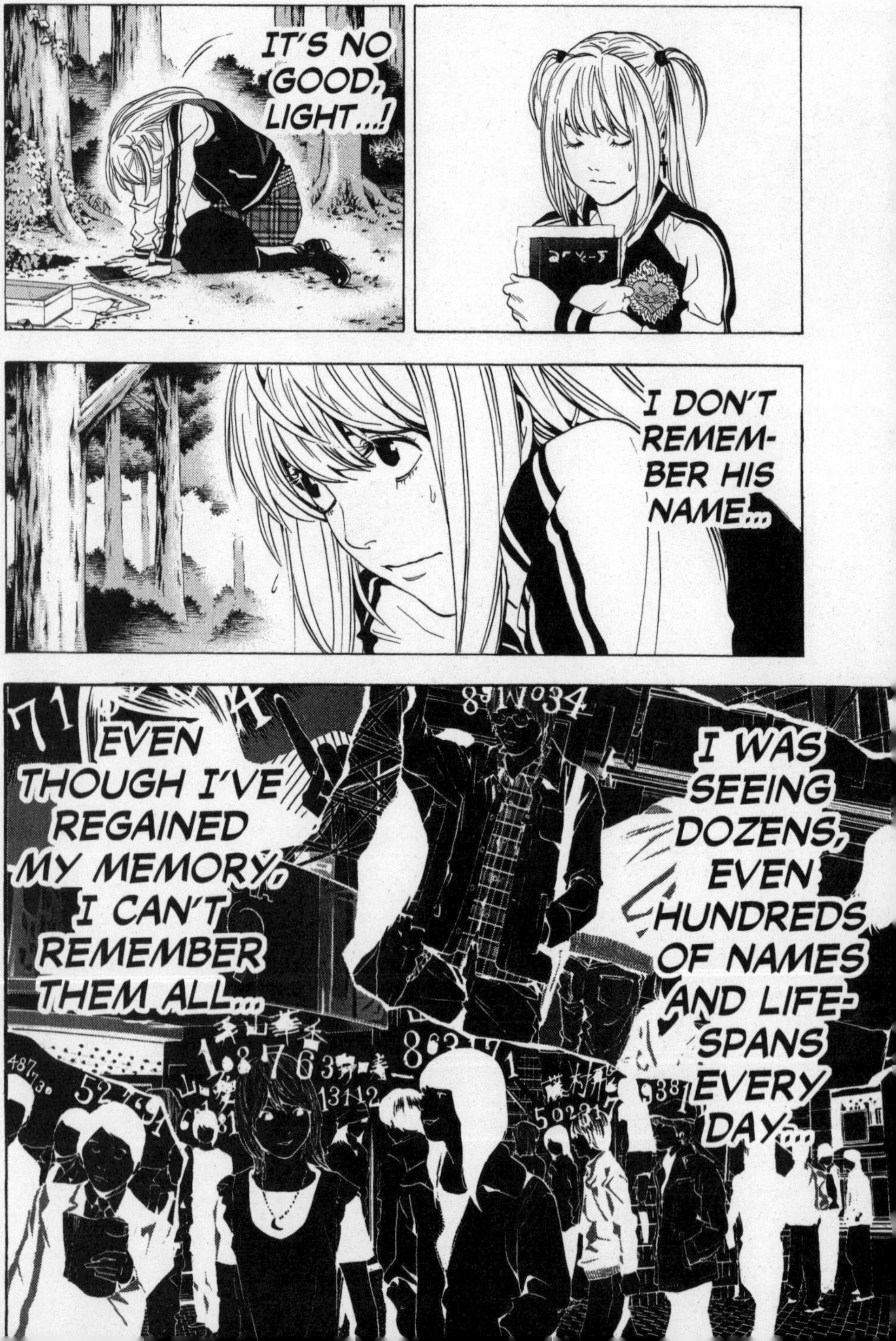
IT'S NO GOOD, LIGHT...!
I DON'T REMEMBER HIS NAME...
I WAS SEEING DOZENS, EVEN HUNDREDS OF NAMES AND LIFESPANS EVERY DAY...
EVEN THOUGH I'VE REGAINED MY MEMORY, I CAN'T REMEMBER THEM ALL...

READ THIS WAY

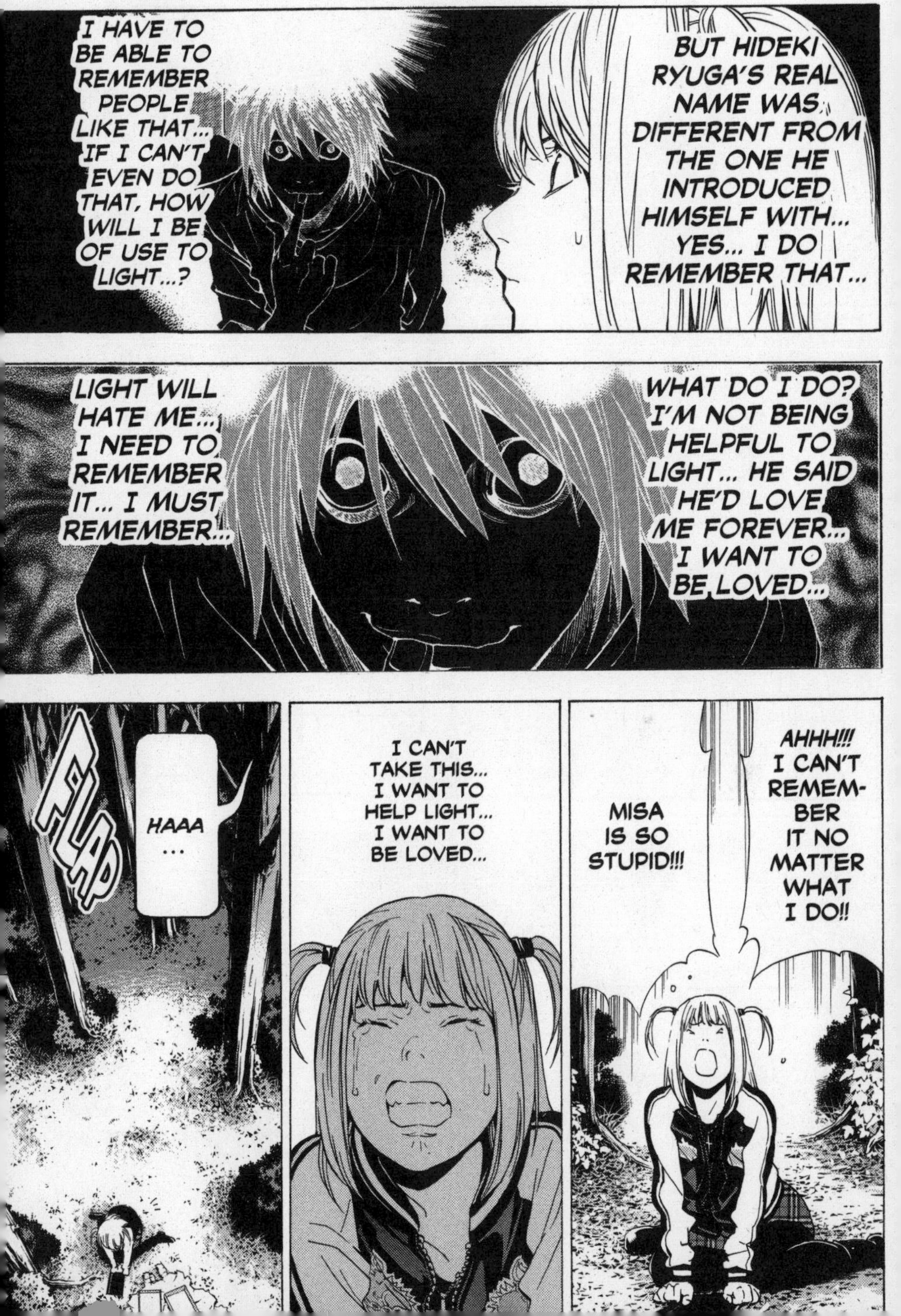
BUT HIDEKI RYUGA'S REAL NAME WAS DIFFERENT FROM THE ONE HE INTRODUCED HIMSELF WITH... YES... I DO REMEMBER THAT...
I HAVE TO BE ABLE TO REMEMBER PEOPLE LIKE THAT... IF I CAN'T EVEN DO THAT, HOW WILL I BE OF USE TO LIGHT...?
WHAT DO I DO? I'M NOT BEING HELPFUL TO LIGHT... HE SAID HE'D LOVE ME FOREVER... I WANT TO BE LOVED...
LIGHT WILL HATE ME... I NEED TO REMEMBER IT... I MUST REMEMBER...
AHHH!!! I CAN'T REMEM-BER IT NO MATTER WHAT I DO!!
MISA IS SO STUPID!!!
I CAN'T TAKE THIS... I WANT TO HELP LIGHT... I WANT TO BE LOVED...
FLAP
HAAA...

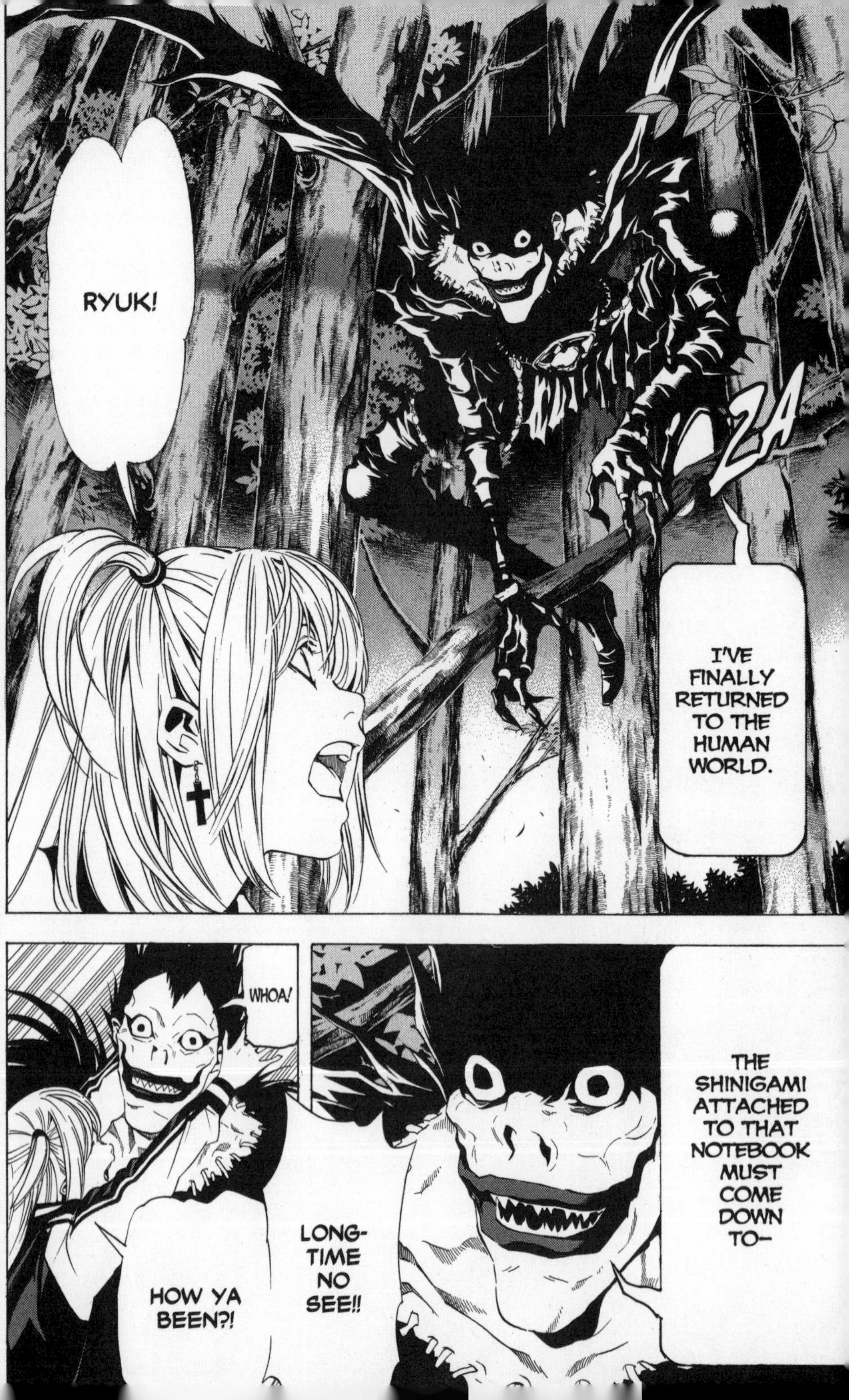
ZA
RYUK!
I'VE FINALLY RETURNED TO THE HUMAN WORLD.
THE SHINIGAMI ATTACHED TO THAT NOTEBOOK MUST COME DOWN TO—
LONG-TIME NO SEE!!
HOW YA BEEN?!
WHOA!

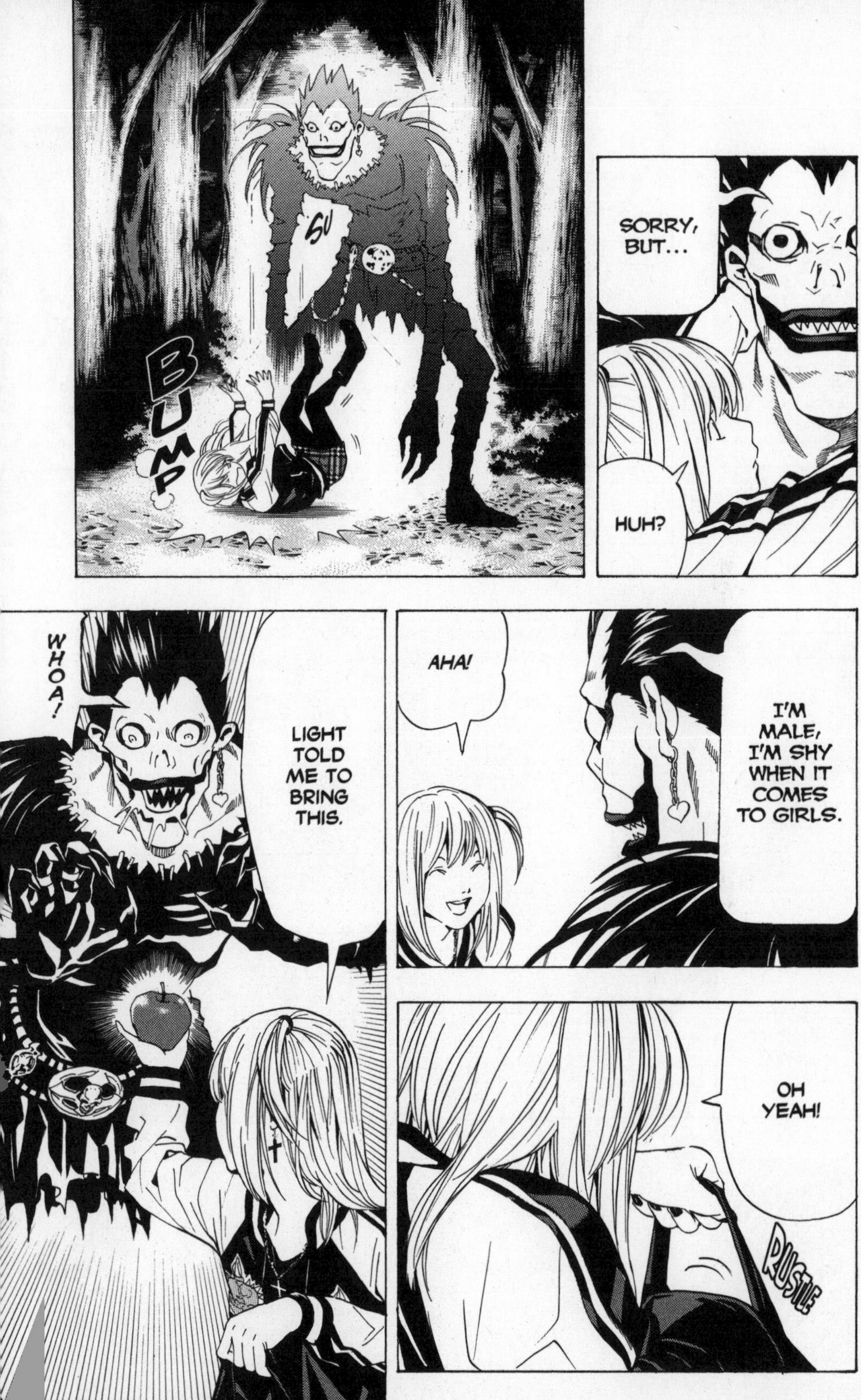
SORRY, BUT...
HUH?
SU
BUMP
I'M MALE, I'M SHY WHEN IT COMES TO GIRLS.
AHA!
OH YEAH!
RUSTLE
LIGHT TOLD ME TO BRING THIS.
WHOA!

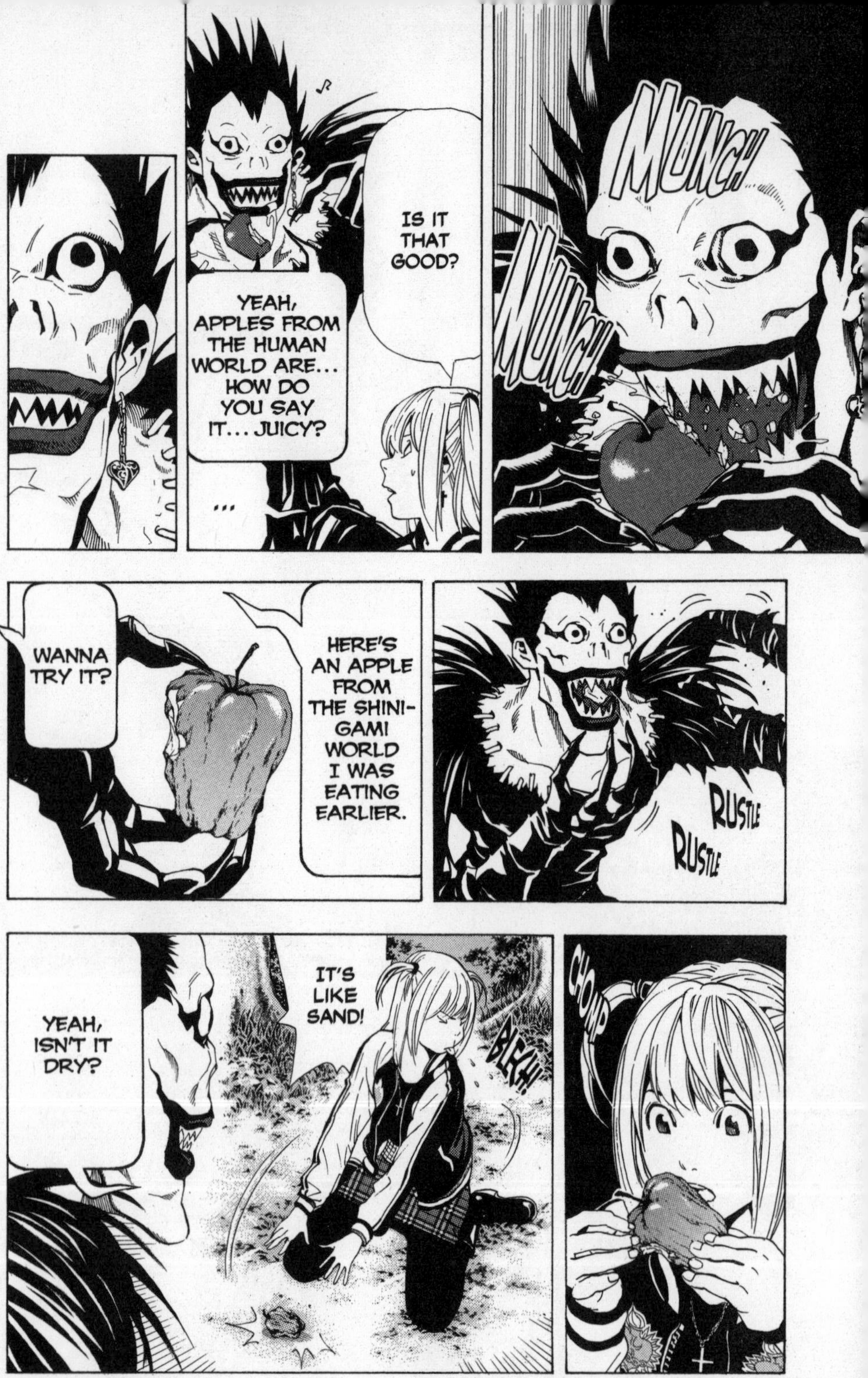
MUNCH
MUNCH
IS IT THAT GOOD?
YEAH, APPLES FROM THE HUMAN WORLD ARE... HOW DO YOU SAY IT... JUICY?
...
RUSTLE
RUSTLE
HERE'S AN APPLE FROM THE SHINI-GAMI WORLD I WAS EATING EARLIER.
WANNA TRY IT?
CHOMP
BLEH!!
IT'S LIKE SAND!
YEAH, ISN'T IT DRY?

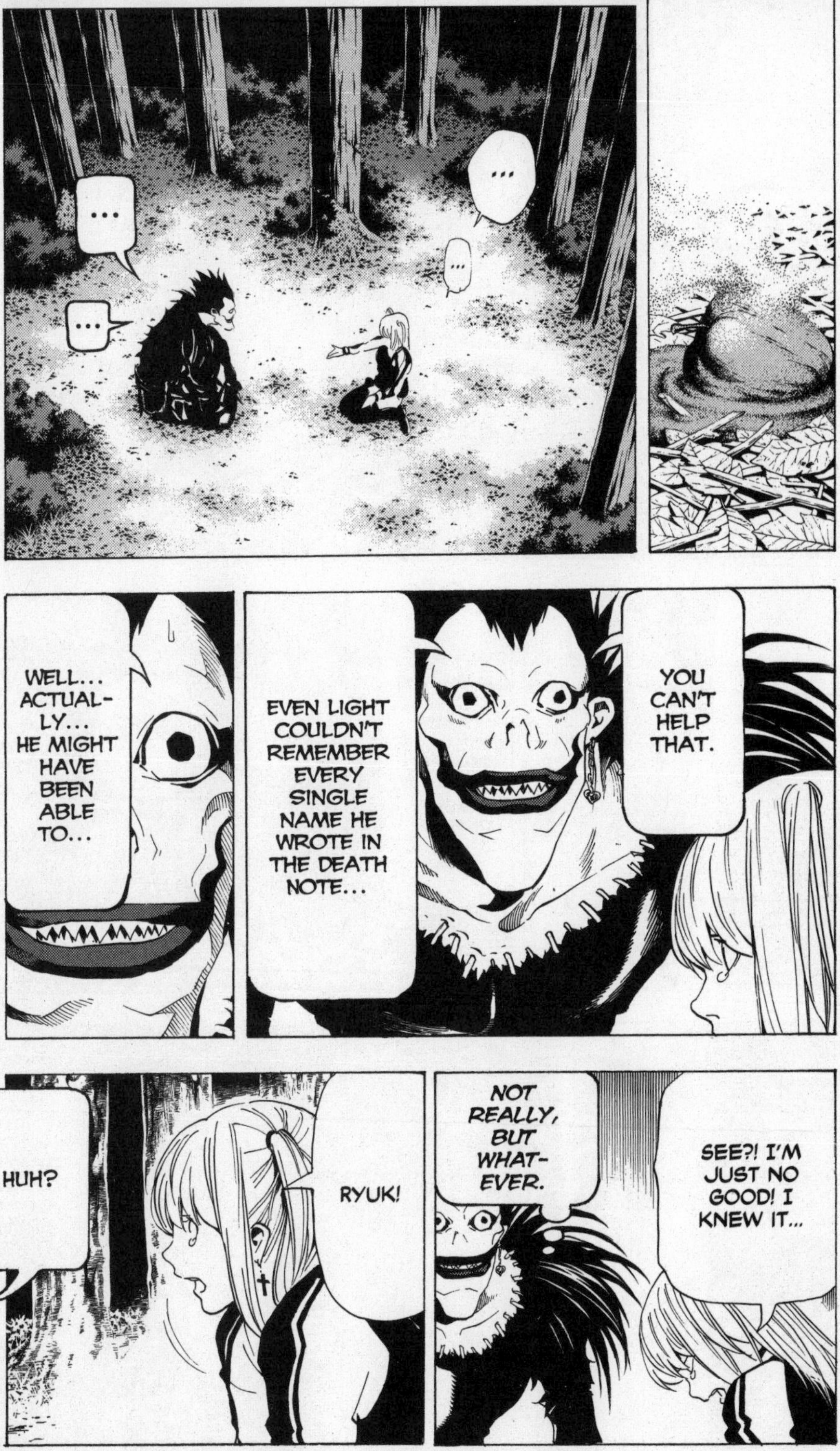
...
...
....
....
YOU CAN'T HELP THAT.
EVEN LIGHT COULDN'T REMEMBER EVERY SINGLE NAME HE WROTE IN THE DEATH NOTE...
WELL... ACTUAL-LY... HE MIGHT HAVE BEEN ABLE TO...
SEE?! I'M JUST NO GOOD! I KNEW IT...
NOT REALLY, BUT WHAT-EVER.
RYUK!
HUH?

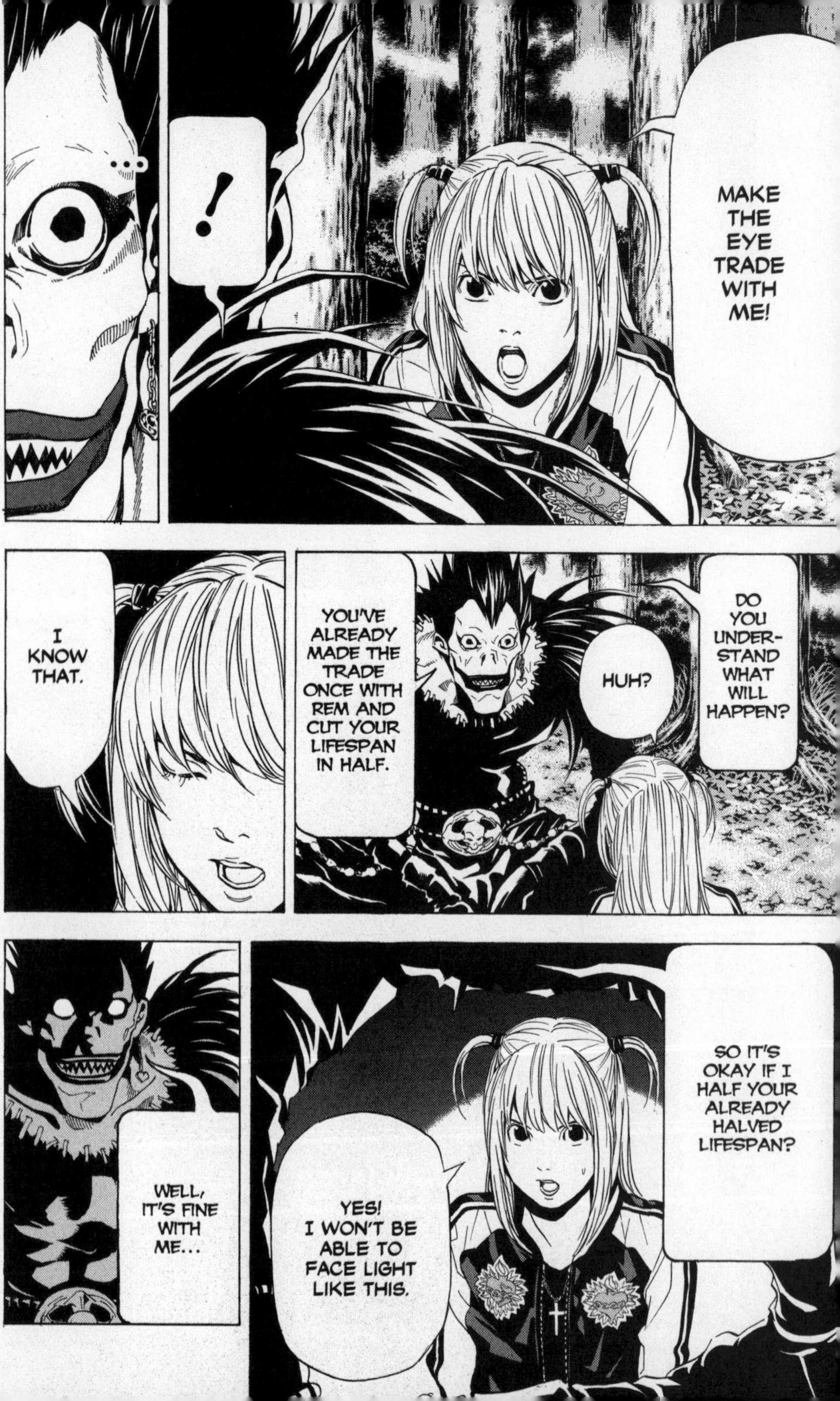
MAKE THE EYE TRADE WITH ME!
!
...
DO YOU UNDER-STAND WHAT WILL HAPPEN?
HUH?
YOU'VE ALREADY MADE THE TRADE ONCE WITH REM AND CUT YOUR LIFESPAN IN HALF.
I KNOW THAT.
SO IT'S OKAY IF I HALF YOUR ALREADY HALVED LIFESPAN?
YES! I WON'T BE ABLE TO FACE LIGHT LIKE THIS.
WELL, IT'S FINE WITH ME...

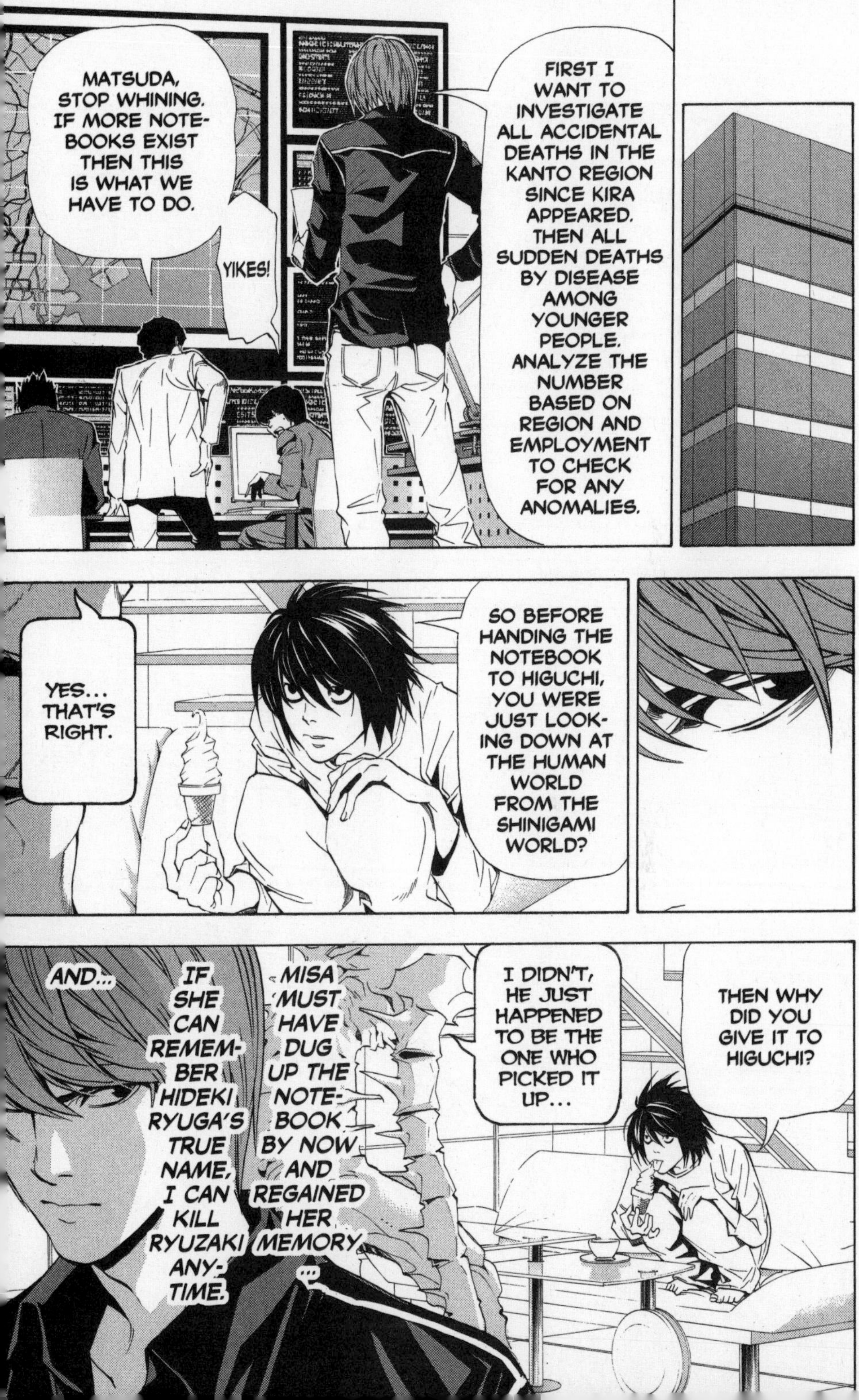
FIRST I WANT TO INVESTIGATE ALL ACCIDENTAL DEATHS IN THE KANTO REGION SINCE KIRA APPEARED. THEN ALL SUDDEN DEATHS BY DISEASE AMONG YOUNGER PEOPLE. ANALYZE THE NUMBER BASED ON REGION AND EMPLOYMENT TO CHECK FOR ANY ANOMALIES.
YIKES!
MATSUDA, STOP WHINING. IF MORE NOTE-BOOKS EXIST THEN THIS IS WHAT WE HAVE TO DO.
SO BEFORE HANDING THE NOTEBOOK TO HIGUCHI, YOU WERE JUST LOOK-ING DOWN AT THE HUMAN WORLD FROM THE SHINIGAMI WORLD?
YES... THAT'S RIGHT.
THEN WHY DID YOU GIVE IT TO HIGUCHI?
I DIDN'T, HE JUST HAPPENED TO BE THE ONE WHO PICKED IT UP...
MISA MUST HAVE DUG UP THE NOTE-BOOK BY NOW AND REGAINED HER MEMORY...
IF SHE CAN REMEM-BER HIDEKI RYUGA'S TRUE NAME, I CAN KILL RYUZAKI ANY-TIME.
AND...

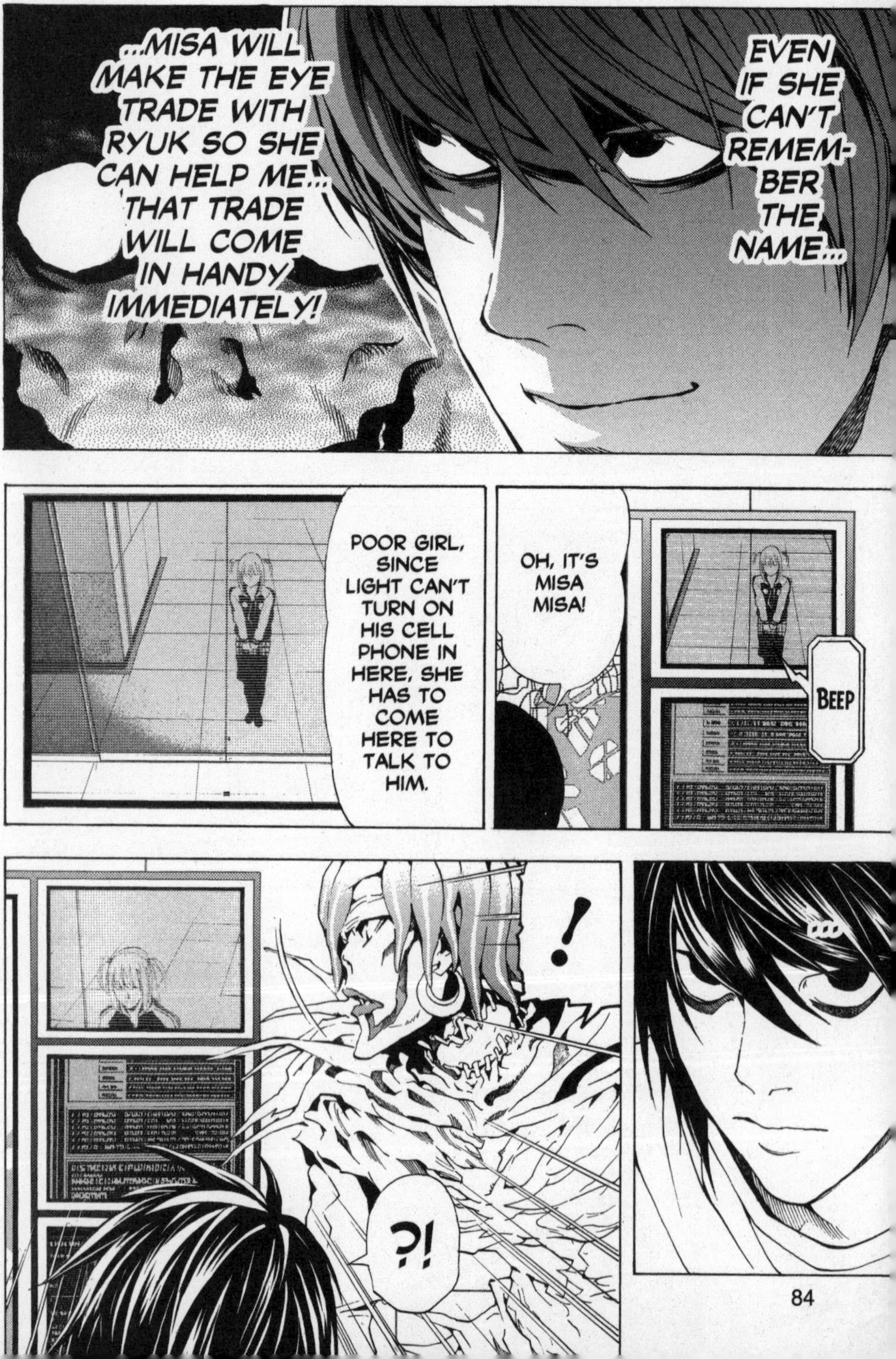
EVEN IF SHE CAN'T REMEMBER THE NAME...
...MISA WILL MAKE THE EYE TRADE WITH RYUK SO SHE CAN HELP ME... THAT TRADE WILL COME IN HANDY IMMEDIATELY!
OH, IT'S MISA MISA!
BEEP
POOR GIRL, SINCE LIGHT CAN'T TURN ON HIS CELL PHONE IN HERE, SHE HAS TO COME HERE TO TALK TO HIM.
...
!
?!

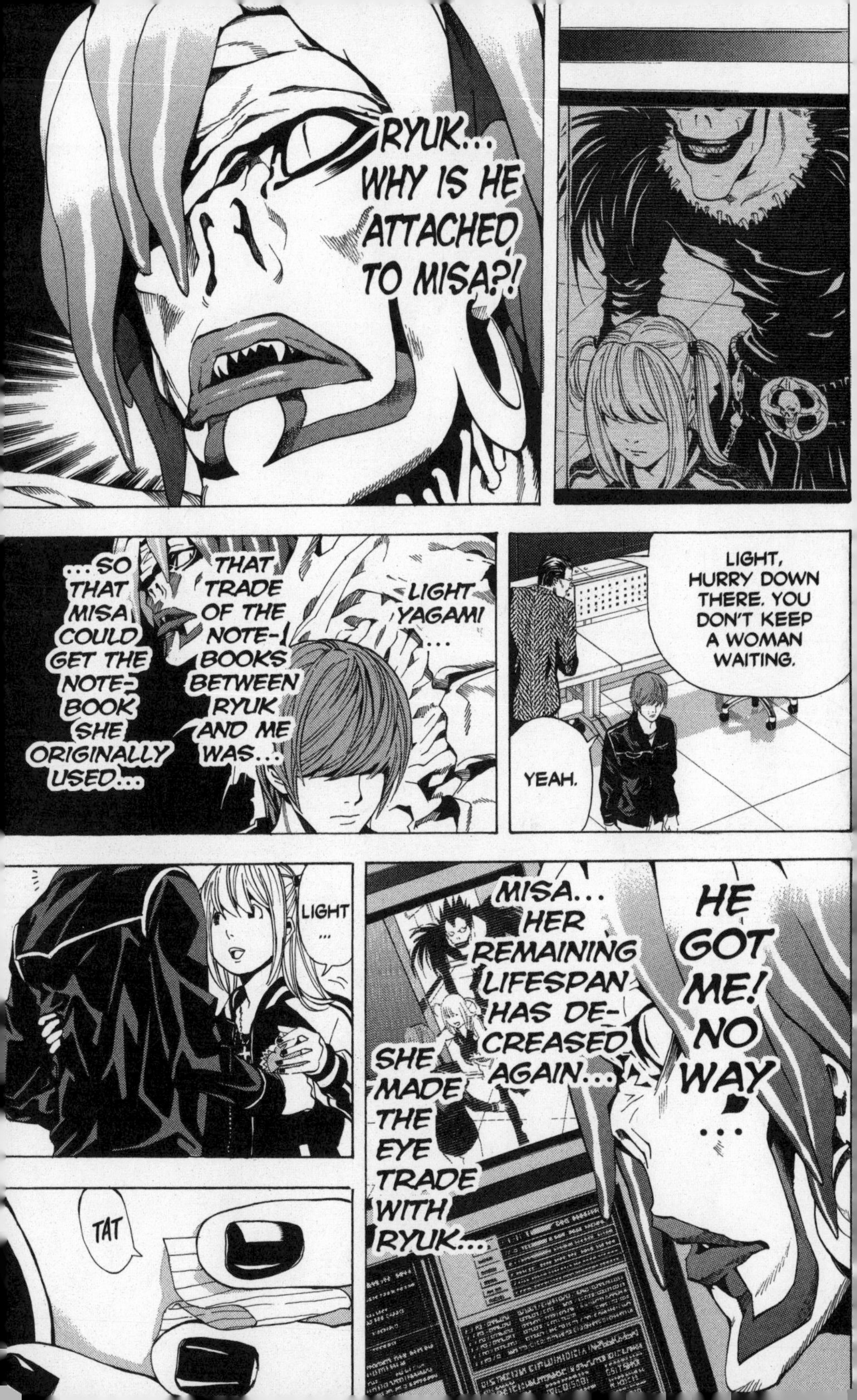
RYUK... WHY IS HE ATTACHED TO MISA?!
LIGHT, HURRY DOWN THERE. YOU DON'T KEEP A WOMAN WAITING.
YEAH.
LIGHT YAGAMI...
THAT TRADE OF THE NOTE-BOOKS BETWEEN RYUK AND ME WAS...
...SO THAT MISA COULD GET THE NOTE-BOOK SHE ORIGINALLY USED...
HE GOT ME! NO WAY...
MISA... HER REMAINING LIFESPAN HAS DE-CREASED AGAIN...
SHE MADE THE EYE TRADE WITH RYUK...
LIGHT...
TAT

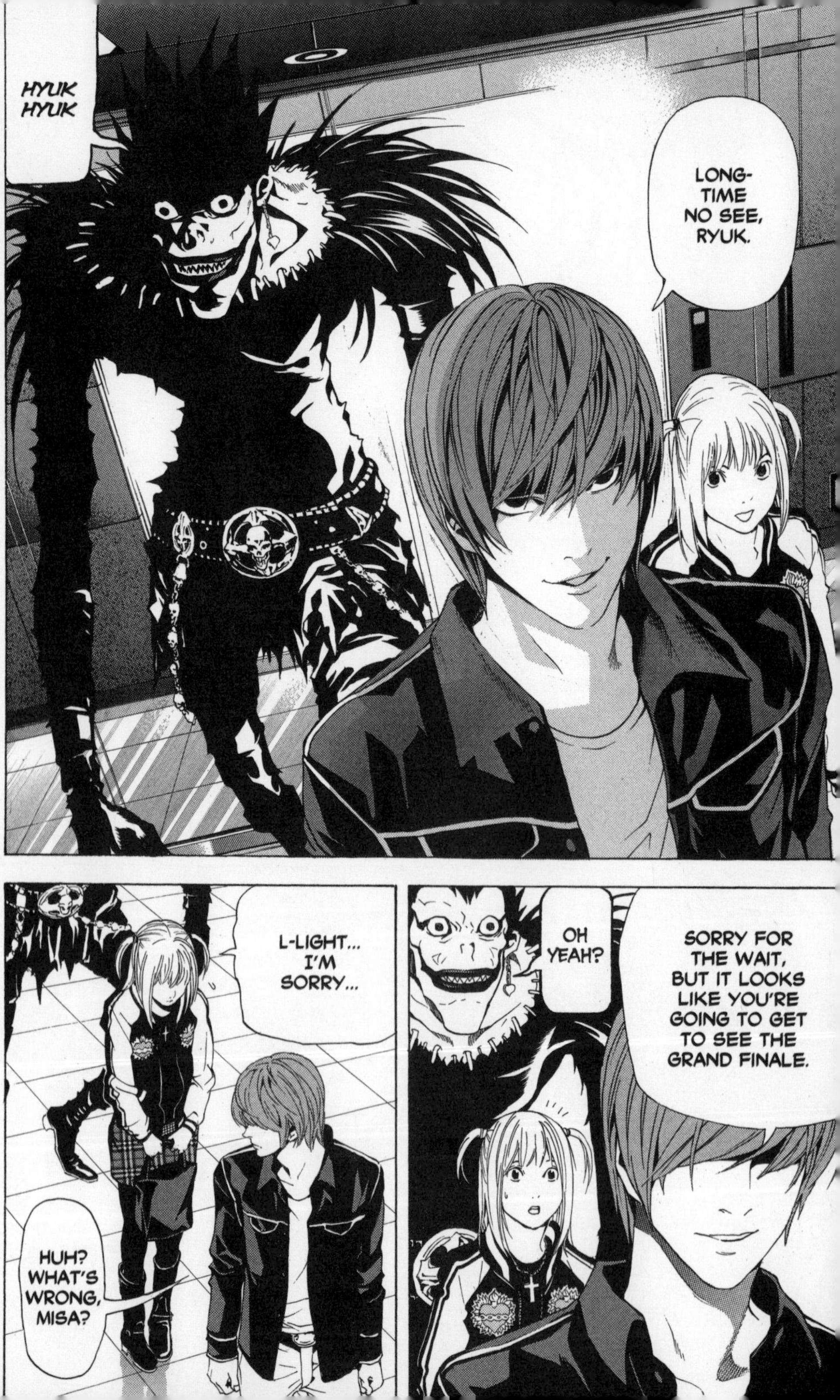
LONG-TIME NO SEE, RYUK.
HYUK HYUK
SORRY FOR THE WAIT, BUT IT LOOKS LIKE YOU'RE GOING TO GET TO SEE THE GRAND FINALE.
OH YEAH?
L-LIGHT... I'M SORRY...
HUH? WHAT'S WRONG, MISA?

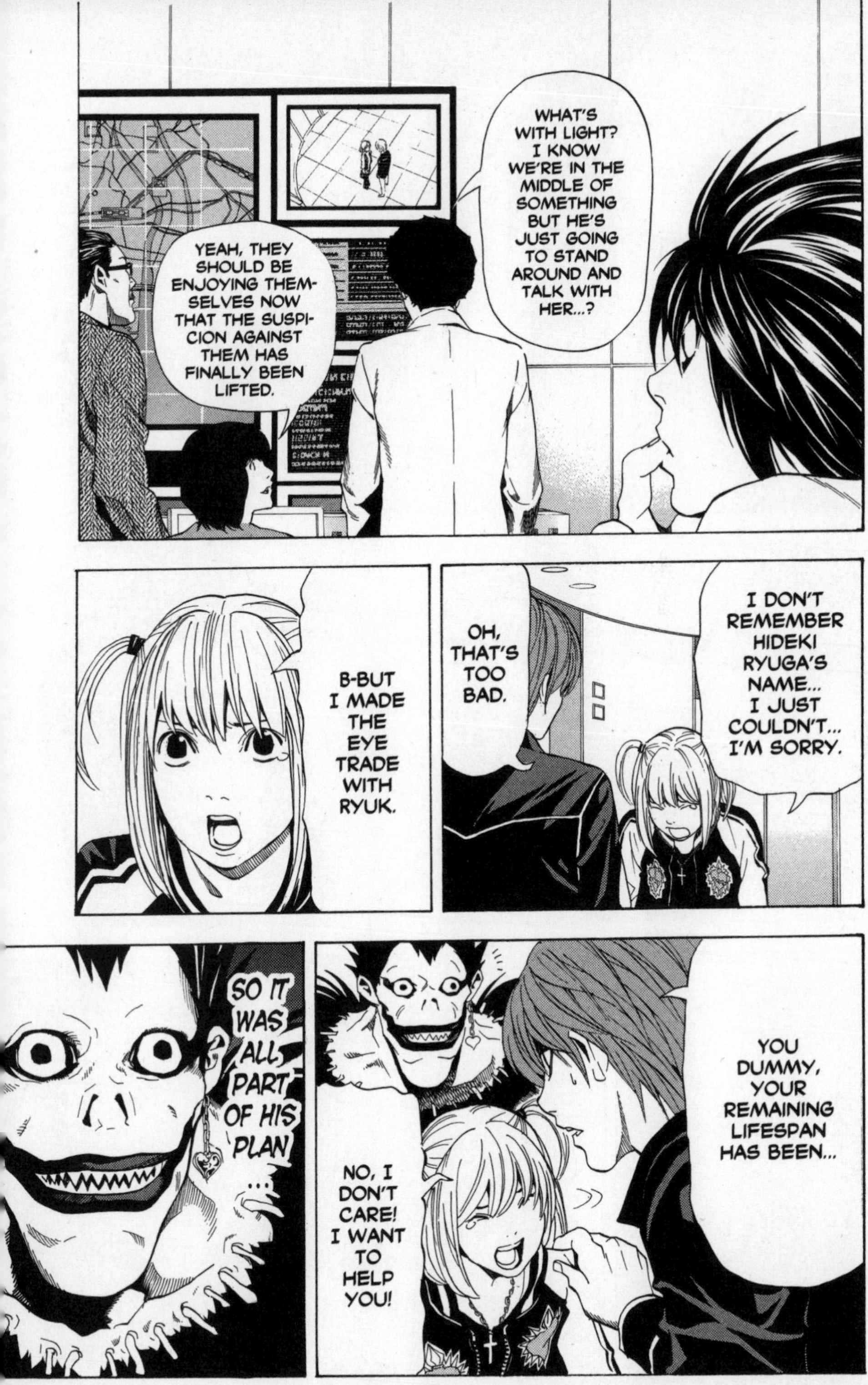
WHAT'S WITH LIGHT? I KNOW WE'RE IN THE MIDDLE OF SOMETHING BUT HE'S JUST GOING TO STAND AROUND AND TALK WITH HER...?
YEAH, THEY SHOULD BE ENJOYING THEMSELVES NOW THAT THE SUSPICION AGAINST THEM HAS FINALLY BEEN LIFTED.
I DON'T REMEMBER HIDEKI RYUGA'S NAME... I JUST COULDN'T... I'M SORRY.
OH, THAT'S TOO BAD.
B-BUT I MADE THE EYE TRADE WITH RYUK.
YOU DUMMY, YOUR REMAINING LIFESPAN HAS BEEN...
NO, I DON'T CARE! I WANT TO HELP YOU!
SO IT WAS ALL PART OF HIS PLAN...

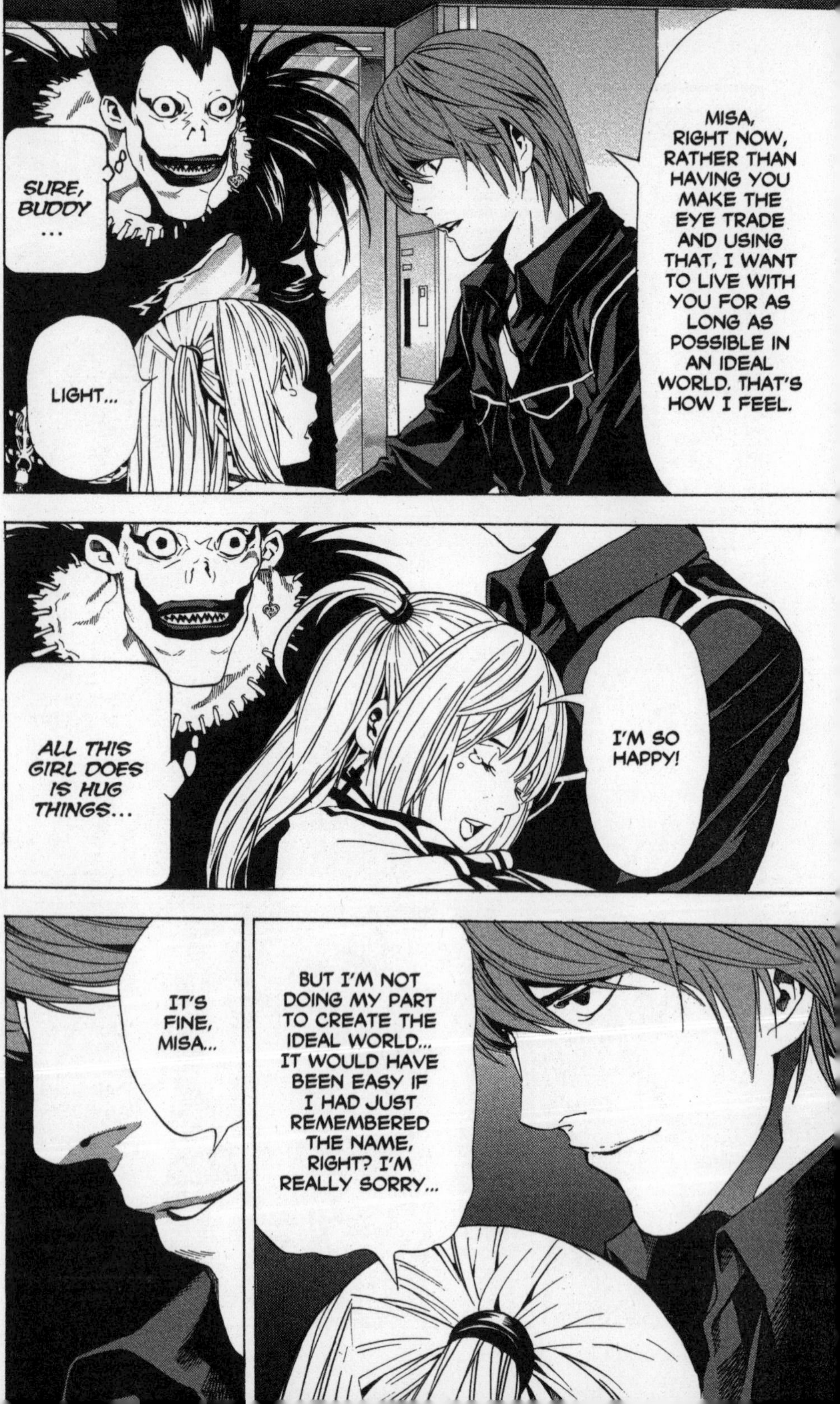
MISA, RIGHT NOW, RATHER THAN HAVING YOU MAKE THE EYE TRADE AND USING THAT, I WANT TO LIVE WITH YOU FOR AS LONG AS POSSIBLE IN AN IDEAL WORLD. THAT'S HOW I FEEL.
SURE, BUDDY ...
LIGHT...
I'M SO HAPPY!
ALL THIS GIRL DOES IS HUG THINGS...
BUT I'M NOT DOING MY PART TO CREATE THE IDEAL WORLD... IT WOULD HAVE BEEN EASY IF I HAD JUST REMEMBERED THE NAME, RIGHT? I'M REALLY SORRY...
IT'S FINE, MISA...

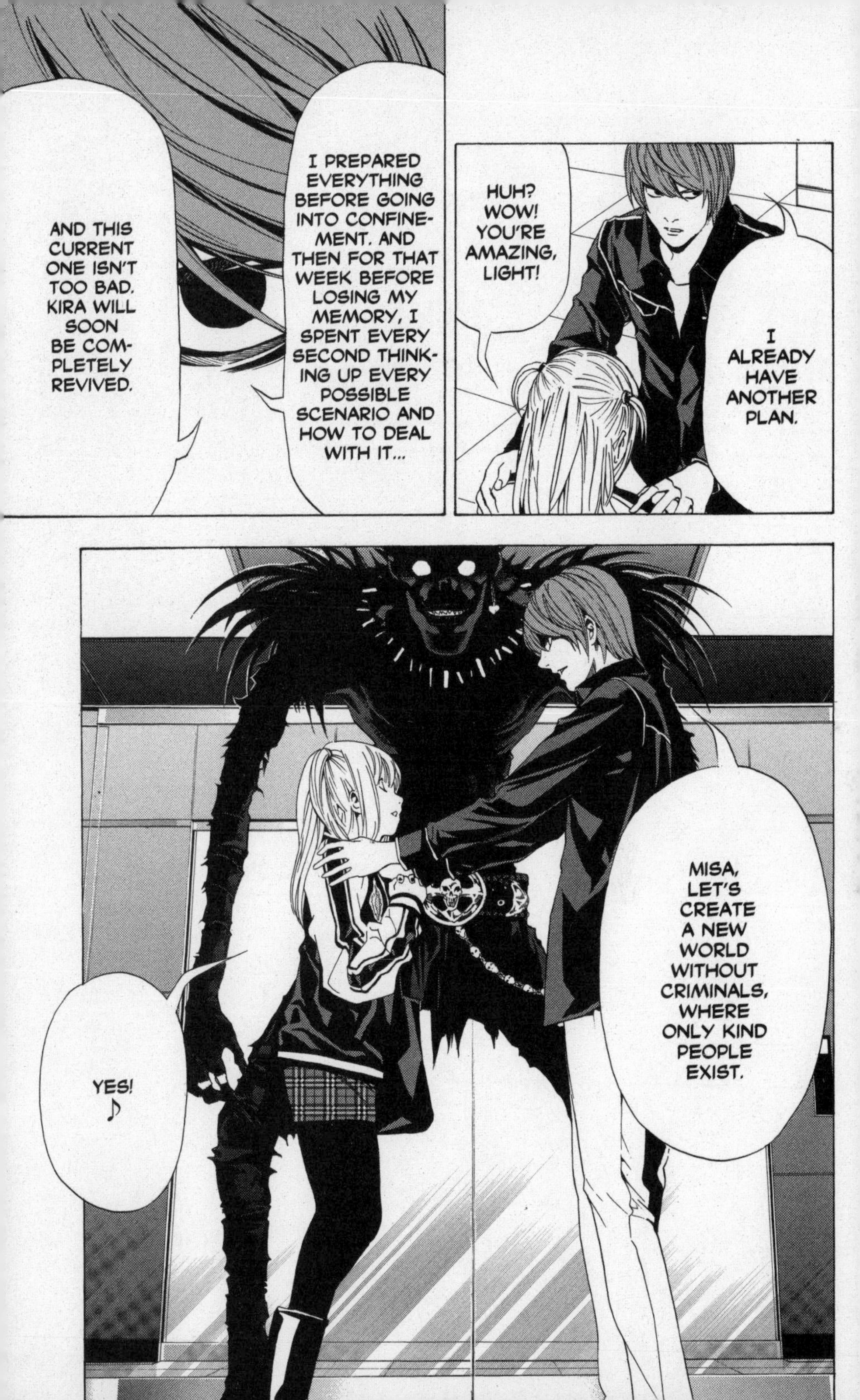
I ALREADY HAVE ANOTHER PLAN.
HUH? WOW! YOU'RE AMAZING, LIGHT!
I PREPARED EVERYTHING BEFORE GOING INTO CONFINE-MENT. AND THEN FOR THAT WEEK BEFORE LOSING MY MEMORY, I SPENT EVERY SECOND THINK-ING UP EVERY POSSIBLE SCENARIO AND HOW TO DEAL WITH IT...
AND THIS CURRENT ONE ISN'T TOO BAD. KIRA WILL SOON BE COM-PLETELY REVIVED.
MISA, LET'S CREATE A NEW WORLD WITHOUT CRIMINALS, WHERE ONLY KIND PEOPLE EXIST.
YES! ♪

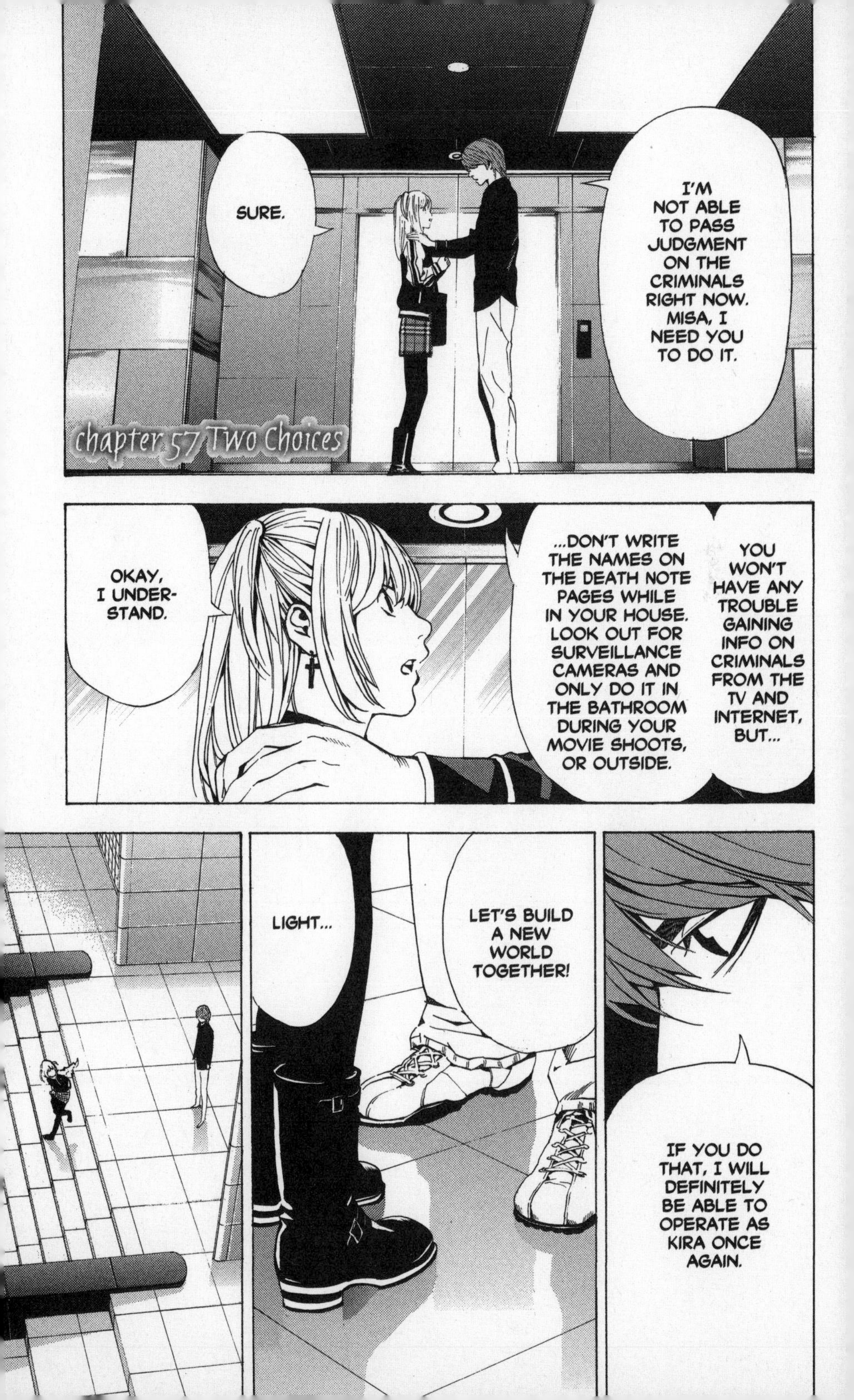
I'M NOT ABLE TO PASS JUDGMENT ON THE CRIMINALS RIGHT NOW. MISA, I NEED YOU TO DO IT.
SURE.
chapter 57 Two Choices
YOU WON'T HAVE ANY TROUBLE GAINING INFO ON CRIMINALS FROM THE TV AND INTERNET, BUT...
...DON'T WRITE THE NAMES ON THE DEATH NOTE PAGES WHILE IN YOUR HOUSE. LOOK OUT FOR SURVEILLANCE CAMERAS AND ONLY DO IT IN THE BATHROOM DURING YOUR MOVIE SHOOTS, OR OUTSIDE.
OKAY, I UNDER-STAND.
IF YOU DO THAT, I WILL DEFINITELY BE ABLE TO OPERATE AS KIRA ONCE AGAIN.
LET'S BUILD A NEW WORLD TOGETHER!
LIGHT...

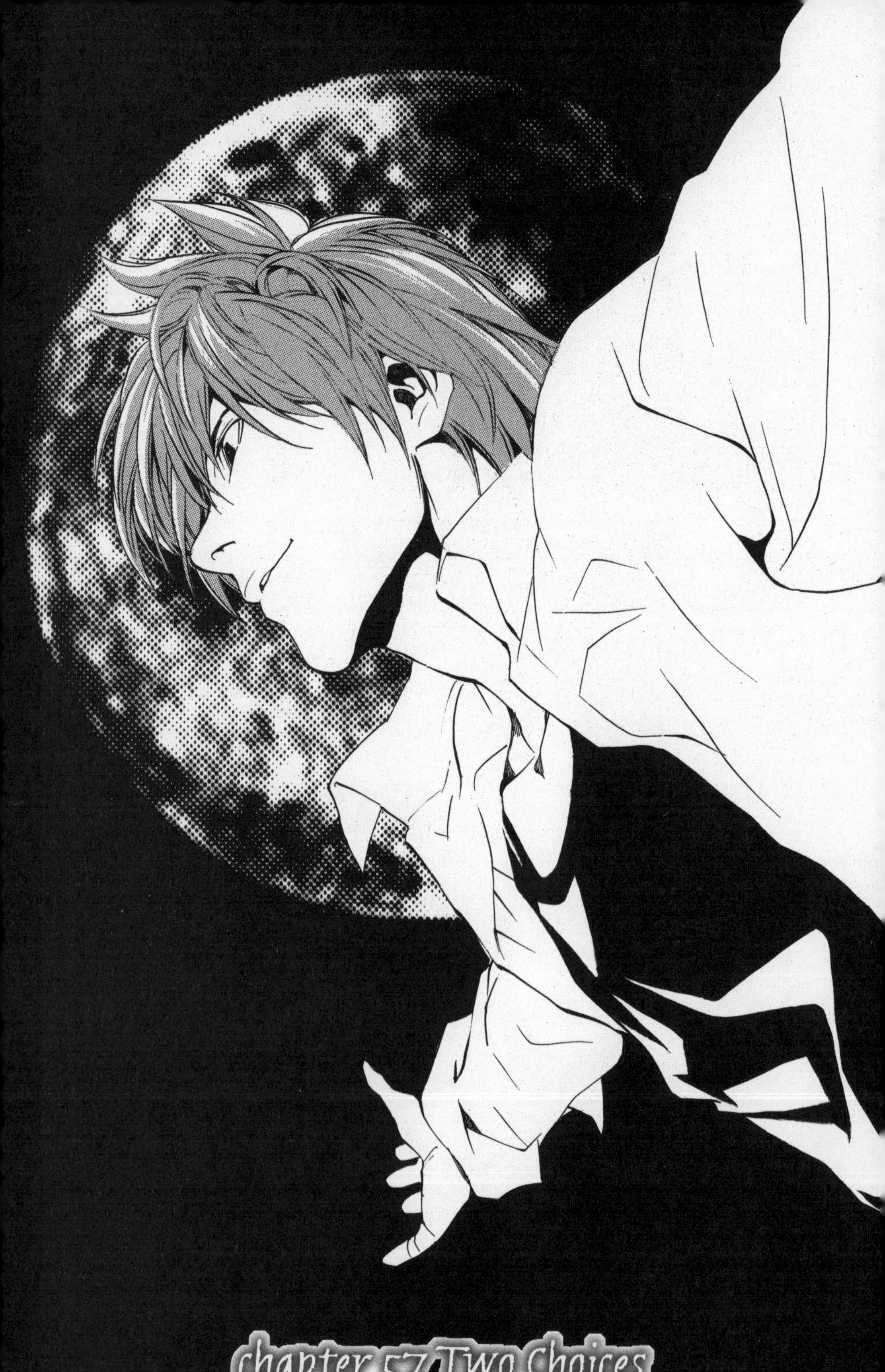

## chapter 57 Two Choices

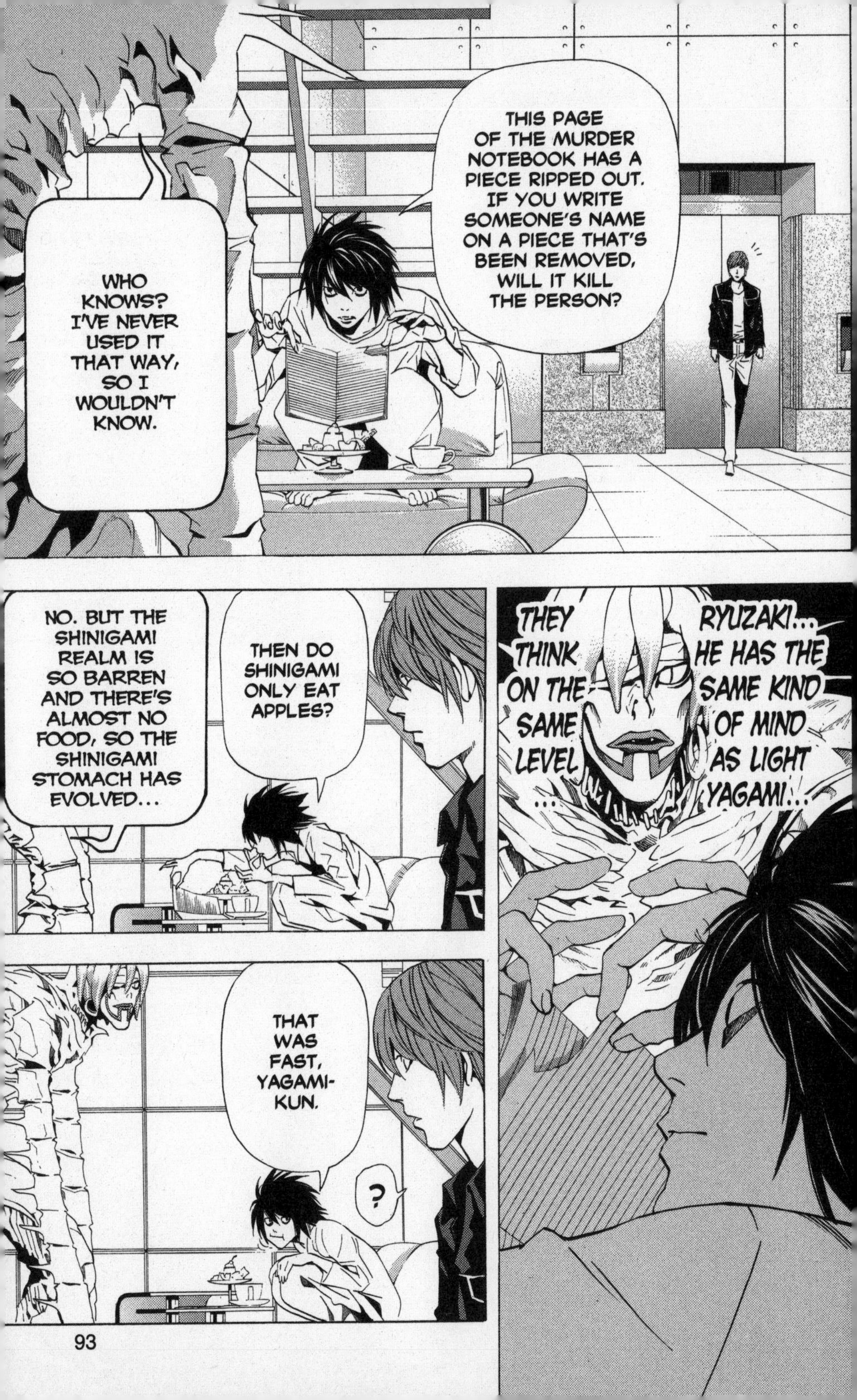
THIS PAGE OF THE MURDER NOTEBOOK HAS A PIECE RIPPED OUT. IF YOU WRITE SOMEONE'S NAME ON A PIECE THAT'S BEEN REMOVED, WILL IT KILL THE PERSON?
WHO KNOWS? I'VE NEVER USED IT THAT WAY, SO I WOULDN'T KNOW.
RYUZAKI... HE HAS THE SAME KIND OF MIND AS LIGHT YAGAMI...
THEY THINK ON THE SAME LEVEL...
THEN DO SHINIGAMI ONLY EAT APPLES?
NO. BUT THE SHINIGAMI REALM IS SO BARREN AND THERE'S ALMOST NO FOOD, SO THE SHINIGAMI STOMACH HAS EVOLVED...
THAT WAS FAST, YAGAMI-KUN.
?

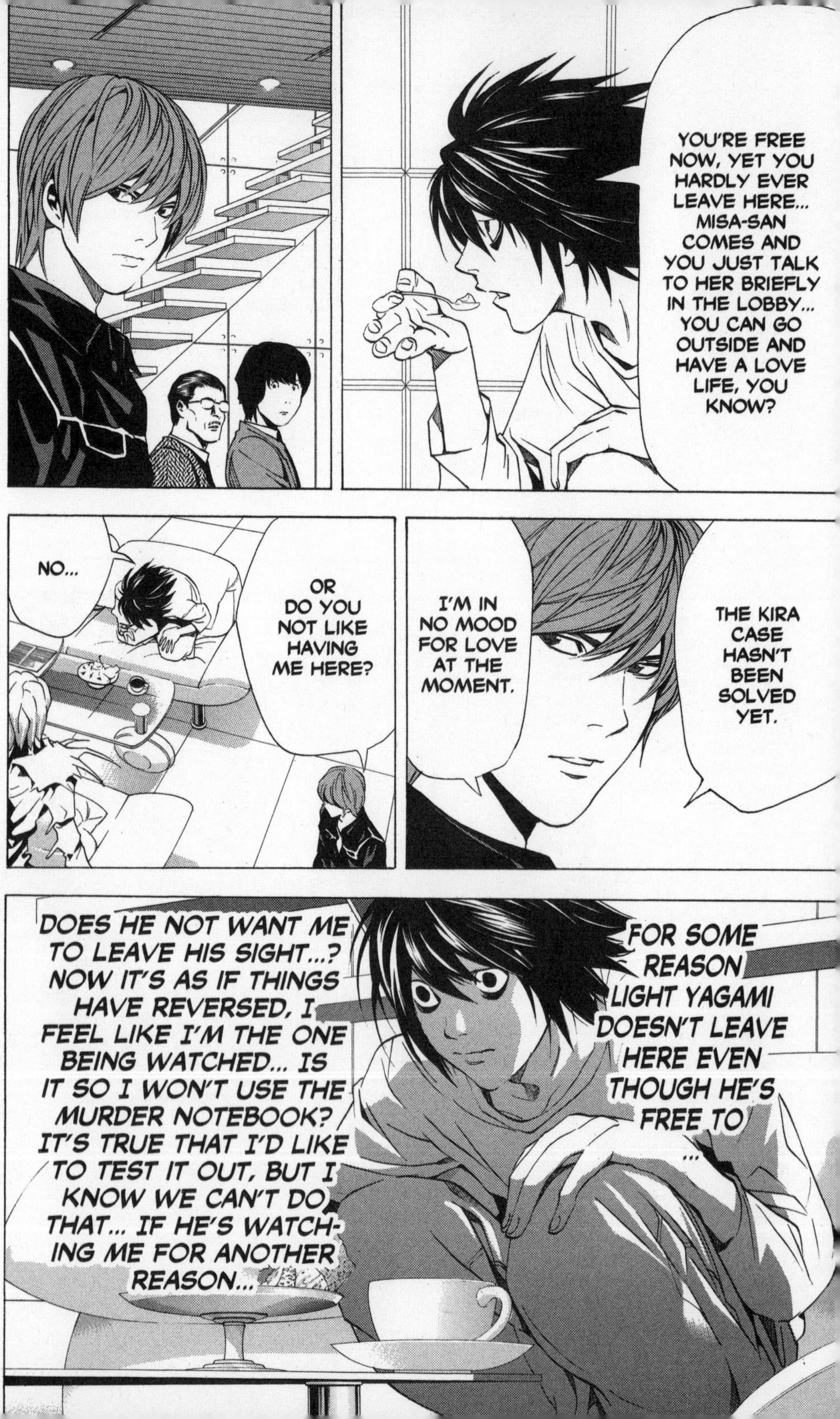
YOU'RE FREE NOW, YET YOU HARDLY EVER LEAVE HERE... MISA-SAN COMES AND YOU JUST TALK TO HER BRIEFLY IN THE LOBBY... YOU CAN GO OUTSIDE AND HAVE A LOVE LIFE, YOU KNOW?
THE KIRA CASE HASN'T BEEN SOLVED YET.
I'M IN NO MOOD FOR LOVE AT THE MOMENT.
OR DO YOU NOT LIKE HAVING ME HERE?
NO...
FOR SOME REASON LIGHT YAGAMI DOESN'T LEAVE HERE EVEN THOUGH HE'S FREE TO ...
DOES HE NOT WANT ME TO LEAVE HIS SIGHT...? NOW IT'S AS IF THINGS HAVE REVERSED, I FEEL LIKE I'M THE ONE BEING WATCHED... IS IT SO I WON'T USE THE MURDER NOTEBOOK? IT'S TRUE THAT I'D LIKE TO TEST IT OUT, BUT I KNOW WE CAN'T DO THAT... IF HE'S WATCHING ME FOR ANOTHER REASON...

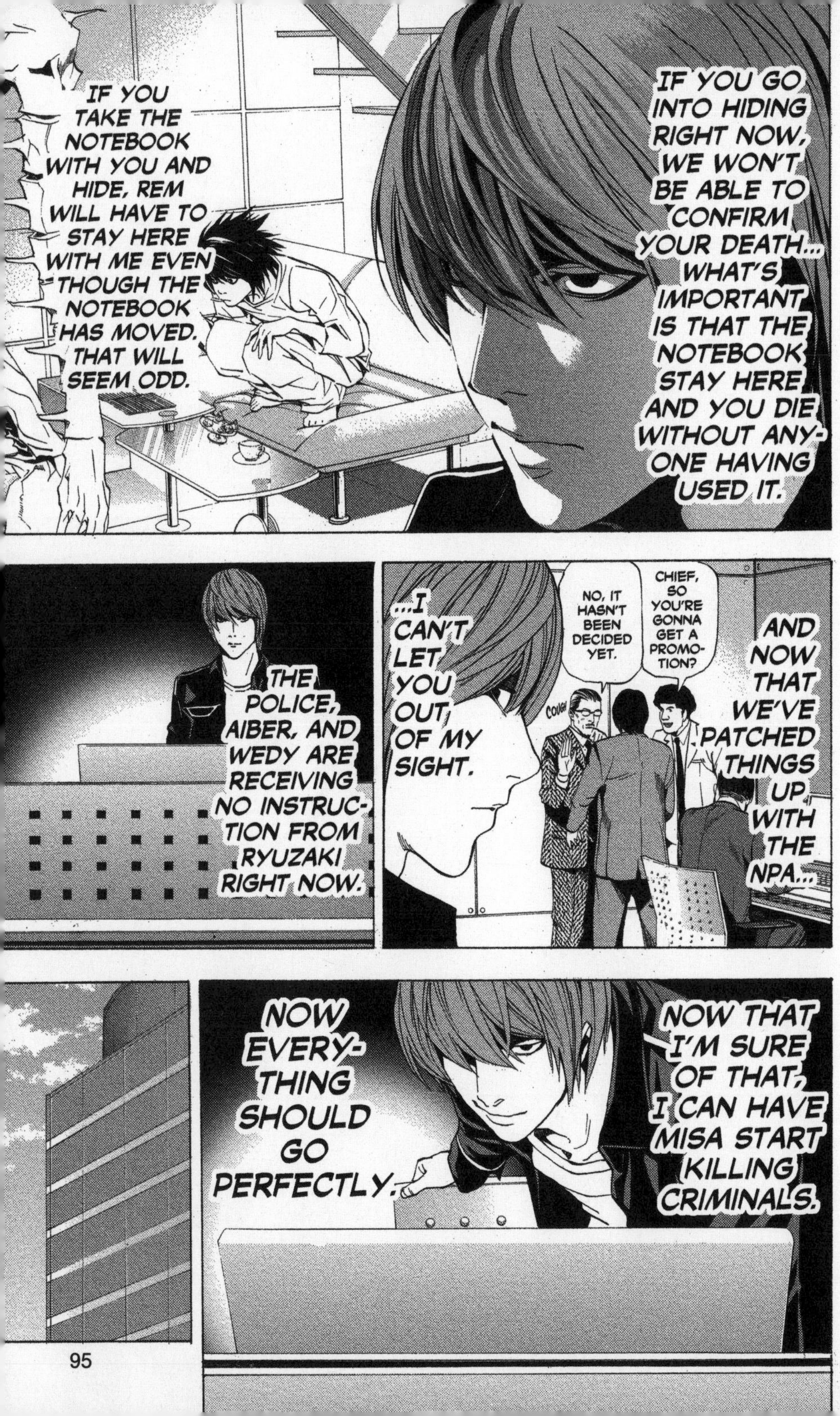
IF YOU GO INTO HIDING RIGHT NOW, WE WON'T BE ABLE TO CONFIRM YOUR DEATH... WHAT'S IMPORTANT IS THAT THE NOTEBOOK STAY HERE AND YOU DIE WITHOUT ANYONE HAVING USED IT.
IF YOU TAKE THE NOTEBOOK WITH YOU AND HIDE, REM WILL HAVE TO STAY HERE WITH ME EVEN THOUGH THE NOTEBOOK HAS MOVED. THAT WILL SEEM ODD.
AND NOW THAT WE'VE PATCHED THINGS UP WITH THE NPA...
CHIEF, SO YOU'RE GONNA GET A PROMOTION?
NO, IT HASN'T BEEN DECIDED YET.
COUGH
...I CAN'T LET YOU OUT OF MY SIGHT.
THE POLICE, AIBER, AND WEDY ARE RECEIVING NO INSTRUCTION FROM RYUZAKI RIGHT NOW.
NOW THAT I'M SURE OF THAT, I CAN HAVE MISA START KILLING CRIMINALS.
NOW EVERYTHING SHOULD GO PERFECTLY.

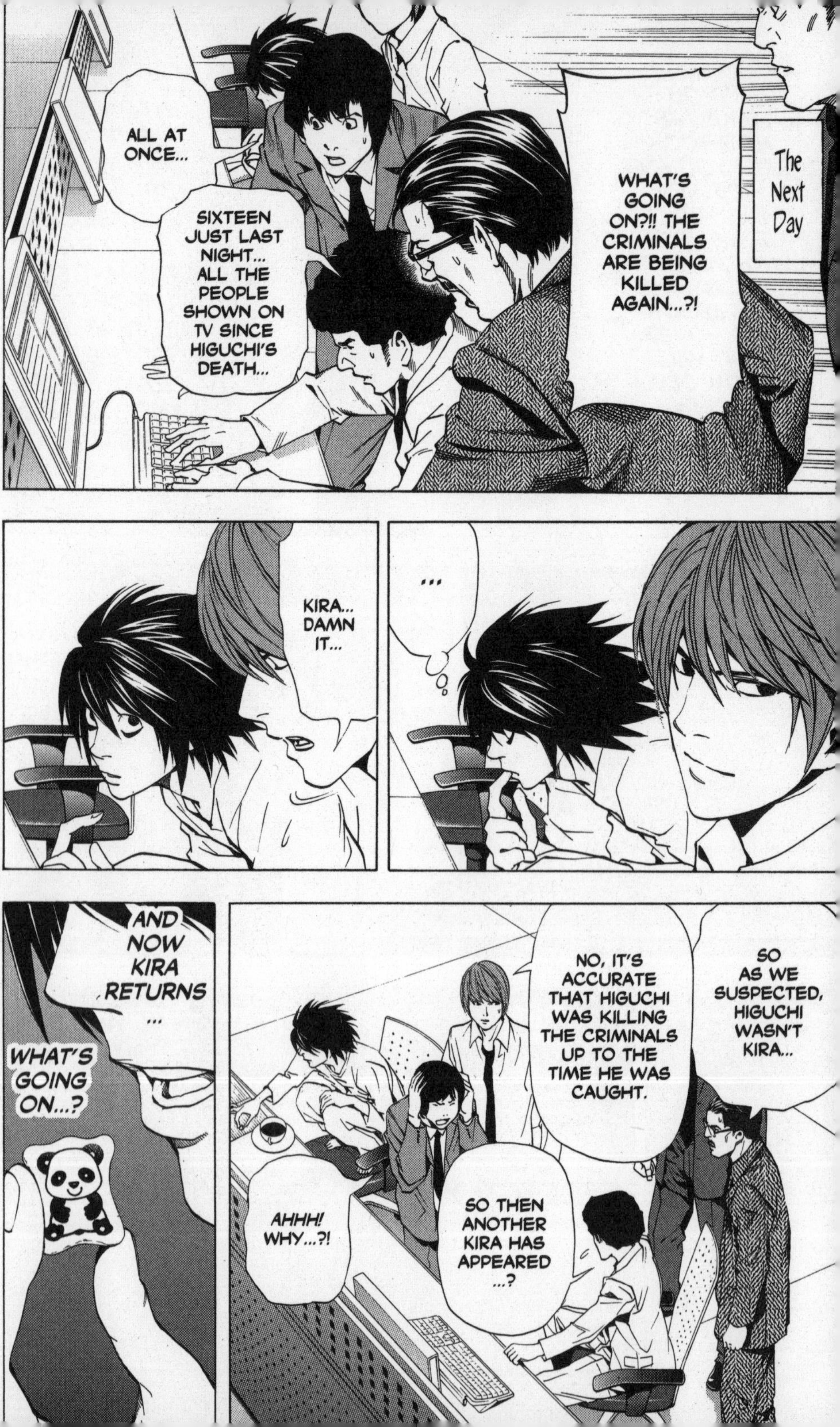
The Next Day
WHAT'S GOING ON?!! THE CRIMINALS ARE BEING KILLED AGAIN...?!
SIXTEEN JUST LAST NIGHT... ALL THE PEOPLE SHOWN ON TV SINCE HIGUCHI'S DEATH...
ALL AT ONCE...
...
KIRA... DAMN IT...
SO AS WE SUSPECTED, HIGUCHI WASN'T KIRA...
NO, IT'S ACCURATE THAT HIGUCHI WAS KILLING THE CRIMINALS UP TO THE TIME HE WAS CAUGHT.
SO THEN ANOTHER KIRA HAS APPEARED ...?
AHHH! WHY...?!
AND NOW KIRA RETURNS ...
WHAT'S GOING ON...?

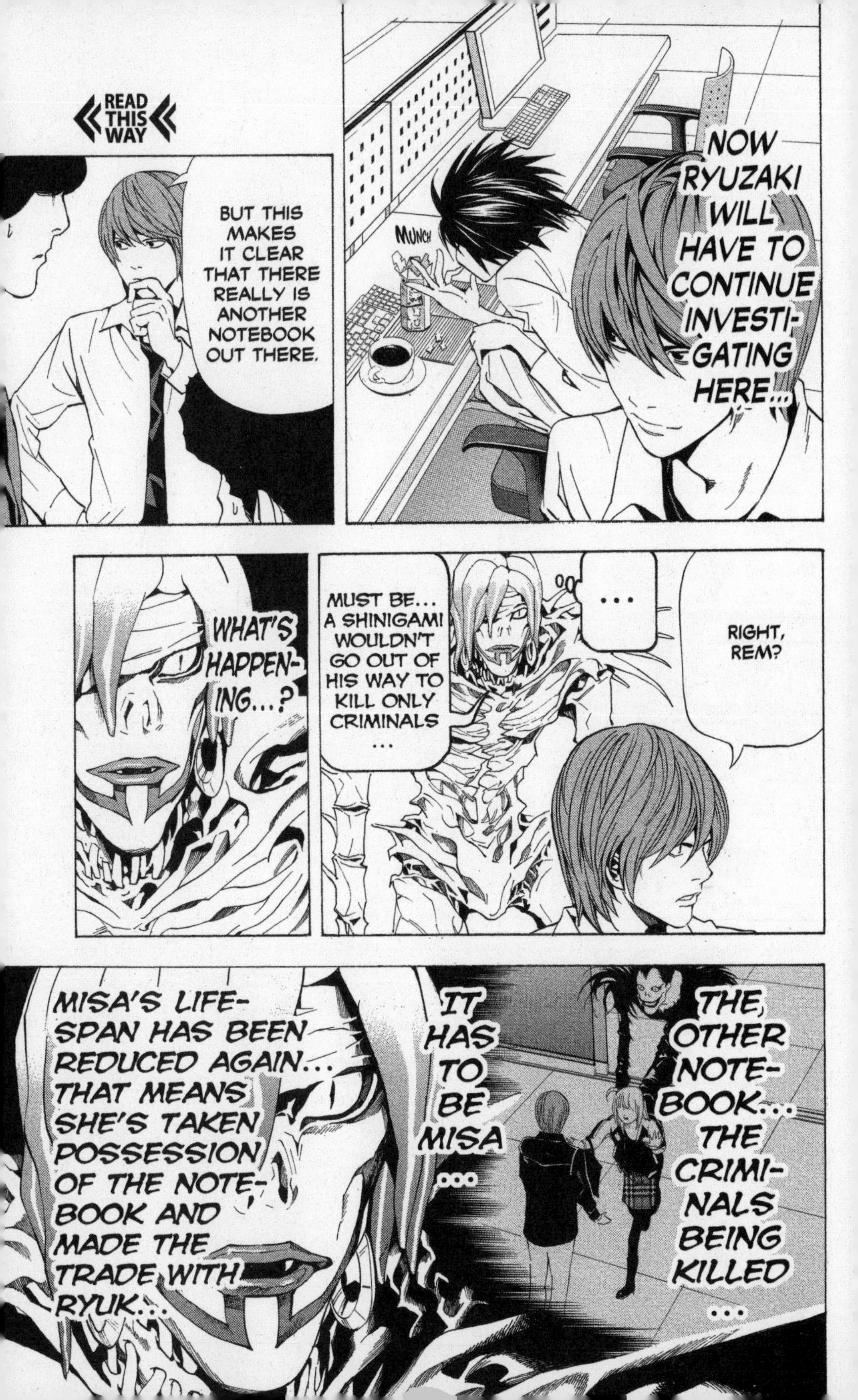
READ THIS WAY
NOW RYUZAKI WILL HAVE TO CONTINUE INVESTI-GATING HERE...
MUNCH
BUT THIS MAKES IT CLEAR THAT THERE REALLY IS ANOTHER NOTEBOOK OUT THERE.
RIGHT, REM?
...
MUST BE... A SHINIGAMI WOULDN'T GO OUT OF HIS WAY TO KILL ONLY CRIMINALS ...
WHAT'S HAPPEN-ING...?
THE OTHER NOTE-BOOK... THE CRIMI-NALS BEING KILLED ...
IT HAS TO BE MISA ...
MISA'S LIFE-SPAN HAS BEEN REDUCED AGAIN... THAT MEANS SHE'S TAKEN POSSESSION OF THE NOTE-BOOK AND MADE THE TRADE WITH RYUK...

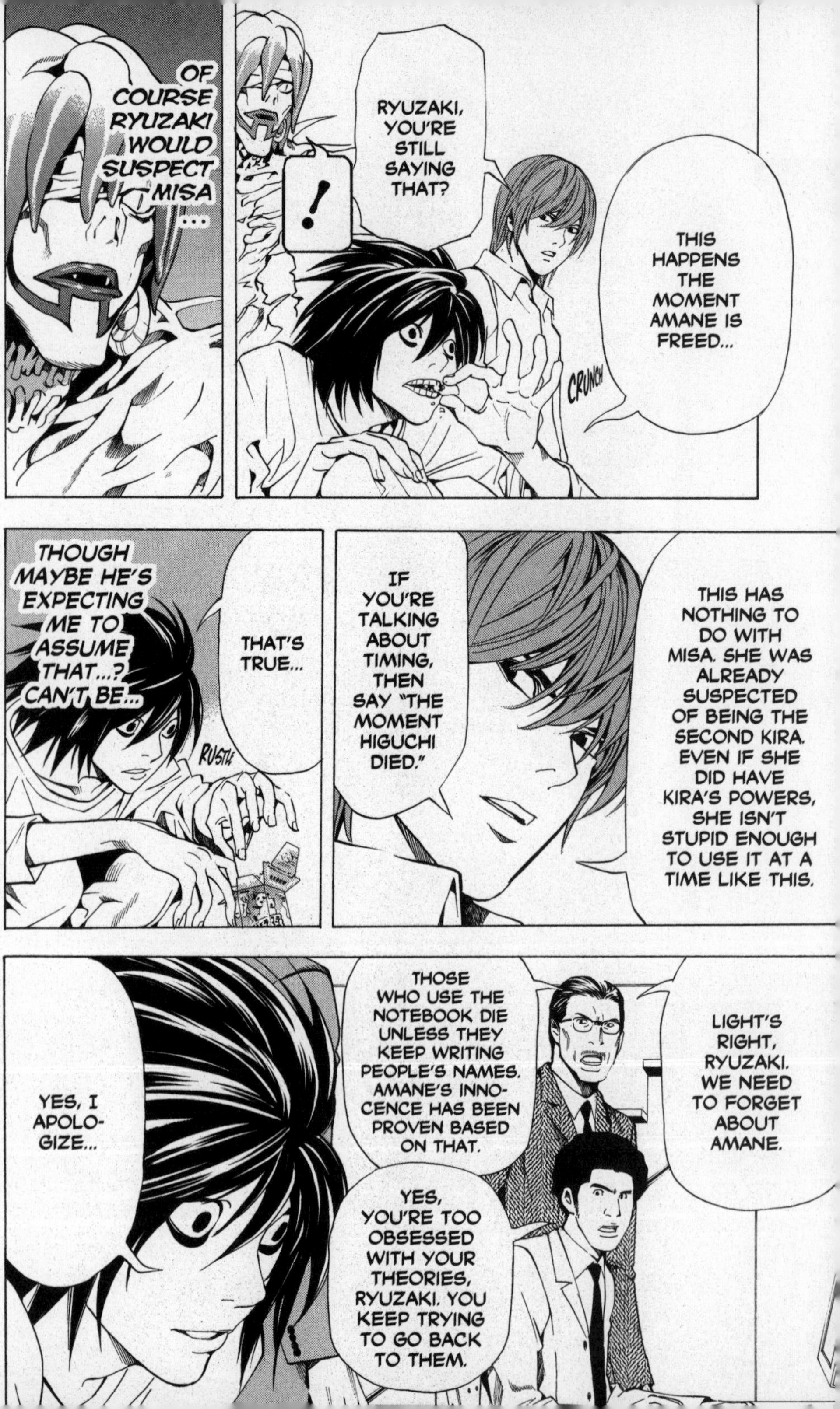
THIS HAPPENS THE MOMENT AMANE IS FREED...
CRUNCH
RYUZAKI, YOU'RE STILL SAYING THAT?
!
OF COURSE RYUZAKI WOULD SUSPECT MISA...
THIS HAS NOTHING TO DO WITH MISA. SHE WAS ALREADY SUSPECTED OF BEING THE SECOND KIRA. EVEN IF SHE DID HAVE KIRA'S POWERS, SHE ISN'T STUPID ENOUGH TO USE IT AT A TIME LIKE THIS.
IF YOU'RE TALKING ABOUT TIMING, THEN SAY "THE MOMENT HIGUCHI DIED."
THAT'S TRUE...
THOUGH MAYBE HE'S EXPECTING ME TO ASSUME THAT...? CAN'T BE...
RUSTLE
LIGHT'S RIGHT, RYUZAKI. WE NEED TO FORGET ABOUT AMANE.
THOSE WHO USE THE NOTEBOOK DIE UNLESS THEY KEEP WRITING PEOPLE'S NAMES. AMANE'S INNOCENCE HAS BEEN PROVEN BASED ON THAT.
YES, YOU'RE TOO OBSESSED WITH YOUR THEORIES, RYUZAKI. YOU KEEP TRYING TO GO BACK TO THEM.
YES, I APOLOGIZE...

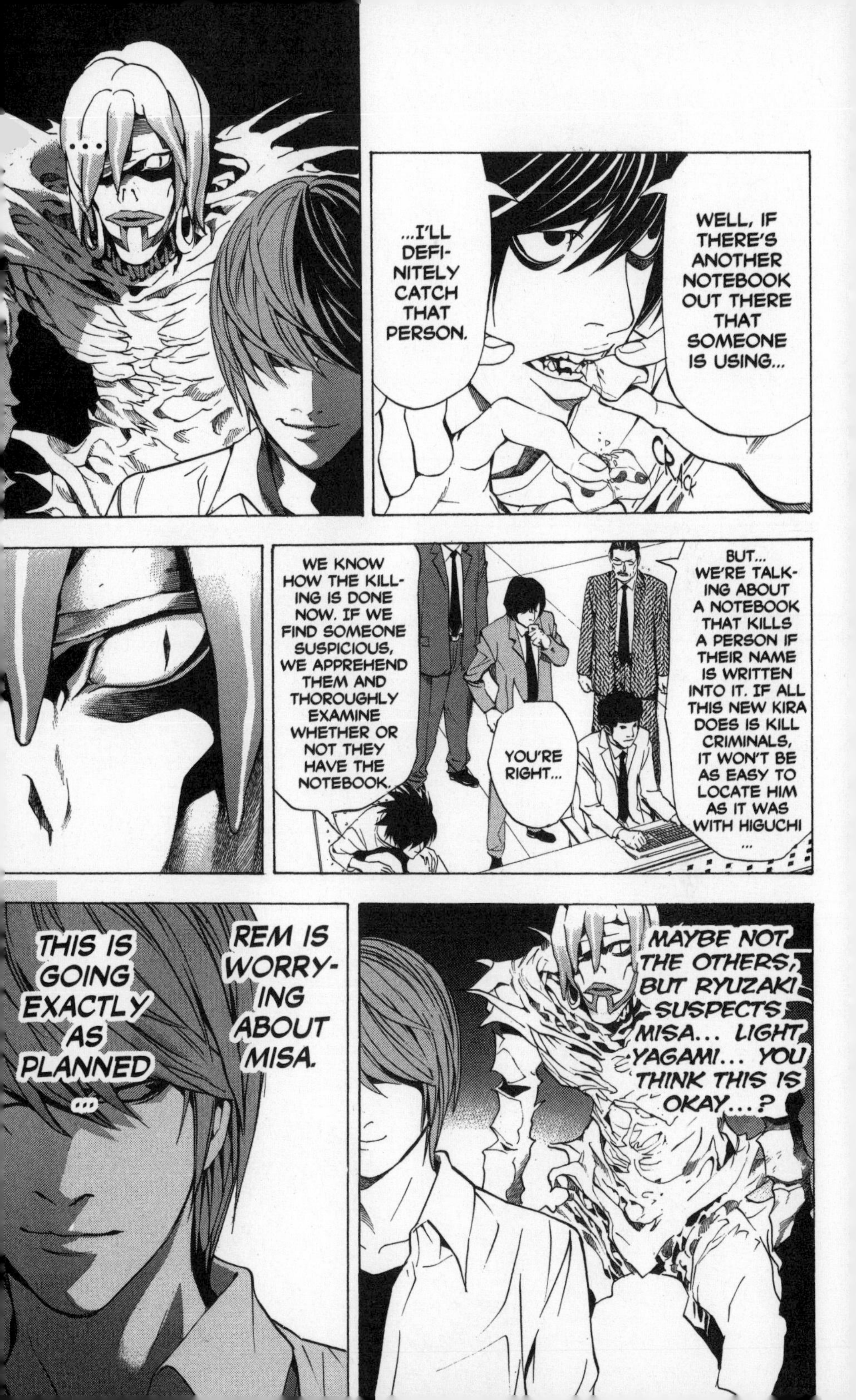

WELL, IF THERE'S ANOTHER NOTEBOOK OUT THERE THAT SOMEONE IS USING...
...I'LL DEFINITELY CATCH THAT PERSON.
CRACK
...
BUT... WE'RE TALKING ABOUT A NOTEBOOK THAT KILLS A PERSON IF THEIR NAME IS WRITTEN INTO IT. IF ALL THIS NEW KIRA DOES IS KILL CRIMINALS, IT WON'T BE AS EASY TO LOCATE HIM AS IT WAS WITH HIGUCHI ...
WE KNOW HOW THE KILLING IS DONE NOW. IF WE FIND SOMEONE SUSPICIOUS, WE APPREHEND THEM AND THOROUGHLY EXAMINE WHETHER OR NOT THEY HAVE THE NOTEBOOK.
YOU'RE RIGHT...
MAYBE NOT THE OTHERS, BUT RYUZAKI SUSPECTS MISA... LIGHT YAGAMI... YOU THINK THIS IS OKAY...?
REM IS WORRYING ABOUT MISA.
THIS IS GOING EXACTLY AS PLANNED ...

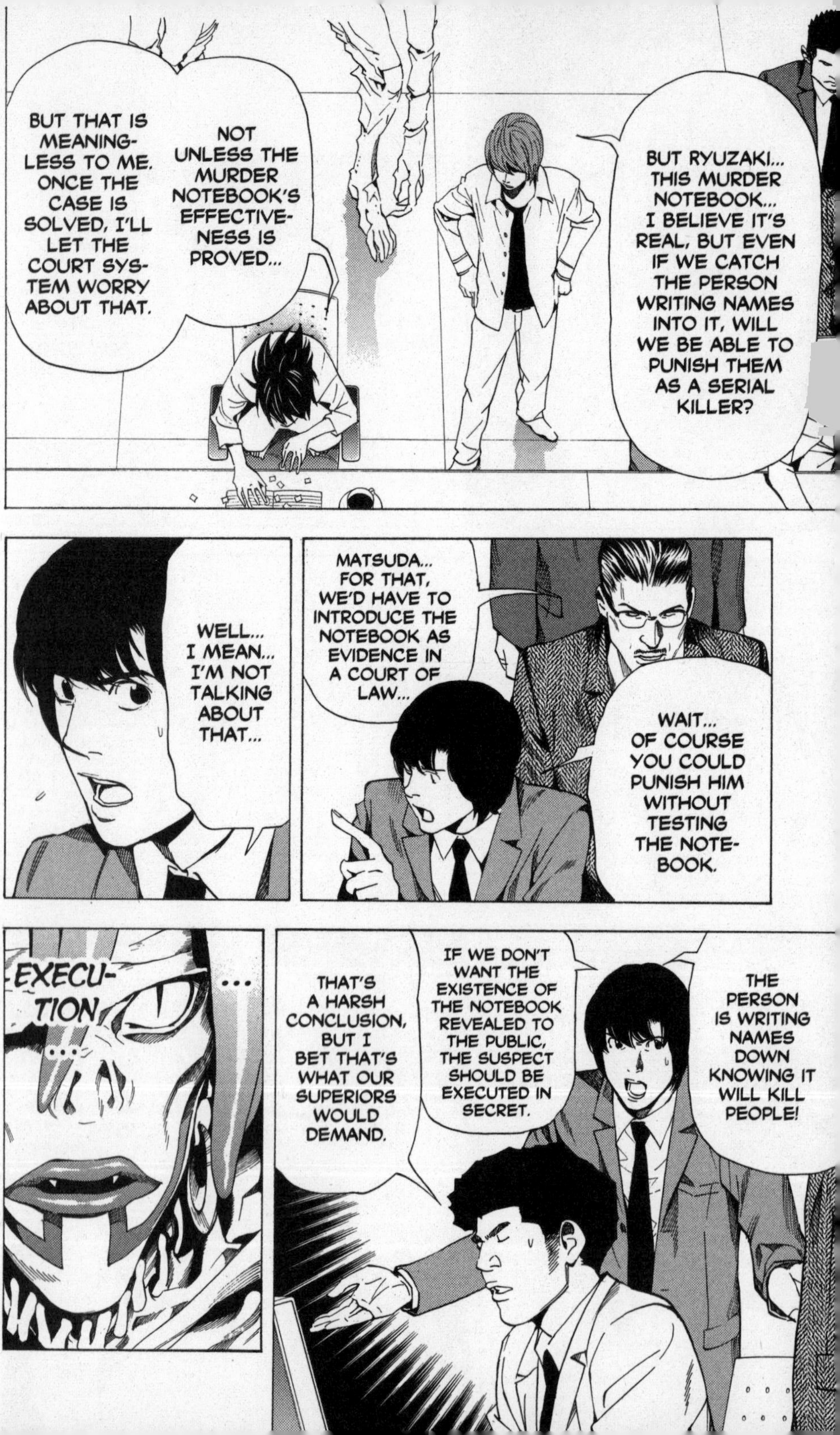
BUT RYUZAKI... THIS MURDER NOTEBOOK... I BELIEVE IT'S REAL, BUT EVEN IF WE CATCH THE PERSON WRITING NAMES INTO IT, WILL WE BE ABLE TO PUNISH THEM AS A SERIAL KILLER?
NOT UNLESS THE MURDER NOTEBOOK'S EFFECTIVE-NESS IS PROVED...
BUT THAT IS MEANING-LESS TO ME. ONCE THE CASE IS SOLVED, I'LL LET THE COURT SYS-TEM WORRY ABOUT THAT.
MATSUDA... FOR THAT, WE'D HAVE TO INTRODUCE THE NOTEBOOK AS EVIDENCE IN A COURT OF LAW...
WAIT... OF COURSE YOU COULD PUNISH HIM WITHOUT TESTING THE NOTE-BOOK.
WELL... I MEAN... I'M NOT TALKING ABOUT THAT...
THE PERSON IS WRITING NAMES DOWN KNOWING IT WILL KILL PEOPLE!
IF WE DON'T WANT THE EXISTENCE OF THE NOTEBOOK REVEALED TO THE PUBLIC, THE SUSPECT SHOULD BE EXECUTED IN SECRET.
THAT'S A HARSH CONCLUSION, BUT I BET THAT'S WHAT OUR SUPERIORS WOULD DEMAND.
...
EXECU-TION ...

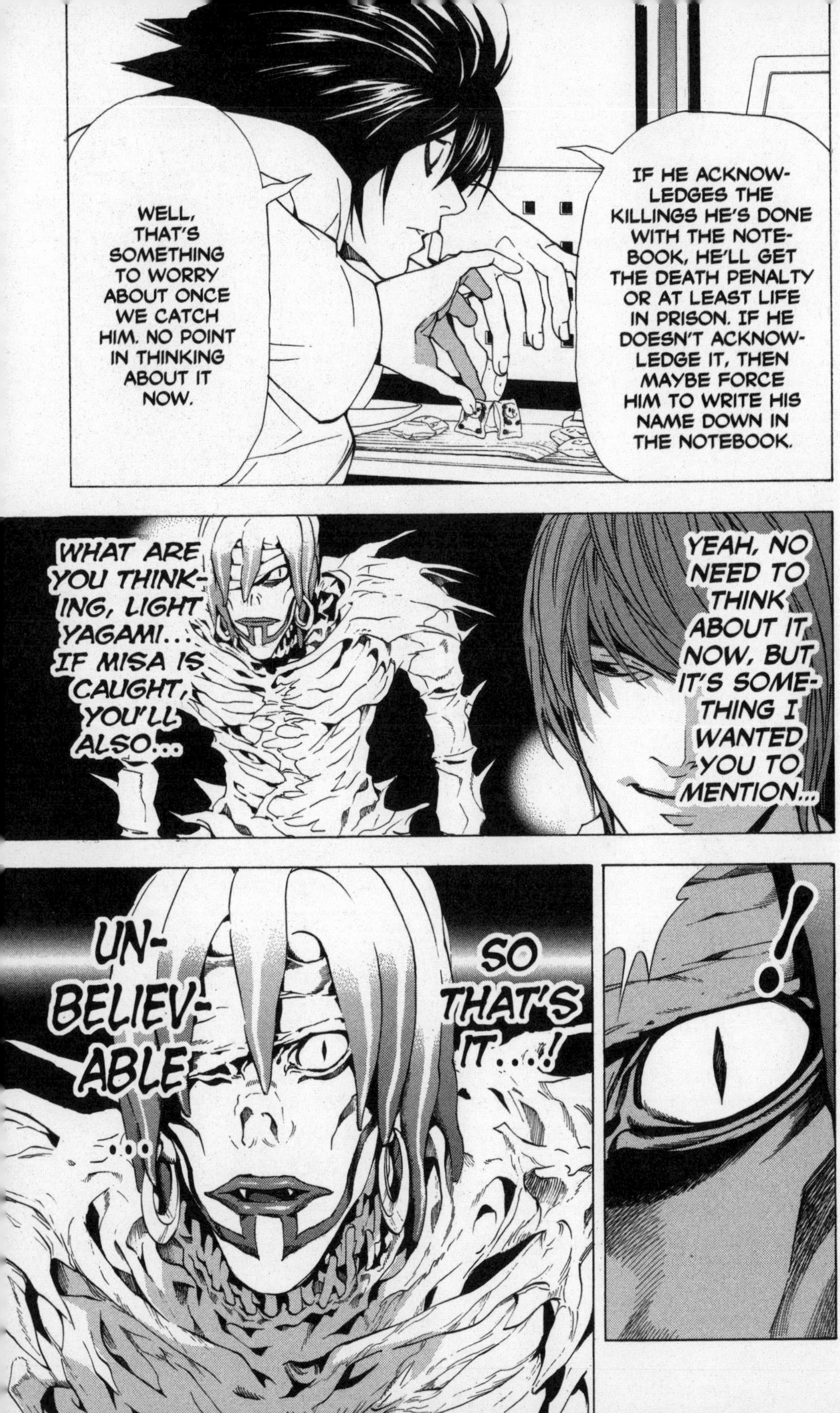
IF HE ACKNOWLEDGES THE KILLINGS HE'S DONE WITH THE NOTEBOOK, HE'LL GET THE DEATH PENALTY OR AT LEAST LIFE IN PRISON. IF HE DOESN'T ACKNOWLEDGE IT, THEN MAYBE FORCE HIM TO WRITE HIS NAME DOWN IN THE NOTEBOOK.
WELL, THAT'S SOMETHING TO WORRY ABOUT ONCE WE CATCH HIM. NO POINT IN THINKING ABOUT IT NOW.
YEAH, NO NEED TO THINK ABOUT IT NOW, BUT IT'S SOMETHING I WANTED YOU TO MENTION...
WHAT ARE YOU THINKING, LIGHT YAGAMI... IF MISA IS CAUGHT, YOU'LL ALSO...
!
SO THAT'S IT...!
UN-BELIEV-ABLE
...

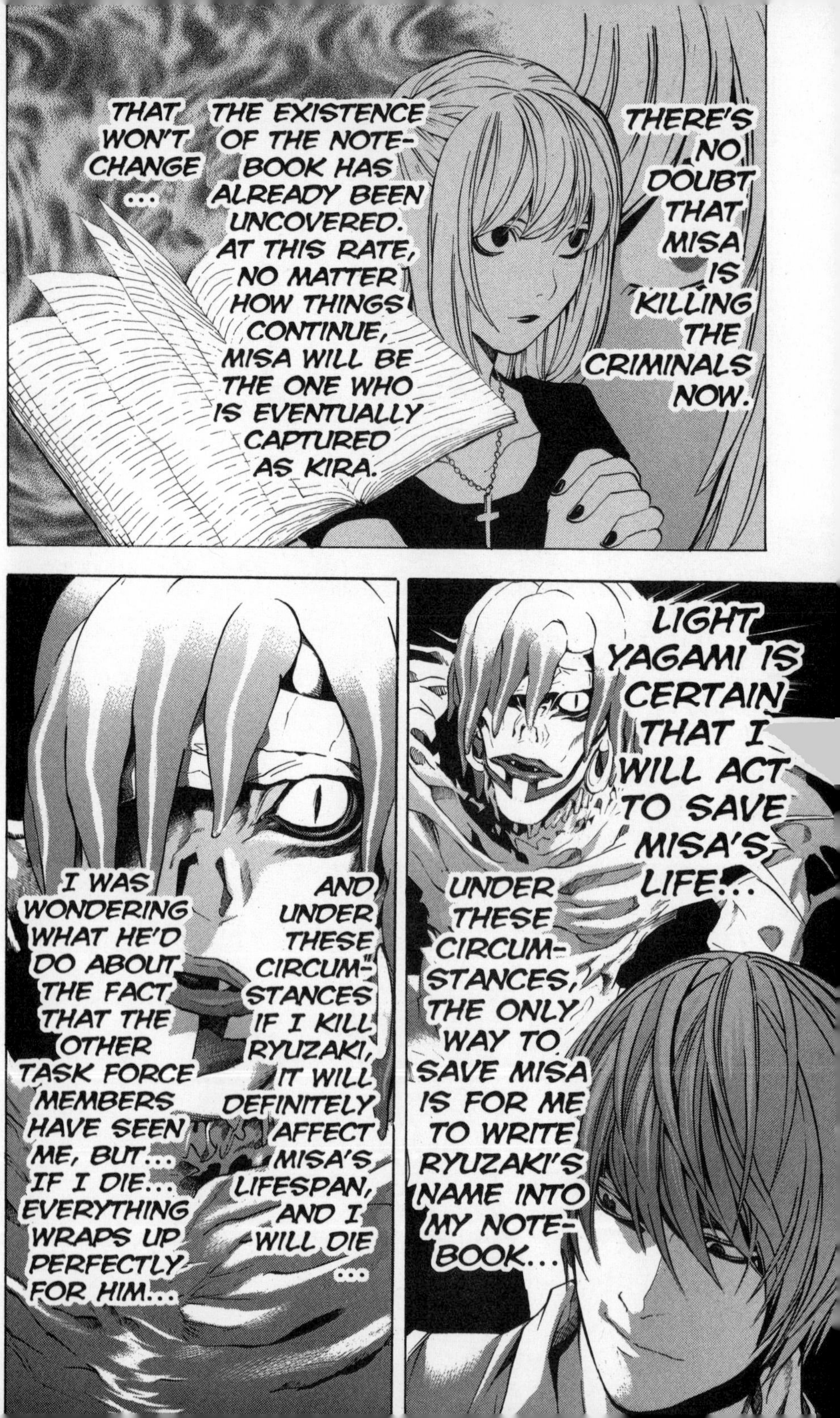
THERE'S NO DOUBT THAT MISA IS KILLING THE CRIMINALS NOW.
THE EXISTENCE OF THE NOTE-BOOK HAS ALREADY BEEN UNCOVERED. AT THIS RATE, NO MATTER HOW THINGS CONTINUE, MISA WILL BE THE ONE WHO IS EVENTUALLY CAPTURED AS KIRA.
THAT WON'T CHANGE...
LIGHT YAGAMI IS CERTAIN THAT I WILL ACT TO SAVE MISA'S LIFE...
UNDER THESE CIRCUM-STANCES, THE ONLY WAY TO SAVE MISA IS FOR ME TO WRITE RYUZAKI'S NAME INTO MY NOTE-BOOK...
AND UNDER THESE CIRCUM-STANCES IF I KILL RYUZAKI, IT WILL DEFINITELY AFFECT MISA'S LIFESPAN, AND I WILL DIE...
I WAS WONDERING WHAT HE'D DO ABOUT THE FACT THAT THE OTHER TASK FORCE MEMBERS HAVE SEEN ME, BUT... IF I DIE... EVERYTHING WRAPS UP PERFECTLY FOR HIM...

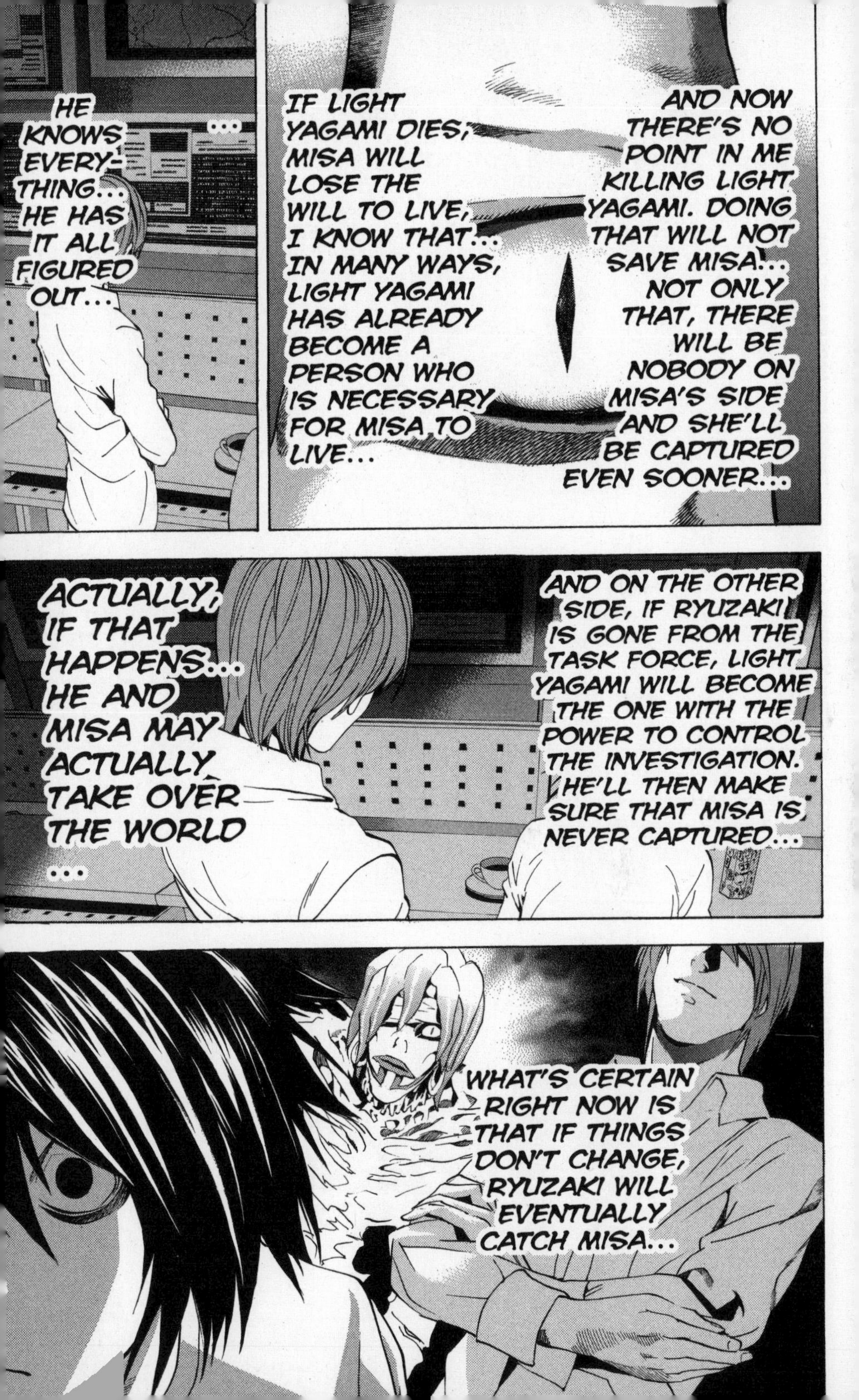
IF LIGHT YAGAMI DIES, MISA WILL LOSE THE WILL TO LIVE, I KNOW THAT... IN MANY WAYS, LIGHT YAGAMI HAS ALREADY BECOME A PERSON WHO IS NECESSARY FOR MISA TO LIVE...
AND NOW THERE'S NO POINT IN ME KILLING LIGHT YAGAMI. DOING THAT WILL NOT SAVE MISA... NOT ONLY THAT, THERE WILL BE NOBODY ON MISA'S SIDE AND SHE'LL BE CAPTURED EVEN SOONER...
...
HE KNOWS EVERY-THING... HE HAS IT ALL FIGURED OUT...
AND ON THE OTHER SIDE, IF RYUZAKI IS GONE FROM THE TASK FORCE, LIGHT YAGAMI WILL BECOME THE ONE WITH THE POWER TO CONTROL THE INVESTIGATION. HE'LL THEN MAKE SURE THAT MISA IS NEVER CAPTURED...
ACTUALLY, IF THAT HAPPENS... HE AND MISA MAY ACTUALLY TAKE OVER THE WORLD ...
WHAT'S CERTAIN RIGHT NOW IS THAT IF THINGS DON'T CHANGE, RYUZAKI WILL EVENTUALLY CATCH MISA...

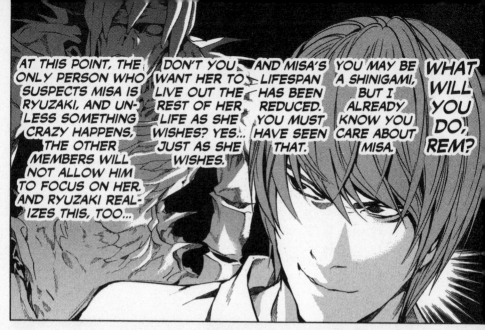

WHAT WILL YOU DO, REM?
YOU MAY BE A SHINIGAMI, BUT I ALREADY KNOW YOU CARE ABOUT MISA.
AND MISA'S LIFESPAN HAS BEEN REDUCED. YOU MUST HAVE SEEN THAT.
DON'T YOU WANT HER TO LIVE OUT THE REST OF HER LIFE AS SHE WISHES? YES... JUST AS SHE WISHES.
AT THIS POINT, THE ONLY PERSON WHO SUSPECTS MISA IS RYUZAKI, AND UNLESS SOMETHING CRAZY HAPPENS, THE OTHER MEMBERS WILL NOT ALLOW HIM TO FOCUS ON HER. AND RYUZAKI REALIZES THIS, TOO...
BUT AS MORE TIME PASSES, THERE'S NO DOUBT HE'LL CONTINUE CLOSING IN ON HER.
YOU CAN'T JUST WATCH AS MISA IS KILLED. THINK ABOUT MISA'S HAPPINESS.
...
AND IT'S NOT LIKE REVEALING EVERYTHING I KNOW NOW WILL CHANGE ANYTHING FOR MISA. SHE'S GUILTY HERE, SHE'LL BE PUT TO DEATH OR GET LIFE IN PRISON...
WHO WILL DIE... MISA OR ME...?
SO SINCE THAT DAY...
...LIGHT YAGAMI WAS THINKING ABOUT THIS VERY MOMENT...

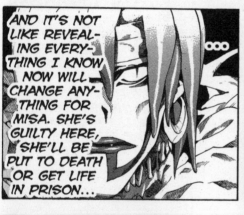

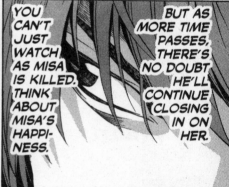

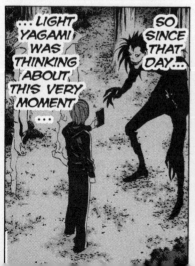

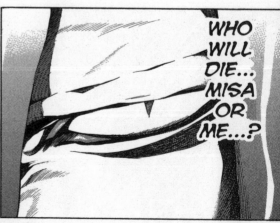

READ THIS WAY

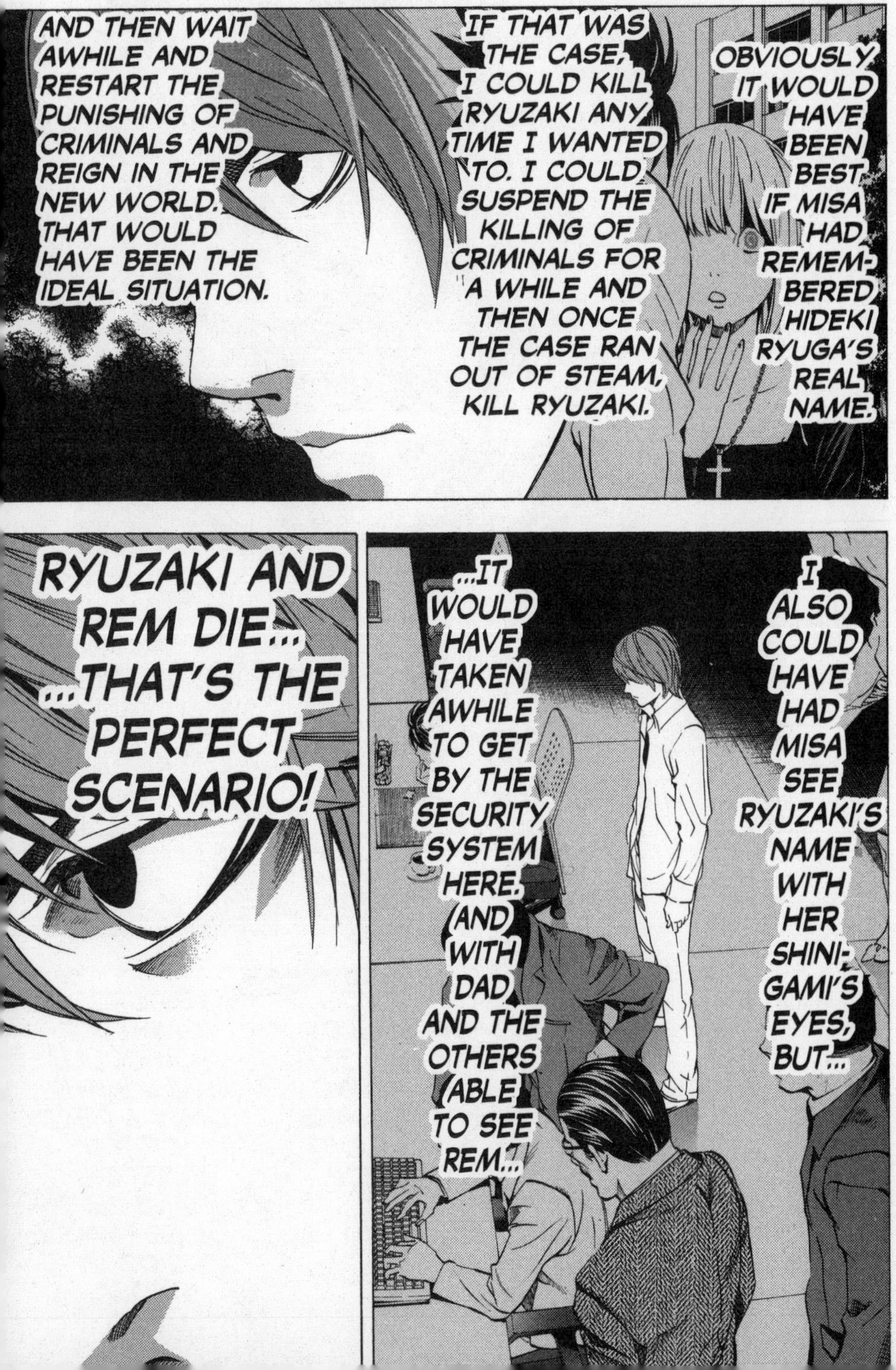
OBVIOUSLY IT WOULD HAVE BEEN BEST IF MISA HAD REMEMBERED HIDEKI RYUGA'S REAL NAME.
IF THAT WAS THE CASE, I COULD KILL RYUZAKI ANY TIME I WANTED TO. I COULD SUSPEND THE KILLING OF CRIMINALS FOR A WHILE AND THEN ONCE THE CASE RAN OUT OF STEAM, KILL RYUZAKI.
AND THEN WAIT AWHILE AND RESTART THE PUNISHING OF CRIMINALS AND REIGN IN THE NEW WORLD. THAT WOULD HAVE BEEN THE IDEAL SITUATION.
I ALSO COULD HAVE HAD MISA SEE RYUZAKI'S NAME WITH HER SHINIGAMI'S EYES, BUT...
...IT WOULD HAVE TAKEN AWHILE TO GET BY THE SECURITY SYSTEM HERE. AND WITH DAD AND THE OTHERS ABLE TO SEE REM...
RYUZAKI AND REM DIE... ...THAT'S THE PERFECT SCENARIO!

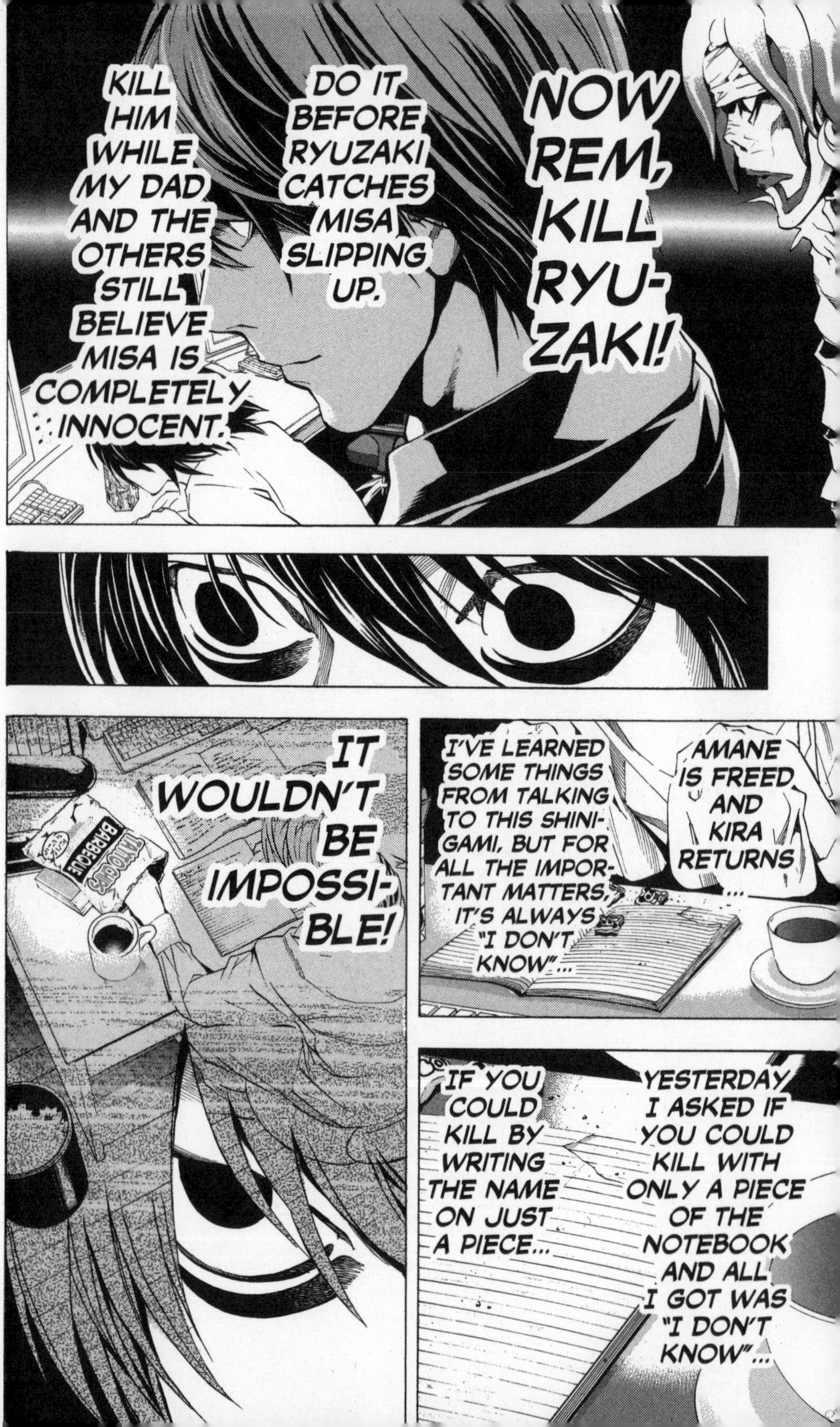

NOW REM, KILL RYU-ZAKI!
DO IT BEFORE RYUZAKI CATCHES MISA SLIPPING UP.
KILL HIM WHILE MY DAD AND THE OTHERS STILL BELIEVE MISA IS COMPLETELY INNOCENT.
AMANE IS FREED AND KIRA RETURNS...
I'VE LEARNED SOME THINGS FROM TALKING TO THIS SHINI-GAMI, BUT FOR ALL THE IMPOR-TANT MATTERS, IT'S ALWAYS "I DON'T KNOW"...
YESTERDAY I ASKED IF YOU COULD KILL WITH ONLY A PIECE OF THE NOTEBOOK AND ALL I GOT WAS "I DON'T KNOW"...
IF YOU COULD KILL BY WRITING THE NAME ON JUST A PIECE...
BARBECUE
IT WOULDN'T BE IMPOSSI-BLE!

READ THIS WAY

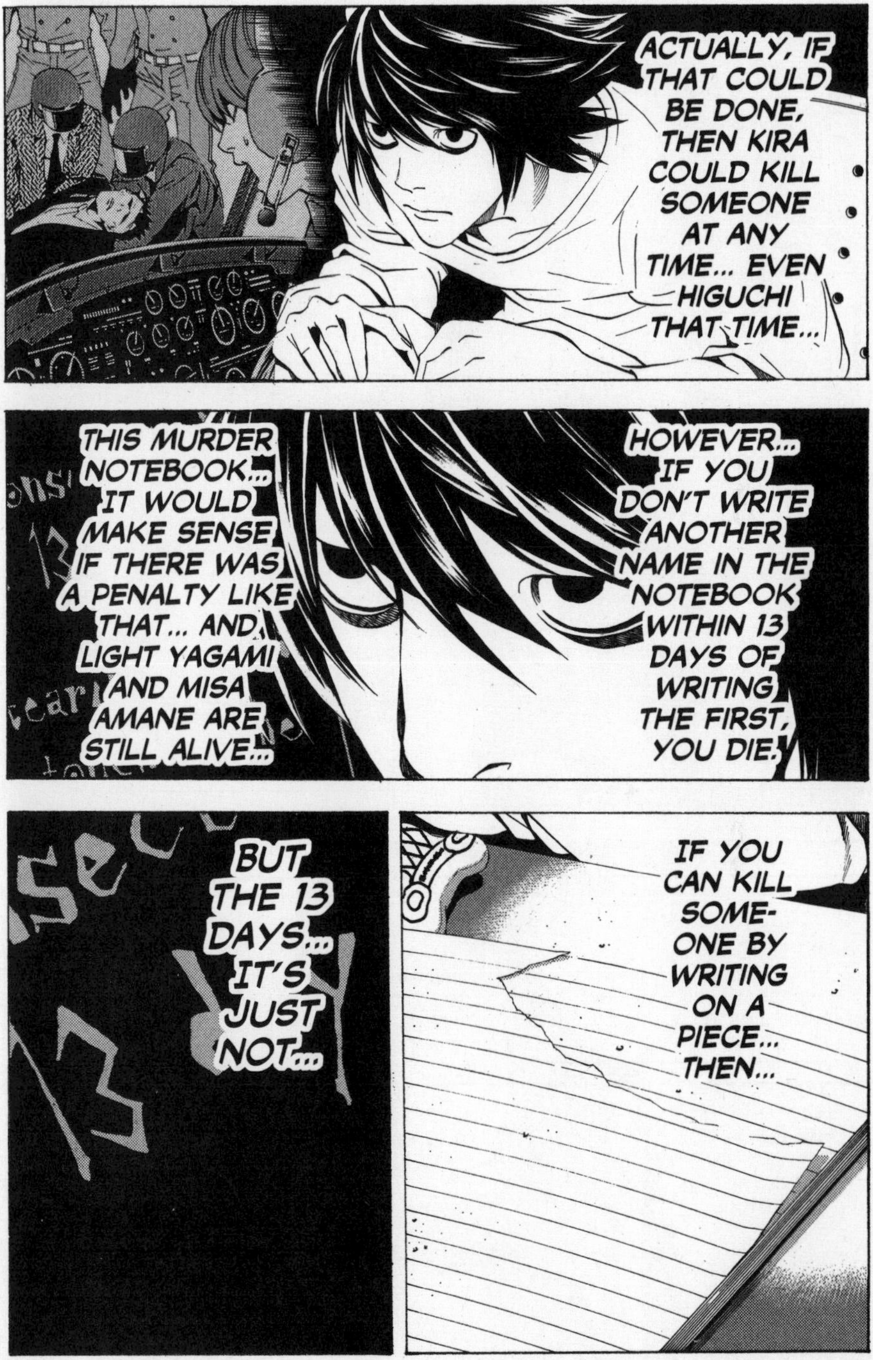

ACTUALLY, IF THAT COULD BE DONE, THEN KIRA COULD KILL SOMEONE AT ANY TIME... EVEN HIGUCHI THAT TIME...
HOWEVER... IF YOU DON'T WRITE ANOTHER NAME IN THE NOTEBOOK WITHIN 13 DAYS OF WRITING THE FIRST, YOU DIE.
THIS MURDER NOTEBOOK... IT WOULD MAKE SENSE IF THERE WAS A PENALTY LIKE THAT... AND, LIGHT YAGAMI AND MISA AMANE ARE STILL ALIVE...
IF YOU CAN KILL SOME-ONE BY WRITING ON A PIECE... THEN...
BUT THE 13 DAYS... IT'S JUST NOT...

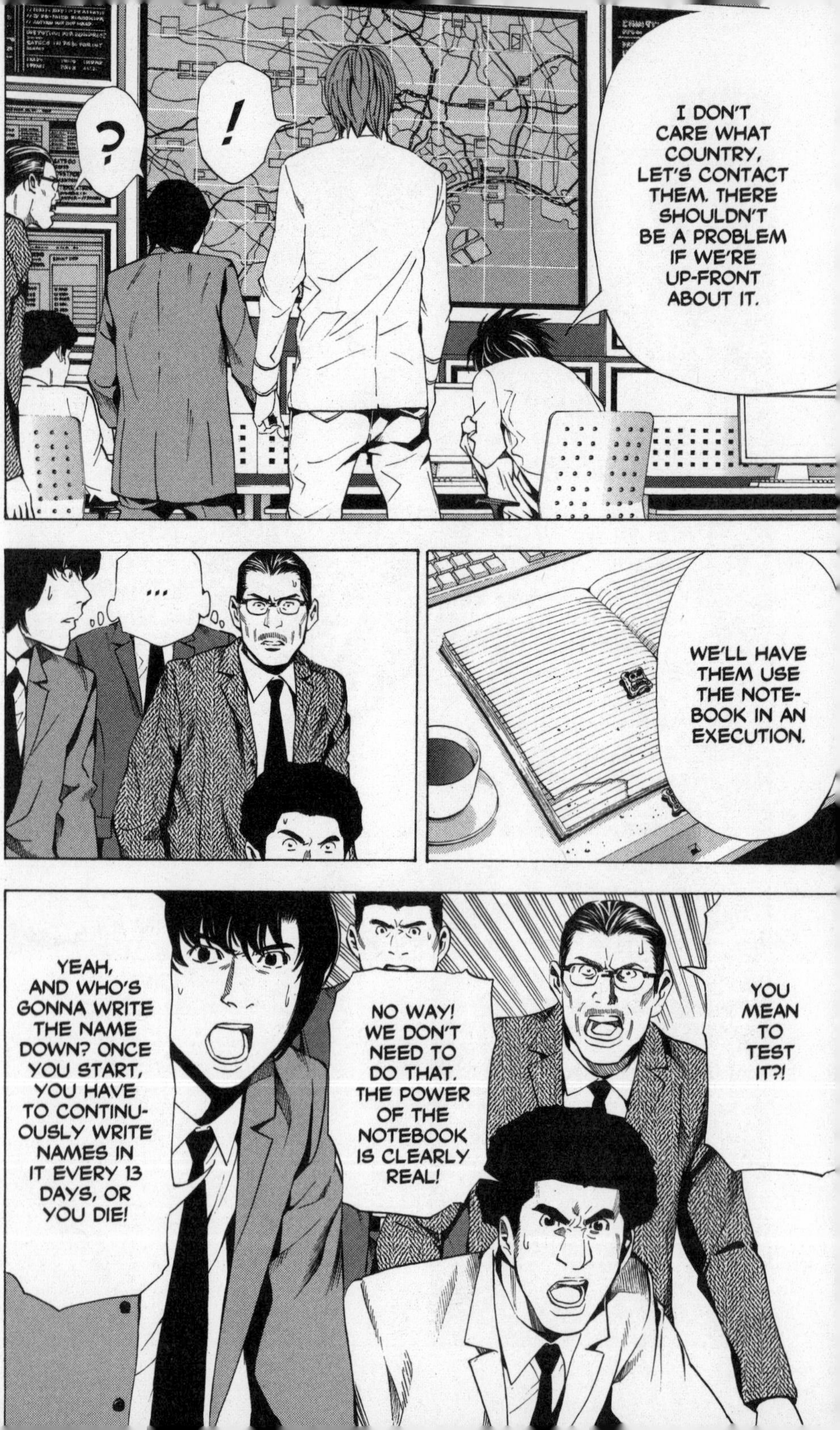

I DON'T CARE WHAT COUNTRY, LET'S CONTACT THEM. THERE SHOULDN'T BE A PROBLEM IF WE'RE UP-FRONT ABOUT IT.
!
?
WE'LL HAVE THEM USE THE NOTE-BOOK IN AN EXECUTION.
...
YOU MEAN TO TEST IT?!
NO WAY! WE DON'T NEED TO DO THAT. THE POWER OF THE NOTEBOOK IS CLEARLY REAL!
YEAH, AND WHO'S GONNA WRITE THE NAME DOWN? ONCE YOU START, YOU HAVE TO CONTINU-OUSLY WRITE NAMES IN IT EVERY 13 DAYS, OR YOU DIE!

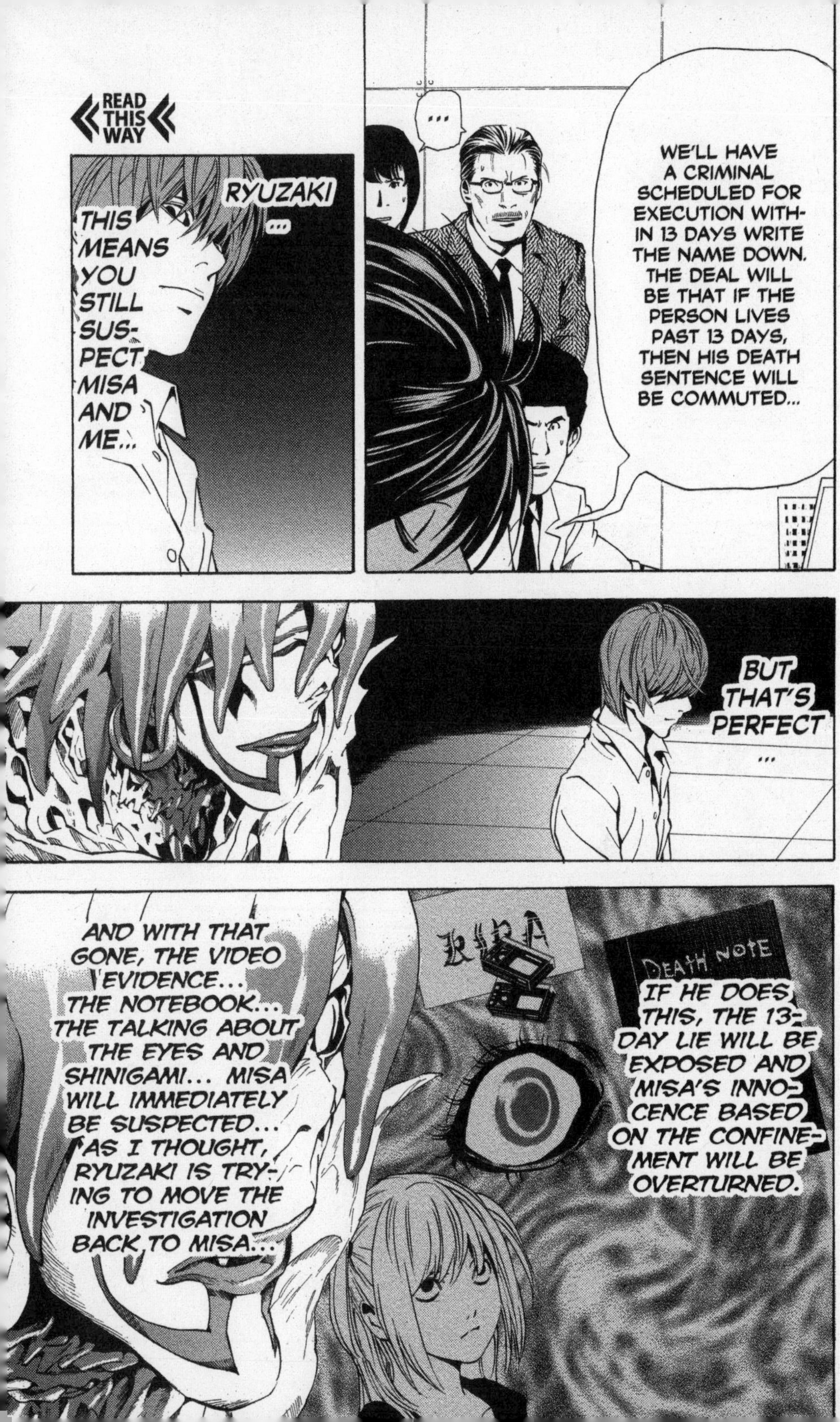
READ THIS WAY
WE'LL HAVE A CRIMINAL SCHEDULED FOR EXECUTION WITHIN 13 DAYS WRITE THE NAME DOWN. THE DEAL WILL BE THAT IF THE PERSON LIVES PAST 13 DAYS, THEN HIS DEATH SENTENCE WILL BE COMMUTED...
...
RYUZAKI ...
THIS MEANS YOU STILL SUSPECT MISA AND ME...
BUT THAT'S PERFECT ...
DEATH NOTE
IF HE DOES THIS, THE 13-DAY LIE WILL BE EXPOSED AND MISA'S INNOCENCE BASED ON THE CONFINEMENT WILL BE OVERTURNED.
AND WITH THAT GONE, THE VIDEO EVIDENCE... THE NOTEBOOK... THE TALKING ABOUT THE EYES AND SHINIGAMI... MISA WILL IMMEDIATELY BE SUSPECTED... AS I THOUGHT, RYUZAKI IS TRYING TO MOVE THE INVESTIGATION BACK TO MISA...

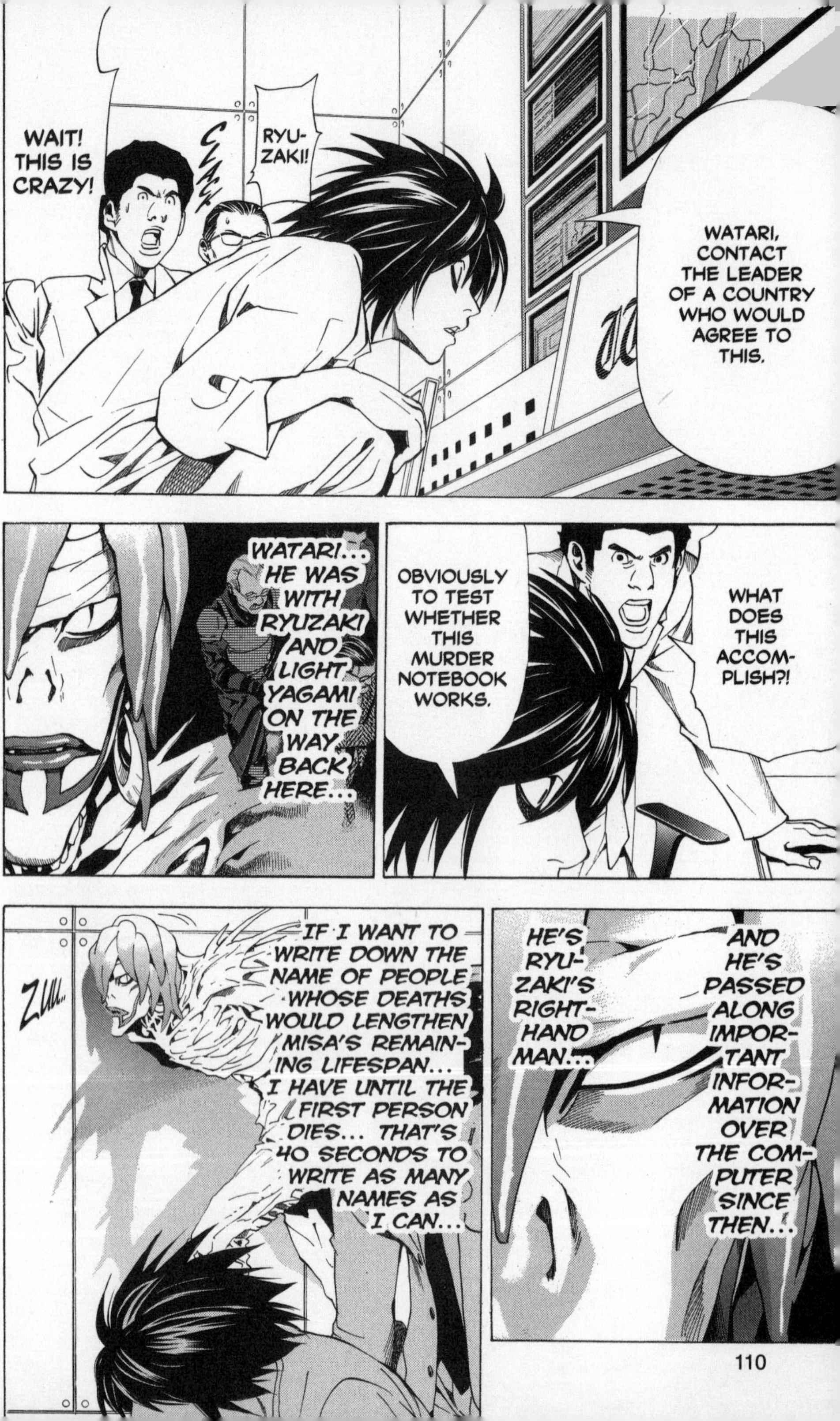
WATARI, CONTACT THE LEADER OF A COUNTRY WHO WOULD AGREE TO THIS.
RYU-ZAKI!
CLACK
WAIT! THIS IS CRAZY!
WHAT DOES THIS ACCOMPLISH?!
OBVIOUSLY TO TEST WHETHER THIS MURDER NOTEBOOK WORKS.
WATARI... HE WAS WITH RYUZAKI AND LIGHT YAGAMI ON THE WAY BACK HERE...
AND HE'S PASSED ALONG IMPORTANT INFORMATION OVER THE COMPUTER SINCE THEN...
HE'S RYUZAKI'S RIGHT-HAND MAN...
IF I WANT TO WRITE DOWN THE NAME OF PEOPLE WHOSE DEATHS WOULD LENGTHEN MISA'S REMAINING LIFESPAN... I HAVE UNTIL THE FIRST PERSON DIES... THAT'S 40 SECONDS TO WRITE AS MANY NAMES AS I CAN...
ZUU..

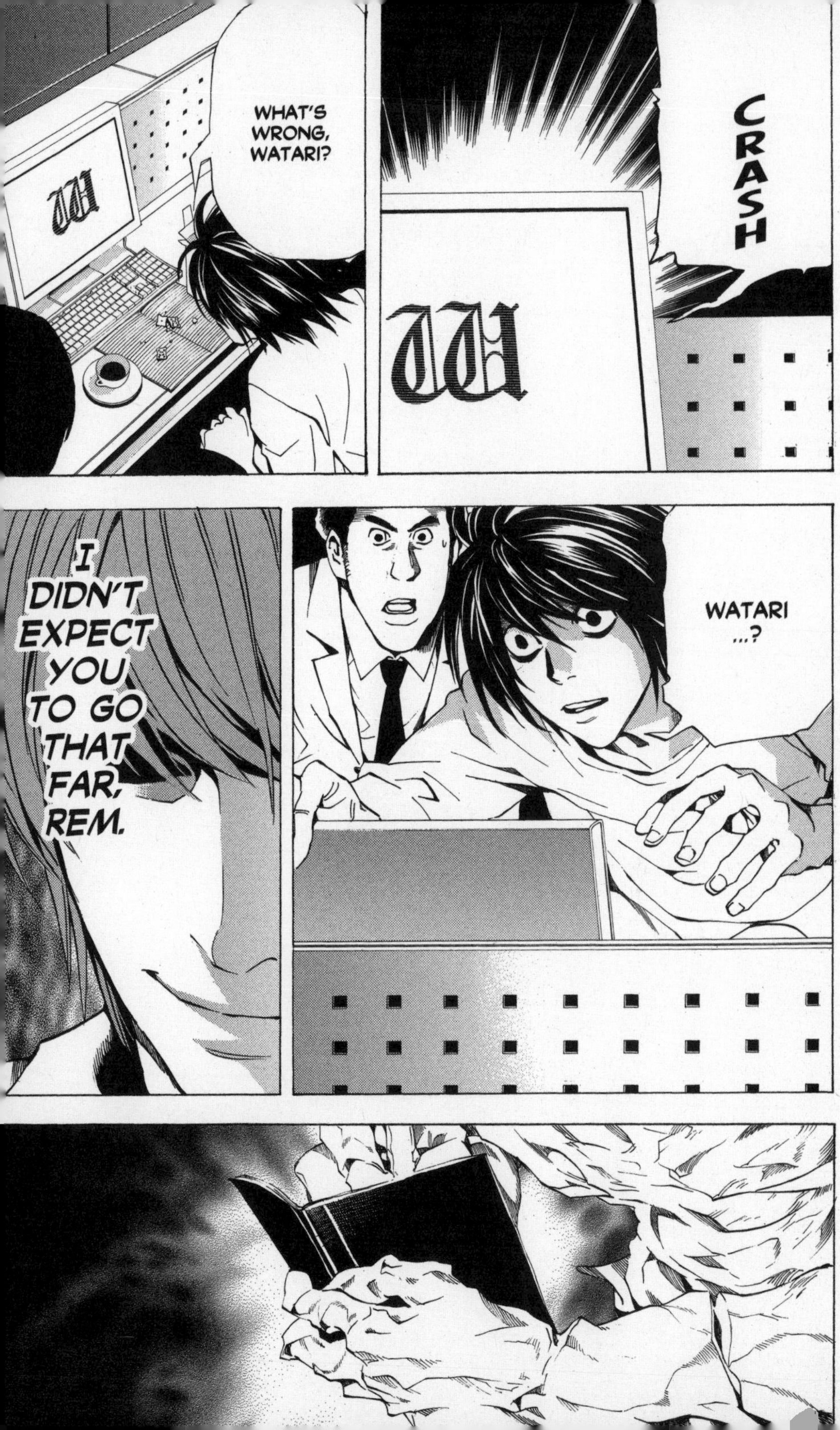
CRASH
WHAT'S WRONG, WATARI?
WATARI ...?
I DIDN'T EXPECT YOU TO GO THAT FAR, REM.

# DEATH NOTE
## How to use it
## XXXIX

○ Humans that have traded for the eye power of a god of death cannot see the name or life-span of humans who have already passed away by looking at their photos.

死神の目を取引した人間は、写真等で既に死んでいる人間の顔を見ても、名前も寿命も見えない。

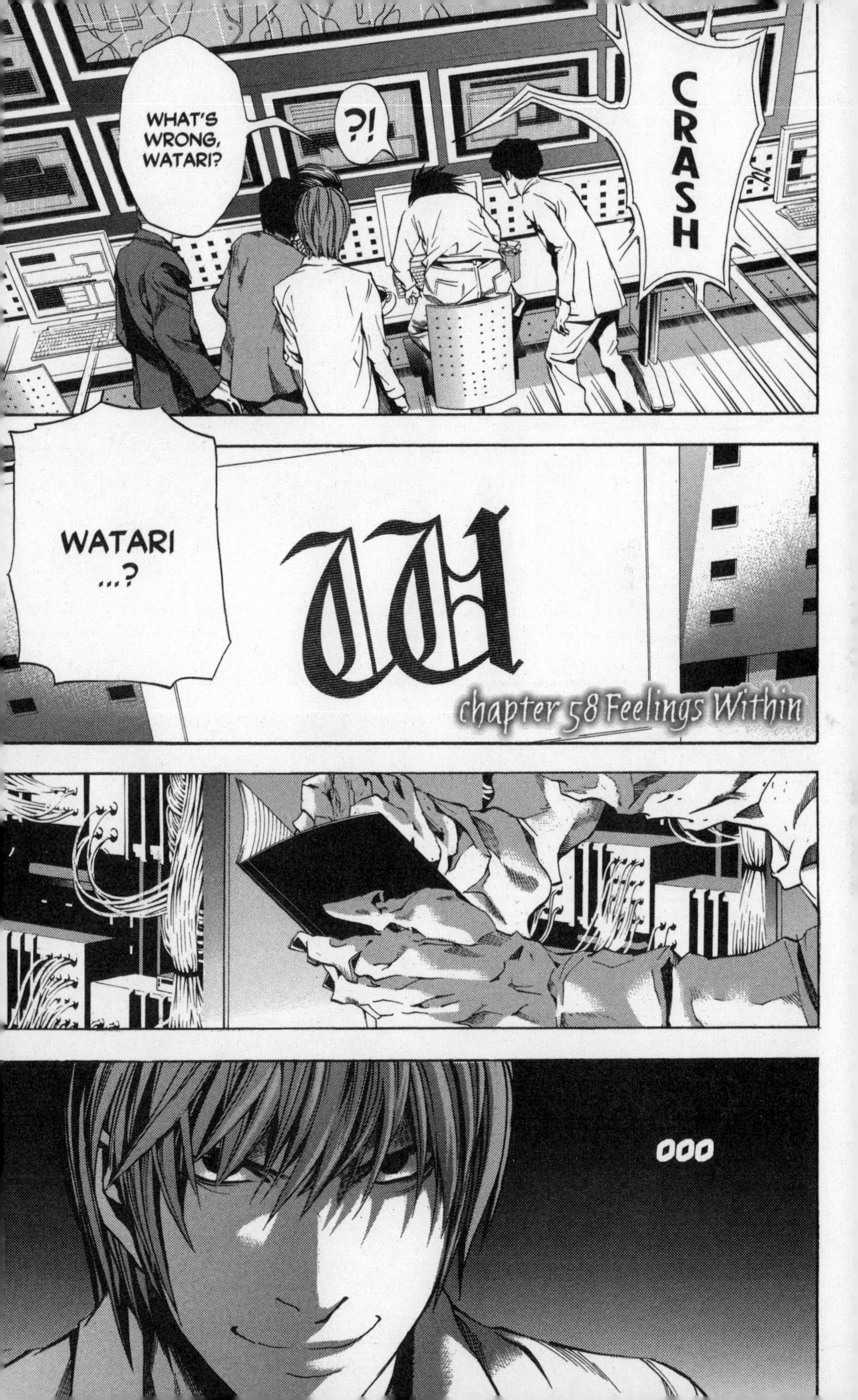
CRASH
?!
WHAT'S WRONG, WATARI?
W
chapter 58 Feelings Within
WATARI ...?

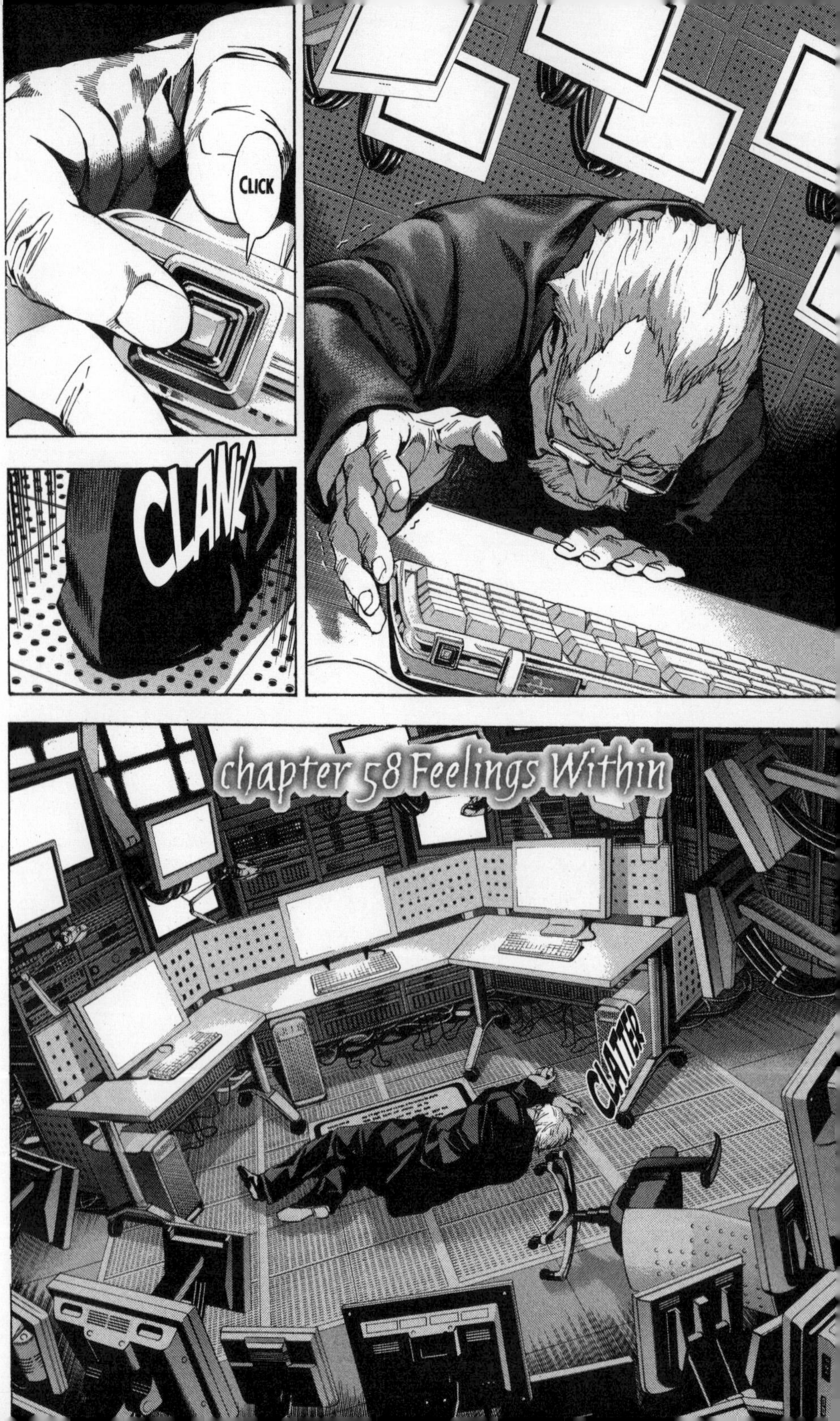
CLICK
CLANK
chapter 58 Feelings Within
CLATTER

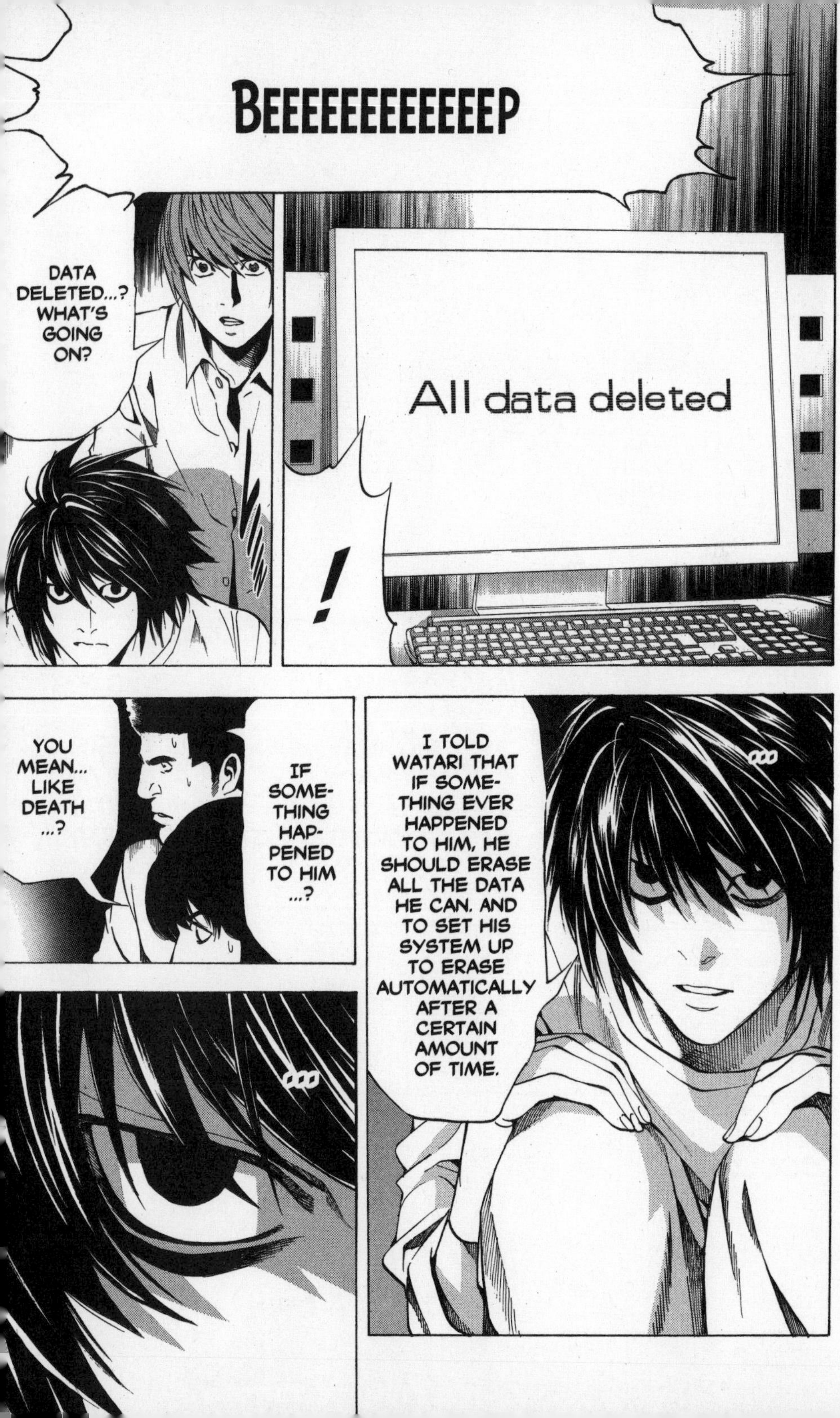
BEEEEEEEEEEEEP
All data deleted
!
DATA DELETED...? WHAT'S GOING ON?
I TOLD WATARI THAT IF SOME-THING EVER HAPPENED TO HIM, HE SHOULD ERASE ALL THE DATA HE CAN. AND TO SET HIS SYSTEM UP TO ERASE AUTOMATICALLY AFTER A CERTAIN AMOUNT OF TIME.
IF SOME-THING HAP-PENED TO HIM ...?
YOU MEAN... LIKE DEATH ...?

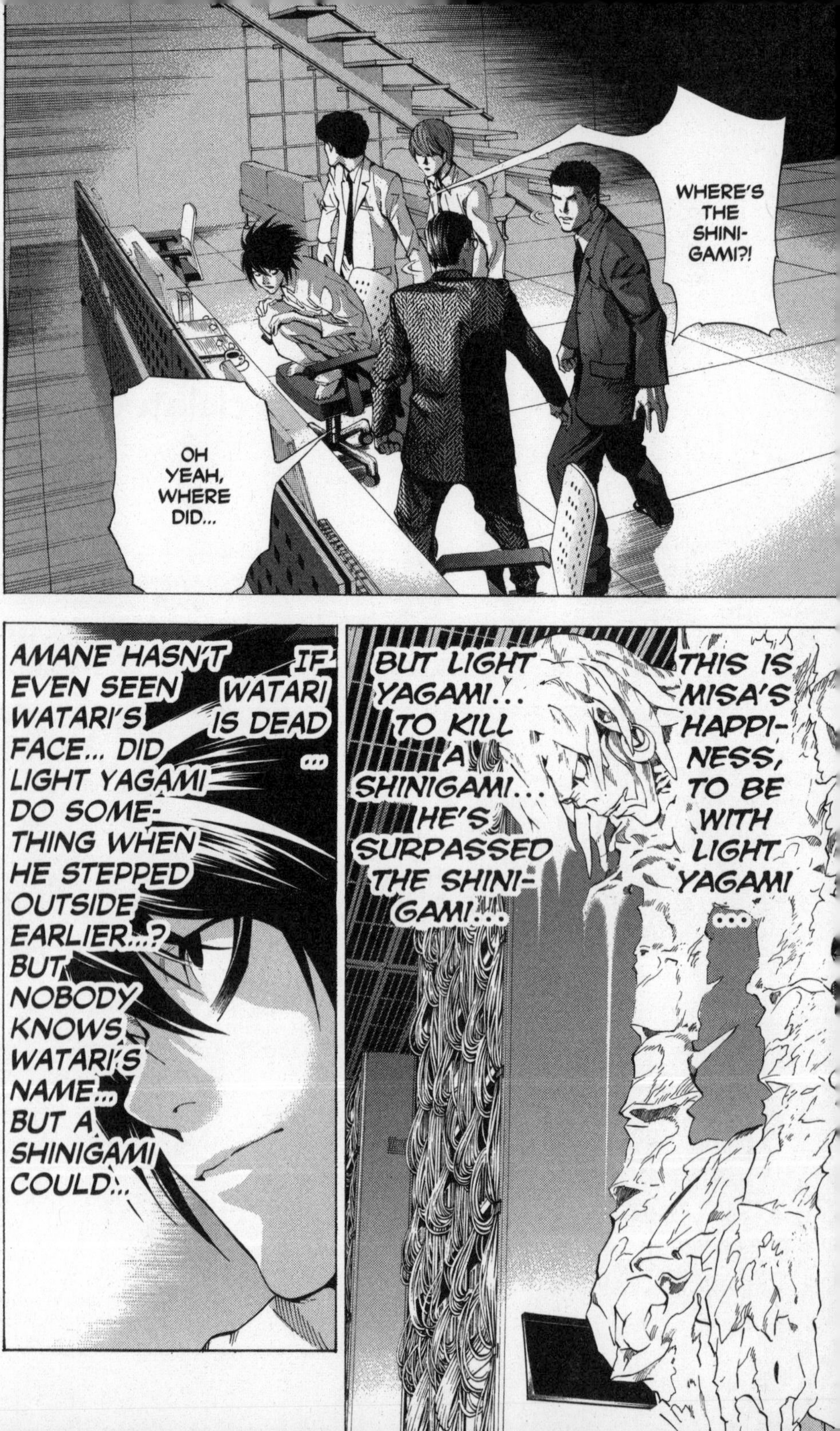
WHERE'S THE SHINI-GAMI?!
OH YEAH, WHERE DID...
THIS IS MISA'S HAPPI-NESS, TO BE WITH LIGHT YAGAMI...
BUT LIGHT YAGAMI... TO KILL A SHINIGAMI... HE'S SURPASSED THE SHINI-GAMI...
IF WATARI IS DEAD...
AMANE HASN'T EVEN SEEN WATARI'S FACE... DID LIGHT YAGAMI DO SOME-THING WHEN HE STEPPED OUTSIDE EARLIER...? BUT NOBODY KNOWS WATARI'S NAME... BUT A SHINIGAMI COULD...

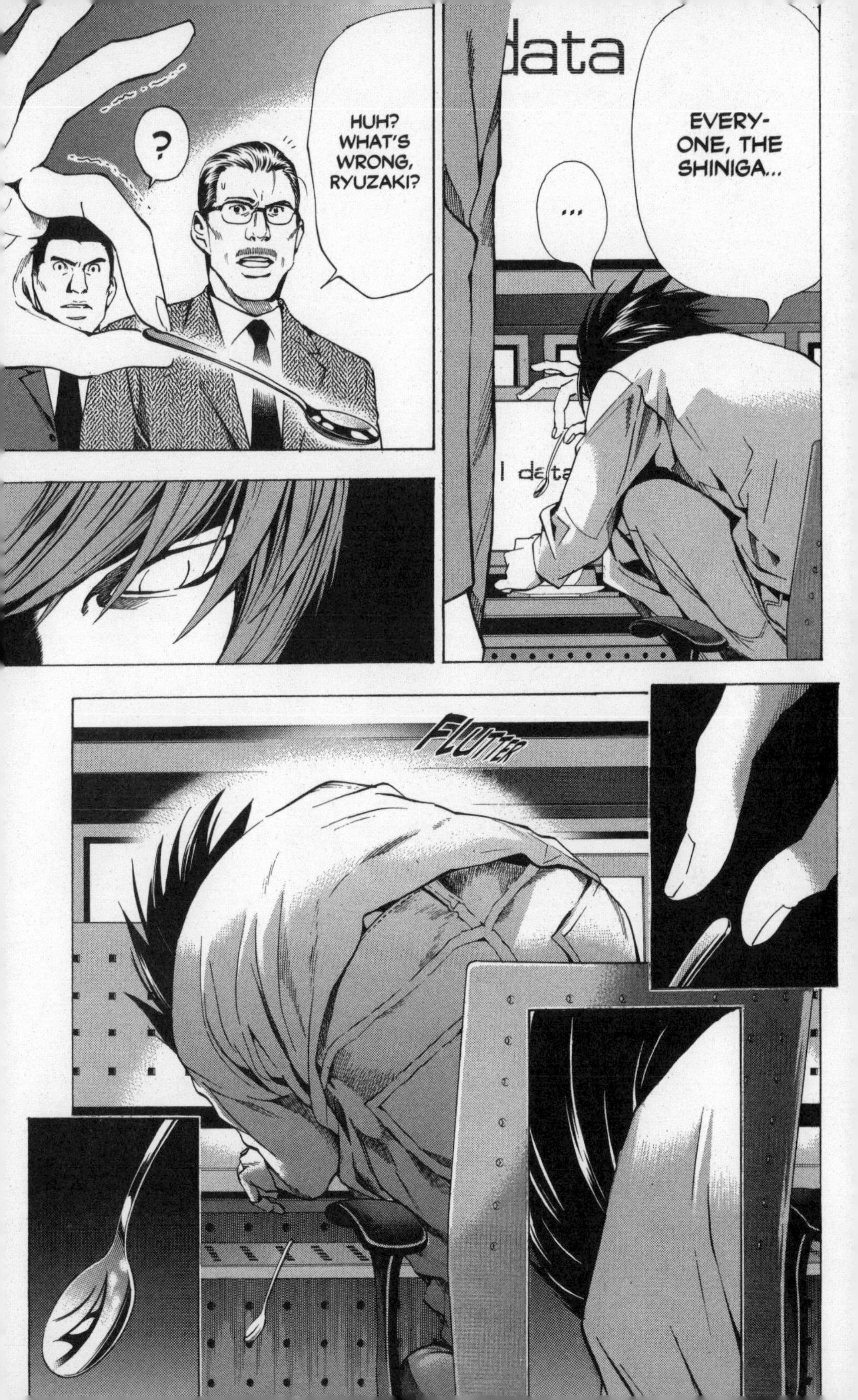
data
EVERY-ONE, THE SHINIGA...
...
l da
HUH? WHAT'S WRONG, RYUZAKI?
?
FLUTTER

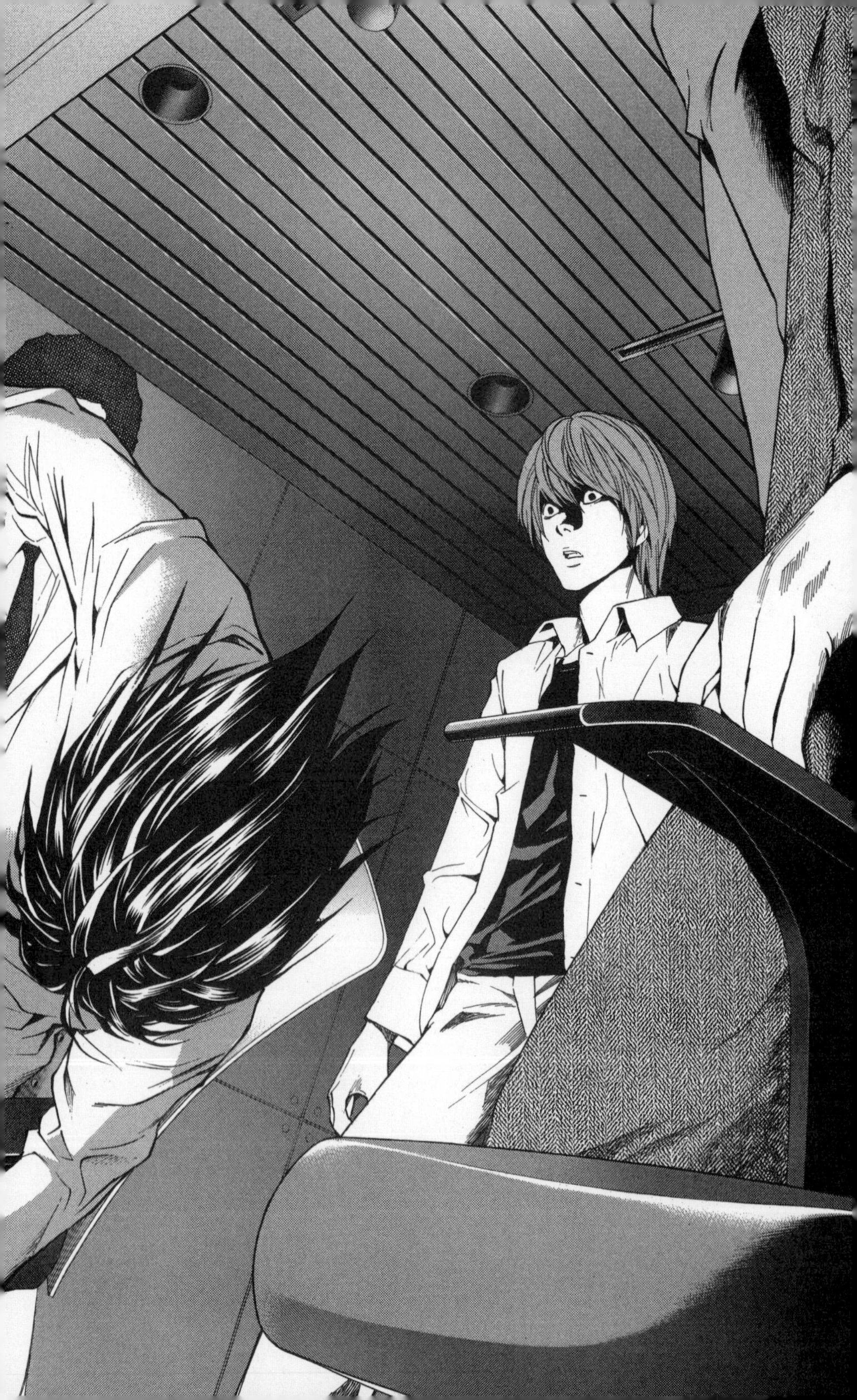

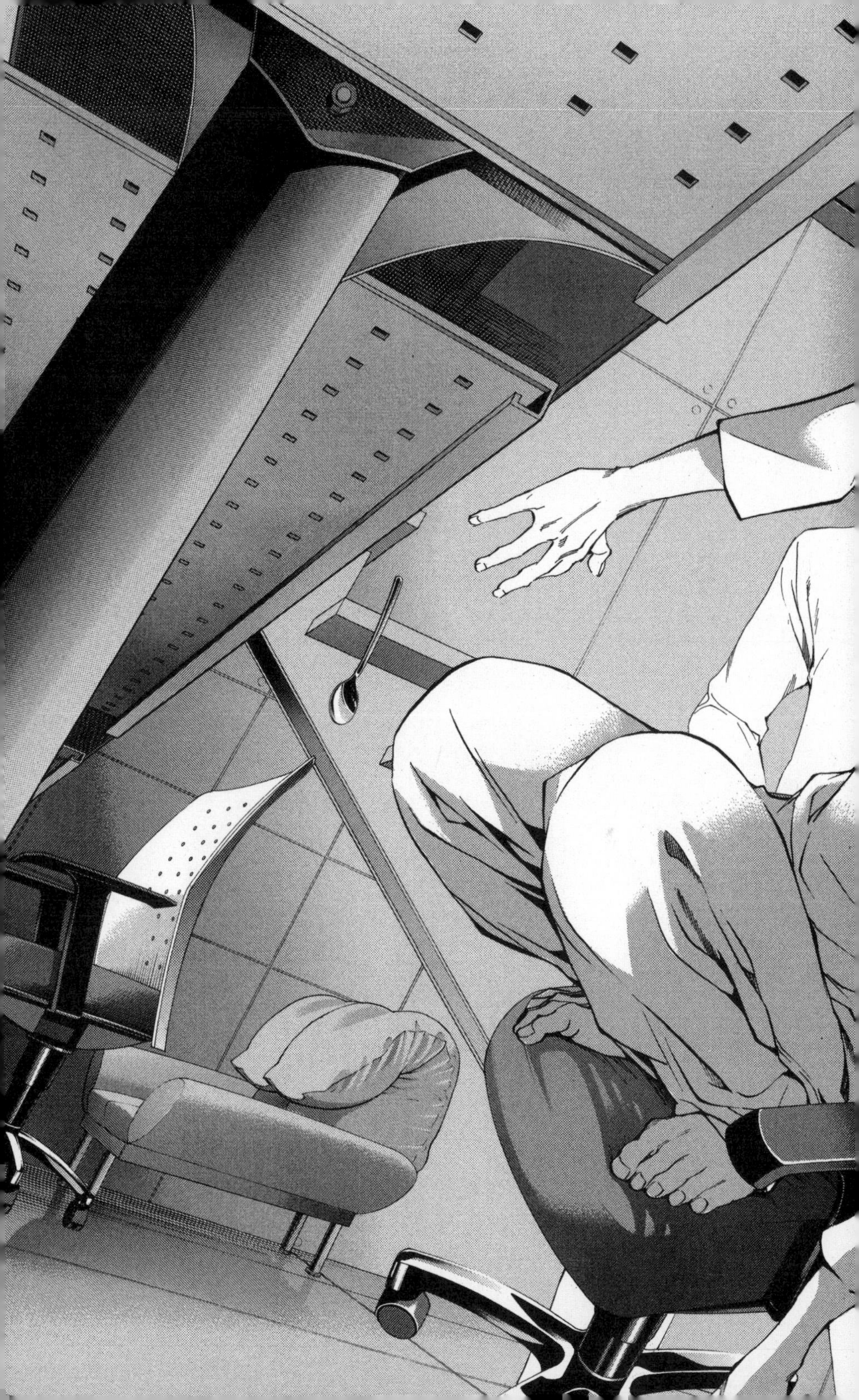

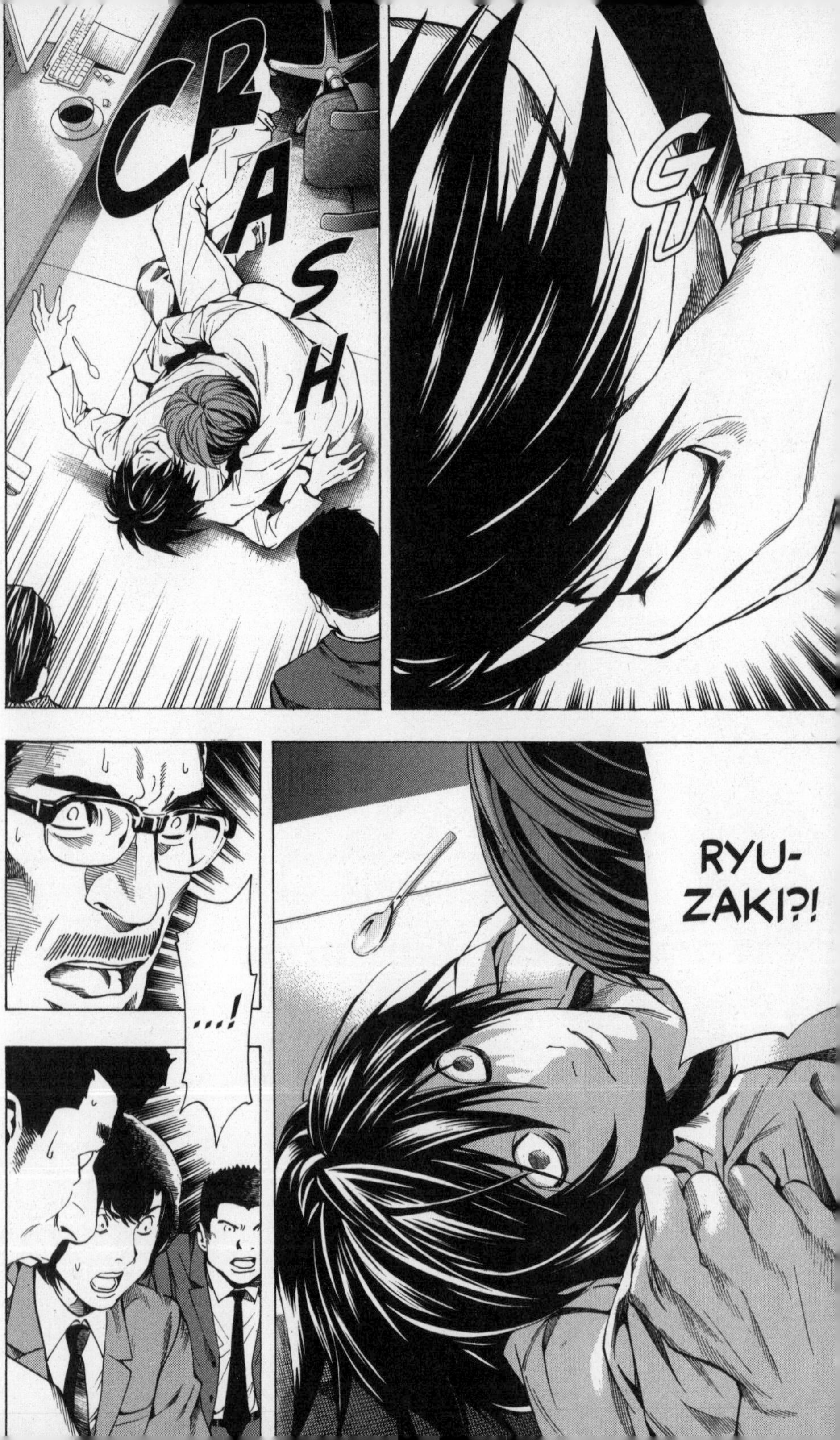
GU
CRASH
RYU-ZAKI?!
...!

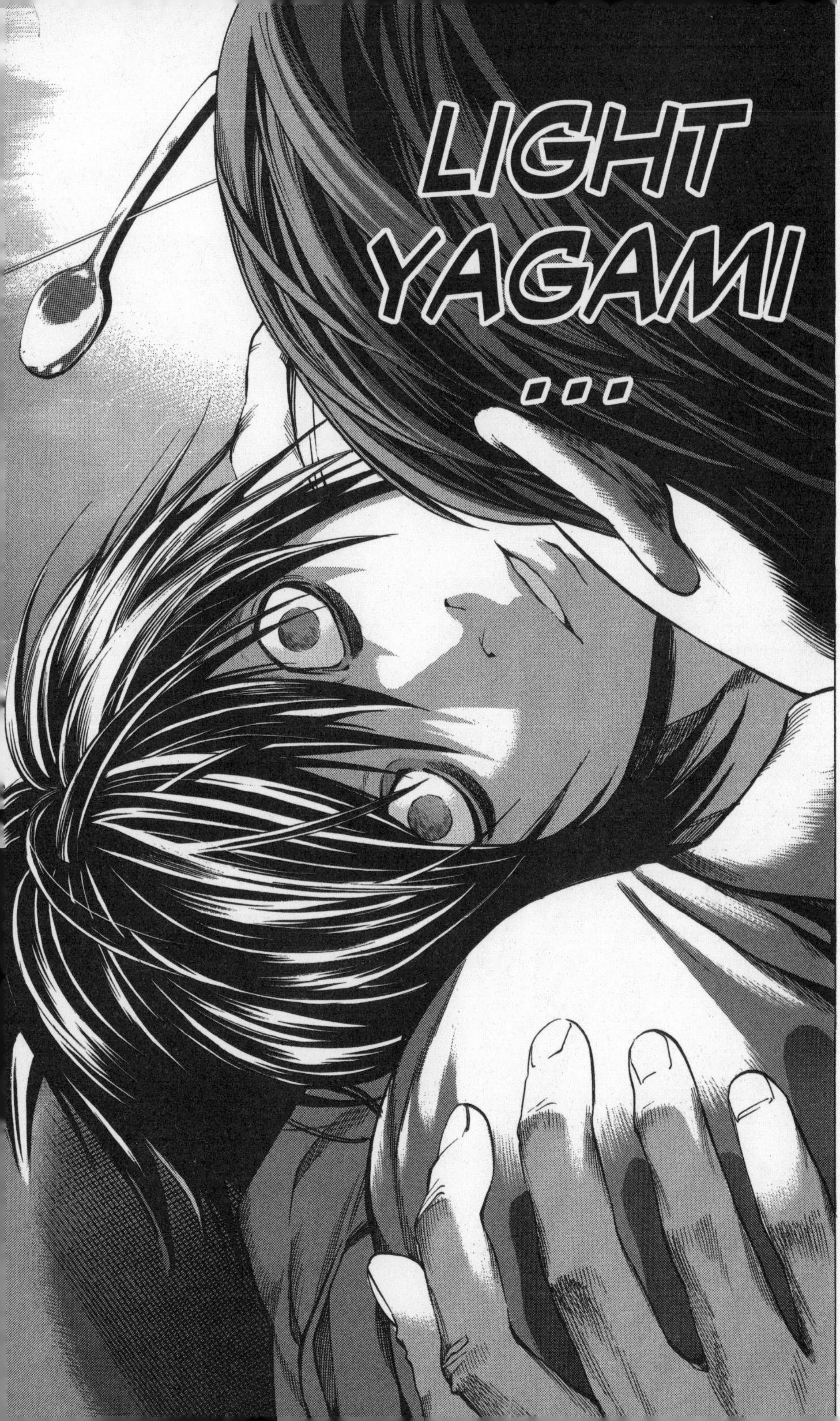
LIGHT YAGAMI
...

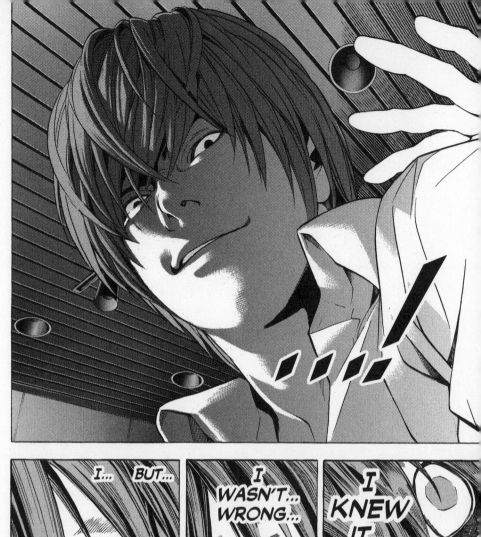

I... BUT...

I WASN'T... WRONG...

I KNEW IT...

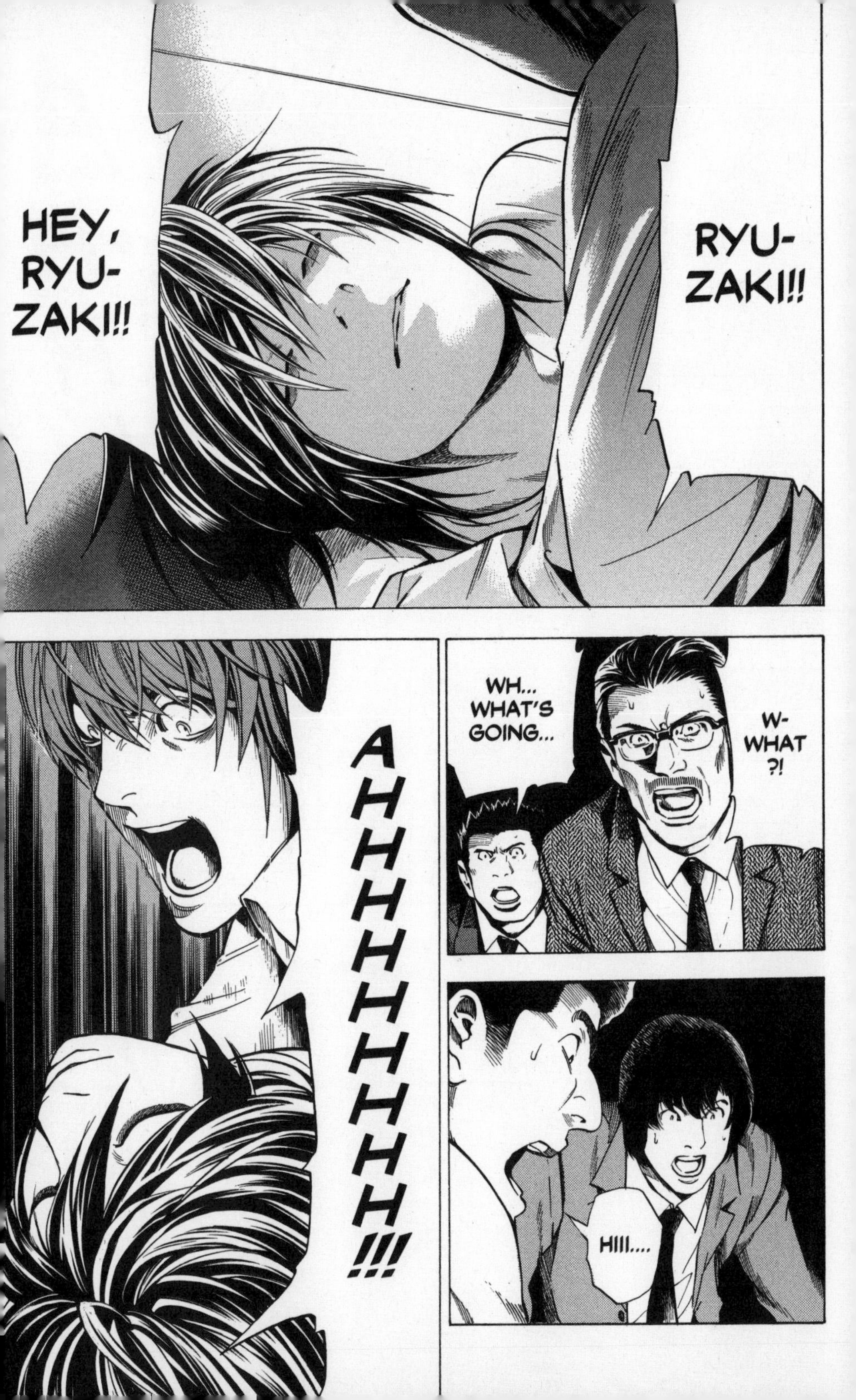
RYU-ZAKI!!!
HEY, RYU-ZAKI!!
W-WHAT?!
WH... WHAT'S GOING...
HIII....
AHHHHHHHHH!!!

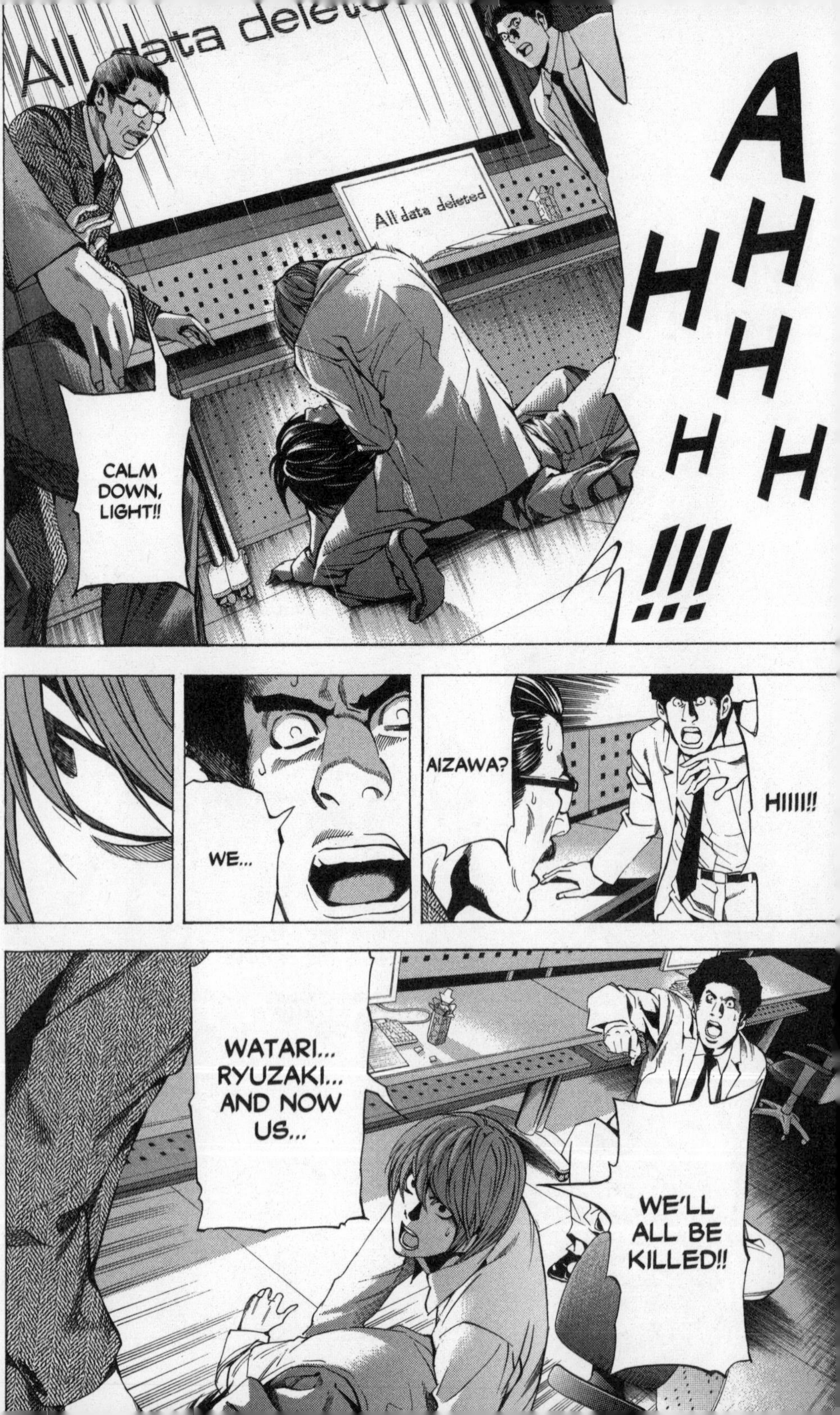
AHHHHH!!!
All data deleted
CALM DOWN, LIGHT!!
HIIII!!
AIZAWA?
WE...
WATARI... RYUZAKI... AND NOW US...
WE'LL ALL BE KILLED!!

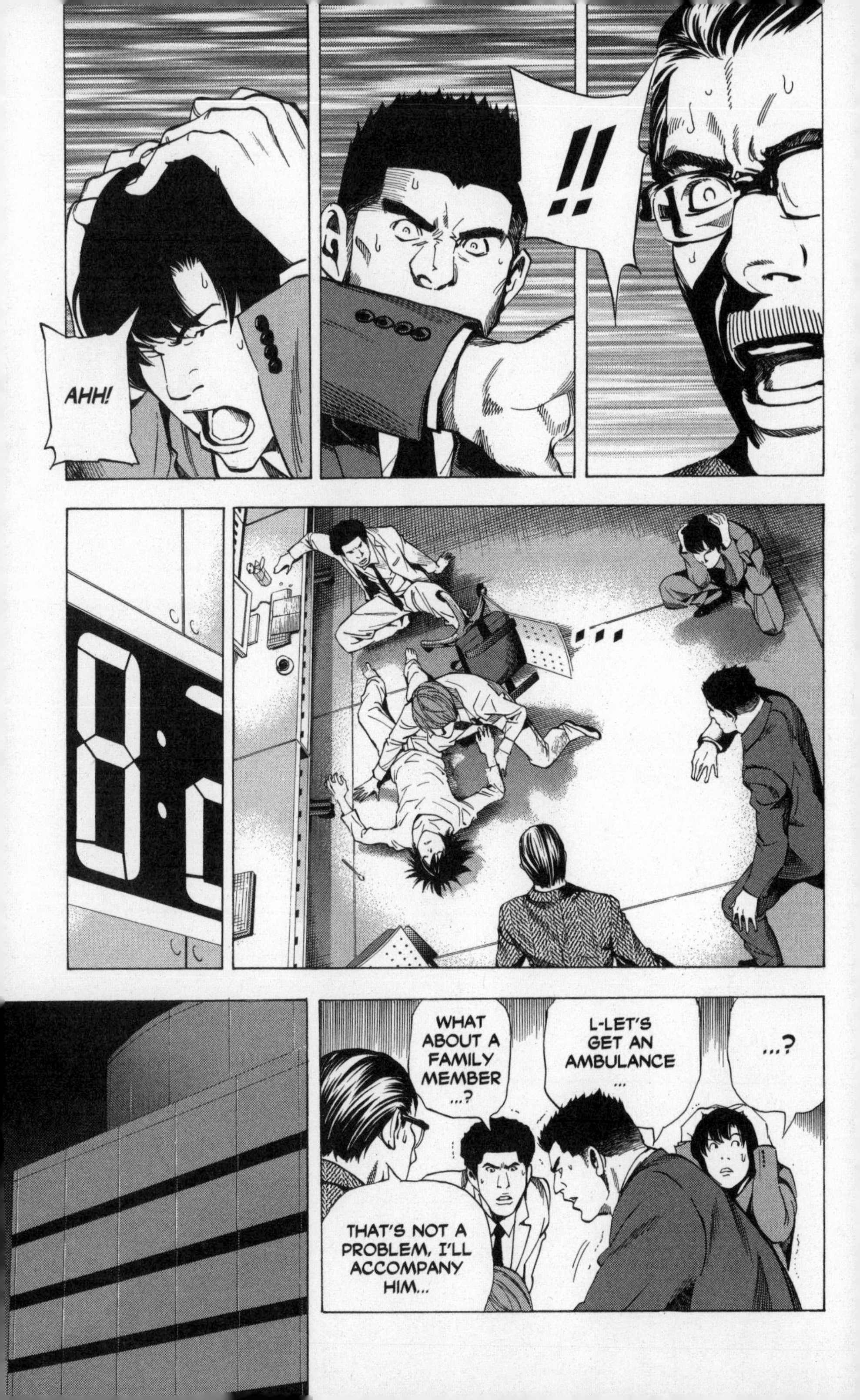
!!
AHH!
...
...?
L-LET'S GET AN AMBULANCE ...
WHAT ABOUT A FAMILY MEMBER ...?
THAT'S NOT A PROBLEM, I'LL ACCOMPANY HIM...

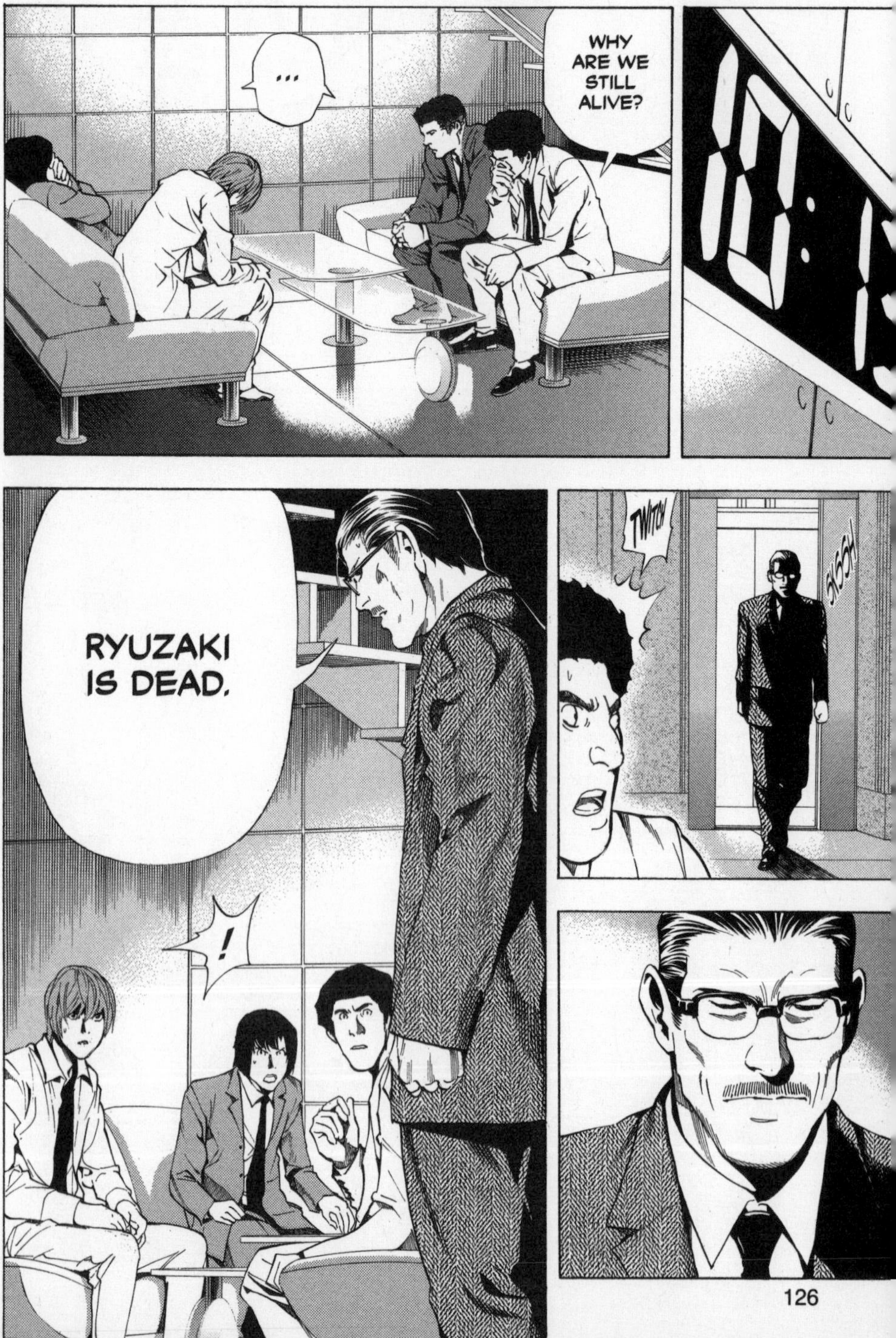
WHY ARE WE STILL ALIVE?
...
TWITCH
SHSSH
RYUZAKI IS DEAD.
!

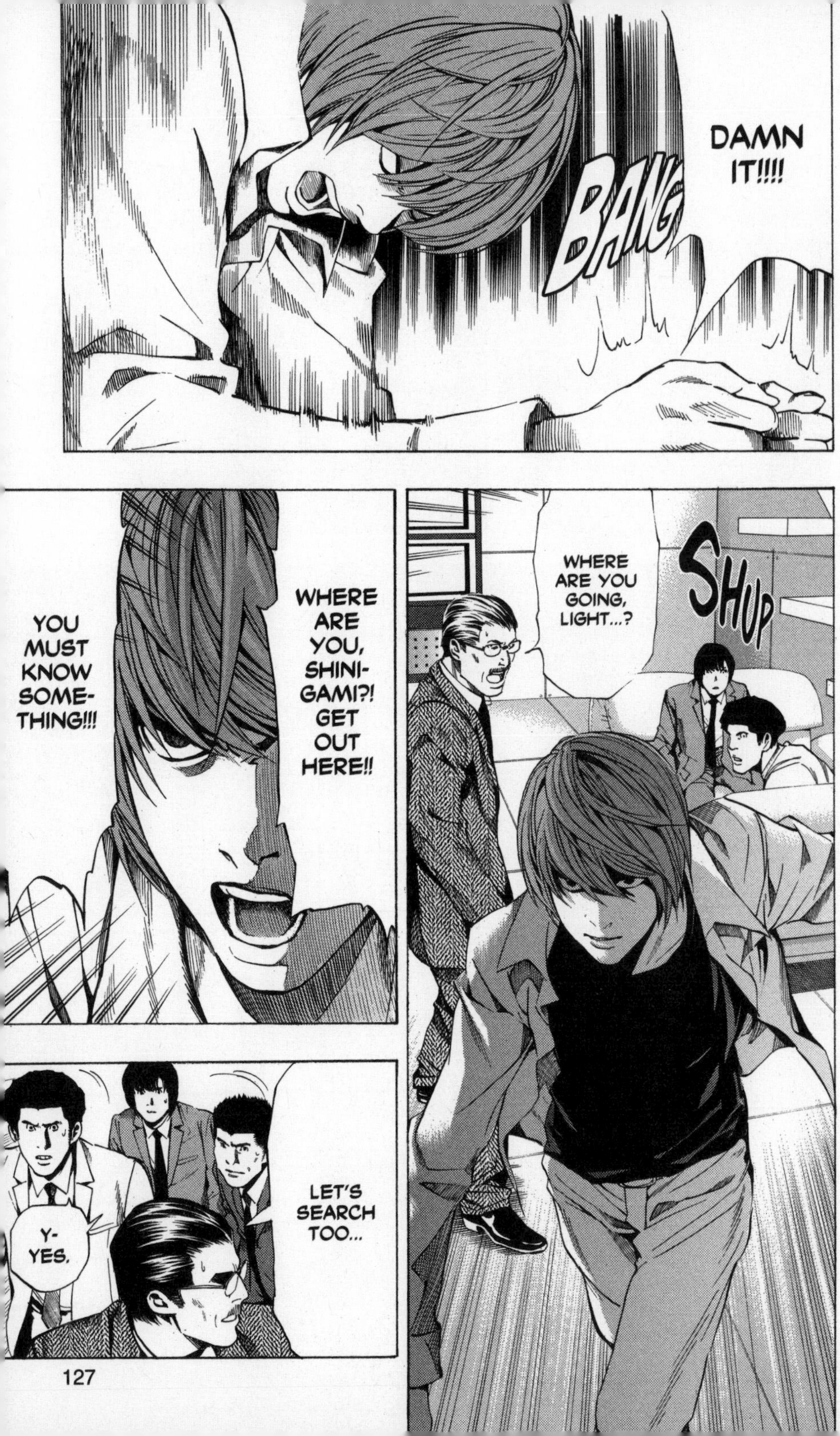
DAMN IT!!!!
BANG
WHERE ARE YOU GOING, LIGHT...?
SHUP
WHERE ARE YOU, SHINIGAMI?! GET OUT HERE!!
YOU MUST KNOW SOMETHING!!!
LET'S SEARCH TOO...
Y-YES.

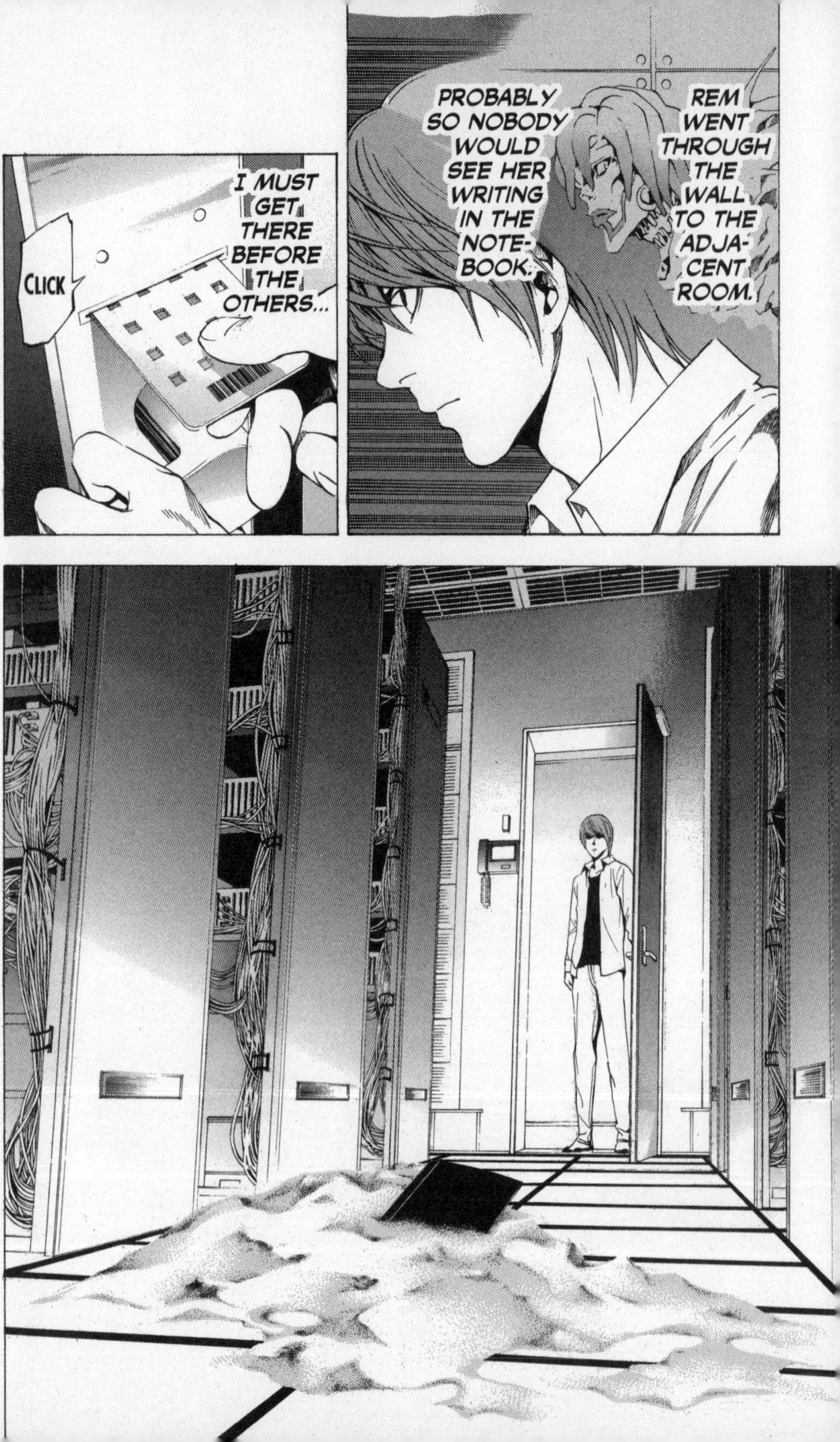
REM WENT THROUGH THE WALL TO THE ADJA-CENT ROOM.
PROBABLY SO NOBODY WOULD SEE HER WRITING IN THE NOTE-BOOK.
I MUST GET THERE BEFORE THE OTHERS...
CLICK

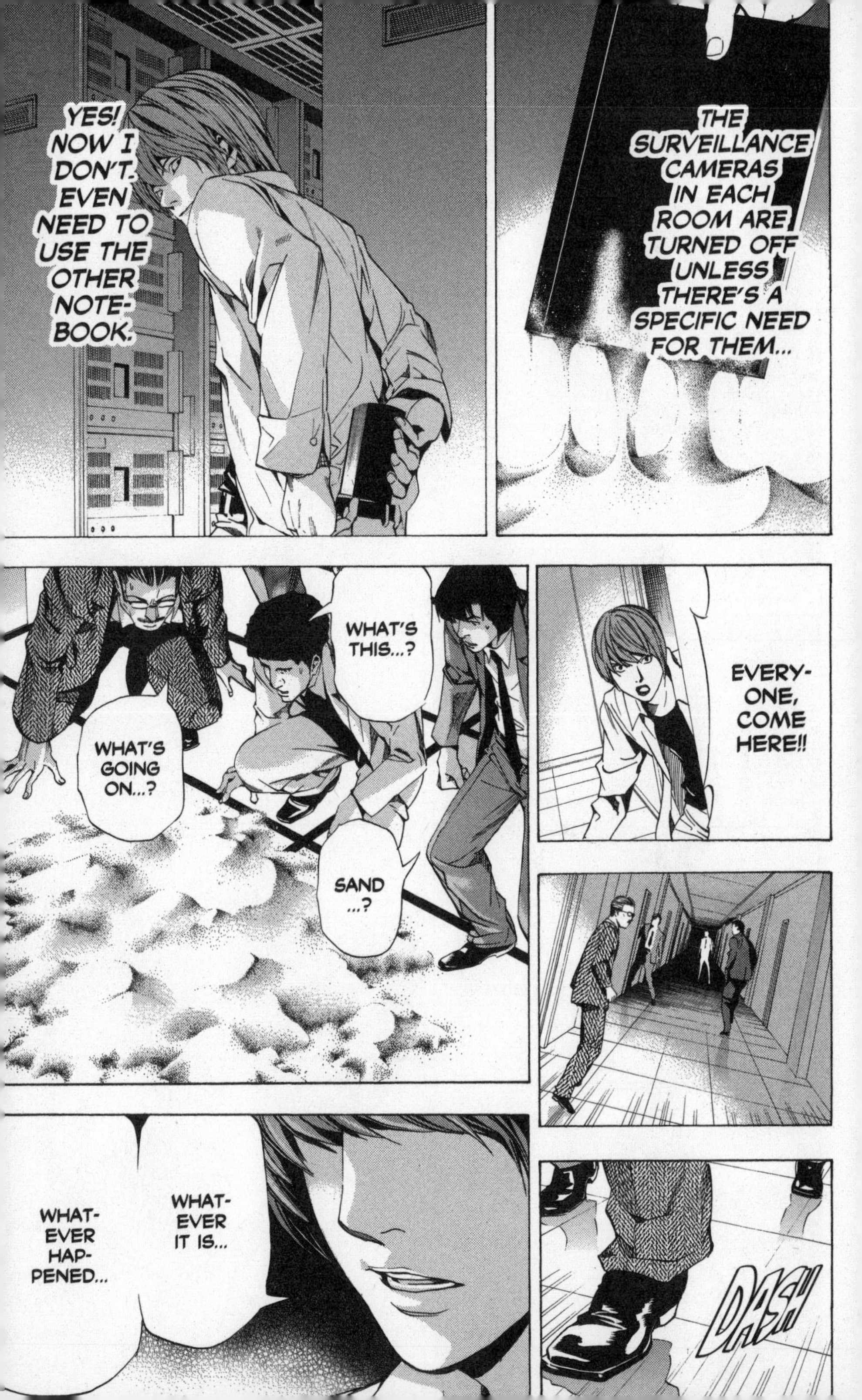
THE SURVEILLANCE CAMERAS IN EACH ROOM ARE TURNED OFF UNLESS THERE'S A SPECIFIC NEED FOR THEM...
YES! NOW I DON'T EVEN NEED TO USE THE OTHER NOTE-BOOK.
EVERY-ONE, COME HERE!!
DASH
WHAT'S THIS...?
WHAT'S GOING ON...?
SAND ...?
WHAT-EVER IT IS...
WHAT-EVER HAP-PENED...

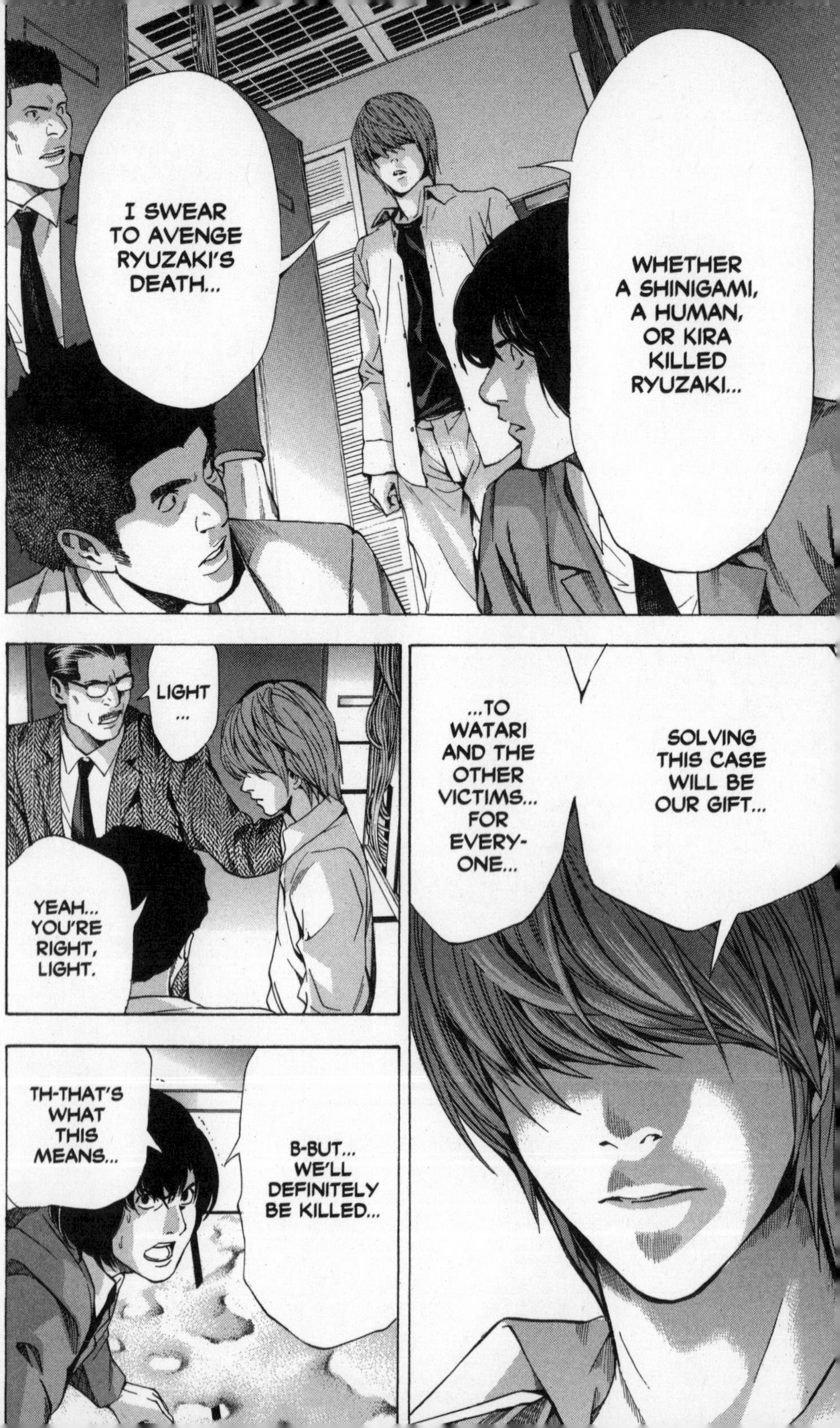
WHETHER A SHINIGAMI, A HUMAN, OR KIRA KILLED RYUZAKI...
I SWEAR TO AVENGE RYUZAKI'S DEATH...
SOLVING THIS CASE WILL BE OUR GIFT...
...TO WATARI AND THE OTHER VICTIMS... FOR EVERY-ONE...
LIGHT ...
YEAH... YOU'RE RIGHT, LIGHT.
B-BUT... WE'LL DEFINITELY BE KILLED...
TH-THAT'S WHAT THIS MEANS...

READ THIS WAY

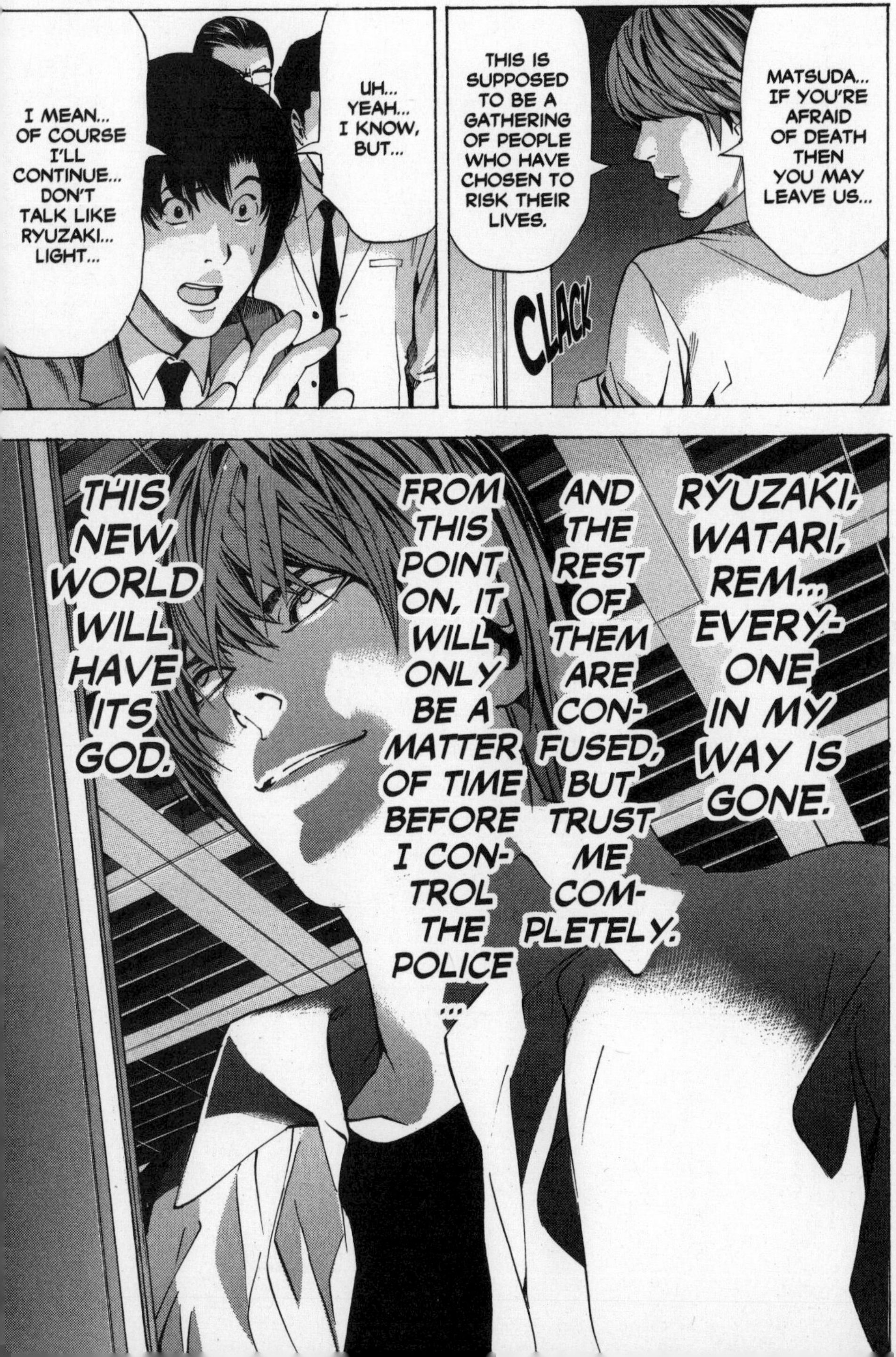

MATSUDA... IF YOU'RE AFRAID OF DEATH THEN YOU MAY LEAVE US...
THIS IS SUPPOSED TO BE A GATHERING OF PEOPLE WHO HAVE CHOSEN TO RISK THEIR LIVES.
CLACK
UH... YEAH... I KNOW, BUT...
I MEAN... OF COURSE I'LL CONTINUE... DON'T TALK LIKE RYUZAKI... LIGHT...
RYUZAKI, WATARI, REM... EVERYONE IN MY WAY IS GONE.
AND THE REST OF THEM ARE CONFUSED, BUT TRUST ME COMPLETELY.
FROM THIS POINT ON, IT WILL ONLY BE A MATTER OF TIME BEFORE I CONTROL THE POLICE...
THIS NEW WORLD WILL HAVE ITS GOD.

# DEATH NOTE
## How to use it
### XL

◦ Whenever a god of death who had been in the human world dies and the DEATH NOTE is left behind and is picked up by a human, that person becomes the owner.

人間界にいた死神が死に、人間界に残されたデスノートは、
人間が拾えばその人間のものとなる。

◦ However, in this case, only the human that can recognize the god of death and its voice is able to see and touch the DEATH NOTE.

しかしこの場合、その死神の姿や声を認知できていた人間でなければ、
ノートを見る事も触る事もできない。

◦ It is very unlikely, but if by any chance a god of death picks up the DEATH NOTE, that god of death becomes the owner.

可能性として極めて低いが、死神が拾えばその死神の物となる。

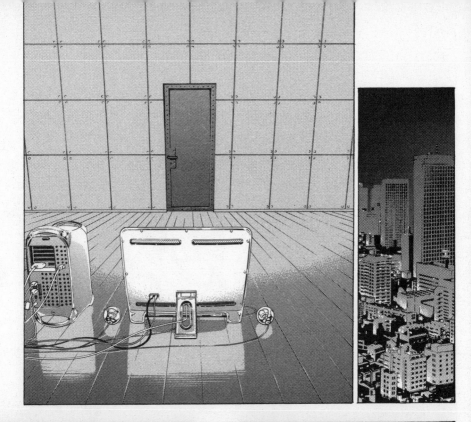

20d 18h 31m 31s

20d 18h 31m 30s

20d 18h 31m 32s

chapter 59 Zero

# chapter 59 Zero

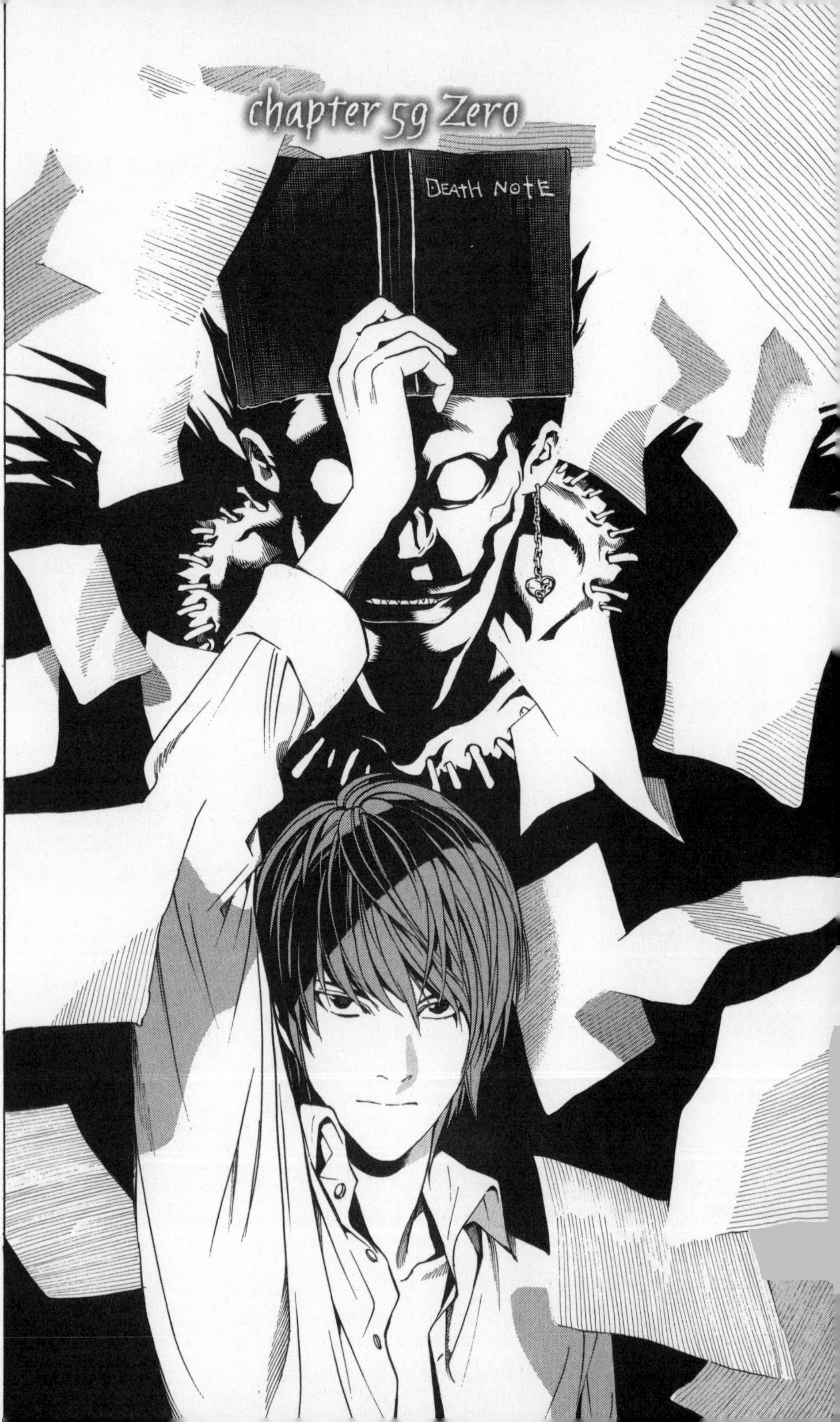
DEATH NOTE

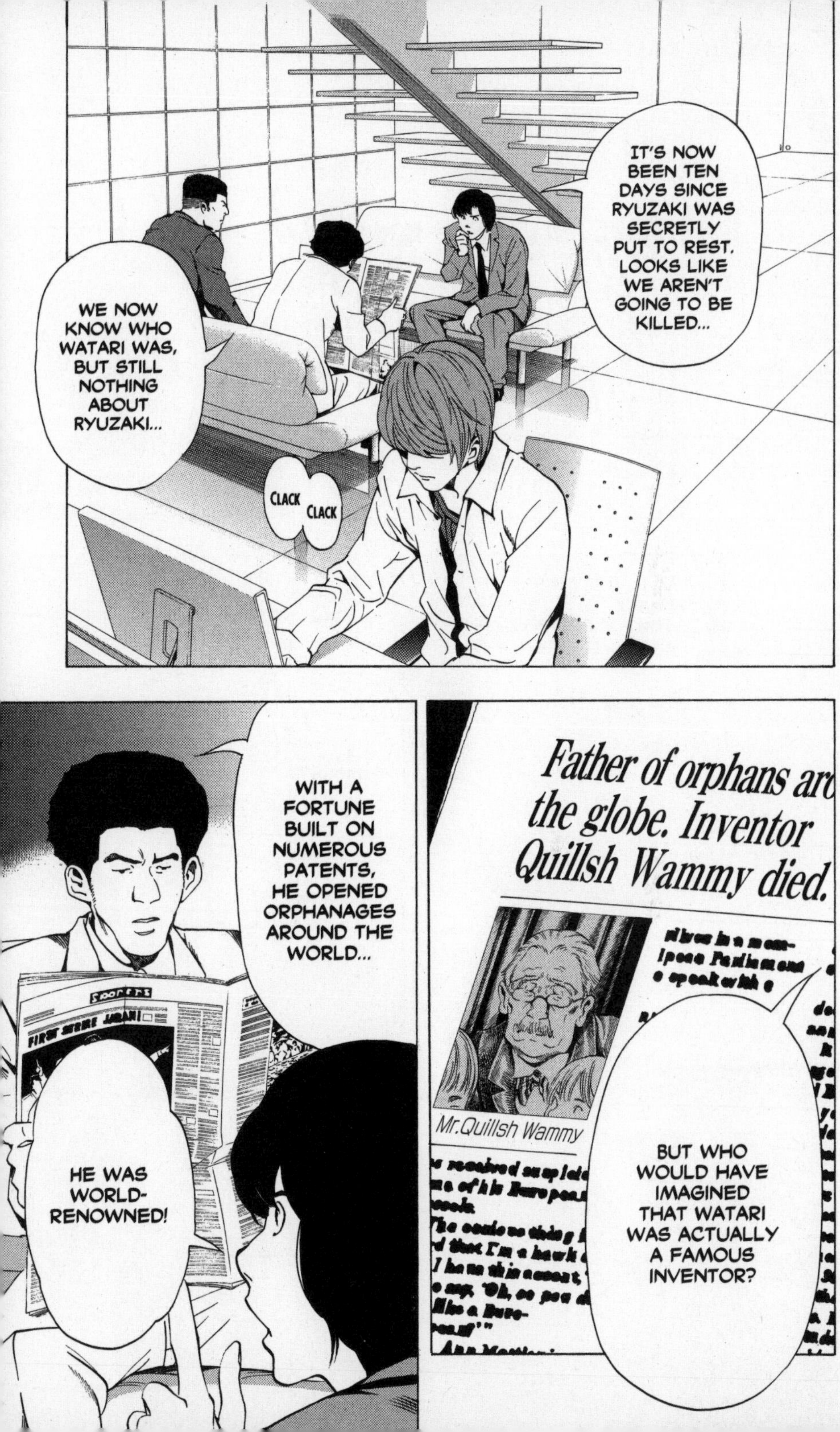
IT'S NOW BEEN TEN DAYS SINCE RYUZAKI WAS SECRETLY PUT TO REST. LOOKS LIKE WE AREN'T GOING TO BE KILLED...
WE NOW KNOW WHO WATARI WAS, BUT STILL NOTHING ABOUT RYUZAKI...
CLACK
CLACK
Father of orphans aro the globe. Inventor Quillsh Wammy died.
Mr.Quillsh Wammy
BUT WHO WOULD HAVE IMAGINED THAT WATARI WAS ACTUALLY A FAMOUS INVENTOR?
WITH A FORTUNE BUILT ON NUMEROUS PATENTS, HE OPENED ORPHANAGES AROUND THE WORLD...
HE WAS WORLD-RENOWNED!

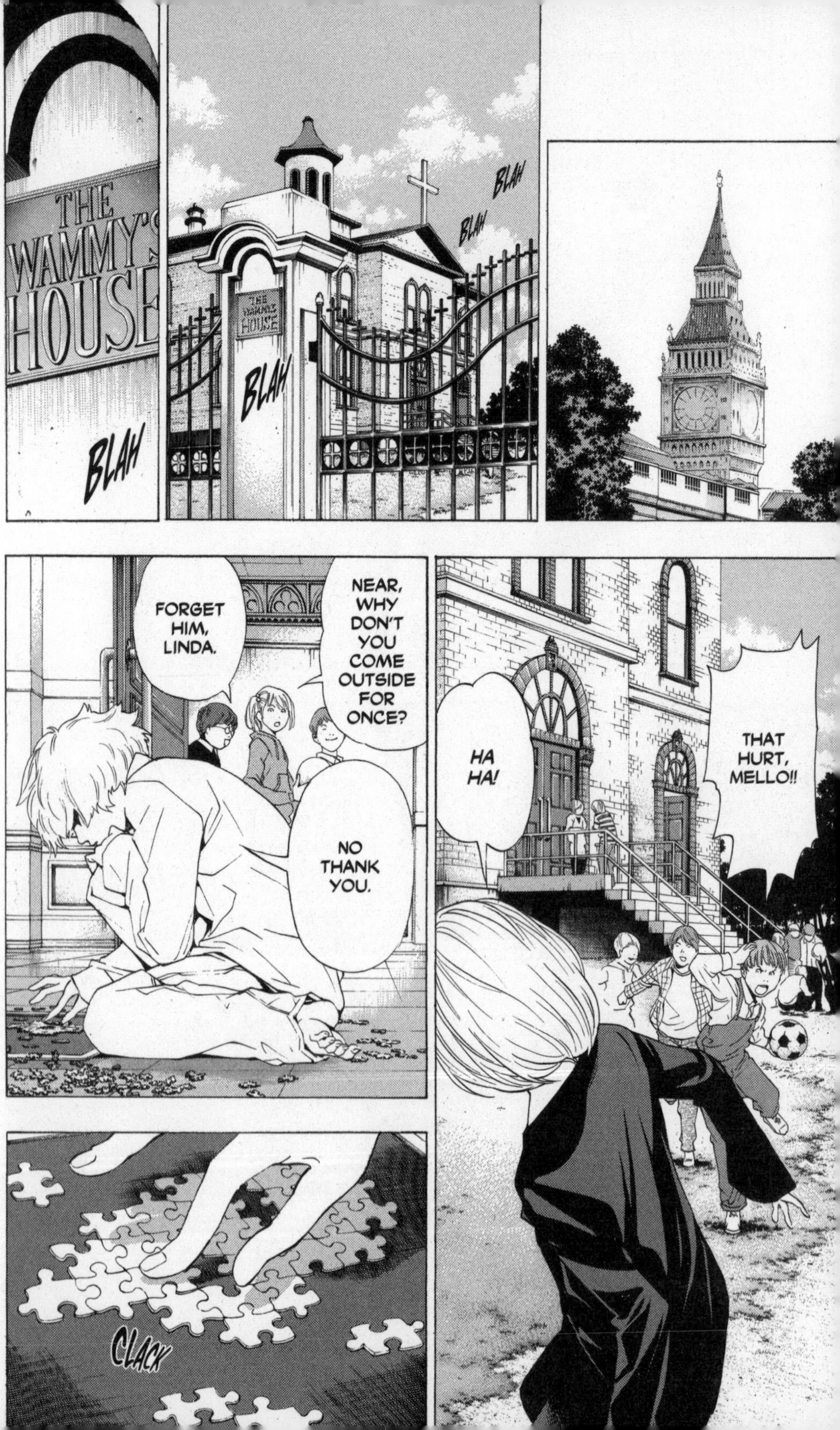
BLAH
BLAH
THE WAMMY'S HOUSE
BLAH
THE WAMMY'S HOUSE
BLAH
THAT HURT, MELLO!!
HA HA!
NEAR, WHY DON'T YOU COME OUTSIDE FOR ONCE?
FORGET HIM, LINDA.
NO THANK YOU.
CLACK

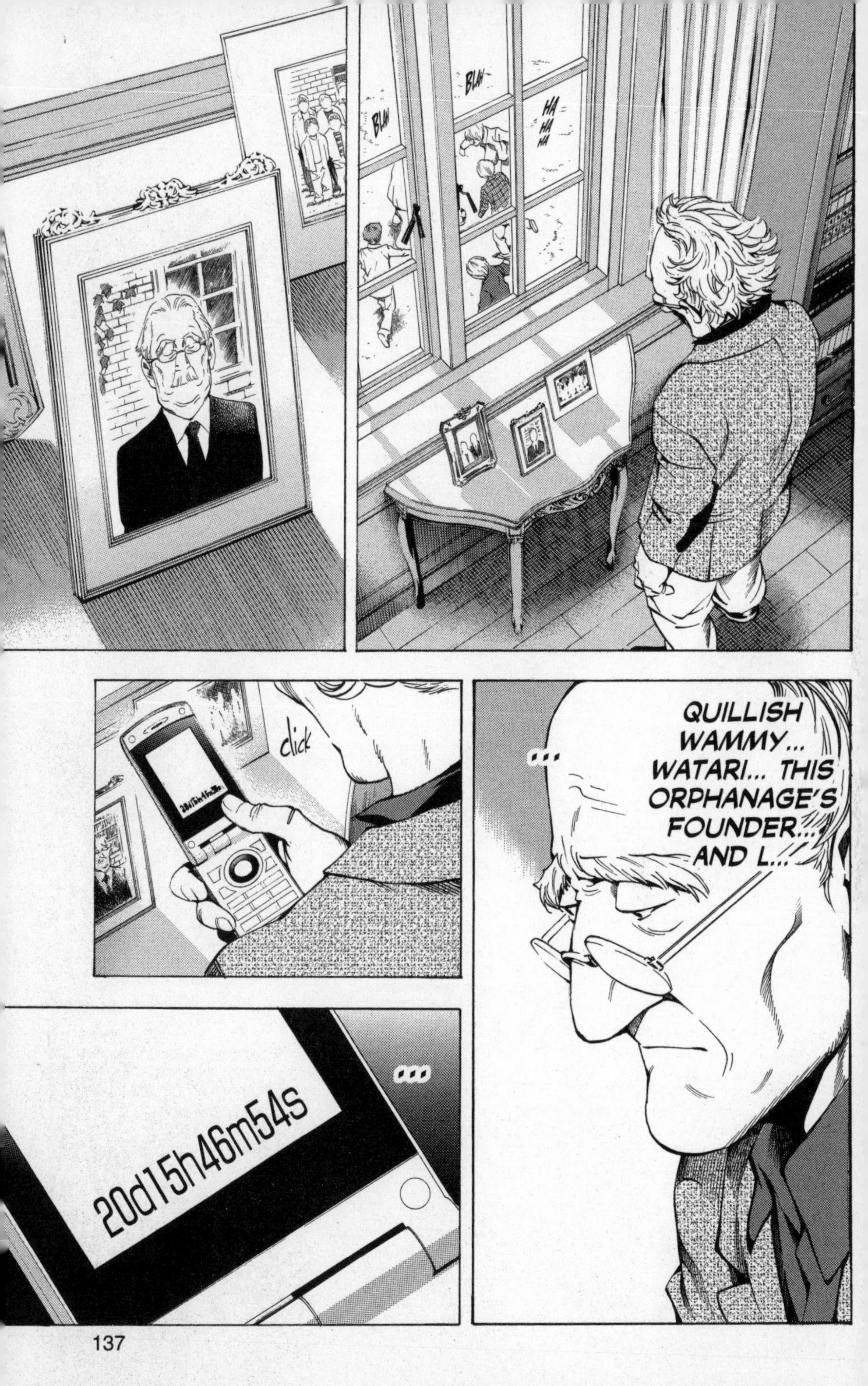
BLAH
BLAH
HA HA HA
...
QUILLISH WAMMY... WATARI... THIS ORPHANAGE'S FOUNDER... AND L...
click
20d15h46m54s
...

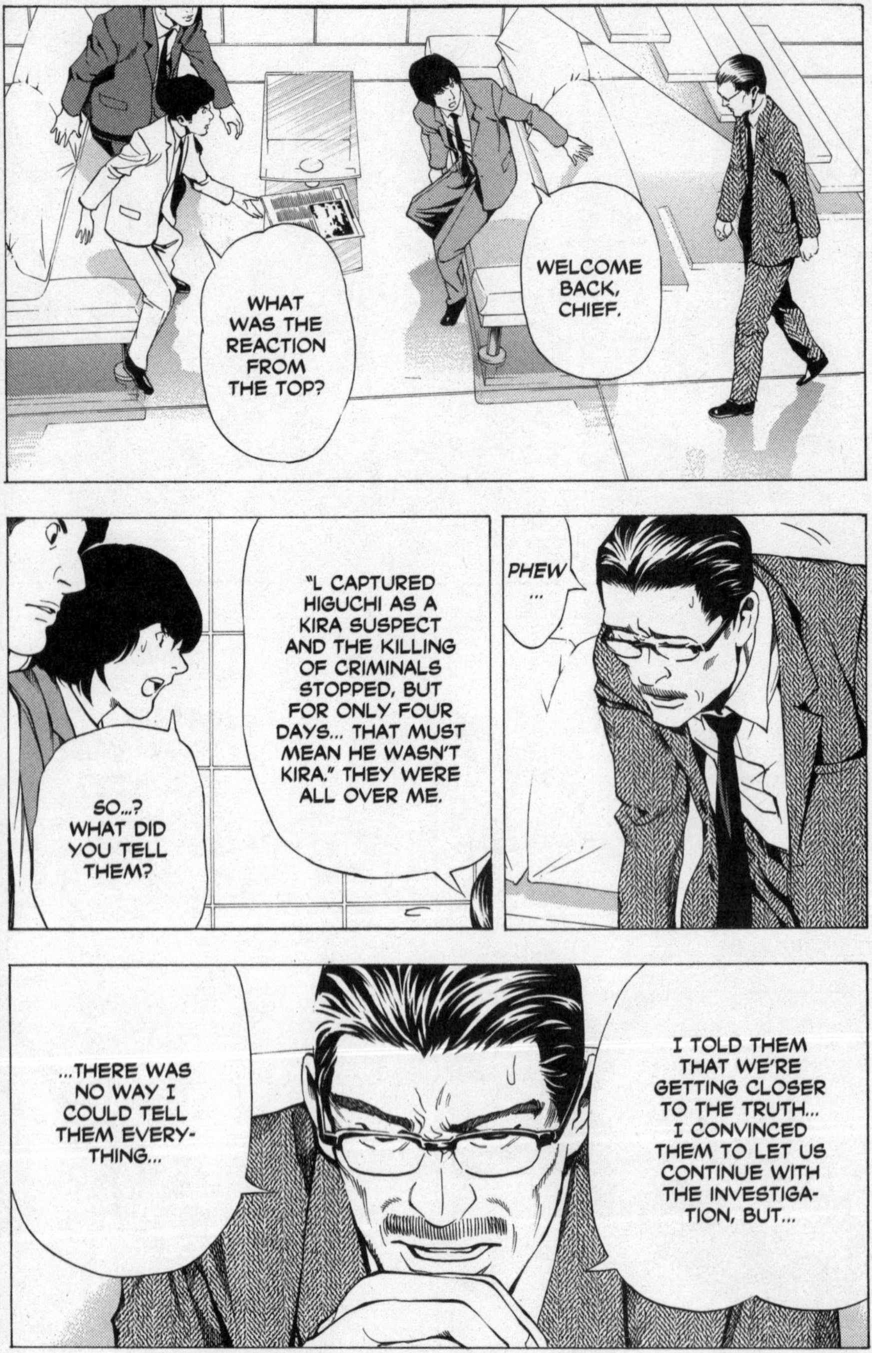
WELCOME BACK, CHIEF.
WHAT WAS THE REACTION FROM THE TOP?
PHEW...
"L CAPTURED HIGUCHI AS A KIRA SUSPECT AND THE KILLING OF CRIMINALS STOPPED, BUT FOR ONLY FOUR DAYS... THAT MUST MEAN HE WASN'T KIRA." THEY WERE ALL OVER ME.
SO...? WHAT DID YOU TELL THEM?
I TOLD THEM THAT WE'RE GETTING CLOSER TO THE TRUTH... I CONVINCED THEM TO LET US CONTINUE WITH THE INVESTIGA-TION, BUT...
...THERE WAS NO WAY I COULD TELL THEM EVERY-THING...

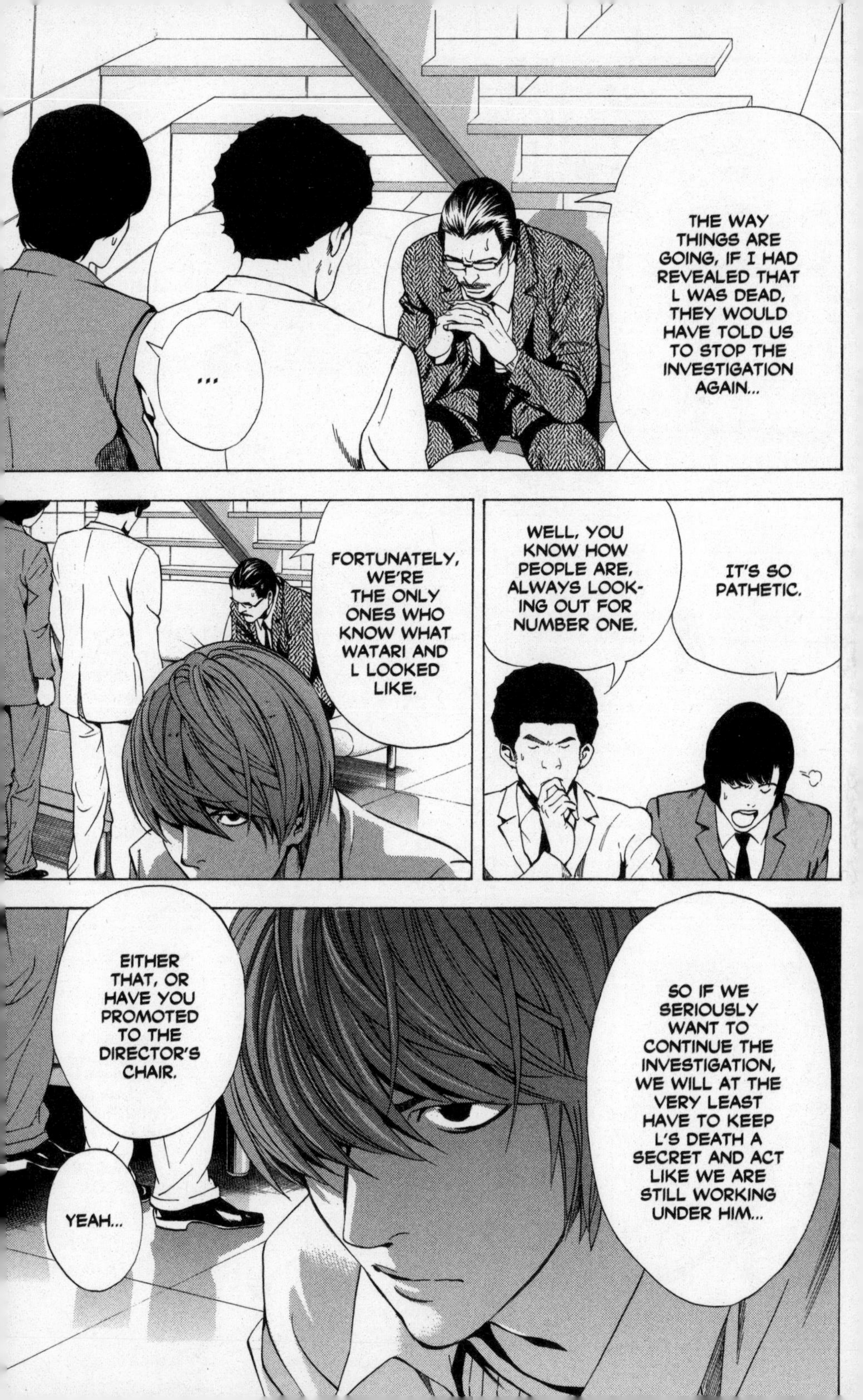
THE WAY THINGS ARE GOING, IF I HAD REVEALED THAT L WAS DEAD, THEY WOULD HAVE TOLD US TO STOP THE INVESTIGATION AGAIN...
...
IT'S SO PATHETIC.
WELL, YOU KNOW HOW PEOPLE ARE, ALWAYS LOOK-ING OUT FOR NUMBER ONE.
FORTUNATELY, WE'RE THE ONLY ONES WHO KNOW WHAT WATARI AND L LOOKED LIKE.
SO IF WE SERIOUSLY WANT TO CONTINUE THE INVESTIGATION, WE WILL AT THE VERY LEAST HAVE TO KEEP L'S DEATH A SECRET AND ACT LIKE WE ARE STILL WORKING UNDER HIM...
EITHER THAT, OR HAVE YOU PROMOTED TO THE DIRECTOR'S CHAIR.
YEAH...

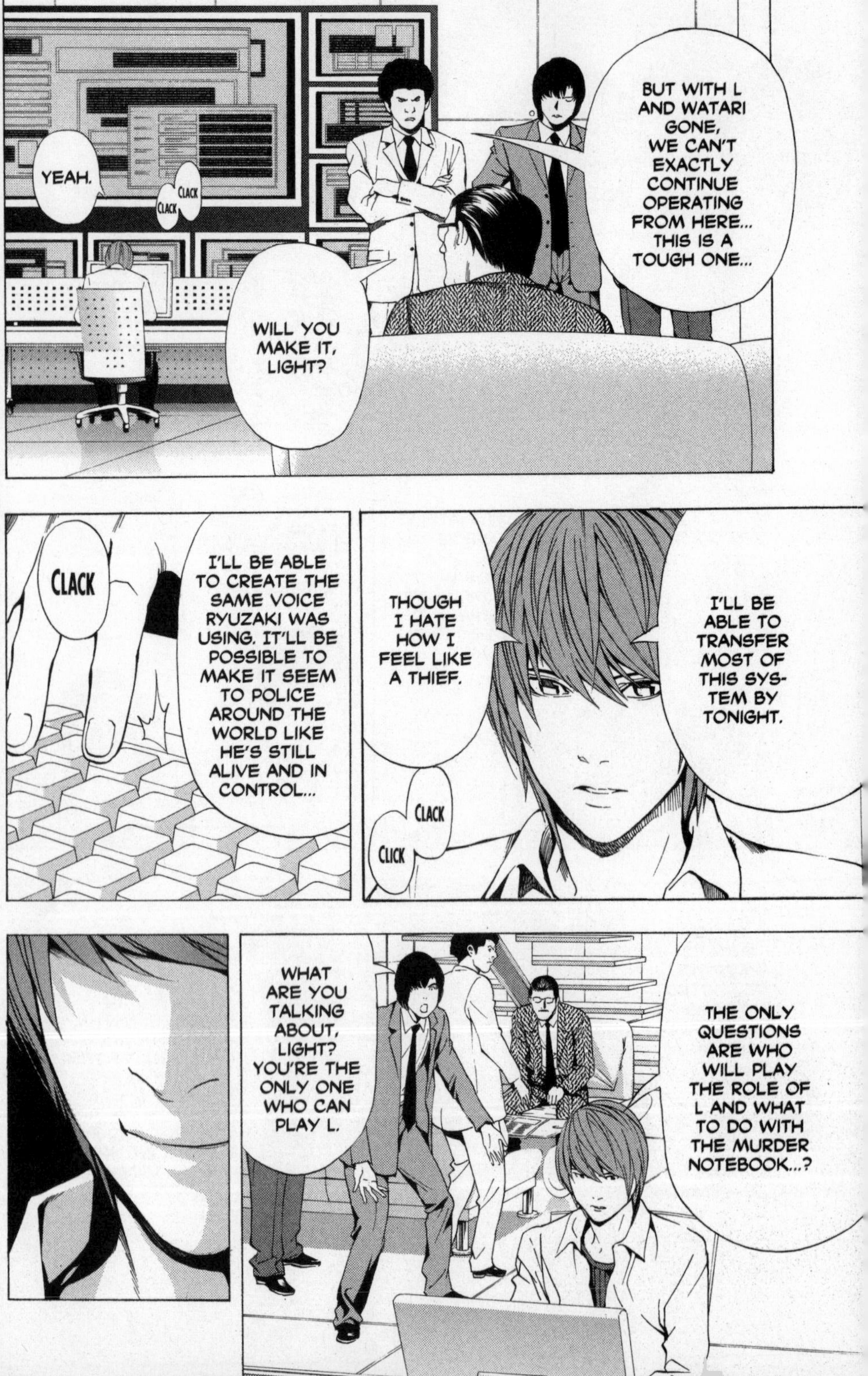
BUT WITH L AND WATARI GONE, WE CAN'T EXACTLY CONTINUE OPERATING FROM HERE... THIS IS A TOUGH ONE...
WILL YOU MAKE IT, LIGHT?
CLACK
CLACK
YEAH.
I'LL BE ABLE TO TRANSFER MOST OF THIS SYS-TEM BY TONIGHT.
THOUGH I HATE HOW I FEEL LIKE A THIEF.
CLACK
CLICK
I'LL BE ABLE TO CREATE THE SAME VOICE RYUZAKI WAS USING. IT'LL BE POSSIBLE TO MAKE IT SEEM TO POLICE AROUND THE WORLD LIKE HE'S STILL ALIVE AND IN CONTROL...
CLACK
THE ONLY QUESTIONS ARE WHO WILL PLAY THE ROLE OF L AND WHAT TO DO WITH THE MURDER NOTEBOOK...?
WHAT ARE YOU TALKING ABOUT, LIGHT? YOU'RE THE ONLY ONE WHO CAN PLAY L.

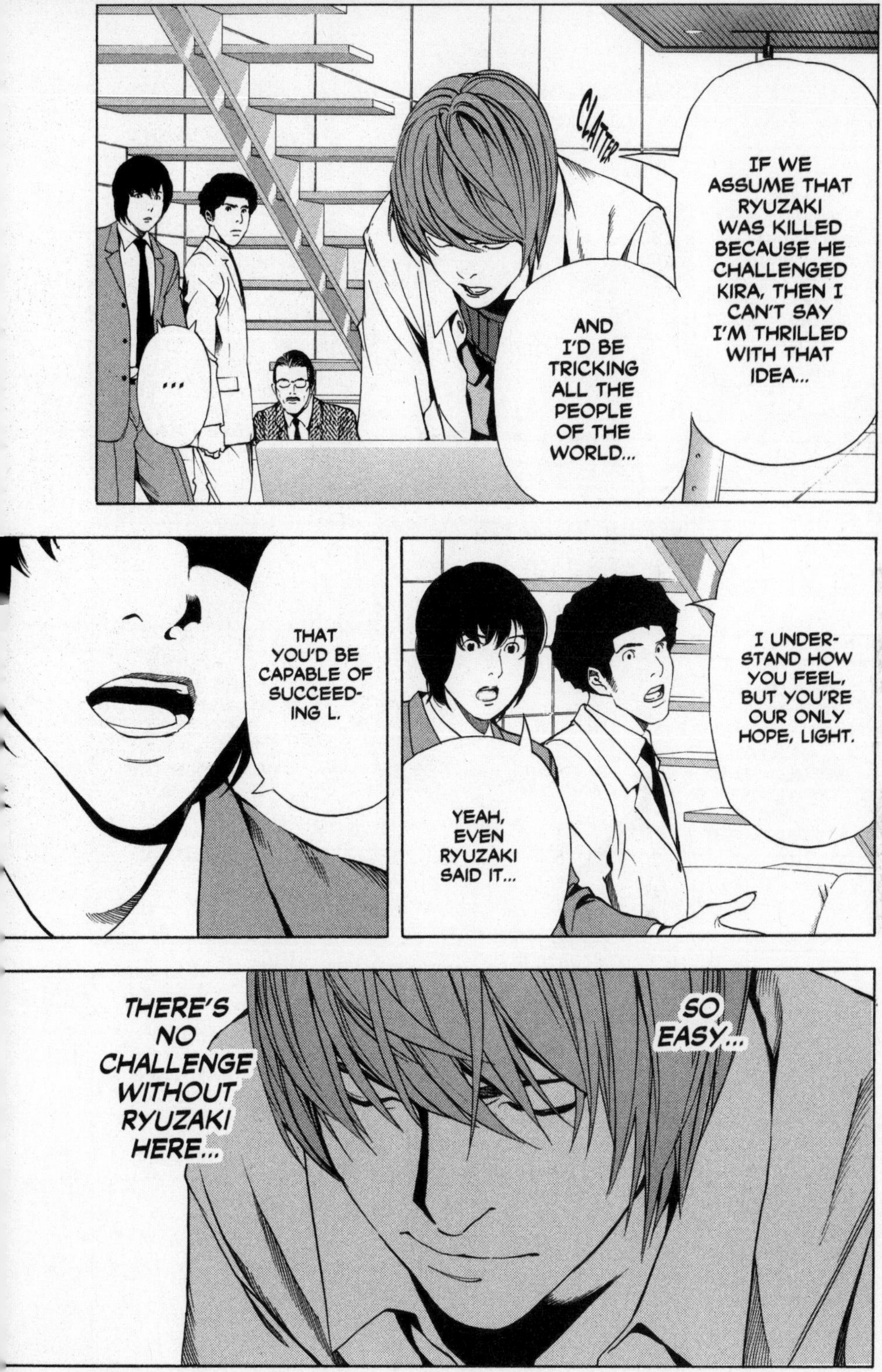
CLATTER
IF WE ASSUME THAT RYUZAKI WAS KILLED BECAUSE HE CHALLENGED KIRA, THEN I CAN'T SAY I'M THRILLED WITH THAT IDEA...
AND I'D BE TRICKING ALL THE PEOPLE OF THE WORLD...
...
I UNDERSTAND HOW YOU FEEL, BUT YOU'RE OUR ONLY HOPE, LIGHT.
YEAH, EVEN RYUZAKI SAID IT...
THAT YOU'D BE CAPABLE OF SUCCEEDING L.
SO EASY...
THERE'S NO CHALLENGE WITHOUT RYUZAKI HERE...

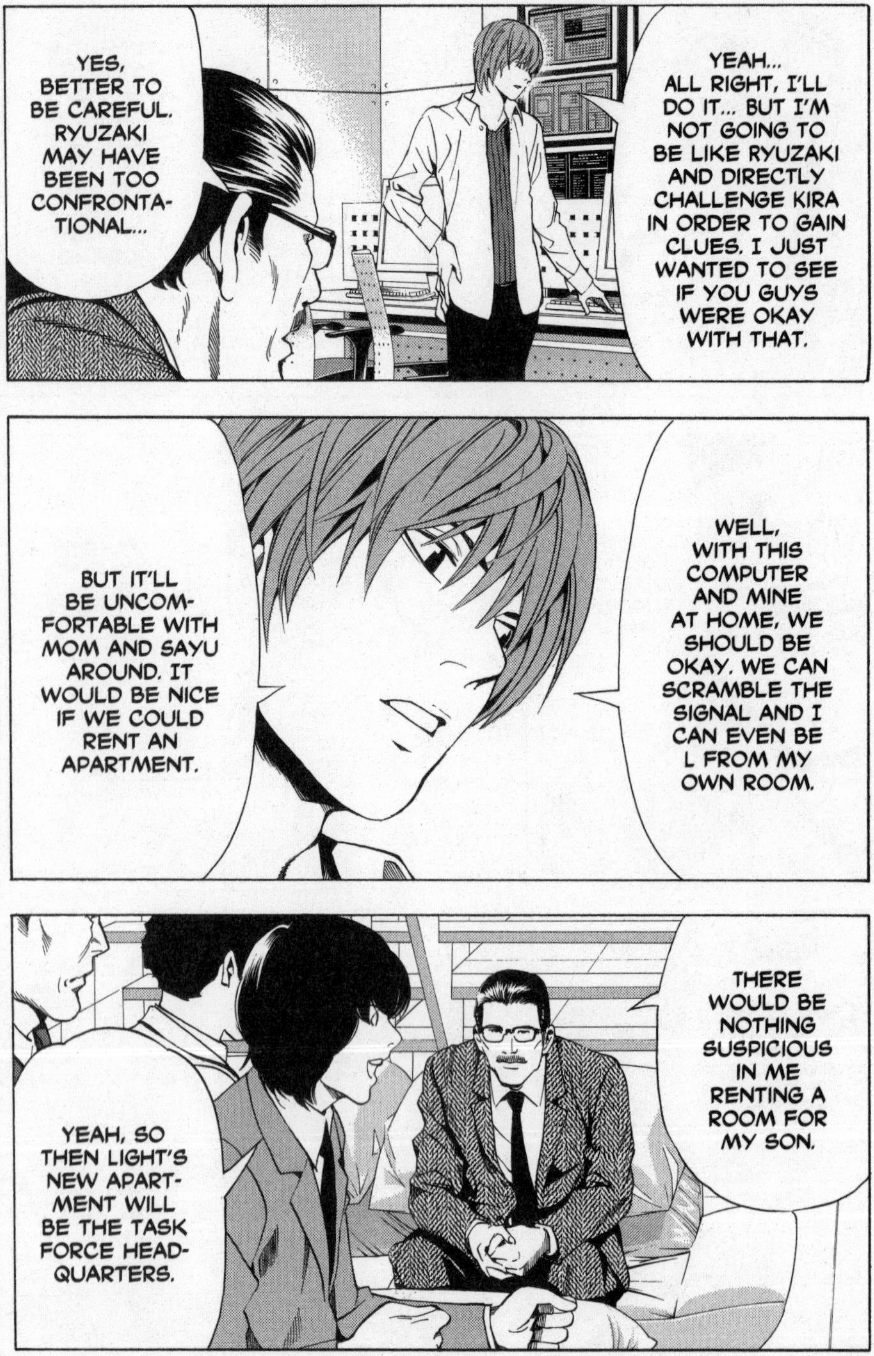
YEAH... ALL RIGHT, I'LL DO IT... BUT I'M NOT GOING TO BE LIKE RYUZAKI AND DIRECTLY CHALLENGE KIRA IN ORDER TO GAIN CLUES. I JUST WANTED TO SEE IF YOU GUYS WERE OKAY WITH THAT.
YES, BETTER TO BE CAREFUL. RYUZAKI MAY HAVE BEEN TOO CONFRONTA-TIONAL...
WELL, WITH THIS COMPUTER AND MINE AT HOME, WE SHOULD BE OKAY. WE CAN SCRAMBLE THE SIGNAL AND I CAN EVEN BE L FROM MY OWN ROOM.
BUT IT'LL BE UNCOM-FORTABLE WITH MOM AND SAYU AROUND. IT WOULD BE NICE IF WE COULD RENT AN APARTMENT.
THERE WOULD BE NOTHING SUSPICIOUS IN ME RENTING A ROOM FOR MY SON.
YEAH, SO THEN LIGHT'S NEW APART-MENT WILL BE THE TASK FORCE HEAD-QUARTERS.

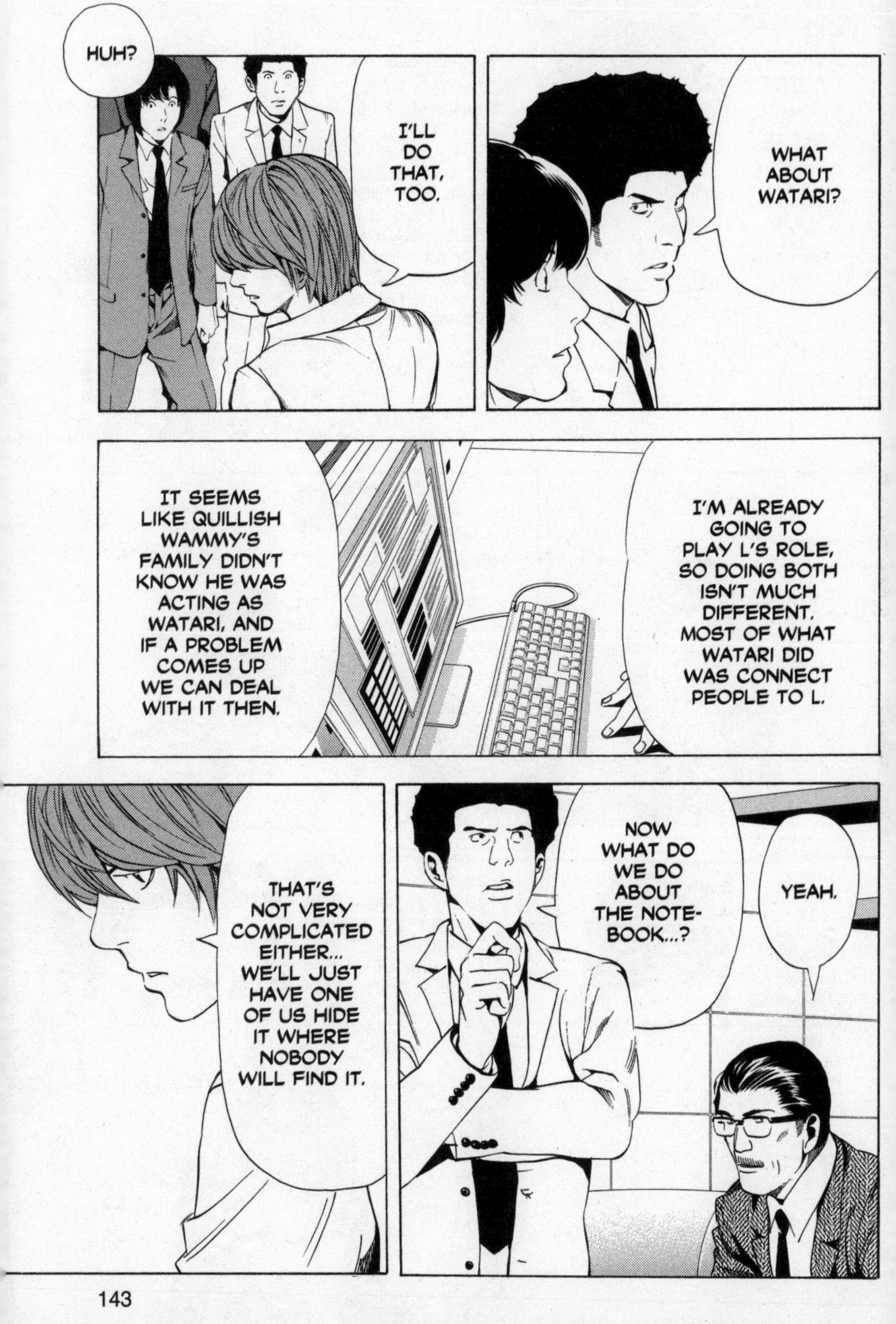
WHAT ABOUT WATARI?
I'LL DO THAT, TOO.
HUH?
I'M ALREADY GOING TO PLAY L'S ROLE, SO DOING BOTH ISN'T MUCH DIFFERENT. MOST OF WHAT WATARI DID WAS CONNECT PEOPLE TO L.
IT SEEMS LIKE QUILLISH WAMMY'S FAMILY DIDN'T KNOW HE WAS ACTING AS WATARI, AND IF A PROBLEM COMES UP WE CAN DEAL WITH IT THEN.
YEAH.
NOW WHAT DO WE DO ABOUT THE NOTE-BOOK...?
THAT'S NOT VERY COMPLICATED EITHER... WE'LL JUST HAVE ONE OF US HIDE IT WHERE NOBODY WILL FIND IT.

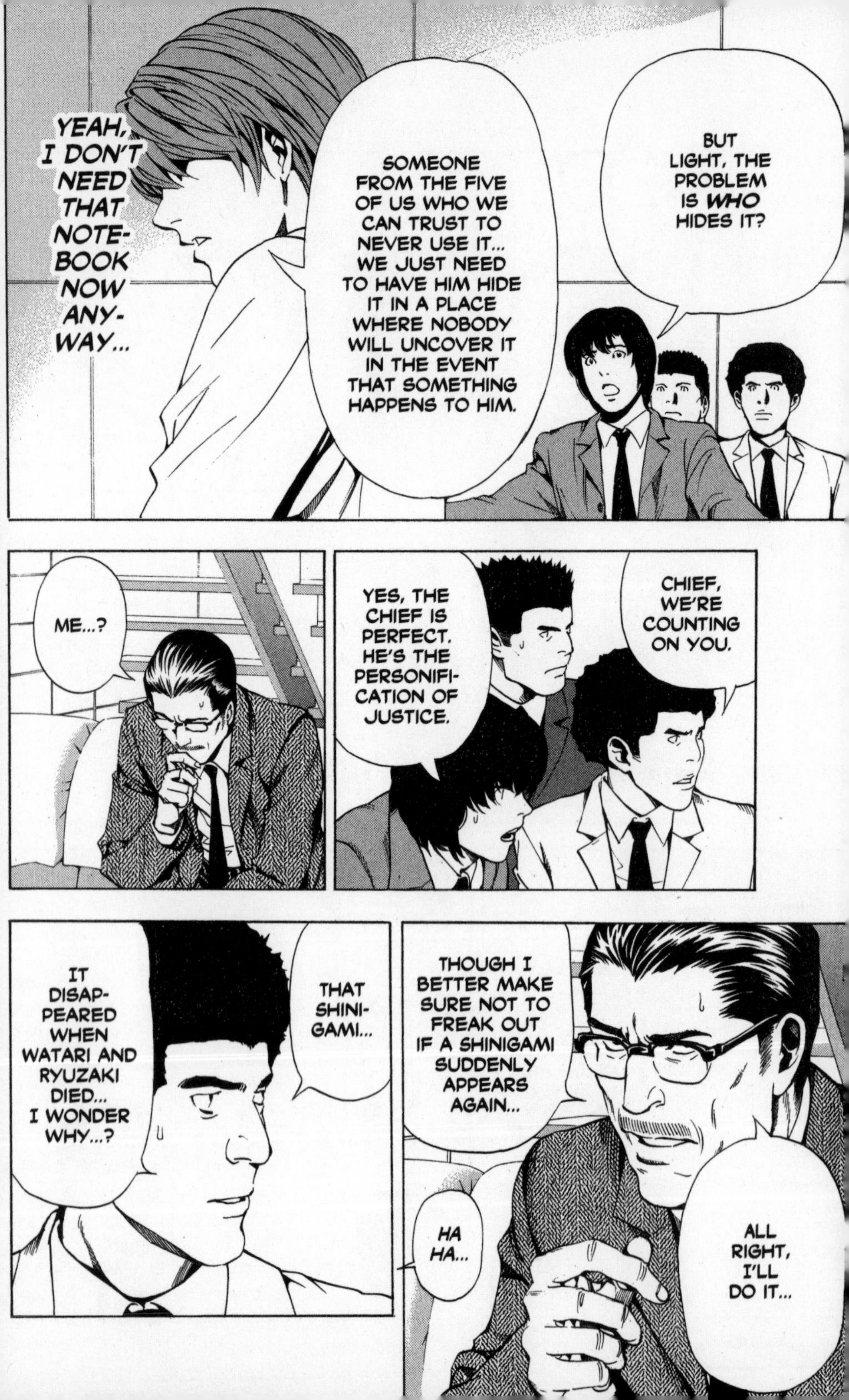
SOMEONE FROM THE FIVE OF US WHO WE CAN TRUST TO NEVER USE IT... WE JUST NEED TO HAVE HIM HIDE IT IN A PLACE WHERE NOBODY WILL UNCOVER IT IN THE EVENT THAT SOMETHING HAPPENS TO HIM.
BUT LIGHT, THE PROBLEM IS *WHO* HIDES IT?
YEAH, I DON'T NEED THAT NOTE-BOOK NOW ANY-WAY...
CHIEF, WE'RE COUNTING ON YOU.
YES, THE CHIEF IS PERFECT. HE'S THE PERSONIFI-CATION OF JUSTICE.
ME...?
ALL RIGHT, I'LL DO IT...
HA HA...
THOUGH I BETTER MAKE SURE NOT TO FREAK OUT IF A SHINIGAMI SUDDENLY APPEARS AGAIN...
THAT SHINI-GAMI...
IT DISAP-PEARED WHEN WATARI AND RYUZAKI DIED... I WONDER WHY...?

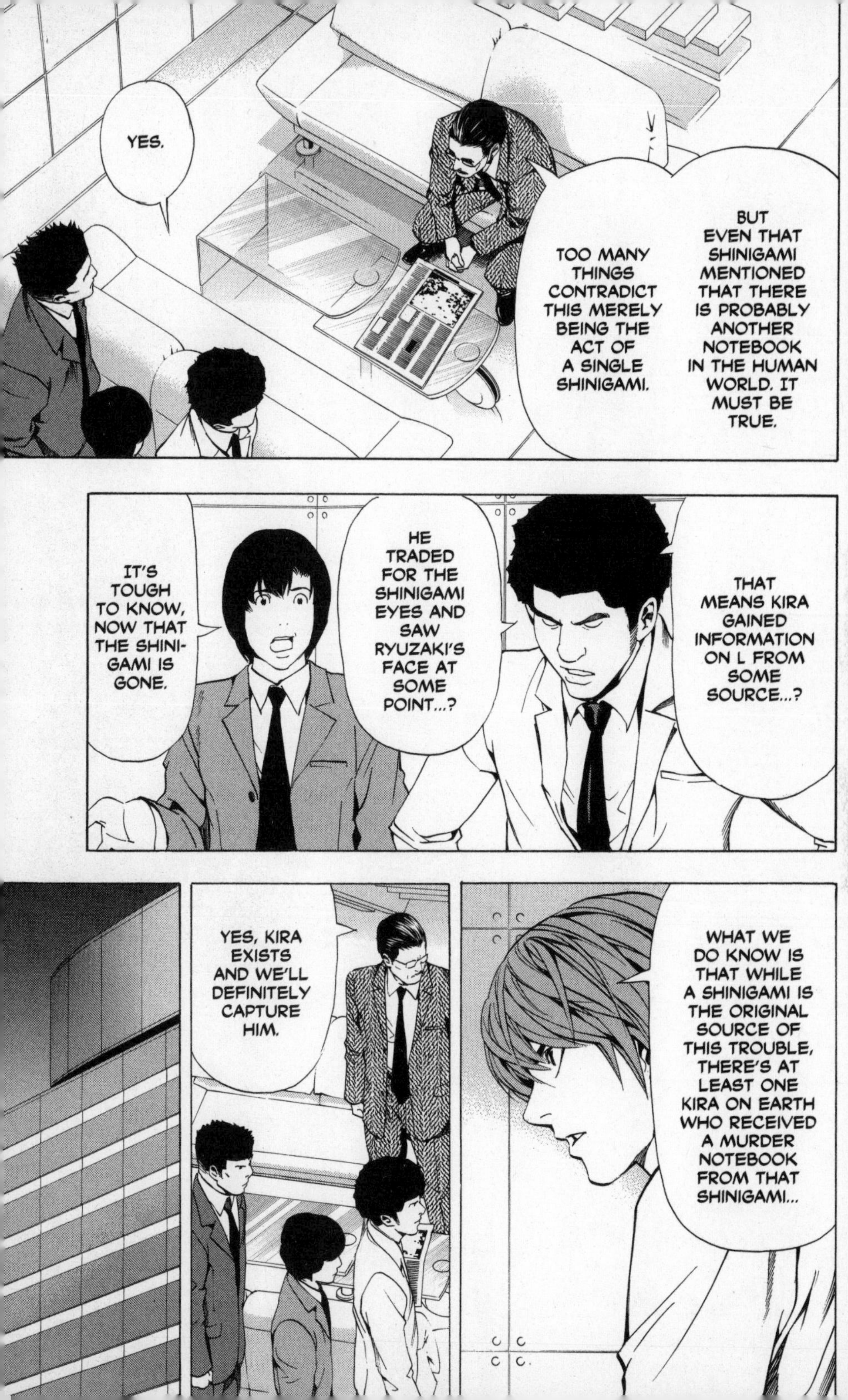
BUT EVEN THAT SHINIGAMI MENTIONED THAT THERE IS PROBABLY ANOTHER NOTEBOOK IN THE HUMAN WORLD. IT MUST BE TRUE.
TOO MANY THINGS CONTRADICT THIS MERELY BEING THE ACT OF A SINGLE SHINIGAMI.
YES.
THAT MEANS KIRA GAINED INFORMATION ON L FROM SOME SOURCE...?
HE TRADED FOR THE SHINIGAMI EYES AND SAW RYUZAKI'S FACE AT SOME POINT...?
IT'S TOUGH TO KNOW, NOW THAT THE SHINI-GAMI IS GONE.
WHAT WE DO KNOW IS THAT WHILE A SHINIGAMI IS THE ORIGINAL SOURCE OF THIS TROUBLE, THERE'S AT LEAST ONE KIRA ON EARTH WHO RECEIVED A MURDER NOTEBOOK FROM THAT SHINIGAMI...
YES, KIRA EXISTS AND WE'LL DEFINITELY CAPTURE HIM.

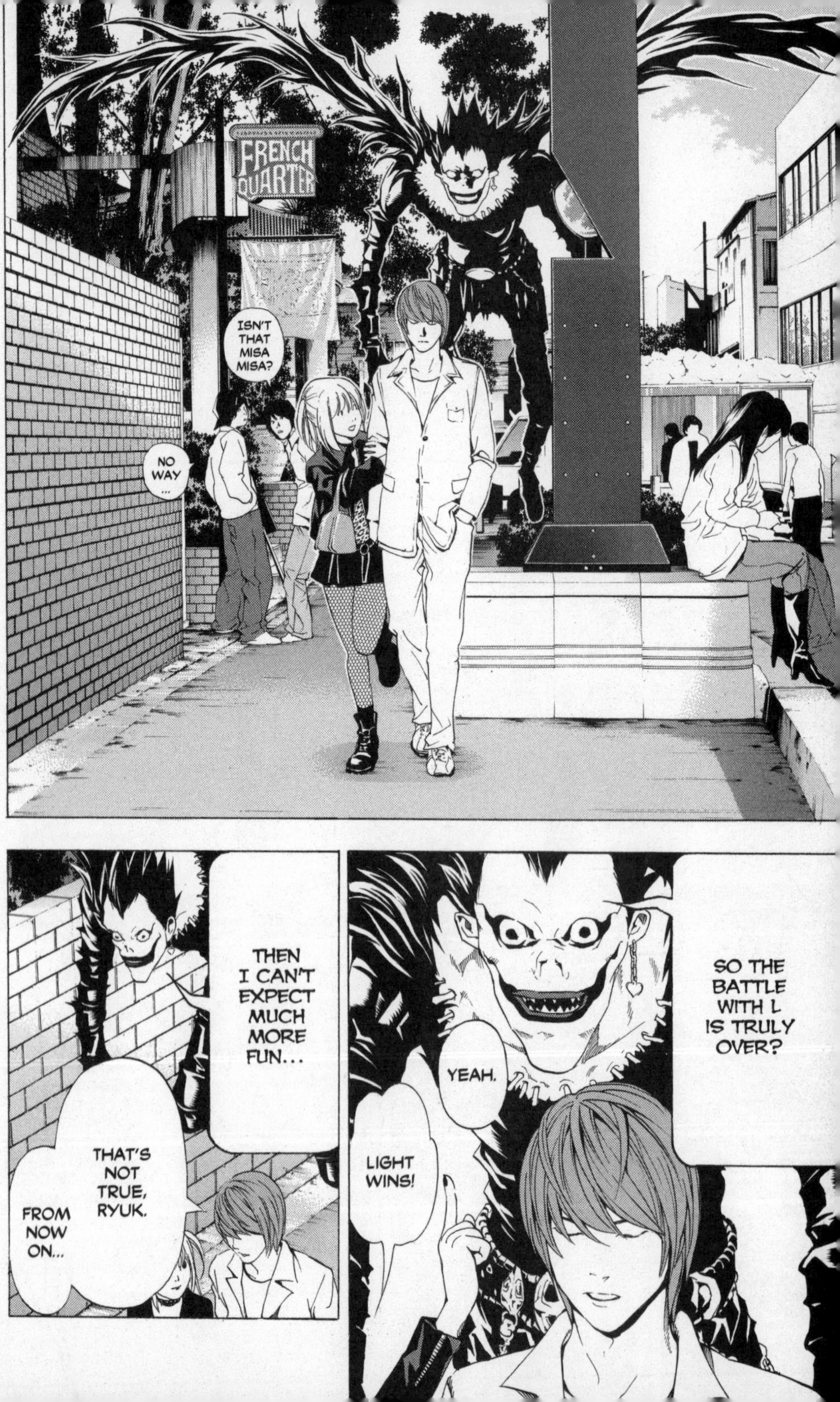
FRENCH QUARTER
ISN'T THAT MISA MISA?
NO WAY …
SO THE BATTLE WITH L IS TRULY OVER?
YEAH.
LIGHT WINS!
THEN I CAN'T EXPECT MUCH MORE FUN…
THAT'S NOT TRUE, RYUK.
FROM NOW ON…

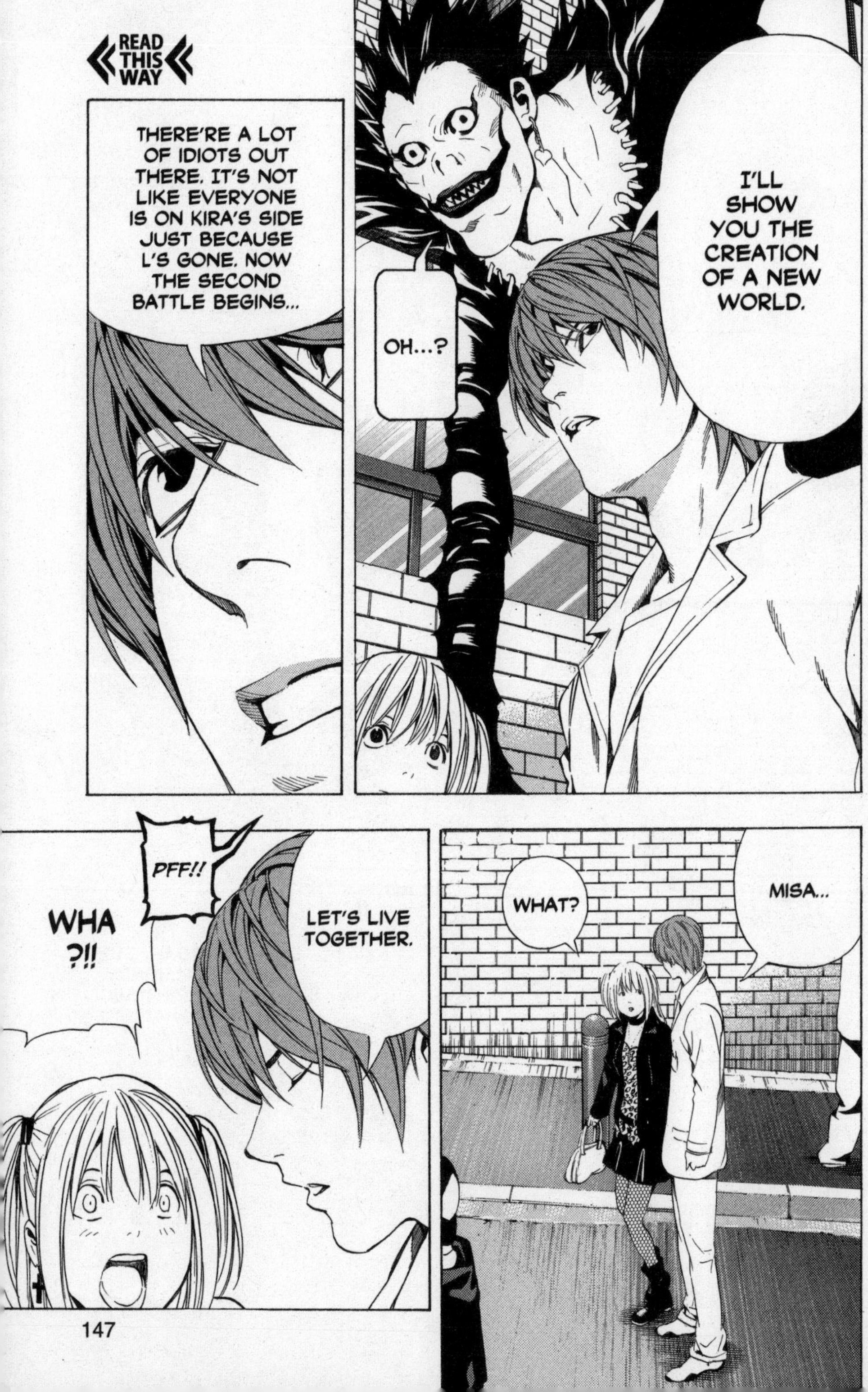
READ THIS WAY
I'LL SHOW YOU THE CREATION OF A NEW WORLD.
OH...?
THERE'RE A LOT OF IDIOTS OUT THERE. IT'S NOT LIKE EVERYONE IS ON KIRA'S SIDE JUST BECAUSE L'S GONE. NOW THE SECOND BATTLE BEGINS...
MISA...
WHAT?
LET'S LIVE TOGETHER.
PFF!!
WHA ?!!

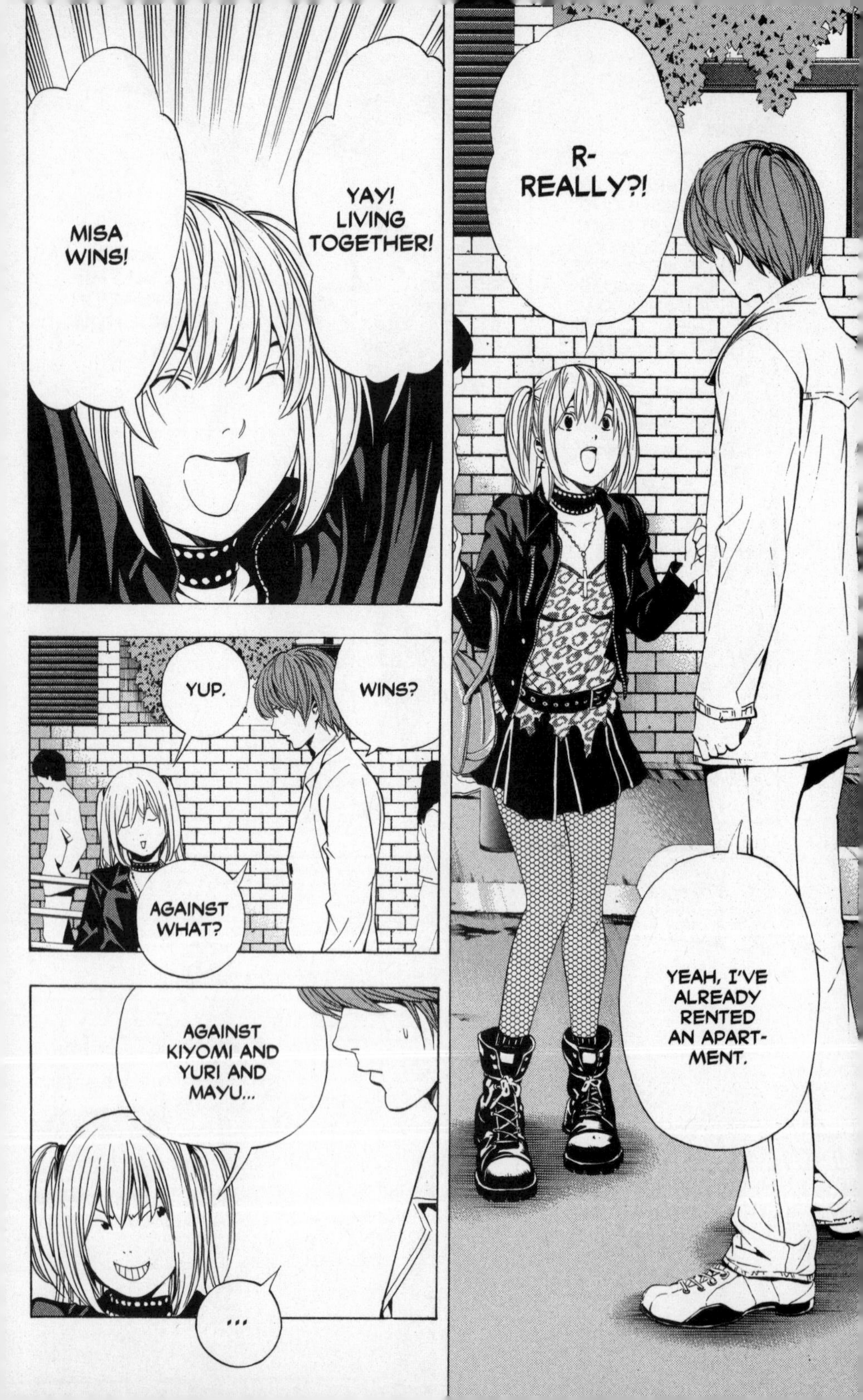
R-REALLY?!
YEAH, I'VE ALREADY RENTED AN APARTMENT.
YAY! LIVING TOGETHER!
MISA WINS!
WINS?
YUP.
AGAINST WHAT?
AGAINST KIYOMI AND YURI AND MAYU...
...

READ THIS WAY

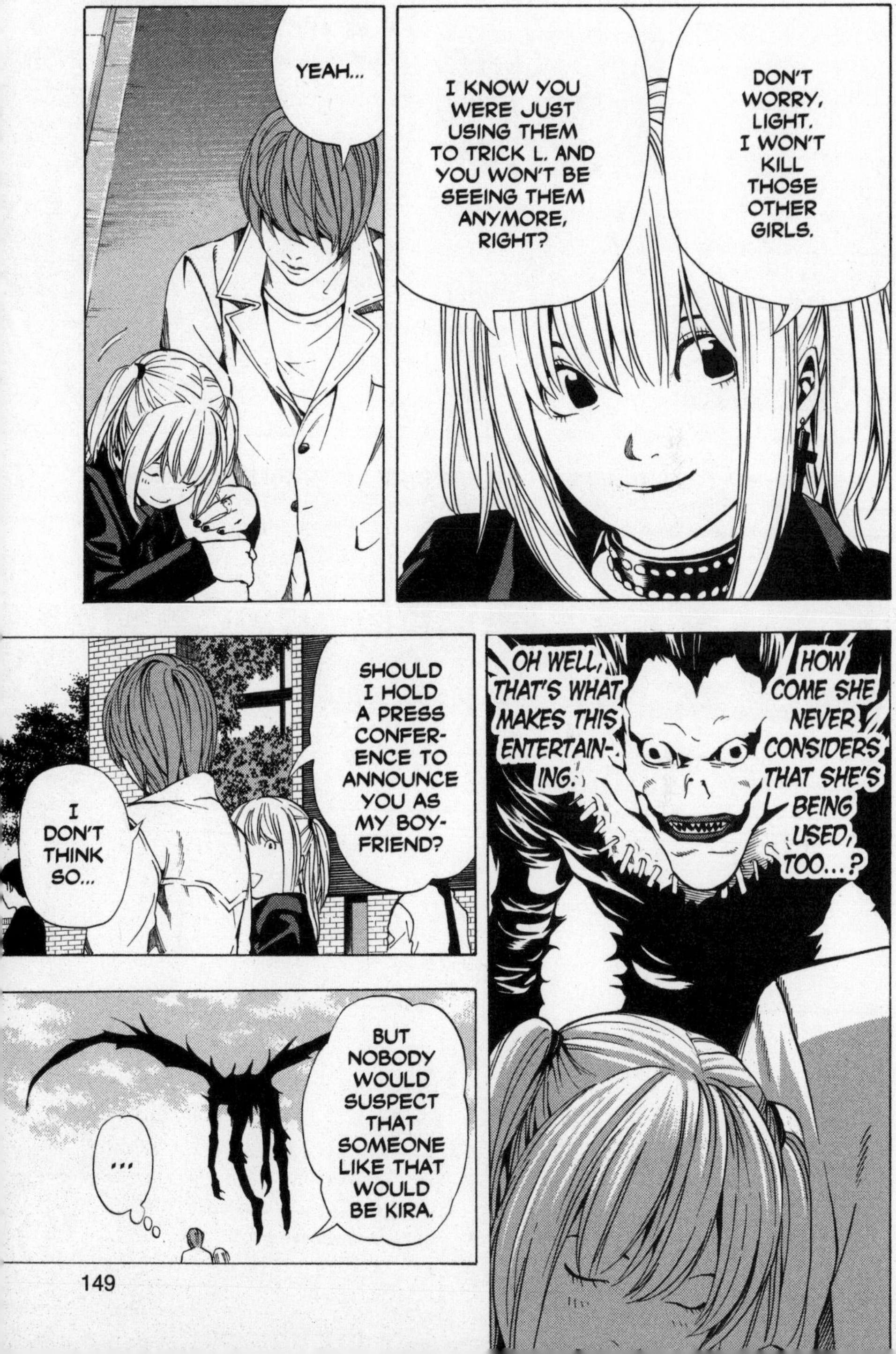

DON'T WORRY, LIGHT. I WON'T KILL THOSE OTHER GIRLS.
I KNOW YOU WERE JUST USING THEM TO TRICK L. AND YOU WON'T BE SEEING THEM ANYMORE, RIGHT?
YEAH...
HOW COME SHE NEVER CONSIDERS THAT SHE'S BEING USED, TOO...?
OH WELL, THAT'S WHAT MAKES THIS ENTERTAIN-ING.
SHOULD I HOLD A PRESS CONFER-ENCE TO ANNOUNCE YOU AS MY BOY-FRIEND?
I DON'T THINK SO...
BUT NOBODY WOULD SUSPECT THAT SOMEONE LIKE THAT WOULD BE KIRA.
...

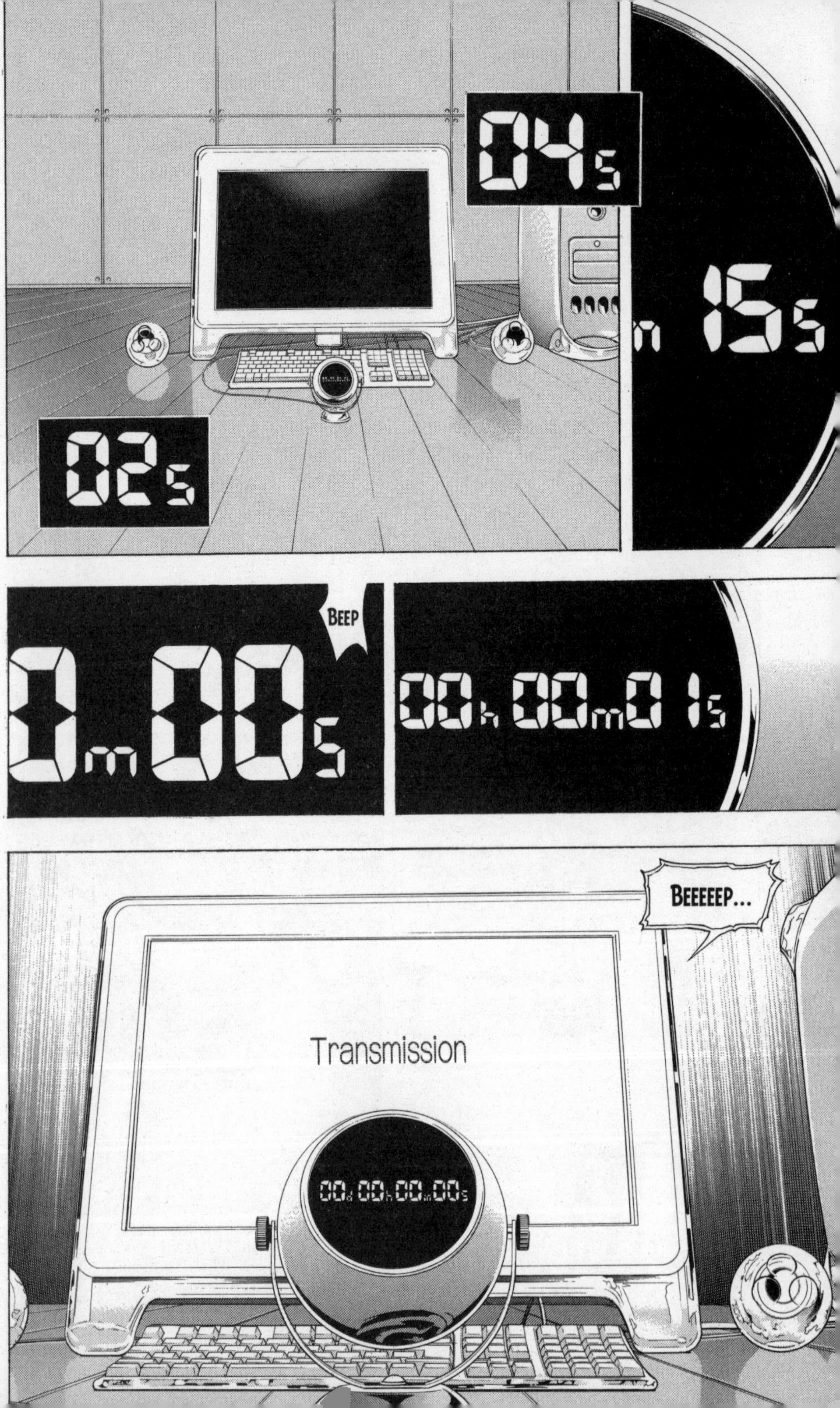
15s
04s
02s
00h00m01s
BEEP
0m00s
BEEEEEP...
Transmission
00d00h00m00s

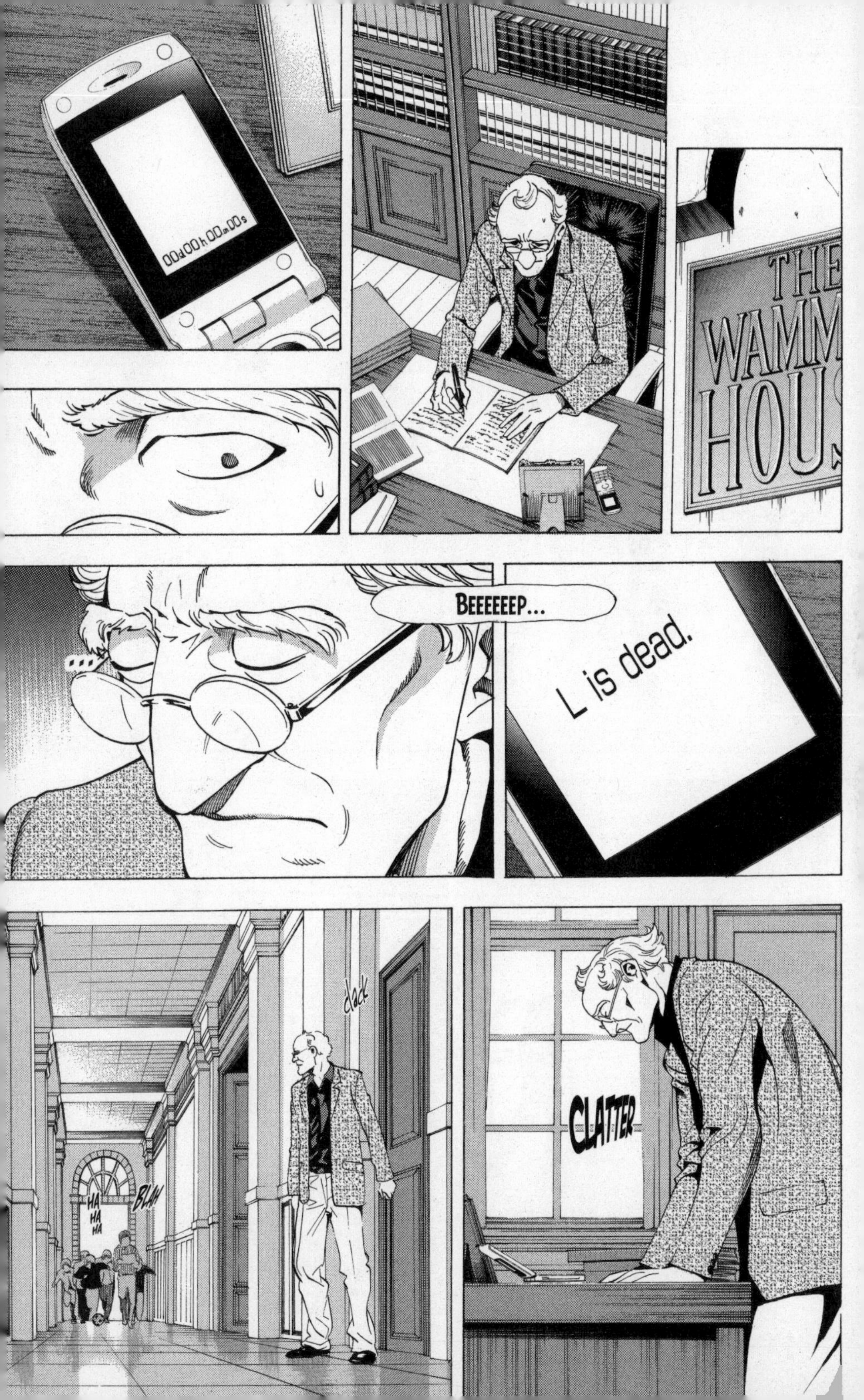
THE
WAMM
HOUS
00d00h00m00s
L is dead.
BEEEEEEP...
...
CLATTER
clack
HA
HA
HA
BLAH

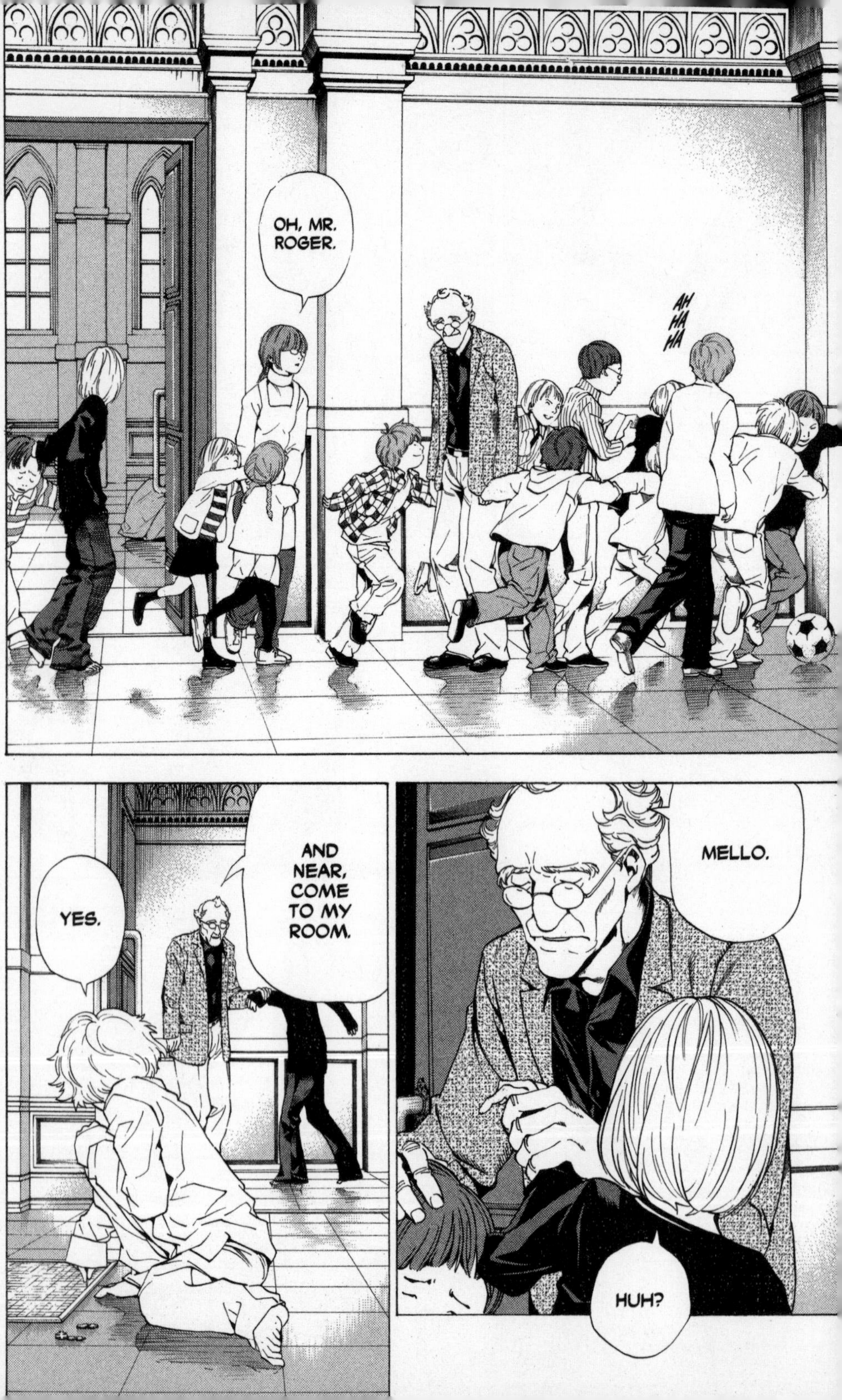
OH, MR. ROGER.
AH HA HA
MELLO.
HUH?
AND NEAR, COME TO MY ROOM.
YES.

WHAT
IS IT,
ROGER?

L IS
DEAD.

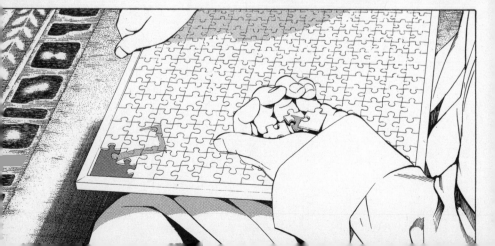

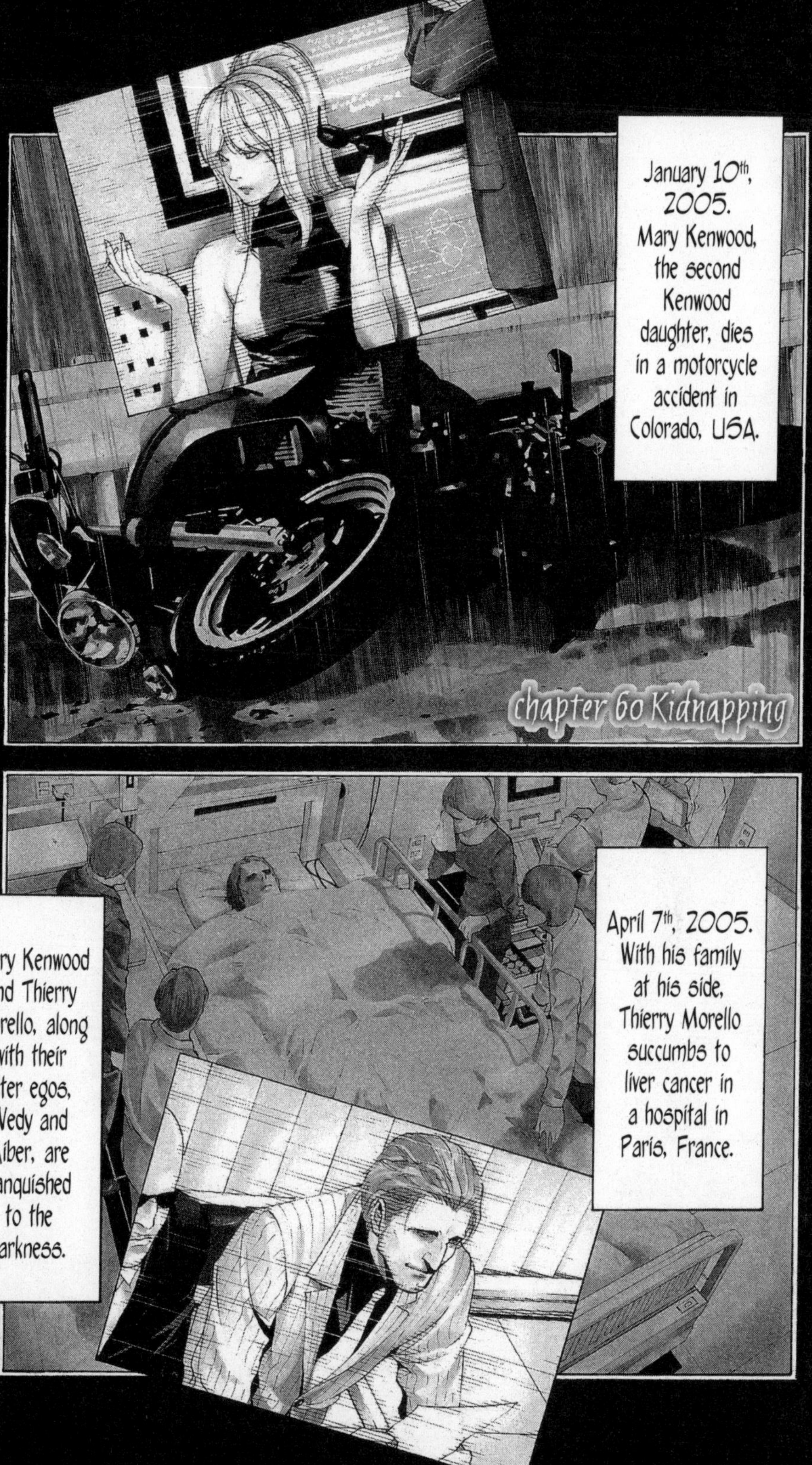
January 10th, 2005. Mary Kenwood, the second Kenwood daughter, dies in a motorcycle accident in Colorado, USA.
chapter 60 Kidnapping
April 7th, 2005. With his family at his side, Thierry Morello succumbs to liver cancer in a hospital in Paris, France.
Mary Kenwood and Thierry Morello, along with their alter egos, Wedy and Aiber, are vanquished to the darkness.

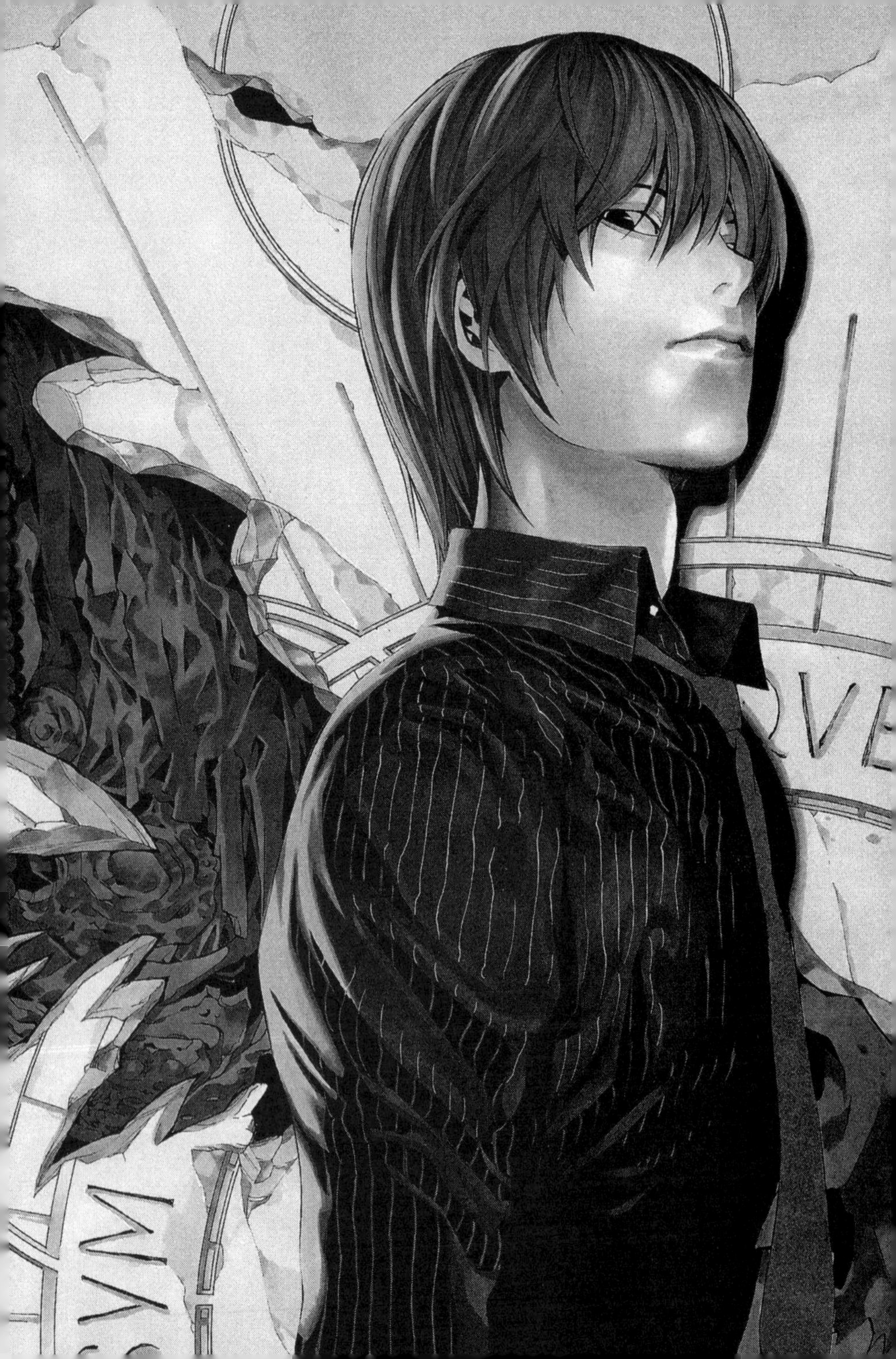

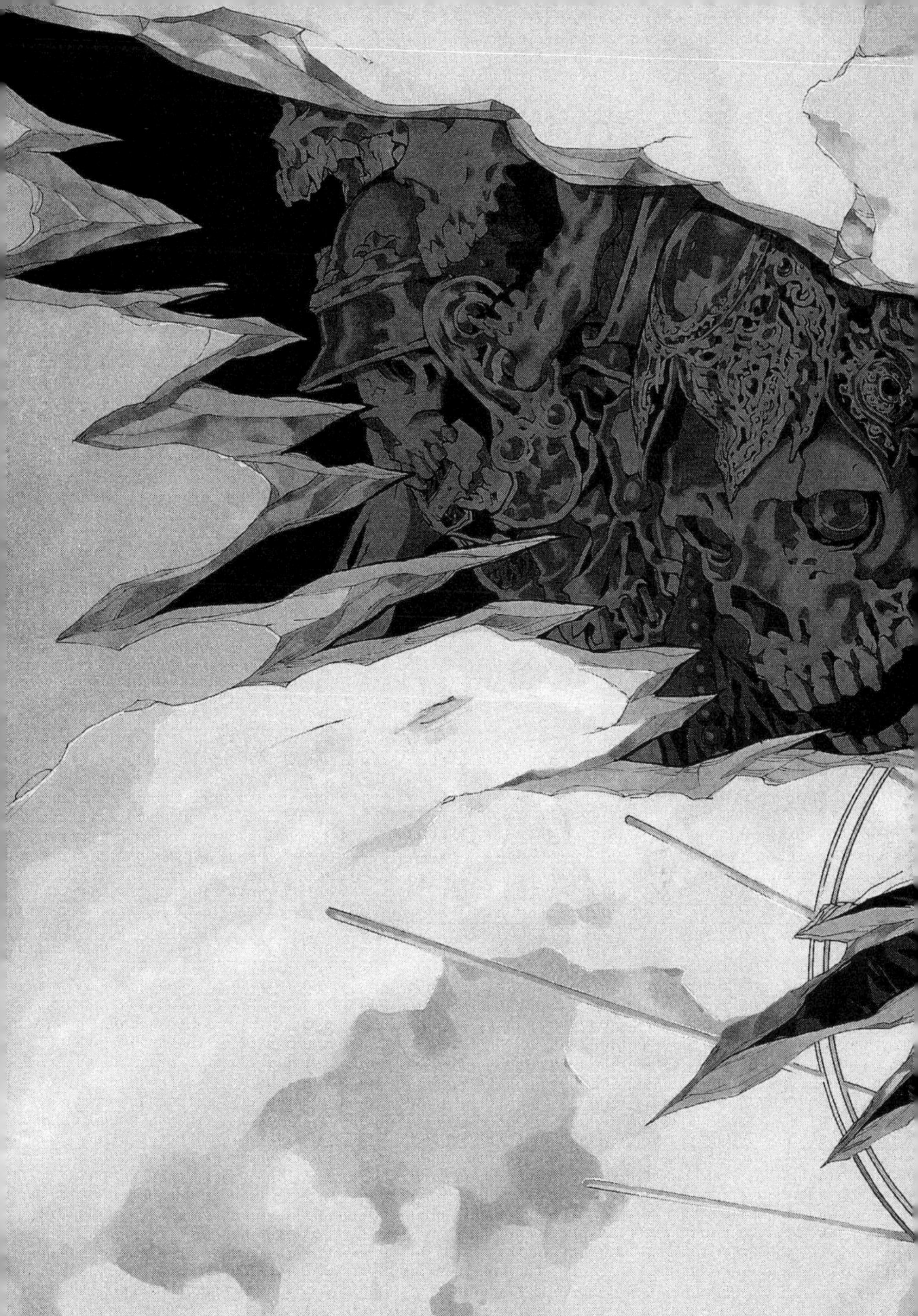

# chapter 60 Kidnapping

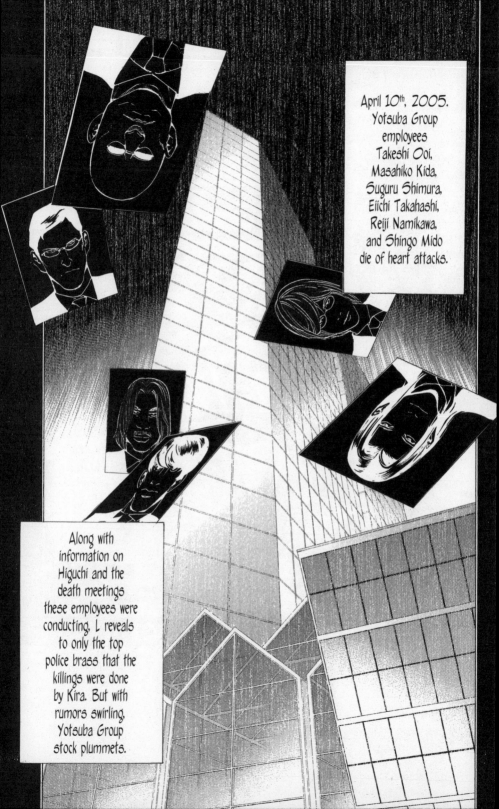

April 10th, 2005. Yotsuba Group employees Takeshi Ooi, Masahiko Kida, Suguru Shimura, Eiichi Takahashi, Reiji Namikawa, and Shingo Mido die of heart attacks.

Along with information on Higuchi and the death meetings these employees were conducting, L reveals to only the top police brass that the killings were done by Kira. But with rumors swirling, Yotsuba Group stock plummets.

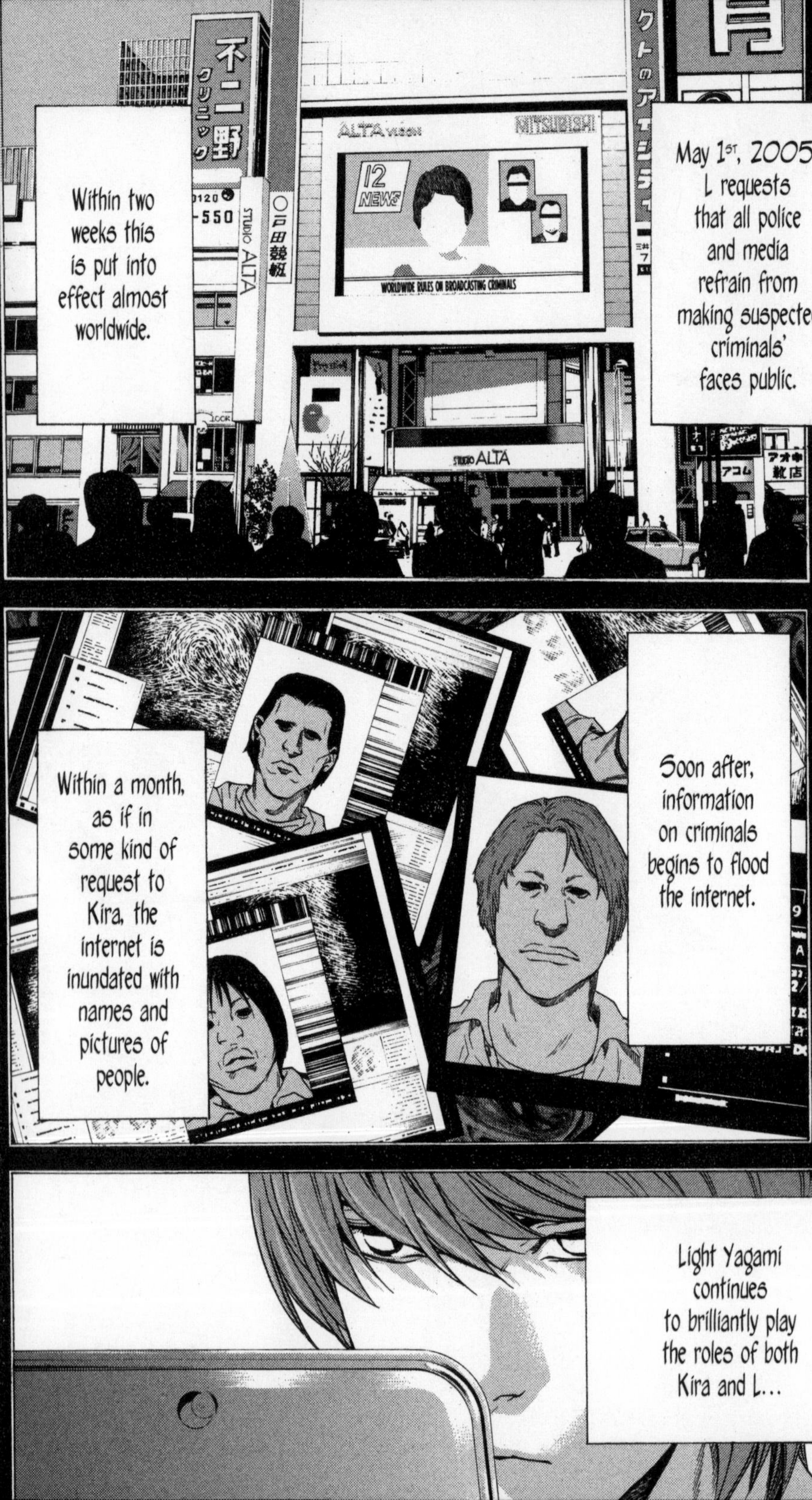

May 1st, 2005. L requests that all police and media refrain from making suspected criminals' faces public.
MITSUBISHI
ALTA VISION
12 NEWS
WORLDWIDE RULES ON BROADCASTING CRIMINALS
STUDIO ALTA
Within two weeks this is put into effect almost worldwide.
Soon after, information on criminals begins to flood the internet.
Within a month, as if in some kind of request to Kira, the internet is inundated with names and pictures of people.
Light Yagami continues to brilliantly play the roles of both Kira and L...

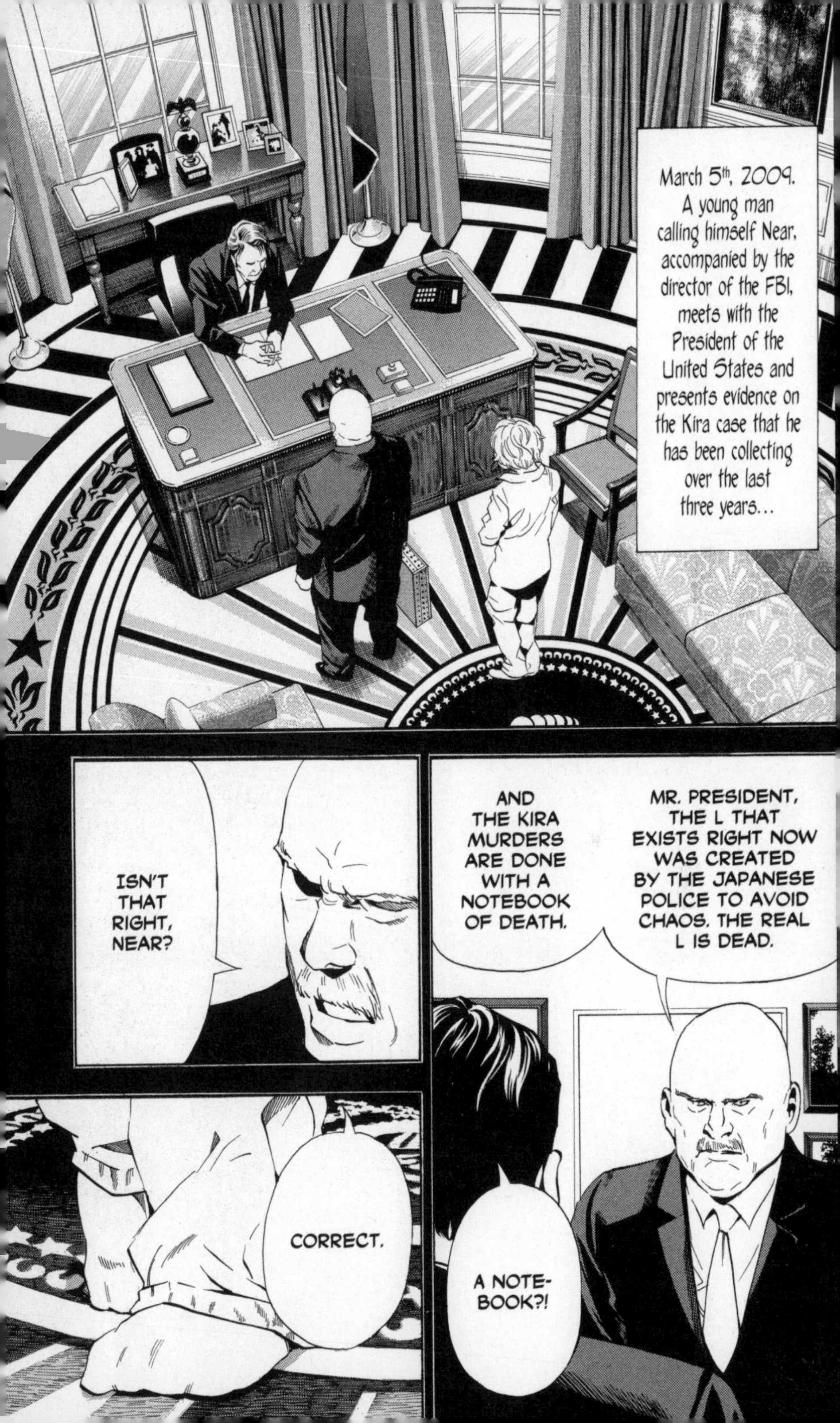
March 5th, 2009. A young man calling himself Near, accompanied by the director of the FBI, meets with the President of the United States and presents evidence on the Kira case that he has been collecting over the last three years...
MR. PRESIDENT, THE L THAT EXISTS RIGHT NOW WAS CREATED BY THE JAPANESE POLICE TO AVOID CHAOS. THE REAL L IS DEAD.
AND THE KIRA MURDERS ARE DONE WITH A NOTEBOOK OF DEATH.
A NOTE-BOOK?!
ISN'T THAT RIGHT, NEAR?
CORRECT.

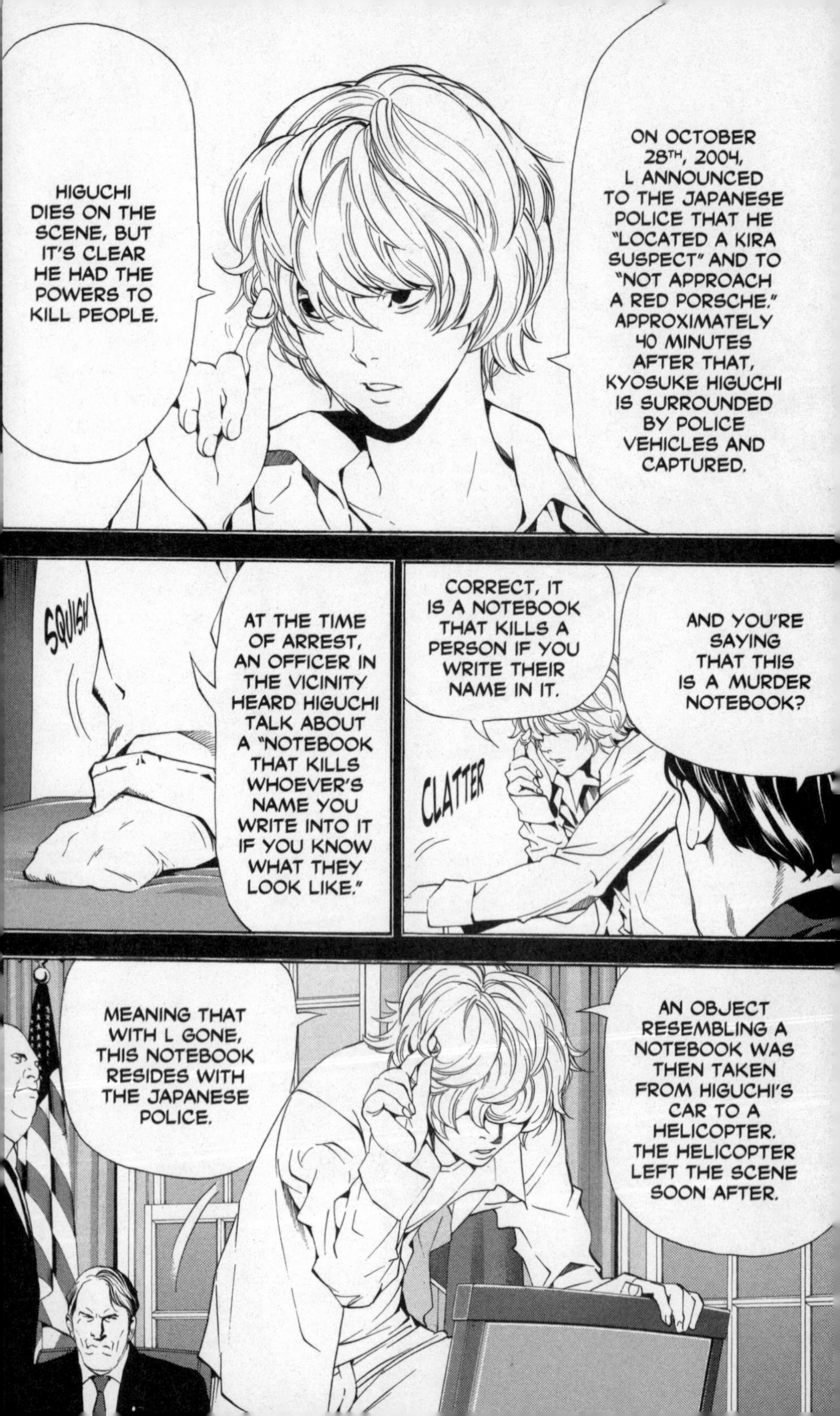
ON OCTOBER 28TH, 2004, L ANNOUNCED TO THE JAPANESE POLICE THAT HE "LOCATED A KIRA SUSPECT" AND TO "NOT APPROACH A RED PORSCHE." APPROXIMATELY 40 MINUTES AFTER THAT, KYOSUKE HIGUCHI IS SURROUNDED BY POLICE VEHICLES AND CAPTURED.
HIGUCHI DIES ON THE SCENE, BUT IT'S CLEAR HE HAD THE POWERS TO KILL PEOPLE.
AND YOU'RE SAYING THAT THIS IS A MURDER NOTEBOOK?
CORRECT, IT IS A NOTEBOOK THAT KILLS A PERSON IF YOU WRITE THEIR NAME IN IT.
CLATTER
AT THE TIME OF ARREST, AN OFFICER IN THE VICINITY HEARD HIGUCHI TALK ABOUT A "NOTEBOOK THAT KILLS WHOEVER'S NAME YOU WRITE INTO IT IF YOU KNOW WHAT THEY LOOK LIKE."
SQUISH
AN OBJECT RESEMBLING A NOTEBOOK WAS THEN TAKEN FROM HIGUCHI'S CAR TO A HELICOPTER. THE HELICOPTER LEFT THE SCENE SOON AFTER.
MEANING THAT WITH L GONE, THIS NOTEBOOK RESIDES WITH THE JAPANESE POLICE.

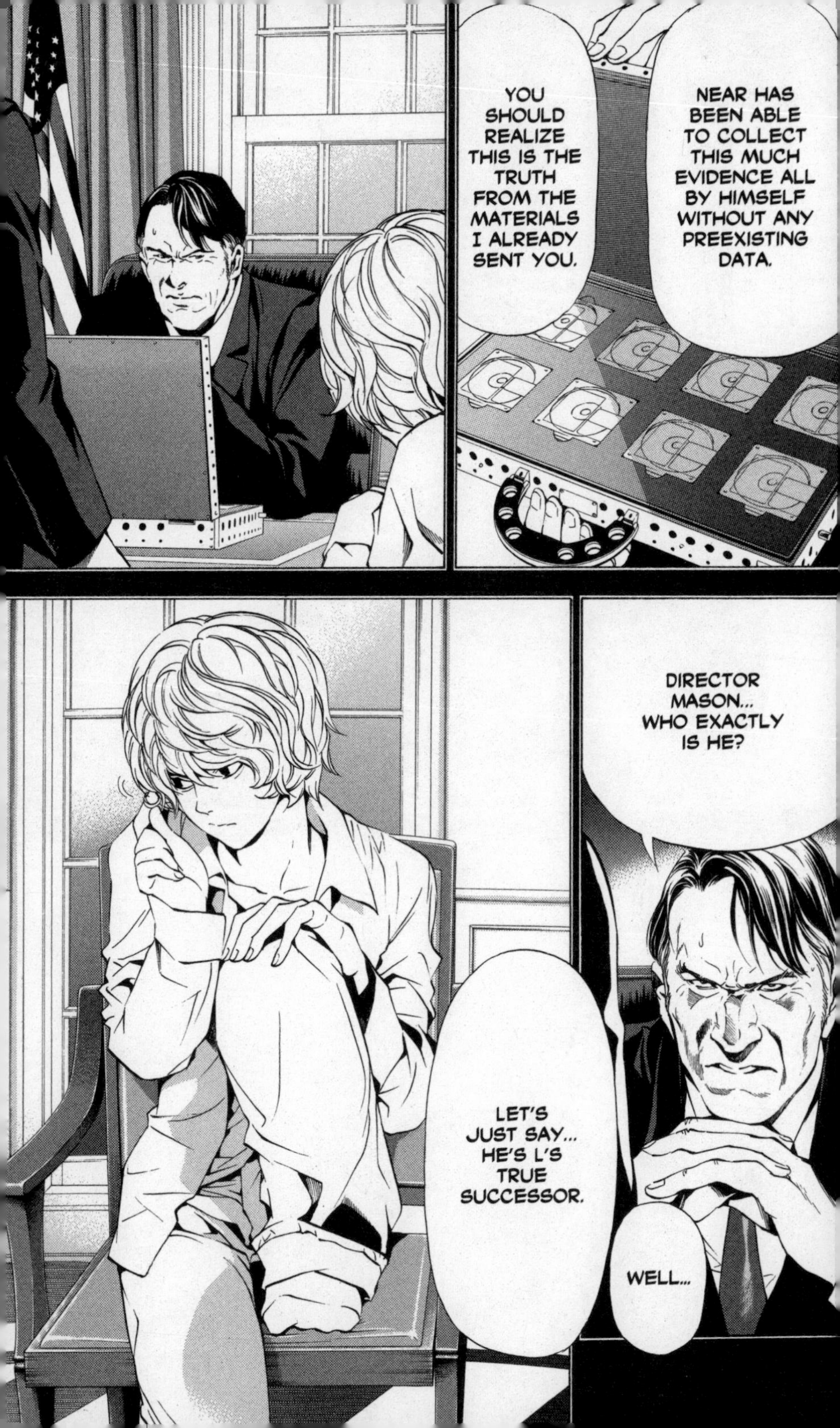
NEAR HAS BEEN ABLE TO COLLECT THIS MUCH EVIDENCE ALL BY HIMSELF WITHOUT ANY PREEXISTING DATA.
YOU SHOULD REALIZE THIS IS THE TRUTH FROM THE MATERIALS I ALREADY SENT YOU.
DIRECTOR MASON... WHO EXACTLY IS HE?
WELL...
LET'S JUST SAY... HE'S L'S TRUE SUCCESSOR.

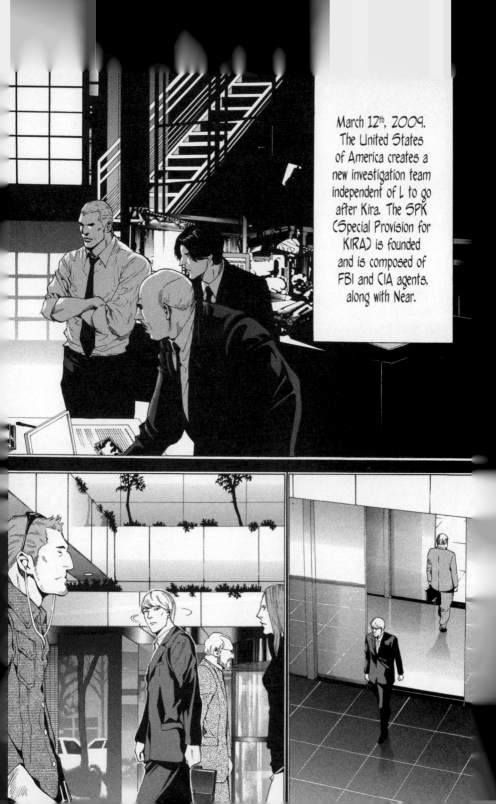

March 12th, 2009.
The United States
of America creates a
new investigation team
independent of L to go
after Kira. The SPK
(Special Provision for
KIRA) is founded
and is composed of
FBI and CIA agents,
along with Near.

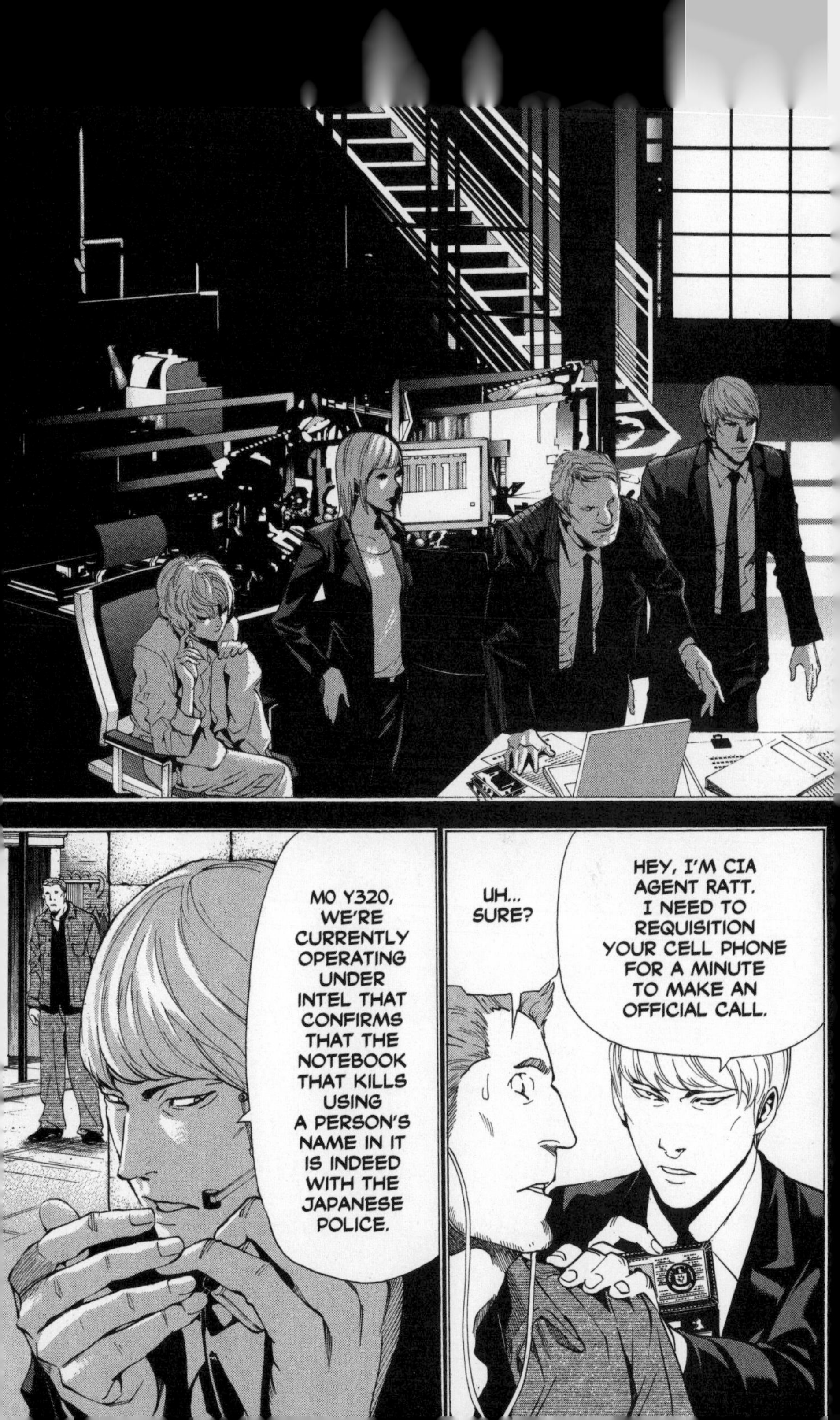
HEY, I'M CIA AGENT RATT. I NEED TO REQUISITION YOUR CELL PHONE FOR A MINUTE TO MAKE AN OFFICIAL CALL.
UH... SURE?
M0 Y320, WE'RE CURRENTLY OPERATING UNDER INTEL THAT CONFIRMS THAT THE NOTEBOOK THAT KILLS USING A PERSON'S NAME IN IT IS INDEED WITH THE JAPANESE POLICE.

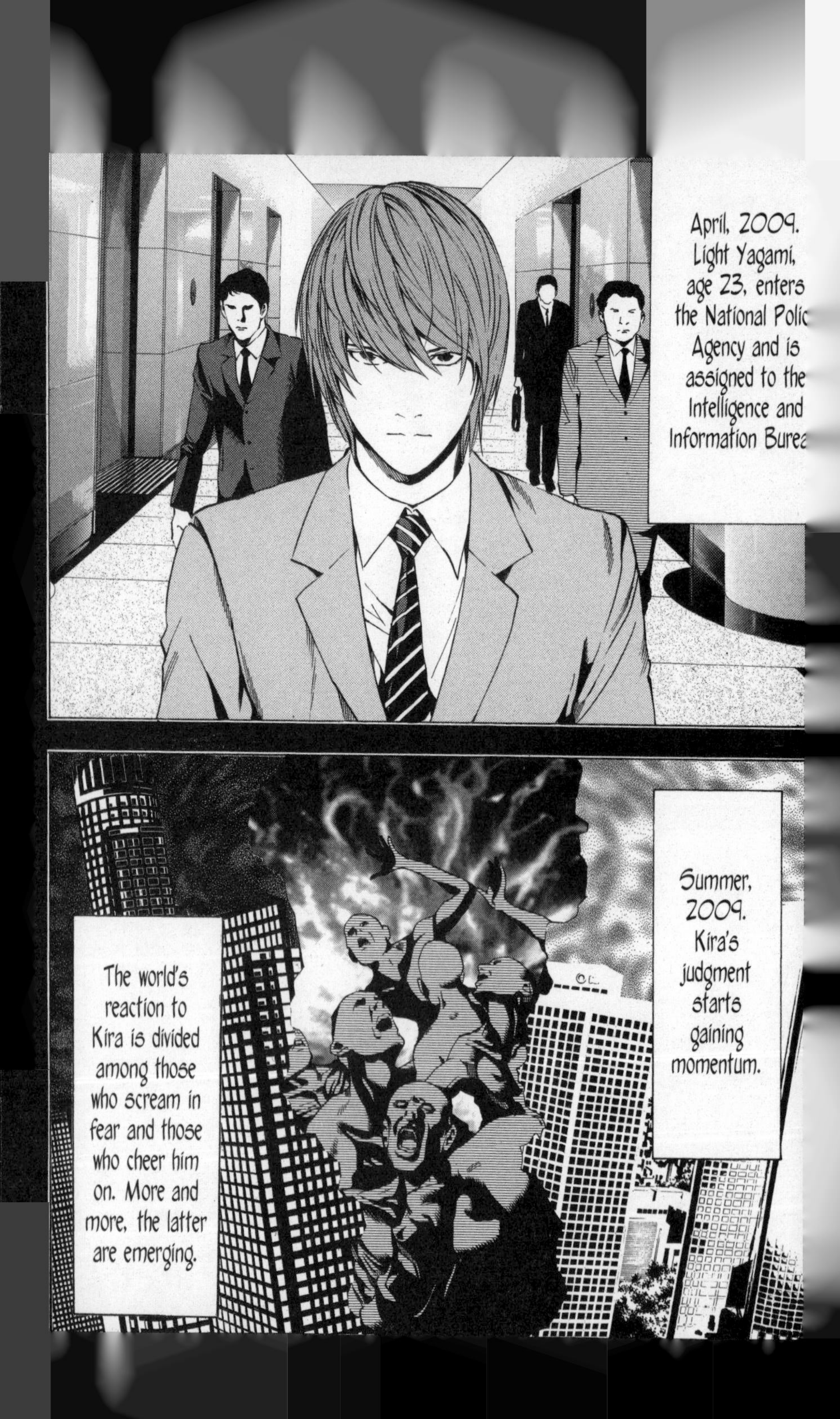
April, 2009. Light Yagami, age 23, enters the National Polic Agency and is assigned to the Intelligence and Information Burea
Summer, 2009. Kira's judgment starts gaining momentum.
The world's reaction to Kira is divided among those who scream in fear and those who cheer him on. More and more, the latter are emerging.

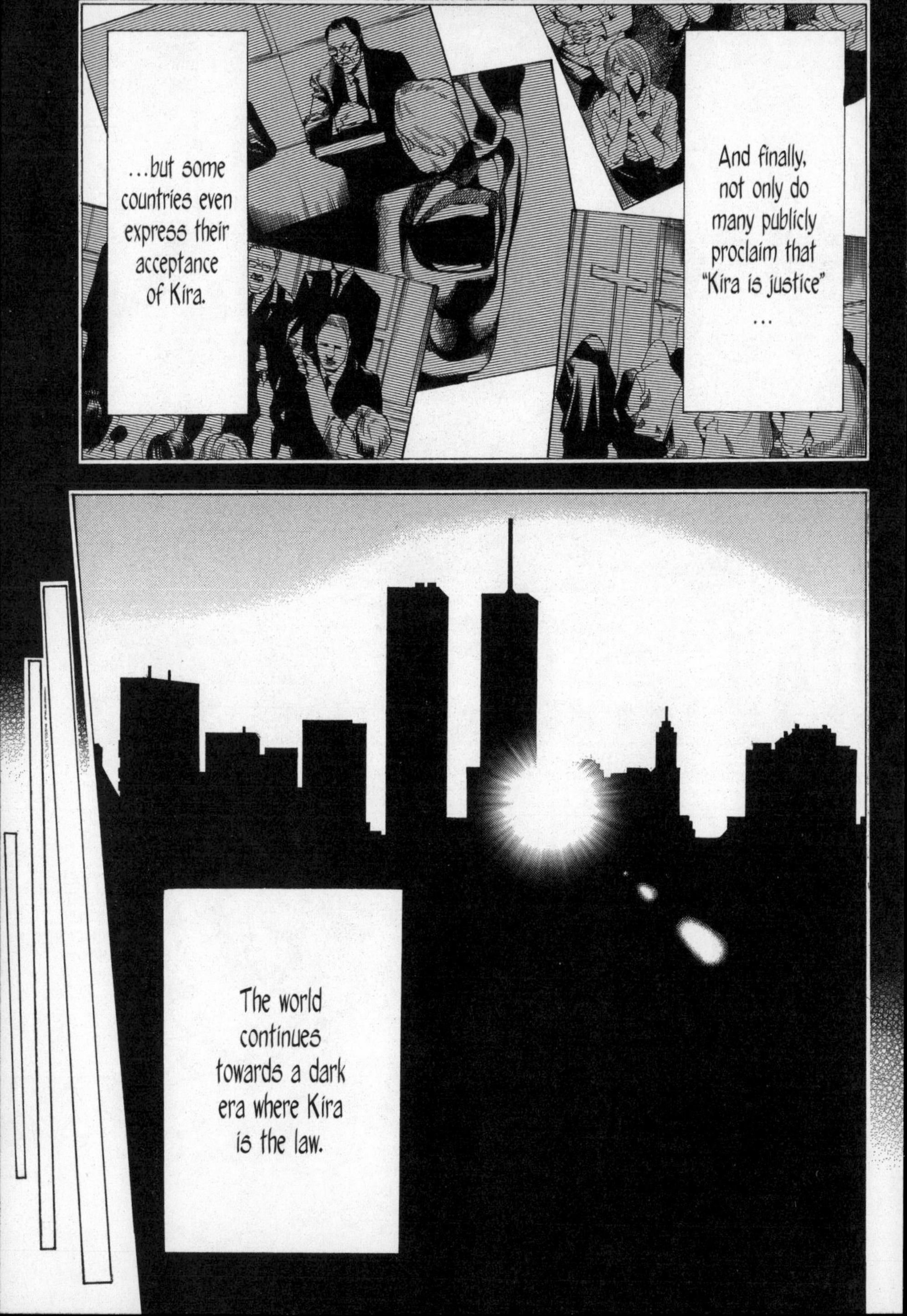
And finally, not only do many publicly proclaim that "Kira is justice" ...
...but some countries even express their acceptance of Kira.
The world continues towards a dark era where Kira is the law.

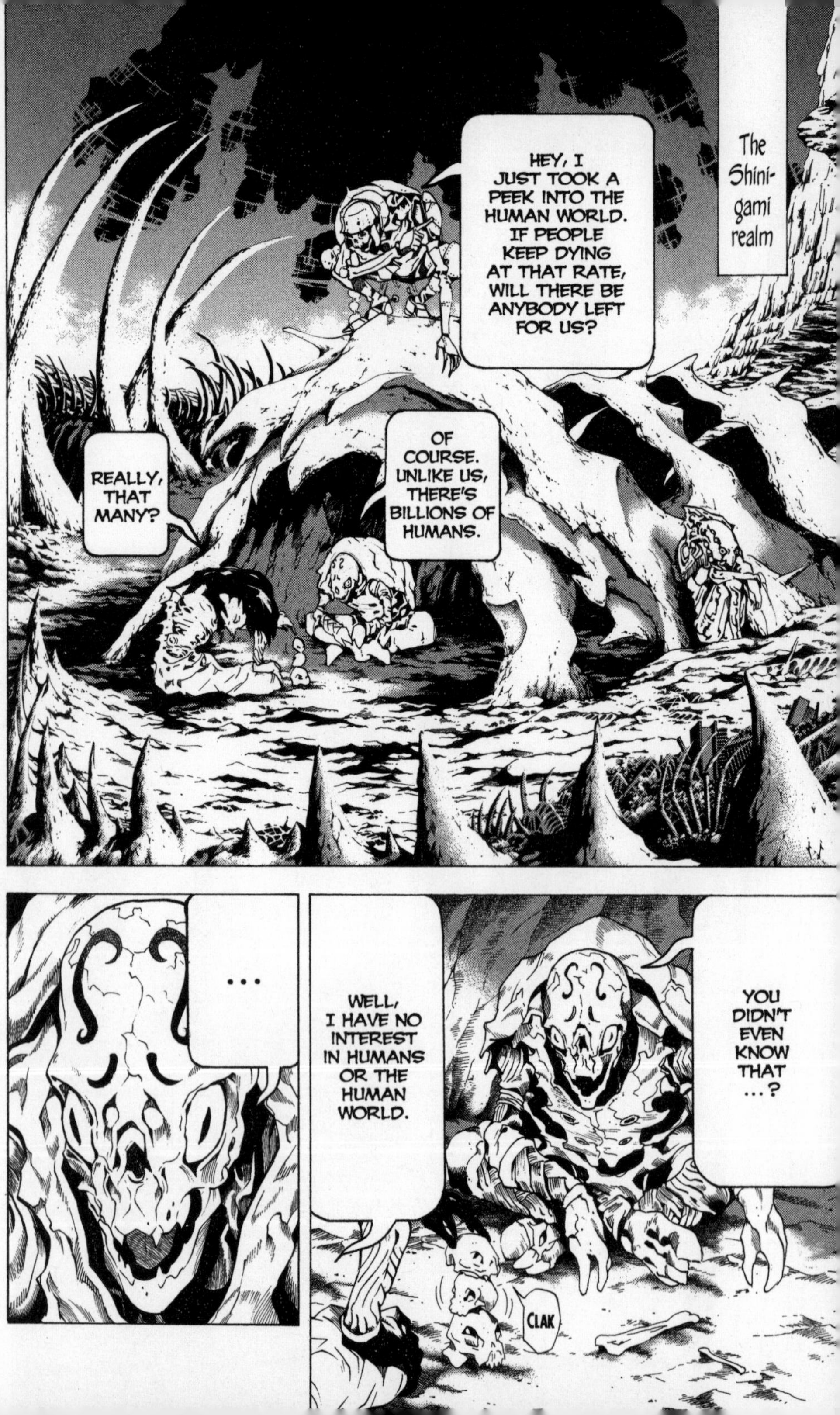
The Shinigami realm
HEY, I JUST TOOK A PEEK INTO THE HUMAN WORLD. IF PEOPLE KEEP DYING AT THAT RATE, WILL THERE BE ANYBODY LEFT FOR US?
OF COURSE. UNLIKE US, THERE'S BILLIONS OF HUMANS.
REALLY, THAT MANY?
YOU DIDN'T EVEN KNOW THAT ...?
WELL, I HAVE NO INTEREST IN HUMANS OR THE HUMAN WORLD.
CLAK
...

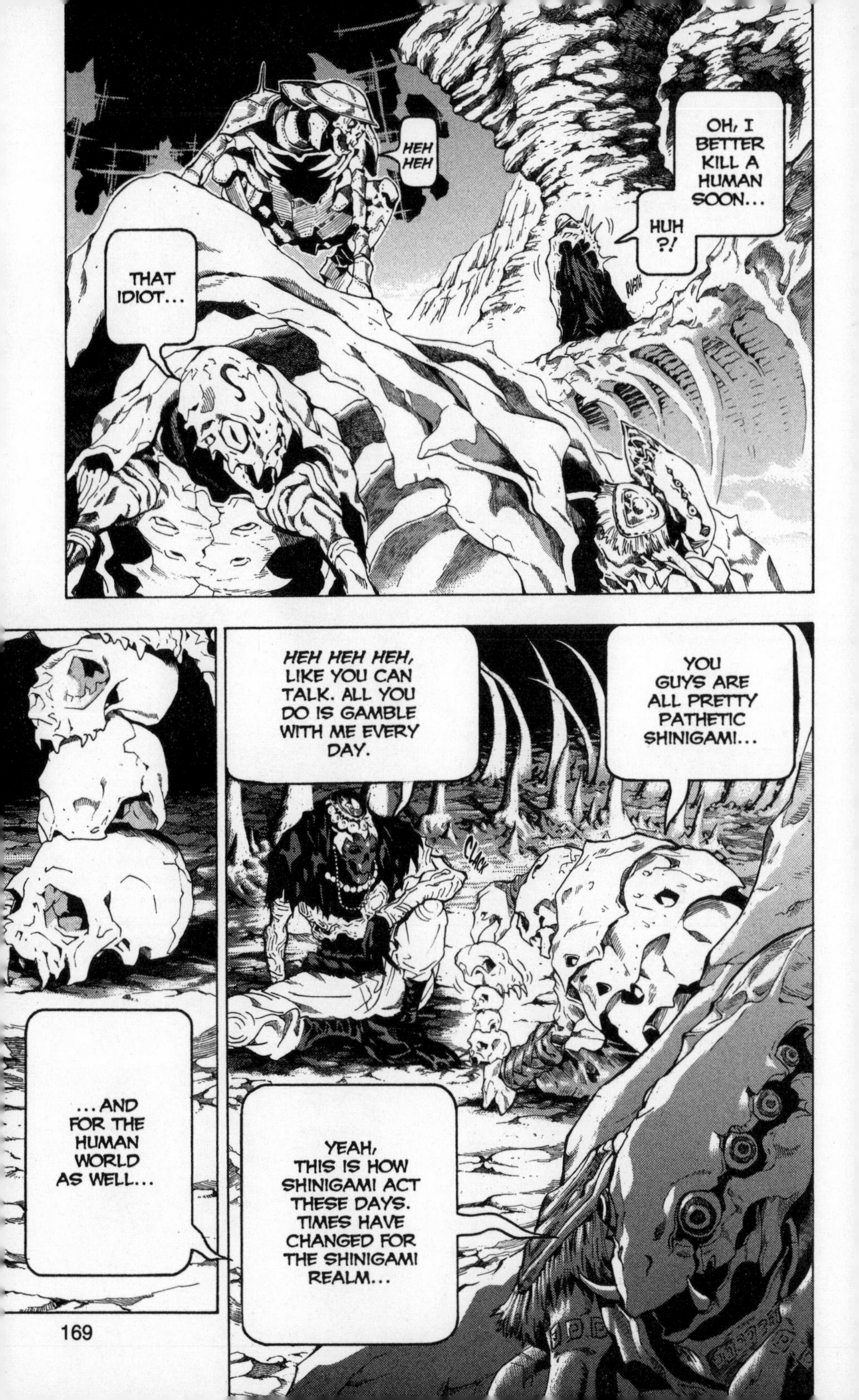
OH, I BETTER KILL A HUMAN SOON...
HUH?!
HEH HEH
THAT IDIOT...
YOU GUYS ARE ALL PRETTY PATHETIC SHINIGAMI...
*HEH HEH HEH,* LIKE YOU CAN TALK. ALL YOU DO IS GAMBLE WITH ME EVERY DAY.
CLACK
YEAH, THIS IS HOW SHINIGAMI ACT THESE DAYS. TIMES HAVE CHANGED FOR THE SHINIGAMI REALM...
...AND FOR THE HUMAN WORLD AS WELL...

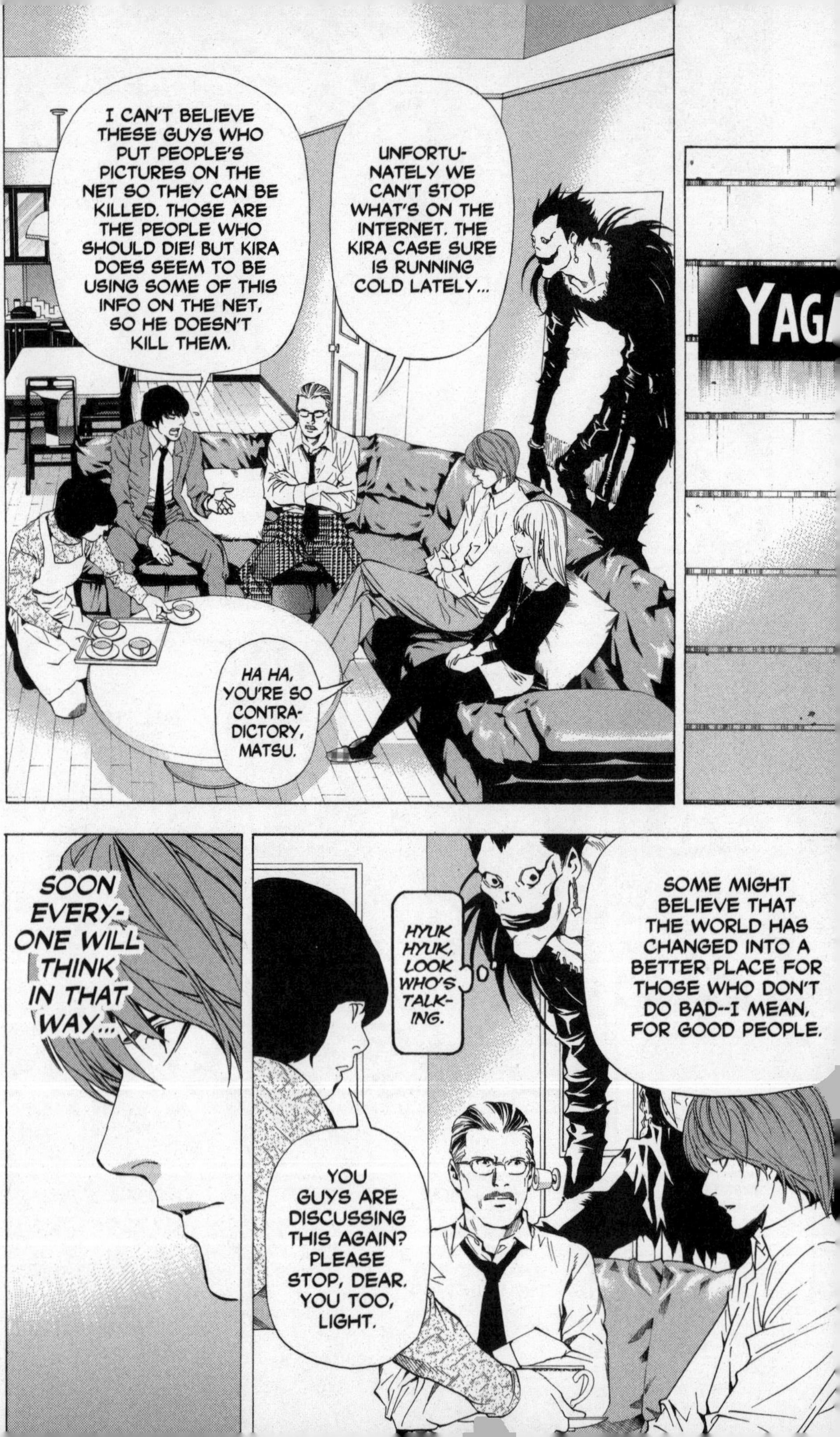
YAGA
I CAN'T BELIEVE THESE GUYS WHO PUT PEOPLE'S PICTURES ON THE NET SO THEY CAN BE KILLED. THOSE ARE THE PEOPLE WHO SHOULD DIE! BUT KIRA DOES SEEM TO BE USING SOME OF THIS INFO ON THE NET, SO HE DOESN'T KILL THEM.
UNFORTU-NATELY WE CAN'T STOP WHAT'S ON THE INTERNET. THE KIRA CASE SURE IS RUNNING COLD LATELY...
HA HA, YOU'RE SO CONTRA-DICTORY, MATSU.
SOME MIGHT BELIEVE THAT THE WORLD HAS CHANGED INTO A BETTER PLACE FOR THOSE WHO DON'T DO BAD--I MEAN, FOR GOOD PEOPLE.
HYUK HYUK, LOOK WHO'S TALK-ING.
YOU GUYS ARE DISCUSSING THIS AGAIN? PLEASE STOP, DEAR. YOU TOO, LIGHT.
SOON EVERY-ONE WILL THINK IN THAT WAY...

READ THIS WAY

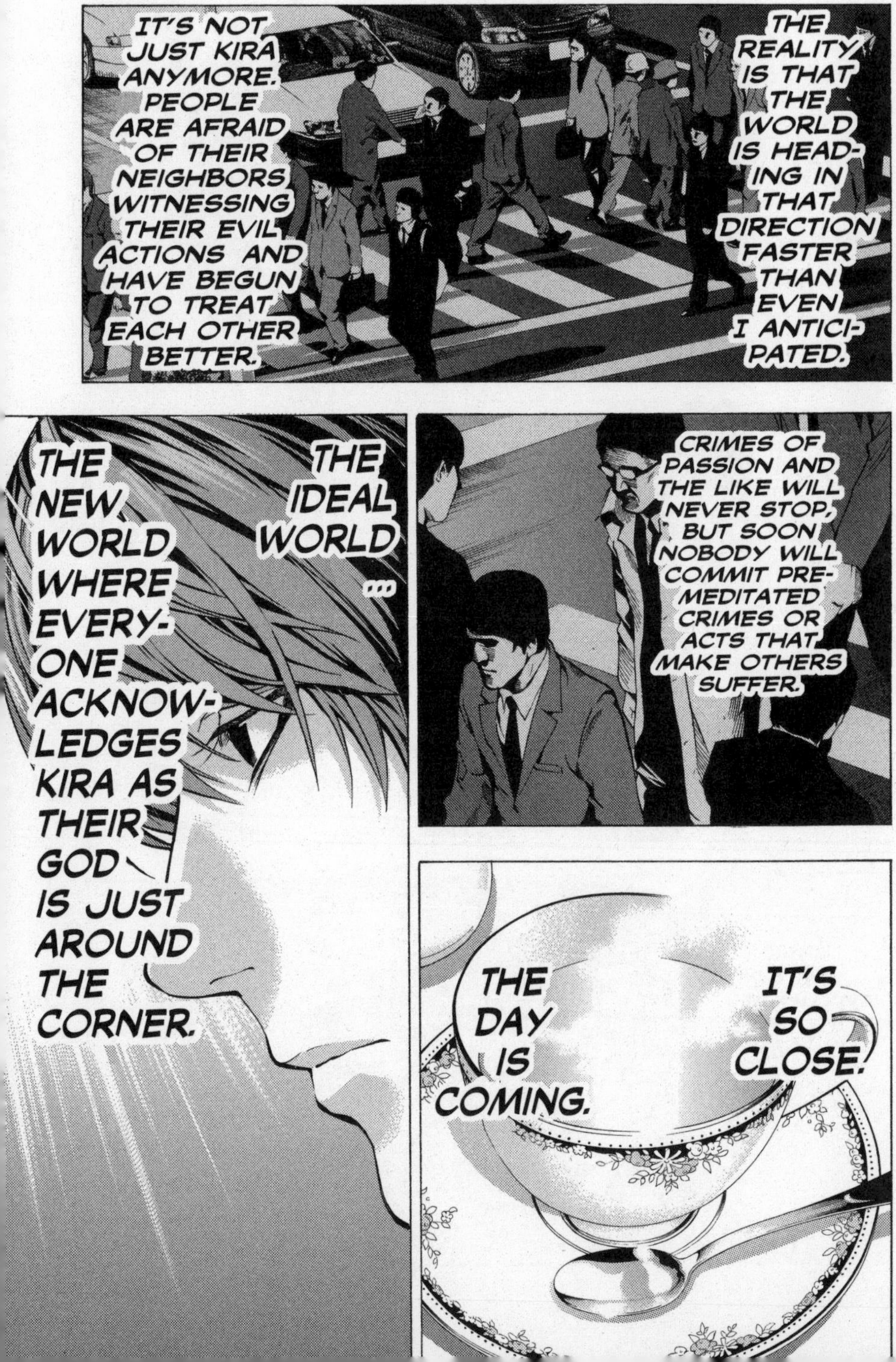
THE REALITY IS THAT THE WORLD IS HEADING IN THAT DIRECTION FASTER THAN EVEN I ANTICIPATED.
IT'S NOT JUST KIRA ANYMORE. PEOPLE ARE AFRAID OF THEIR NEIGHBORS WITNESSING THEIR EVIL ACTIONS AND HAVE BEGUN TO TREAT EACH OTHER BETTER.
CRIMES OF PASSION AND THE LIKE WILL NEVER STOP, BUT SOON NOBODY WILL COMMIT PRE-MEDITATED CRIMES OR ACTS THAT MAKE OTHERS SUFFER.
IT'S SO CLOSE.
THE DAY IS COMING.
THE IDEAL WORLD...
THE NEW WORLD WHERE EVERYONE ACKNOWLEDGES KIRA AS THEIR GOD IS JUST AROUND THE CORNER.

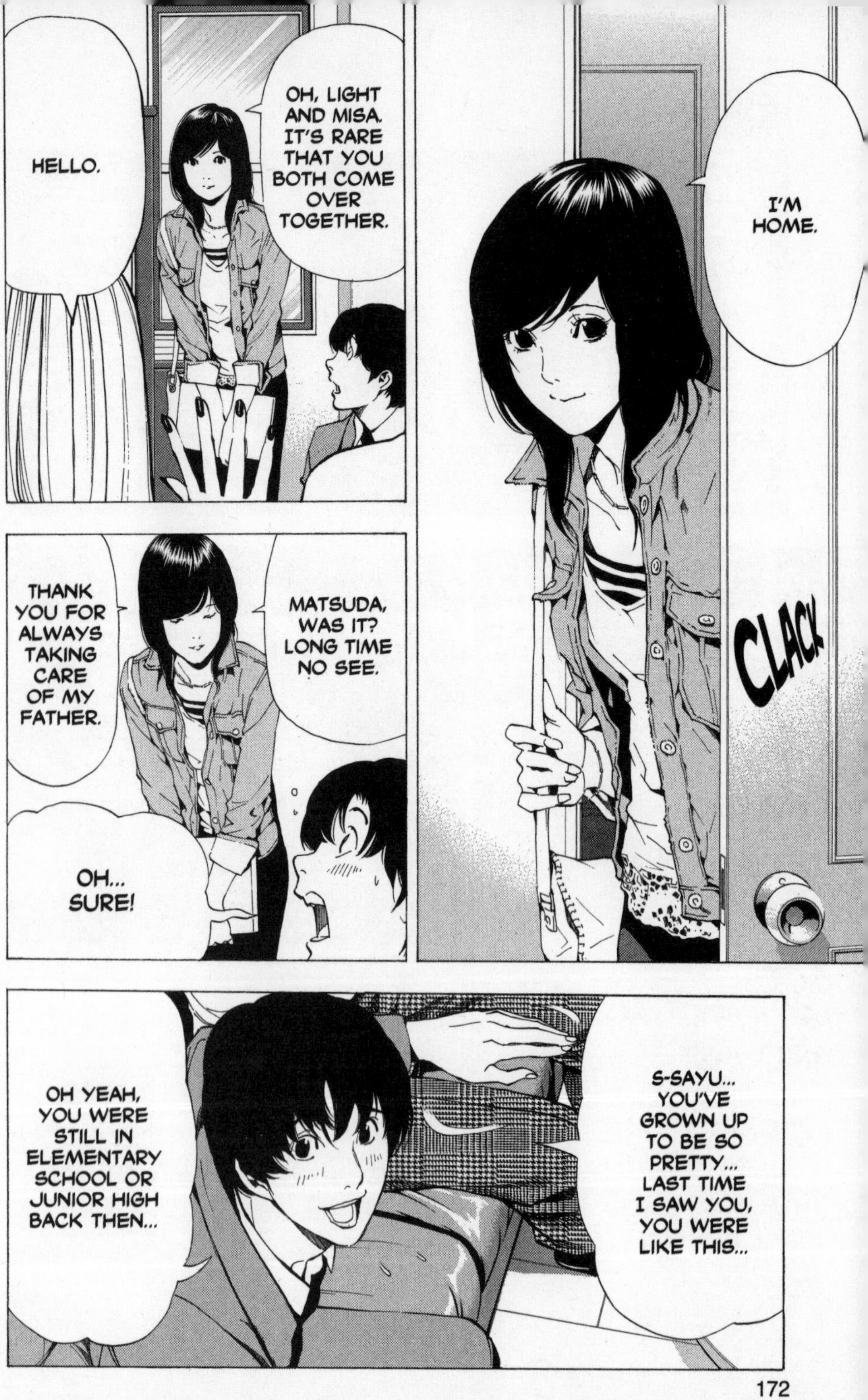
I'M HOME.
CLACK
OH, LIGHT AND MISA. IT'S RARE THAT YOU BOTH COME OVER TOGETHER.
HELLO.
MATSUDA, WAS IT? LONG TIME NO SEE.
THANK YOU FOR ALWAYS TAKING CARE OF MY FATHER.
OH... SURE!
S-SAYU... YOU'VE GROWN UP TO BE SO PRETTY... LAST TIME I SAW YOU, YOU WERE LIKE THIS...
OH YEAH, YOU WERE STILL IN ELEMENTARY SCHOOL OR JUNIOR HIGH BACK THEN...

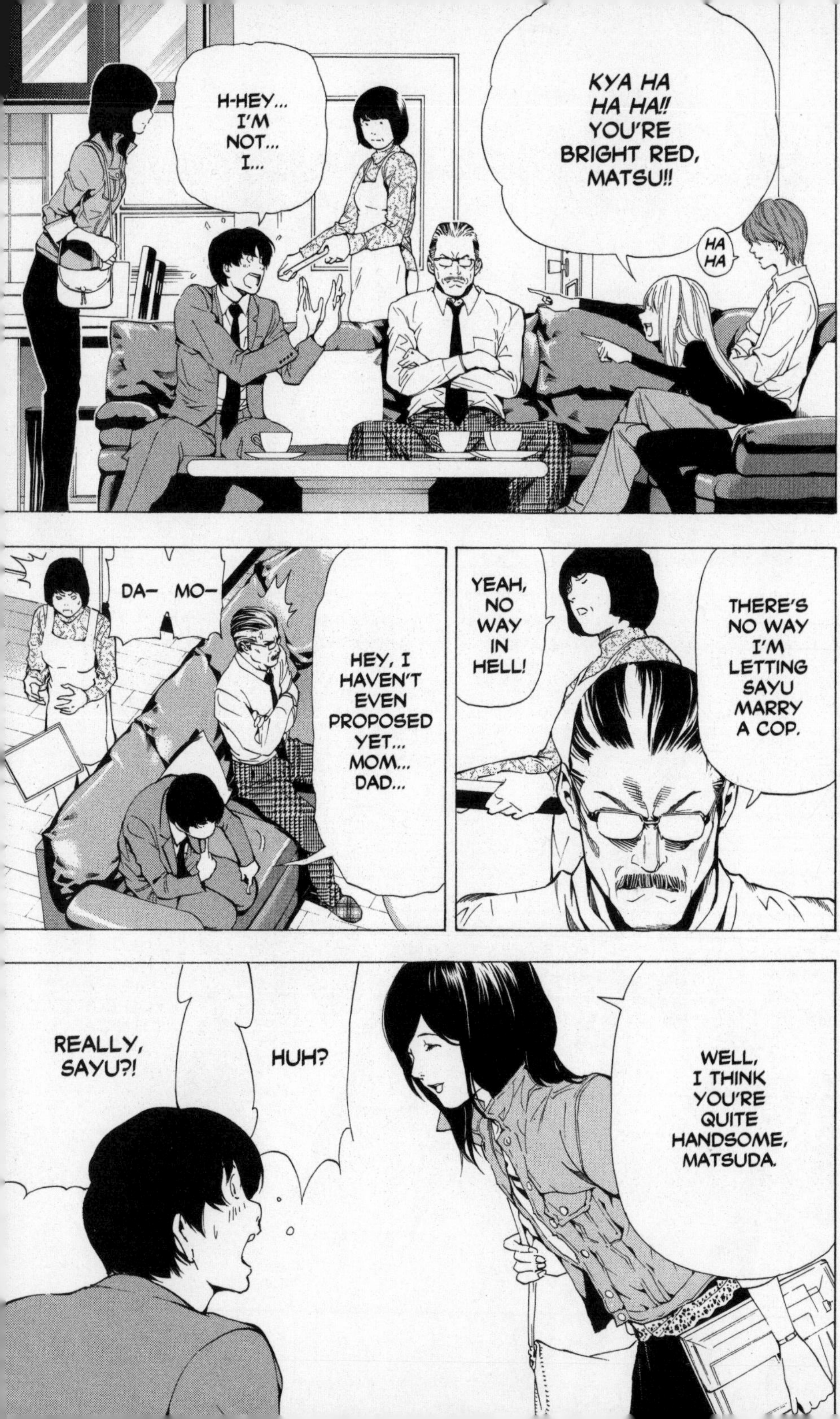
KYA HA HA HA!! YOU'RE BRIGHT RED, MATSU!!
HA HA
H-HEY... I'M NOT... I...
THERE'S NO WAY I'M LETTING SAYU MARRY A COP.
YEAH, NO WAY IN HELL!
HEY, I HAVEN'T EVEN PROPOSED YET... MOM... DAD...
DA- MO-
WELL, I THINK YOU'RE QUITE HANDSOME, MATSUDA.
HUH?
REALLY, SAYU?!

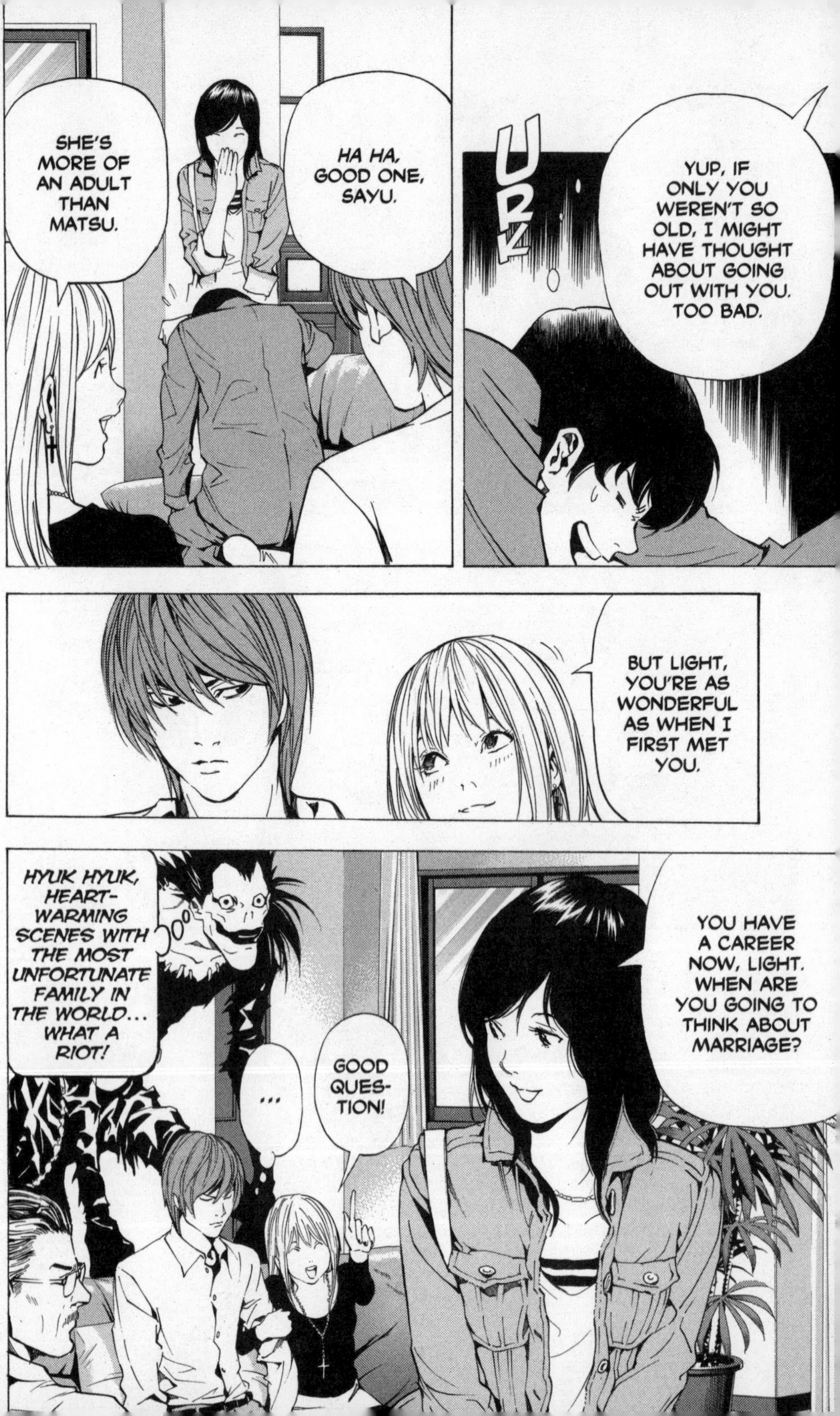
YUP, IF ONLY YOU WEREN'T SO OLD, I MIGHT HAVE THOUGHT ABOUT GOING OUT WITH YOU. TOO BAD.
URK
HA HA, GOOD ONE, SAYU.
SHE'S MORE OF AN ADULT THAN MATSU.
BUT LIGHT, YOU'RE AS WONDERFUL AS WHEN I FIRST MET YOU.
YOU HAVE A CAREER NOW, LIGHT. WHEN ARE YOU GOING TO THINK ABOUT MARRIAGE?
GOOD QUES-TION!
...
HYUK HYUK, HEART-WARMING SCENES WITH THE MOST UNFORTUNATE FAMILY IN THE WORLD... WHAT A RIOT!

READ THIS WAY

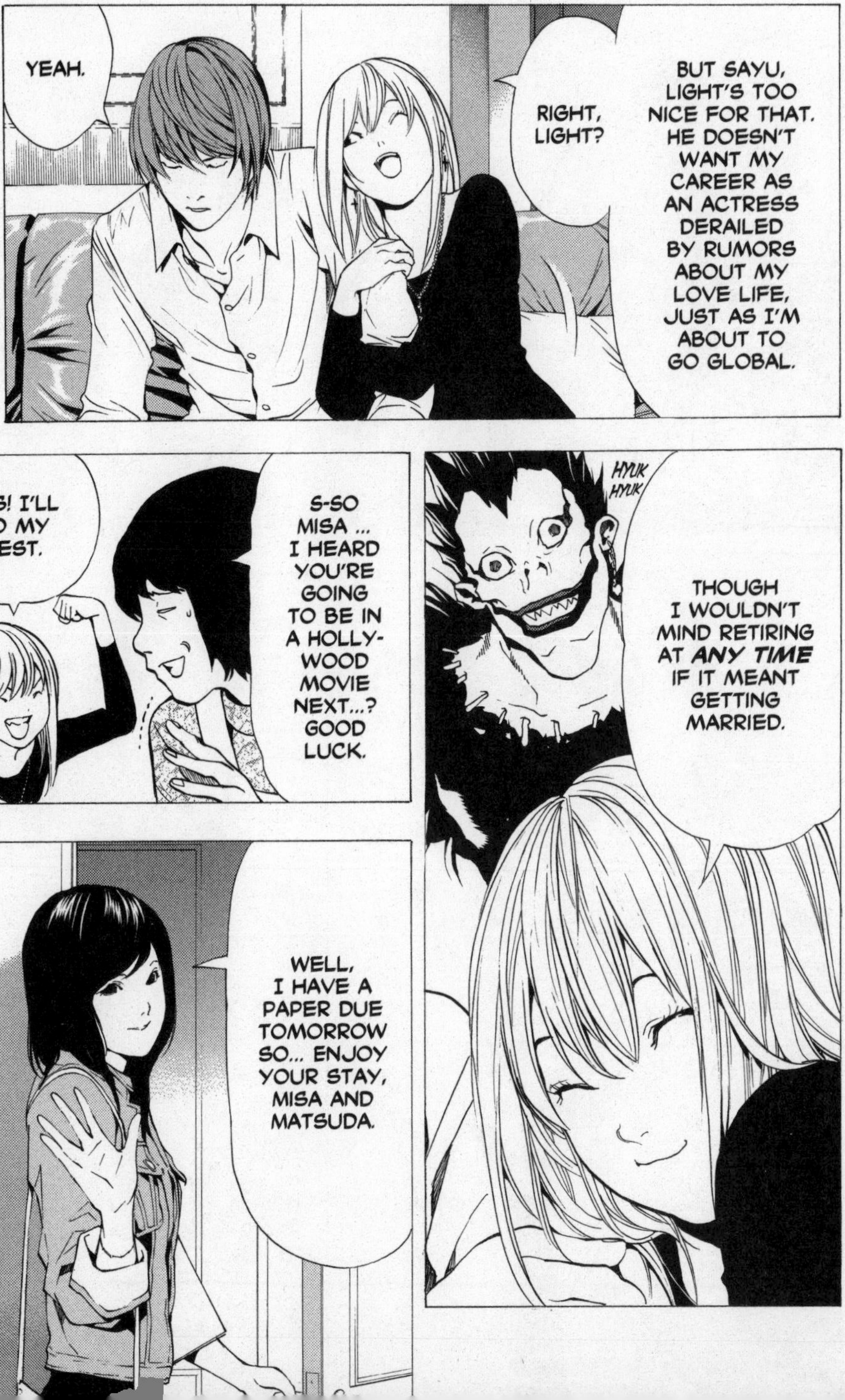
BUT SAYU, LIGHT'S TOO NICE FOR THAT. HE DOESN'T WANT MY CAREER AS AN ACTRESS DERAILED BY RUMORS ABOUT MY LOVE LIFE, JUST AS I'M ABOUT TO GO GLOBAL.
RIGHT, LIGHT?
YEAH.
HYUK HYUK
THOUGH I WOULDN'T MIND RETIRING AT *ANY TIME* IF IT MEANT GETTING MARRIED.
S-SO MISA ... I HEARD YOU'RE GOING TO BE IN A HOLLY-WOOD MOVIE NEXT...? GOOD LUCK.
YES! I'LL DO MY BEST.
WELL, I HAVE A PAPER DUE TOMORROW SO... ENJOY YOUR STAY, MISA AND MATSUDA.

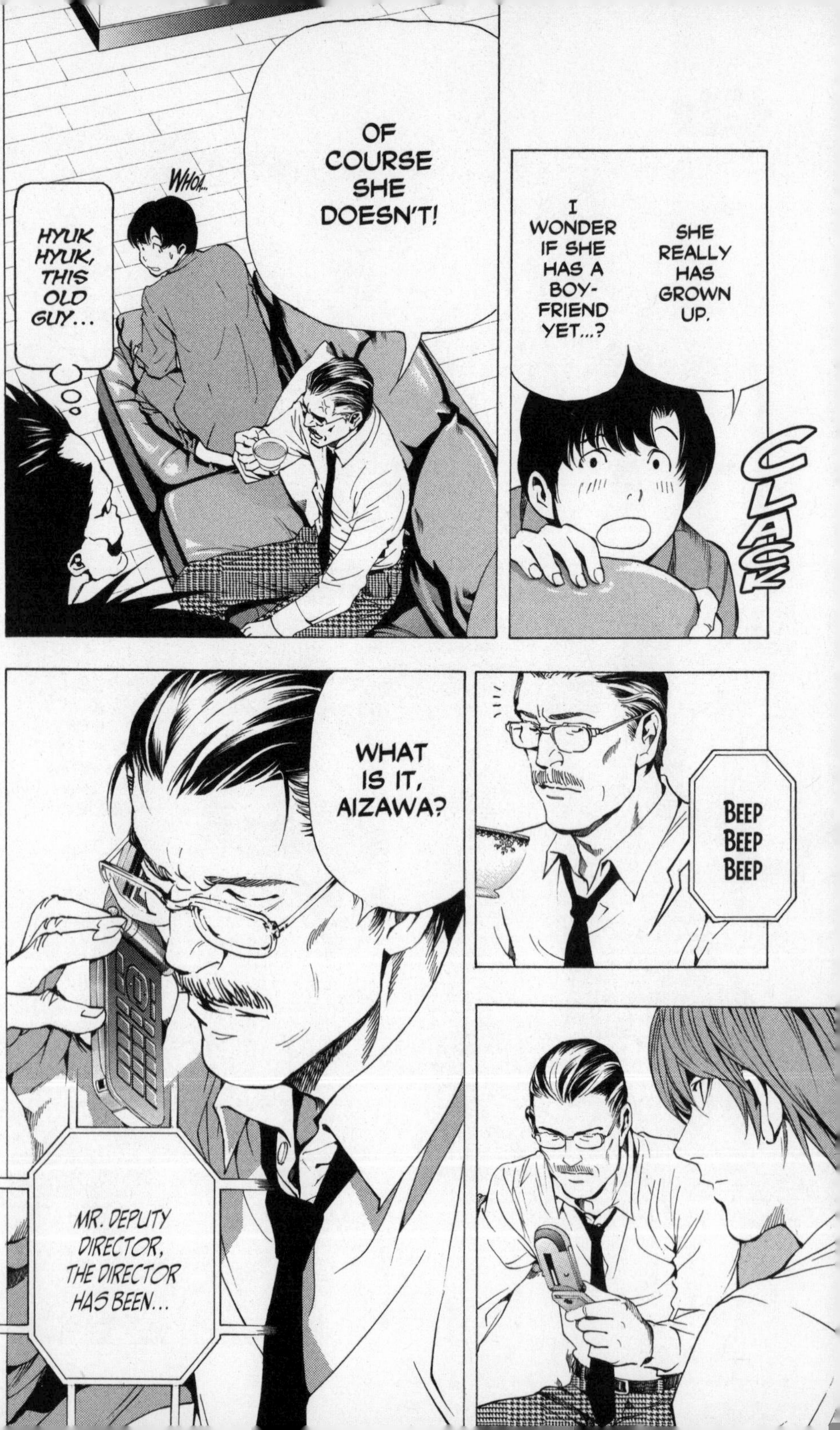
SHE REALLY HAS GROWN UP.
I WONDER IF SHE HAS A BOY-FRIEND YET...?
CLACK
OF COURSE SHE DOESN'T!
WHOA...
HYUK HYUK, THIS OLD GUY...
BEEP BEEP BEEP
WHAT IS IT, AIZAWA?
MR. DEPUTY DIRECTOR, THE DIRECTOR HAS BEEN...

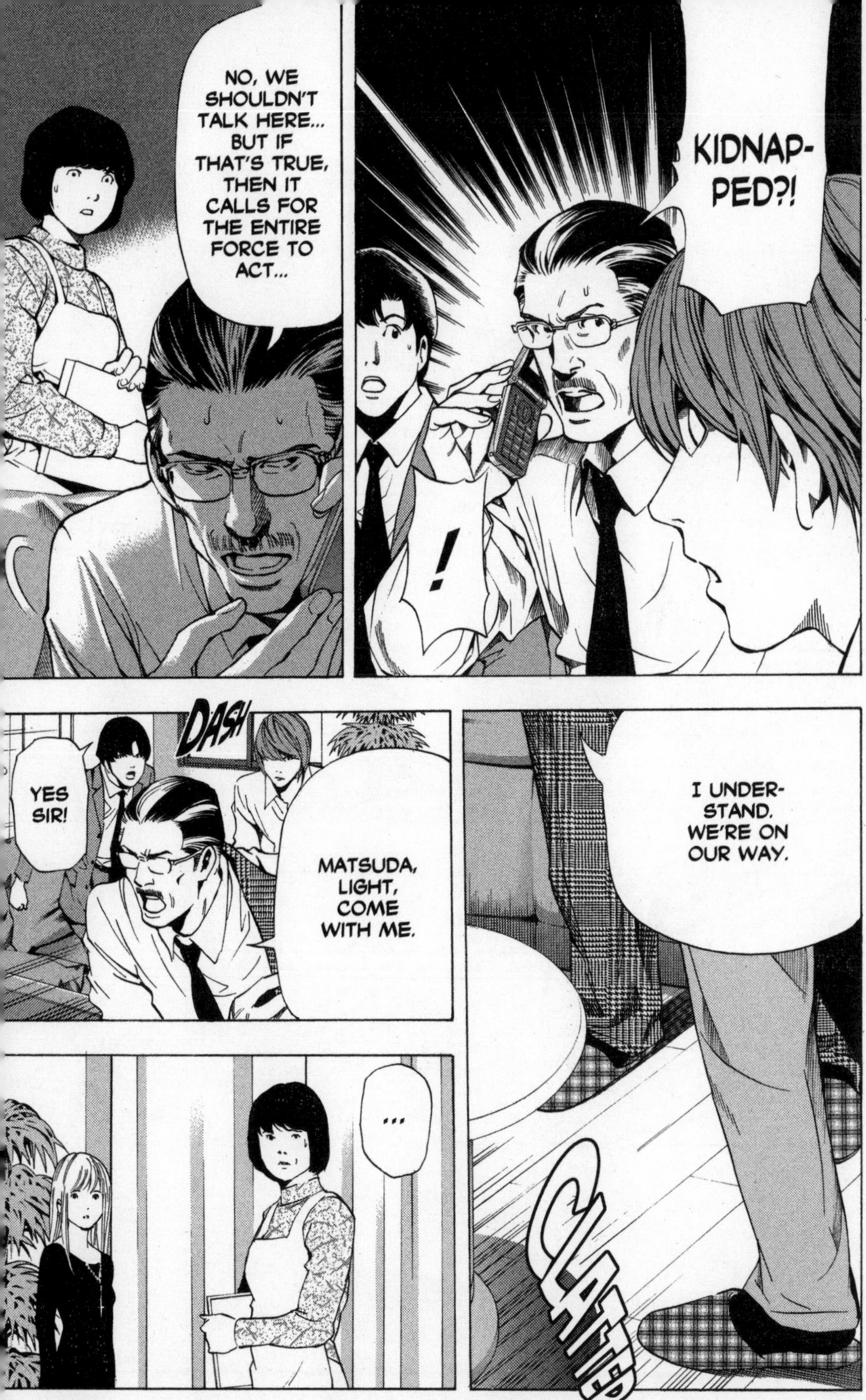
KIDNAP-PED?!
!
NO, WE SHOULDN'T TALK HERE... BUT IF THAT'S TRUE, THEN IT CALLS FOR THE ENTIRE FORCE TO ACT...
I UNDER-STAND. WE'RE ON OUR WAY.
CLATTER
MATSUDA, LIGHT, COME WITH ME.
DASH
YES SIR!
...

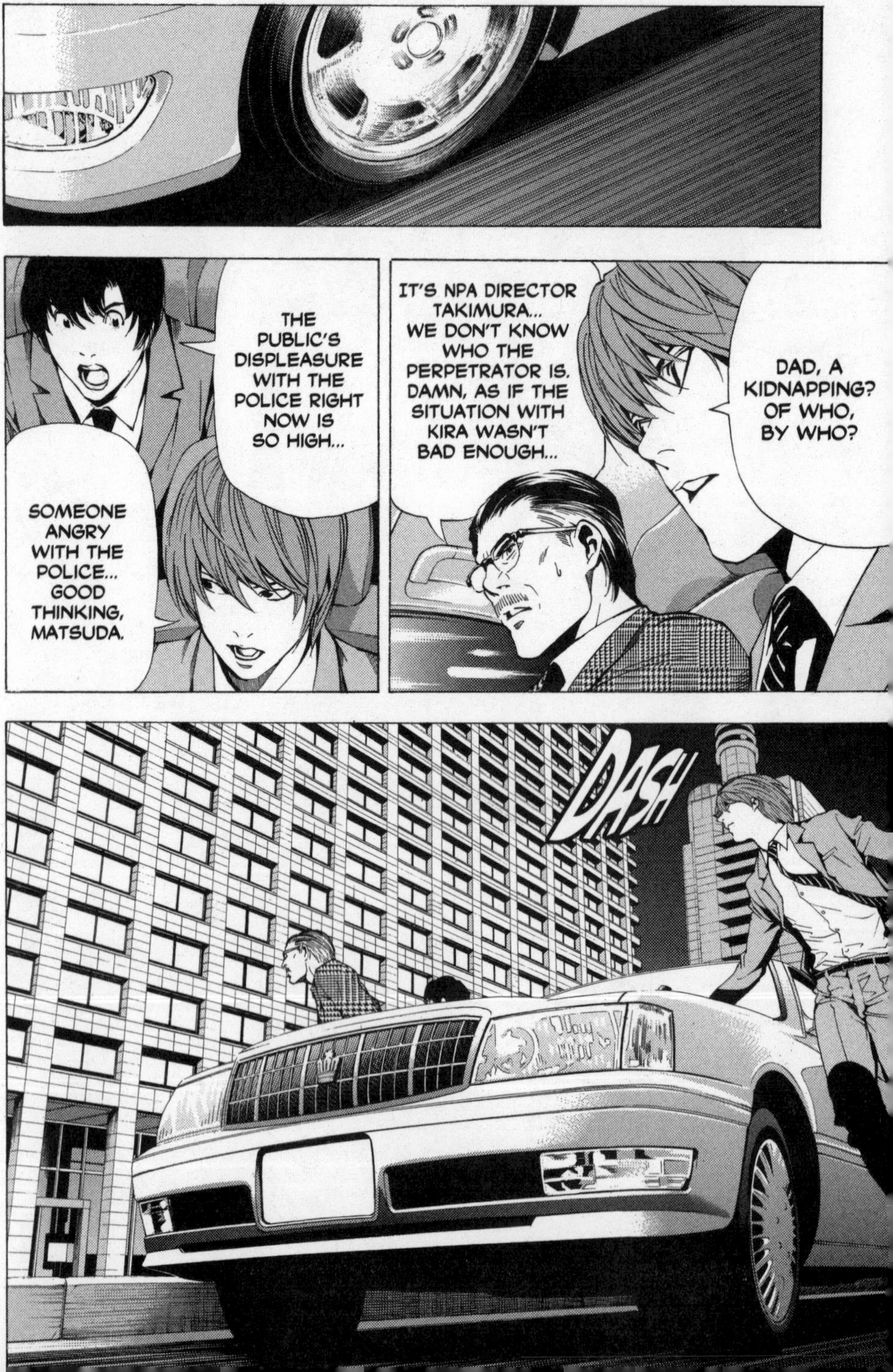
DAD, A KIDNAPPING? OF WHO, BY WHO?
IT'S NPA DIRECTOR TAKIMURA... WE DON'T KNOW WHO THE PERPETRATOR IS. DAMN, AS IF THE SITUATION WITH KIRA WASN'T BAD ENOUGH...
THE PUBLIC'S DISPLEASURE WITH THE POLICE RIGHT NOW IS SO HIGH...
SOMEONE ANGRY WITH THE POLICE... GOOD THINKING, MATSUDA.
DASH

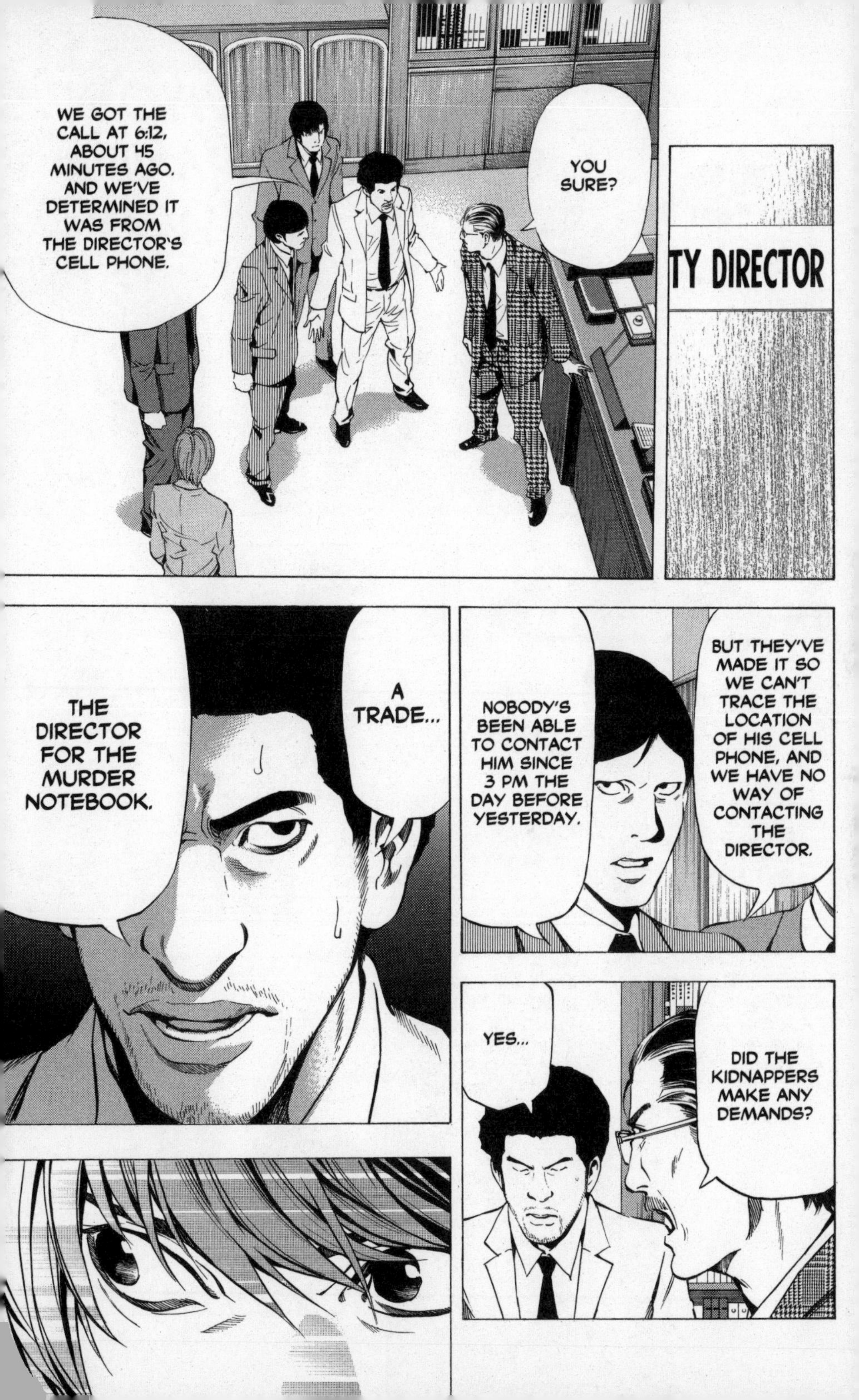
TY DIRECTOR
YOU SURE?
WE GOT THE CALL AT 6:12, ABOUT 45 MINUTES AGO. AND WE'VE DETERMINED IT WAS FROM THE DIRECTOR'S CELL PHONE.
BUT THEY'VE MADE IT SO WE CAN'T TRACE THE LOCATION OF HIS CELL PHONE, AND WE HAVE NO WAY OF CONTACTING THE DIRECTOR.
NOBODY'S BEEN ABLE TO CONTACT HIM SINCE 3 PM THE DAY BEFORE YESTERDAY.
DID THE KIDNAPPERS MAKE ANY DEMANDS?
YES...
A TRADE...
THE DIRECTOR FOR THE MURDER NOTEBOOK.

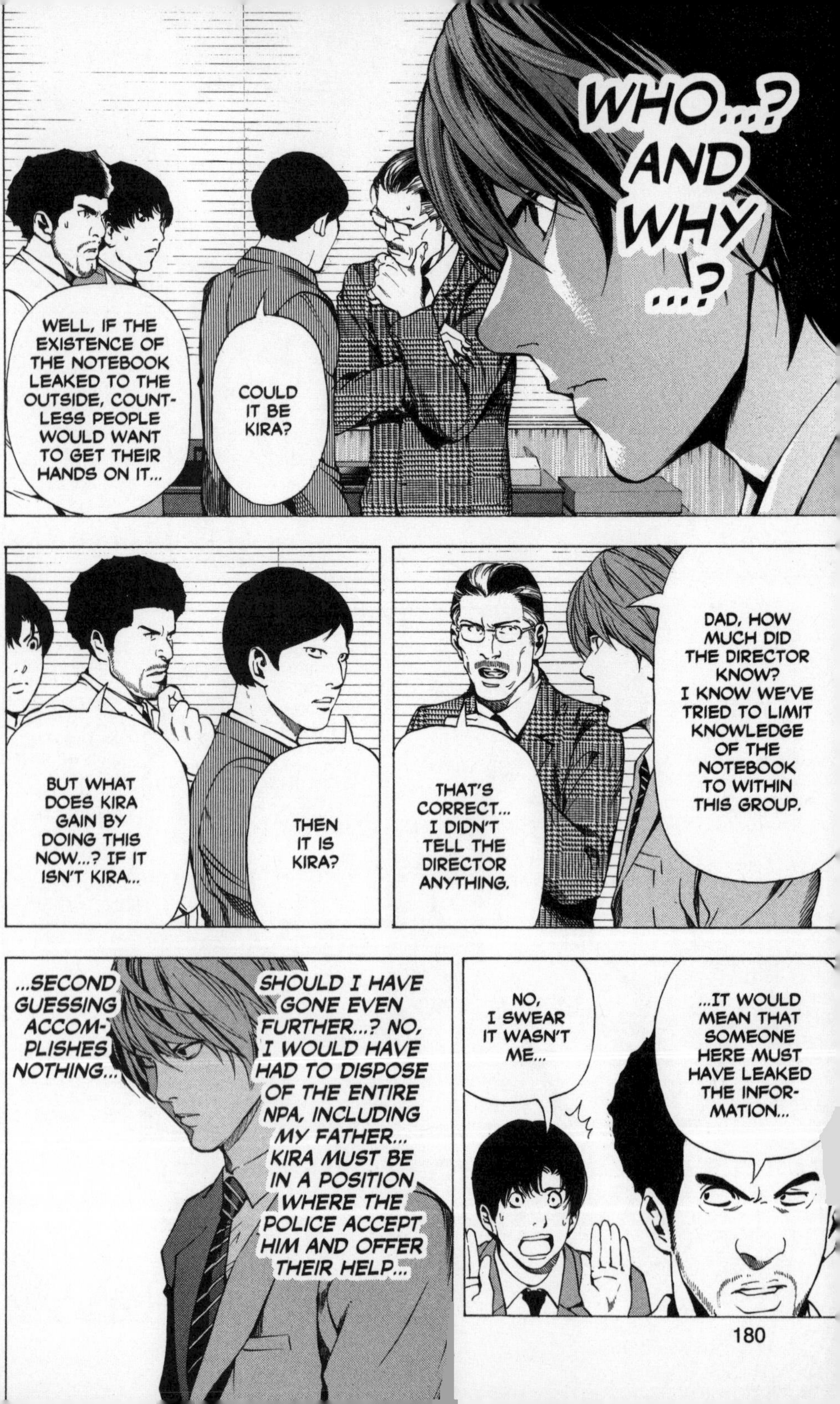
WHO...? AND WHY ...?
COULD IT BE KIRA?
WELL, IF THE EXISTENCE OF THE NOTEBOOK LEAKED TO THE OUTSIDE, COUNTLESS PEOPLE WOULD WANT TO GET THEIR HANDS ON IT...
DAD, HOW MUCH DID THE DIRECTOR KNOW? I KNOW WE'VE TRIED TO LIMIT KNOWLEDGE OF THE NOTEBOOK TO WITHIN THIS GROUP.
THAT'S CORRECT... I DIDN'T TELL THE DIRECTOR ANYTHING.
THEN IT IS KIRA?
BUT WHAT DOES KIRA GAIN BY DOING THIS NOW...? IF IT ISN'T KIRA...
...IT WOULD MEAN THAT SOMEONE HERE MUST HAVE LEAKED THE INFORMATION...
NO, I SWEAR IT WASN'T ME...
SHOULD I HAVE GONE EVEN FURTHER...? NO, I WOULD HAVE HAD TO DISPOSE OF THE ENTIRE NPA, INCLUDING MY FATHER... KIRA MUST BE IN A POSITION WHERE THE POLICE ACCEPT HIM AND OFFER THEIR HELP...
...SECOND GUESSING ACCOMPLISHES NOTHING...

READ THIS WAY

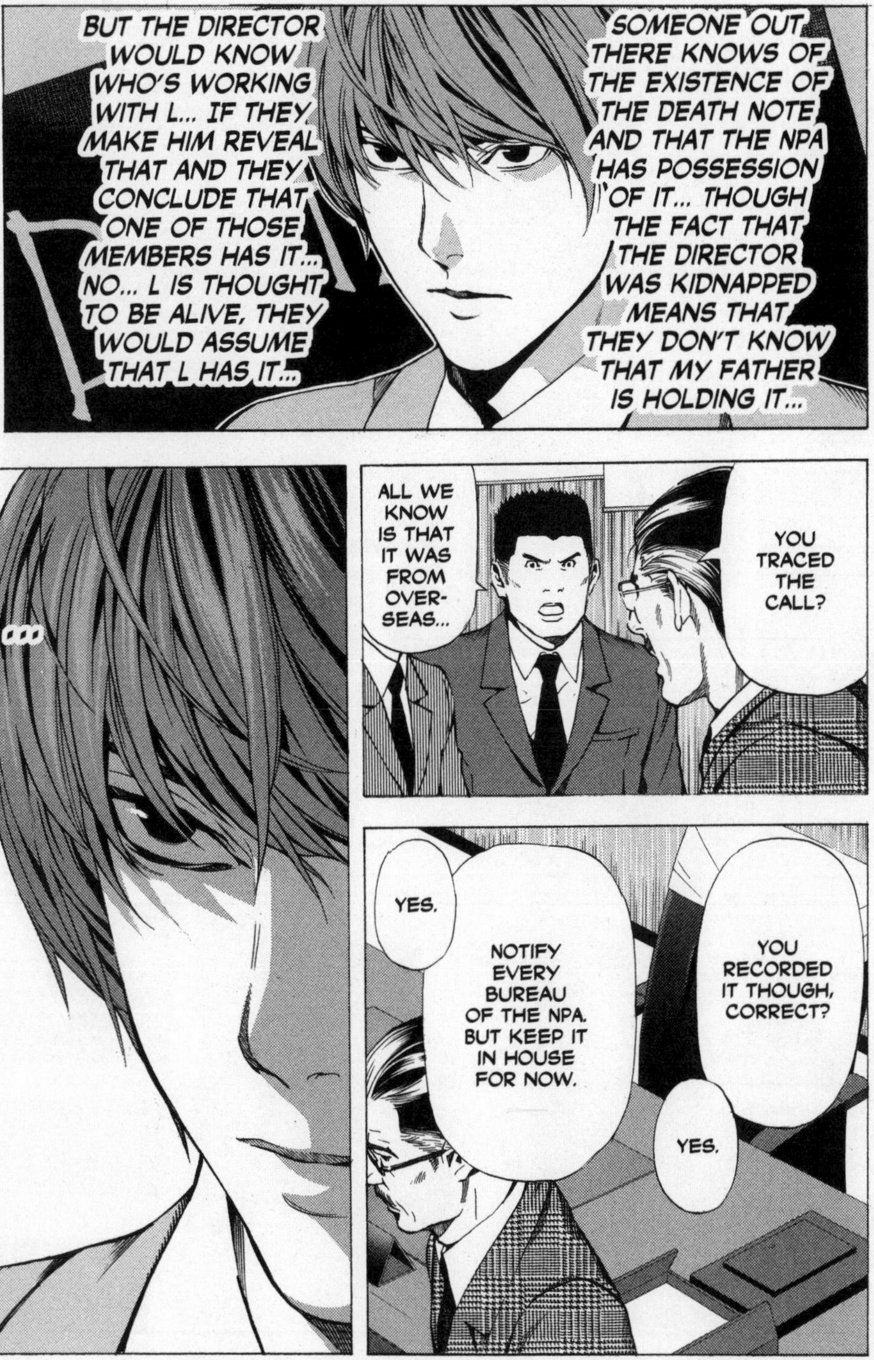
SOMEONE OUT THERE KNOWS OF THE EXISTENCE OF THE DEATH NOTE AND THAT THE NPA HAS POSSESSION OF IT... THOUGH THE FACT THAT THE DIRECTOR WAS KIDNAPPED MEANS THAT THEY DON'T KNOW THAT MY FATHER IS HOLDING IT...
BUT THE DIRECTOR WOULD KNOW WHO'S WORKING WITH L... IF THEY MAKE HIM REVEAL THAT AND THEY CONCLUDE THAT ONE OF THOSE MEMBERS HAS IT... NO... L IS THOUGHT TO BE ALIVE, THEY WOULD ASSUME THAT L HAS IT...
YOU TRACED THE CALL?
ALL WE KNOW IS THAT IT WAS FROM OVER-SEAS...
YOU RECORDED IT THOUGH, CORRECT?
YES.
NOTIFY EVERY BUREAU OF THE NPA. BUT KEEP IT IN HOUSE FOR NOW.
YES.
...

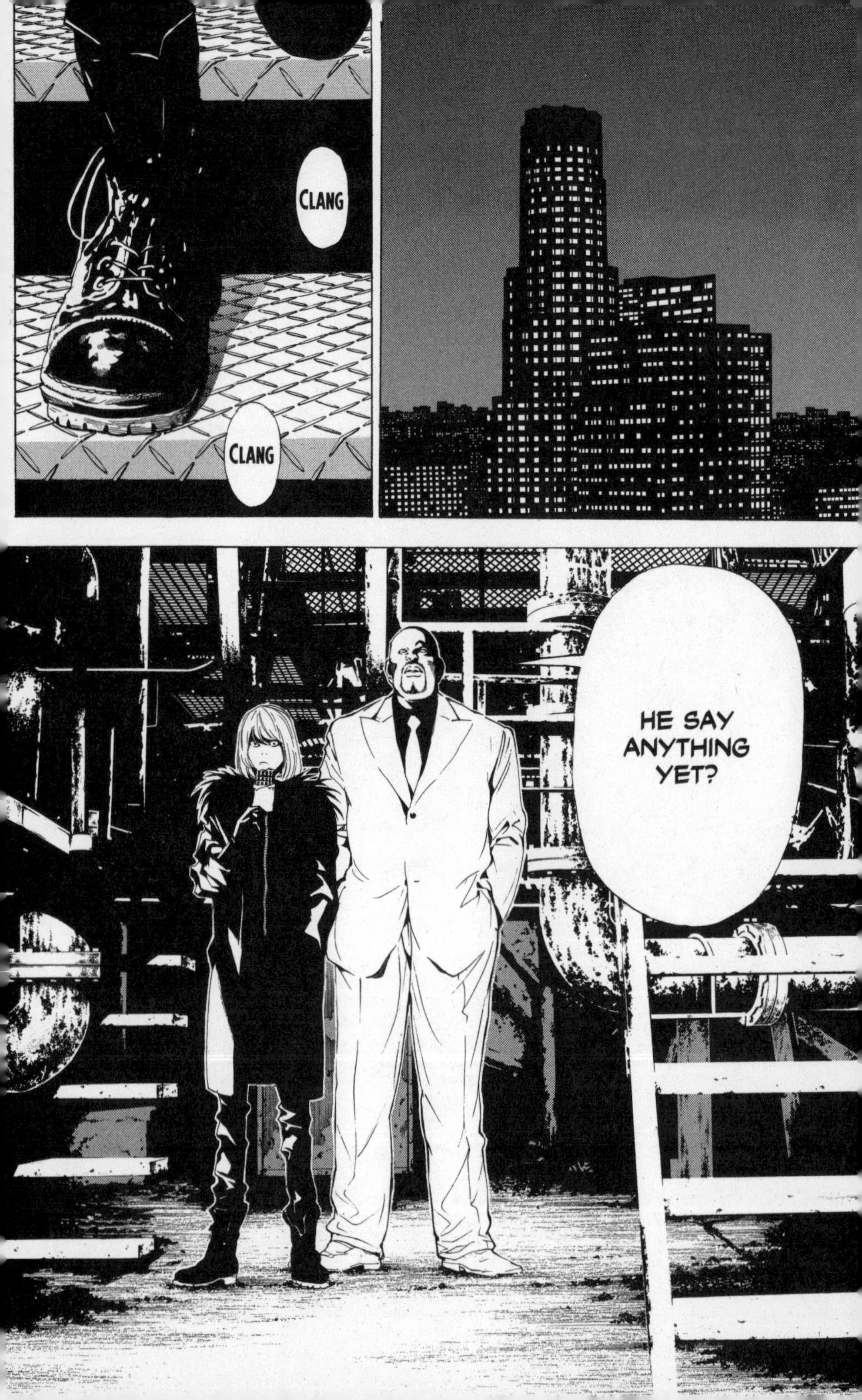
CLANG
CLANG
HE SAY ANYTHING YET?

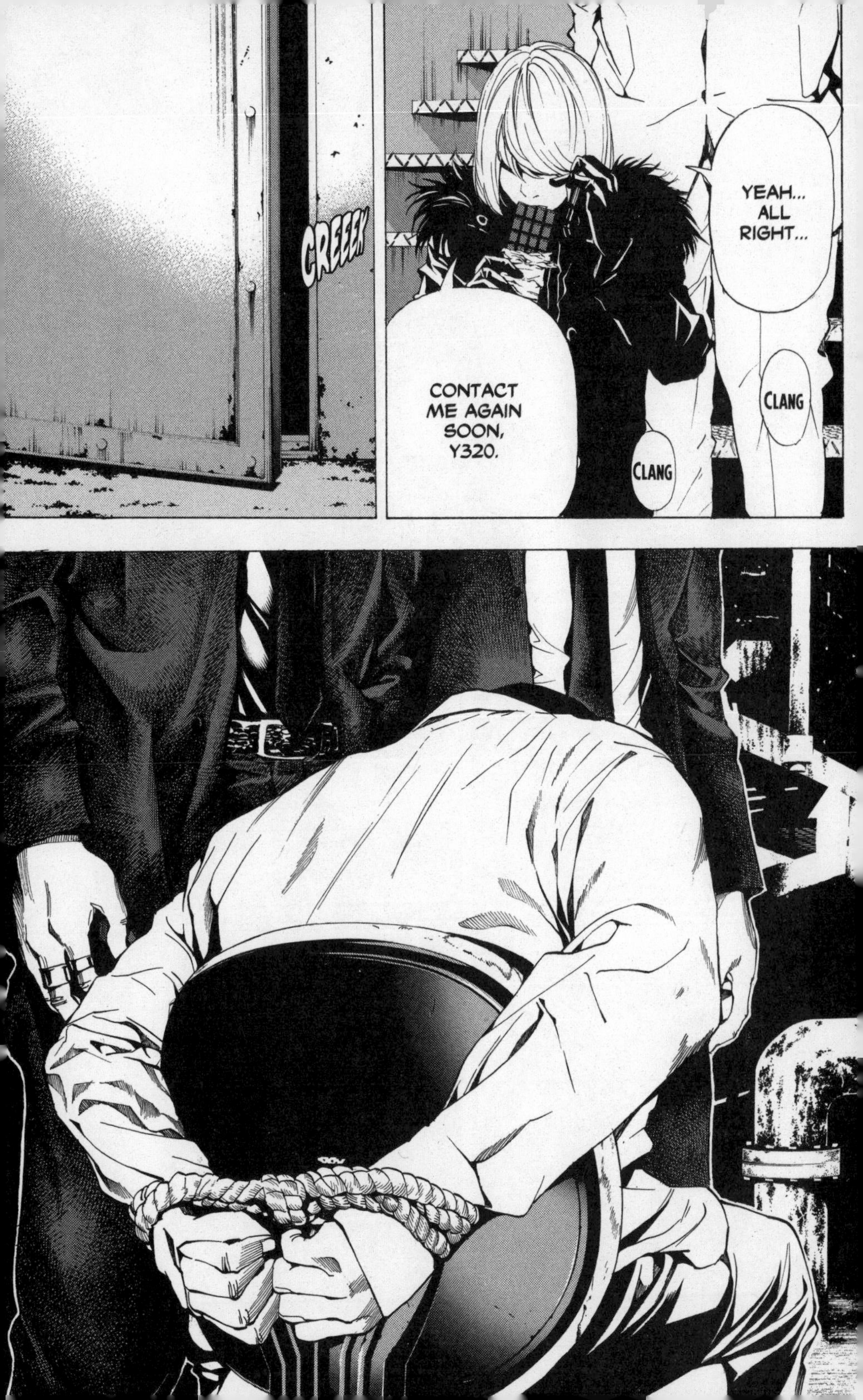
YEAH... ALL RIGHT...
CLANG
CONTACT ME AGAIN SOON, Y320.
CLANG
CREEEK

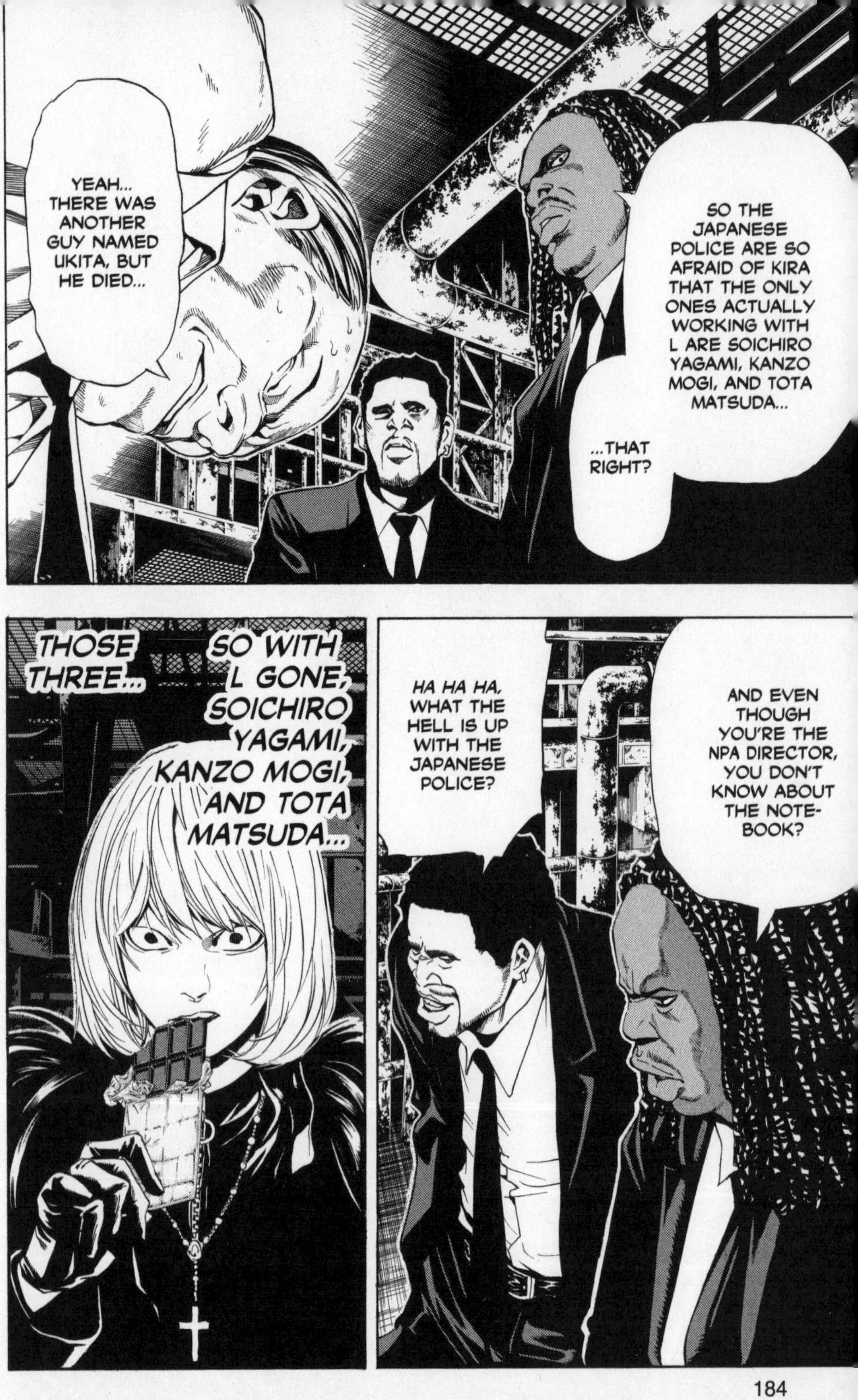
SO THE JAPANESE POLICE ARE SO AFRAID OF KIRA THAT THE ONLY ONES ACTUALLY WORKING WITH L ARE SOICHIRO YAGAMI, KANZO MOGI, AND TOTA MATSUDA...
...THAT RIGHT?
YEAH... THERE WAS ANOTHER GUY NAMED UKITA, BUT HE DIED...
AND EVEN THOUGH YOU'RE THE NPA DIRECTOR, YOU DON'T KNOW ABOUT THE NOTE-BOOK?
HA HA HA, WHAT THE HELL IS UP WITH THE JAPANESE POLICE?
SO WITH L GONE, SOICHIRO YAGAMI, KANZO MOGI, AND TOTA MATSUDA...
THOSE THREE...

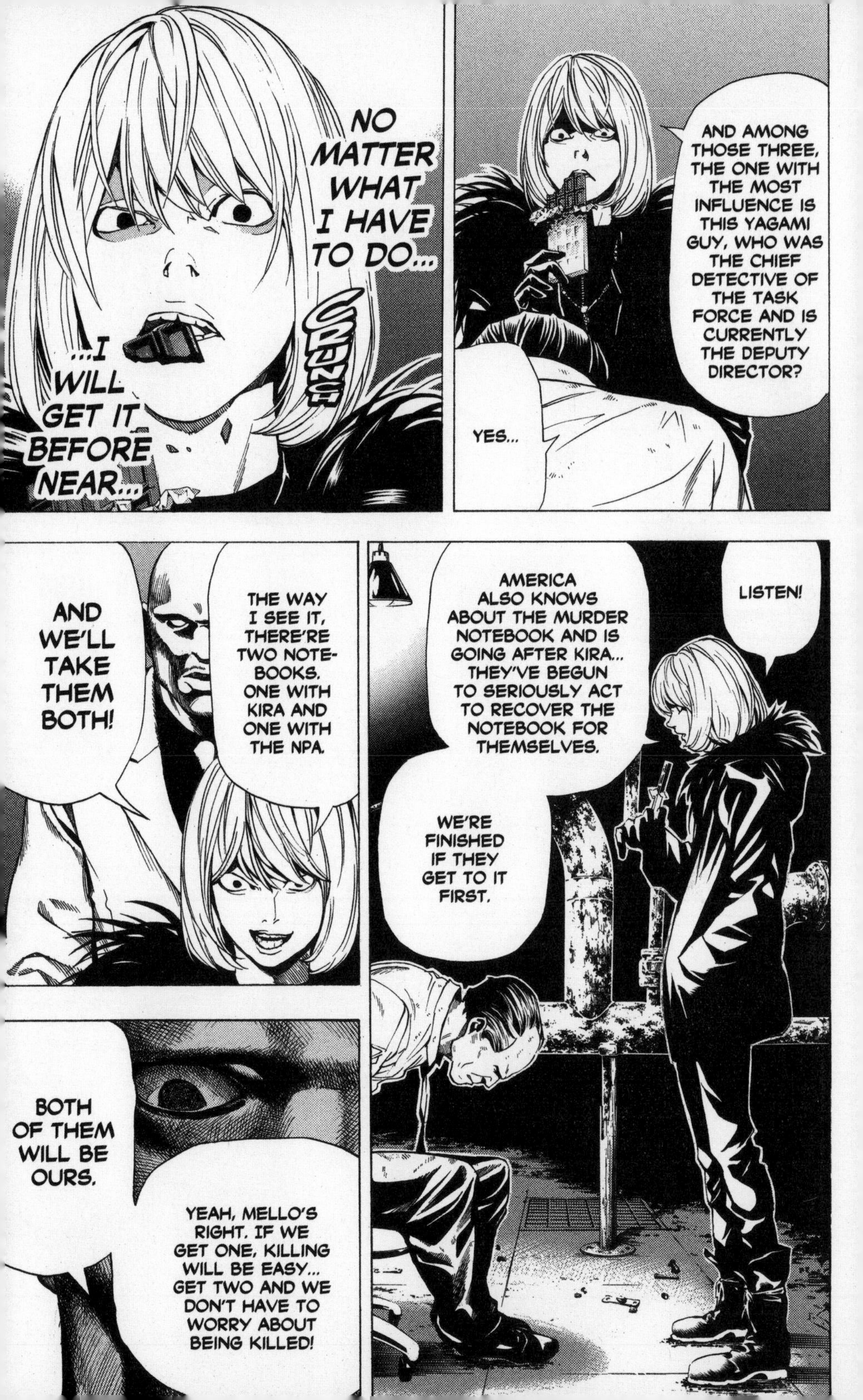
AND AMONG THOSE THREE, THE ONE WITH THE MOST INFLUENCE IS THIS YAGAMI GUY, WHO WAS THE CHIEF DETECTIVE OF THE TASK FORCE AND IS CURRENTLY THE DEPUTY DIRECTOR?
YES...
NO MATTER WHAT I HAVE TO DO...
CRUNCH
...I WILL GET IT BEFORE NEAR...
LISTEN!
AMERICA ALSO KNOWS ABOUT THE MURDER NOTEBOOK AND IS GOING AFTER KIRA... THEY'VE BEGUN TO SERIOUSLY ACT TO RECOVER THE NOTEBOOK FOR THEMSELVES.
WE'RE FINISHED IF THEY GET TO IT FIRST.
THE WAY I SEE IT, THERE'RE TWO NOTE-BOOKS. ONE WITH KIRA AND ONE WITH THE NPA.
AND WE'LL TAKE THEM BOTH!
BOTH OF THEM WILL BE OURS.
YEAH, MELLO'S RIGHT. IF WE GET ONE, KILLING WILL BE EASY... GET TWO AND WE DON'T HAVE TO WORRY ABOUT BEING KILLED!

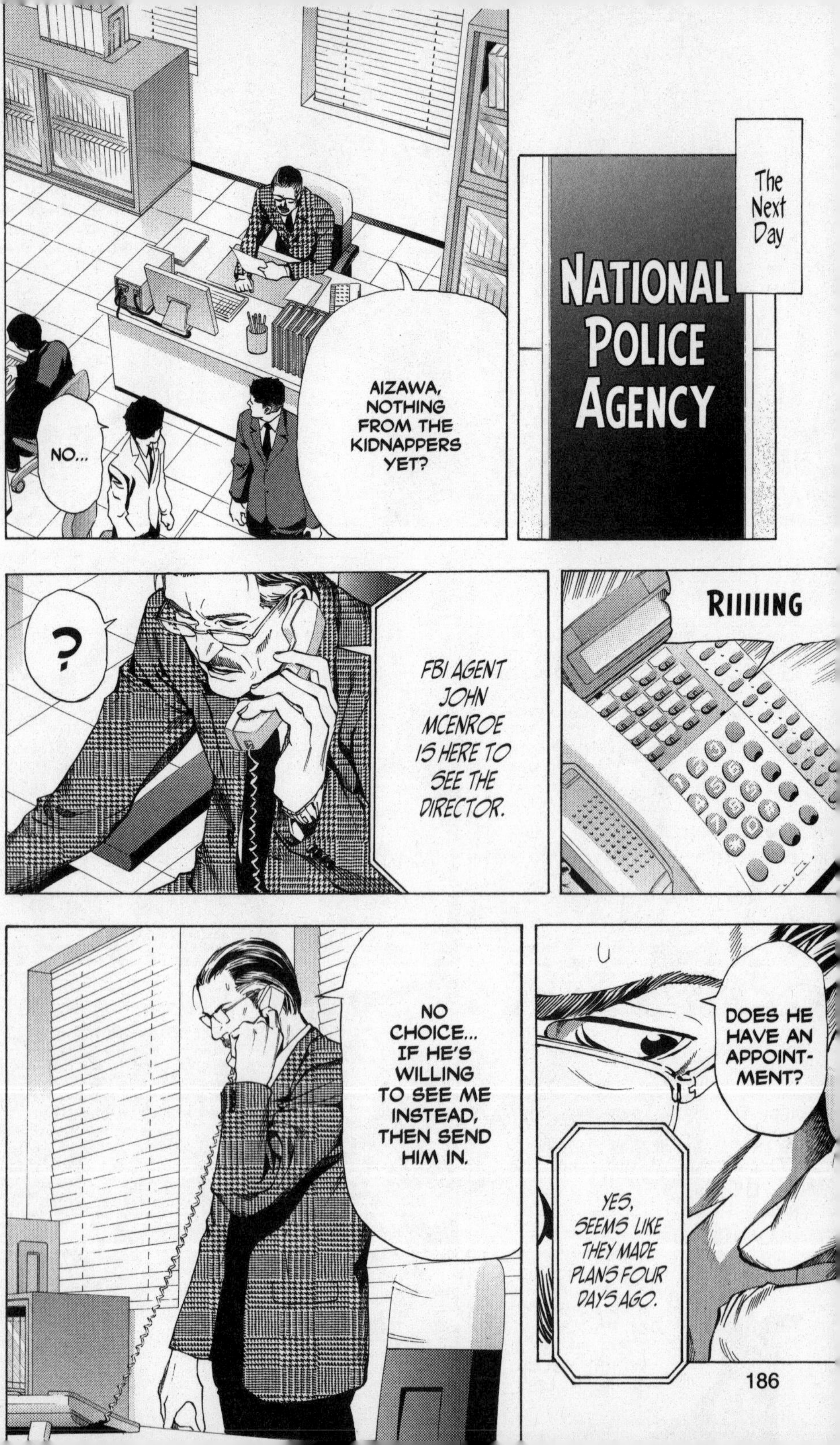
The Next Day
NATIONAL POLICE AGENCY
AIZAWA, NOTHING FROM THE KIDNAPPERS YET?
NO...
RIIIIING
FBI AGENT JOHN MCENROE IS HERE TO SEE THE DIRECTOR.
?
DOES HE HAVE AN APPOINT-MENT?
YES, SEEMS LIKE THEY MADE PLANS FOUR DAYS AGO.
NO CHOICE... IF HE'S WILLING TO SEE ME INSTEAD, THEN SEND HIM IN.

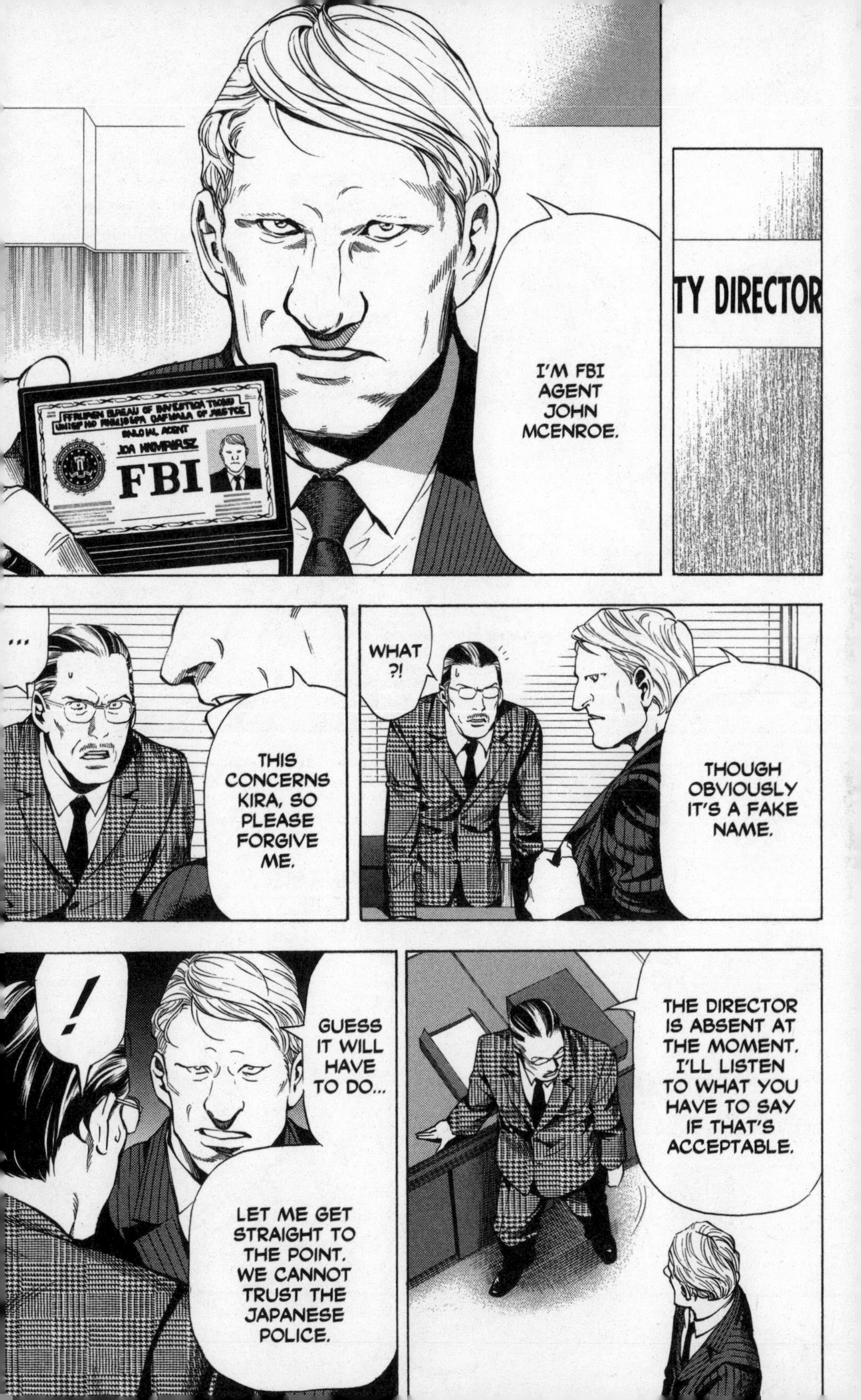
TY DIRECTOR
I'M FBI AGENT JOHN MCENROE.
FBI
THOUGH OBVIOUSLY IT'S A FAKE NAME.
WHAT ?!
THIS CONCERNS KIRA, SO PLEASE FORGIVE ME.
...
THE DIRECTOR IS ABSENT AT THE MOMENT. I'LL LISTEN TO WHAT YOU HAVE TO SAY IF THAT'S ACCEPTABLE.
GUESS IT WILL HAVE TO DO...
!
LET ME GET STRAIGHT TO THE POINT. WE CANNOT TRUST THE JAPANESE POLICE.

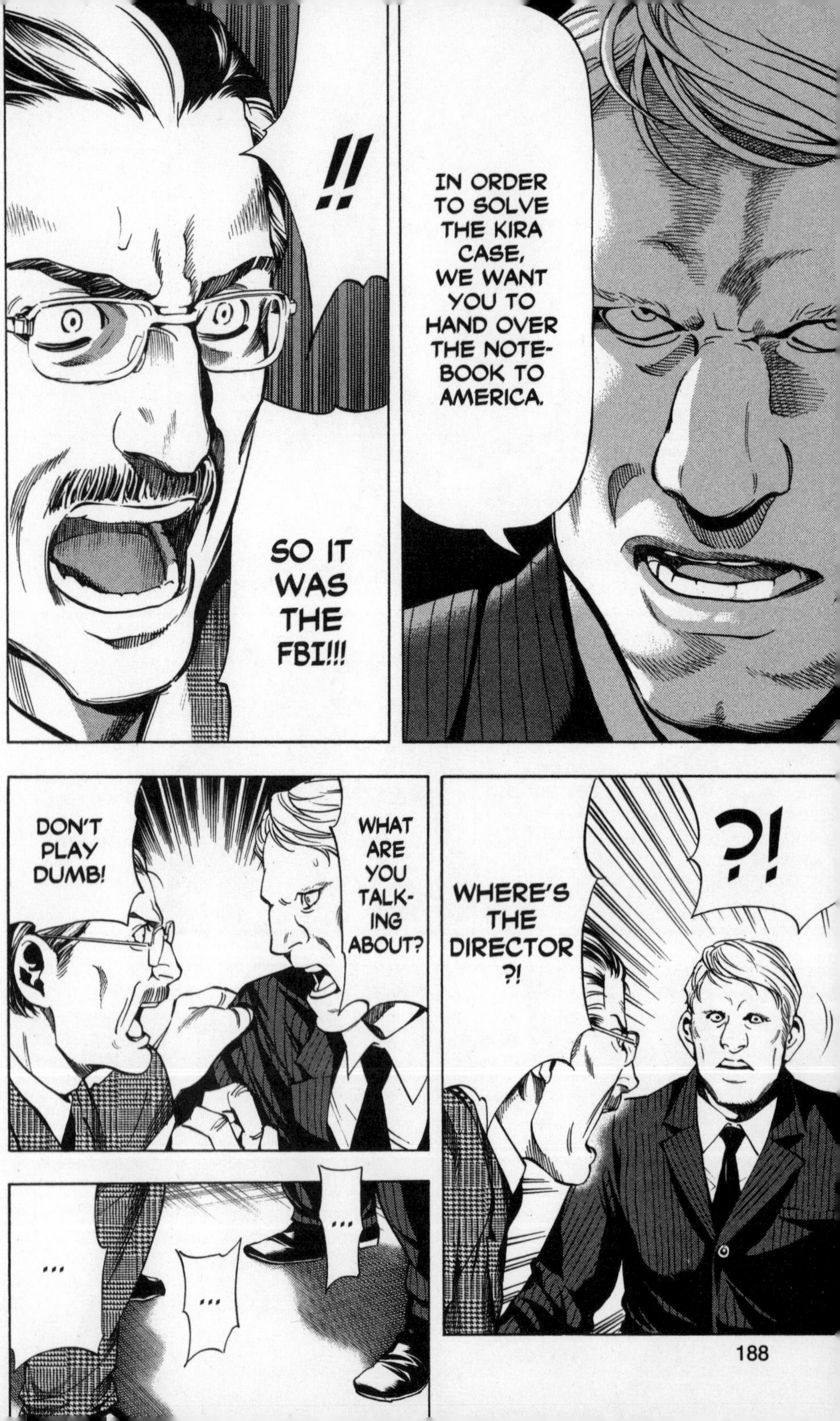
IN ORDER TO SOLVE THE KIRA CASE, WE WANT YOU TO HAND OVER THE NOTE-BOOK TO AMERICA.
!!
SO IT WAS THE FBI!!!
?!
WHERE'S THE DIRECTOR ?!
WHAT ARE YOU TALK-ING ABOUT?
DON'T PLAY DUMB!
...
...
...

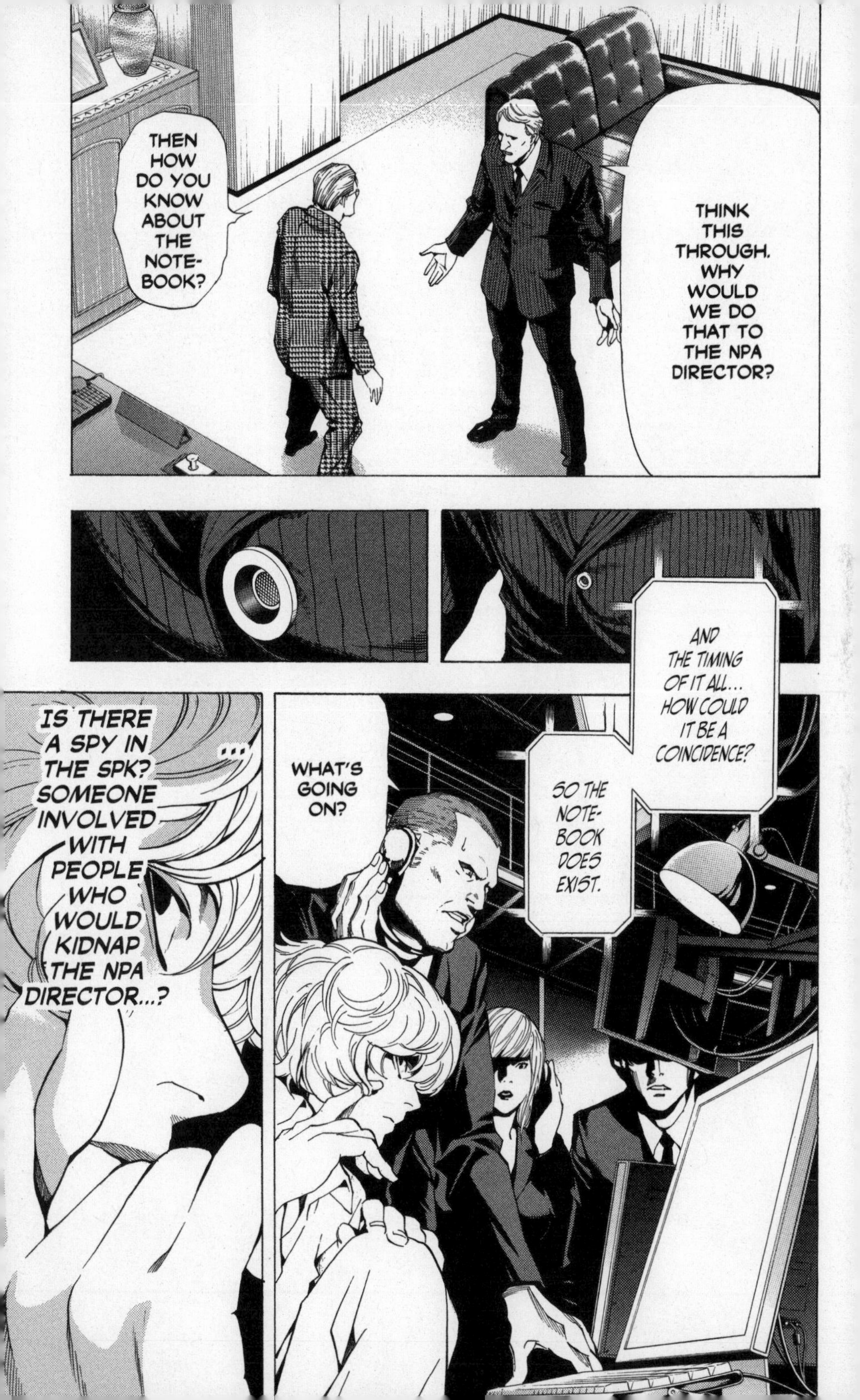
THINK THIS THROUGH. WHY WOULD WE DO THAT TO THE NPA DIRECTOR?
THEN HOW DO YOU KNOW ABOUT THE NOTE-BOOK?
AND THE TIMING OF IT ALL... HOW COULD IT BE A COINCIDENCE?
SO THE NOTE-BOOK DOES EXIST.
WHAT'S GOING ON?
...
IS THERE A SPY IN THE SPK? SOMEONE INVOLVED WITH PEOPLE WHO WOULD KIDNAP THE NPA DIRECTOR...?

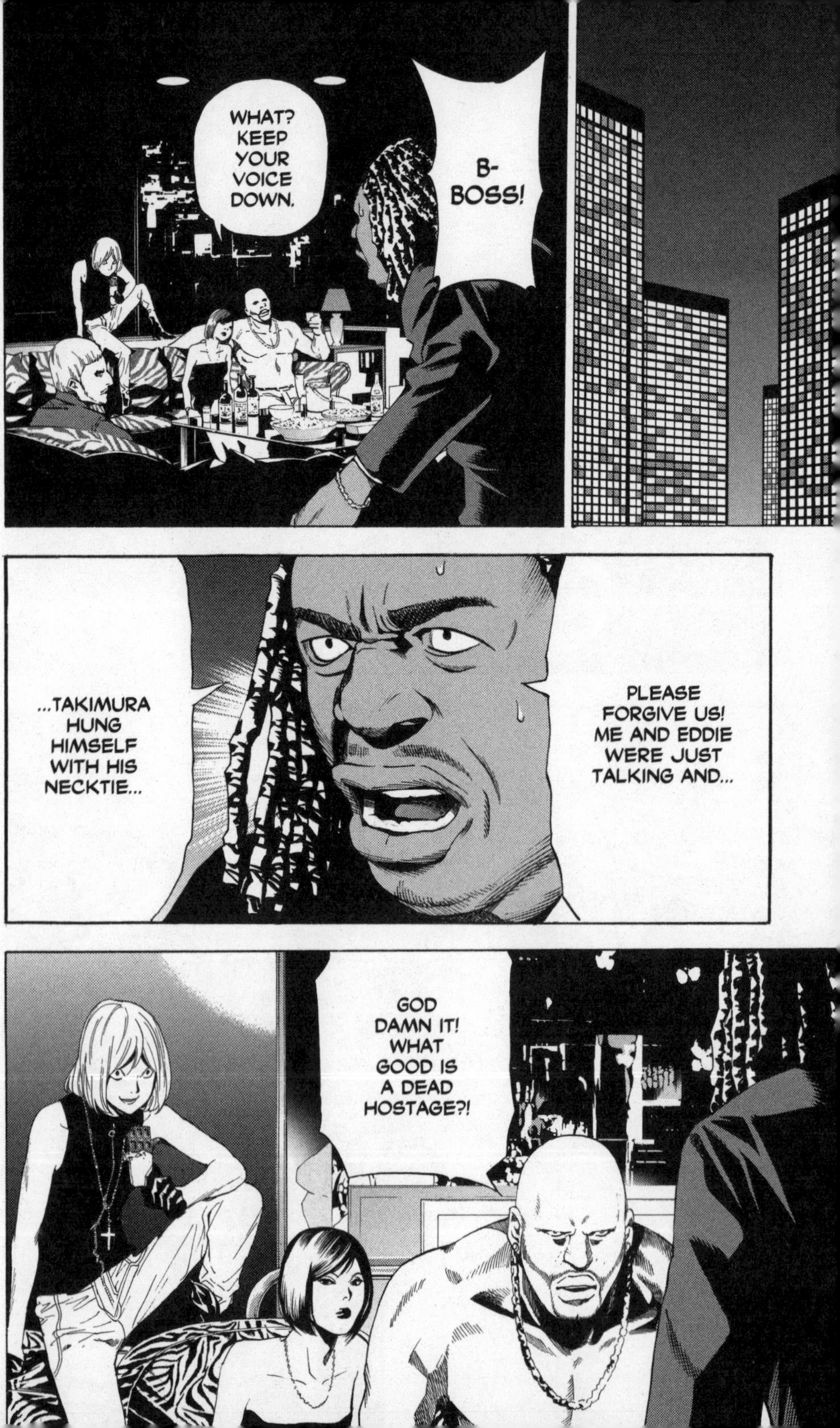
B-BOSS!
WHAT? KEEP YOUR VOICE DOWN.
PLEASE FORGIVE US! ME AND EDDIE WERE JUST TALKING AND...
...TAKIMURA HUNG HIMSELF WITH HIS NECKTIE...
GOD DAMN IT! WHAT GOOD IS A DEAD HOSTAGE?!

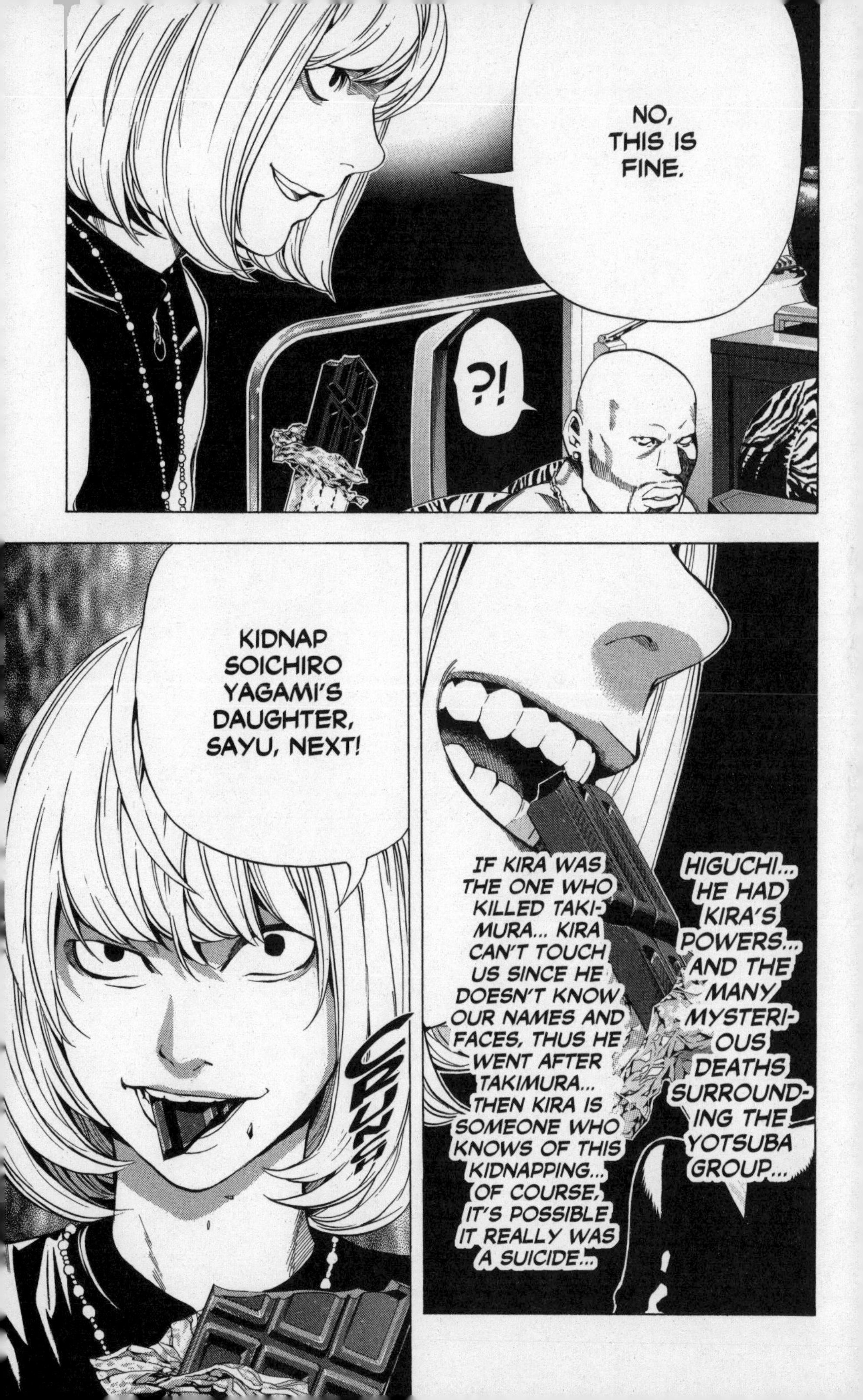
NO, THIS IS FINE.
?!
HIGUCHI... HE HAD KIRA'S POWERS... AND THE MANY MYSTERIOUS DEATHS SURROUNDING THE YOTSUBA GROUP...
IF KIRA WAS THE ONE WHO KILLED TAKIMURA... KIRA CAN'T TOUCH US SINCE HE DOESN'T KNOW OUR NAMES AND FACES, THUS HE WENT AFTER TAKIMURA... THEN KIRA IS SOMEONE WHO KNOWS OF THIS KIDNAPPING... OF COURSE, IT'S POSSIBLE IT REALLY WAS A SUICIDE...
KIDNAP SOICHIRO YAGAMI'S DAUGHTER, SAYU, NEXT!

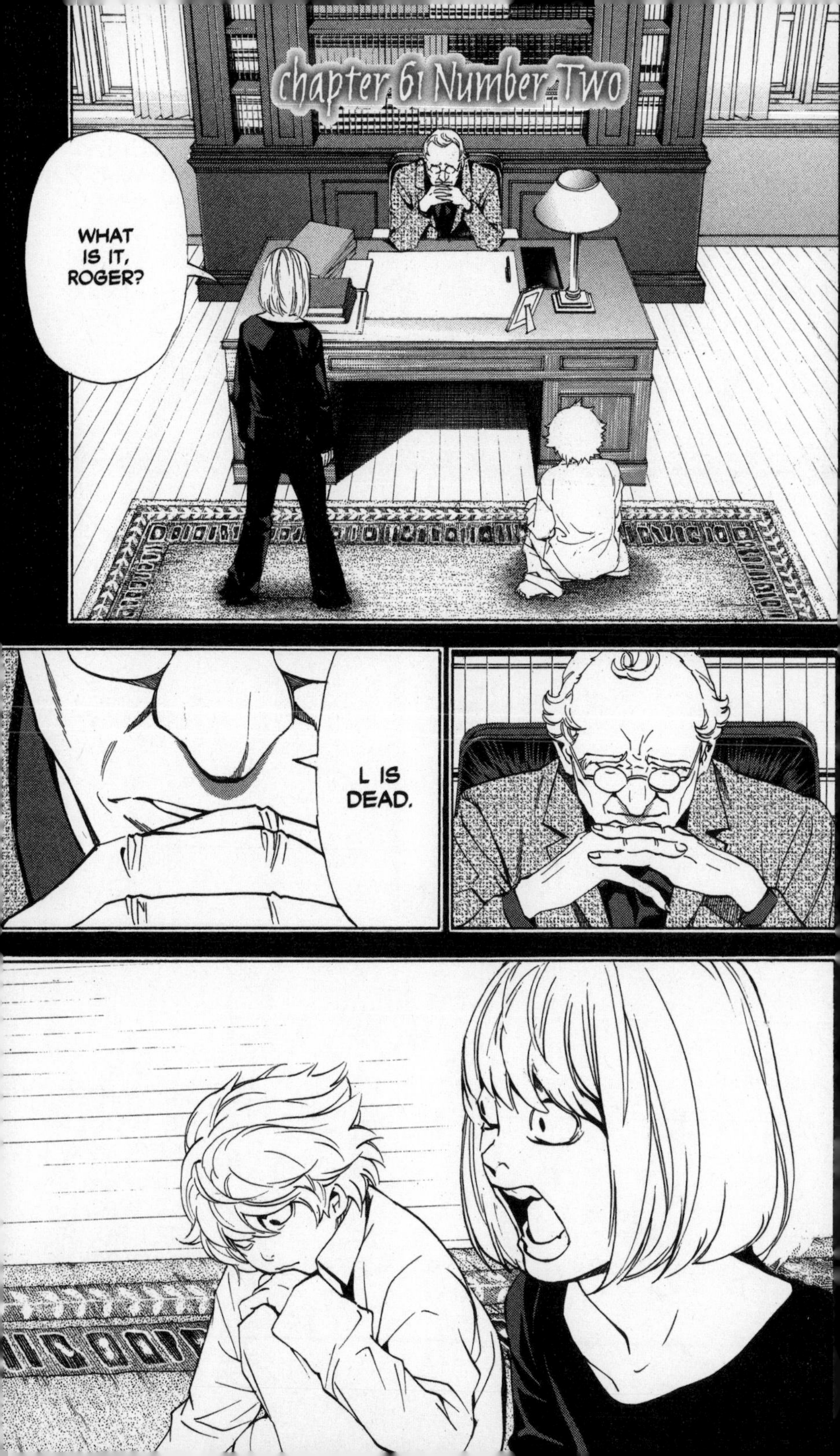
chapter 61 Number Two
WHAT IS IT, ROGER?
L IS DEAD.

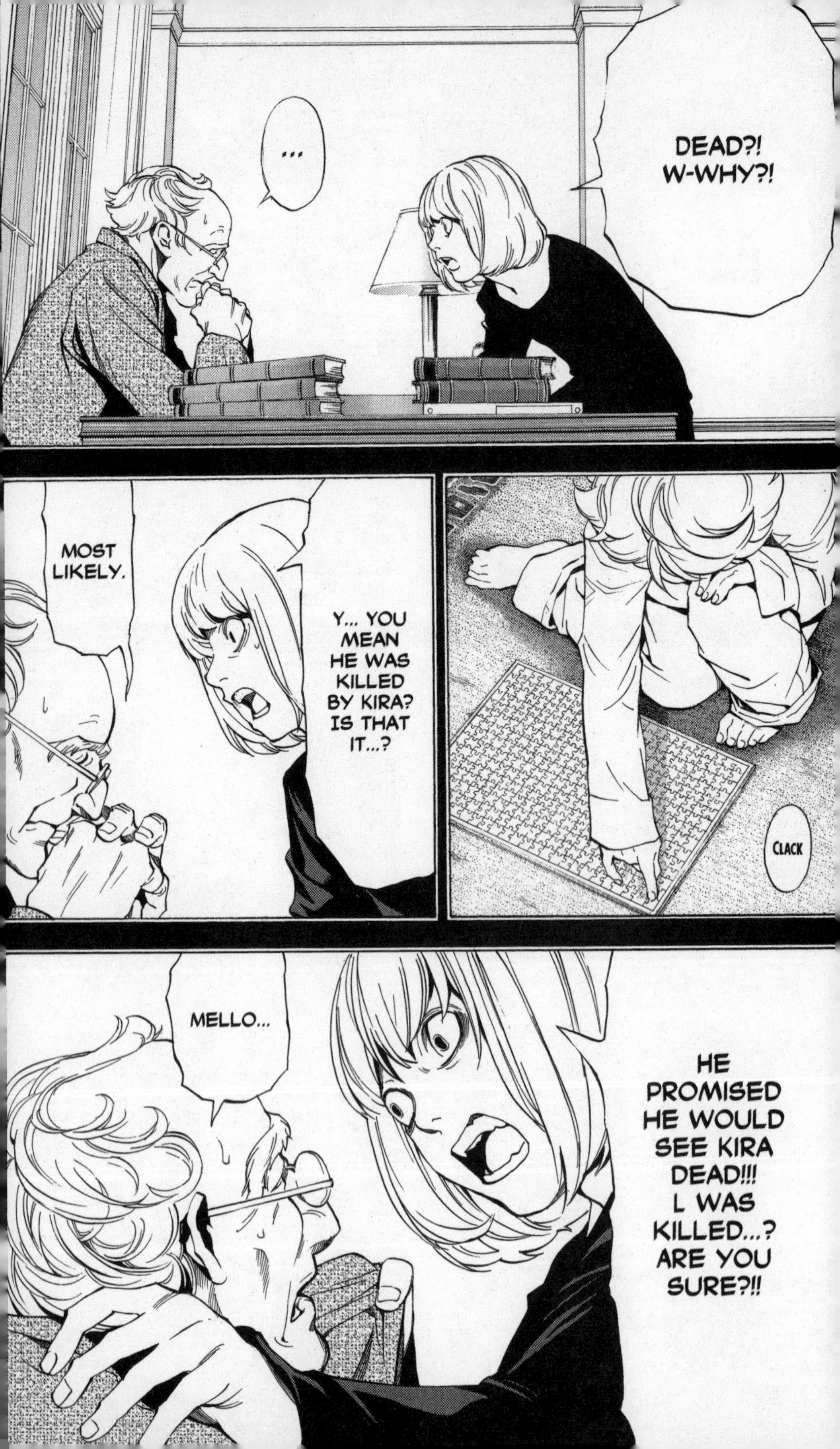
DEAD?! W-WHY?!
...
CLACK
Y... YOU MEAN HE WAS KILLED BY KIRA? IS THAT IT...?
MOST LIKELY.
HE PROMISED HE WOULD SEE KIRA DEAD!!! L WAS KILLED...? ARE YOU SURE?!!
MELLO...

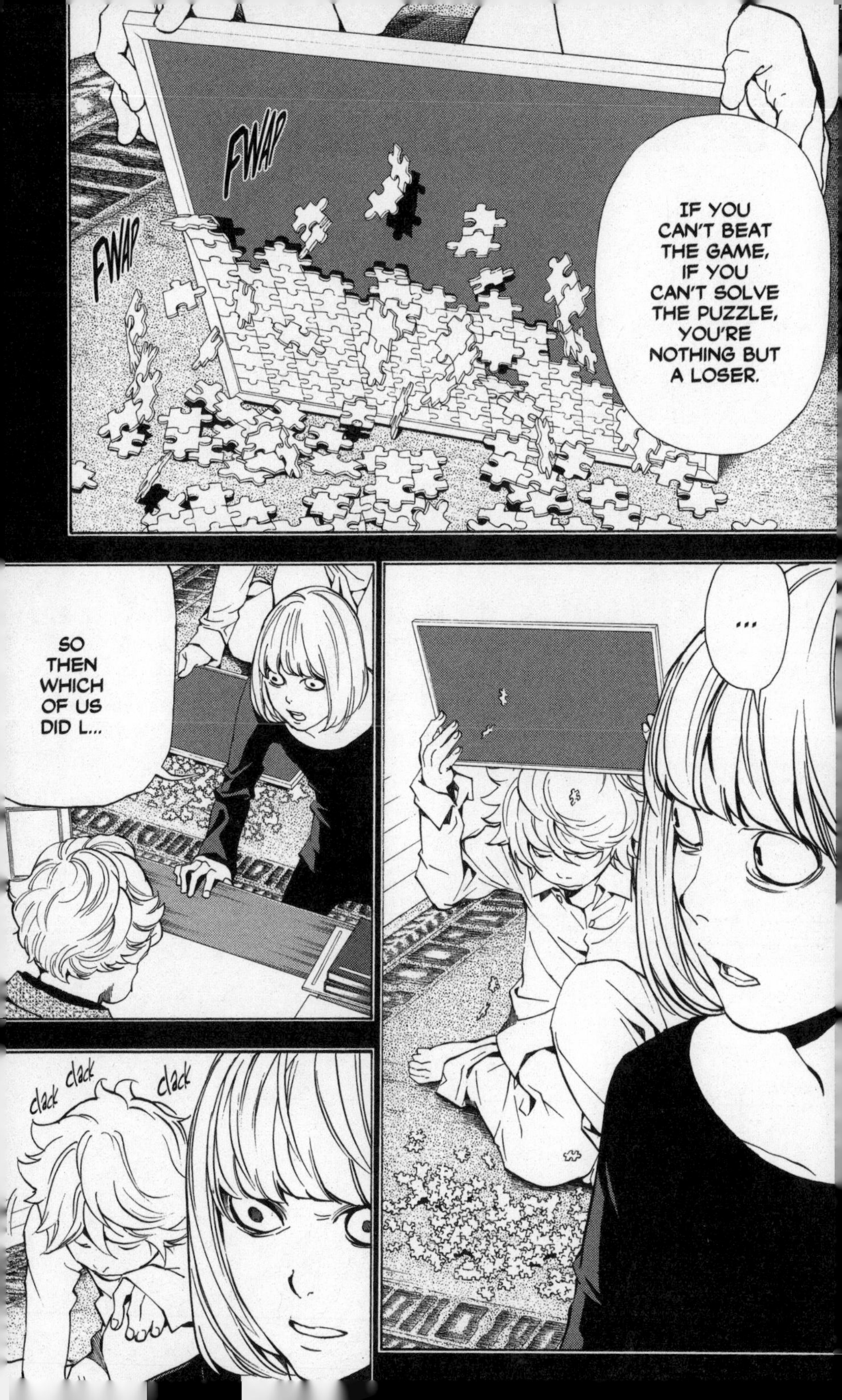
IF YOU CAN'T BEAT THE GAME, IF YOU CAN'T SOLVE THE PUZZLE, YOU'RE NOTHING BUT A LOSER.
FWAP
FWAP
...
SO THEN WHICH OF US DID L...
clack
clack
clack

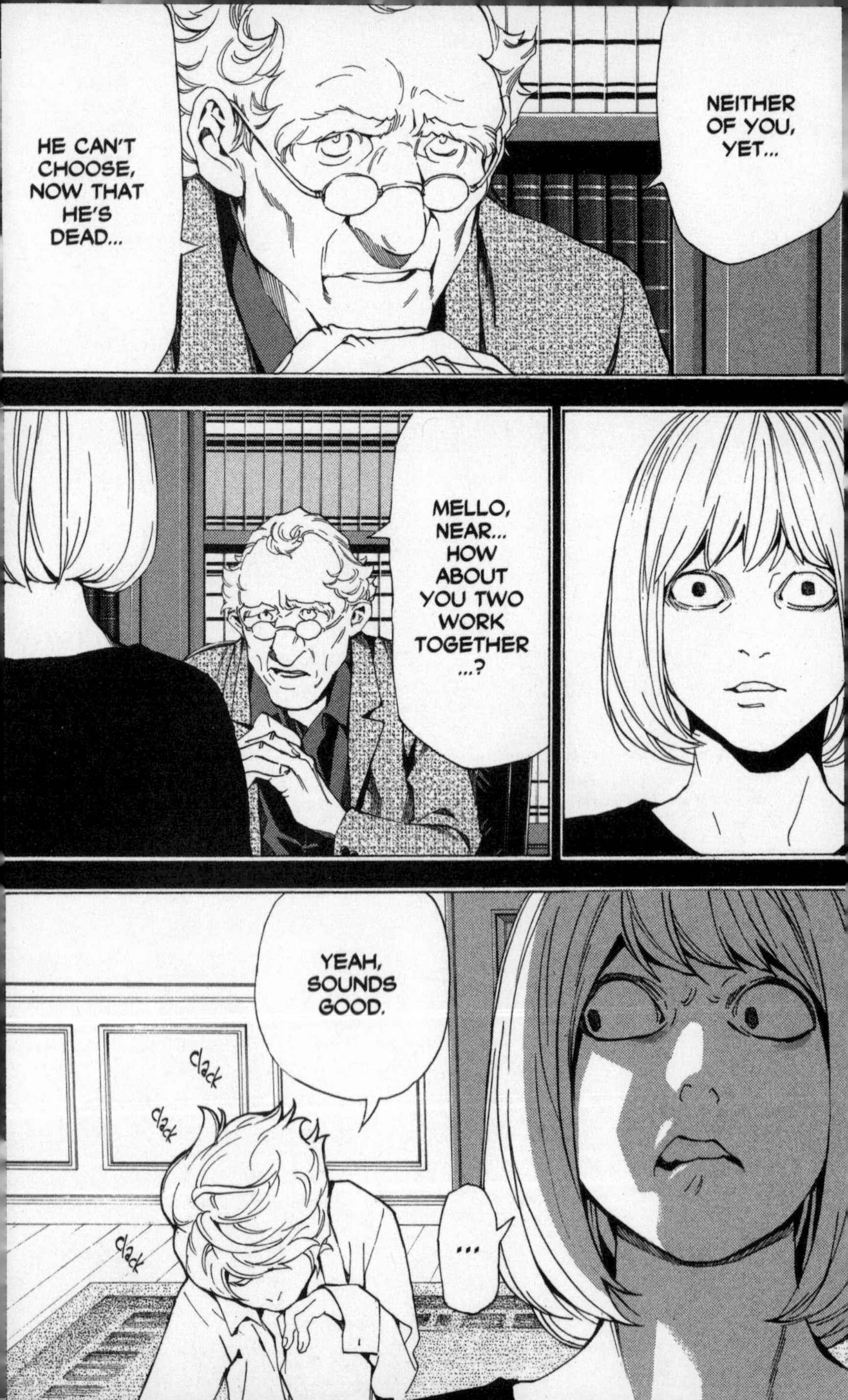
NEITHER OF YOU, YET...
HE CAN'T CHOOSE, NOW THAT HE'S DEAD...
MELLO, NEAR... HOW ABOUT YOU TWO WORK TOGETHER ...?
YEAH, SOUNDS GOOD.
clack
clack
...
clack

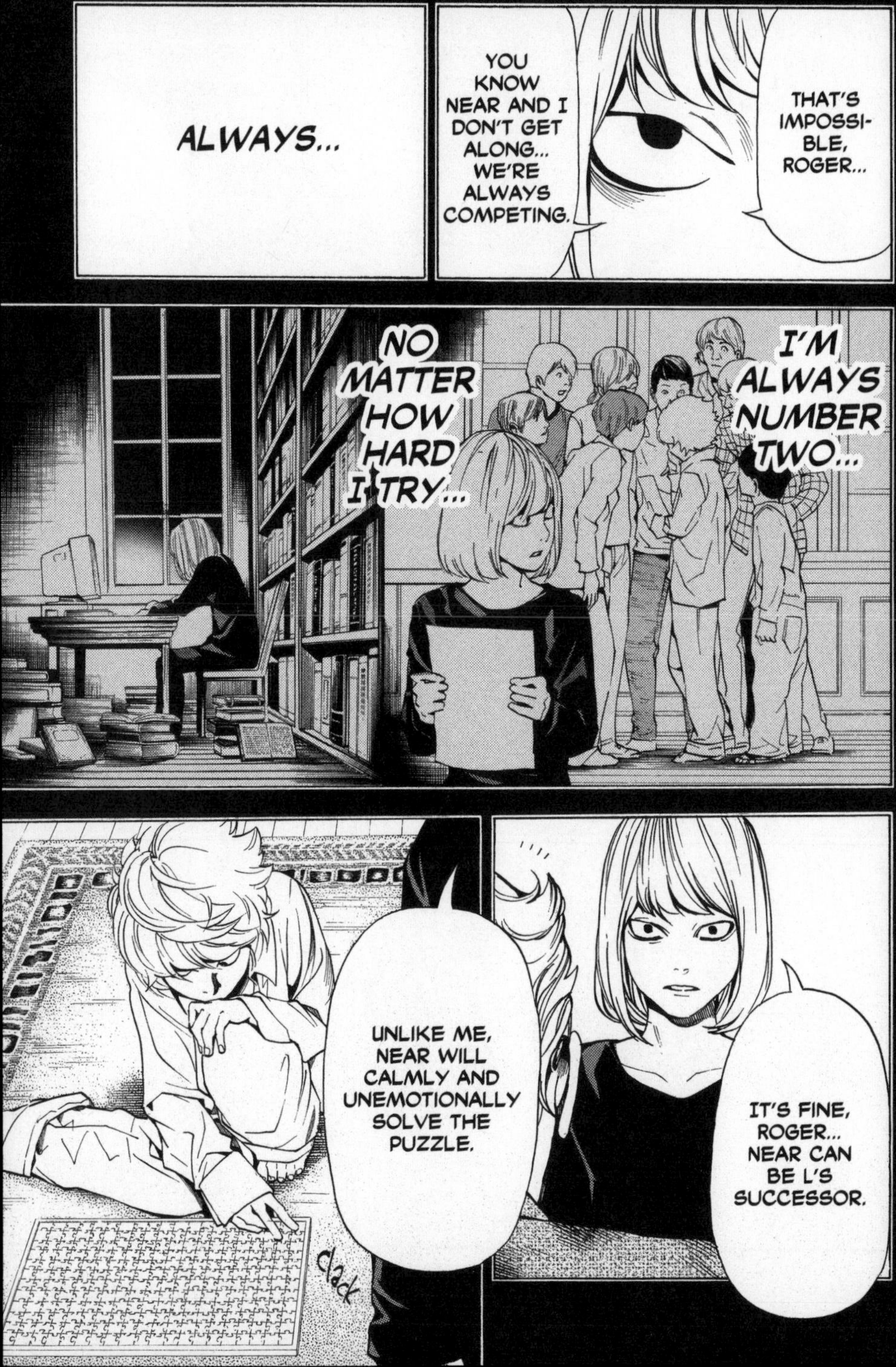
THAT'S IMPOSSIBLE, ROGER...
YOU KNOW NEAR AND I DON'T GET ALONG... WE'RE ALWAYS COMPETING.
ALWAYS...
I'M ALWAYS NUMBER TWO...
NO MATTER HOW HARD I TRY...
IT'S FINE, ROGER... NEAR CAN BE L'S SUCCESSOR.
UNLIKE ME, NEAR WILL CALMLY AND UNEMOTIONALLY SOLVE THE PUZZLE.
clack

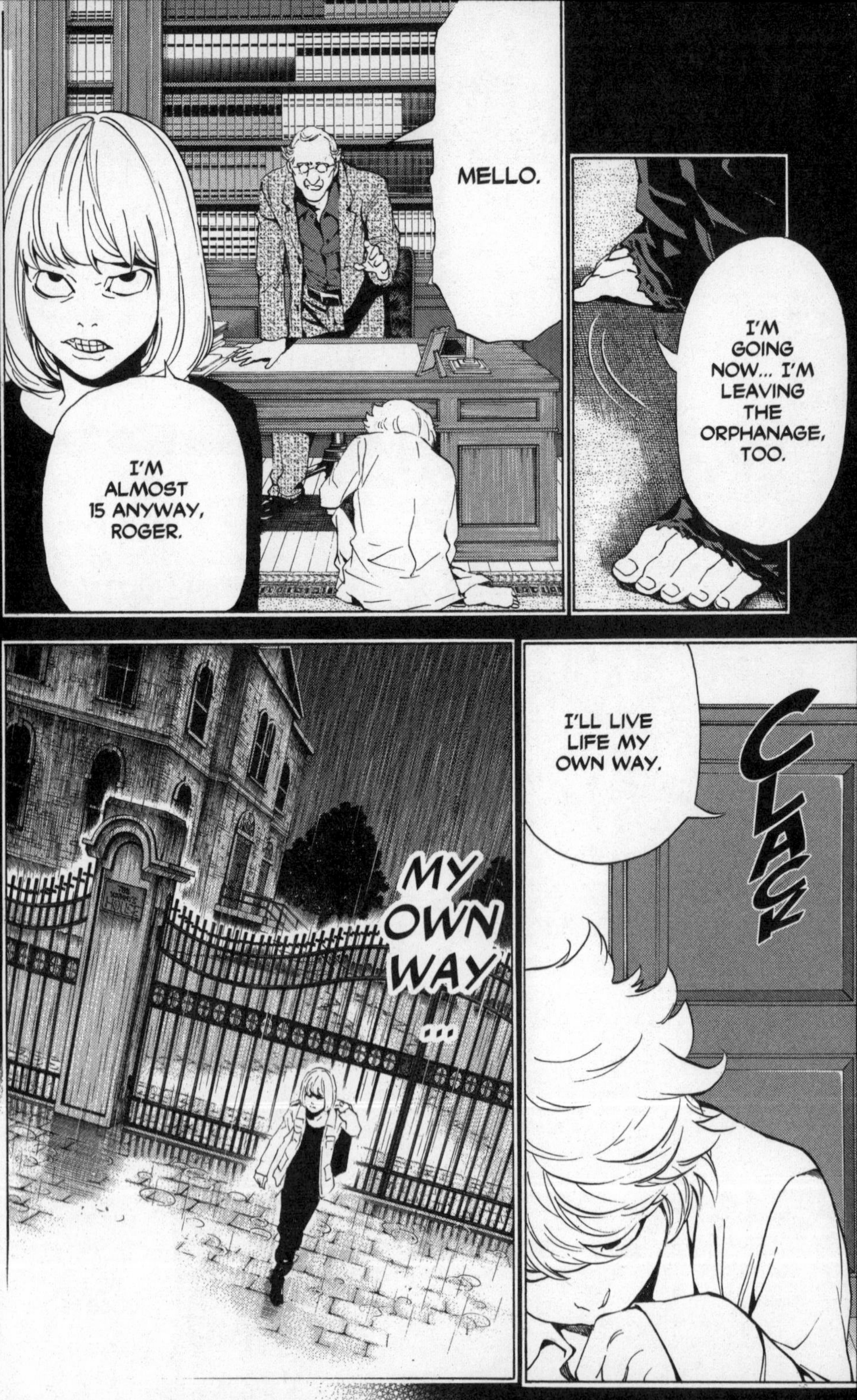
I'M GOING NOW... I'M LEAVING THE ORPHANAGE, TOO.
MELLO.
I'M ALMOST 15 ANYWAY, ROGER.
I'LL LIVE LIFE MY OWN WAY.
CLACK
MY OWN WAY...

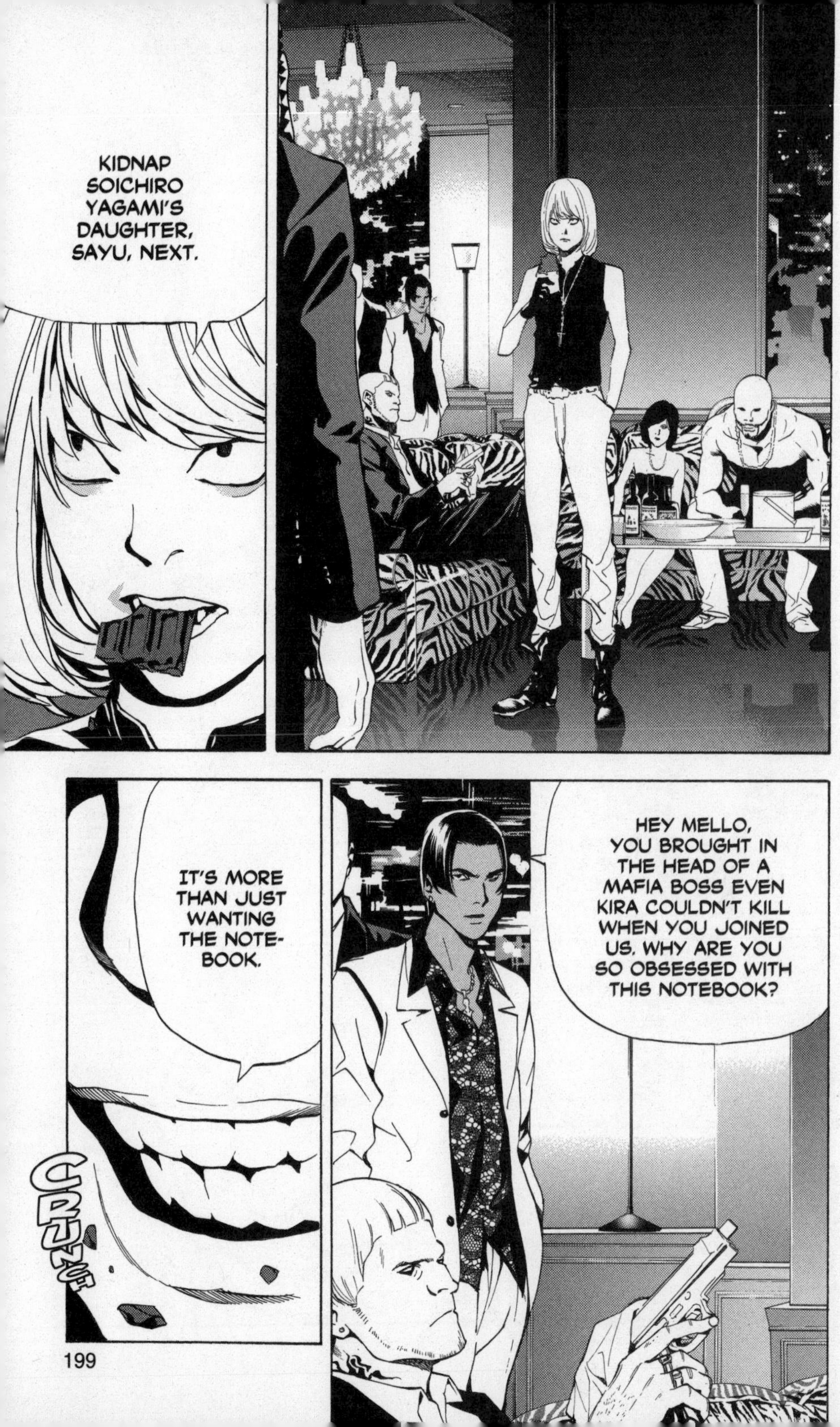
KIDNAP SOICHIRO YAGAMI'S DAUGHTER, SAYU, NEXT.
HEY MELLO, YOU BROUGHT IN THE HEAD OF A MAFIA BOSS EVEN KIRA COULDN'T KILL WHEN YOU JOINED US. WHY ARE YOU SO OBSESSED WITH THIS NOTEBOOK?
IT'S MORE THAN JUST WANTING THE NOTE-BOOK.
CRUNCH

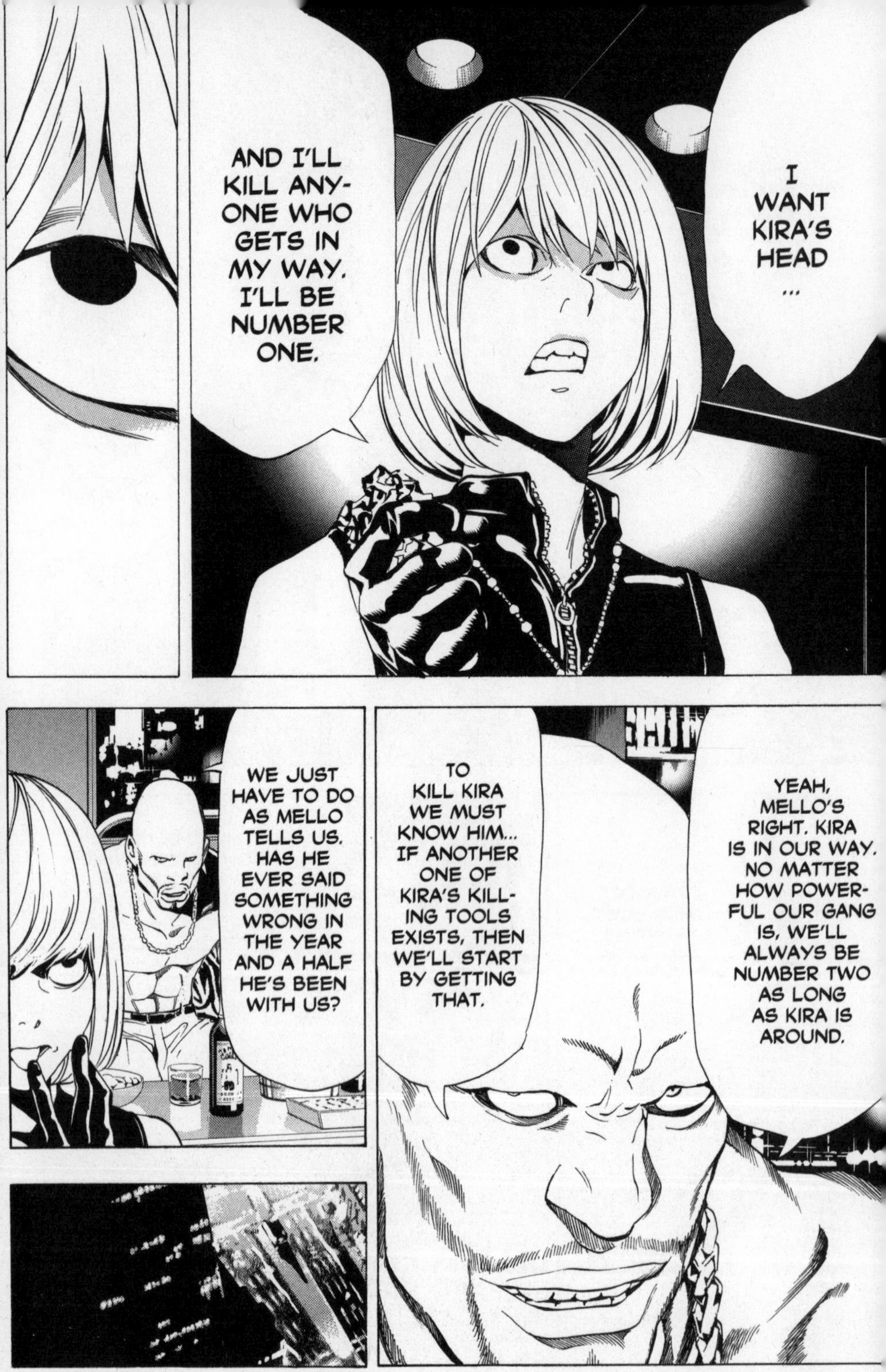
I WANT KIRA'S HEAD ...
AND I'LL KILL ANYONE WHO GETS IN MY WAY. I'LL BE NUMBER ONE.
YEAH, MELLO'S RIGHT. KIRA IS IN OUR WAY. NO MATTER HOW POWERFUL OUR GANG IS, WE'LL ALWAYS BE NUMBER TWO AS LONG AS KIRA IS AROUND.
TO KILL KIRA WE MUST KNOW HIM... IF ANOTHER ONE OF KIRA'S KILLING TOOLS EXISTS, THEN WE'LL START BY GETTING THAT.
WE JUST HAVE TO DO AS MELLO TELLS US. HAS HE EVER SAID SOMETHING WRONG IN THE YEAR AND A HALF HE'S BEEN WITH US?

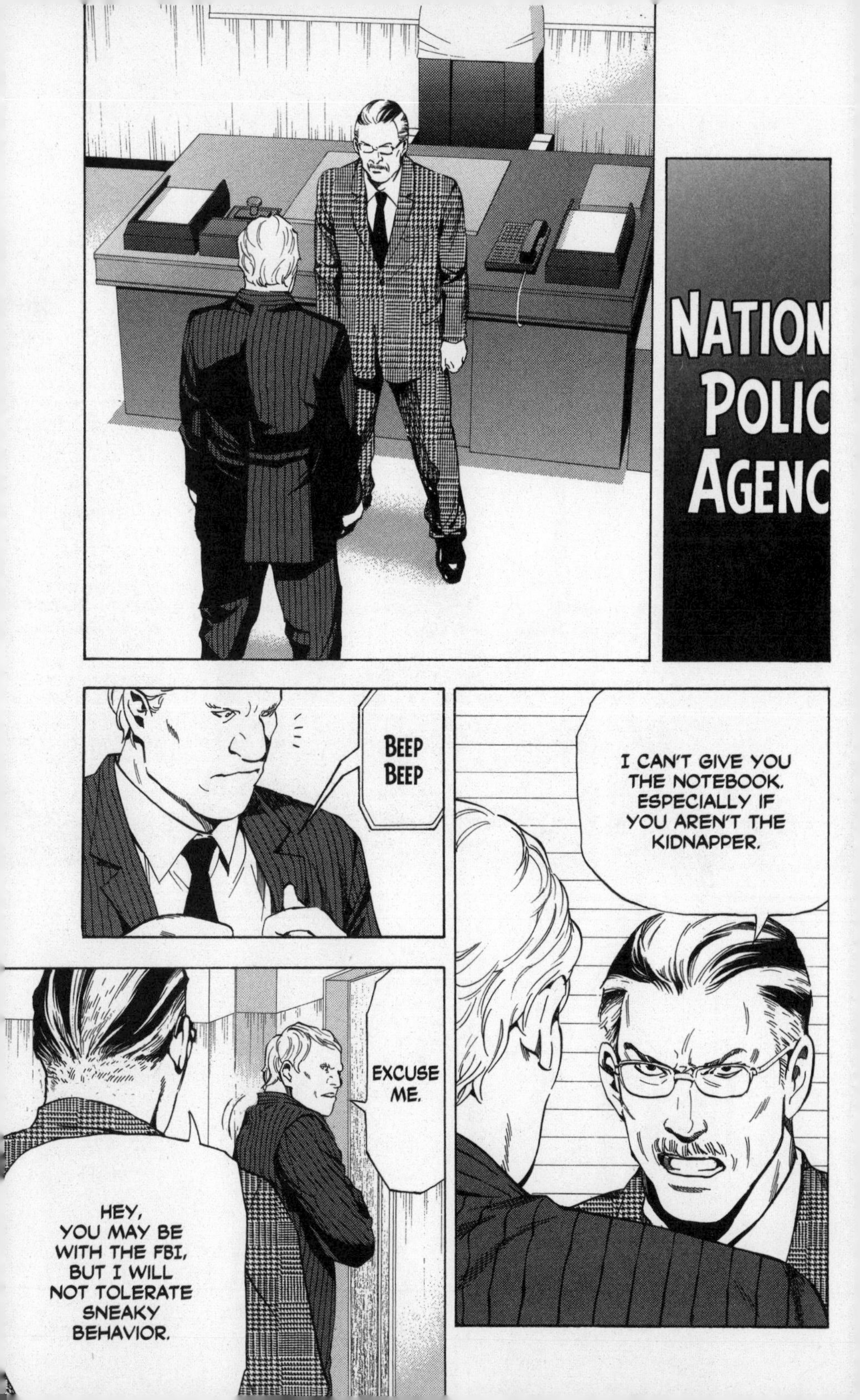
NATION POLIC AGENC
I CAN'T GIVE YOU THE NOTEBOOK. ESPECIALLY IF YOU AREN'T THE KIDNAPPER.
BEEP BEEP
EXCUSE ME.
HEY, YOU MAY BE WITH THE FBI, BUT I WILL NOT TOLERATE SNEAKY BEHAVIOR.

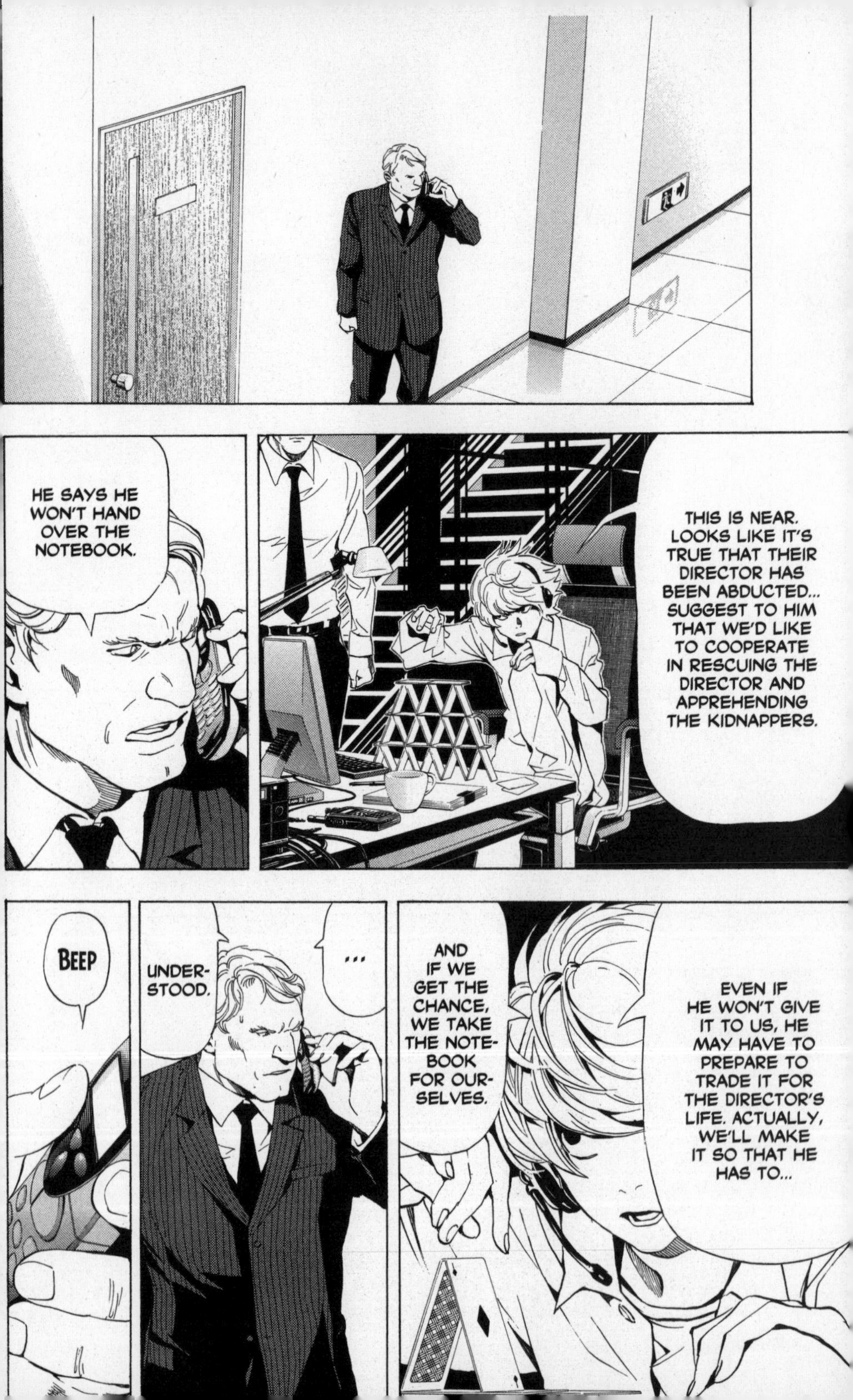
THIS IS NEAR. LOOKS LIKE IT'S TRUE THAT THEIR DIRECTOR HAS BEEN ABDUCTED... SUGGEST TO HIM THAT WE'D LIKE TO COOPERATE IN RESCUING THE DIRECTOR AND APPREHENDING THE KIDNAPPERS.
HE SAYS HE WON'T HAND OVER THE NOTEBOOK.
EVEN IF HE WON'T GIVE IT TO US, HE MAY HAVE TO PREPARE TO TRADE IT FOR THE DIRECTOR'S LIFE. ACTUALLY, WE'LL MAKE IT SO THAT HE HAS TO...
AND IF WE GET THE CHANCE, WE TAKE THE NOTE-BOOK FOR OUR-SELVES.
...
UNDER-STOOD.
BEEP

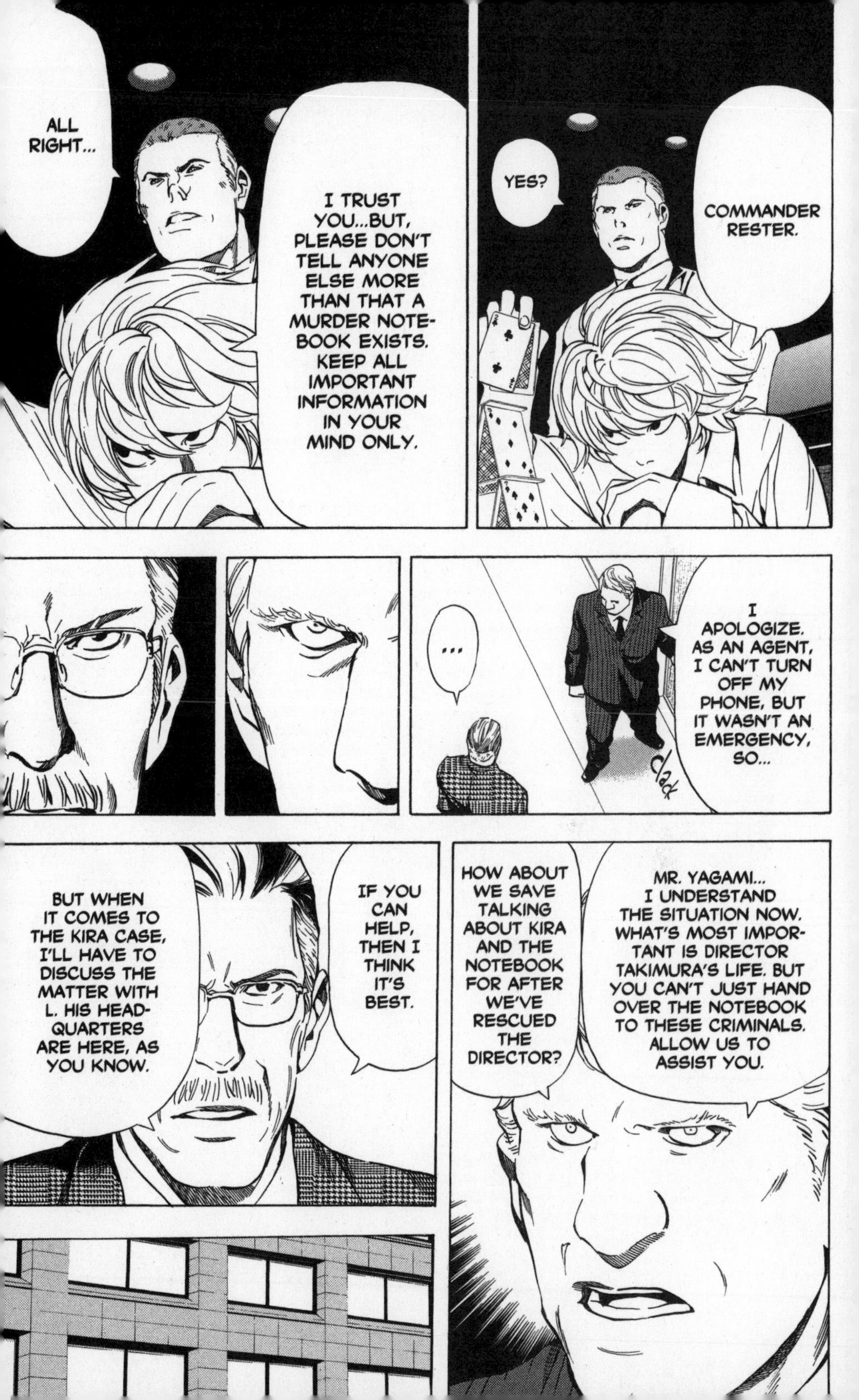

COMMANDER RESTER.
YES?
I TRUST YOU...BUT, PLEASE DON'T TELL ANYONE ELSE MORE THAN THAT A MURDER NOTE-BOOK EXISTS. KEEP ALL IMPORTANT INFORMATION IN YOUR MIND ONLY.
ALL RIGHT...
I APOLOGIZE. AS AN AGENT, I CAN'T TURN OFF MY PHONE, BUT IT WASN'T AN EMERGENCY, SO...
clack
...
MR. YAGAMI... I UNDERSTAND THE SITUATION NOW. WHAT'S MOST IMPOR-TANT IS DIRECTOR TAKIMURA'S LIFE. BUT YOU CAN'T JUST HAND OVER THE NOTEBOOK TO THESE CRIMINALS. ALLOW US TO ASSIST YOU.
HOW ABOUT WE SAVE TALKING ABOUT KIRA AND THE NOTEBOOK FOR AFTER WE'VE RESCUED THE DIRECTOR?
IF YOU CAN HELP, THEN I THINK IT'S BEST.
BUT WHEN IT COMES TO THE KIRA CASE, I'LL HAVE TO DISCUSS THE MATTER WITH L. HIS HEAD-QUARTERS ARE HERE, AS YOU KNOW.

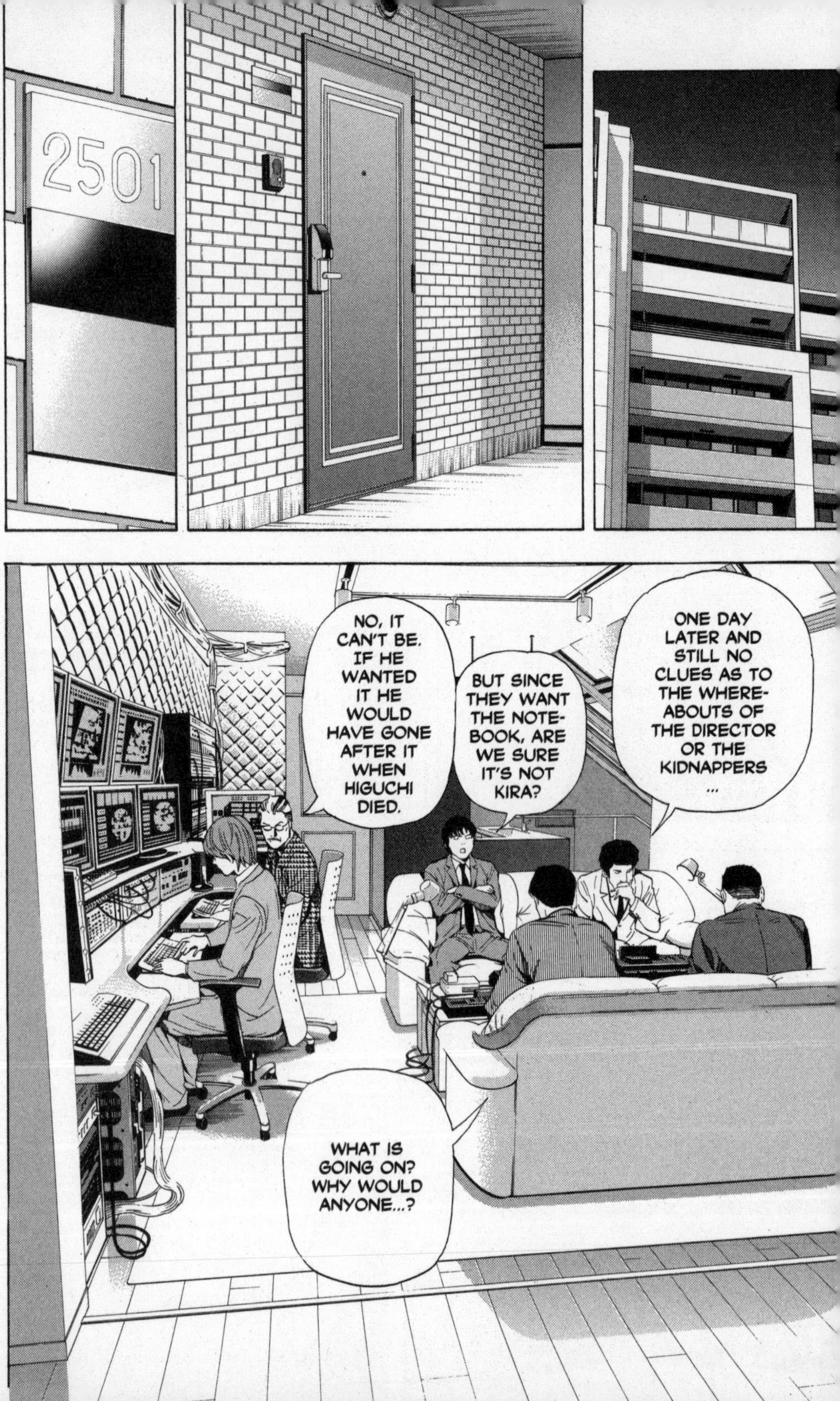
2501
ONE DAY LATER AND STILL NO CLUES AS TO THE WHEREABOUTS OF THE DIRECTOR OR THE KIDNAPPERS...
BUT SINCE THEY WANT THE NOTEBOOK, ARE WE SURE IT'S NOT KIRA?
NO, IT CAN'T BE. IF HE WANTED IT HE WOULD HAVE GONE AFTER IT WHEN HIGUCHI DIED.
WHAT IS GOING ON? WHY WOULD ANYONE...?

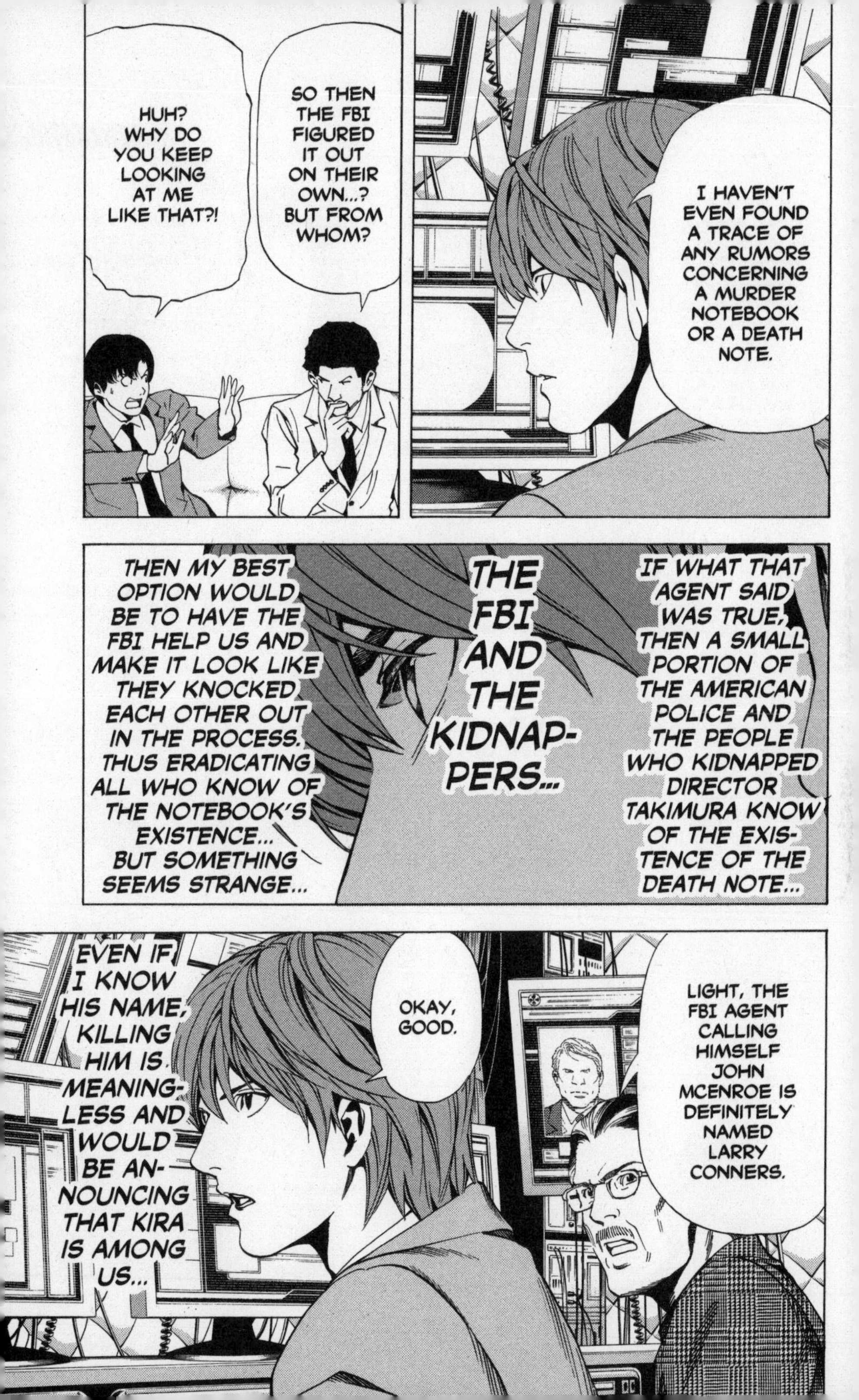
I HAVEN'T EVEN FOUND A TRACE OF ANY RUMORS CONCERNING A MURDER NOTEBOOK OR A DEATH NOTE.
SO THEN THE FBI FIGURED IT OUT ON THEIR OWN...? BUT FROM WHOM?
HUH? WHY DO YOU KEEP LOOKING AT ME LIKE THAT?!
IF WHAT THAT AGENT SAID WAS TRUE, THEN A SMALL PORTION OF THE AMERICAN POLICE AND THE PEOPLE WHO KIDNAPPED DIRECTOR TAKIMURA KNOW OF THE EXISTENCE OF THE DEATH NOTE...
THE FBI AND THE KIDNAPPERS...
THEN MY BEST OPTION WOULD BE TO HAVE THE FBI HELP US AND MAKE IT LOOK LIKE THEY KNOCKED EACH OTHER OUT IN THE PROCESS. THUS ERADICATING ALL WHO KNOW OF THE NOTEBOOK'S EXISTENCE... BUT SOMETHING SEEMS STRANGE...
LIGHT, THE FBI AGENT CALLING HIMSELF JOHN MCENROE IS DEFINITELY NAMED LARRY CONNERS.
OKAY, GOOD.
EVEN IF I KNOW HIS NAME, KILLING HIM IS MEANINGLESS AND WOULD BE ANNOUNCING THAT KIRA IS AMONG US...

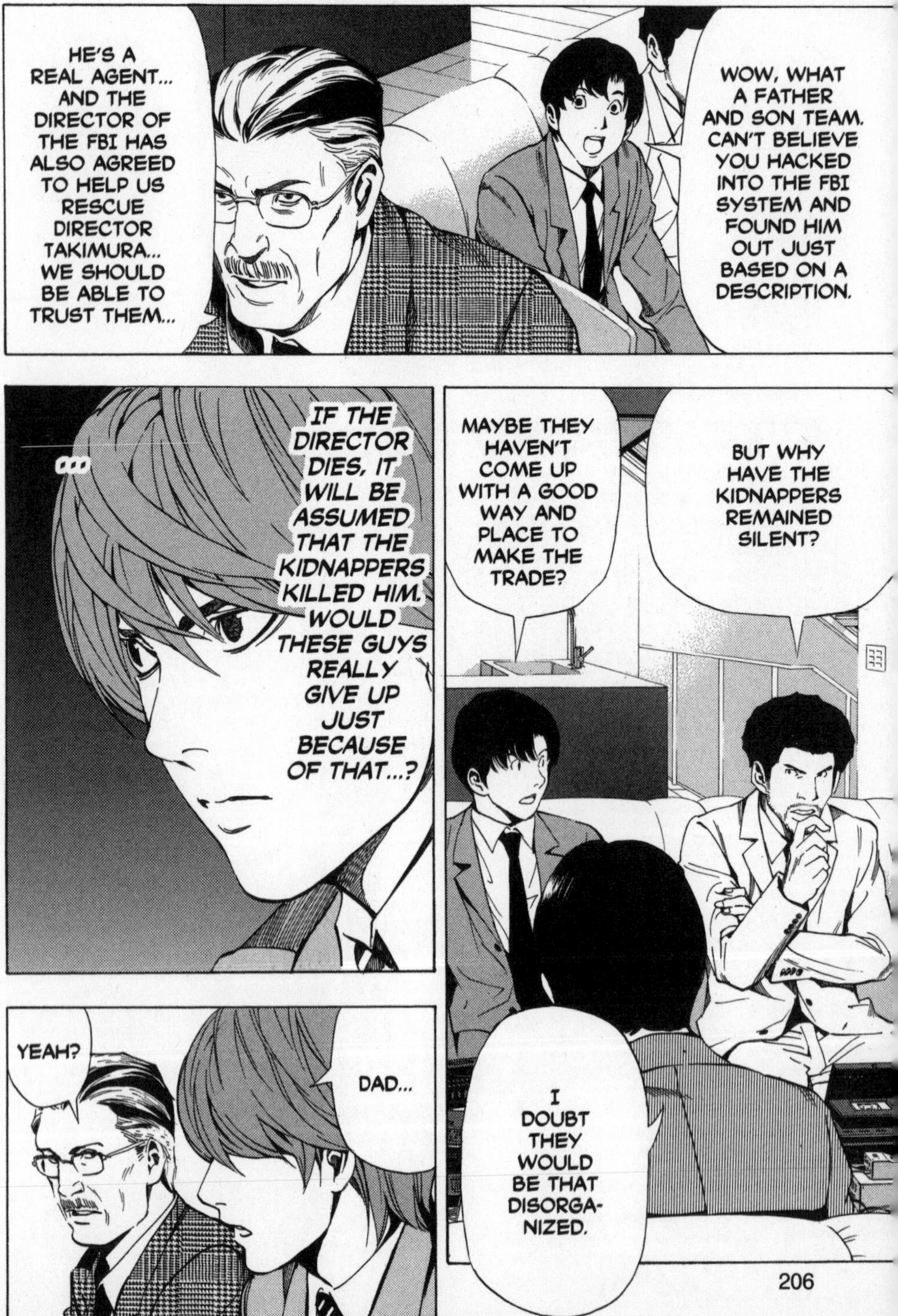
WOW, WHAT A FATHER AND SON TEAM. CAN'T BELIEVE YOU HACKED INTO THE FBI SYSTEM AND FOUND HIM OUT JUST BASED ON A DESCRIPTION.
HE'S A REAL AGENT... AND THE DIRECTOR OF THE FBI HAS ALSO AGREED TO HELP US RESCUE DIRECTOR TAKIMURA... WE SHOULD BE ABLE TO TRUST THEM...
BUT WHY HAVE THE KIDNAPPERS REMAINED SILENT?
MAYBE THEY HAVEN'T COME UP WITH A GOOD WAY AND PLACE TO MAKE THE TRADE?
I DOUBT THEY WOULD BE THAT DISORGANIZED.
IF THE DIRECTOR DIES, IT WILL BE ASSUMED THAT THE KIDNAPPERS KILLED HIM. WOULD THESE GUYS REALLY GIVE UP JUST BECAUSE OF THAT...?
...
DAD...
YEAH?

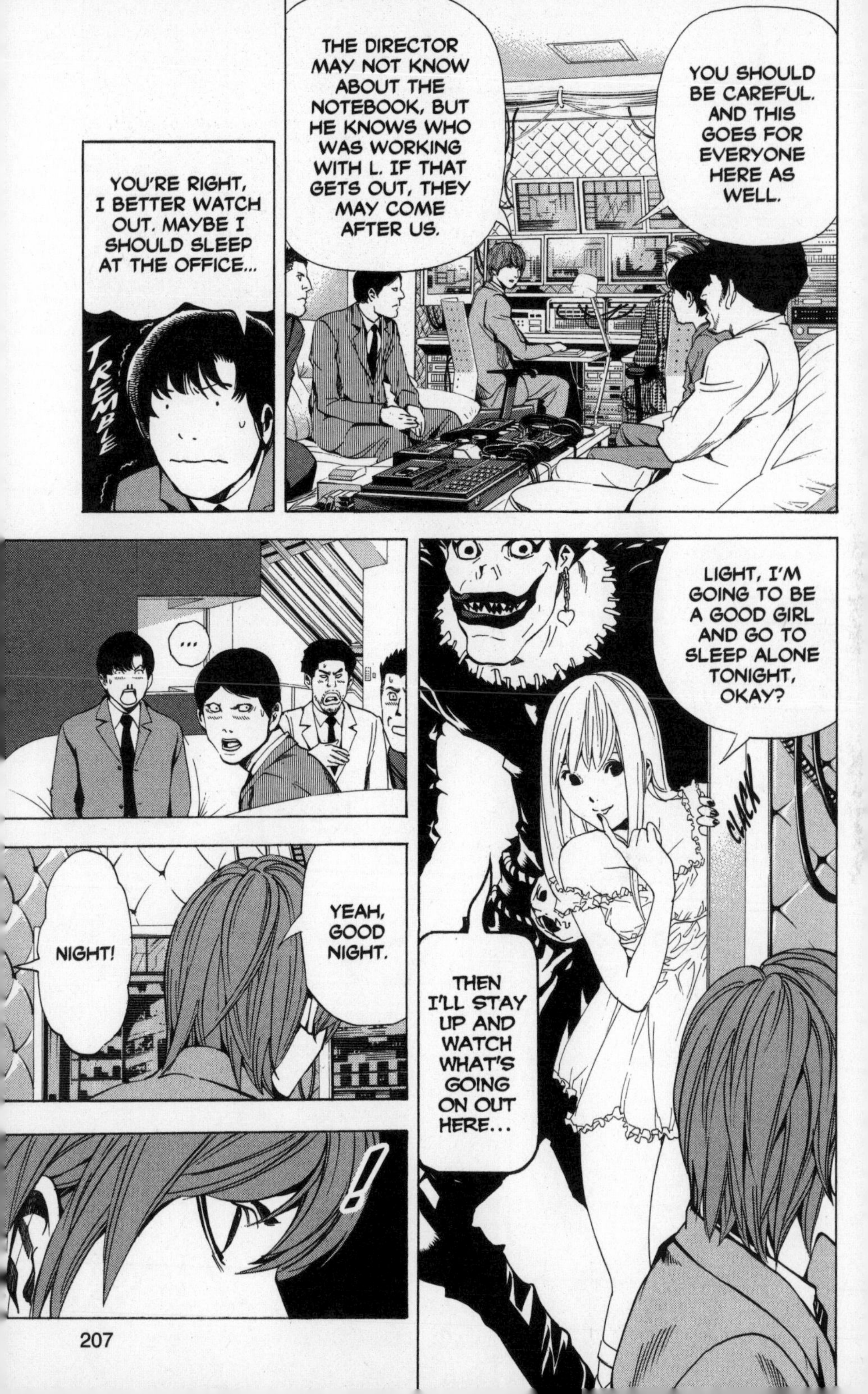
YOU SHOULD BE CAREFUL. AND THIS GOES FOR EVERYONE HERE AS WELL.
THE DIRECTOR MAY NOT KNOW ABOUT THE NOTEBOOK, BUT HE KNOWS WHO WAS WORKING WITH L. IF THAT GETS OUT, THEY MAY COME AFTER US.
YOU'RE RIGHT, I BETTER WATCH OUT. MAYBE I SHOULD SLEEP AT THE OFFICE...
TREMBLE
LIGHT, I'M GOING TO BE A GOOD GIRL AND GO TO SLEEP ALONE TONIGHT, OKAY?
CLACK
THEN I'LL STAY UP AND WATCH WHAT'S GOING ON OUT HERE...
...
YEAH, GOOD NIGHT.
NIGHT!
!

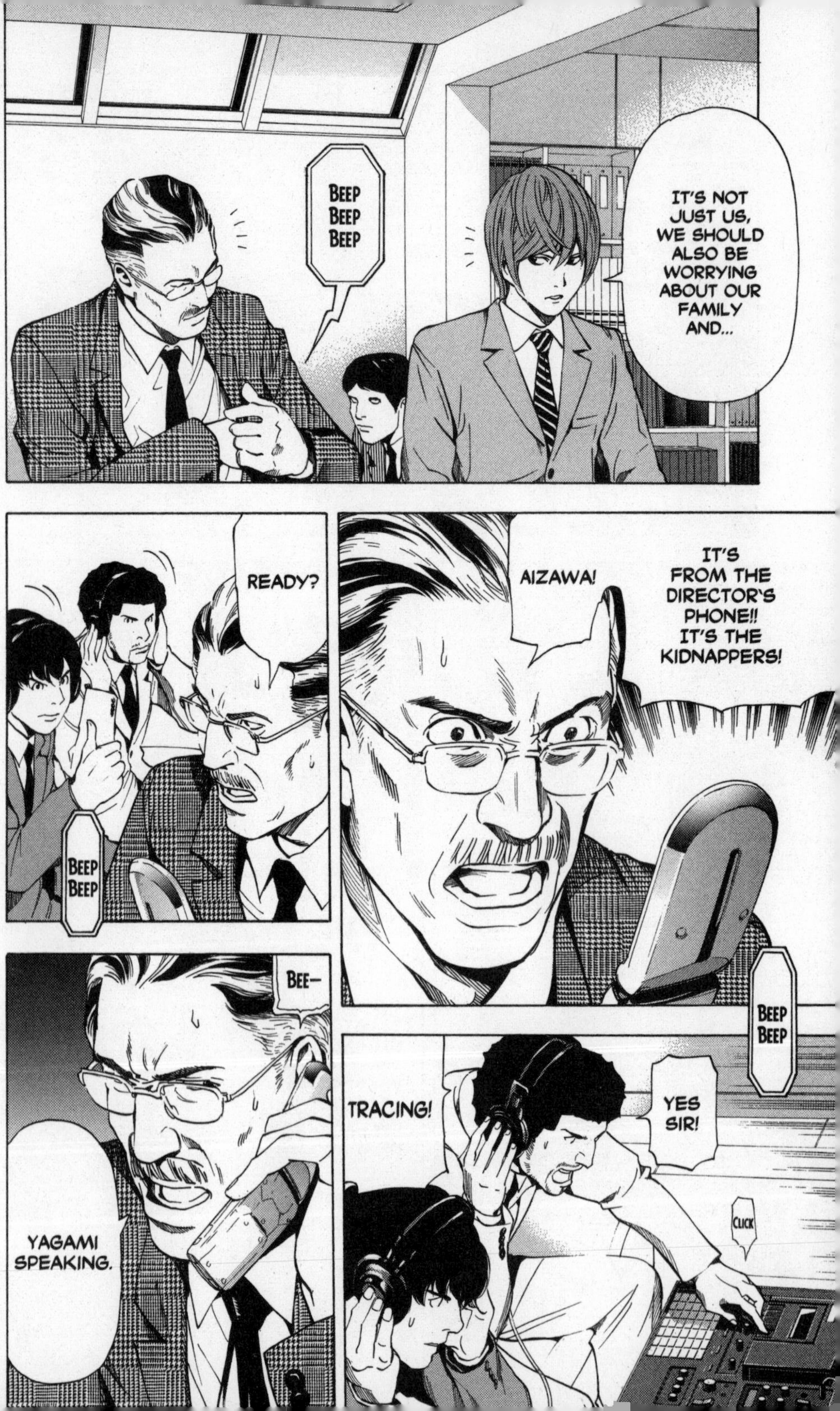
IT'S NOT JUST US, WE SHOULD ALSO BE WORRYING ABOUT OUR FAMILY AND...
BEEP BEEP BEEP
IT'S FROM THE DIRECTOR'S PHONE!! IT'S THE KIDNAPPERS!
AIZAWA!
READY?
BEEP BEEP
BEEP BEEP
YES SIR!
TRACING!
CLICK
BEE—
YAGAMI SPEAKING.

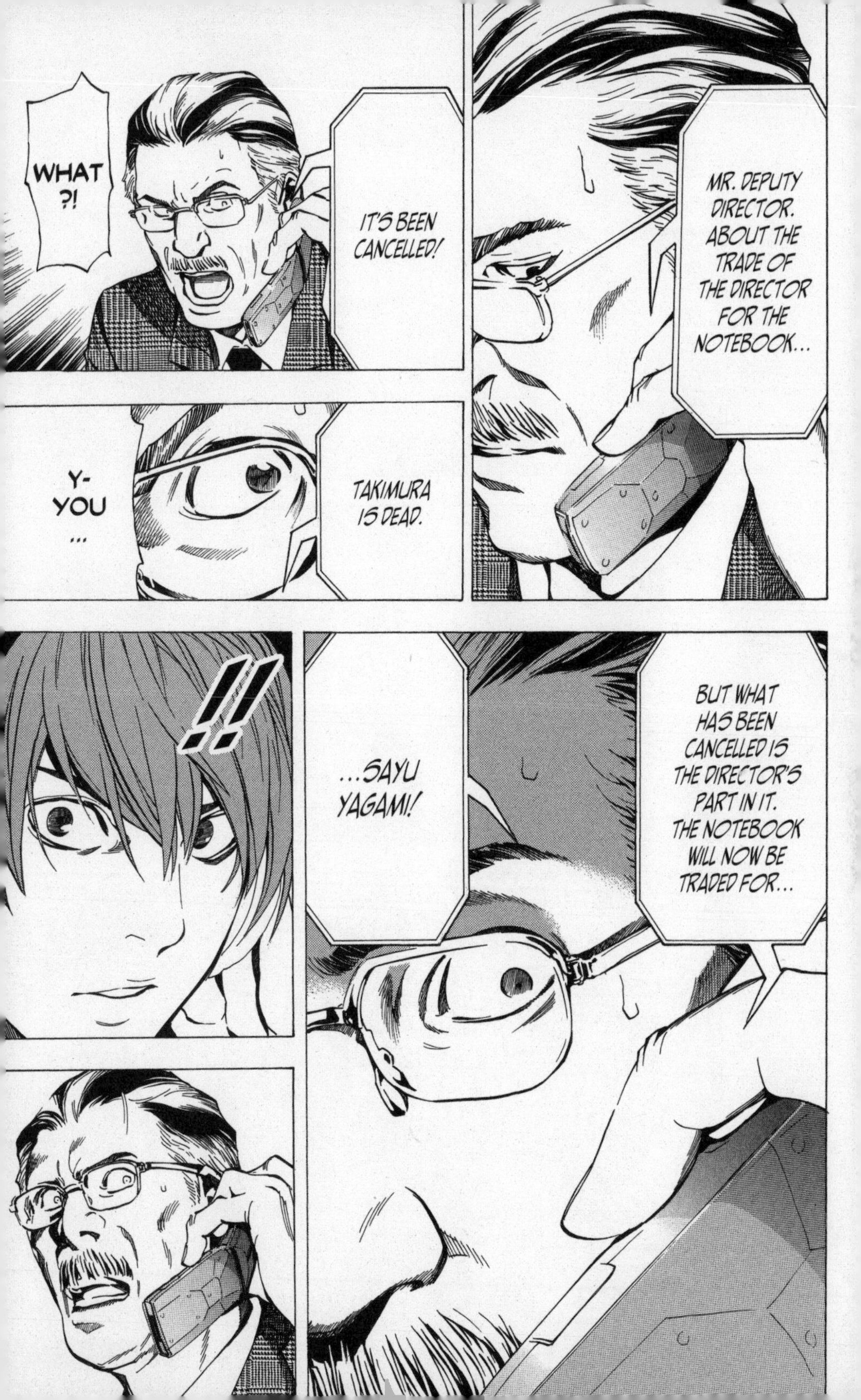
MR. DEPUTY DIRECTOR. ABOUT THE TRADE OF THE DIRECTOR FOR THE NOTEBOOK...
IT'S BEEN CANCELLED!
WHAT ?!
TAKIMURA IS DEAD.
Y- YOU ...
BUT WHAT HAS BEEN CANCELLED IS THE DIRECTOR'S PART IN IT. THE NOTEBOOK WILL NOW BE TRADED FOR...
...SAYU YAGAMI!
!!

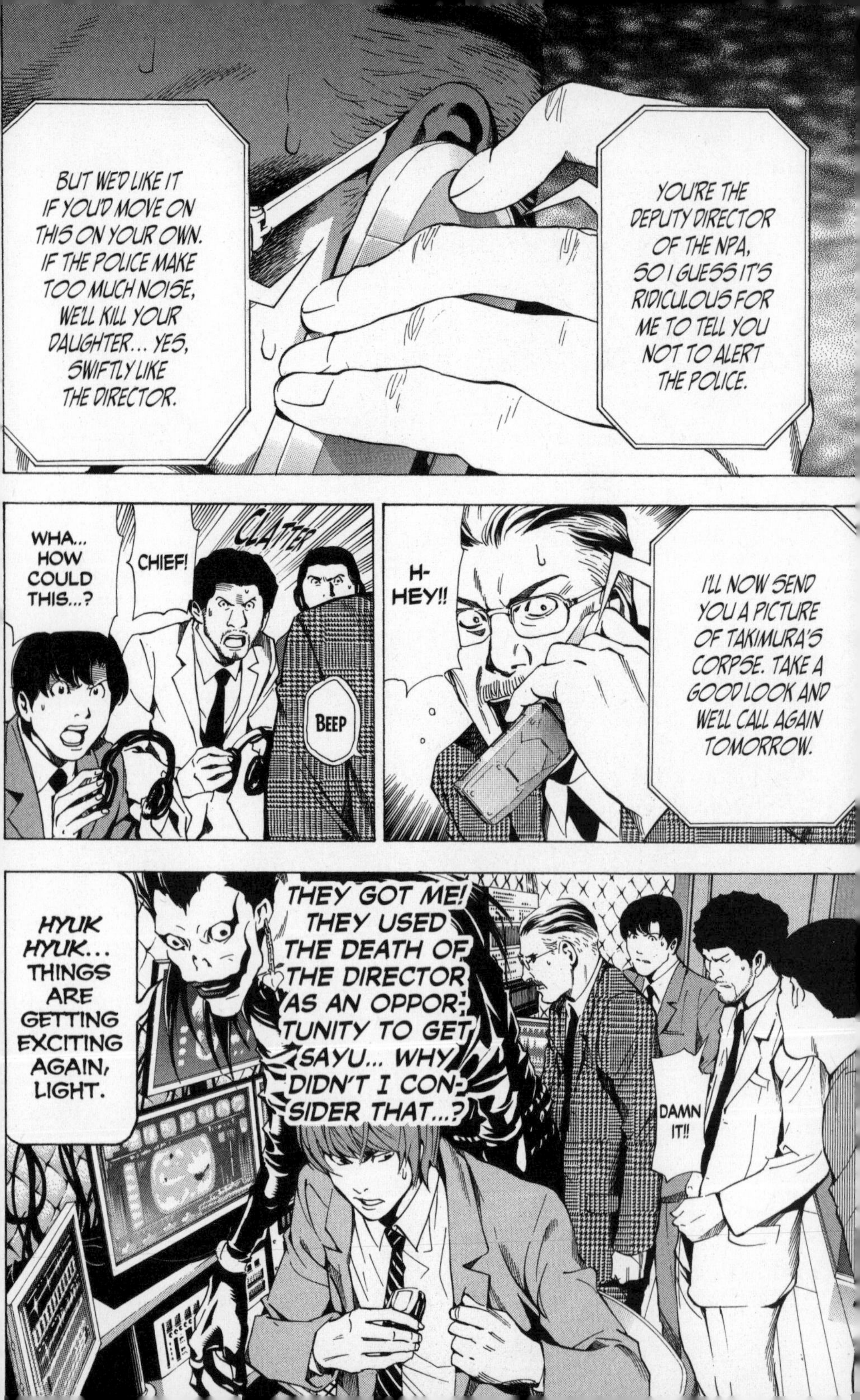
YOU'RE THE DEPUTY DIRECTOR OF THE NPA, SO I GUESS IT'S RIDICULOUS FOR ME TO TELL YOU NOT TO ALERT THE POLICE.
BUT WE'D LIKE IT IF YOU'D MOVE ON THIS ON YOUR OWN. IF THE POLICE MAKE TOO MUCH NOISE, WE'LL KILL YOUR DAUGHTER... YES, SWIFTLY LIKE THE DIRECTOR.
I'LL NOW SEND YOU A PICTURE OF TAKIMURA'S CORPSE. TAKE A GOOD LOOK AND WE'LL CALL AGAIN TOMORROW.
H-HEY!!
CLATTER
BEEP
CHIEF!
WHA... HOW COULD THIS...?
DAMN IT!!
THEY GOT ME! THEY USED THE DEATH OF THE DIRECTOR AS AN OPPORTUNITY TO GET SAYU... WHY DIDN'T I CONSIDER THAT...?
HYUK HYUK... THINGS ARE GETTING EXCITING AGAIN, LIGHT.

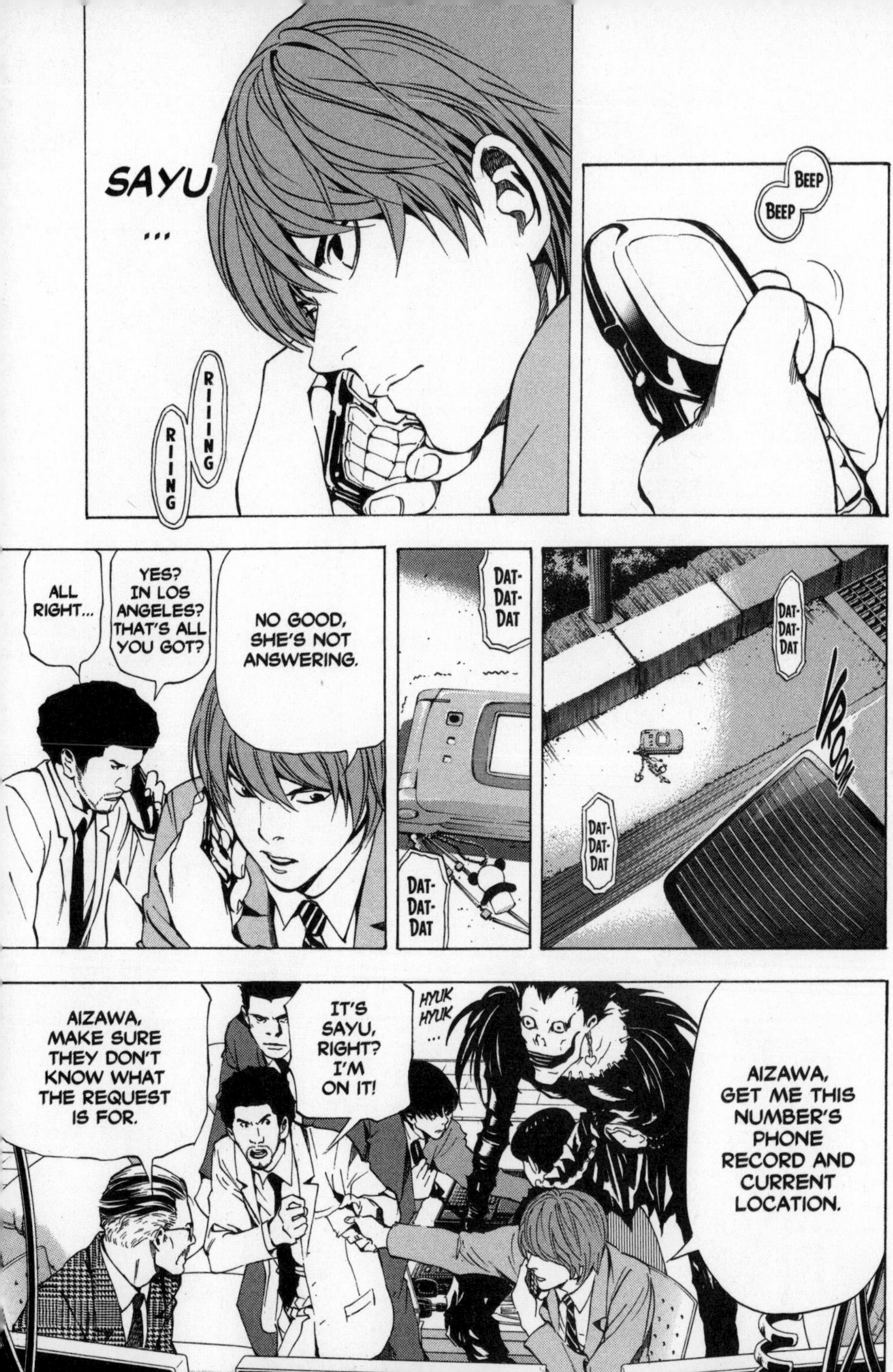
BEEP
BEEP
SAYU
...
RIIING
RIIING
DAT-DAT-DAT
VROOM
DAT-DAT-DAT
DAT-DAT-DAT
DAT-DAT-DAT
NO GOOD, SHE'S NOT ANSWERING.
YES? IN LOS ANGELES? THAT'S ALL YOU GOT?
ALL RIGHT...
AIZAWA, GET ME THIS NUMBER'S PHONE RECORD AND CURRENT LOCATION.
HYUK HYUK ...
IT'S SAYU, RIGHT? I'M ON IT!
AIZAWA, MAKE SURE THEY DON'T KNOW WHAT THE REQUEST IS FOR.

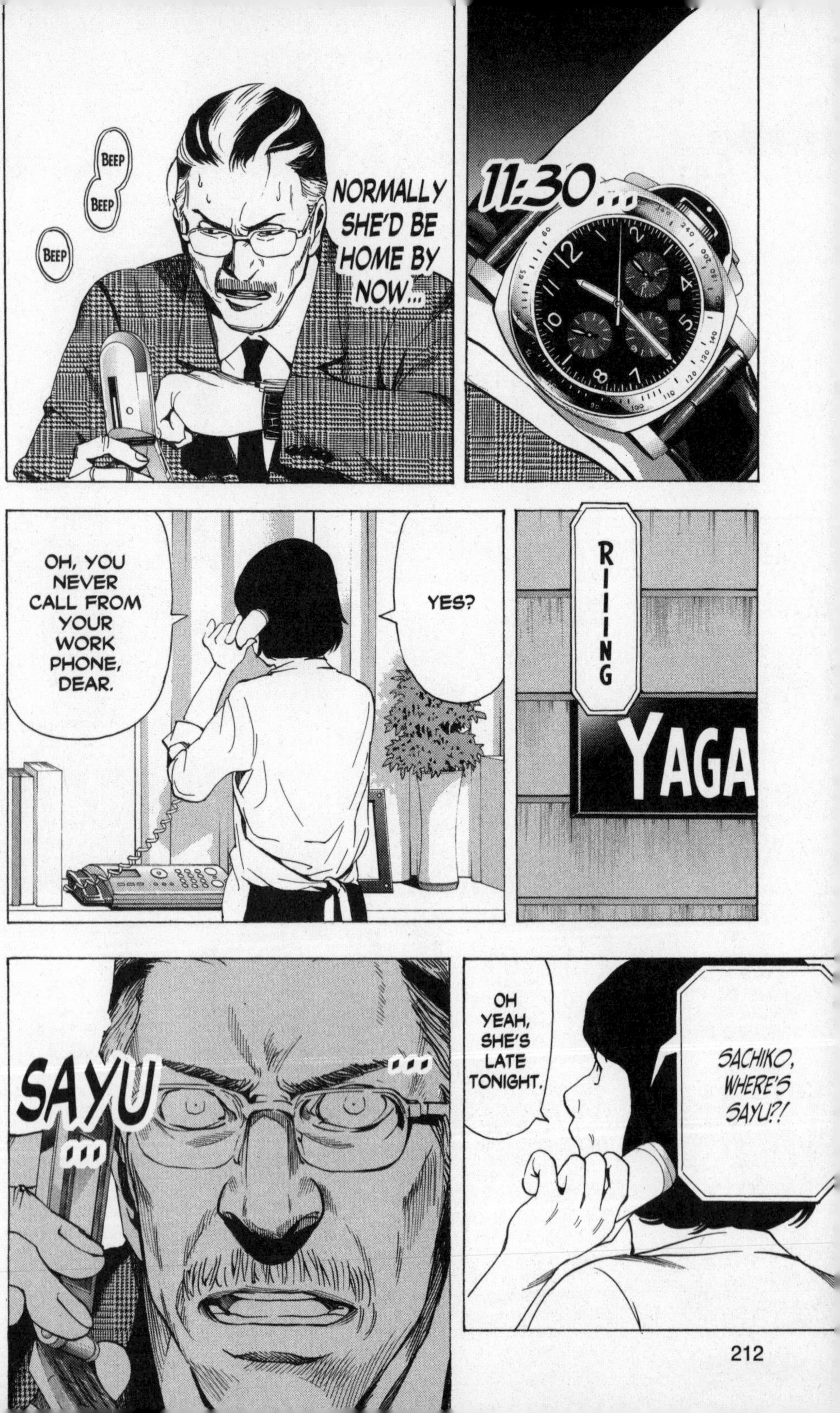
11:30...
NORMALLY SHE'D BE HOME BY NOW...
BEEP
BEEP
BEEP
RIIING
YAGA
YES?
OH, YOU NEVER CALL FROM YOUR WORK PHONE, DEAR.
SACHIKO, WHERE'S SAYU?!
OH YEAH, SHE'S LATE TONIGHT.
...
SAYU
...

# DEATH NOTE
## How to use it
## XLI

○ It is useless trying to erase names written in the DEATH NOTE with erasers or white-out.

デスノートに書いた名前・文字等を
消しゴム・インク消し・修正液等で消しても何の意味もなさない。

I recently moved and couldn't locate any of my art supplies.
Though for some reason I had origami paper, so that's where
I got the red for the apple in this picture.

-Tsugumi Ohba

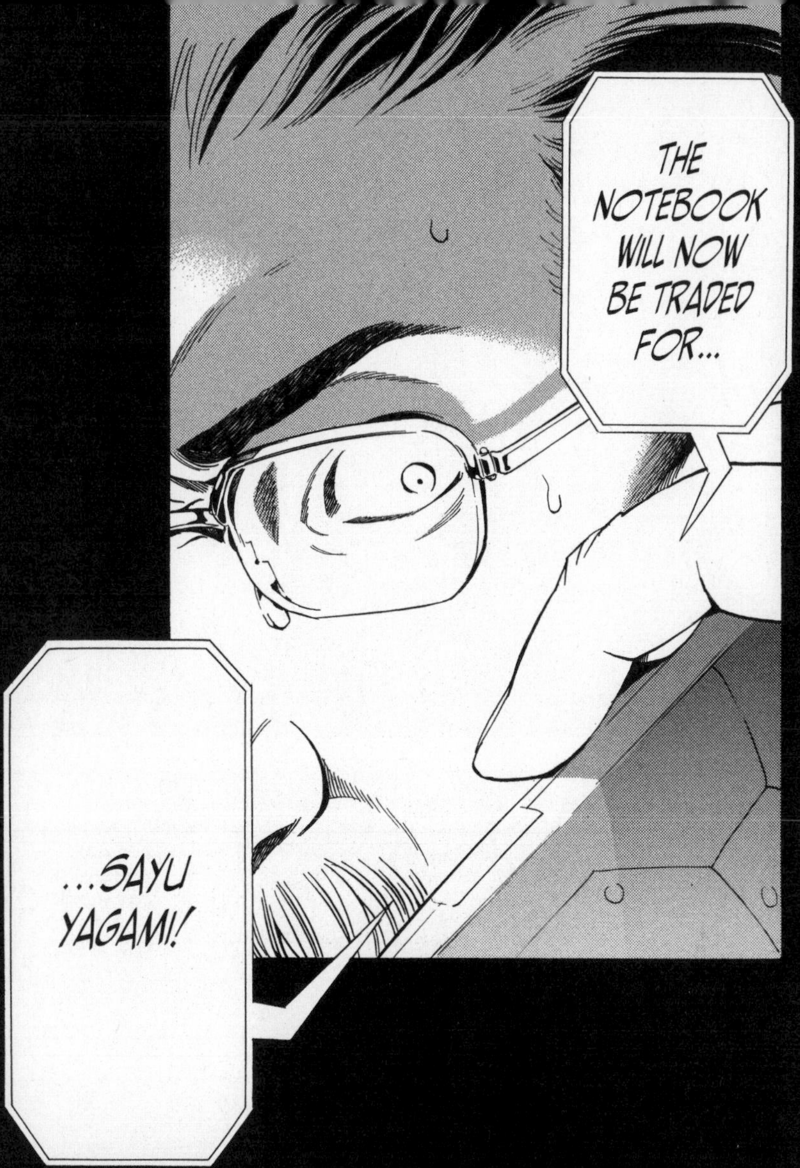
THE NOTEBOOK WILL NOW BE TRADED FOR...
...SAYU YAGAMI!

## chapter 62 Decision

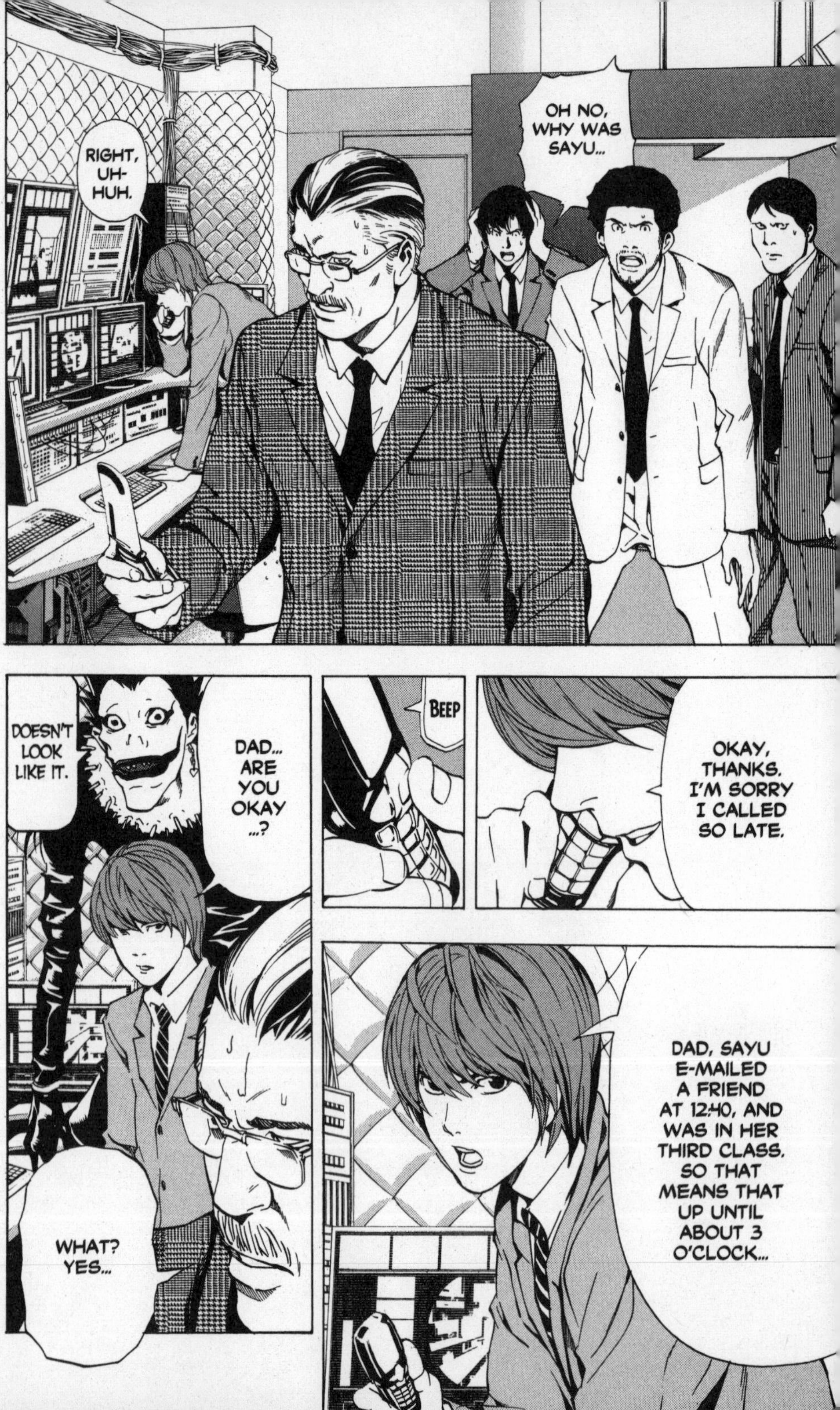
OH NO, WHY WAS SAYU...
RIGHT, UH-HUH.
OKAY, THANKS. I'M SORRY I CALLED SO LATE.
BEEP
DAD, SAYU E-MAILED A FRIEND AT 12:40, AND WAS IN HER THIRD CLASS. SO THAT MEANS THAT UP UNTIL ABOUT 3 O'CLOCK...
DAD... ARE YOU OKAY ...?
DOESN'T LOOK LIKE IT.
WHAT? YES...

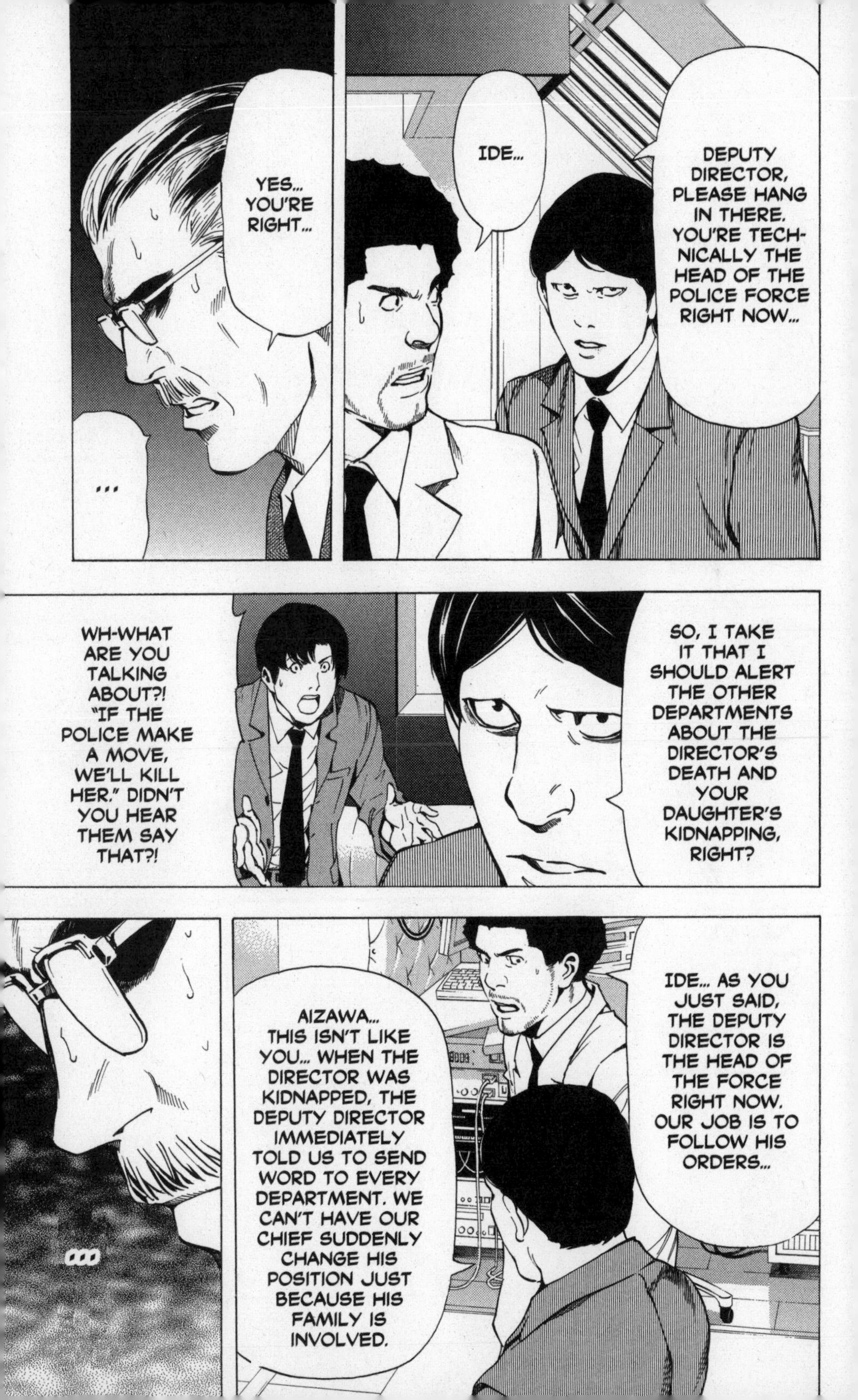
DEPUTY DIRECTOR, PLEASE HANG IN THERE. YOU'RE TECHNICALLY THE HEAD OF THE POLICE FORCE RIGHT NOW...
IDE...
YES... YOU'RE RIGHT...
...
SO, I TAKE IT THAT I SHOULD ALERT THE OTHER DEPARTMENTS ABOUT THE DIRECTOR'S DEATH AND YOUR DAUGHTER'S KIDNAPPING, RIGHT?
WH-WHAT ARE YOU TALKING ABOUT?! "IF THE POLICE MAKE A MOVE, WE'LL KILL HER." DIDN'T YOU HEAR THEM SAY THAT?!
IDE... AS YOU JUST SAID, THE DEPUTY DIRECTOR IS THE HEAD OF THE FORCE RIGHT NOW. OUR JOB IS TO FOLLOW HIS ORDERS...
AIZAWA... THIS ISN'T LIKE YOU... WHEN THE DIRECTOR WAS KIDNAPPED, THE DEPUTY DIRECTOR IMMEDIATELY TOLD US TO SEND WORD TO EVERY DEPARTMENT. WE CAN'T HAVE OUR CHIEF SUDDENLY CHANGE HIS POSITION JUST BECAUSE HIS FAMILY IS INVOLVED.
...

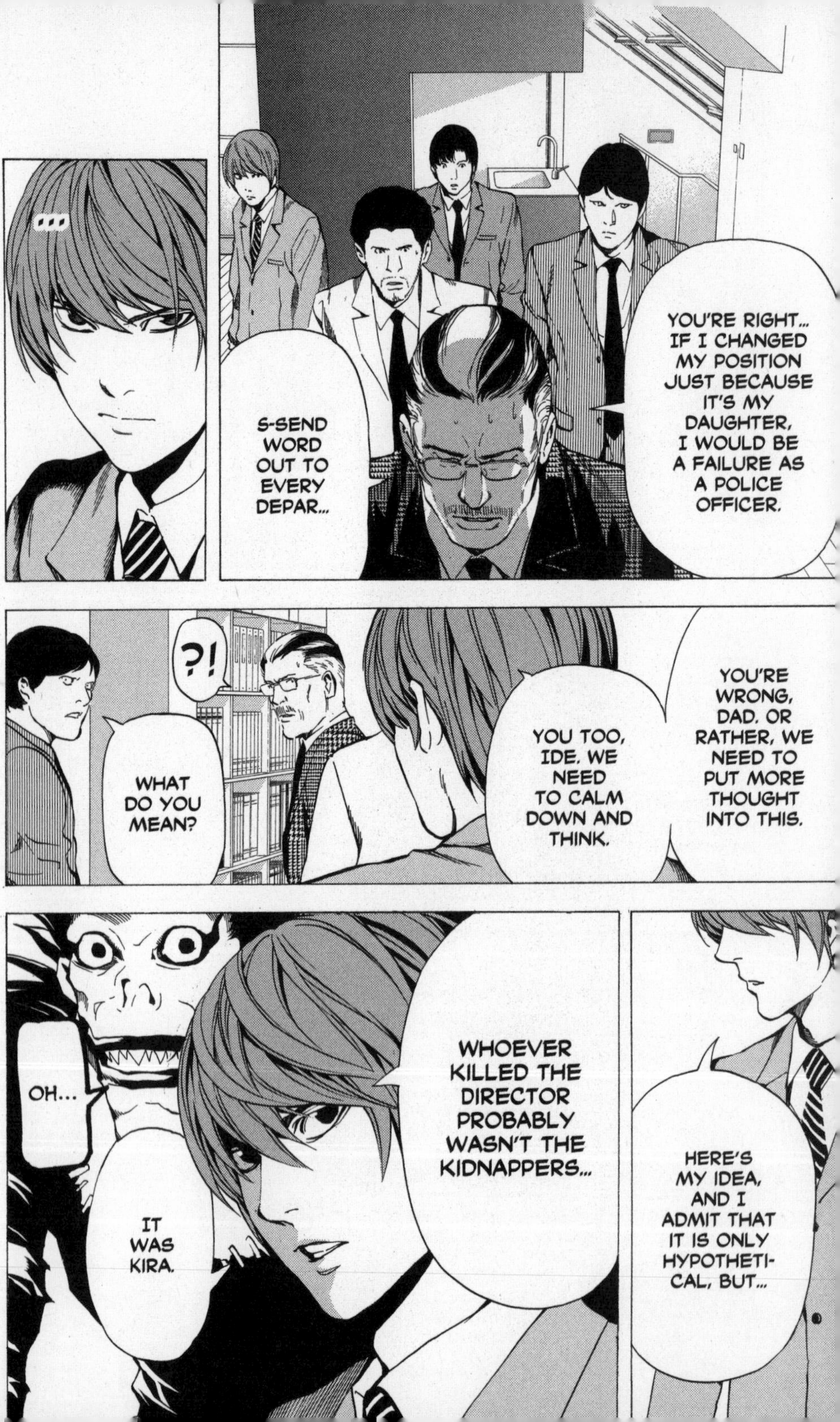
YOU'RE RIGHT... IF I CHANGED MY POSITION JUST BECAUSE IT'S MY DAUGHTER, I WOULD BE A FAILURE AS A POLICE OFFICER.
S-SEND WORD OUT TO EVERY DEPAR...
...
YOU'RE WRONG, DAD. OR RATHER, WE NEED TO PUT MORE THOUGHT INTO THIS.
YOU TOO, IDE. WE NEED TO CALM DOWN AND THINK.
?!
WHAT DO YOU MEAN?
HERE'S MY IDEA, AND I ADMIT THAT IT IS ONLY HYPOTHETICAL, BUT...
WHOEVER KILLED THE DIRECTOR PROBABLY WASN'T THE KIDNAPPERS...
OH...
IT WAS KIRA.

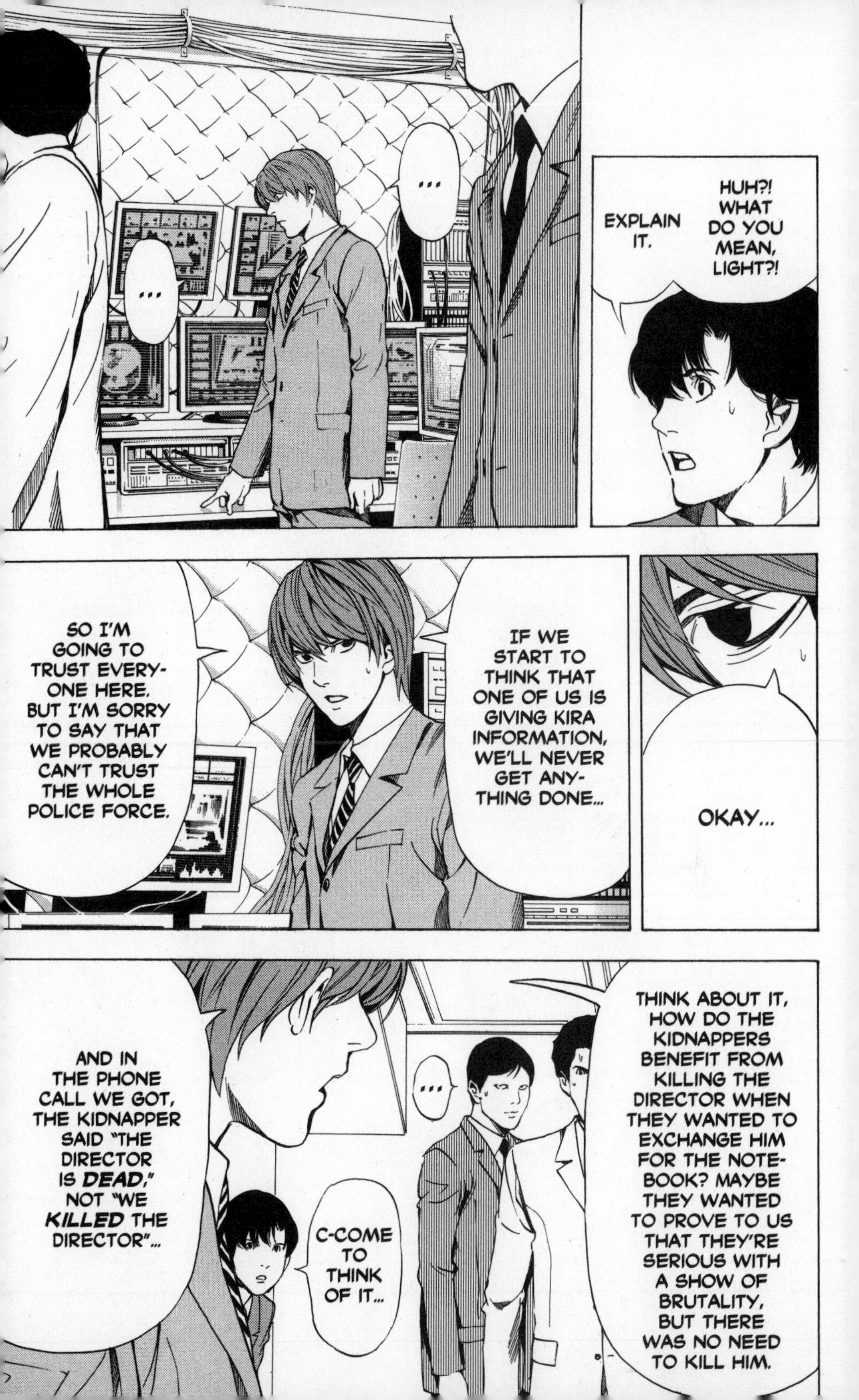
HUH?! WHAT DO YOU MEAN, LIGHT?!
EXPLAIN IT.
...
...
OKAY...
IF WE START TO THINK THAT ONE OF US IS GIVING KIRA INFORMATION, WE'LL NEVER GET ANY-THING DONE...
SO I'M GOING TO TRUST EVERY-ONE HERE. BUT I'M SORRY TO SAY THAT WE PROBABLY CAN'T TRUST THE WHOLE POLICE FORCE.
THINK ABOUT IT, HOW DO THE KIDNAPPERS BENEFIT FROM KILLING THE DIRECTOR WHEN THEY WANTED TO EXCHANGE HIM FOR THE NOTE-BOOK? MAYBE THEY WANTED TO PROVE TO US THAT THEY'RE SERIOUS WITH A SHOW OF BRUTALITY, BUT THERE WAS NO NEED TO KILL HIM.
AND IN THE PHONE CALL WE GOT, THE KIDNAPPER SAID "THE DIRECTOR IS *DEAD*," NOT "WE *KILLED* THE DIRECTOR"...
...
C-COME TO THINK OF IT...

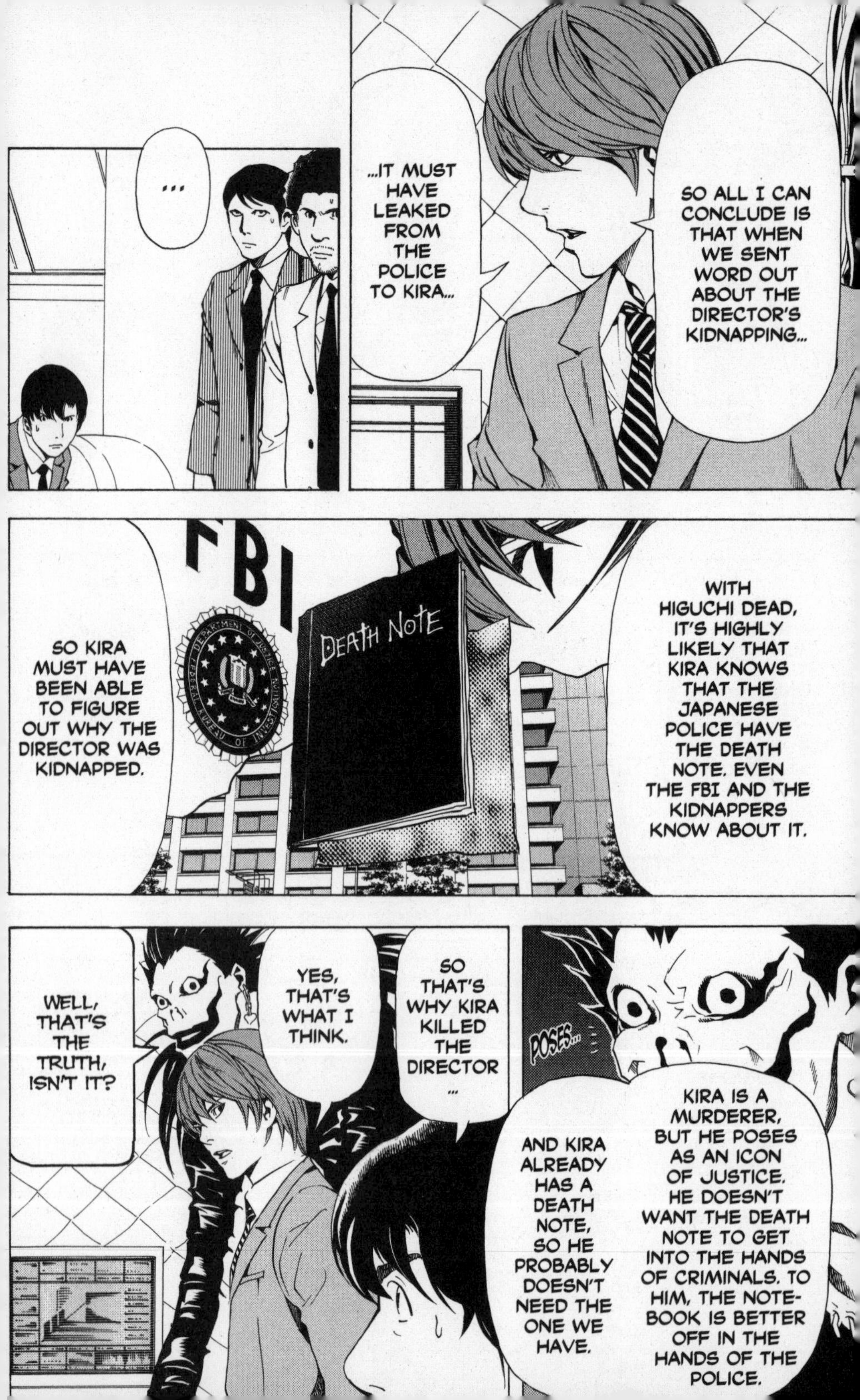
SO ALL I CAN CONCLUDE IS THAT WHEN WE SENT WORD OUT ABOUT THE DIRECTOR'S KIDNAPPING...
...IT MUST HAVE LEAKED FROM THE POLICE TO KIRA...
...
WITH HIGUCHI DEAD, IT'S HIGHLY LIKELY THAT KIRA KNOWS THAT THE JAPANESE POLICE HAVE THE DEATH NOTE. EVEN THE FBI AND THE KIDNAPPERS KNOW ABOUT IT.
DEATH NOTE
FBI
SO KIRA MUST HAVE BEEN ABLE TO FIGURE OUT WHY THE DIRECTOR WAS KIDNAPPED.
POSES...
KIRA IS A MURDERER, BUT HE POSES AS AN ICON OF JUSTICE. HE DOESN'T WANT THE DEATH NOTE TO GET INTO THE HANDS OF CRIMINALS. TO HIM, THE NOTE-BOOK IS BETTER OFF IN THE HANDS OF THE POLICE.
AND KIRA ALREADY HAS A DEATH NOTE, SO HE PROBABLY DOESN'T NEED THE ONE WE HAVE.
SO THAT'S WHY KIRA KILLED THE DIRECTOR...
YES, THAT'S WHAT I THINK.
WELL, THAT'S THE TRUTH, ISN'T IT?

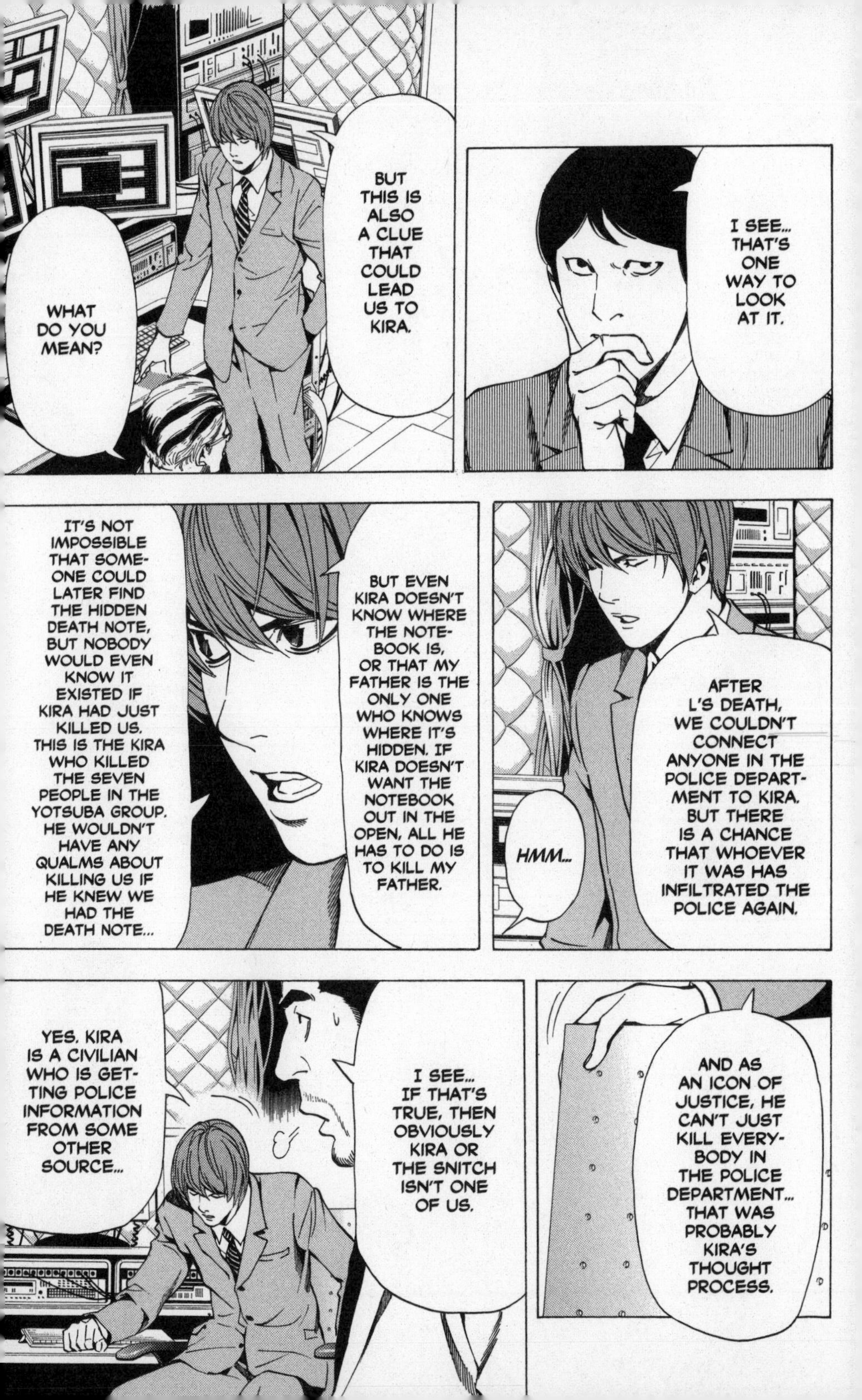
I SEE... THAT'S ONE WAY TO LOOK AT IT.
BUT THIS IS ALSO A CLUE THAT COULD LEAD US TO KIRA.
WHAT DO YOU MEAN?
AFTER L'S DEATH, WE COULDN'T CONNECT ANYONE IN THE POLICE DEPARTMENT TO KIRA. BUT THERE IS A CHANCE THAT WHOEVER IT WAS HAS INFILTRATED THE POLICE AGAIN.
HMM...
BUT EVEN KIRA DOESN'T KNOW WHERE THE NOTEBOOK IS, OR THAT MY FATHER IS THE ONLY ONE WHO KNOWS WHERE IT'S HIDDEN. IF KIRA DOESN'T WANT THE NOTEBOOK OUT IN THE OPEN, ALL HE HAS TO DO IS TO KILL MY FATHER.
IT'S NOT IMPOSSIBLE THAT SOMEONE COULD LATER FIND THE HIDDEN DEATH NOTE, BUT NOBODY WOULD EVEN KNOW IT EXISTED IF KIRA HAD JUST KILLED US. THIS IS THE KIRA WHO KILLED THE SEVEN PEOPLE IN THE YOTSUBA GROUP. HE WOULDN'T HAVE ANY QUALMS ABOUT KILLING US IF HE KNEW WE HAD THE DEATH NOTE...
AND AS AN ICON OF JUSTICE, HE CAN'T JUST KILL EVERYBODY IN THE POLICE DEPARTMENT... THAT WAS PROBABLY KIRA'S THOUGHT PROCESS.
I SEE... IF THAT'S TRUE, THEN OBVIOUSLY KIRA OR THE SNITCH ISN'T ONE OF US.
YES. KIRA IS A CIVILIAN WHO IS GETTING POLICE INFORMATION FROM SOME OTHER SOURCE...

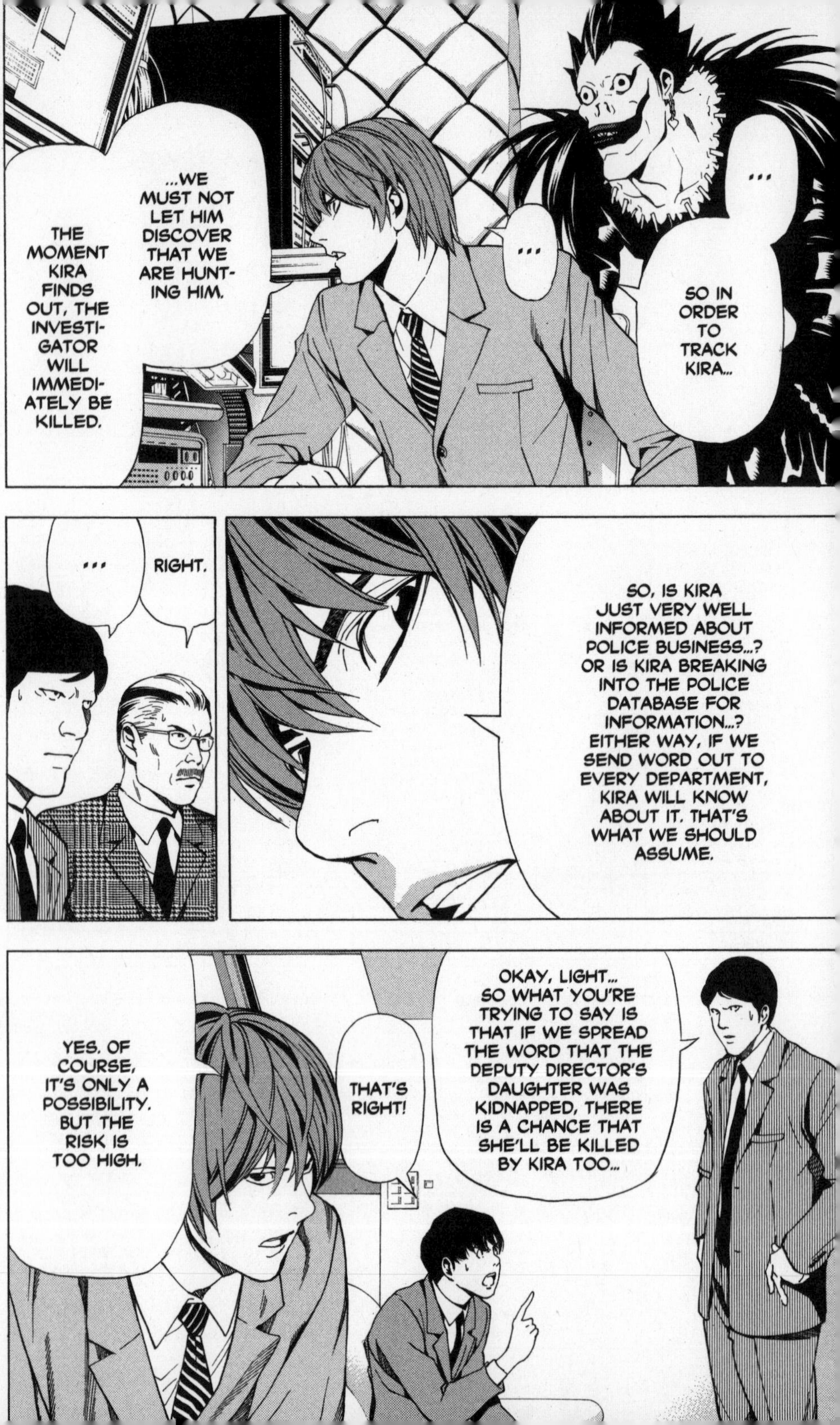

...
SO IN ORDER TO TRACK KIRA...
...
...WE MUST NOT LET HIM DISCOVER THAT WE ARE HUNTING HIM.
THE MOMENT KIRA FINDS OUT, THE INVESTIGATOR WILL IMMEDIATELY BE KILLED.
SO, IS KIRA JUST VERY WELL INFORMED ABOUT POLICE BUSINESS...? OR IS KIRA BREAKING INTO THE POLICE DATABASE FOR INFORMATION...? EITHER WAY, IF WE SEND WORD OUT TO EVERY DEPARTMENT, KIRA WILL KNOW ABOUT IT. THAT'S WHAT WE SHOULD ASSUME.
RIGHT.
...
OKAY, LIGHT... SO WHAT YOU'RE TRYING TO SAY IS THAT IF WE SPREAD THE WORD THAT THE DEPUTY DIRECTOR'S DAUGHTER WAS KIDNAPPED, THERE IS A CHANCE THAT SHE'LL BE KILLED BY KIRA TOO...
THAT'S RIGHT!
YES. OF COURSE, IT'S ONLY A POSSIBILITY. BUT THE RISK IS TOO HIGH.

READ THIS WAY

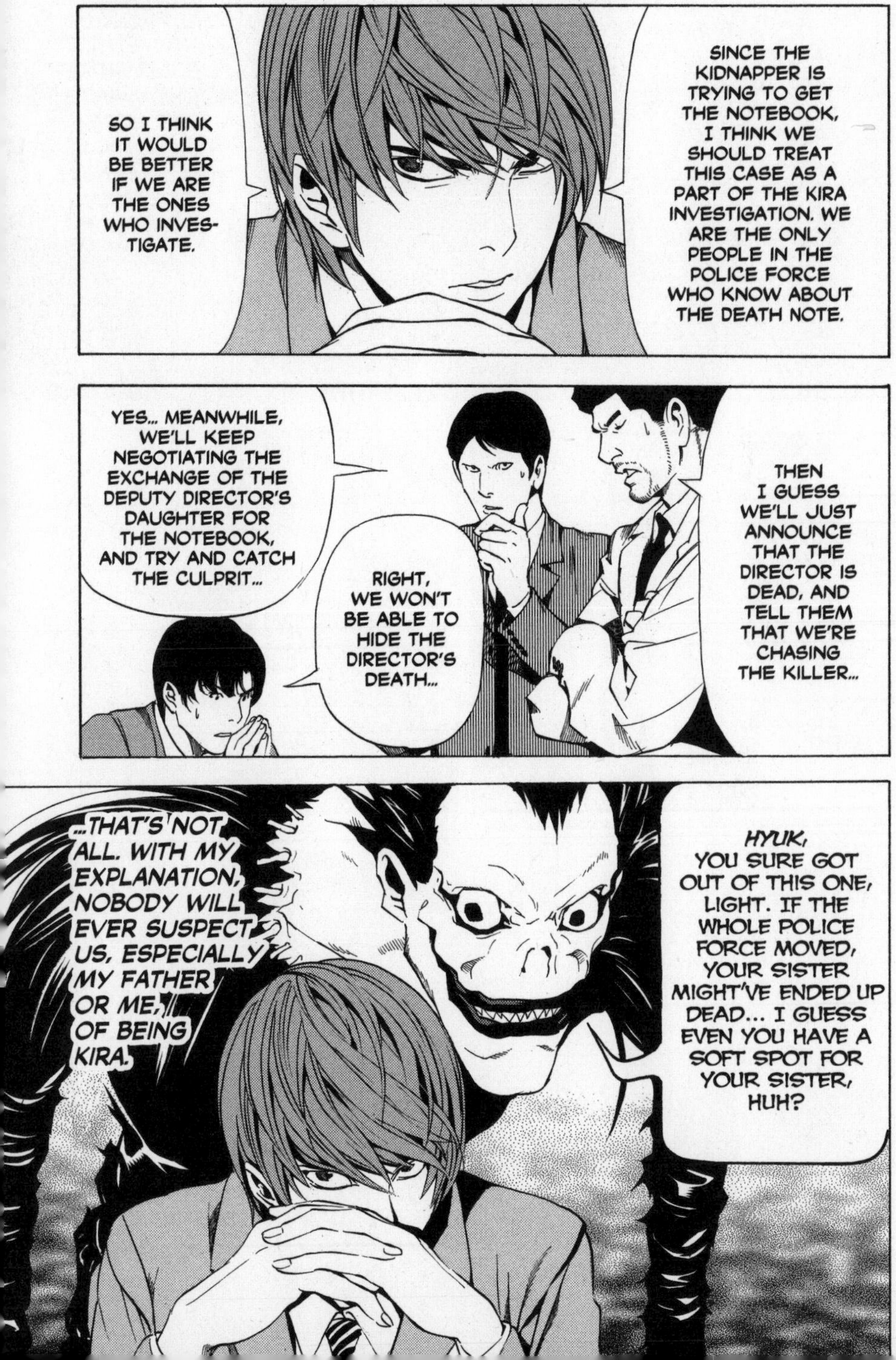

SINCE THE KIDNAPPER IS TRYING TO GET THE NOTEBOOK, I THINK WE SHOULD TREAT THIS CASE AS A PART OF THE KIRA INVESTIGATION. WE ARE THE ONLY PEOPLE IN THE POLICE FORCE WHO KNOW ABOUT THE DEATH NOTE.
SO I THINK IT WOULD BE BETTER IF WE ARE THE ONES WHO INVES-TIGATE.
THEN I GUESS WE'LL JUST ANNOUNCE THAT THE DIRECTOR IS DEAD, AND TELL THEM THAT WE'RE CHASING THE KILLER...
RIGHT, WE WON'T BE ABLE TO HIDE THE DIRECTOR'S DEATH...
YES... MEANWHILE, WE'LL KEEP NEGOTIATING THE EXCHANGE OF THE DEPUTY DIRECTOR'S DAUGHTER FOR THE NOTEBOOK, AND TRY AND CATCH THE CULPRIT...
*HYUK,* YOU SURE GOT OUT OF THIS ONE, LIGHT. IF THE WHOLE POLICE FORCE MOVED, YOUR SISTER MIGHT'VE ENDED UP DEAD... I GUESS EVEN YOU HAVE A SOFT SPOT FOR YOUR SISTER, HUH?
...THAT'S NOT ALL. WITH MY EXPLANATION, NOBODY WILL EVER SUSPECT US, ESPECIALLY MY FATHER OR ME, OF BEING KIRA.

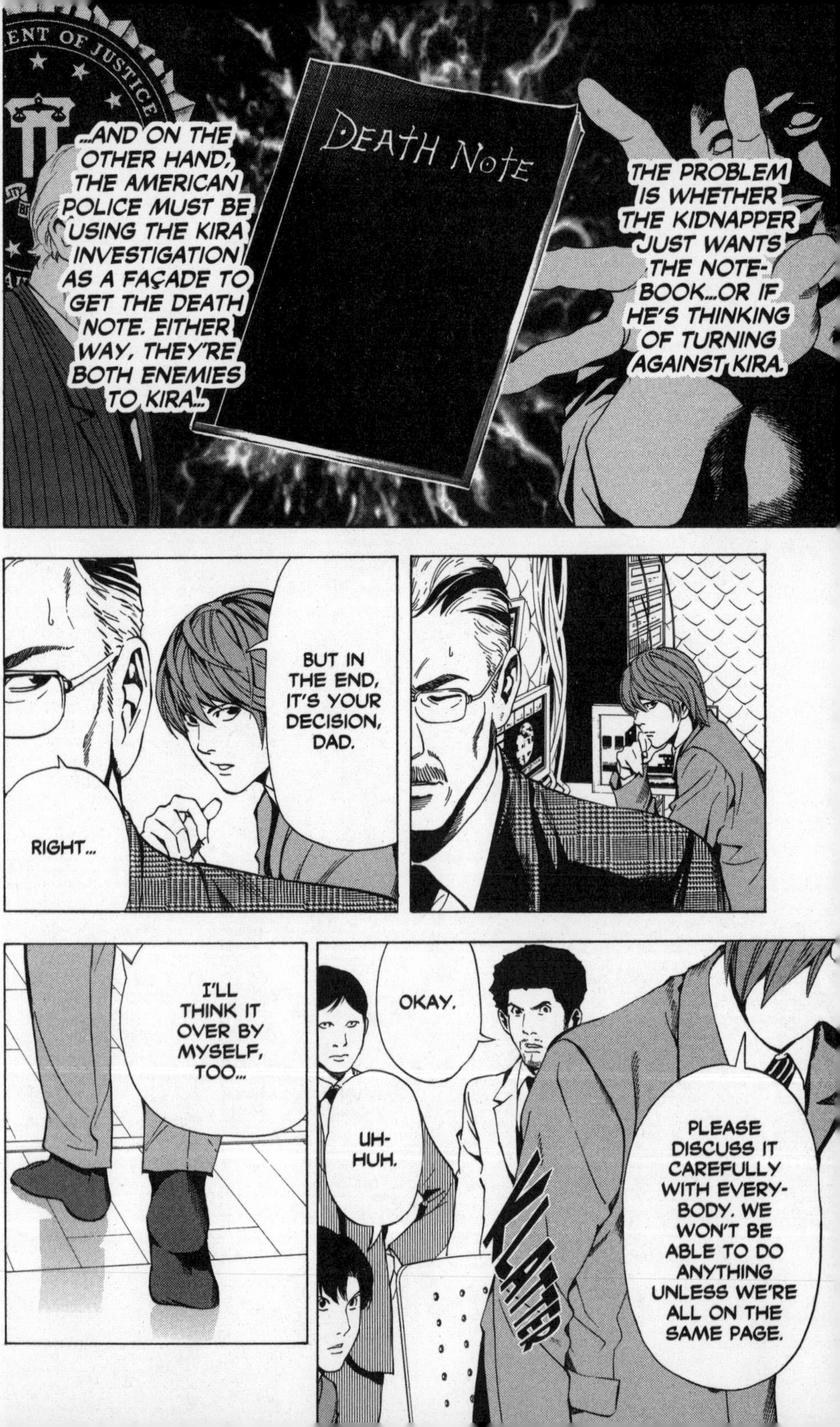

DEATH NOTE
THE PROBLEM IS WHETHER THE KIDNAPPER JUST WANTS THE NOTE-BOOK...OR IF HE'S THINKING OF TURNING AGAINST KIRA.
...AND ON THE OTHER HAND, THE AMERICAN POLICE MUST BE USING THE KIRA INVESTIGATION AS A FAÇADE TO GET THE DEATH NOTE. EITHER WAY, THEY'RE BOTH ENEMIES TO KIRA!...
BUT IN THE END, IT'S YOUR DECISION, DAD.
RIGHT...
PLEASE DISCUSS IT CAREFULLY WITH EVERY-BODY. WE WON'T BE ABLE TO DO ANYTHING UNLESS WE'RE ALL ON THE SAME PAGE.
KLATTER
OKAY.
UH-HUH.
I'LL THINK IT OVER BY MYSELF, TOO...

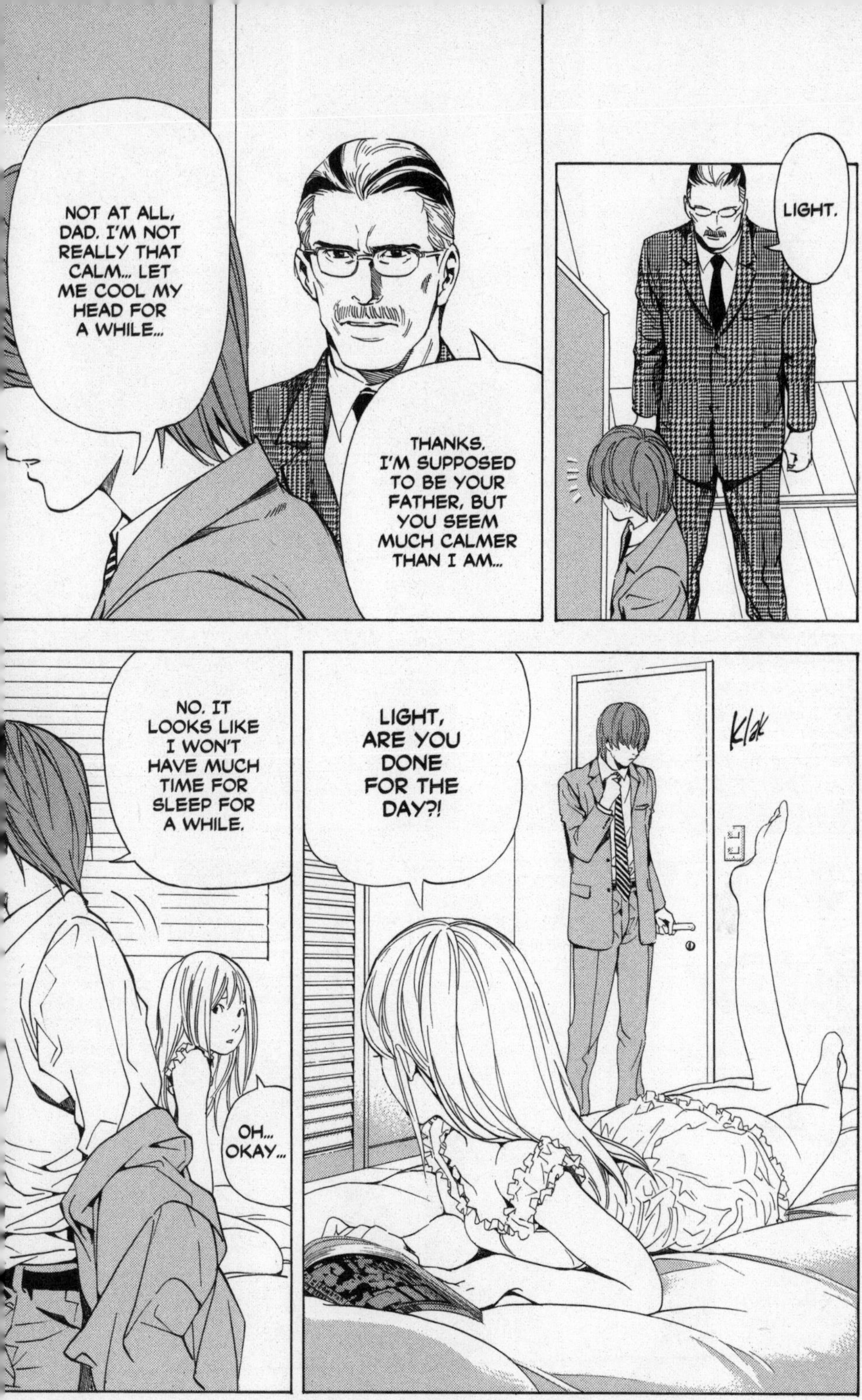
LIGHT.
THANKS. I'M SUPPOSED TO BE YOUR FATHER, BUT YOU SEEM MUCH CALMER THAN I AM...
NOT AT ALL, DAD. I'M NOT REALLY THAT CALM... LET ME COOL MY HEAD FOR A WHILE...
Klak
LIGHT, ARE YOU DONE FOR THE DAY?!
NO. IT LOOKS LIKE I WON'T HAVE MUCH TIME FOR SLEEP FOR A WHILE.
OH... OKAY...

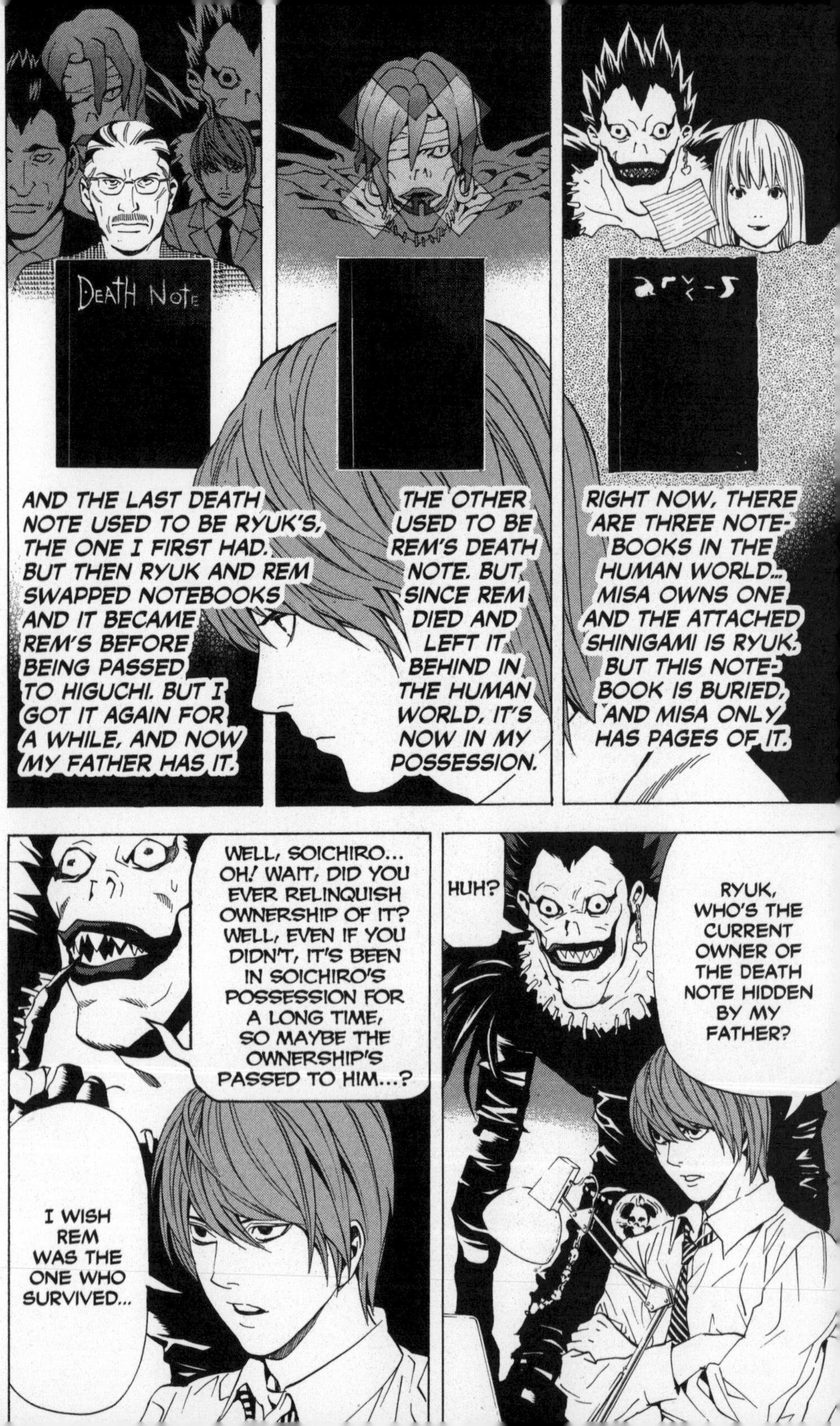
RIGHT NOW, THERE ARE THREE NOTEBOOKS IN THE HUMAN WORLD... MISA OWNS ONE AND THE ATTACHED SHINIGAMI IS RYUK. BUT THIS NOTEBOOK IS BURIED, AND MISA ONLY HAS PAGES OF IT.
THE OTHER USED TO BE REM'S DEATH NOTE. BUT SINCE REM DIED AND LEFT IT BEHIND IN THE HUMAN WORLD, IT'S NOW IN MY POSSESSION.
DEATH NOTE
AND THE LAST DEATH NOTE USED TO BE RYUK'S, THE ONE I FIRST HAD. BUT THEN RYUK AND REM SWAPPED NOTEBOOKS AND IT BECAME REM'S BEFORE BEING PASSED TO HIGUCHI. BUT I GOT IT AGAIN FOR A WHILE, AND NOW MY FATHER HAS IT.
RYUK, WHO'S THE CURRENT OWNER OF THE DEATH NOTE HIDDEN BY MY FATHER?
HUH?
WELL, SOICHIRO... OH! WAIT, DID YOU EVER RELINQUISH OWNERSHIP OF IT? WELL, EVEN IF YOU DIDN'T, IT'S BEEN IN SOICHIRO'S POSSESSION FOR A LONG TIME, SO MAYBE THE OWNERSHIP'S PASSED TO HIM...?
I WISH REM WAS THE ONE WHO SURVIVED...

READ THIS WAY

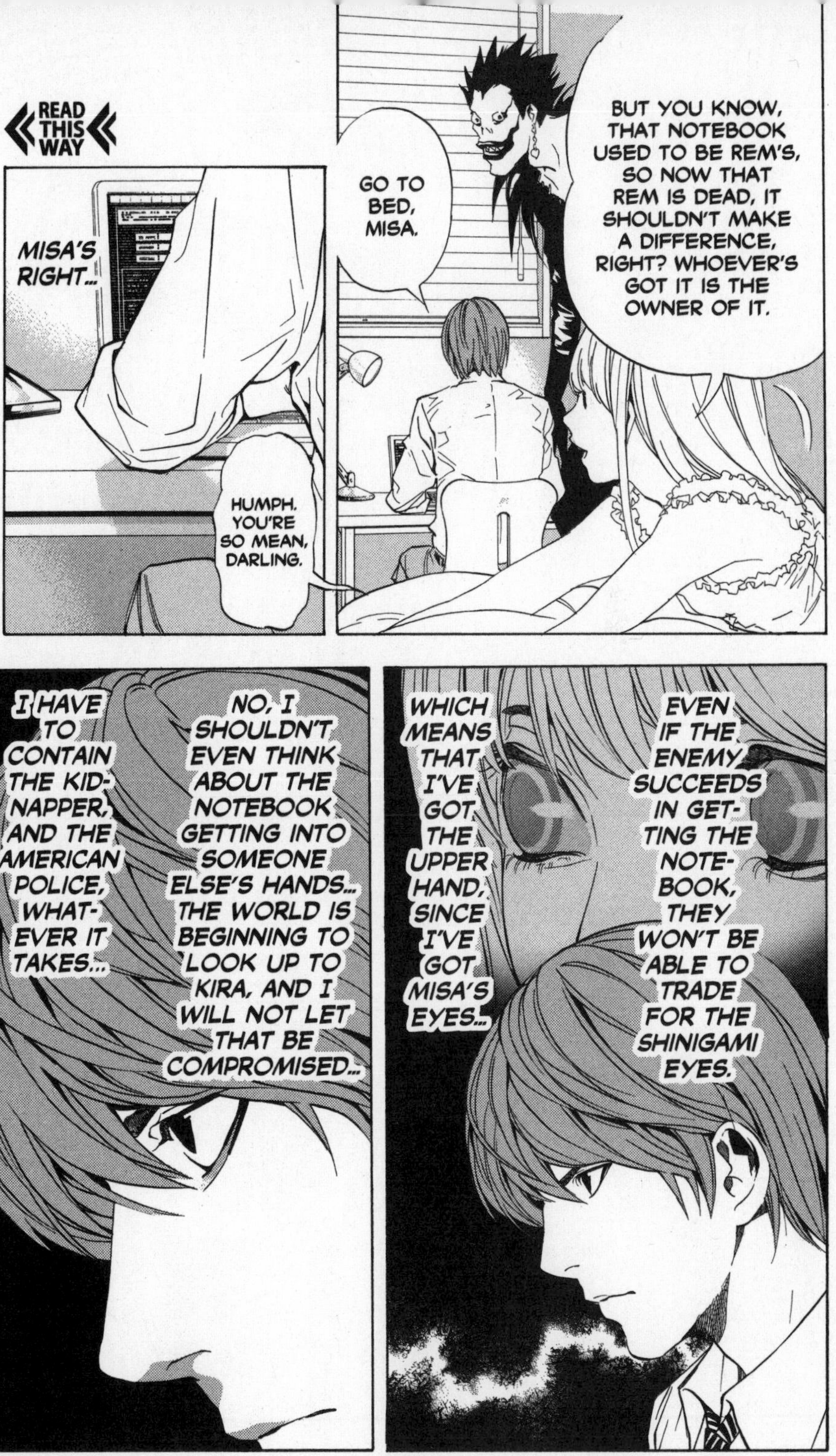

BUT YOU KNOW, THAT NOTEBOOK USED TO BE REM'S, SO NOW THAT REM IS DEAD, IT SHOULDN'T MAKE A DIFFERENCE, RIGHT? WHOEVER'S GOT IT IS THE OWNER OF IT.
GO TO BED, MISA.
HUMPH. YOU'RE SO MEAN, DARLING.
MISA'S RIGHT...
EVEN IF THE ENEMY SUCCEEDS IN GETTING THE NOTEBOOK, THEY WON'T BE ABLE TO TRADE FOR THE SHINIGAMI EYES.
WHICH MEANS THAT I'VE GOT THE UPPER HAND, SINCE I'VE GOT MISA'S EYES...
NO, I SHOULDN'T EVEN THINK ABOUT THE NOTEBOOK GETTING INTO SOMEONE ELSE'S HANDS... THE WORLD IS BEGINNING TO LOOK UP TO KIRA, AND I WILL NOT LET THAT BE COMPROMISED...
I HAVE TO CONTAIN THE KIDNAPPER, AND THE AMERICAN POLICE, WHATEVER IT TAKES...

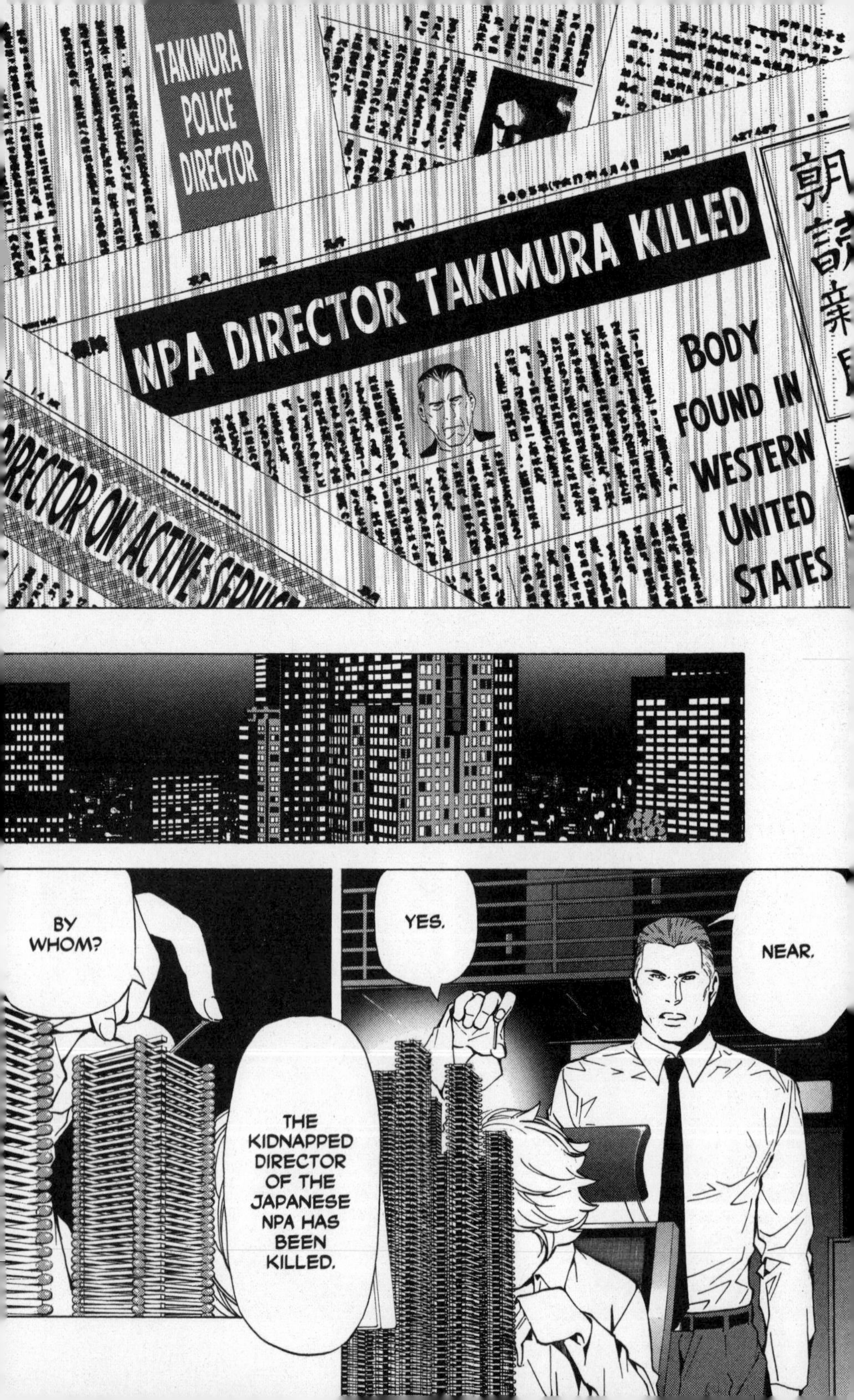

BODY FOUND IN WESTERN UNITED STATES
NPA DIRECTOR TAKIMURA KILLED
TAKIMURA POLICE DIRECTOR
DIRECTOR ON ACTIVE
NEAR.
YES.
THE KIDNAPPED DIRECTOR OF THE JAPANESE NPA HAS BEEN KILLED.
BY WHOM?

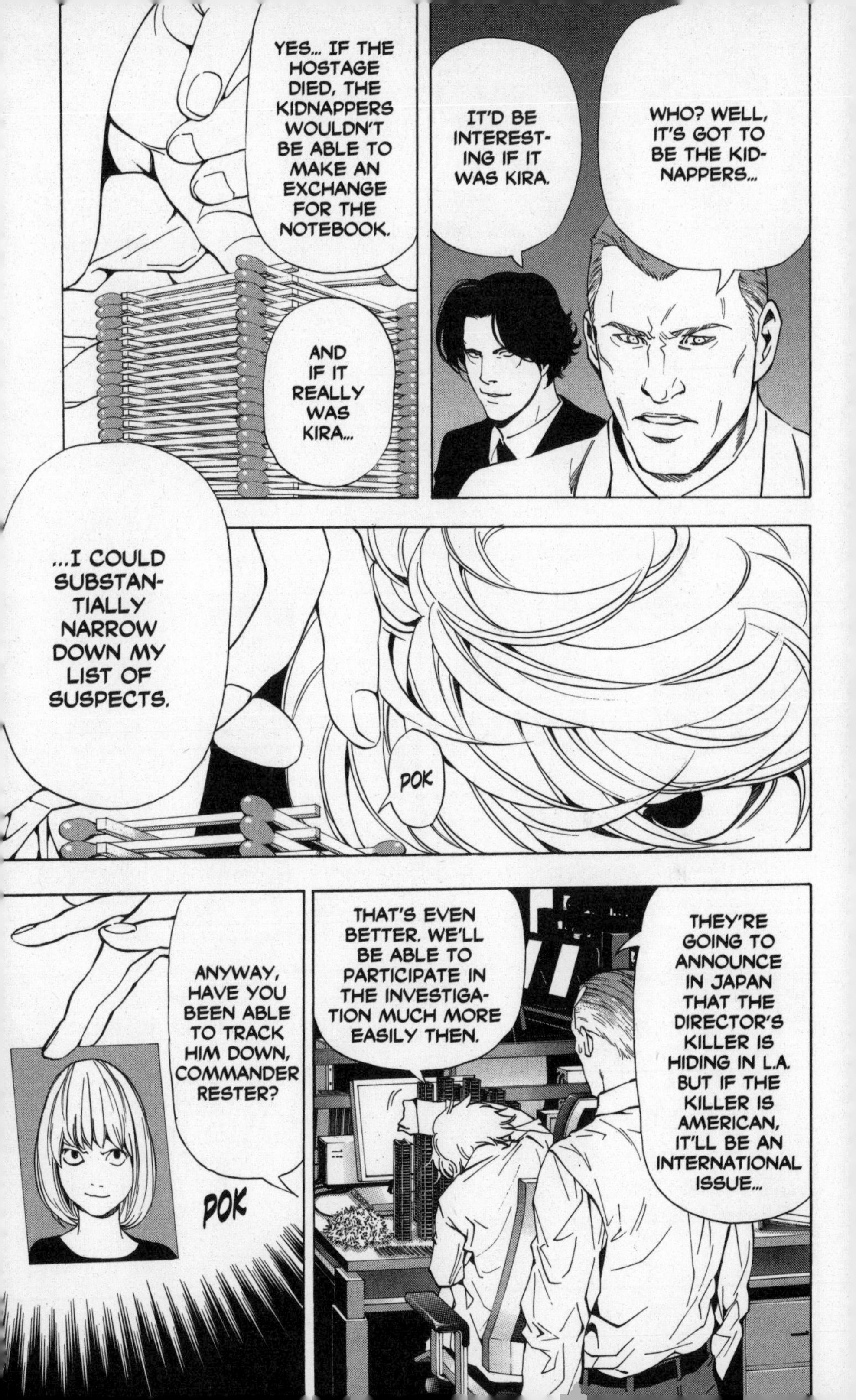
WHO? WELL, IT'S GOT TO BE THE KID-NAPPERS...
IT'D BE INTEREST-ING IF IT WAS KIRA.
YES... IF THE HOSTAGE DIED, THE KIDNAPPERS WOULDN'T BE ABLE TO MAKE AN EXCHANGE FOR THE NOTEBOOK.
AND IF IT REALLY WAS KIRA...
...I COULD SUBSTAN-TIALLY NARROW DOWN MY LIST OF SUSPECTS.
POK
THEY'RE GOING TO ANNOUNCE IN JAPAN THAT THE DIRECTOR'S KILLER IS HIDING IN L.A. BUT IF THE KILLER IS AMERICAN, IT'LL BE AN INTERNATIONAL ISSUE...
THAT'S EVEN BETTER. WE'LL BE ABLE TO PARTICIPATE IN THE INVESTIGA-TION MUCH MORE EASILY THEN.
ANYWAY, HAVE YOU BEEN ABLE TO TRACK HIM DOWN, COMMANDER RESTER?
POK

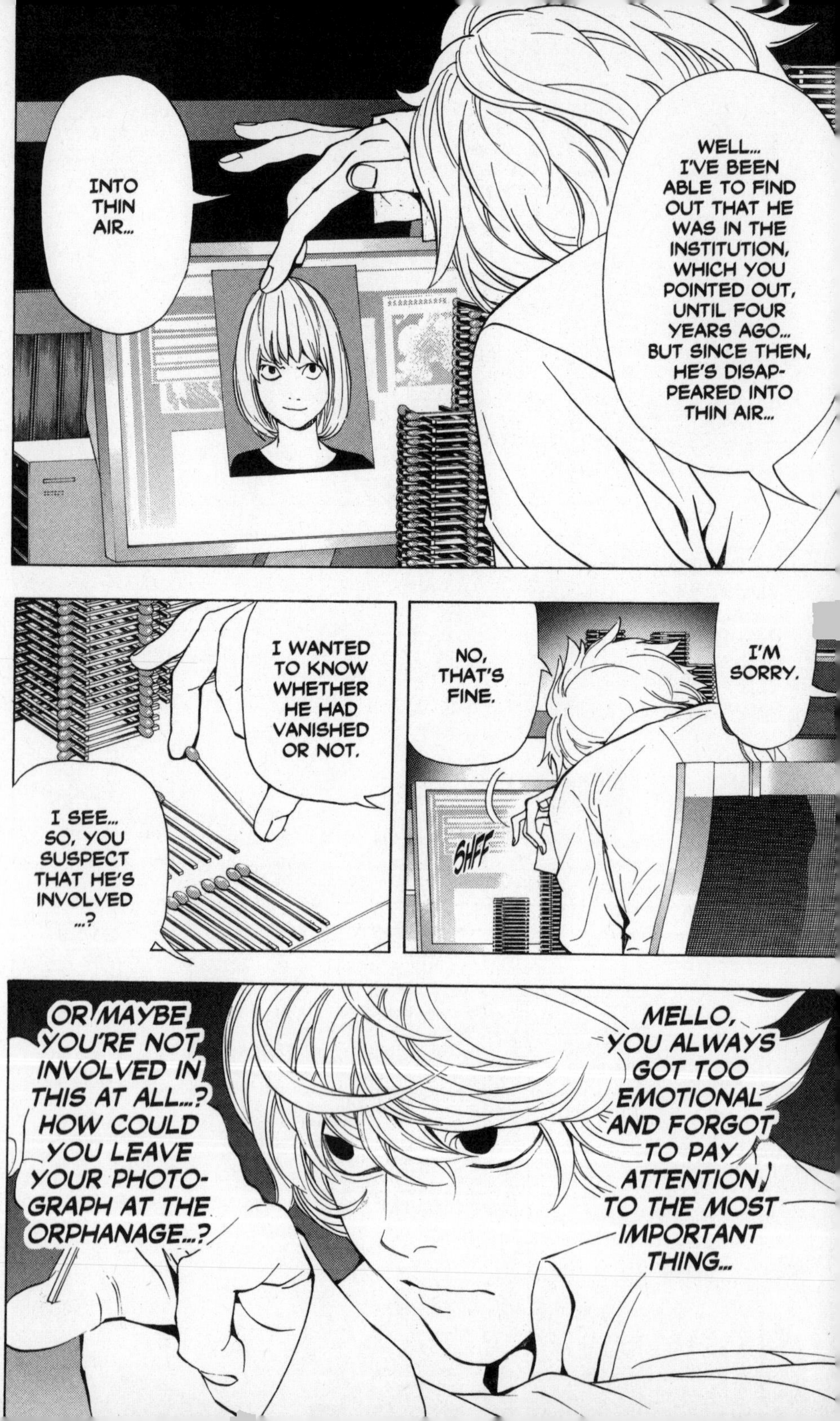
WELL... I'VE BEEN ABLE TO FIND OUT THAT HE WAS IN THE INSTITUTION, WHICH YOU POINTED OUT, UNTIL FOUR YEARS AGO... BUT SINCE THEN, HE'S DISAPPEARED INTO THIN AIR...
INTO THIN AIR...
I'M SORRY.
NO, THAT'S FINE.
SHFF
I WANTED TO KNOW WHETHER HE HAD VANISHED OR NOT.
I SEE... SO, YOU SUSPECT THAT HE'S INVOLVED ...?
MELLO, YOU ALWAYS GOT TOO EMOTIONAL AND FORGOT TO PAY ATTENTION TO THE MOST IMPORTANT THING...
OR MAYBE YOU'RE NOT INVOLVED IN THIS AT ALL...? HOW COULD YOU LEAVE YOUR PHOTOGRAPH AT THE ORPHANAGE...?

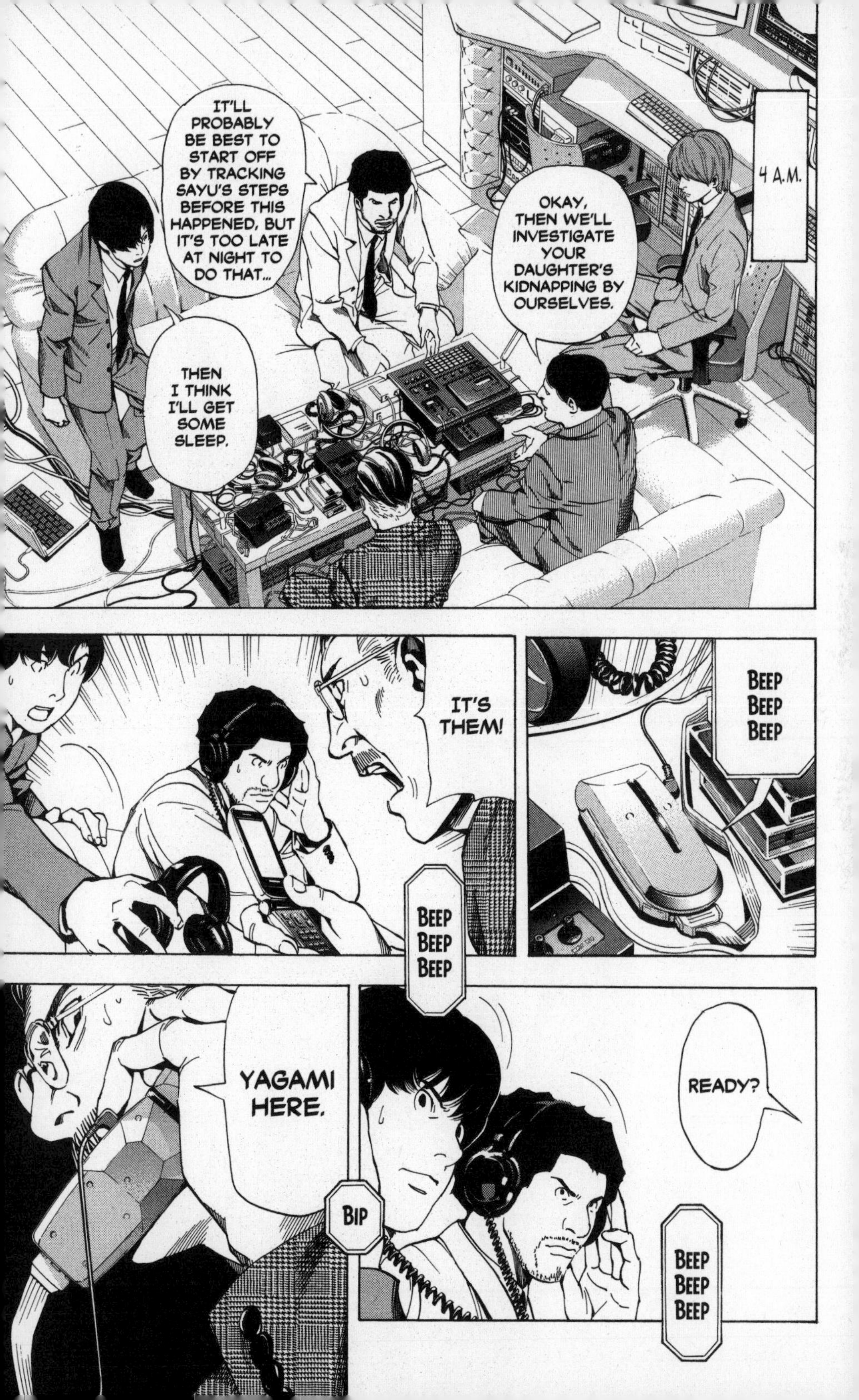
4 A.M.
OKAY, THEN WE'LL INVESTIGATE YOUR DAUGHTER'S KIDNAPPING BY OURSELVES.
IT'LL PROBABLY BE BEST TO START OFF BY TRACKING SAYU'S STEPS BEFORE THIS HAPPENED, BUT IT'S TOO LATE AT NIGHT TO DO THAT...
THEN I THINK I'LL GET SOME SLEEP.
BEEP BEEP BEEP
IT'S THEM!
BEEP BEEP BEEP
READY?
BEEP BEEP BEEP
BIP
YAGAMI HERE.

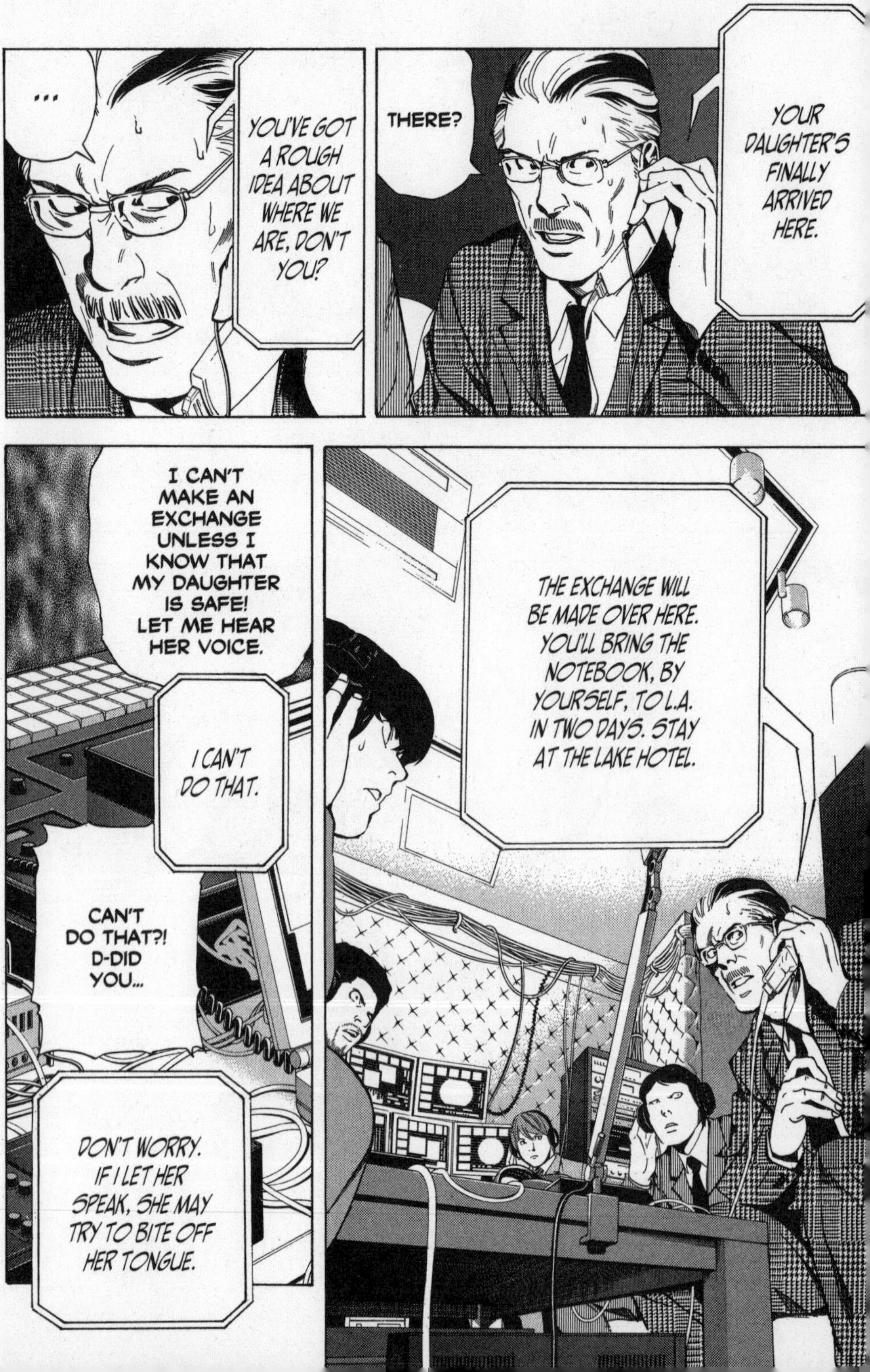
YOUR DAUGHTER'S FINALLY ARRIVED HERE.
THERE?
YOU'VE GOT A ROUGH IDEA ABOUT WHERE WE ARE, DON'T YOU?
...
THE EXCHANGE WILL BE MADE OVER HERE. YOU'LL BRING THE NOTEBOOK, BY YOURSELF, TO L.A. IN TWO DAYS. STAY AT THE LAKE HOTEL.
I CAN'T MAKE AN EXCHANGE UNLESS I KNOW THAT MY DAUGHTER IS SAFE! LET ME HEAR HER VOICE.
I CAN'T DO THAT.
CAN'T DO THAT?! D-DID YOU...
DON'T WORRY. IF I LET HER SPEAK, SHE MAY TRY TO BITE OFF HER TONGUE.

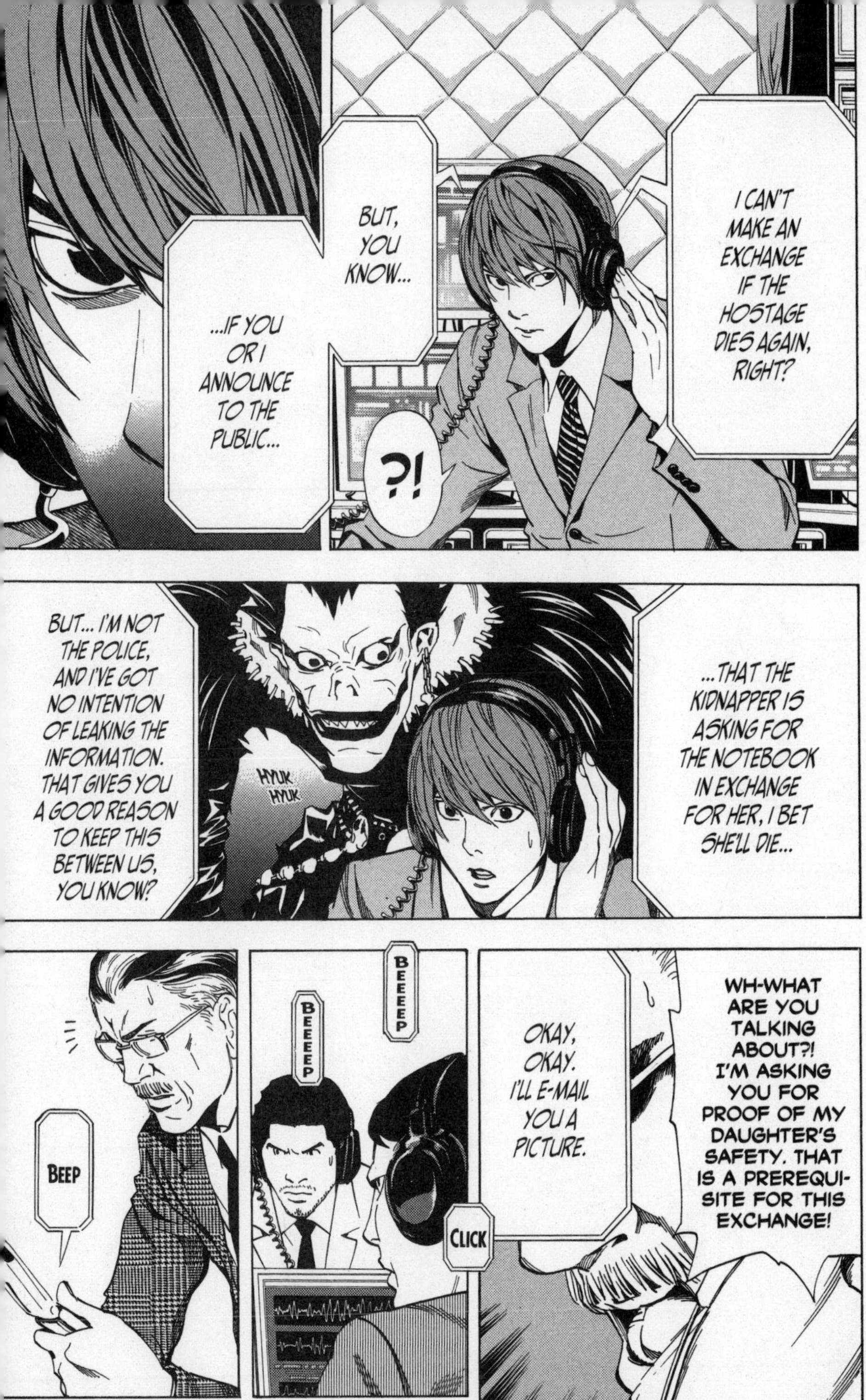

I CAN'T MAKE AN EXCHANGE IF THE HOSTAGE DIES AGAIN, RIGHT?
BUT, YOU KNOW...
?!
...IF YOU OR I ANNOUNCE TO THE PUBLIC...
...THAT THE KIDNAPPER IS ASKING FOR THE NOTEBOOK IN EXCHANGE FOR HER, I BET SHE'LL DIE...
BUT... I'M NOT THE POLICE, AND I'VE GOT NO INTENTION OF LEAKING THE INFORMATION. THAT GIVES YOU A GOOD REASON TO KEEP THIS BETWEEN US, YOU KNOW?
HYUK HYUK
WH-WHAT ARE YOU TALKING ABOUT?! I'M ASKING YOU FOR PROOF OF MY DAUGHTER'S SAFETY. THAT IS A PREREQUISITE FOR THIS EXCHANGE!
OKAY, OKAY. I'LL E-MAIL YOU A PICTURE.
BEEEEP
BEEEEP
CLICK
BEEP

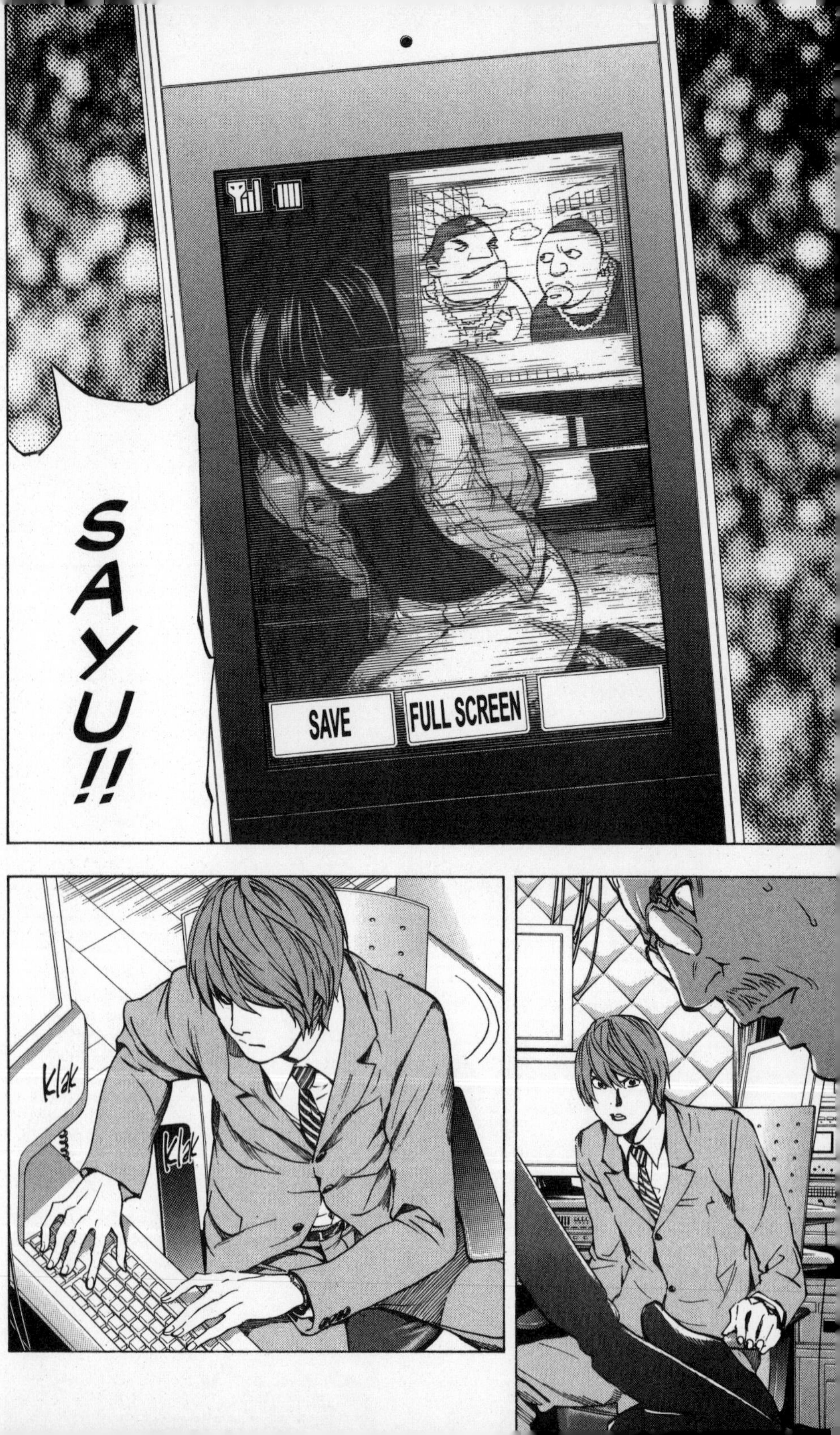
SAYU!!
SAVE
FULL SCREEN
Klak
Klak

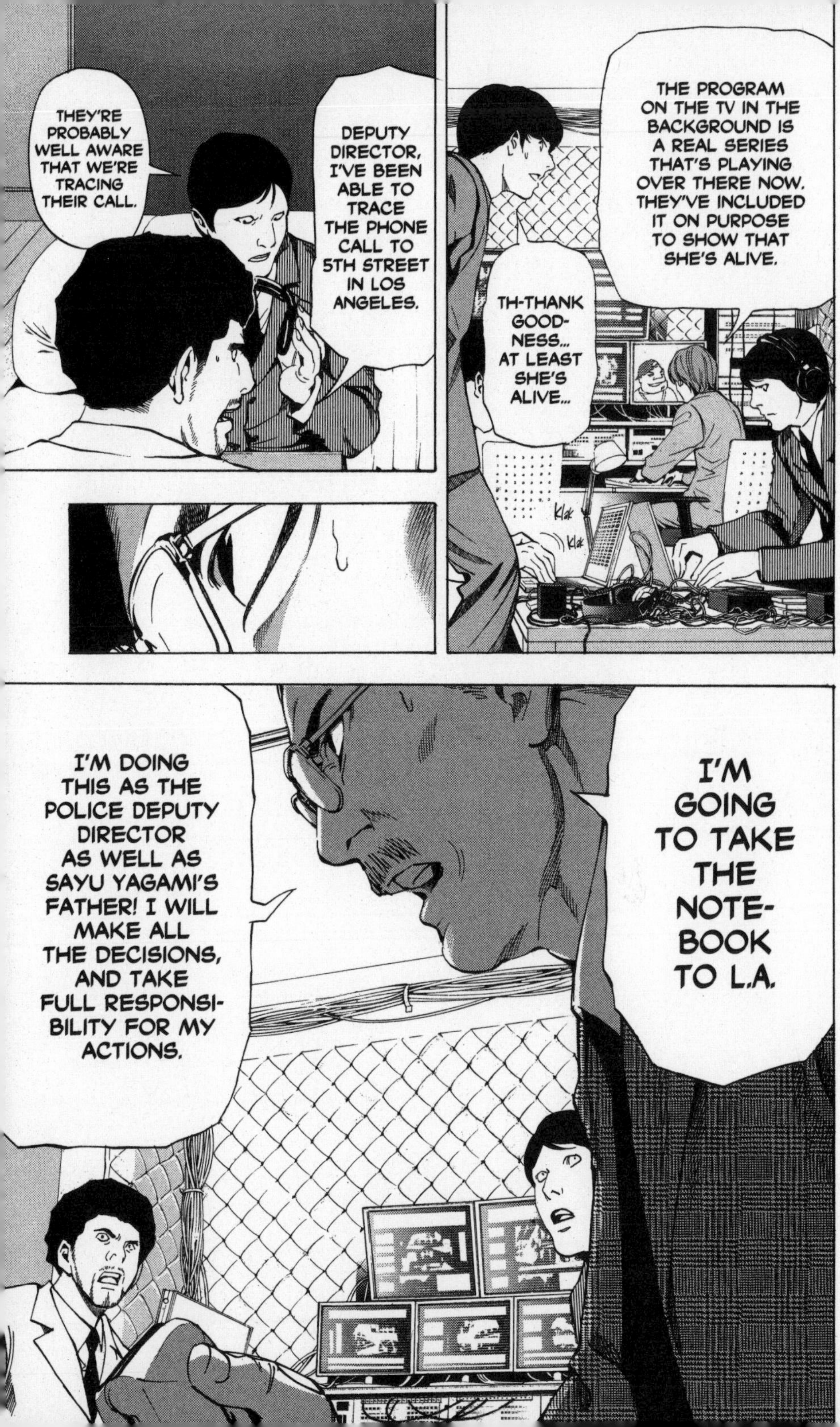
THE PROGRAM ON THE TV IN THE BACKGROUND IS A REAL SERIES THAT'S PLAYING OVER THERE NOW. THEY'VE INCLUDED IT ON PURPOSE TO SHOW THAT SHE'S ALIVE.
TH-THANK GOODNESS... AT LEAST SHE'S ALIVE...
Klak
Klak
DEPUTY DIRECTOR, I'VE BEEN ABLE TO TRACE THE PHONE CALL TO 5TH STREET IN LOS ANGELES.
THEY'RE PROBABLY WELL AWARE THAT WE'RE TRACING THEIR CALL.
I'M GOING TO TAKE THE NOTEBOOK TO L.A.
I'M DOING THIS AS THE POLICE DEPUTY DIRECTOR AS WELL AS SAYU YAGAMI'S FATHER! I WILL MAKE ALL THE DECISIONS, AND TAKE FULL RESPONSIBILITY FOR MY ACTIONS.

# DEATH NOTE
## How to Use It
## XLII

- The use of the DEATH NOTE in the human world sometimes affects other human's lives or shortens their original life-span, even though their names are not actually written in the DEATH NOTE itself. In these cases, no matter the cause, the god of death sees only the original life-span and not the shortened life-span.

人間界にデスノートがある事である人間の人生が変わり、
デスノートに書かれなくとも本来の寿命より前に死んでしまう事はある。
それがどんな死に方であろうと、その場合、やはり死神の目には
縮んだ寿命でなく本来の寿命が見える事になる。

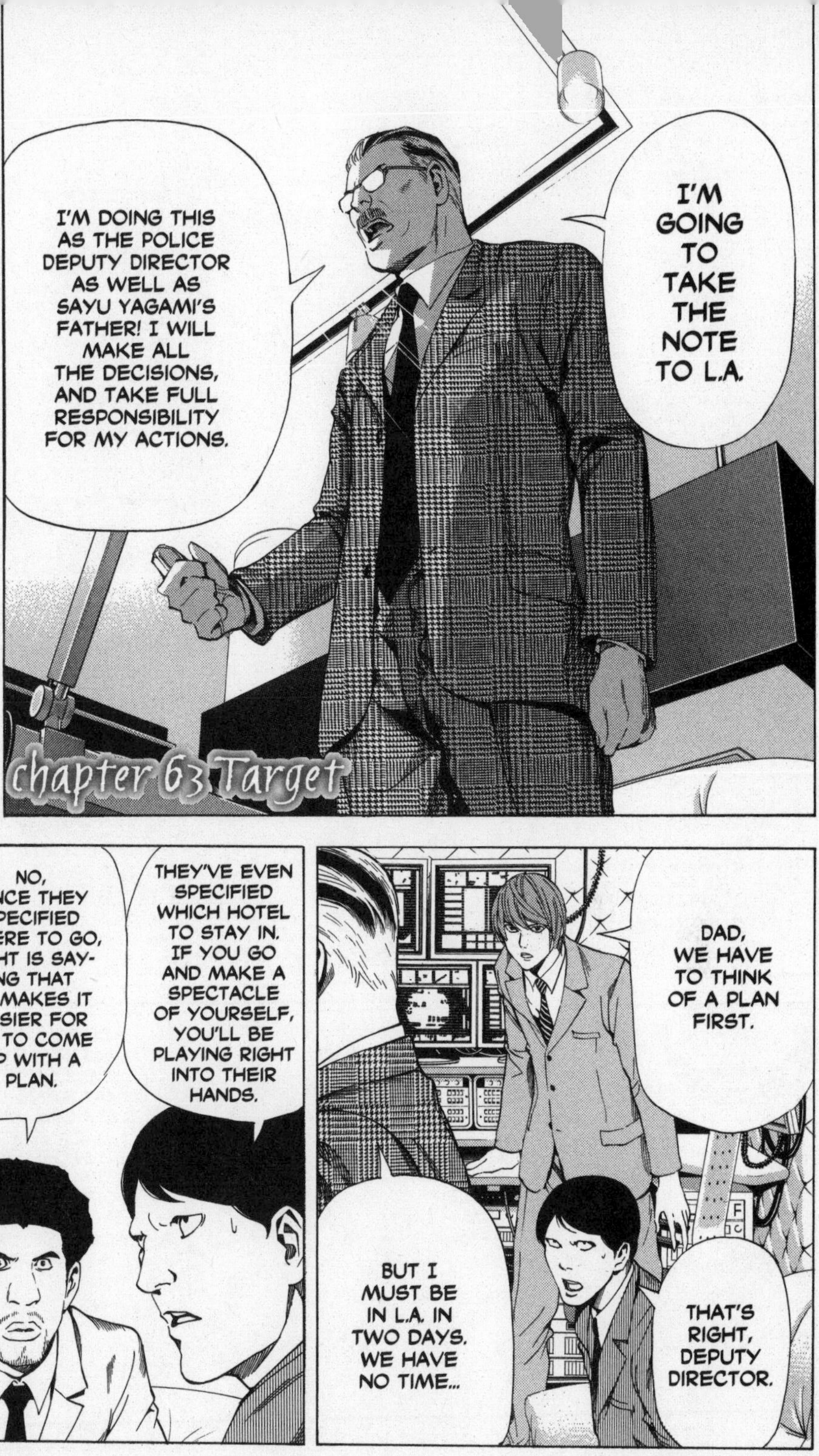
I'M GOING TO TAKE THE NOTE TO L.A.
I'M DOING THIS AS THE POLICE DEPUTY DIRECTOR AS WELL AS SAYU YAGAMI'S FATHER! I WILL MAKE ALL THE DECISIONS, AND TAKE FULL RESPONSIBILITY FOR MY ACTIONS.
chapter 63 Target
DAD, WE HAVE TO THINK OF A PLAN FIRST.
THAT'S RIGHT, DEPUTY DIRECTOR.
BUT I MUST BE IN L.A. IN TWO DAYS. WE HAVE NO TIME...
THEY'VE EVEN SPECIFIED WHICH HOTEL TO STAY IN. IF YOU GO AND MAKE A SPECTACLE OF YOURSELF, YOU'LL BE PLAYING RIGHT INTO THEIR HANDS.
NO, SINCE THEY SPECIFIED WHERE TO GO, LIGHT IS SAYING THAT IT MAKES IT EASIER FOR US TO COME UP WITH A PLAN.

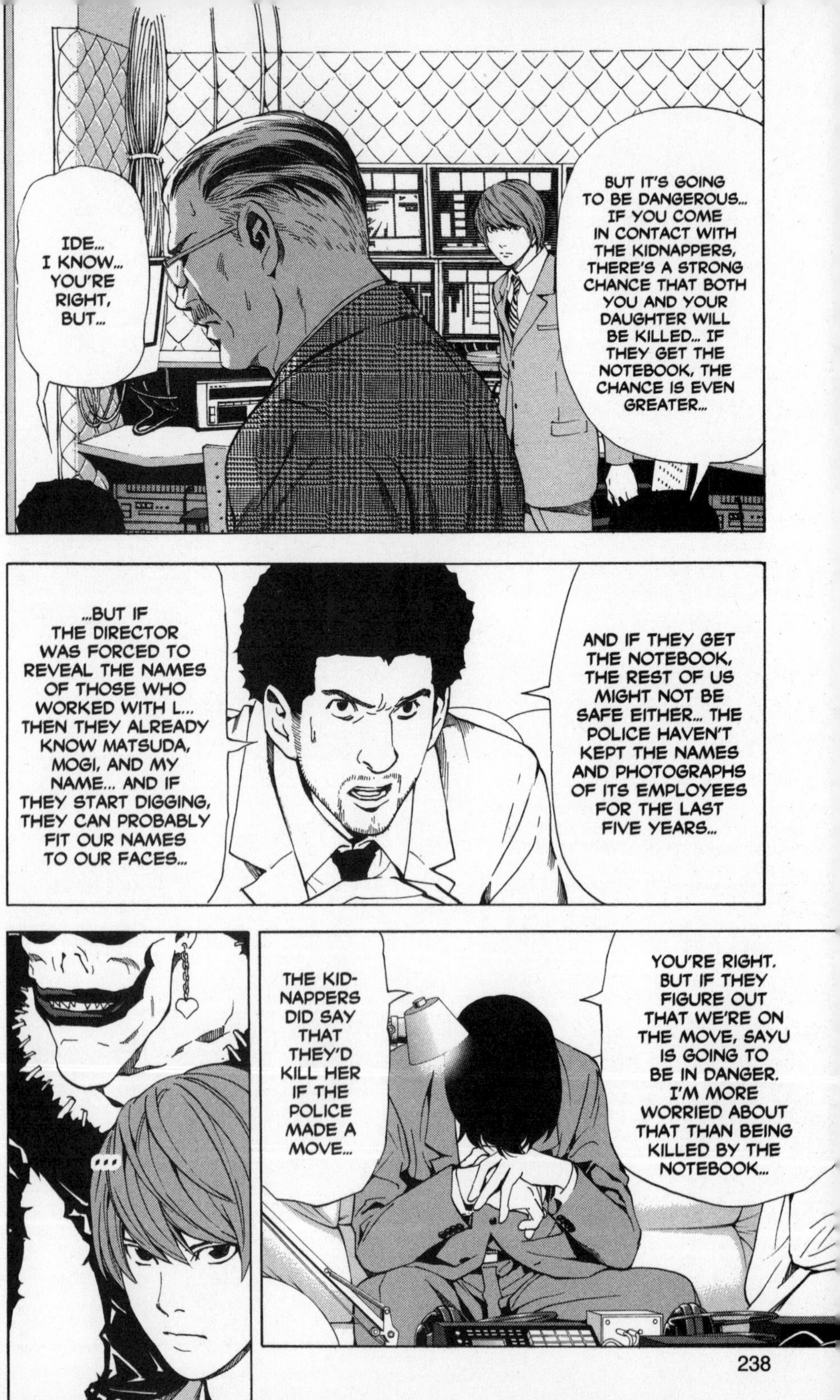
BUT IT'S GOING TO BE DANGEROUS... IF YOU COME IN CONTACT WITH THE KIDNAPPERS, THERE'S A STRONG CHANCE THAT BOTH YOU AND YOUR DAUGHTER WILL BE KILLED... IF THEY GET THE NOTEBOOK, THE CHANCE IS EVEN GREATER...
IDE... I KNOW... YOU'RE RIGHT, BUT...
AND IF THEY GET THE NOTEBOOK, THE REST OF US MIGHT NOT BE SAFE EITHER... THE POLICE HAVEN'T KEPT THE NAMES AND PHOTOGRAPHS OF ITS EMPLOYEES FOR THE LAST FIVE YEARS...
...BUT IF THE DIRECTOR WAS FORCED TO REVEAL THE NAMES OF THOSE WHO WORKED WITH L... THEN THEY ALREADY KNOW MATSUDA, MOGI, AND MY NAME... AND IF THEY START DIGGING, THEY CAN PROBABLY FIT OUR NAMES TO OUR FACES...
YOU'RE RIGHT. BUT IF THEY FIGURE OUT THAT WE'RE ON THE MOVE, SAYU IS GOING TO BE IN DANGER. I'M MORE WORRIED ABOUT THAT THAN BEING KILLED BY THE NOTEBOOK...
THE KID-NAPPERS DID SAY THAT THEY'D KILL HER IF THE POLICE MADE A MOVE...
...

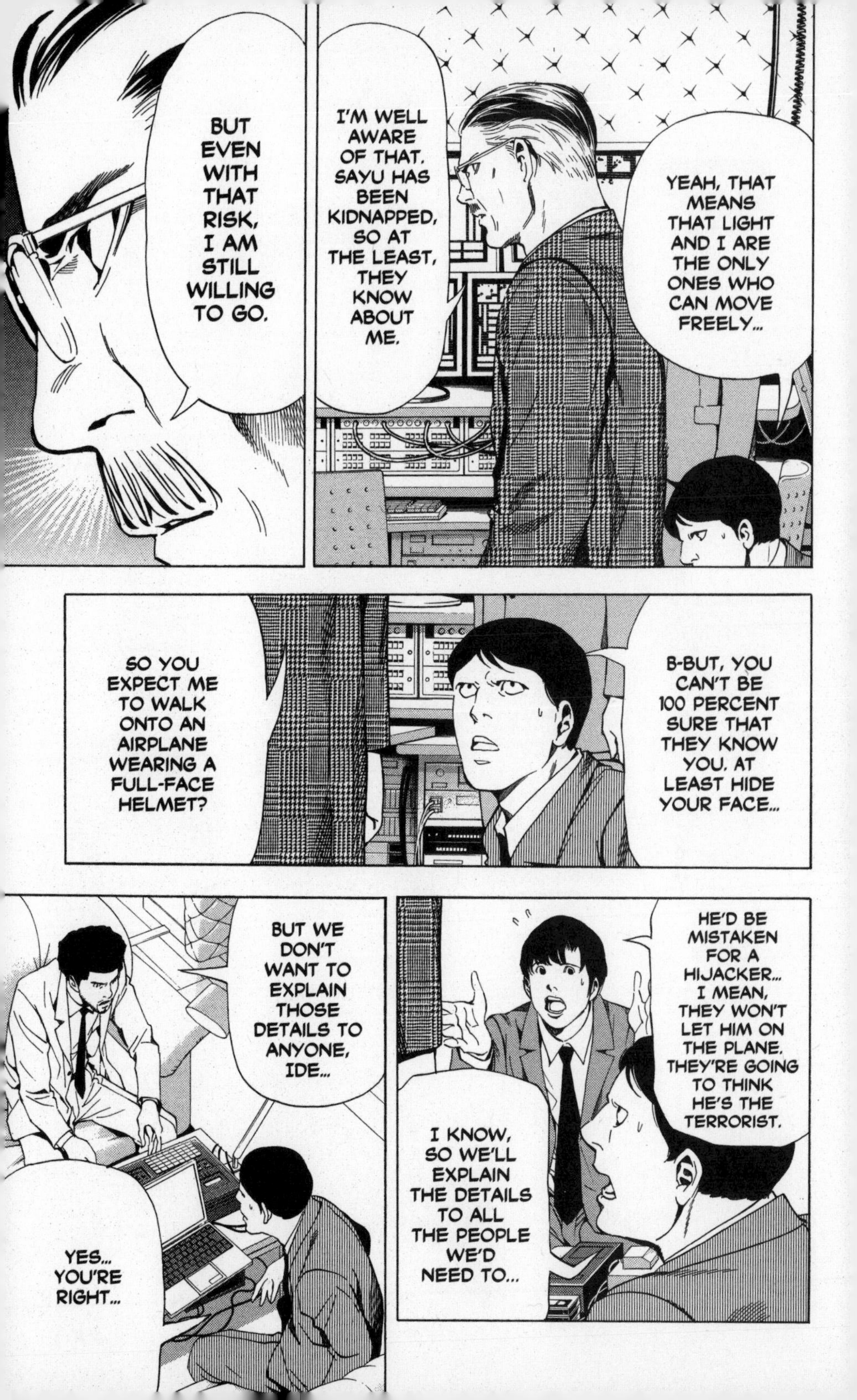
YEAH, THAT MEANS THAT LIGHT AND I ARE THE ONLY ONES WHO CAN MOVE FREELY...
I'M WELL AWARE OF THAT. SAYU HAS BEEN KIDNAPPED, SO AT THE LEAST, THEY KNOW ABOUT ME.
BUT EVEN WITH THAT RISK, I AM STILL WILLING TO GO.
B-BUT, YOU CAN'T BE 100 PERCENT SURE THAT THEY KNOW YOU. AT LEAST HIDE YOUR FACE...
SO YOU EXPECT ME TO WALK ONTO AN AIRPLANE WEARING A FULL-FACE HELMET?
HE'D BE MISTAKEN FOR A HIJACKER... I MEAN, THEY WON'T LET HIM ON THE PLANE. THEY'RE GOING TO THINK HE'S THE TERRORIST.
I KNOW, SO WE'LL EXPLAIN THE DETAILS TO ALL THE PEOPLE WE'D NEED TO...
BUT WE DON'T WANT TO EXPLAIN THOSE DETAILS TO ANYONE, IDE...
YES... YOU'RE RIGHT...

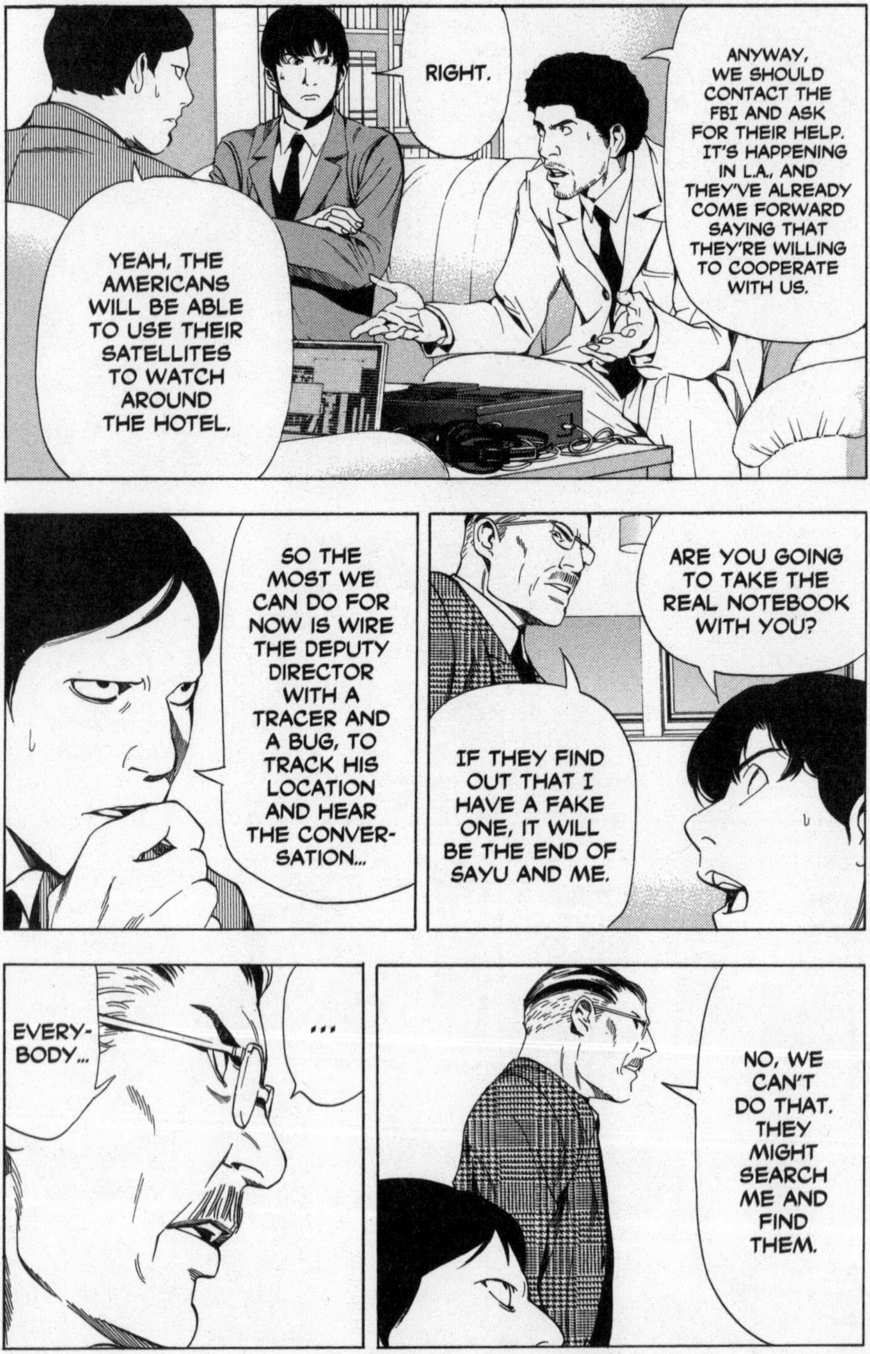
ANYWAY, WE SHOULD CONTACT THE FBI AND ASK FOR THEIR HELP. IT'S HAPPENING IN L.A., AND THEY'VE ALREADY COME FORWARD SAYING THAT THEY'RE WILLING TO COOPERATE WITH US.
RIGHT.
YEAH, THE AMERICANS WILL BE ABLE TO USE THEIR SATELLITES TO WATCH AROUND THE HOTEL.
ARE YOU GOING TO TAKE THE REAL NOTEBOOK WITH YOU?
IF THEY FIND OUT THAT I HAVE A FAKE ONE, IT WILL BE THE END OF SAYU AND ME.
SO THE MOST WE CAN DO FOR NOW IS WIRE THE DEPUTY DIRECTOR WITH A TRACER AND A BUG, TO TRACK HIS LOCATION AND HEAR THE CONVER-SATION...
NO, WE CAN'T DO THAT. THEY MIGHT SEARCH ME AND FIND THEM.
...
EVERY-BODY...

I DON'T WANT TO TRY ANY TRICKS.

OKAY, DAD. AS FOR THE COMMAND OF THE JAPANESE POLICE... WELL, THAT'S JUST EVERYONE HERE...

...AND THE AMERICAN POLICE, I... NO, L WILL TAKE CHARGE OF ALL COMMANDS.

I'LL HEAD FOR L.A. BEFORE YOU, AND MAKE PREPARATIONS WITH THE AMERICAN POLICE.

I'M ONLY LISTED AS A NORMAL GRADUATE STUDENT IN THEIR DATA. THEY MAY KNOW THAT I'M YOUR SON, BUT THERE'S NO REASON FOR THEM TO SUSPECT ME, SO I WON'T NEED A HEAVY DISGUISE.

AIZAWA AND THE OTHERS WILL HEAD FOR L.A. AS WELL, BUT YOU'LL ALL NEED TO TAKE DIFFERENT FLIGHTS...

AND TO BE SAFE, IDE, THE MOST UNKNOWN TO THEM, WILL TAKE THE SAME FLIGHT AS MY FATHER.

OKAY...

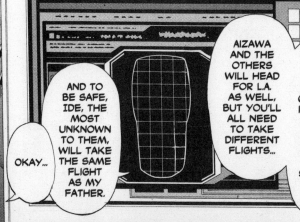

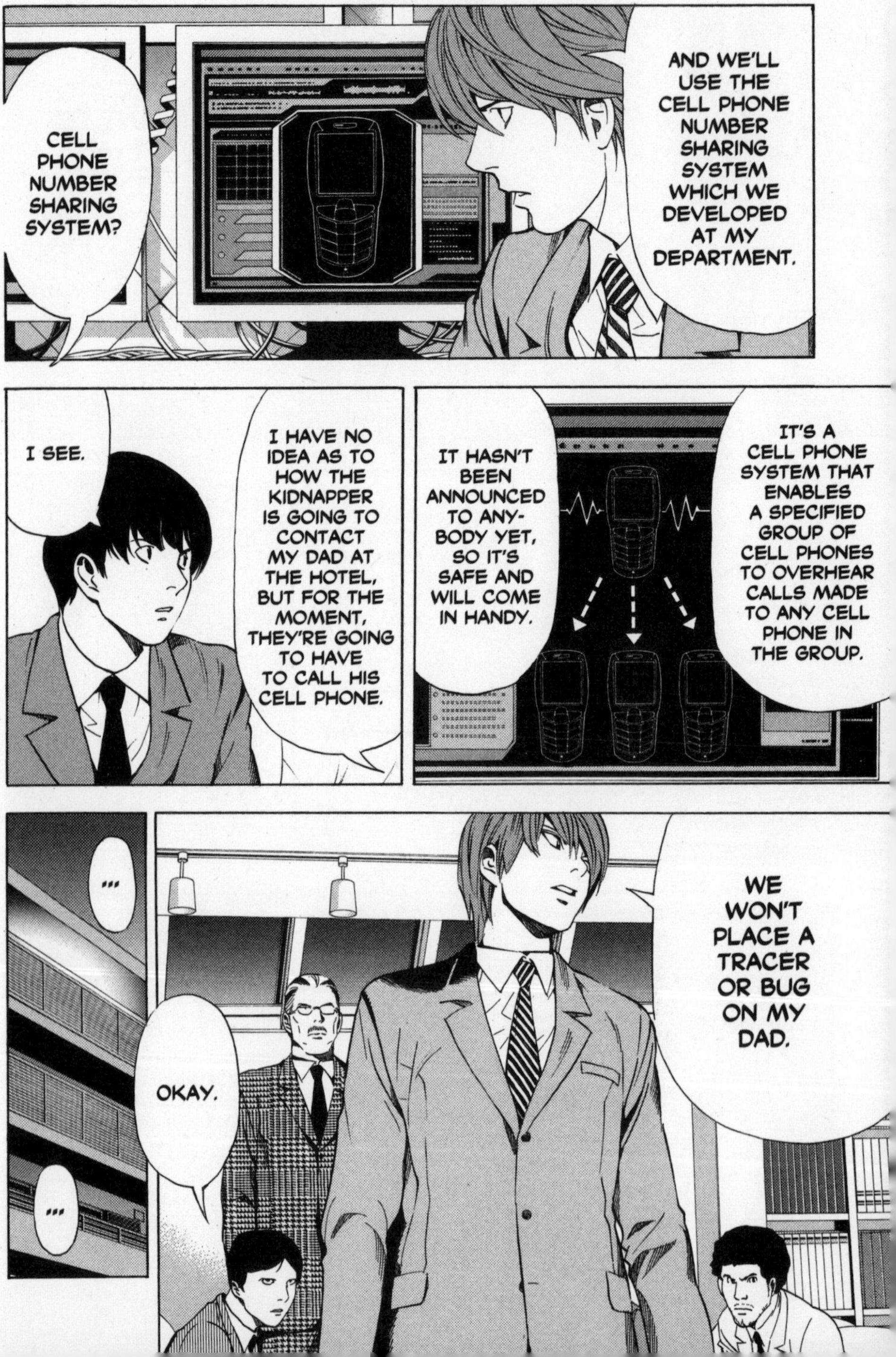
AND WE'LL USE THE CELL PHONE NUMBER SHARING SYSTEM WHICH WE DEVELOPED AT MY DEPARTMENT.
CELL PHONE NUMBER SHARING SYSTEM?
IT'S A CELL PHONE SYSTEM THAT ENABLES A SPECIFIED GROUP OF CELL PHONES TO OVERHEAR CALLS MADE TO ANY CELL PHONE IN THE GROUP.
IT HASN'T BEEN ANNOUNCED TO ANY-BODY YET, SO IT'S SAFE AND WILL COME IN HANDY.
I HAVE NO IDEA AS TO HOW THE KIDNAPPER IS GOING TO CONTACT MY DAD AT THE HOTEL, BUT FOR THE MOMENT, THEY'RE GOING TO HAVE TO CALL HIS CELL PHONE.
I SEE.
WE WON'T PLACE A TRACER OR BUG ON MY DAD.
OKAY.
...
...

READ THIS WAY

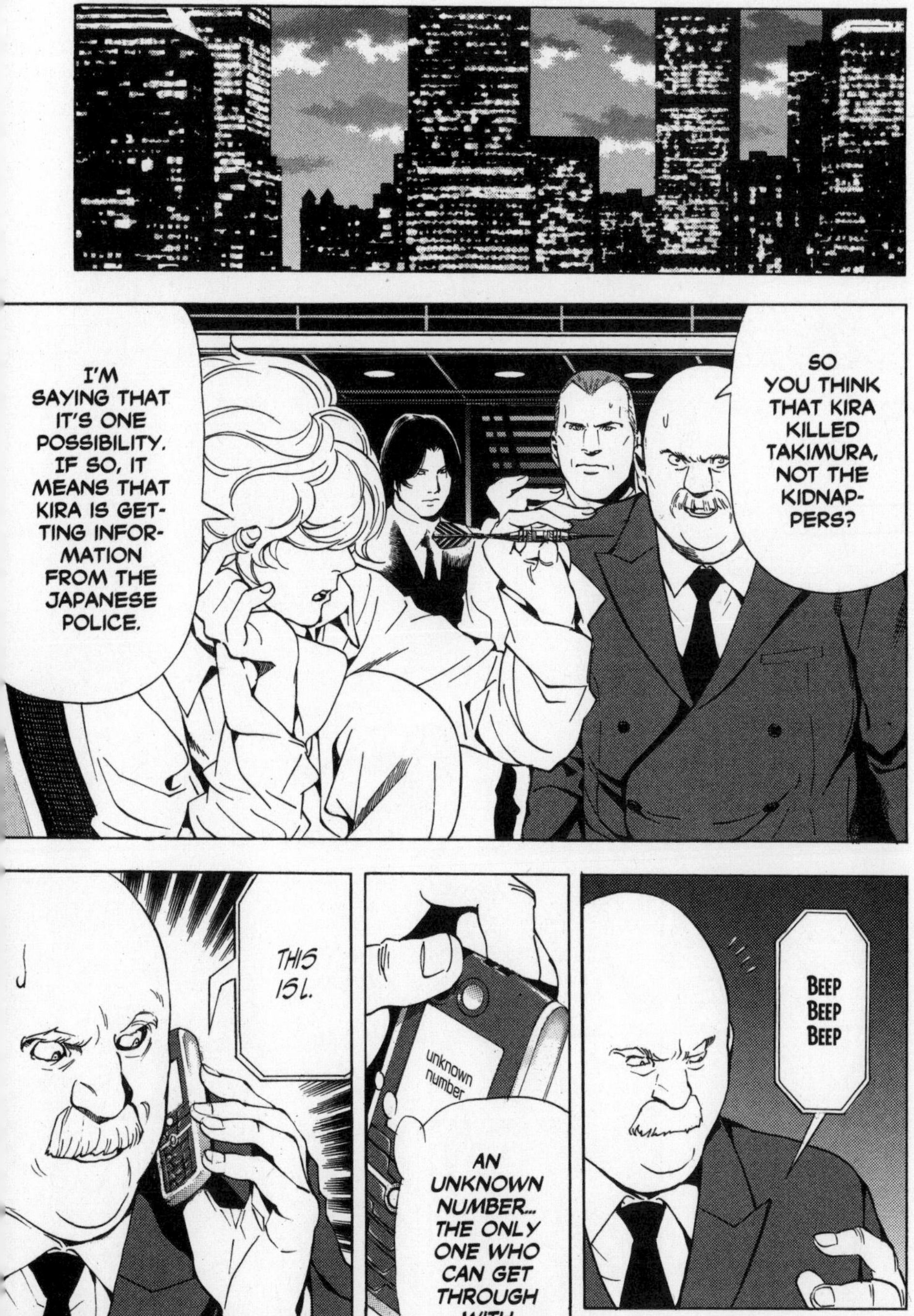
SO YOU THINK THAT KIRA KILLED TAKIMURA, NOT THE KIDNAPPERS?
I'M SAYING THAT IT'S ONE POSSIBILITY. IF SO, IT MEANS THAT KIRA IS GETTING INFORMATION FROM THE JAPANESE POLICE.
BEEP BEEP BEEP
unknown number
AN UNKNOWN NUMBER... THE ONLY ONE WHO CAN GET THROUGH WITH THAT IS...
THIS IS L.

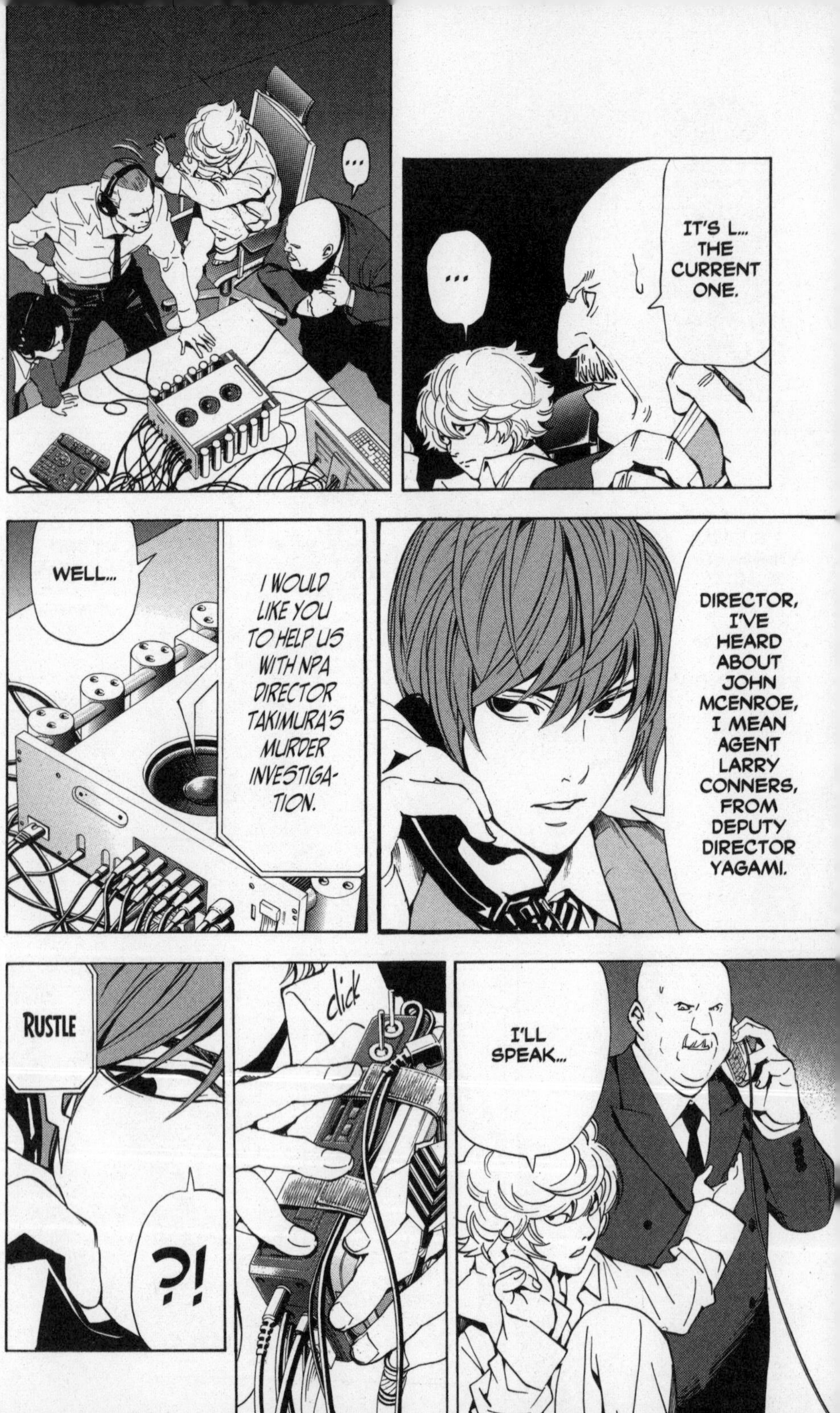
IT'S L... THE CURRENT ONE.
...
...
DIRECTOR, I'VE HEARD ABOUT JOHN MCENROE, I MEAN AGENT LARRY CONNERS, FROM DEPUTY DIRECTOR YAGAMI.
I WOULD LIKE YOU TO HELP US WITH NPA DIRECTOR TAKIMURA'S MURDER INVESTIGATION.
WELL...
I'LL SPEAK...
click
RUSTLE
?!

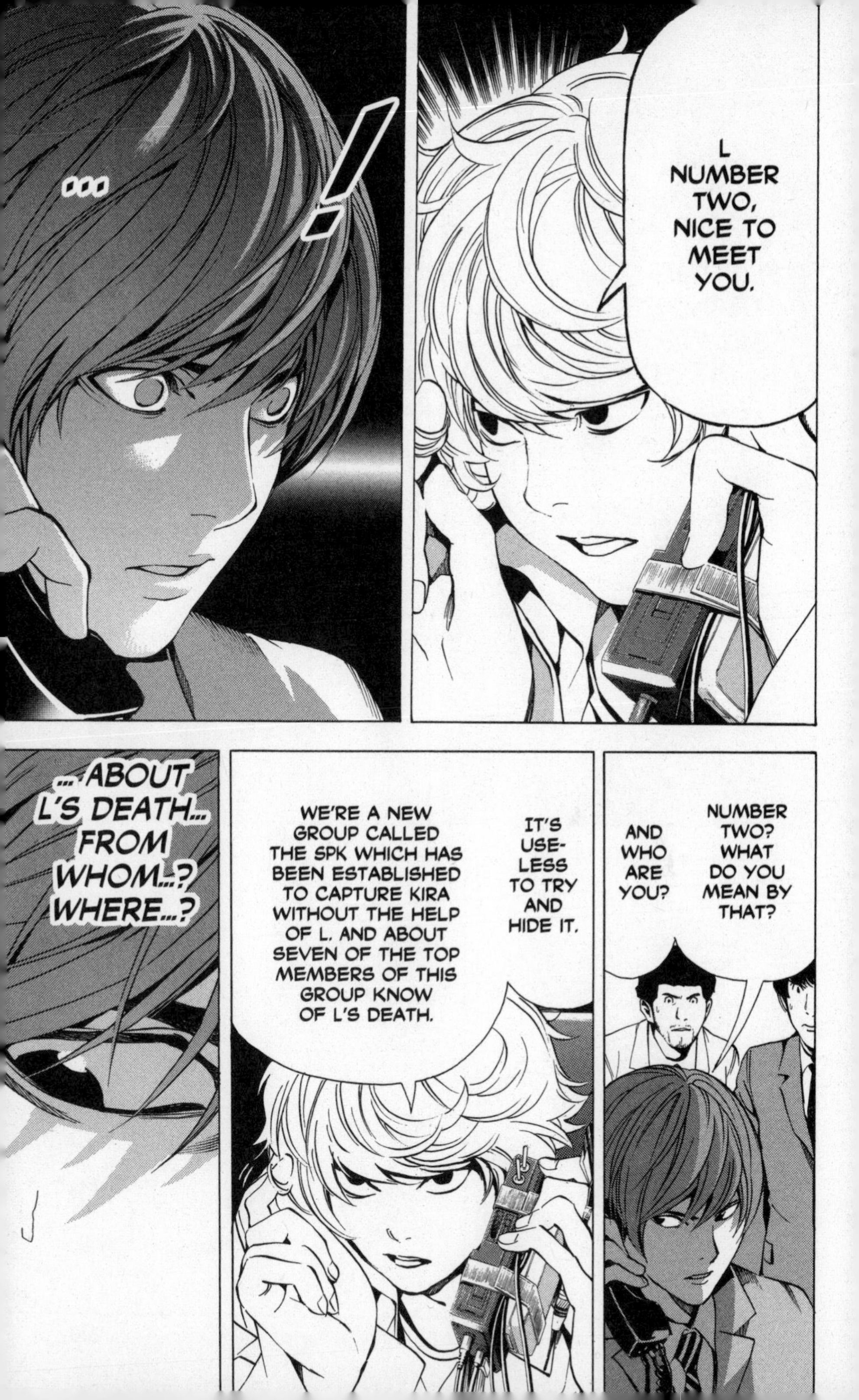
L NUMBER TWO, NICE TO MEET YOU.
...
!
NUMBER TWO? WHAT DO YOU MEAN BY THAT?
AND WHO ARE YOU?
IT'S USE-LESS TO TRY AND HIDE IT.
WE'RE A NEW GROUP CALLED THE SPK WHICH HAS BEEN ESTABLISHED TO CAPTURE KIRA WITHOUT THE HELP OF L. AND ABOUT SEVEN OF THE TOP MEMBERS OF THIS GROUP KNOW OF L'S DEATH.
...ABOUT L'S DEATH... FROM WHOM...? WHERE...?

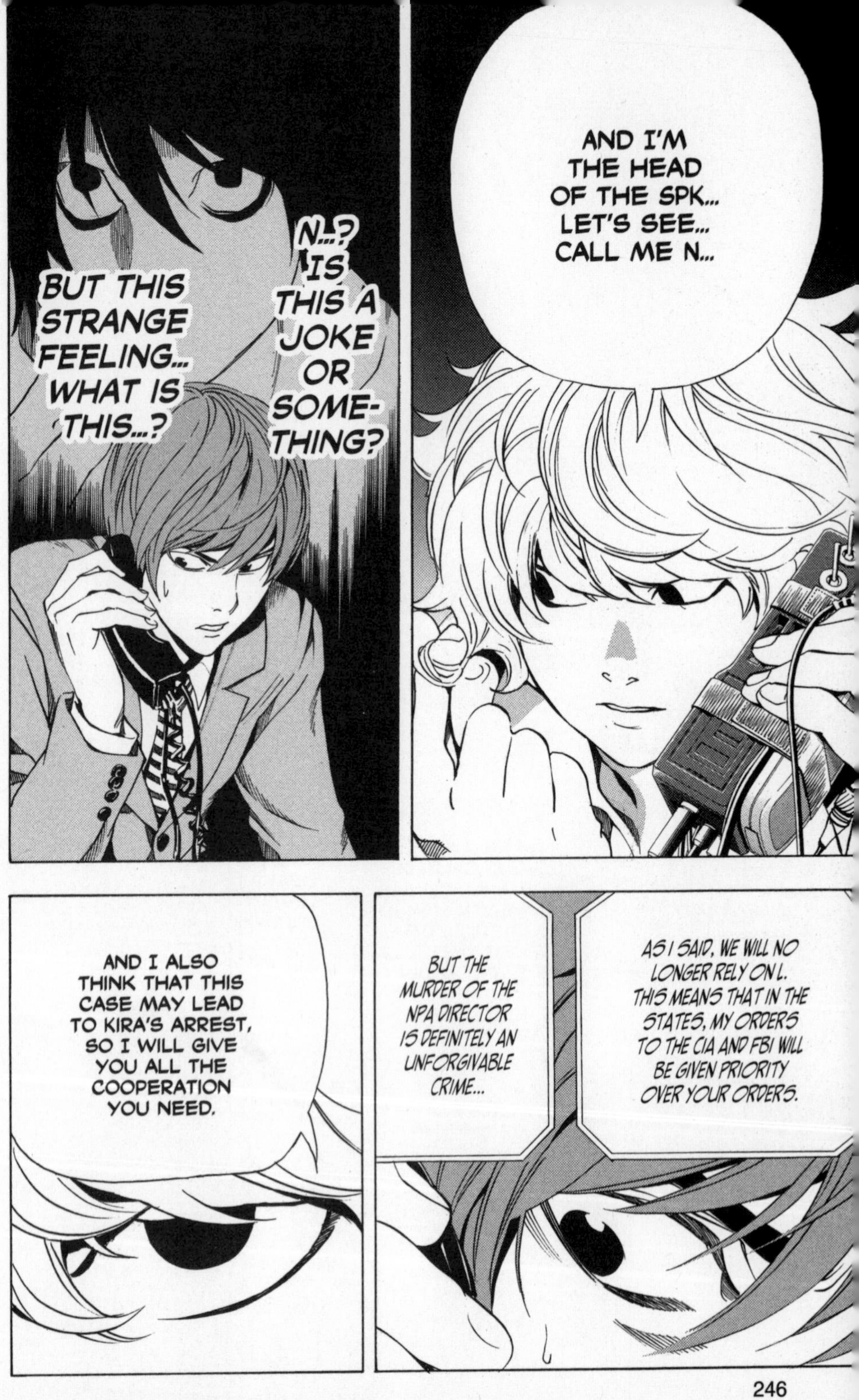
AND I'M THE HEAD OF THE SPK... LET'S SEE... CALL ME N...
N...? IS THIS A JOKE OR SOMETHING?
BUT THIS STRANGE FEELING... WHAT IS THIS...?
AS I SAID, WE WILL NO LONGER RELY ON L. THIS MEANS THAT IN THE STATES, MY ORDERS TO THE CIA AND FBI WILL BE GIVEN PRIORITY OVER YOUR ORDERS.
BUT THE MURDER OF THE NPA DIRECTOR IS DEFINITELY AN UNFORGIVABLE CRIME...
AND I ALSO THINK THAT THIS CASE MAY LEAD TO KIRA'S ARREST, SO I WILL GIVE YOU ALL THE COOPERATION YOU NEED.

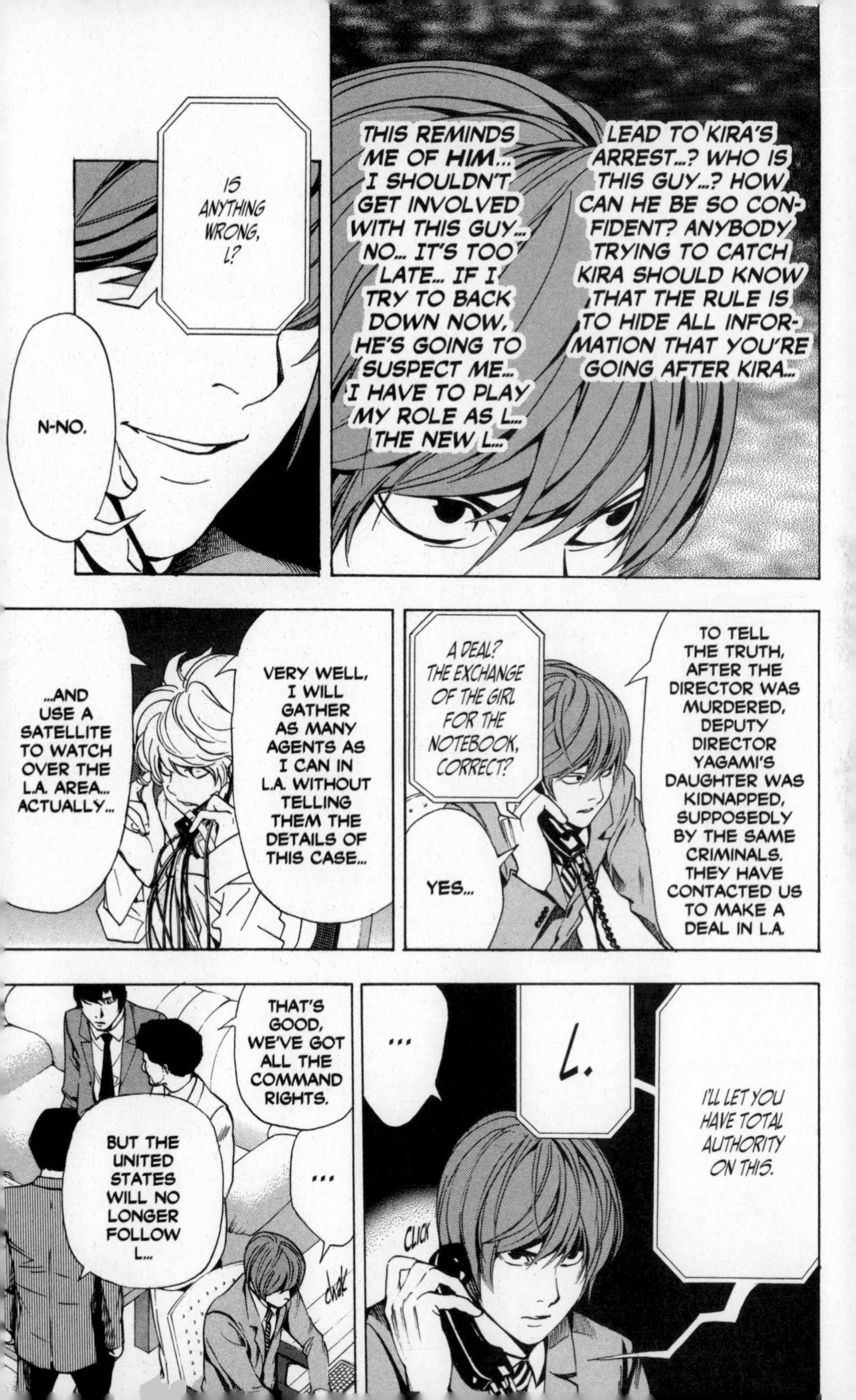
LEAD TO KIRA'S ARREST...? WHO IS THIS GUY...? HOW CAN HE BE SO CON-FIDENT? ANYBODY TRYING TO CATCH KIRA SHOULD KNOW THAT THE RULE IS TO HIDE ALL INFOR-MATION THAT YOU'RE GOING AFTER KIRA...
THIS REMINDS ME OF HIM... I SHOULDN'T GET INVOLVED WITH THIS GUY... NO... IT'S TOO LATE... IF I TRY TO BACK DOWN NOW, HE'S GOING TO SUSPECT ME... I HAVE TO PLAY MY ROLE AS L... THE NEW L...
IS ANYTHING WRONG, L?
N-NO.
TO TELL THE TRUTH, AFTER THE DIRECTOR WAS MURDERED, DEPUTY DIRECTOR YAGAMI'S DAUGHTER WAS KIDNAPPED, SUPPOSEDLY BY THE SAME CRIMINALS. THEY HAVE CONTACTED US TO MAKE A DEAL IN L.A.
A DEAL? THE EXCHANGE OF THE GIRL FOR THE NOTEBOOK, CORRECT?
YES...
VERY WELL, I WILL GATHER AS MANY AGENTS AS I CAN IN L.A. WITHOUT TELLING THEM THE DETAILS OF THIS CASE...
...AND USE A SATELLITE TO WATCH OVER THE L.A. AREA... ACTUALLY...
I'LL LET YOU HAVE TOTAL AUTHORITY ON THIS.
L.
...
CLICK
chak
THAT'S GOOD, WE'VE GOT ALL THE COMMAND RIGHTS.
...
BUT THE UNITED STATES WILL NO LONGER FOLLOW L...

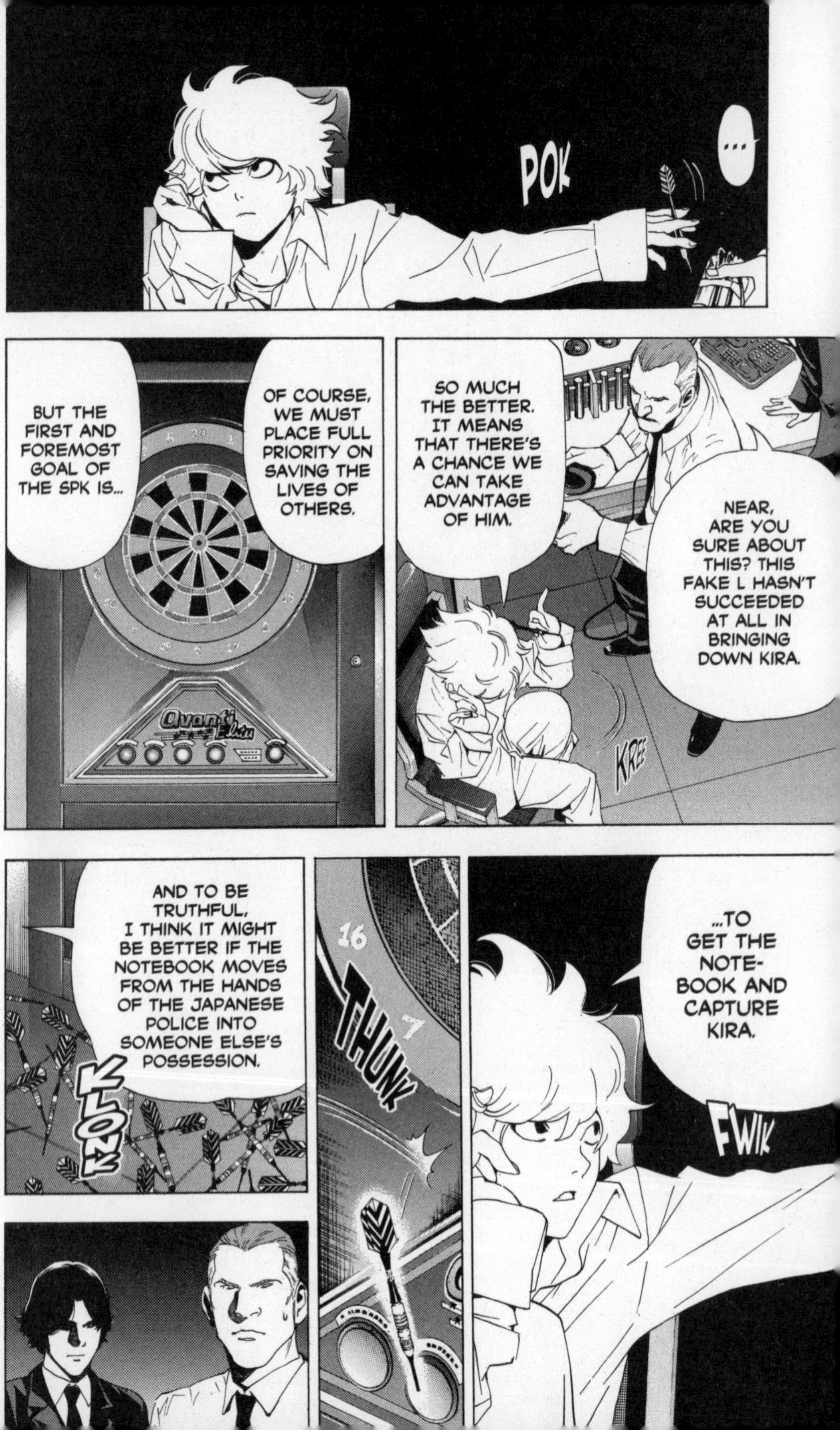
POK
...
NEAR, ARE YOU SURE ABOUT THIS? THIS FAKE L HASN'T SUCCEEDED AT ALL IN BRINGING DOWN KIRA.
SO MUCH THE BETTER. IT MEANS THAT THERE'S A CHANCE WE CAN TAKE ADVANTAGE OF HIM.
KREE
OF COURSE, WE MUST PLACE FULL PRIORITY ON SAVING THE LIVES OF OTHERS.
BUT THE FIRST AND FOREMOST GOAL OF THE SPK IS...
...TO GET THE NOTEBOOK AND CAPTURE KIRA.
FWIK
THUNK
AND TO BE TRUTHFUL, I THINK IT MIGHT BE BETTER IF THE NOTEBOOK MOVES FROM THE HANDS OF THE JAPANESE POLICE INTO SOMEONE ELSE'S POSSESSION.
KLONK

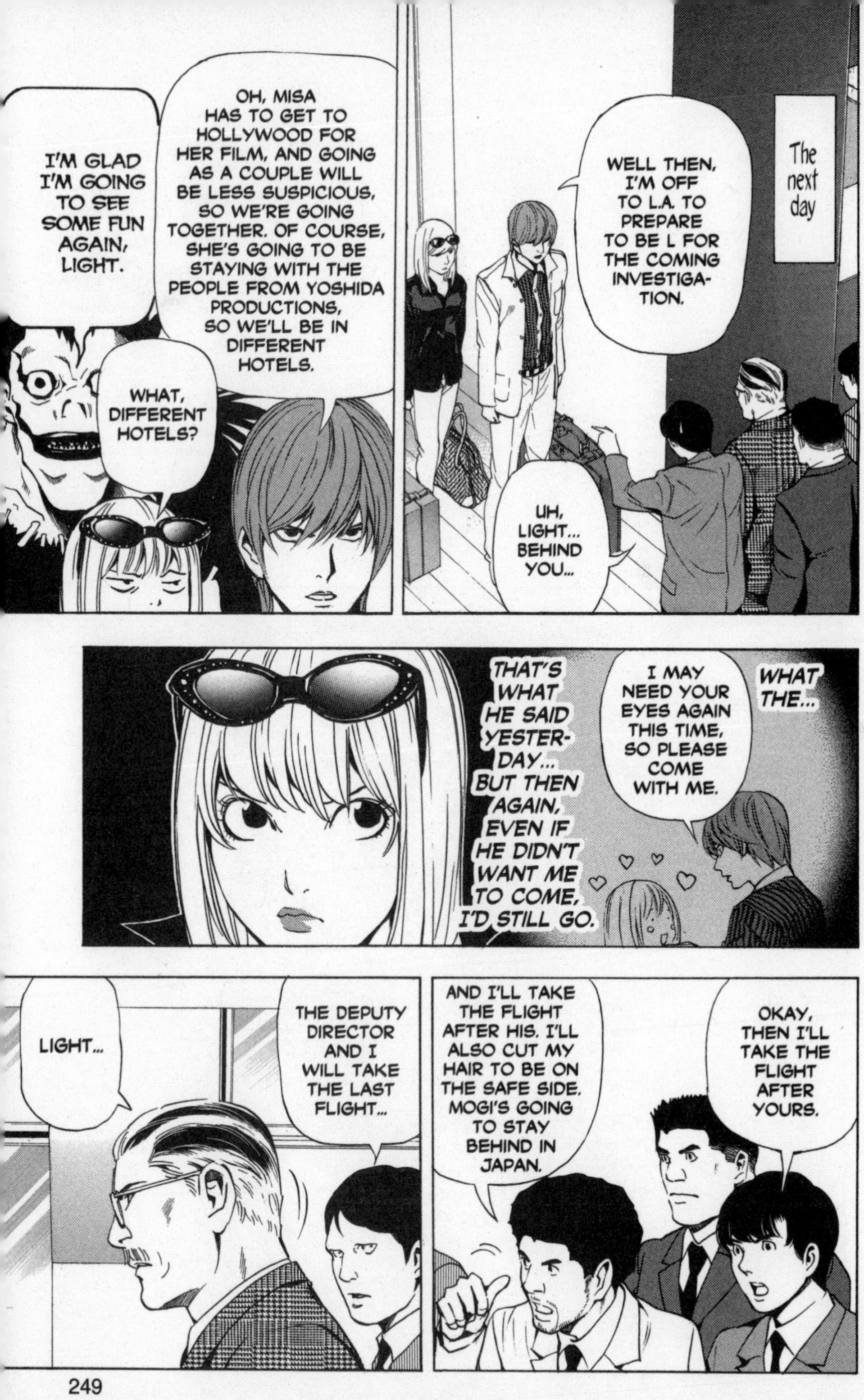
The next day
WELL THEN, I'M OFF TO L.A. TO PREPARE TO BE L FOR THE COMING INVESTIGATION.
UH, LIGHT... BEHIND YOU...
OH, MISA HAS TO GET TO HOLLYWOOD FOR HER FILM, AND GOING AS A COUPLE WILL BE LESS SUSPICIOUS, SO WE'RE GOING TOGETHER. OF COURSE, SHE'S GOING TO BE STAYING WITH THE PEOPLE FROM YOSHIDA PRODUCTIONS, SO WE'LL BE IN DIFFERENT HOTELS.
I'M GLAD I'M GOING TO SEE SOME FUN AGAIN, LIGHT.
WHAT, DIFFERENT HOTELS?
WHAT THE...
I MAY NEED YOUR EYES AGAIN THIS TIME, SO PLEASE COME WITH ME.
THAT'S WHAT HE SAID YESTERDAY... BUT THEN AGAIN, EVEN IF HE DIDN'T WANT ME TO COME, I'D STILL GO.
OKAY, THEN I'LL TAKE THE FLIGHT AFTER YOURS.
AND I'LL TAKE THE FLIGHT AFTER HIS. I'LL ALSO CUT MY HAIR TO BE ON THE SAFE SIDE. MOGI'S GOING TO STAY BEHIND IN JAPAN.
THE DEPUTY DIRECTOR AND I WILL TAKE THE LAST FLIGHT...
LIGHT...

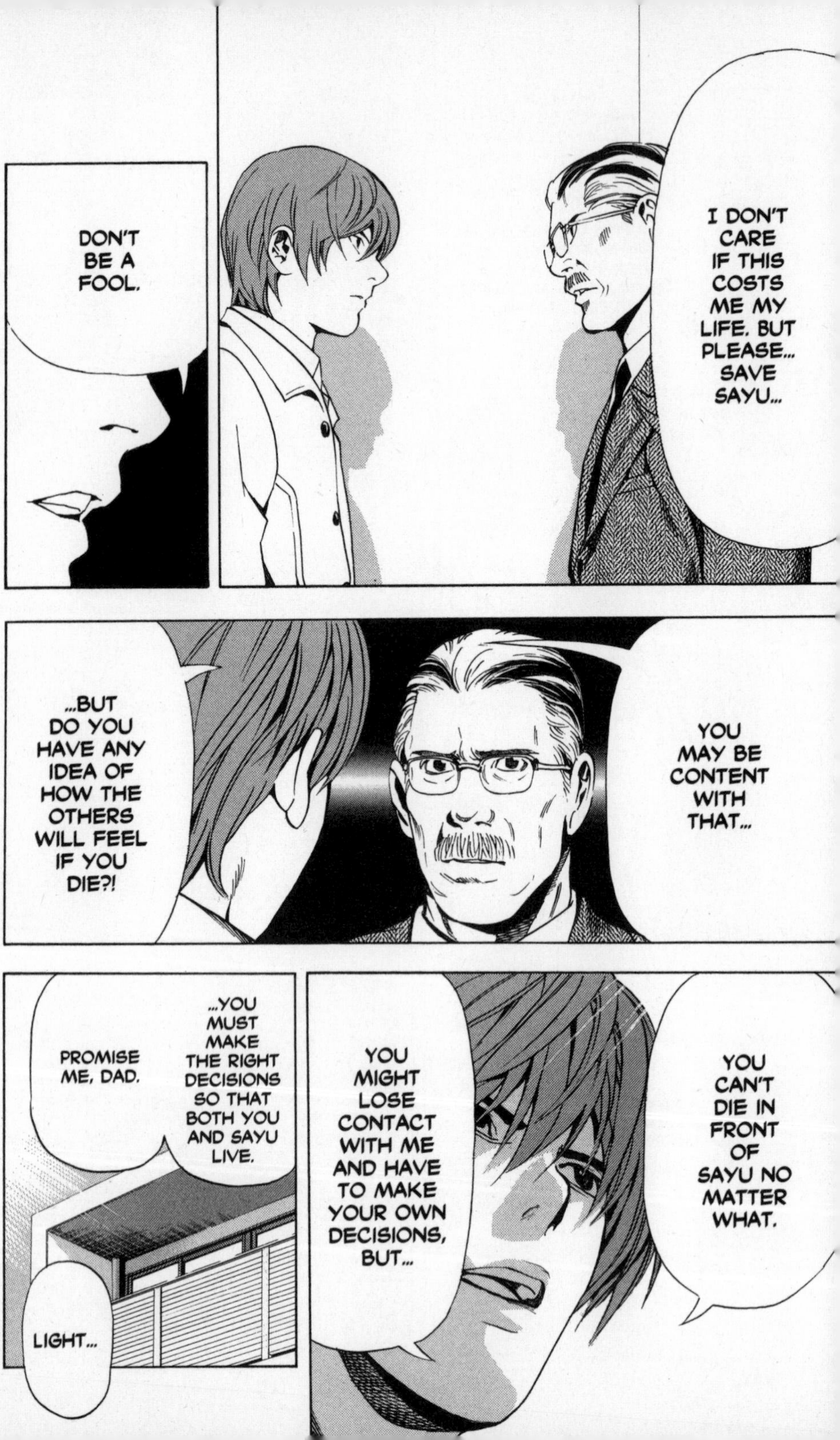
I DON'T CARE IF THIS COSTS ME MY LIFE. BUT PLEASE... SAVE SAYU...
DON'T BE A FOOL.
YOU MAY BE CONTENT WITH THAT...
...BUT DO YOU HAVE ANY IDEA OF HOW THE OTHERS WILL FEEL IF YOU DIE?!
YOU CAN'T DIE IN FRONT OF SAYU NO MATTER WHAT.
YOU MIGHT LOSE CONTACT WITH ME AND HAVE TO MAKE YOUR OWN DECISIONS, BUT...
...YOU MUST MAKE THE RIGHT DECISIONS SO THAT BOTH YOU AND SAYU LIVE.
PROMISE ME, DAD.
LIGHT...

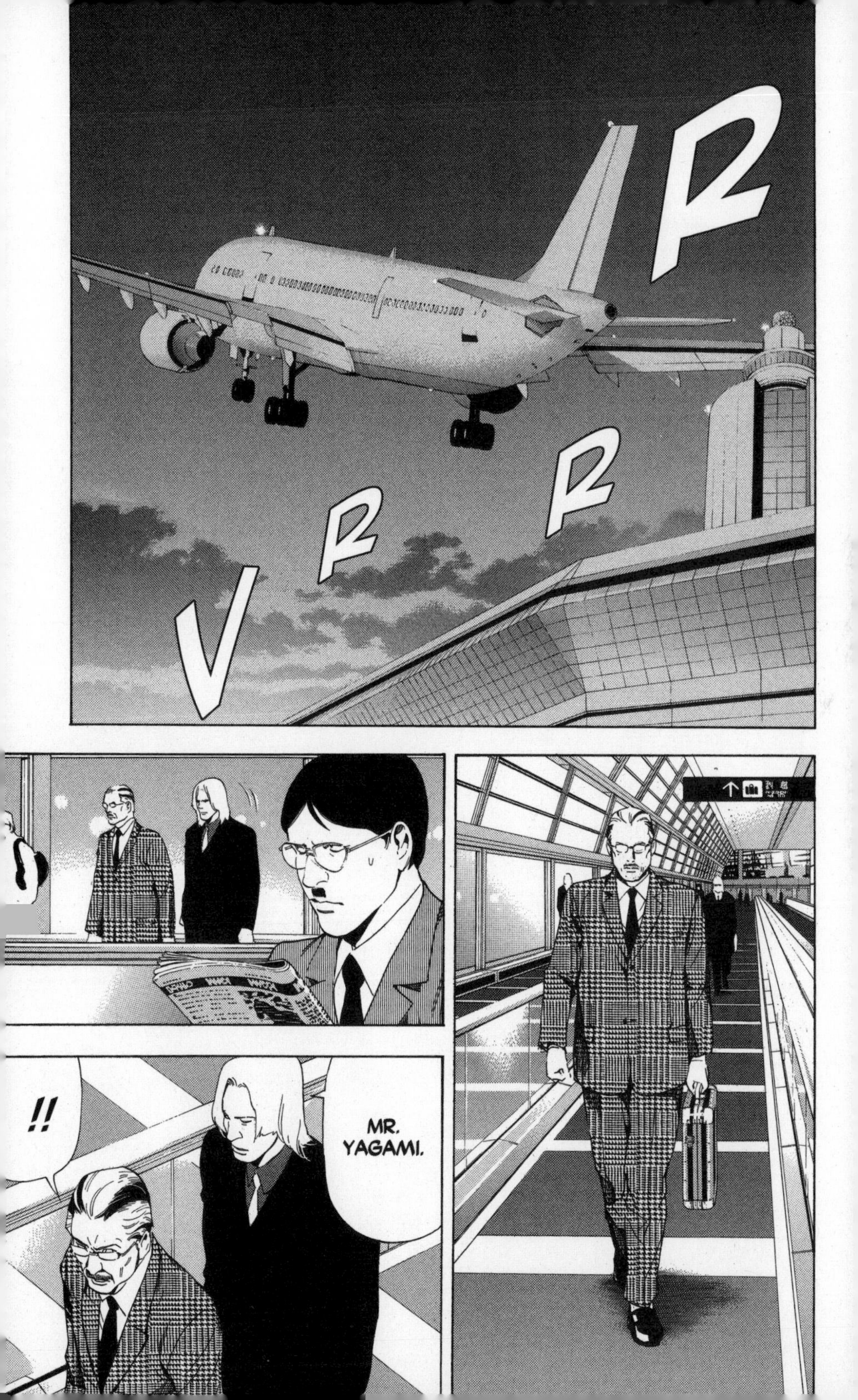
VRRR
MR. YAGAMI.
!!

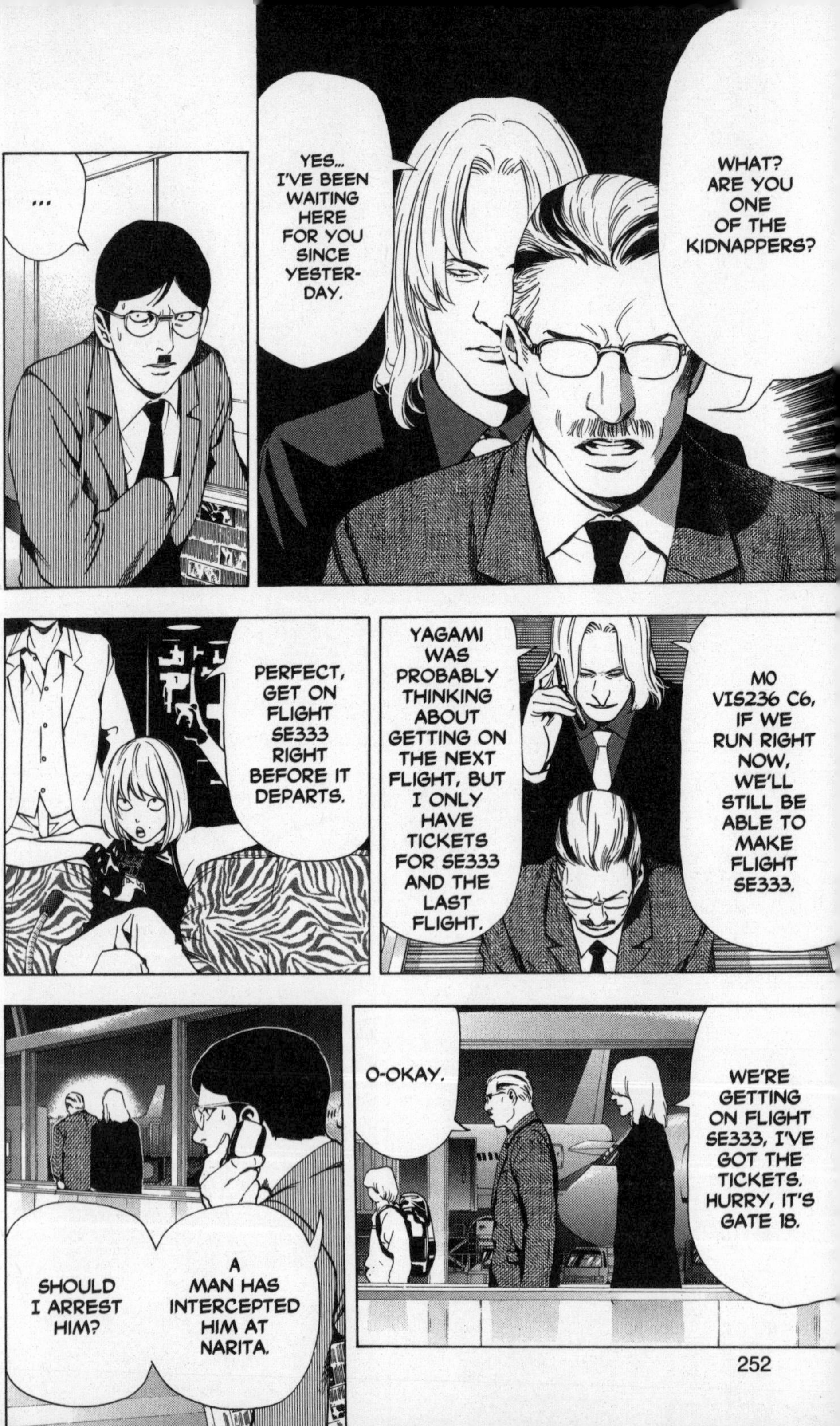
WHAT? ARE YOU ONE OF THE KIDNAPPERS?
YES... I'VE BEEN WAITING HERE FOR YOU SINCE YESTER-DAY.
...
MO VIS236 C6, IF WE RUN RIGHT NOW, WE'LL STILL BE ABLE TO MAKE FLIGHT SE333.
YAGAMI WAS PROBABLY THINKING ABOUT GETTING ON THE NEXT FLIGHT, BUT I ONLY HAVE TICKETS FOR SE333 AND THE LAST FLIGHT.
PERFECT, GET ON FLIGHT SE333 RIGHT BEFORE IT DEPARTS.
WE'RE GETTING ON FLIGHT SE333, I'VE GOT THE TICKETS. HURRY, IT'S GATE 18.
O-OKAY.
A MAN HAS INTERCEPTED HIM AT NARITA.
SHOULD I ARREST HIM?

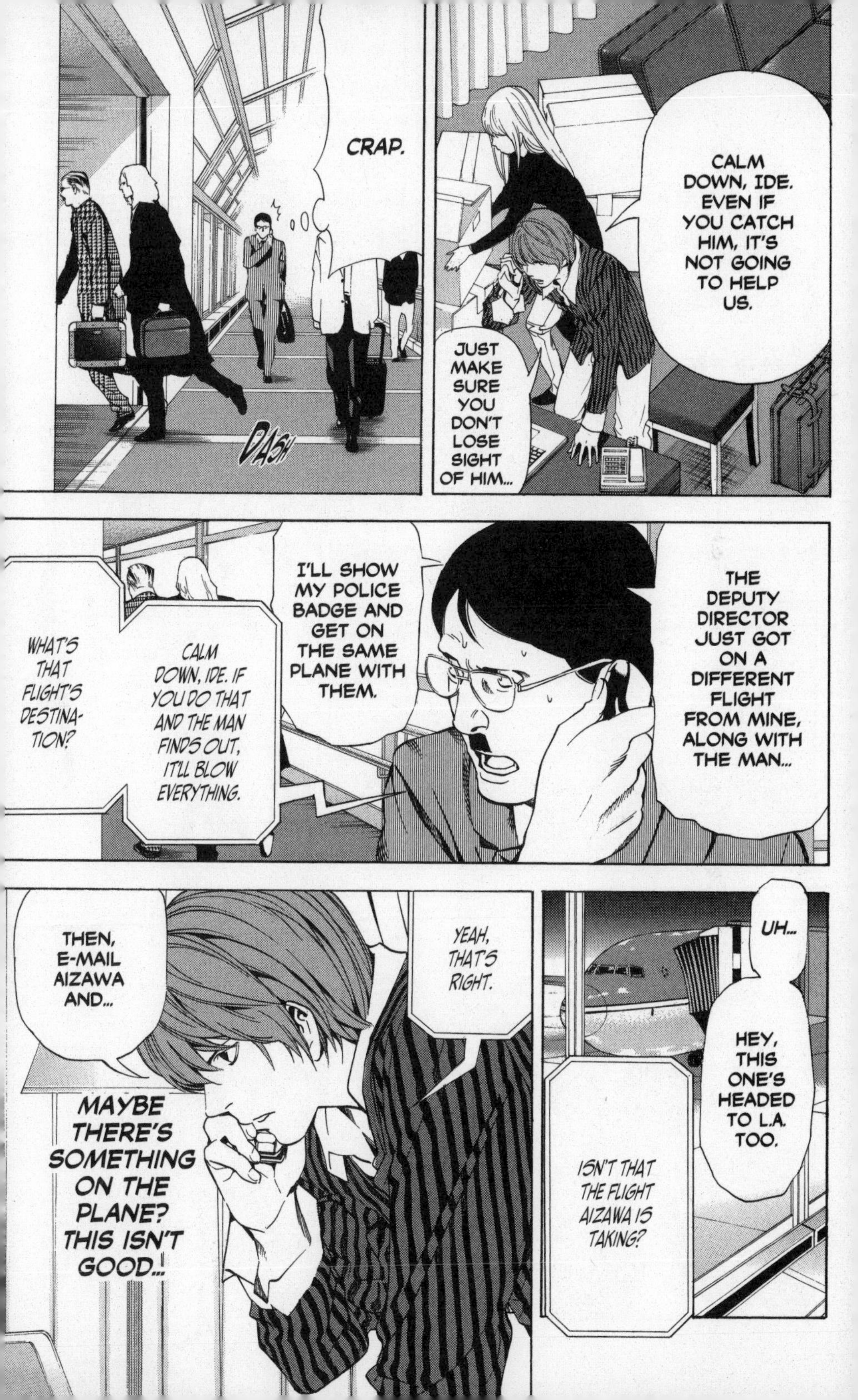
CALM DOWN, IDE. EVEN IF YOU CATCH HIM, IT'S NOT GOING TO HELP US.
JUST MAKE SURE YOU DON'T LOSE SIGHT OF HIM...
CRAP.
DASH
THE DEPUTY DIRECTOR JUST GOT ON A DIFFERENT FLIGHT FROM MINE, ALONG WITH THE MAN...
I'LL SHOW MY POLICE BADGE AND GET ON THE SAME PLANE WITH THEM.
CALM DOWN, IDE. IF YOU DO THAT AND THE MAN FINDS OUT, IT'LL BLOW EVERYTHING.
WHAT'S THAT FLIGHT'S DESTINATION?
UH...
HEY, THIS ONE'S HEADED TO L.A. TOO.
ISN'T THAT THE FLIGHT AIZAWA IS TAKING?
YEAH, THAT'S RIGHT.
THEN, E-MAIL AIZAWA AND...
MAYBE THERE'S SOMETHING ON THE PLANE? THIS ISN'T GOOD...!

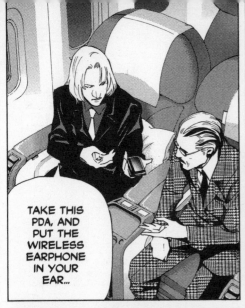

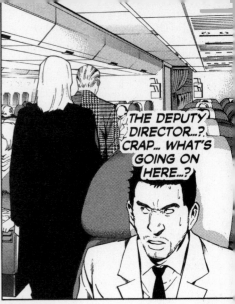

THE DEPUTY DIRECTOR...? CRAP... WHAT'S GOING ON HERE...?
TAKE THIS PDA, AND PUT THE WIRELESS EARPHONE IN YOUR EAR...
YAGAMI, ONLY YOU CAN HEAR MY VOICE. NOT EVEN THE MAN NEXT TO YOU CAN HEAR ME, SO LISTEN CLOSELY.
I'M THE MASTER-MIND BEHIND YOUR DAUGHTER'S KIDNAPPING.
I HAVE NO INTEREST IN THE LIVES OF YOU OR YOUR DAUGHTER.
CRUNCH

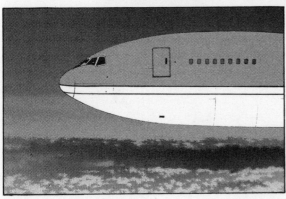

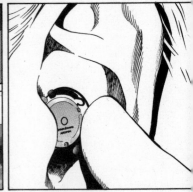

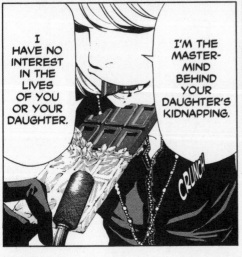

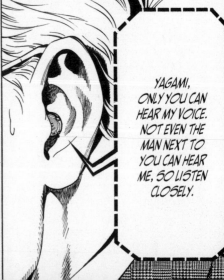

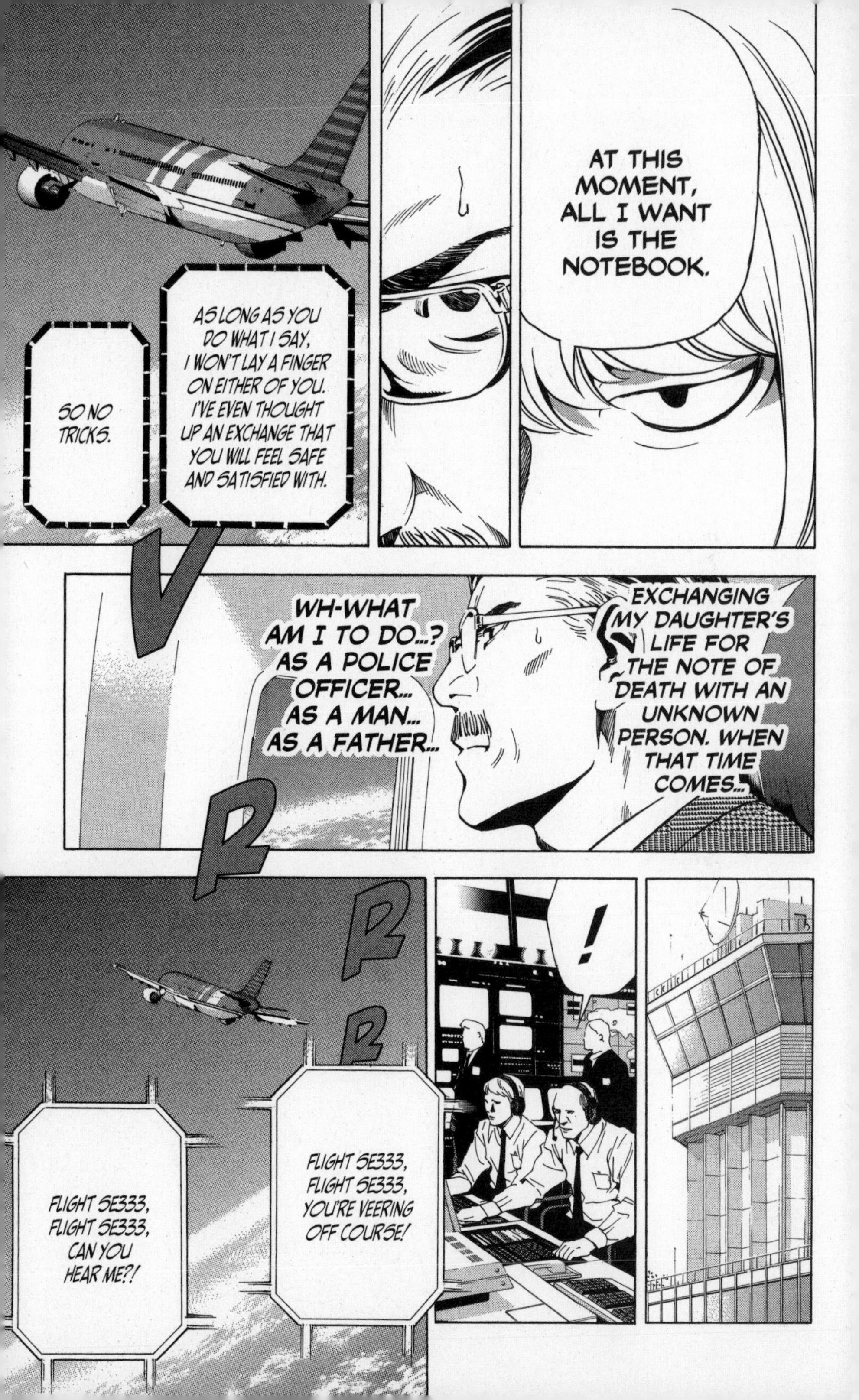
AT THIS MOMENT, ALL I WANT IS THE NOTEBOOK.
AS LONG AS YOU DO WHAT I SAY, I WON'T LAY A FINGER ON EITHER OF YOU. I'VE EVEN THOUGHT UP AN EXCHANGE THAT YOU WILL FEEL SAFE AND SATISFIED WITH.
SO NO TRICKS.
EXCHANGING MY DAUGHTER'S LIFE FOR THE NOTE OF DEATH WITH AN UNKNOWN PERSON. WHEN THAT TIME COMES...
WH-WHAT AM I TO DO...? AS A POLICE OFFICER... AS A MAN... AS A FATHER...
VRRR
!
FLIGHT SE333, FLIGHT SE333, YOU'RE VEERING OFF COURSE!
FLIGHT SE333, FLIGHT SE333, CAN YOU HEAR ME?!

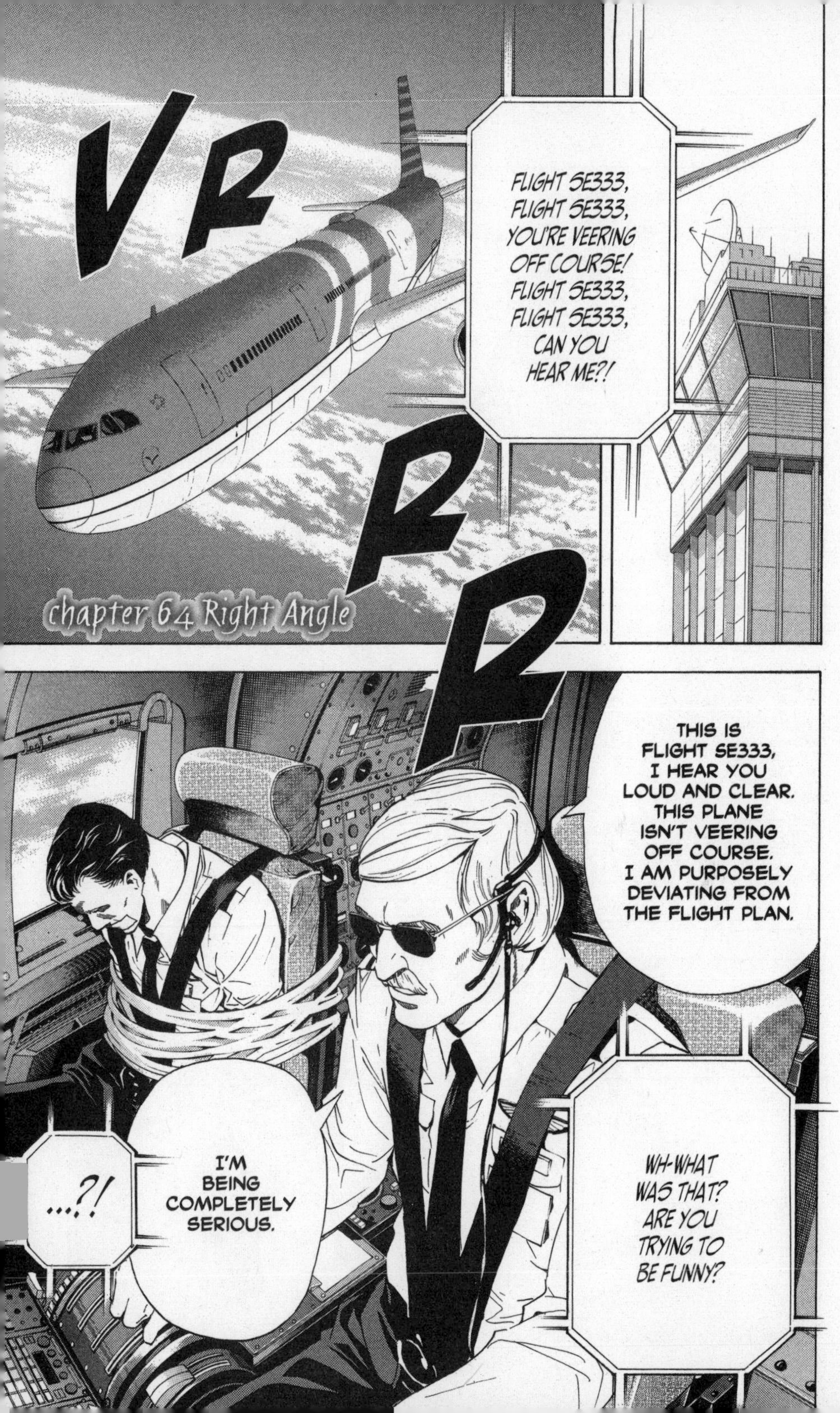
FLIGHT SE333, FLIGHT SE333, YOU'RE VEERING OFF COURSE! FLIGHT SE333, FLIGHT SE333, CAN YOU HEAR ME?!
VRRR
chapter 64 Right Angle
THIS IS FLIGHT SE333, I HEAR YOU LOUD AND CLEAR. THIS PLANE ISN'T VEERING OFF COURSE. I AM PURPOSELY DEVIATING FROM THE FLIGHT PLAN.
WH-WHAT WAS THAT? ARE YOU TRYING TO BE FUNNY?
I'M BEING COMPLETELY SERIOUS.
...?!

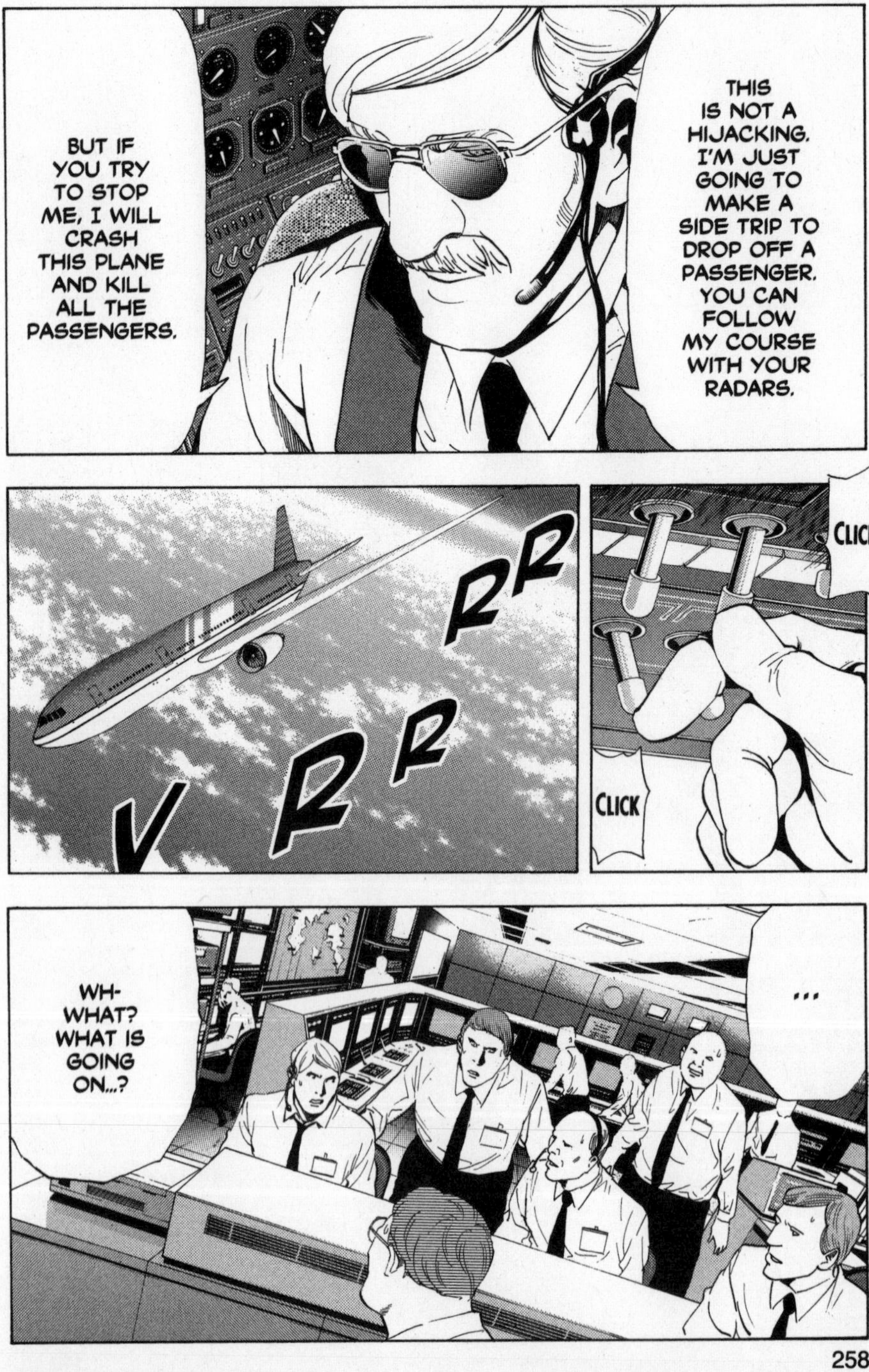
THIS IS NOT A HIJACKING. I'M JUST GOING TO MAKE A SIDE TRIP TO DROP OFF A PASSENGER. YOU CAN FOLLOW MY COURSE WITH YOUR RADARS.
BUT IF YOU TRY TO STOP ME, I WILL CRASH THIS PLANE AND KILL ALL THE PASSENGERS.
CLICK
CLICK
VRRRR
...
WH- WHAT? WHAT IS GOING ON...?

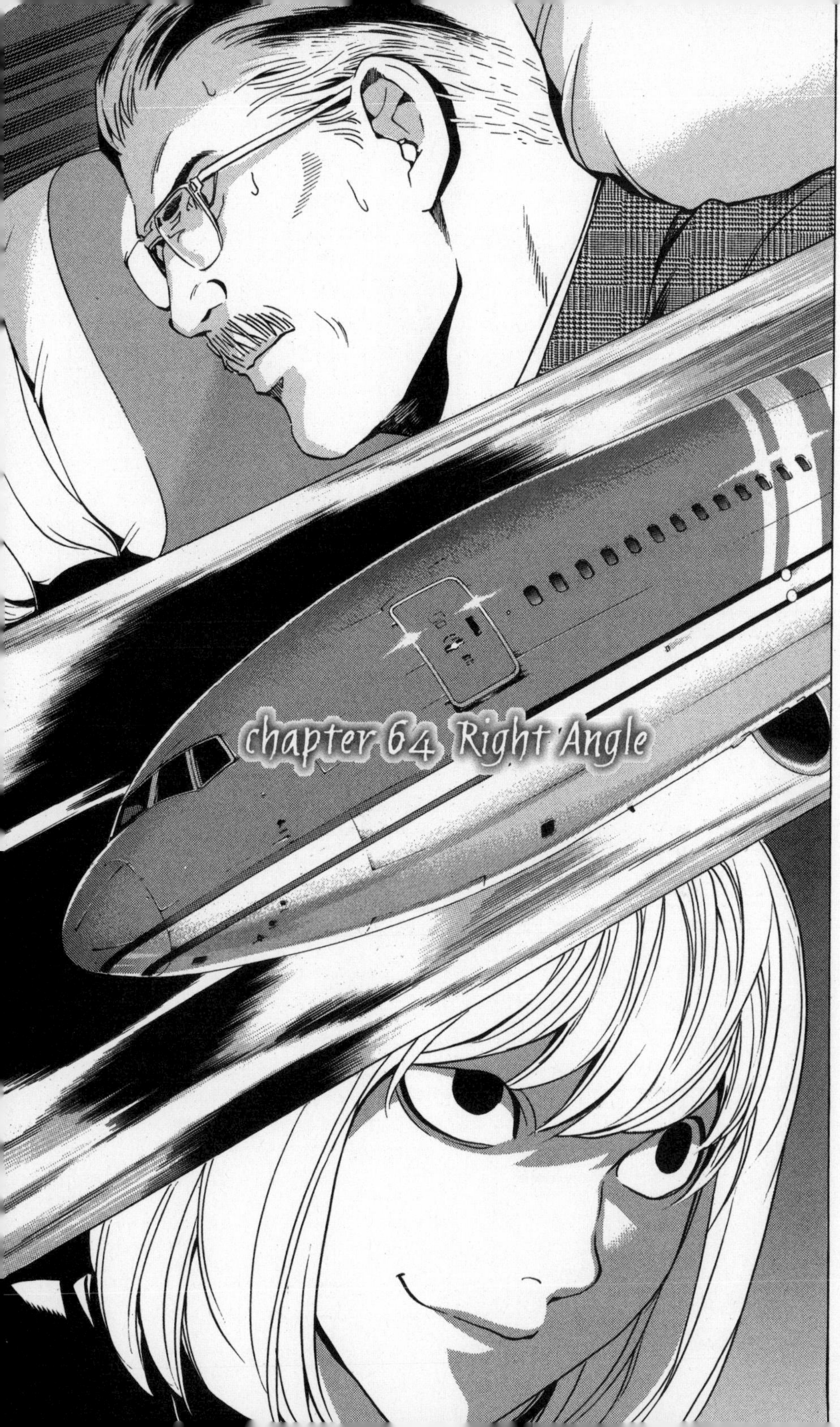
chapter 64 Right Angle

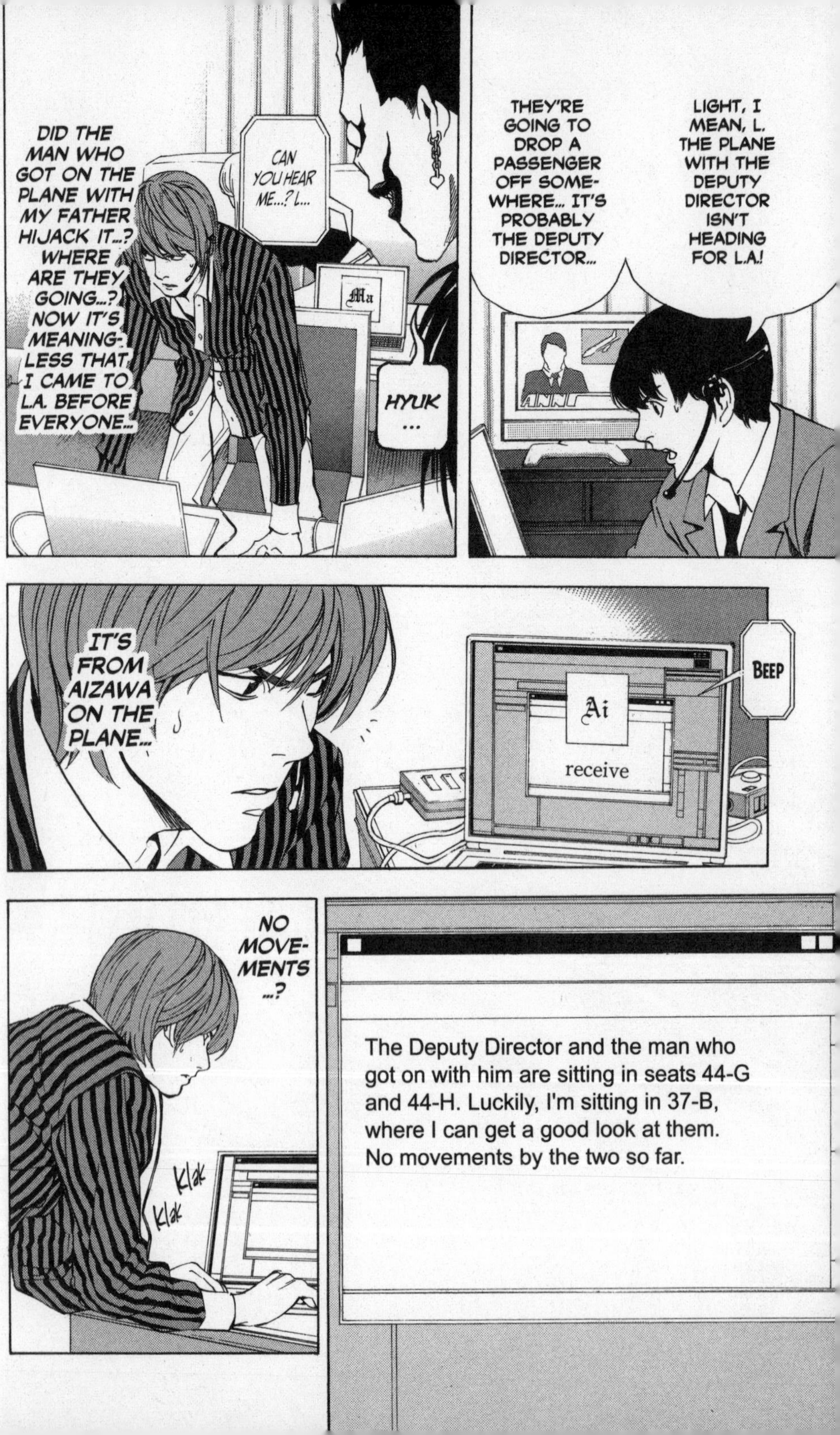
LIGHT, I MEAN, L. THE PLANE WITH THE DEPUTY DIRECTOR ISN'T HEADING FOR L.A.!
THEY'RE GOING TO DROP A PASSENGER OFF SOME-WHERE... IT'S PROBABLY THE DEPUTY DIRECTOR...
ANN
CAN YOU HEAR ME...? L...
DID THE MAN WHO GOT ON THE PLANE WITH MY FATHER HIJACK IT...? WHERE ARE THEY GOING...? NOW IT'S MEANING-LESS THAT I CAME TO L.A. BEFORE EVERYONE...
Ma
HYUK ...
BEEP
Ai
receive
IT'S FROM AIZAWA ON THE PLANE...
The Deputy Director and the man who got on with him are sitting in seats 44-G and 44-H. Luckily, I'm sitting in 37-B, where I can get a good look at them. No movements by the two so far.
NO MOVE-MENTS ...?
Klak
Klak

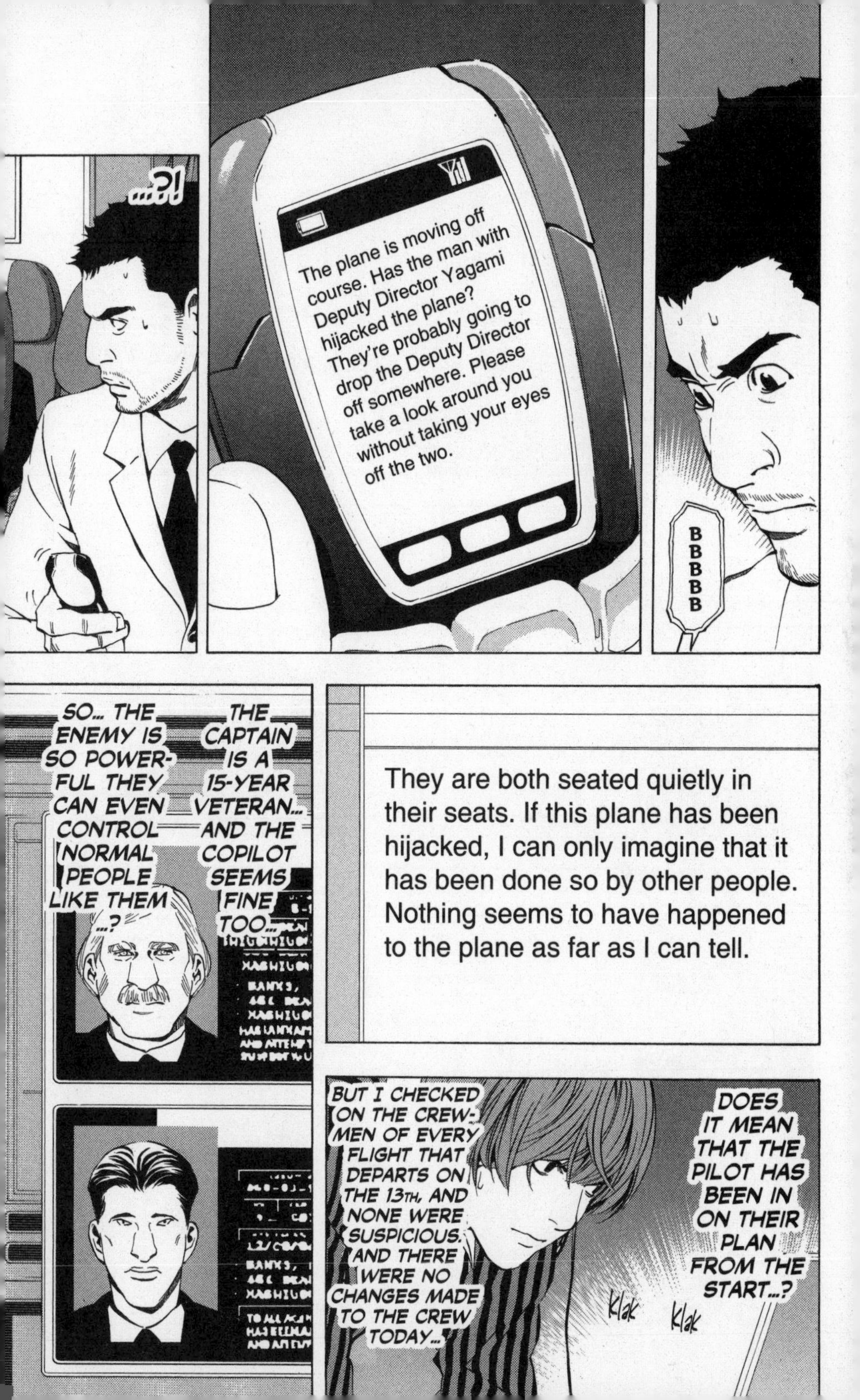
BBBBB
The plane is moving off course. Has the man with Deputy Director Yagami hijacked the plane? They're probably going to drop the Deputy Director off somewhere. Please take a look around you without taking your eyes off the two.
...?!
They are both seated quietly in their seats. If this plane has been hijacked, I can only imagine that it has been done so by other people. Nothing seems to have happened to the plane as far as I can tell.
THE CAPTAIN IS A 15-YEAR VETERAN... AND THE COPILOT SEEMS FINE TOO...
SO... THE ENEMY IS SO POWERFUL THEY CAN EVEN CONTROL NORMAL PEOPLE LIKE THEM ...?
DOES IT MEAN THAT THE PILOT HAS BEEN IN ON THEIR PLAN FROM THE START...?
BUT I CHECKED ON THE CREWMEN OF EVERY FLIGHT THAT DEPARTS ON THE 13TH, AND NONE WERE SUSPICIOUS. AND THERE WERE NO CHANGES MADE TO THE CREW TODAY...
Klak
Klak

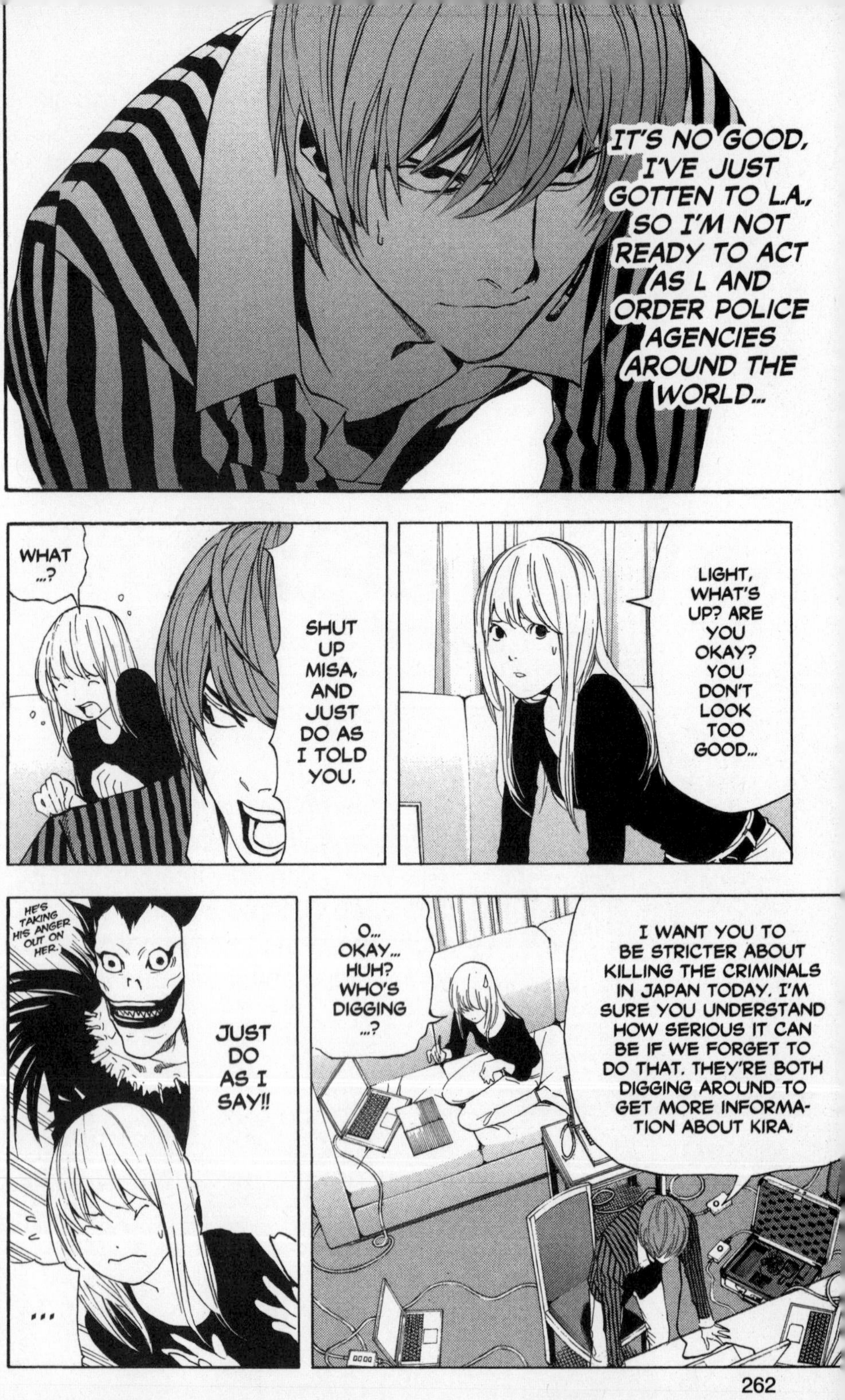
IT'S NO GOOD, I'VE JUST GOTTEN TO L.A., SO I'M NOT READY TO ACT AS L AND ORDER POLICE AGENCIES AROUND THE WORLD...
LIGHT, WHAT'S UP? ARE YOU OKAY? YOU DON'T LOOK TOO GOOD...
SHUT UP MISA, AND JUST DO AS I TOLD YOU.
WHAT ...?
I WANT YOU TO BE STRICTER ABOUT KILLING THE CRIMINALS IN JAPAN TODAY. I'M SURE YOU UNDERSTAND HOW SERIOUS IT CAN BE IF WE FORGET TO DO THAT. THEY'RE BOTH DIGGING AROUND TO GET MORE INFORMATION ABOUT KIRA.
O... OKAY... HUH? WHO'S DIGGING ...?
HE'S TAKING HIS ANGER OUT ON HER.
JUST DO AS I SAY!!
...

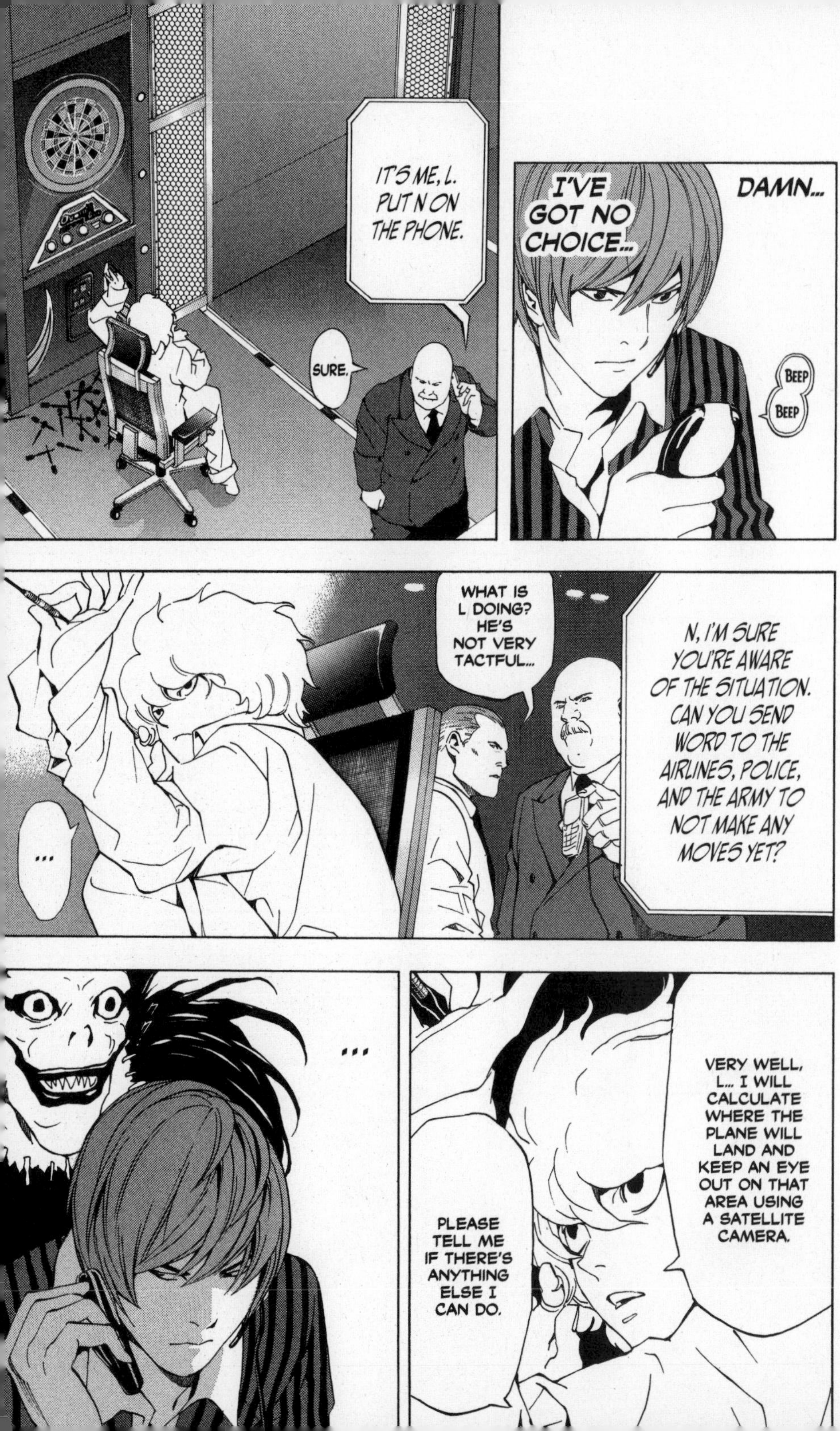
DAMN...
I'VE GOT NO CHOICE...
BEEP
BEEP
IT'S ME, L. PUT N ON THE PHONE.
SURE.
N, I'M SURE YOU'RE AWARE OF THE SITUATION. CAN YOU SEND WORD TO THE AIRLINES, POLICE, AND THE ARMY TO NOT MAKE ANY MOVES YET?
WHAT IS L DOING? HE'S NOT VERY TACTFUL...
...
VERY WELL, L... I WILL CALCULATE WHERE THE PLANE WILL LAND AND KEEP AN EYE OUT ON THAT AREA USING A SATELLITE CAMERA.
PLEASE TELL ME IF THERE'S ANYTHING ELSE I CAN DO.
...

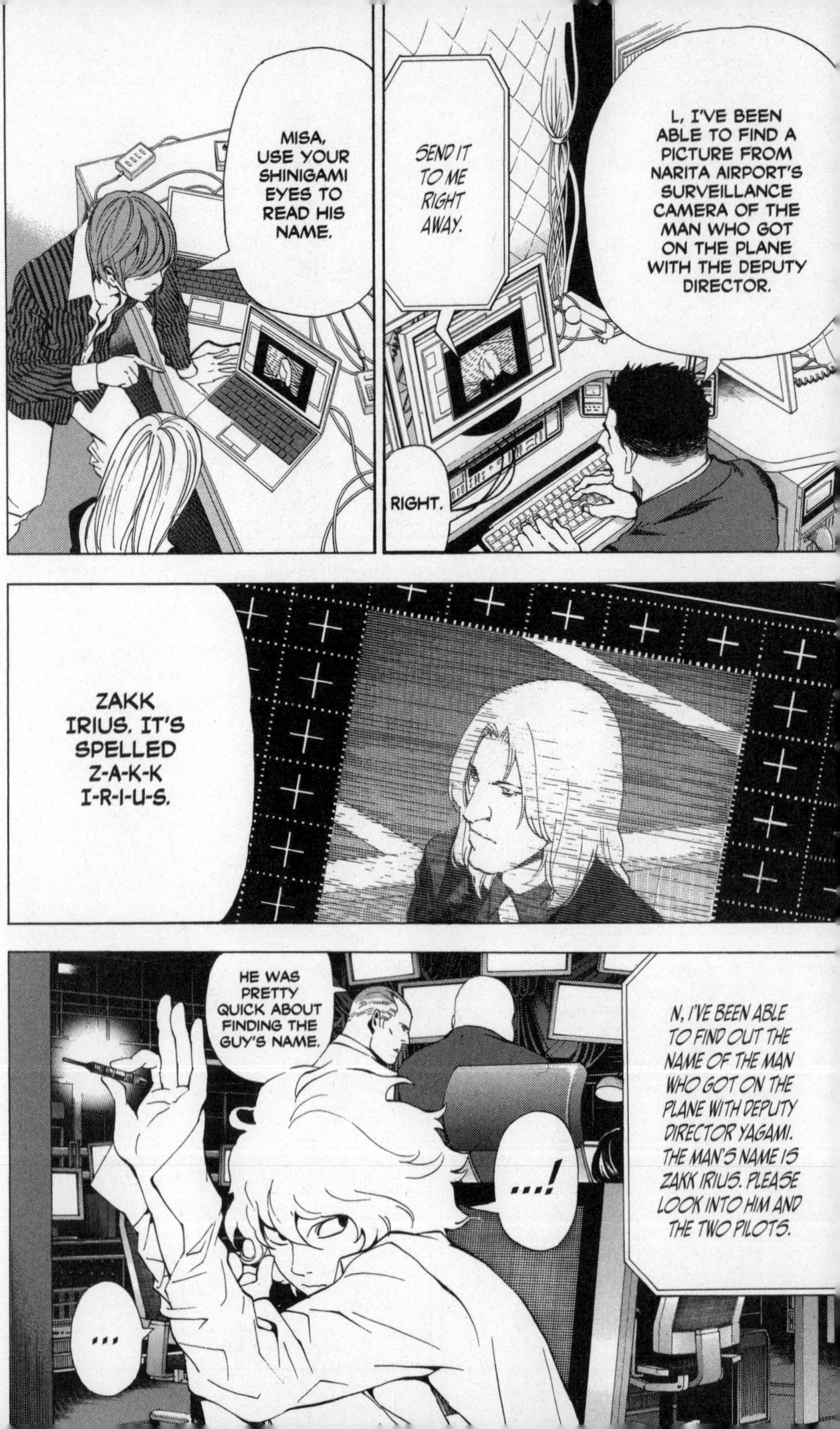
L, I'VE BEEN ABLE TO FIND A PICTURE FROM NARITA AIRPORT'S SURVEILLANCE CAMERA OF THE MAN WHO GOT ON THE PLANE WITH THE DEPUTY DIRECTOR.
SEND IT TO ME RIGHT AWAY.
RIGHT.
MISA, USE YOUR SHINIGAMI EYES TO READ HIS NAME.
ZAKK IRIUS. IT'S SPELLED Z-A-K-K I-R-I-U-S.
N, I'VE BEEN ABLE TO FIND OUT THE NAME OF THE MAN WHO GOT ON THE PLANE WITH DEPUTY DIRECTOR YAGAMI. THE MAN'S NAME IS ZAKK IRIUS. PLEASE LOOK INTO HIM AND THE TWO PILOTS.
HE WAS PRETTY QUICK ABOUT FINDING THE GUY'S NAME.
...!
...

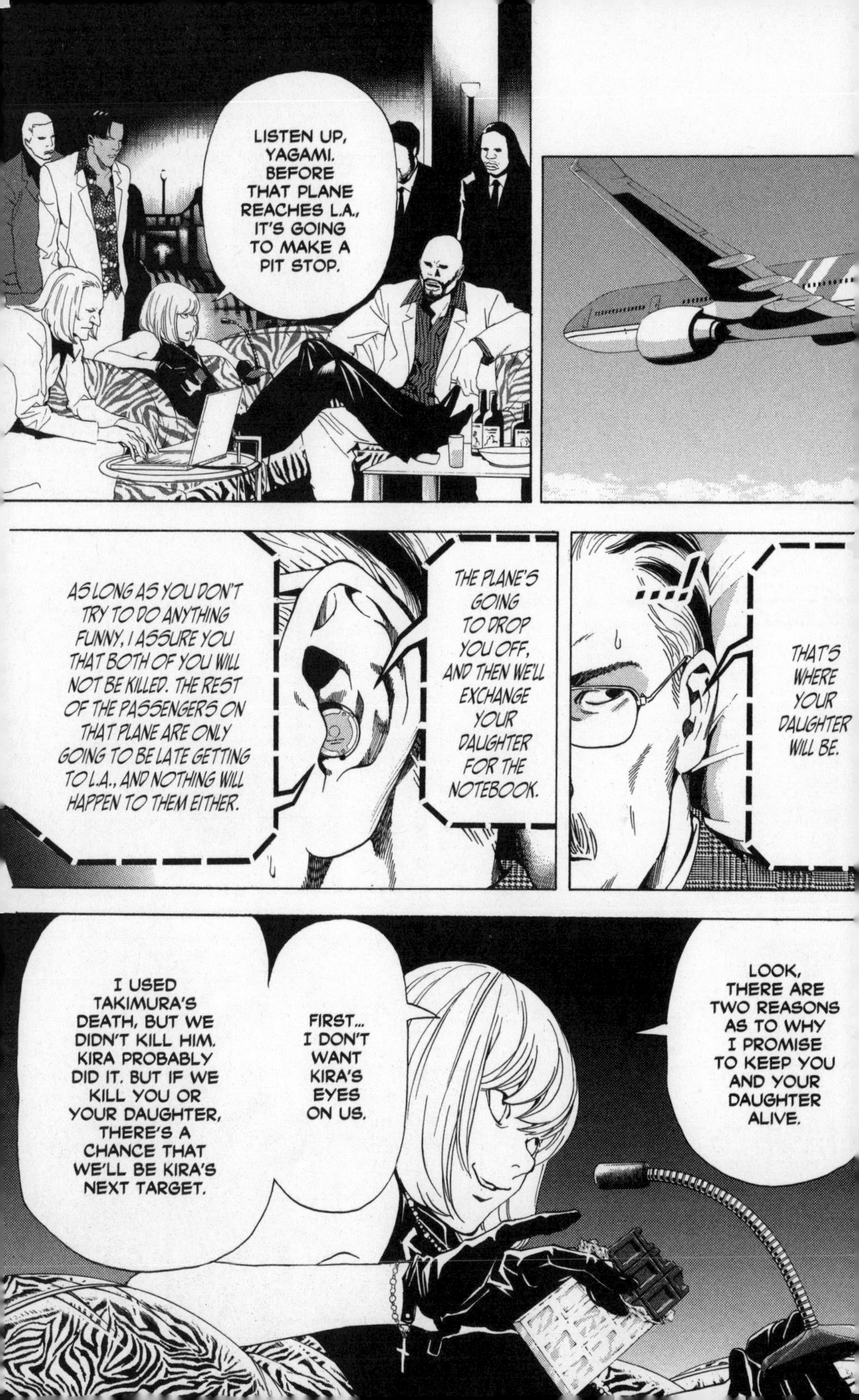
LISTEN UP, YAGAMI. BEFORE THAT PLANE REACHES L.A., IT'S GOING TO MAKE A PIT STOP.
...!!
THAT'S WHERE YOUR DAUGHTER WILL BE.
THE PLANE'S GOING TO DROP YOU OFF, AND THEN WE'LL EXCHANGE YOUR DAUGHTER FOR THE NOTEBOOK.
AS LONG AS YOU DON'T TRY TO DO ANYTHING FUNNY, I ASSURE YOU THAT BOTH OF YOU WILL NOT BE KILLED. THE REST OF THE PASSENGERS ON THAT PLANE ARE ONLY GOING TO BE LATE GETTING TO L.A., AND NOTHING WILL HAPPEN TO THEM EITHER.
LOOK, THERE ARE TWO REASONS AS TO WHY I PROMISE TO KEEP YOU AND YOUR DAUGHTER ALIVE.
FIRST... I DON'T WANT KIRA'S EYES ON US.
I USED TAKIMURA'S DEATH, BUT WE DIDN'T KILL HIM. KIRA PROBABLY DID IT. BUT IF WE KILL YOU OR YOUR DAUGHTER, THERE'S A CHANCE THAT WE'LL BE KIRA'S NEXT TARGET.

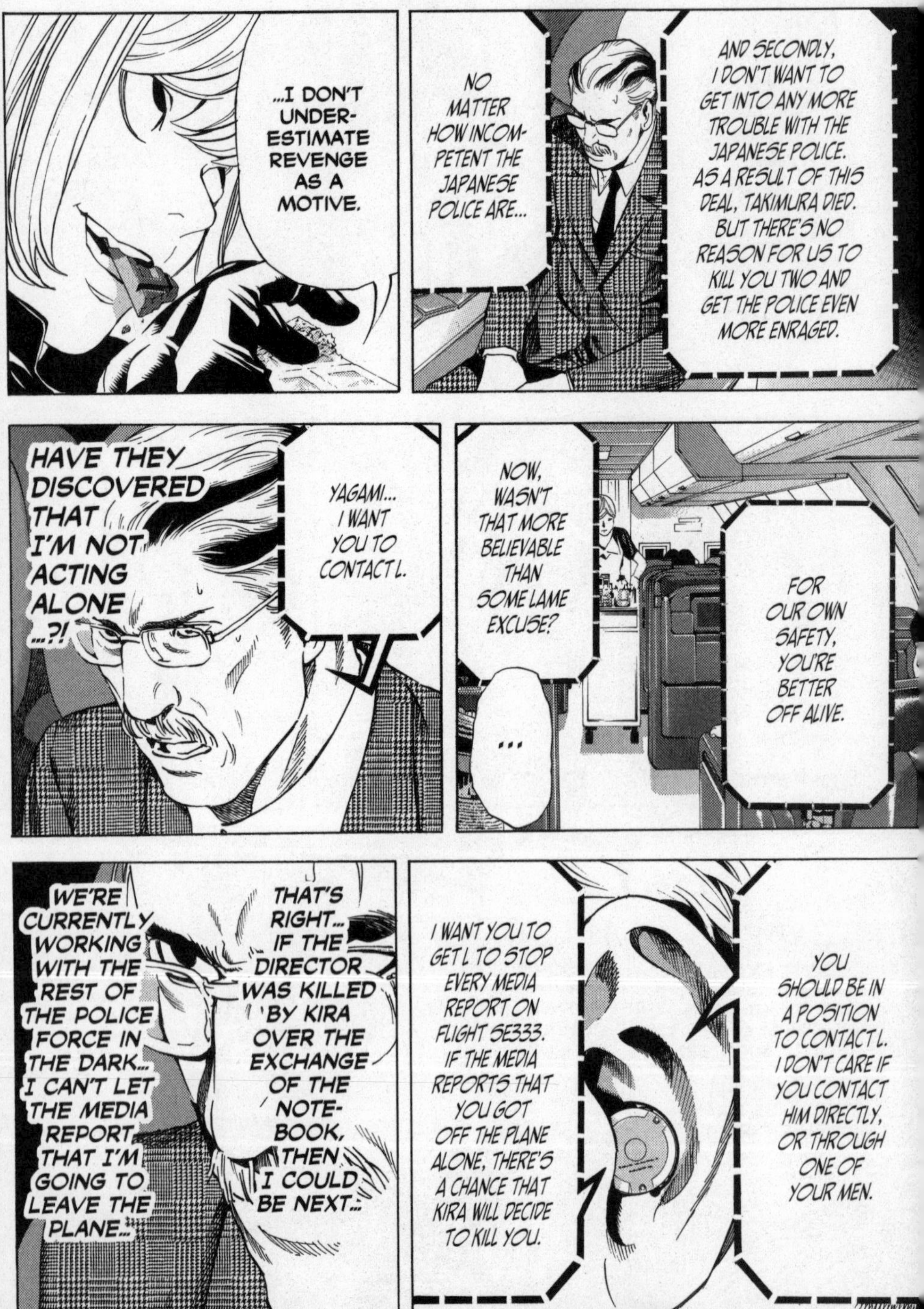
AND SECONDLY, I DON'T WANT TO GET INTO ANY MORE TROUBLE WITH THE JAPANESE POLICE. AS A RESULT OF THIS DEAL, TAKIMURA DIED. BUT THERE'S NO REASON FOR US TO KILL YOU TWO AND GET THE POLICE EVEN MORE ENRAGED.
NO MATTER HOW INCOMPETENT THE JAPANESE POLICE ARE...
...I DON'T UNDERESTIMATE REVENGE AS A MOTIVE.
FOR OUR OWN SAFETY, YOU'RE BETTER OFF ALIVE.
NOW, WASN'T THAT MORE BELIEVABLE THAN SOME LAME EXCUSE?
...
YAGAMI... I WANT YOU TO CONTACT L.
HAVE THEY DISCOVERED THAT I'M NOT ACTING ALONE ...?!
YOU SHOULD BE IN A POSITION TO CONTACT L. I DON'T CARE IF YOU CONTACT HIM DIRECTLY, OR THROUGH ONE OF YOUR MEN.
I WANT YOU TO GET L TO STOP EVERY MEDIA REPORT ON FLIGHT SE333. IF THE MEDIA REPORTS THAT YOU GOT OFF THE PLANE ALONE, THERE'S A CHANCE THAT KIRA WILL DECIDE TO KILL YOU.
THAT'S RIGHT... IF THE DIRECTOR WAS KILLED BY KIRA OVER THE EXCHANGE OF THE NOTEBOOK, THEN I COULD BE NEXT...
WE'RE CURRENTLY WORKING WITH THE REST OF THE POLICE FORCE IN THE DARK... I CAN'T LET THE MEDIA REPORT THAT I'M GOING TO LEAVE THE PLANE...

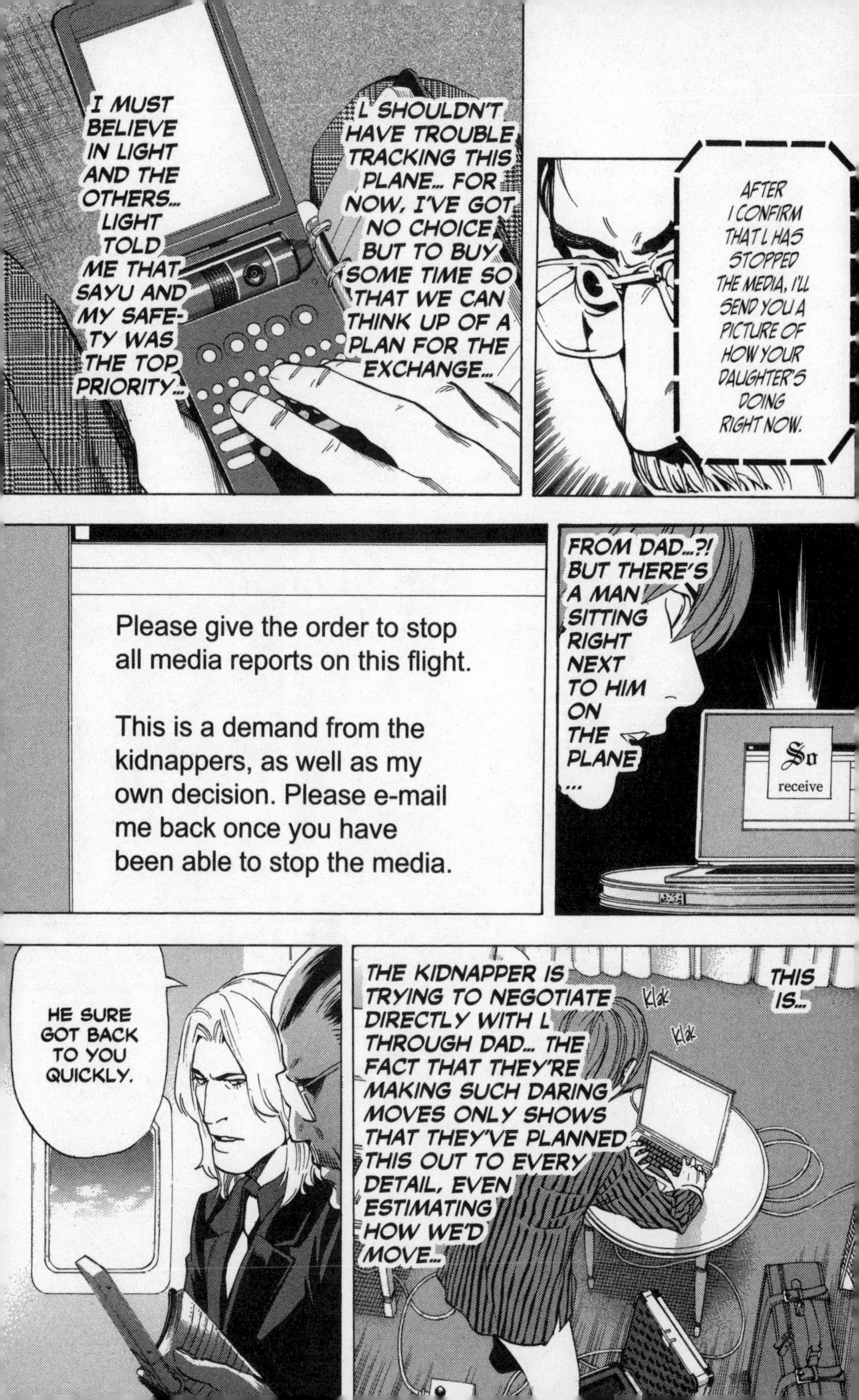
AFTER I CONFIRM THAT L HAS STOPPED THE MEDIA, I'LL SEND YOU A PICTURE OF HOW YOUR DAUGHTER'S DOING RIGHT NOW.
L SHOULDN'T HAVE TROUBLE TRACKING THIS PLANE... FOR NOW, I'VE GOT NO CHOICE BUT TO BUY SOME TIME SO THAT WE CAN THINK UP OF A PLAN FOR THE EXCHANGE...
I MUST BELIEVE IN LIGHT AND THE OTHERS... LIGHT TOLD ME THAT SAYU AND MY SAFETY WAS THE TOP PRIORITY...
FROM DAD...?! BUT THERE'S A MAN SITTING RIGHT NEXT TO HIM ON THE PLANE...
So
receive
Please give the order to stop all media reports on this flight.
This is a demand from the kidnappers, as well as my own decision. Please e-mail me back once you have been able to stop the media.
THIS IS...
THE KIDNAPPER IS TRYING TO NEGOTIATE DIRECTLY WITH L THROUGH DAD... THE FACT THAT THEY'RE MAKING SUCH DARING MOVES ONLY SHOWS THAT THEY'VE PLANNED THIS OUT TO EVERY DETAIL, EVEN ESTIMATING HOW WE'D MOVE...
Klak
Klak
HE SURE GOT BACK TO YOU QUICKLY.

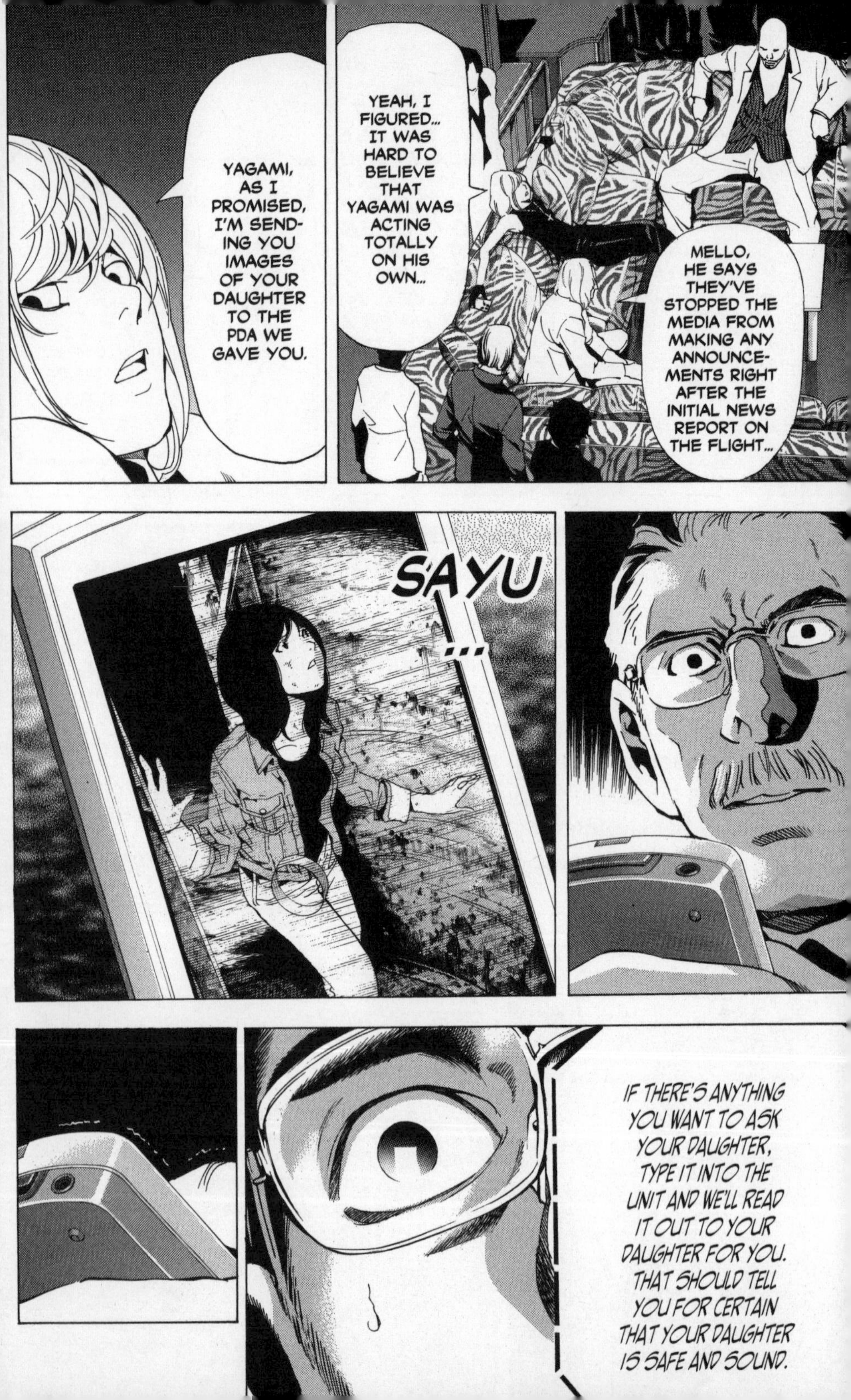
MELLO, HE SAYS THEY'VE STOPPED THE MEDIA FROM MAKING ANY ANNOUNCEMENTS RIGHT AFTER THE INITIAL NEWS REPORT ON THE FLIGHT...
YEAH, I FIGURED... IT WAS HARD TO BELIEVE THAT YAGAMI WAS ACTING TOTALLY ON HIS OWN...
YAGAMI, AS I PROMISED, I'M SENDING YOU IMAGES OF YOUR DAUGHTER TO THE PDA WE GAVE YOU.
SAYU ...
IF THERE'S ANYTHING YOU WANT TO ASK YOUR DAUGHTER, TYPE IT INTO THE UNIT AND WE'LL READ IT OUT TO YOUR DAUGHTER FOR YOU. THAT SHOULD TELL YOU FOR CERTAIN THAT YOUR DAUGHTER IS SAFE AND SOUND.

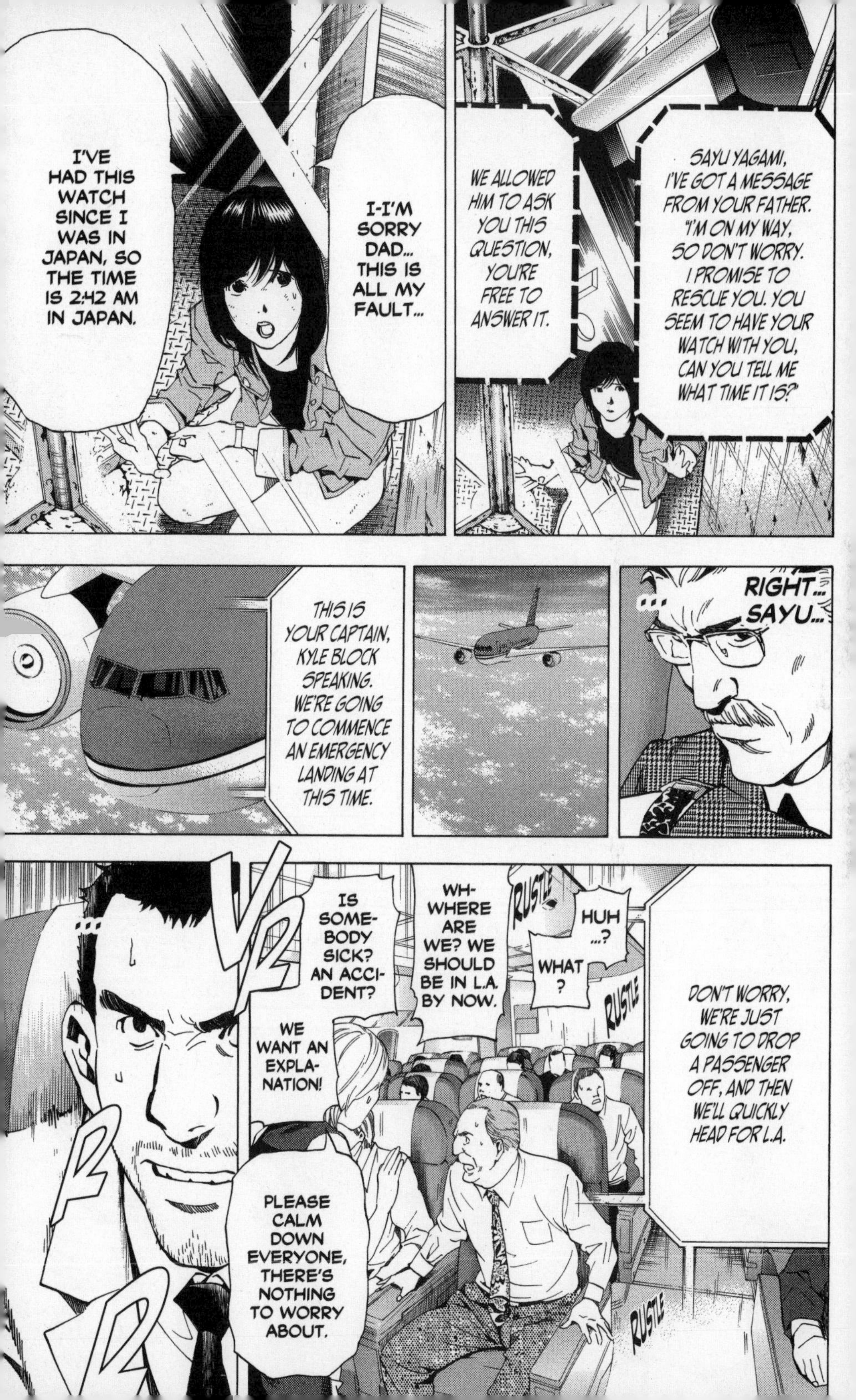
SAYU YAGAMI, I'VE GOT A MESSAGE FROM YOUR FATHER. "I'M ON MY WAY, SO DON'T WORRY. I PROMISE TO RESCUE YOU. YOU SEEM TO HAVE YOUR WATCH WITH YOU, CAN YOU TELL ME WHAT TIME IT IS?"
WE ALLOWED HIM TO ASK YOU THIS QUESTION, YOU'RE FREE TO ANSWER IT.
I-I'M SORRY DAD... THIS IS ALL MY FAULT...
I'VE HAD THIS WATCH SINCE I WAS IN JAPAN, SO THE TIME IS 2:42 AM IN JAPAN.
...
RIGHT... SAYU...
THIS IS YOUR CAPTAIN, KYLE BLOCK SPEAKING. WE'RE GOING TO COMMENCE AN EMERGENCY LANDING AT THIS TIME.
DON'T WORRY, WE'RE JUST GOING TO DROP A PASSENGER OFF, AND THEN WE'LL QUICKLY HEAD FOR L.A.
RUSTLE
HUH ...?
WHAT ?
RUSTLE
WH- WHERE ARE WE? WE SHOULD BE IN L.A. BY NOW.
IS SOME- BODY SICK? AN ACCI- DENT?
WE WANT AN EXPLA- NATION!
PLEASE CALM DOWN EVERYONE, THERE'S NOTHING TO WORRY ABOUT.
RUSTLE
...

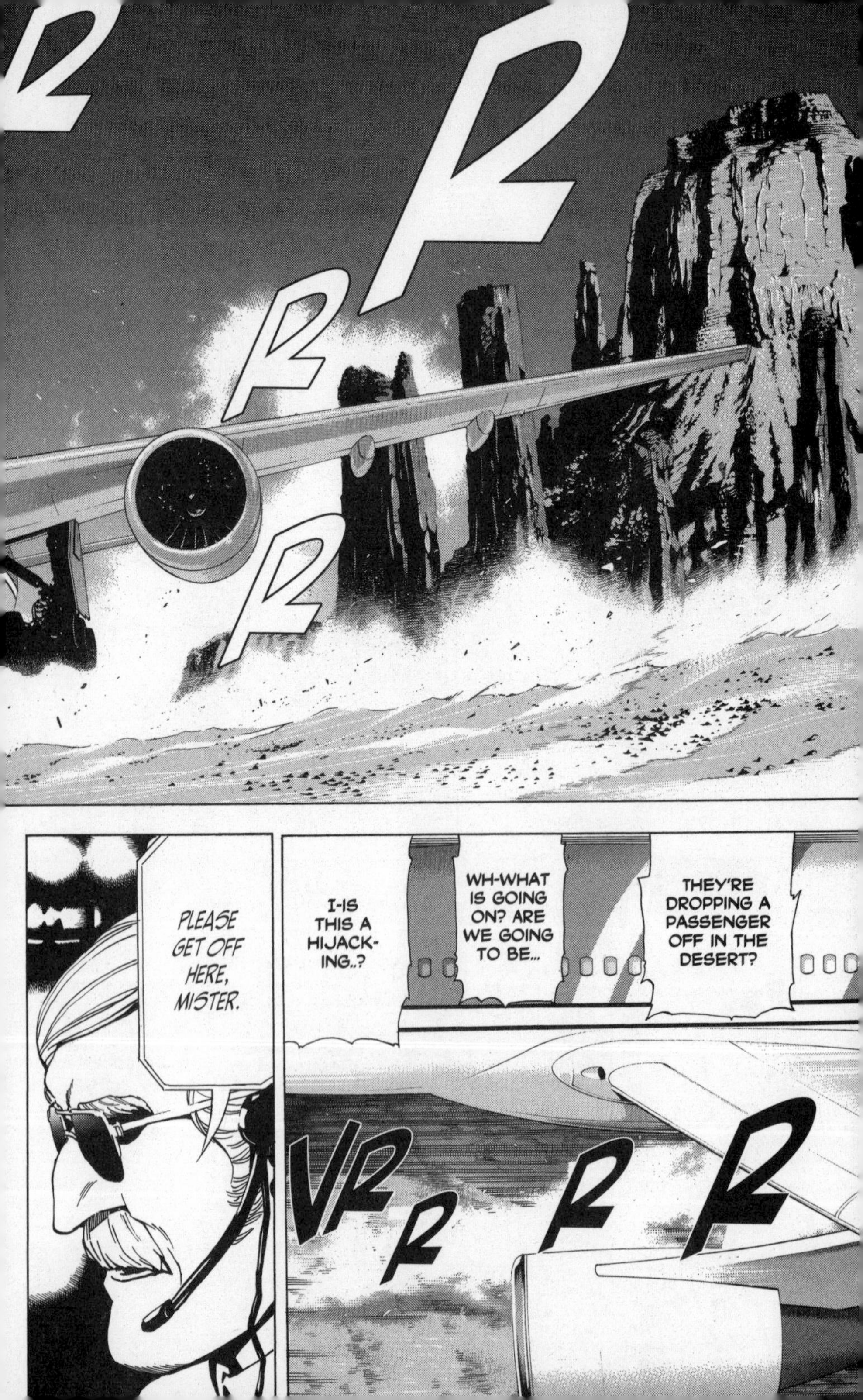
RRRRR
THEY'RE DROPPING A PASSENGER OFF IN THE DESERT?
WH-WHAT IS GOING ON? ARE WE GOING TO BE...
I-IS THIS A HIJACK-ING..?
VRRRR
PLEASE GET OFF HERE, MISTER.

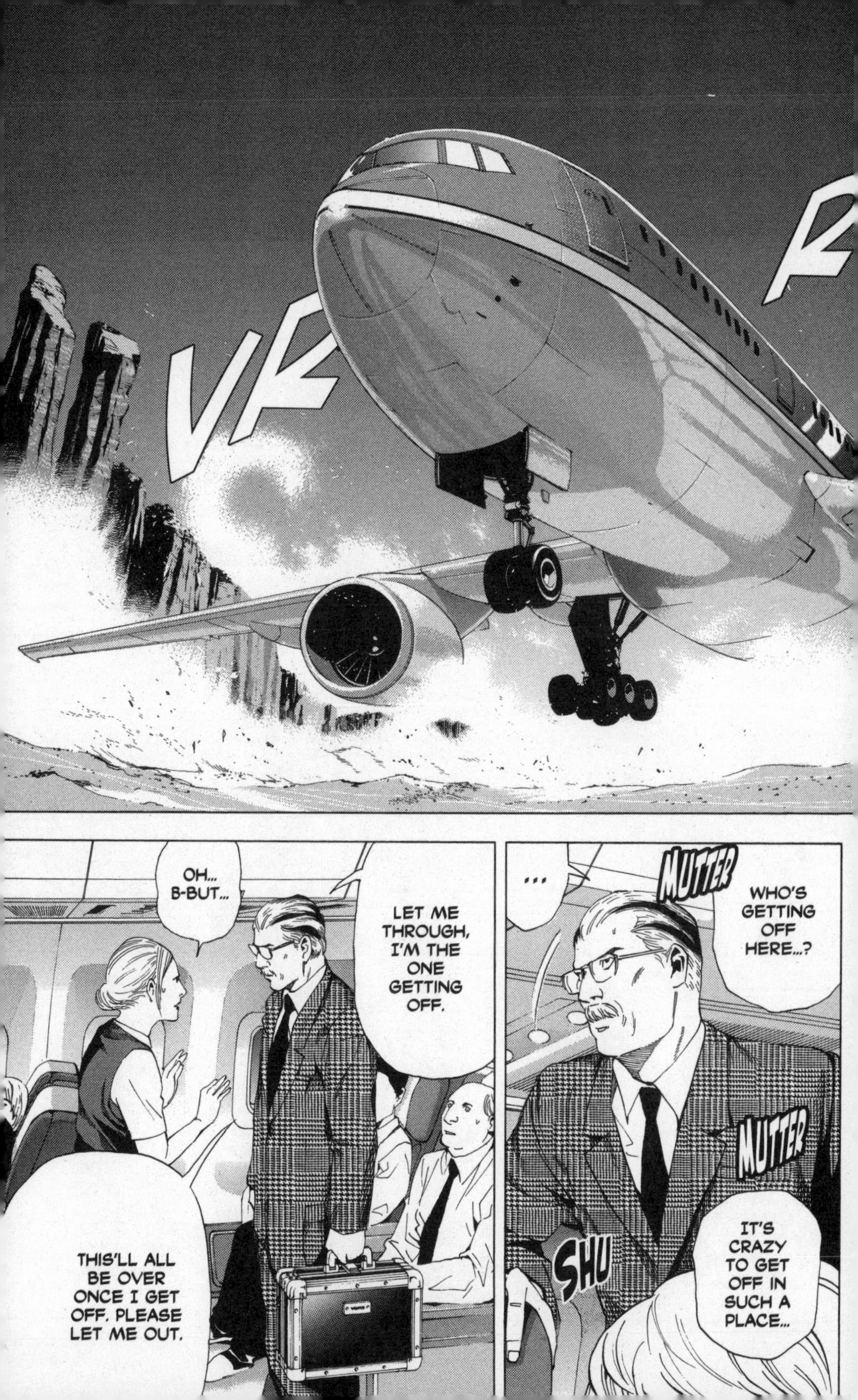
VF
MUTTER
WHO'S GETTING OFF HERE...?
...
MUTTER
IT'S CRAZY TO GET OFF IN SUCH A PLACE...
SHU
LET ME THROUGH, I'M THE ONE GETTING OFF.
OH... B-BUT...
THIS'LL ALL BE OVER ONCE I GET OFF. PLEASE LET ME OUT.

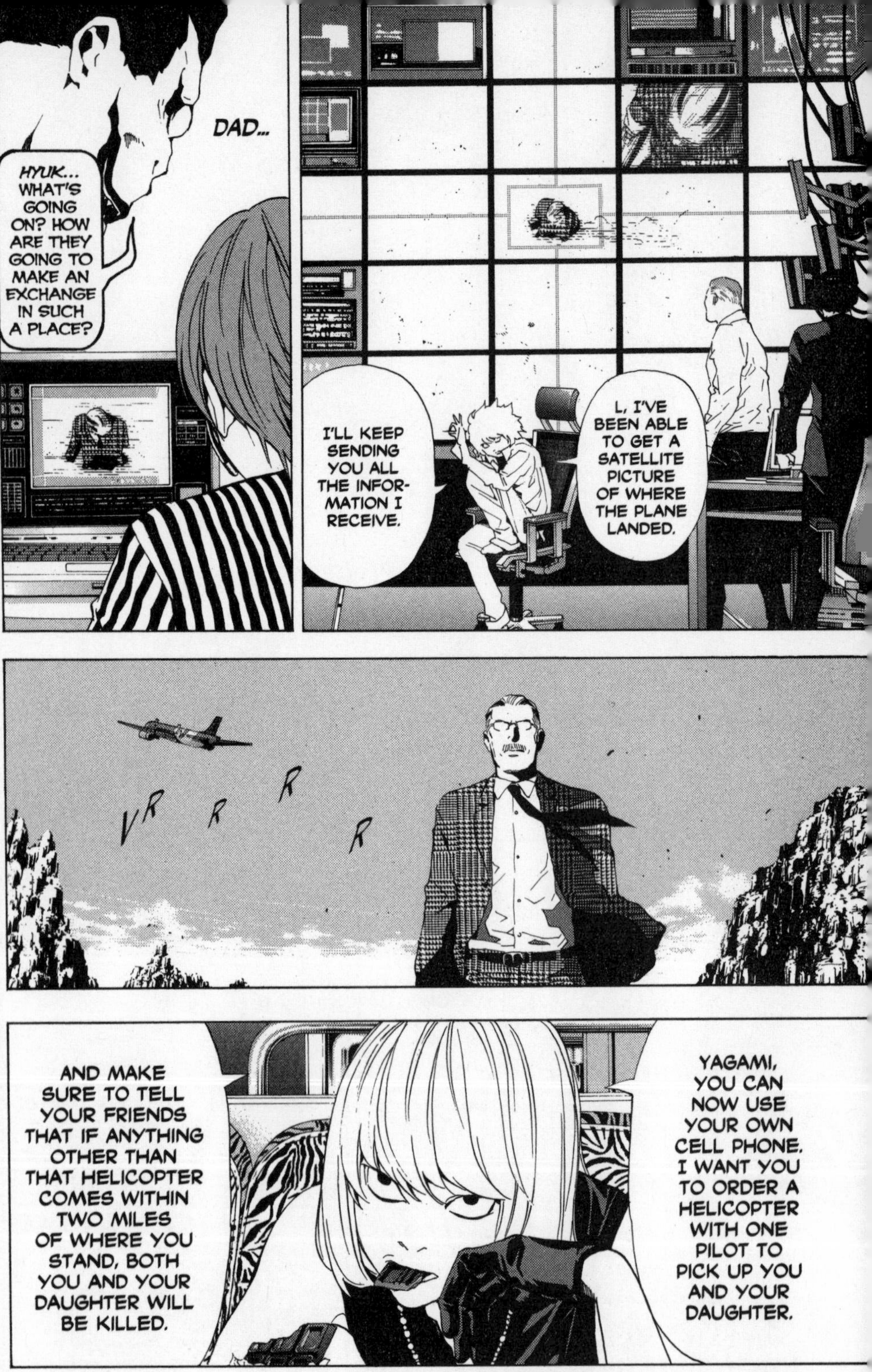
L, I'VE BEEN ABLE TO GET A SATELLITE PICTURE OF WHERE THE PLANE LANDED.
I'LL KEEP SENDING YOU ALL THE INFORMATION I RECEIVE.
DAD...
HYUK... WHAT'S GOING ON? HOW ARE THEY GOING TO MAKE AN EXCHANGE IN SUCH A PLACE?
VRRRR
YAGAMI, YOU CAN NOW USE YOUR OWN CELL PHONE. I WANT YOU TO ORDER A HELICOPTER WITH ONE PILOT TO PICK UP YOU AND YOUR DAUGHTER.
AND MAKE SURE TO TELL YOUR FRIENDS THAT IF ANYTHING OTHER THAN THAT HELICOPTER COMES WITHIN TWO MILES OF WHERE YOU STAND, BOTH YOU AND YOUR DAUGHTER WILL BE KILLED.

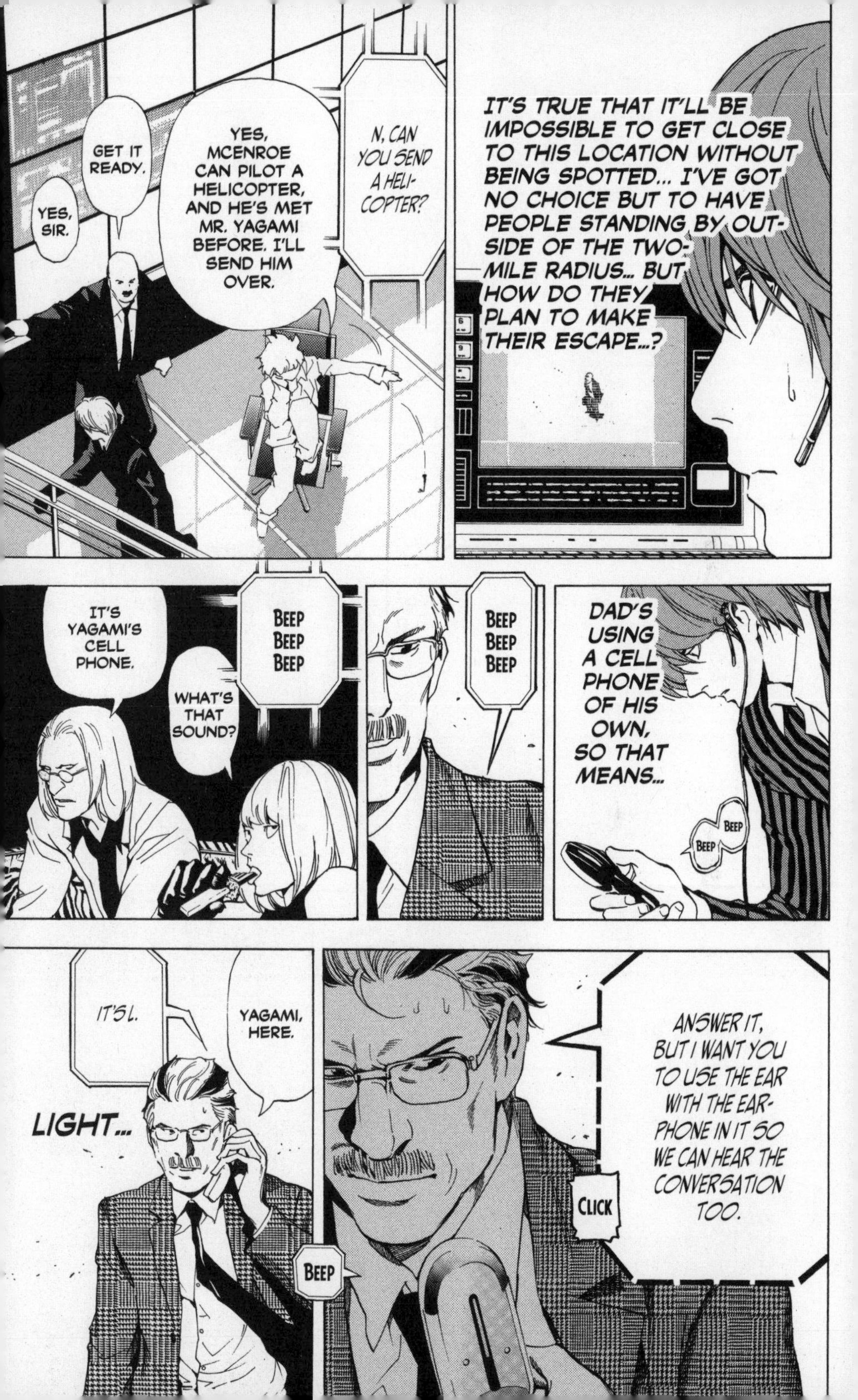
IT'S TRUE THAT IT'LL BE IMPOSSIBLE TO GET CLOSE TO THIS LOCATION WITHOUT BEING SPOTTED... I'VE GOT NO CHOICE BUT TO HAVE PEOPLE STANDING BY OUTSIDE OF THE TWO-MILE RADIUS... BUT HOW DO THEY PLAN TO MAKE THEIR ESCAPE...?
N, CAN YOU SEND A HELICOPTER?
YES, MCENROE CAN PILOT A HELICOPTER, AND HE'S MET MR. YAGAMI BEFORE. I'LL SEND HIM OVER.
GET IT READY.
YES, SIR.
DAD'S USING A CELL PHONE OF HIS OWN, SO THAT MEANS...
BEEP
BEEP
BEEP BEEP BEEP
BEEP BEEP BEEP
WHAT'S THAT SOUND?
IT'S YAGAMI'S CELL PHONE.
ANSWER IT, BUT I WANT YOU TO USE THE EAR WITH THE EARPHONE IN IT SO WE CAN HEAR THE CONVERSATION TOO.
CLICK
BEEP
YAGAMI, HERE.
IT'S L.
LIGHT...

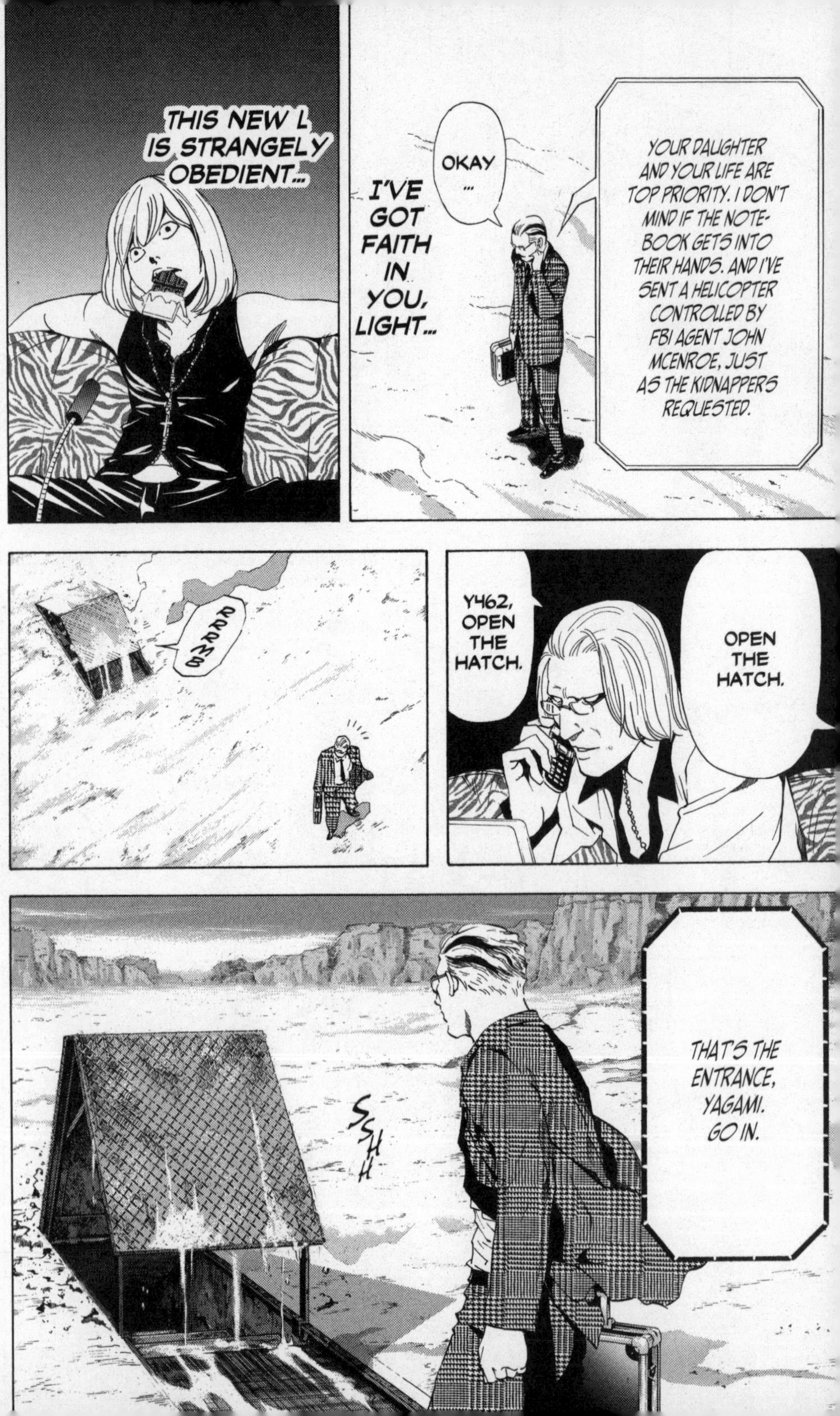
YOUR DAUGHTER AND YOUR LIFE ARE TOP PRIORITY. I DON'T MIND IF THE NOTEBOOK GETS INTO THEIR HANDS. AND I'VE SENT A HELICOPTER CONTROLLED BY FBI AGENT JOHN MCENROE, JUST AS THE KIDNAPPERS REQUESTED.
OKAY ...
I'VE GOT FAITH IN YOU, LIGHT...
THIS NEW L IS STRANGELY OBEDIENT...
Y462, OPEN THE HATCH.
OPEN THE HATCH.
RRRMB
THAT'S THE ENTRANCE, YAGAMI. GO IN.
SSHH

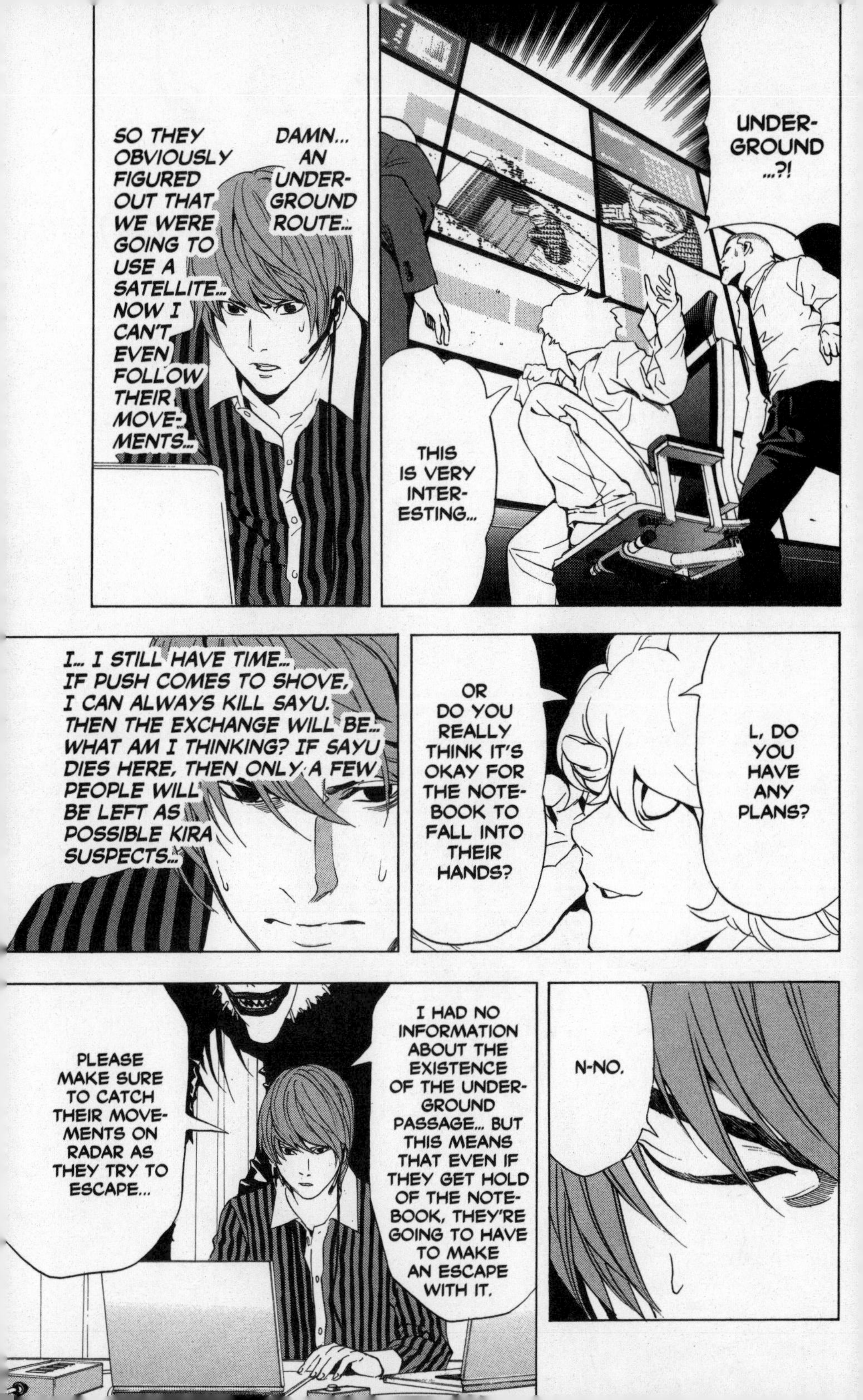
UNDER-GROUND ...?!
THIS IS VERY INTER-ESTING...
DAMN... AN UNDER-GROUND ROUTE...
SO THEY OBVIOUSLY FIGURED OUT THAT WE WERE GOING TO USE A SATELLITE... NOW I CAN'T EVEN FOLLOW THEIR MOVE-MENTS...
L, DO YOU HAVE ANY PLANS?
OR DO YOU REALLY THINK IT'S OKAY FOR THE NOTE-BOOK TO FALL INTO THEIR HANDS?
I... I STILL HAVE TIME... IF PUSH COMES TO SHOVE, I CAN ALWAYS KILL SAYU. THEN THE EXCHANGE WILL BE... WHAT AM I THINKING? IF SAYU DIES HERE, THEN ONLY A FEW PEOPLE WILL BE LEFT AS POSSIBLE KIRA SUSPECTS...
N-NO.
I HAD NO INFORMATION ABOUT THE EXISTENCE OF THE UNDER-GROUND PASSAGE... BUT THIS MEANS THAT EVEN IF THEY GET HOLD OF THE NOTE-BOOK, THEY'RE GOING TO HAVE TO MAKE AN ESCAPE WITH IT.
PLEASE MAKE SURE TO CATCH THEIR MOVE-MENTS ON RADAR AS THEY TRY TO ESCAPE...

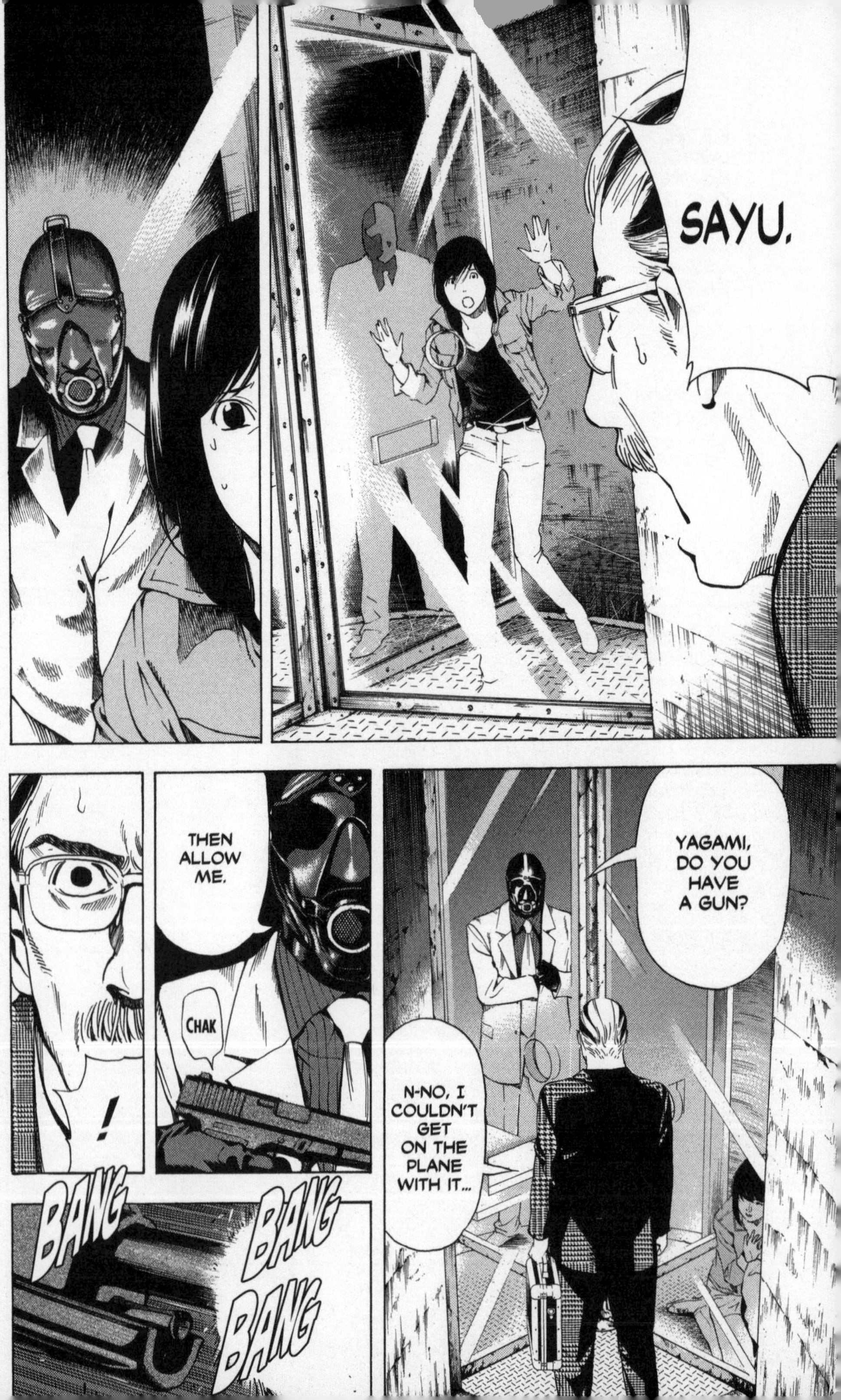
SAYU.
YAGAMI, DO YOU HAVE A GUN?
N-NO, I COULDN'T GET ON THE PLANE WITH IT...
THEN ALLOW ME.
CHAK
!
BANG
BANG
BANG

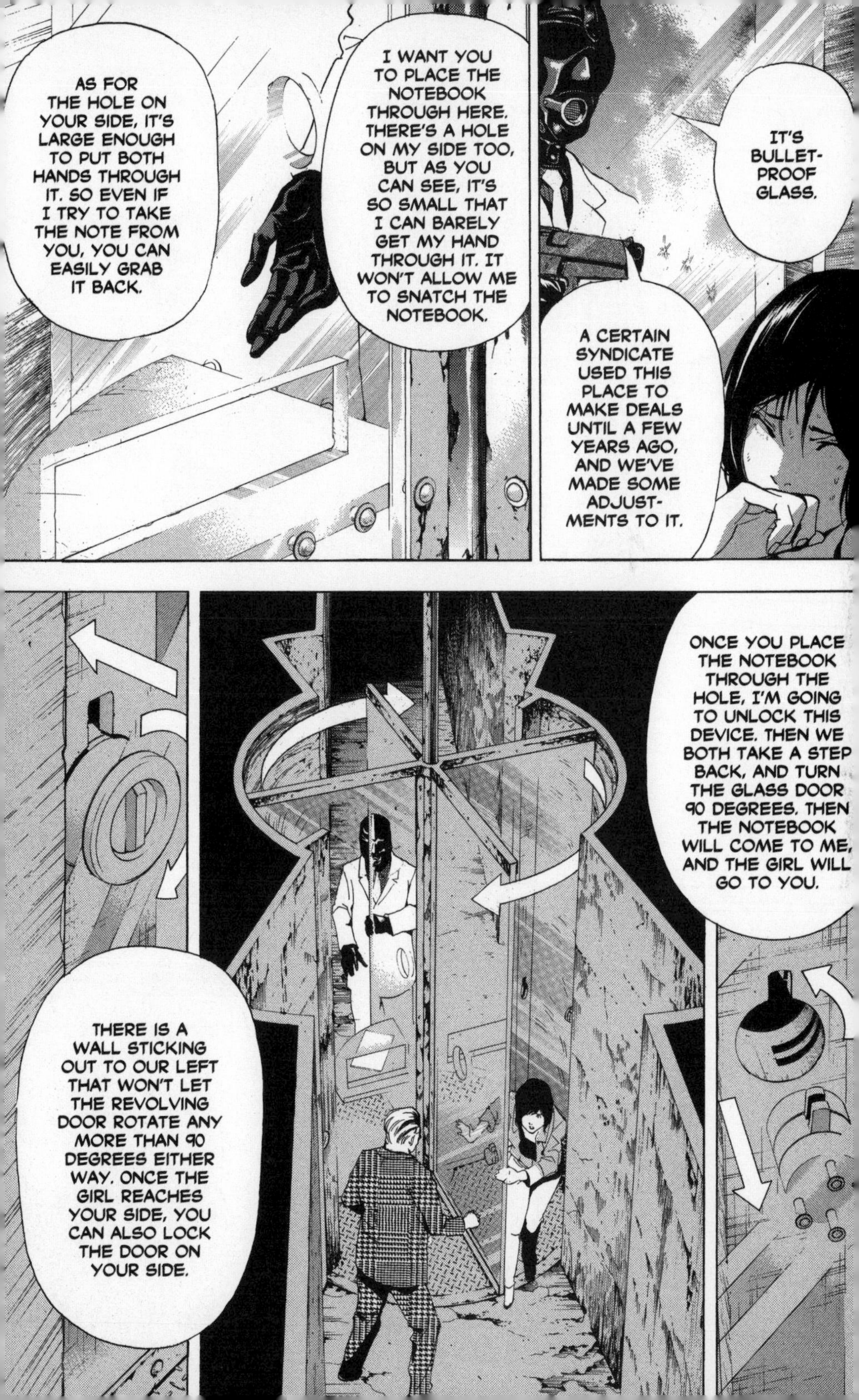
IT'S BULLET-PROOF GLASS.
A CERTAIN SYNDICATE USED THIS PLACE TO MAKE DEALS UNTIL A FEW YEARS AGO, AND WE'VE MADE SOME ADJUST-MENTS TO IT.
I WANT YOU TO PLACE THE NOTEBOOK THROUGH HERE. THERE'S A HOLE ON MY SIDE TOO, BUT AS YOU CAN SEE, IT'S SO SMALL THAT I CAN BARELY GET MY HAND THROUGH IT. IT WON'T ALLOW ME TO SNATCH THE NOTEBOOK.
AS FOR THE HOLE ON YOUR SIDE, IT'S LARGE ENOUGH TO PUT BOTH HANDS THROUGH IT. SO EVEN IF I TRY TO TAKE THE NOTE FROM YOU, YOU CAN EASILY GRAB IT BACK.
ONCE YOU PLACE THE NOTEBOOK THROUGH THE HOLE, I'M GOING TO UNLOCK THIS DEVICE. THEN WE BOTH TAKE A STEP BACK, AND TURN THE GLASS DOOR 90 DEGREES. THEN THE NOTEBOOK WILL COME TO ME, AND THE GIRL WILL GO TO YOU.
THERE IS A WALL STICKING OUT TO OUR LEFT THAT WON'T LET THE REVOLVING DOOR ROTATE ANY MORE THAN 90 DEGREES EITHER WAY. ONCE THE GIRL REACHES YOUR SIDE, YOU CAN ALSO LOCK THE DOOR ON YOUR SIDE.

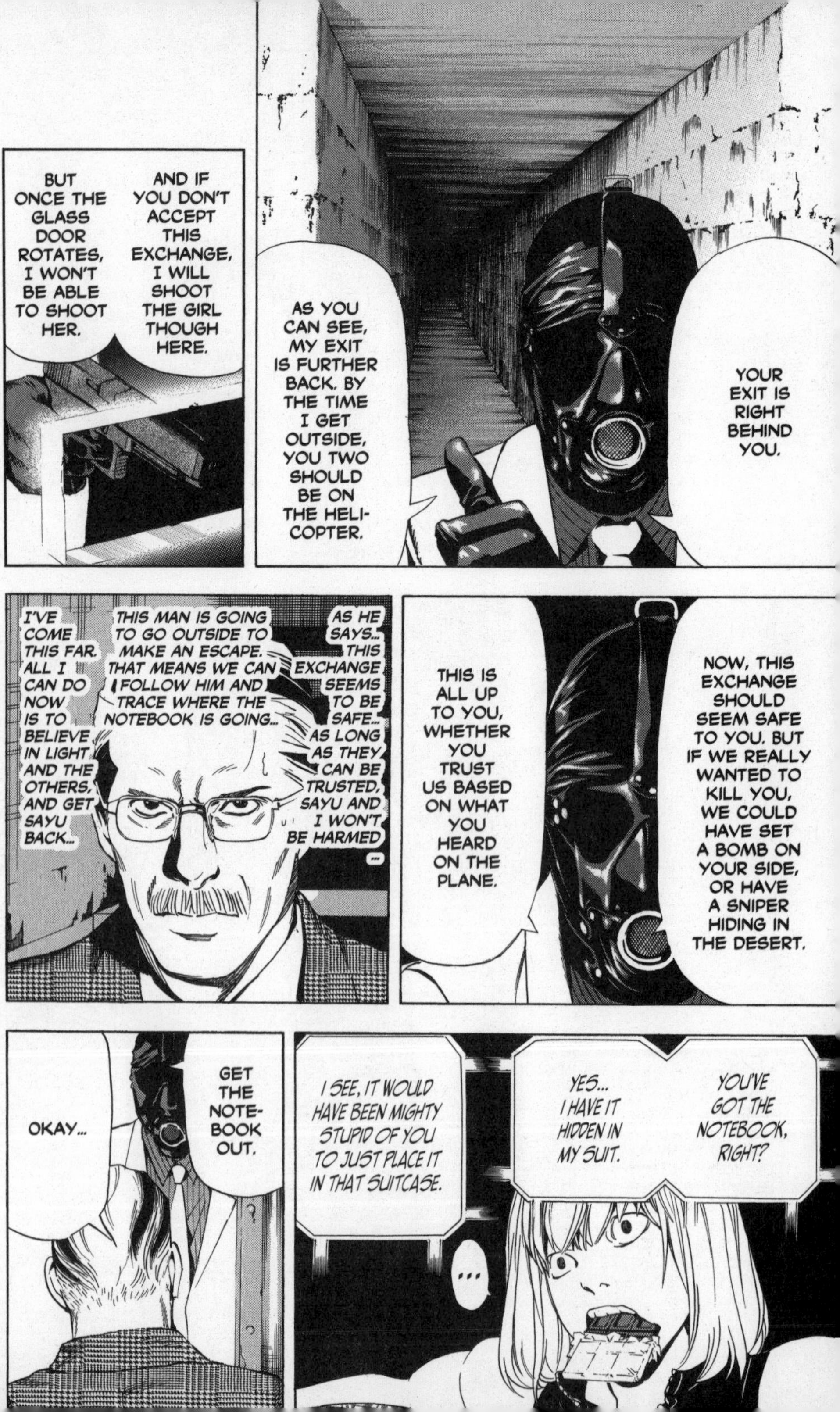
YOUR EXIT IS RIGHT BEHIND YOU.
AS YOU CAN SEE, MY EXIT IS FURTHER BACK. BY THE TIME I GET OUTSIDE, YOU TWO SHOULD BE ON THE HELI-COPTER.
AND IF YOU DON'T ACCEPT THIS EXCHANGE, I WILL SHOOT THE GIRL THOUGH HERE.
BUT ONCE THE GLASS DOOR ROTATES, I WON'T BE ABLE TO SHOOT HER.
NOW, THIS EXCHANGE SHOULD SEEM SAFE TO YOU. BUT IF WE REALLY WANTED TO KILL YOU, WE COULD HAVE SET A BOMB ON YOUR SIDE, OR HAVE A SNIPER HIDING IN THE DESERT.
THIS IS ALL UP TO YOU, WHETHER YOU TRUST US BASED ON WHAT YOU HEARD ON THE PLANE.
AS HE SAYS... THIS EXCHANGE SEEMS TO BE SAFE... AS LONG AS THEY CAN BE TRUSTED, SAYU AND I WON'T BE HARMED...
THIS MAN IS GOING TO GO OUTSIDE TO MAKE AN ESCAPE. THAT MEANS WE CAN FOLLOW HIM AND TRACE WHERE THE NOTEBOOK IS GOING...
I'VE COME THIS FAR. ALL I CAN DO NOW IS TO BELIEVE IN LIGHT AND THE OTHERS, AND GET SAYU BACK...
YOU'VE GOT THE NOTEBOOK, RIGHT?
YES... I HAVE IT HIDDEN IN MY SUIT.
I SEE, IT WOULD HAVE BEEN MIGHTY STUPID OF YOU TO JUST PLACE IT IN THAT SUITCASE.
...
GET THE NOTE-BOOK OUT.
OKAY...

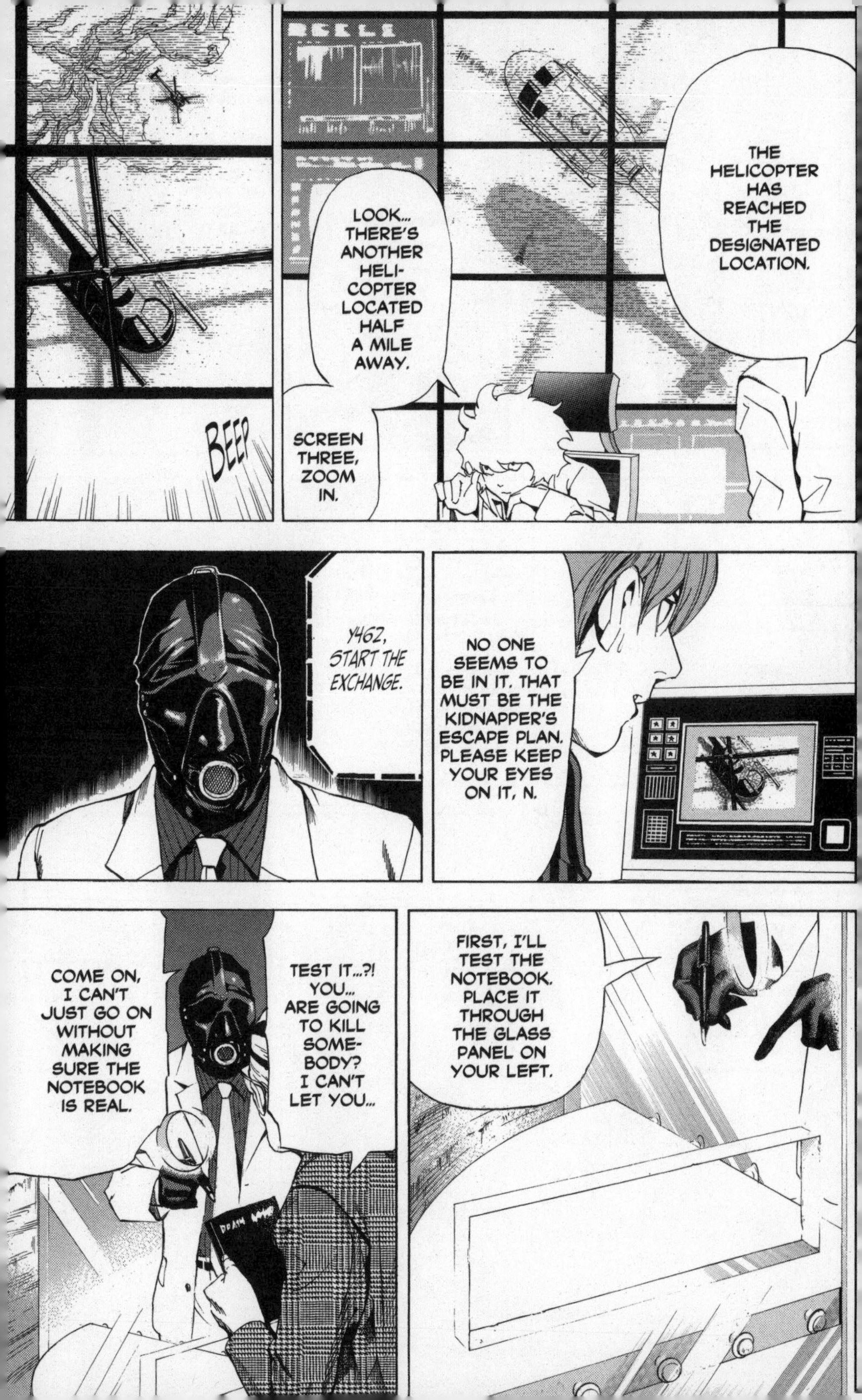
THE HELICOPTER HAS REACHED THE DESIGNATED LOCATION.
LOOK... THERE'S ANOTHER HELI-COPTER LOCATED HALF A MILE AWAY.
SCREEN THREE, ZOOM IN.
BEEP
NO ONE SEEMS TO BE IN IT. THAT MUST BE THE KIDNAPPER'S ESCAPE PLAN. PLEASE KEEP YOUR EYES ON IT, N.
Y462, START THE EXCHANGE.
FIRST, I'LL TEST THE NOTEBOOK. PLACE IT THROUGH THE GLASS PANEL ON YOUR LEFT.
TEST IT...?! YOU... ARE GOING TO KILL SOME-BODY? I CAN'T LET YOU...
COME ON, I CAN'T JUST GO ON WITHOUT MAKING SURE THE NOTEBOOK IS REAL.

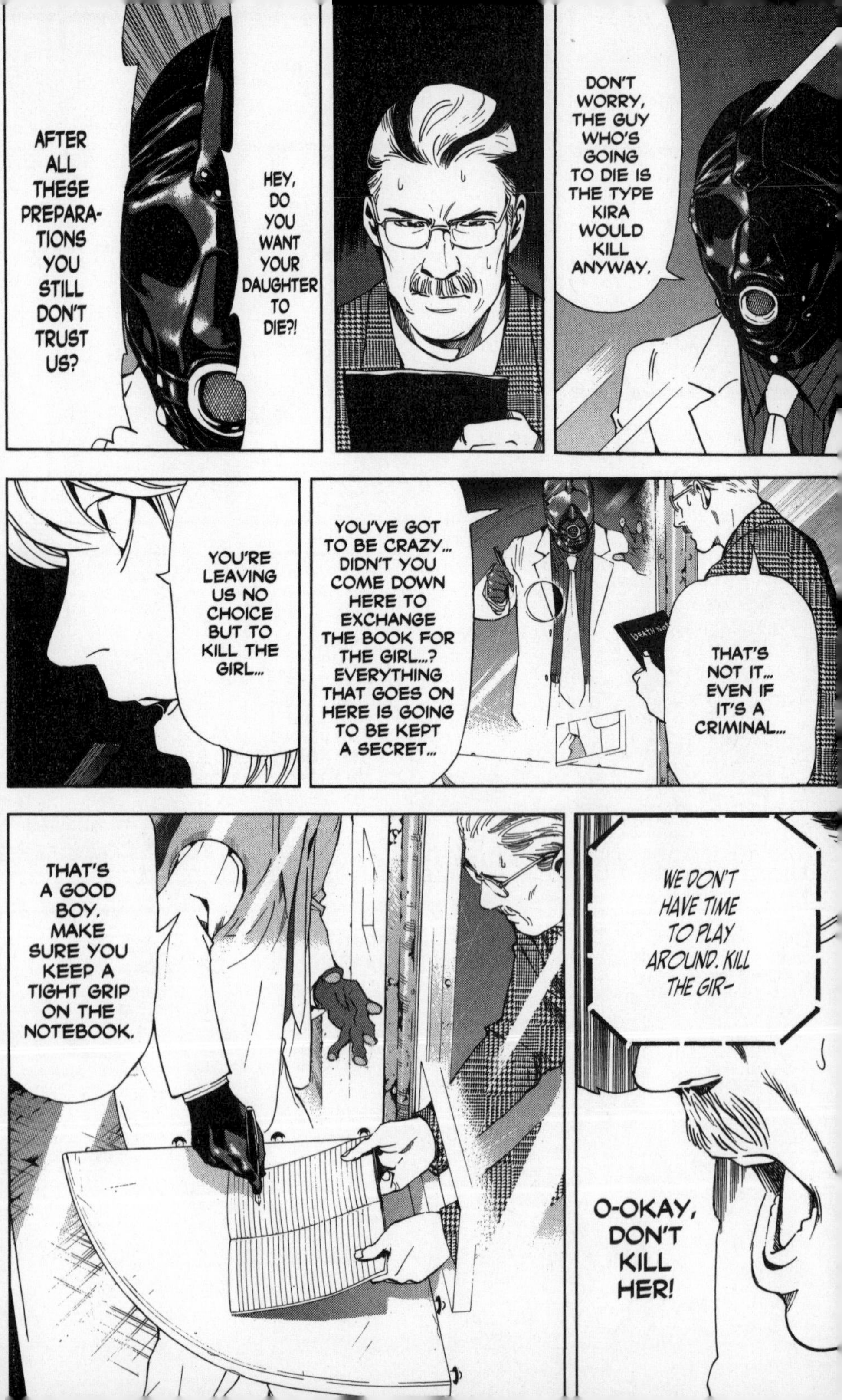
DON'T WORRY, THE GUY WHO'S GOING TO DIE IS THE TYPE KIRA WOULD KILL ANYWAY.
HEY, DO YOU WANT YOUR DAUGHTER TO DIE?!
AFTER ALL THESE PREPARATIONS YOU STILL DON'T TRUST US?
THAT'S NOT IT... EVEN IF IT'S A CRIMINAL...
YOU'VE GOT TO BE CRAZY... DIDN'T YOU COME DOWN HERE TO EXCHANGE THE BOOK FOR THE GIRL...? EVERYTHING THAT GOES ON HERE IS GOING TO BE KEPT A SECRET...
YOU'RE LEAVING US NO CHOICE BUT TO KILL THE GIRL...
WE DON'T HAVE TIME TO PLAY AROUND. KILL THE GIR-
O-OKAY, DON'T KILL HER!
THAT'S A GOOD BOY. MAKE SURE YOU KEEP A TIGHT GRIP ON THE NOTEBOOK.

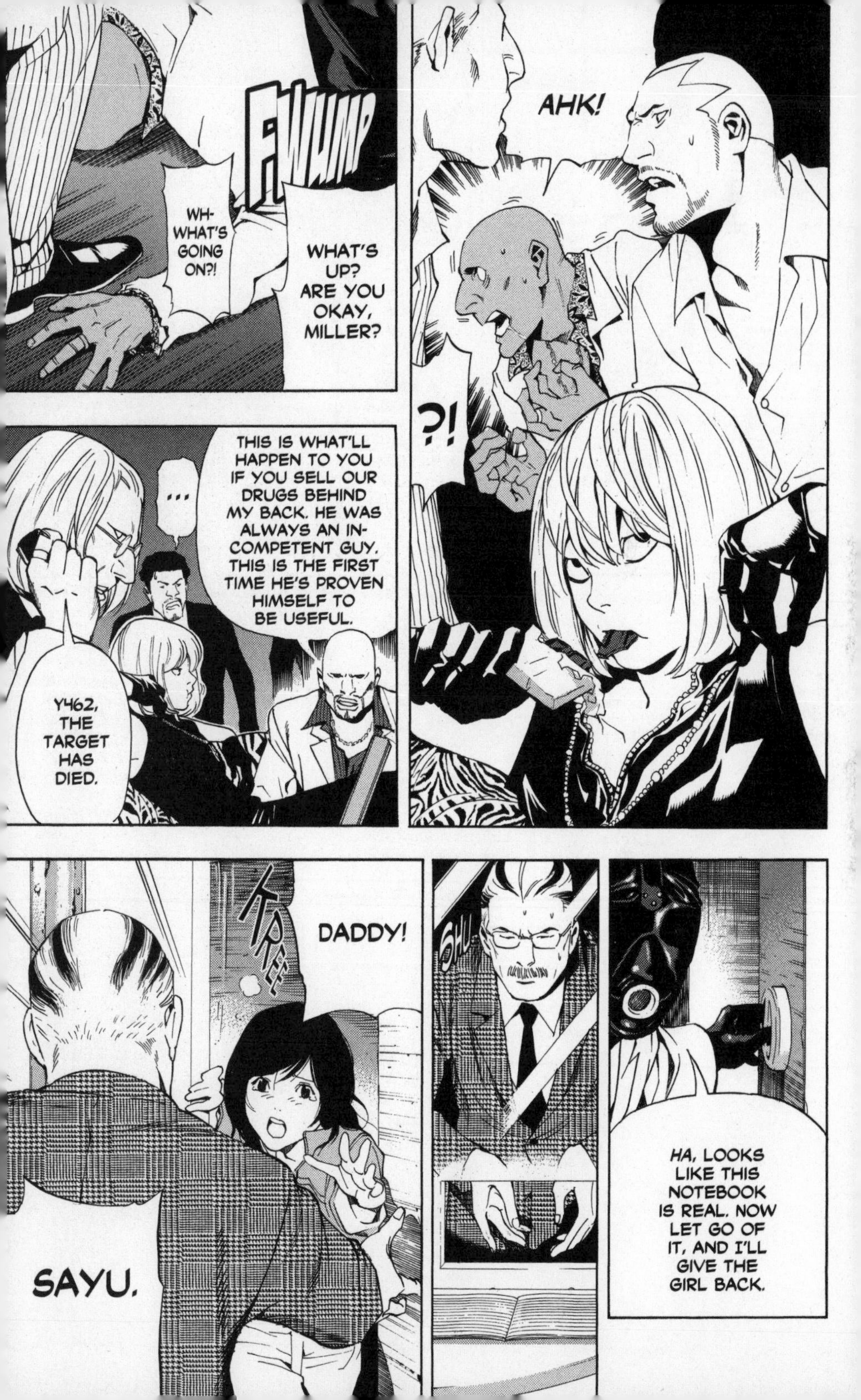
AHK!
?!
FWUMP
WHAT'S UP? ARE YOU OKAY, MILLER?
WH- WHAT'S GOING ON?!
THIS IS WHAT'LL HAPPEN TO YOU IF YOU SELL OUR DRUGS BEHIND MY BACK. HE WAS ALWAYS AN INCOMPETENT GUY. THIS IS THE FIRST TIME HE'S PROVEN HIMSELF TO BE USEFUL.
...
Y462, THE TARGET HAS DIED.
*HA*, LOOKS LIKE THIS NOTEBOOK IS REAL. NOW LET GO OF IT, AND I'LL GIVE THE GIRL BACK.
SHU
KREE
DADDY!
SAYU.

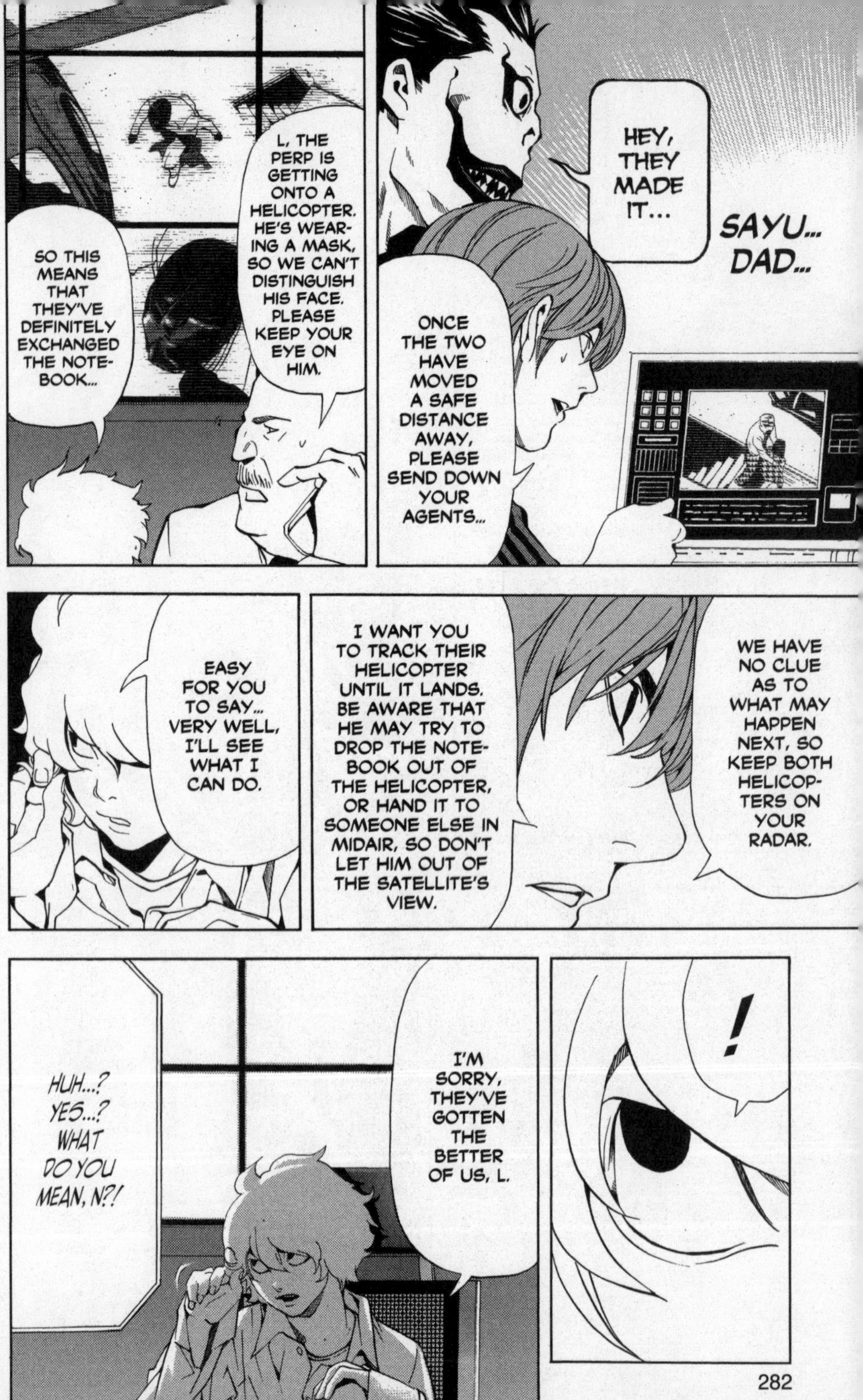
HEY, THEY MADE IT...
SAYU... DAD...
ONCE THE TWO HAVE MOVED A SAFE DISTANCE AWAY, PLEASE SEND DOWN YOUR AGENTS...
L, THE PERP IS GETTING ONTO A HELICOPTER. HE'S WEARING A MASK, SO WE CAN'T DISTINGUISH HIS FACE. PLEASE KEEP YOUR EYE ON HIM.
SO THIS MEANS THAT THEY'VE DEFINITELY EXCHANGED THE NOTEBOOK...
WE HAVE NO CLUE AS TO WHAT MAY HAPPEN NEXT, SO KEEP BOTH HELICOPTERS ON YOUR RADAR.
I WANT YOU TO TRACK THEIR HELICOPTER UNTIL IT LANDS. BE AWARE THAT HE MAY TRY TO DROP THE NOTEBOOK OUT OF THE HELICOPTER, OR HAND IT TO SOMEONE ELSE IN MIDAIR, SO DON'T LET HIM OUT OF THE SATELLITE'S VIEW.
EASY FOR YOU TO SAY... VERY WELL, I'LL SEE WHAT I CAN DO.
!
I'M SORRY, THEY'VE GOTTEN THE BETTER OF US, L.
HUH...? YES...? WHAT DO YOU MEAN, N?!

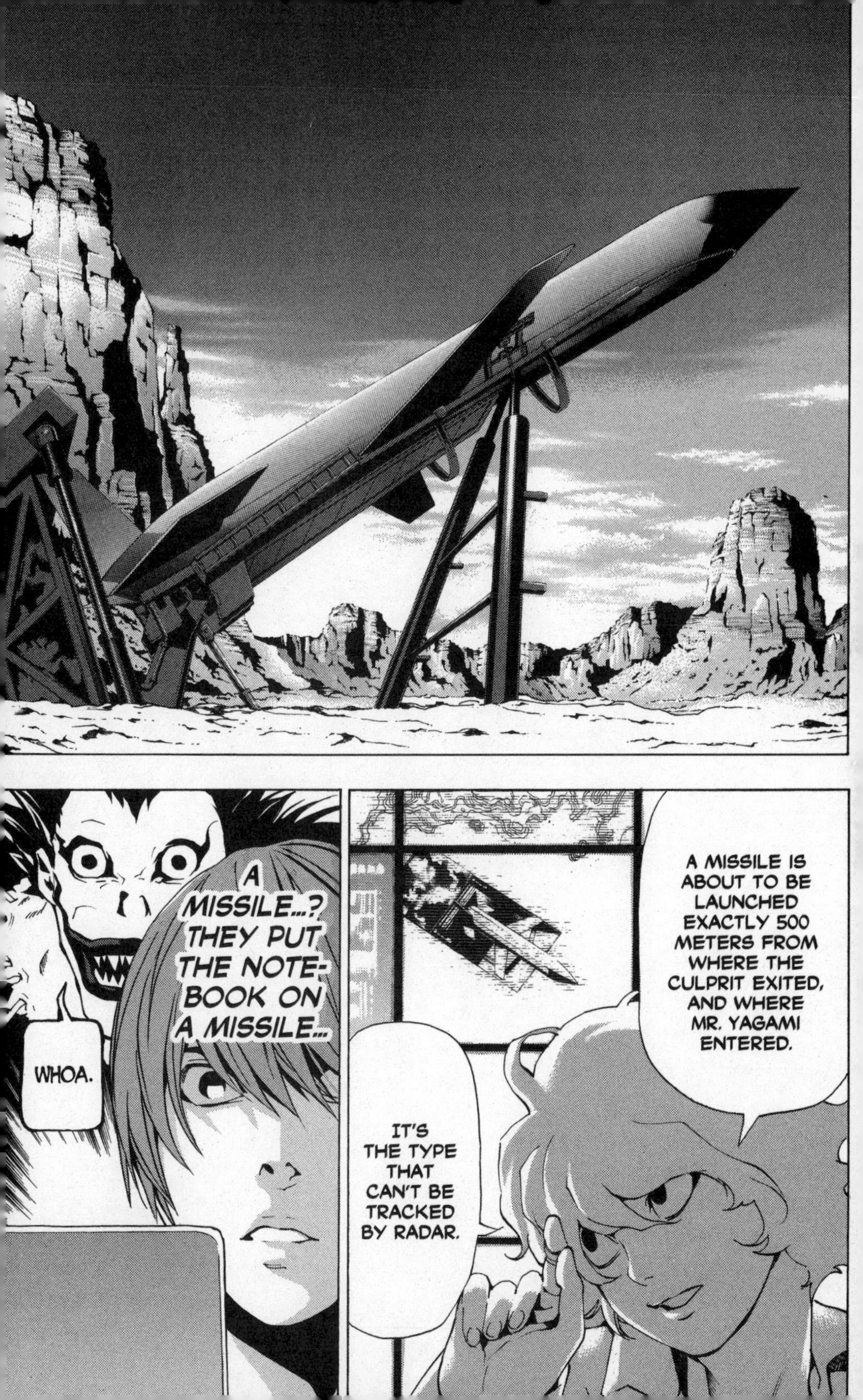
A MISSILE IS ABOUT TO BE LAUNCHED EXACTLY 500 METERS FROM WHERE THE CULPRIT EXITED, AND WHERE MR. YAGAMI ENTERED.
IT'S THE TYPE THAT CAN'T BE TRACKED BY RADAR.
A MISSILE...? THEY PUT THE NOTE-BOOK ON A MISSILE...
WHOA.

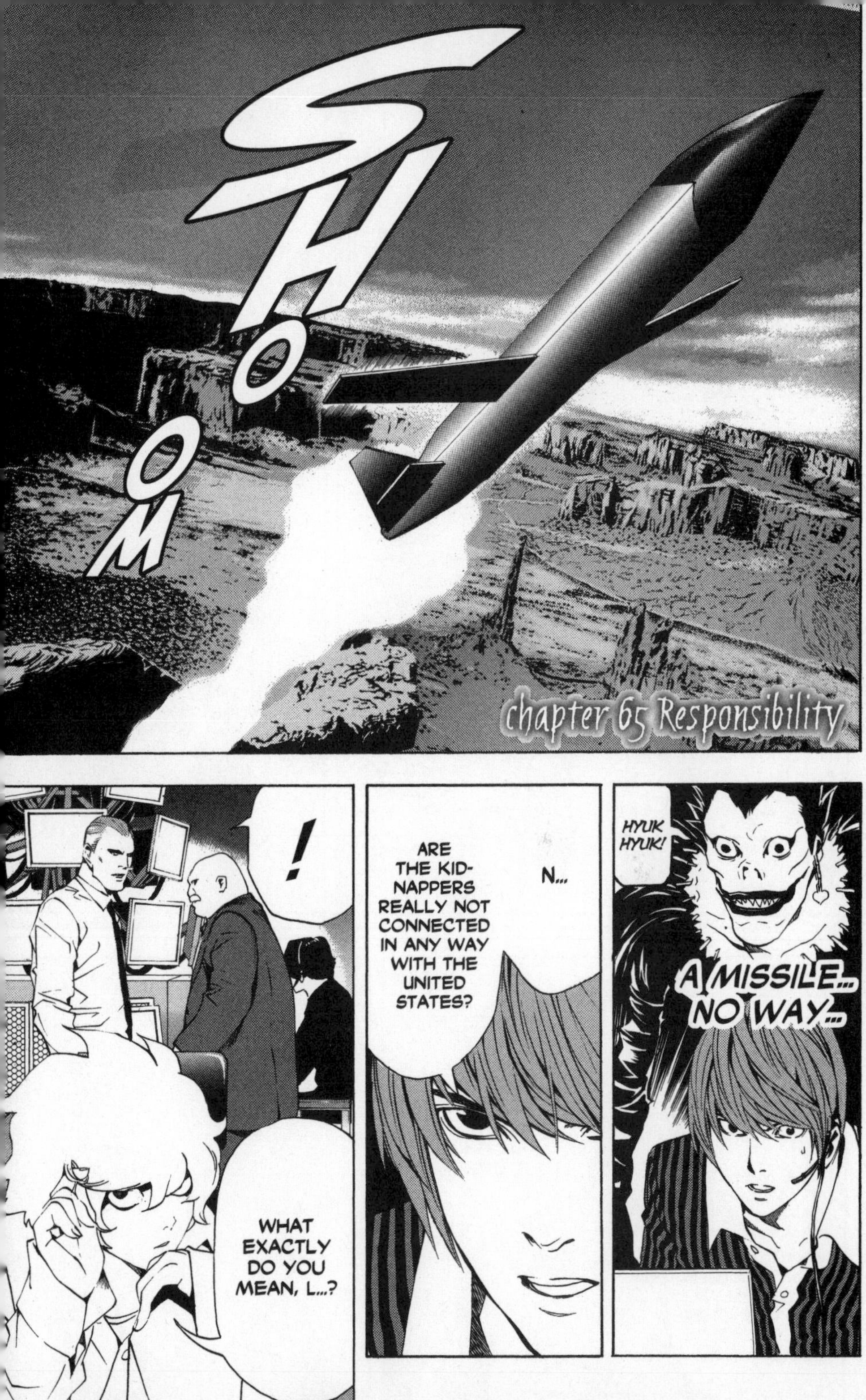
SHOOM
chapter 65 Responsibility
HYUK HYUK!
A MISSILE... NO WAY...
N...
ARE THE KID-NAPPERS REALLY NOT CONNECTED IN ANY WAY WITH THE UNITED STATES?
!
WHAT EXACTLY DO YOU MEAN, L...?

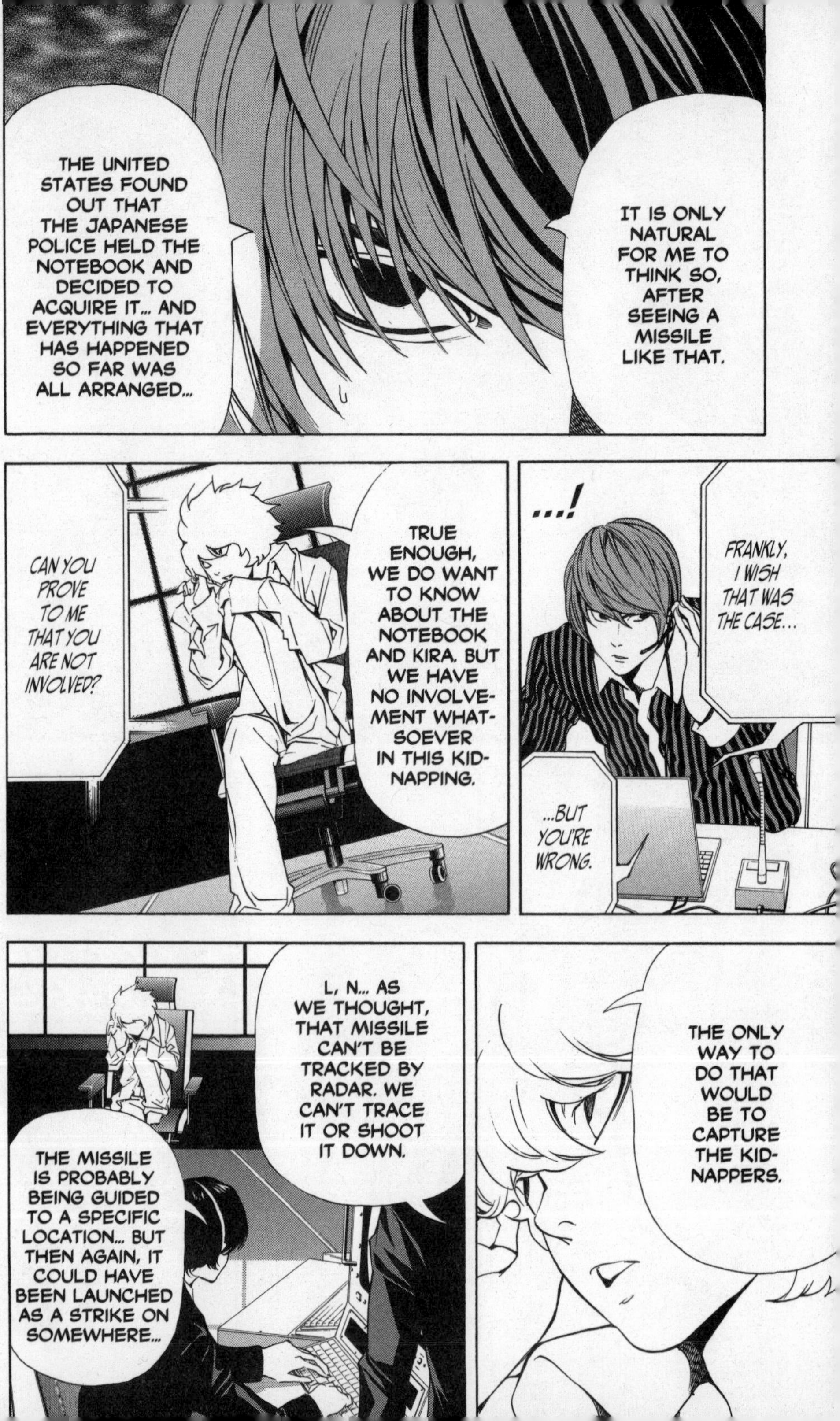
THE UNITED STATES FOUND OUT THAT THE JAPANESE POLICE HELD THE NOTEBOOK AND DECIDED TO ACQUIRE IT... AND EVERYTHING THAT HAS HAPPENED SO FAR WAS ALL ARRANGED...
IT IS ONLY NATURAL FOR ME TO THINK SO, AFTER SEEING A MISSILE LIKE THAT.
...!
FRANKLY, I WISH THAT WAS THE CASE...
...BUT YOU'RE WRONG.
TRUE ENOUGH, WE DO WANT TO KNOW ABOUT THE NOTEBOOK AND KIRA. BUT WE HAVE NO INVOLVEMENT WHATSOEVER IN THIS KIDNAPPING.
CAN YOU PROVE TO ME THAT YOU ARE NOT INVOLVED?
THE ONLY WAY TO DO THAT WOULD BE TO CAPTURE THE KIDNAPPERS.
L, N... AS WE THOUGHT, THAT MISSILE CAN'T BE TRACKED BY RADAR. WE CAN'T TRACE IT OR SHOOT IT DOWN.
THE MISSILE IS PROBABLY BEING GUIDED TO A SPECIFIC LOCATION... BUT THEN AGAIN, IT COULD HAVE BEEN LAUNCHED AS A STRIKE ON SOMEWHERE...

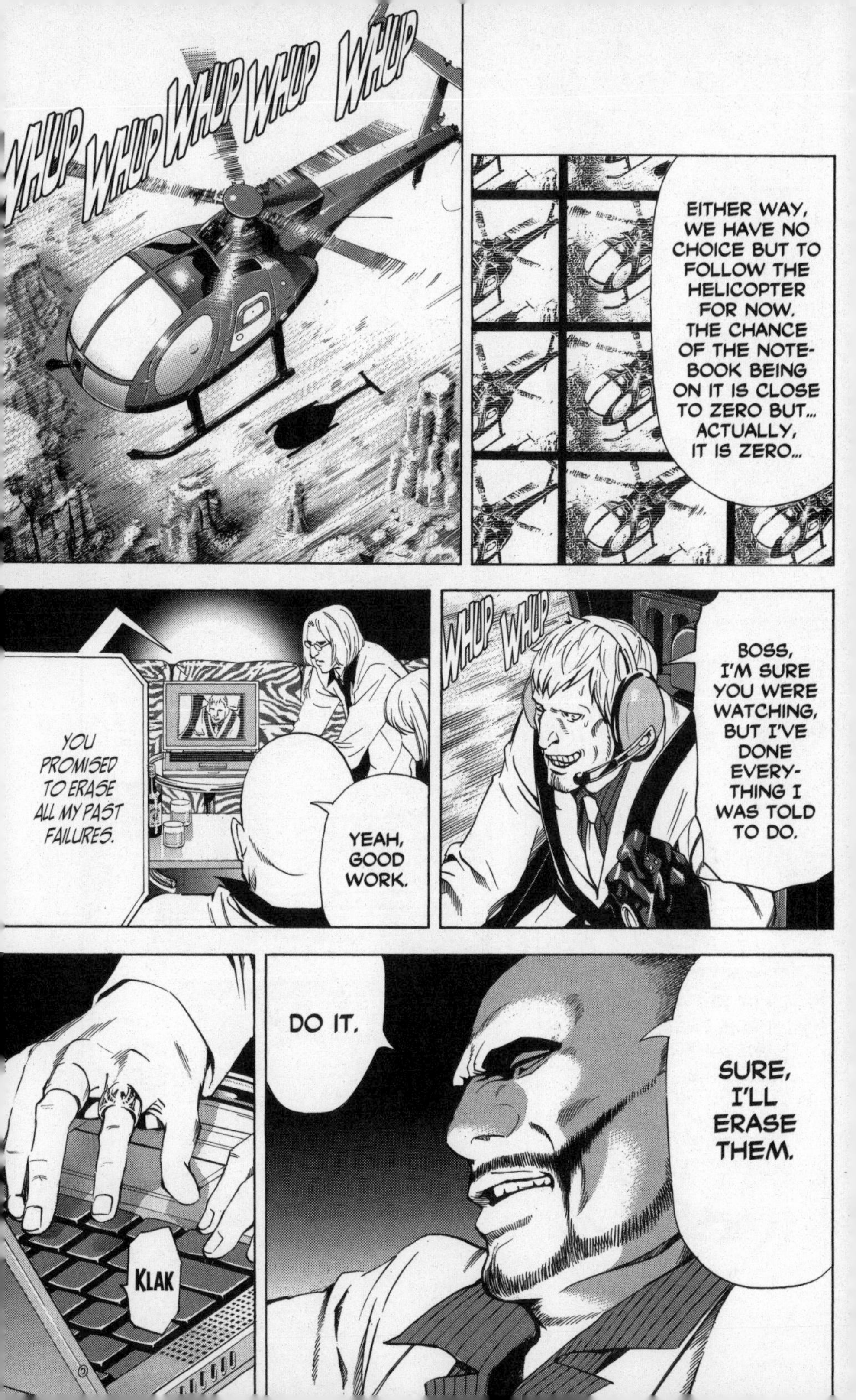
EITHER WAY, WE HAVE NO CHOICE BUT TO FOLLOW THE HELICOPTER FOR NOW. THE CHANCE OF THE NOTE-BOOK BEING ON IT IS CLOSE TO ZERO BUT... ACTUALLY, IT IS ZERO...
WHUP WHUP WHUP WHUP WHUP
WHUP WHUP
BOSS, I'M SURE YOU WERE WATCHING, BUT I'VE DONE EVERY-THING I WAS TOLD TO DO.
YEAH, GOOD WORK.
YOU PROMISED TO ERASE ALL MY PAST FAILURES.
SURE, I'LL ERASE THEM.
DO IT.
KLAK

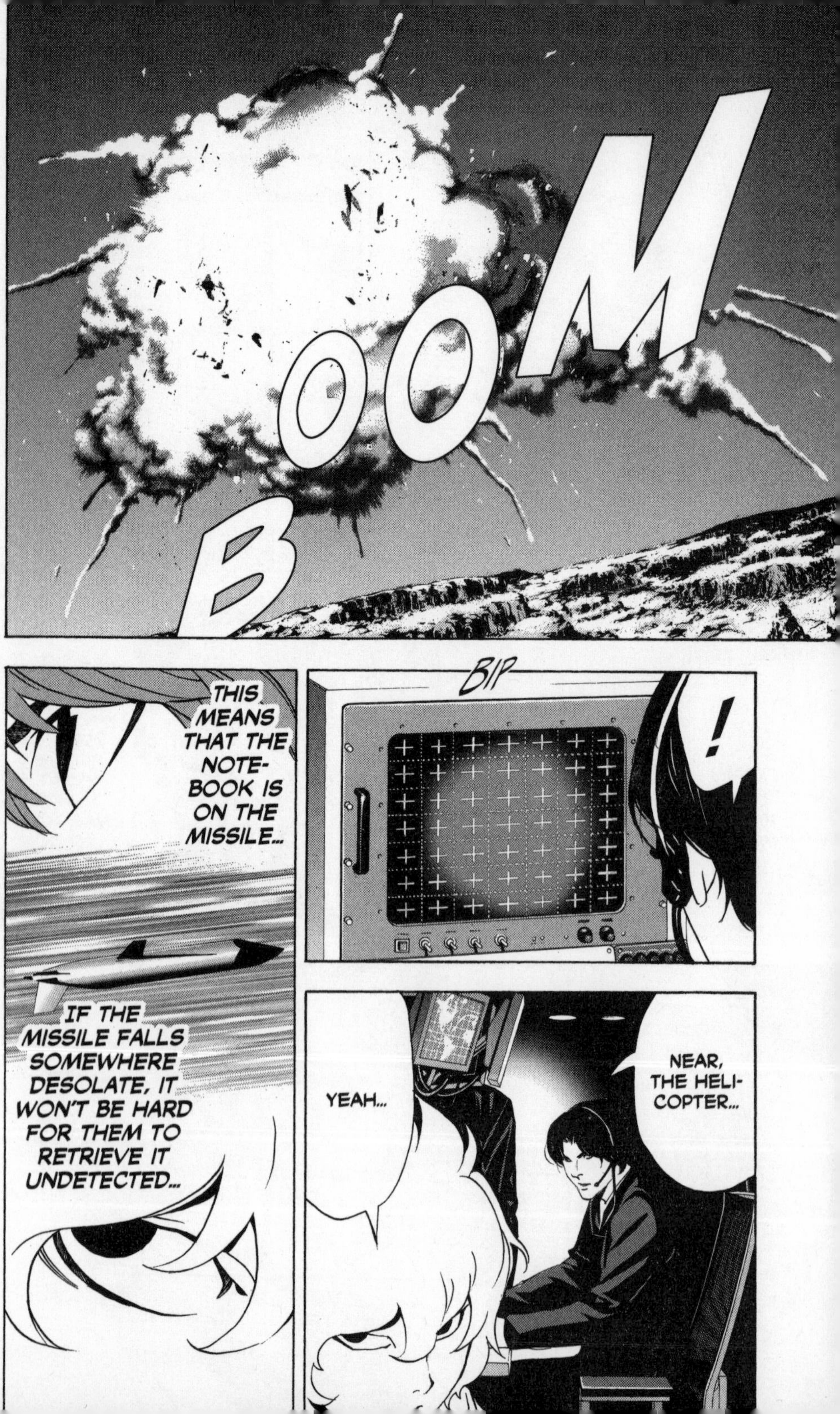
BOOM
BIP
!
NEAR, THE HELICOPTER...
YEAH...
THIS MEANS THAT THE NOTEBOOK IS ON THE MISSILE...
IF THE MISSILE FALLS SOMEWHERE DESOLATE, IT WON'T BE HARD FOR THEM TO RETRIEVE IT UNDETECTED...

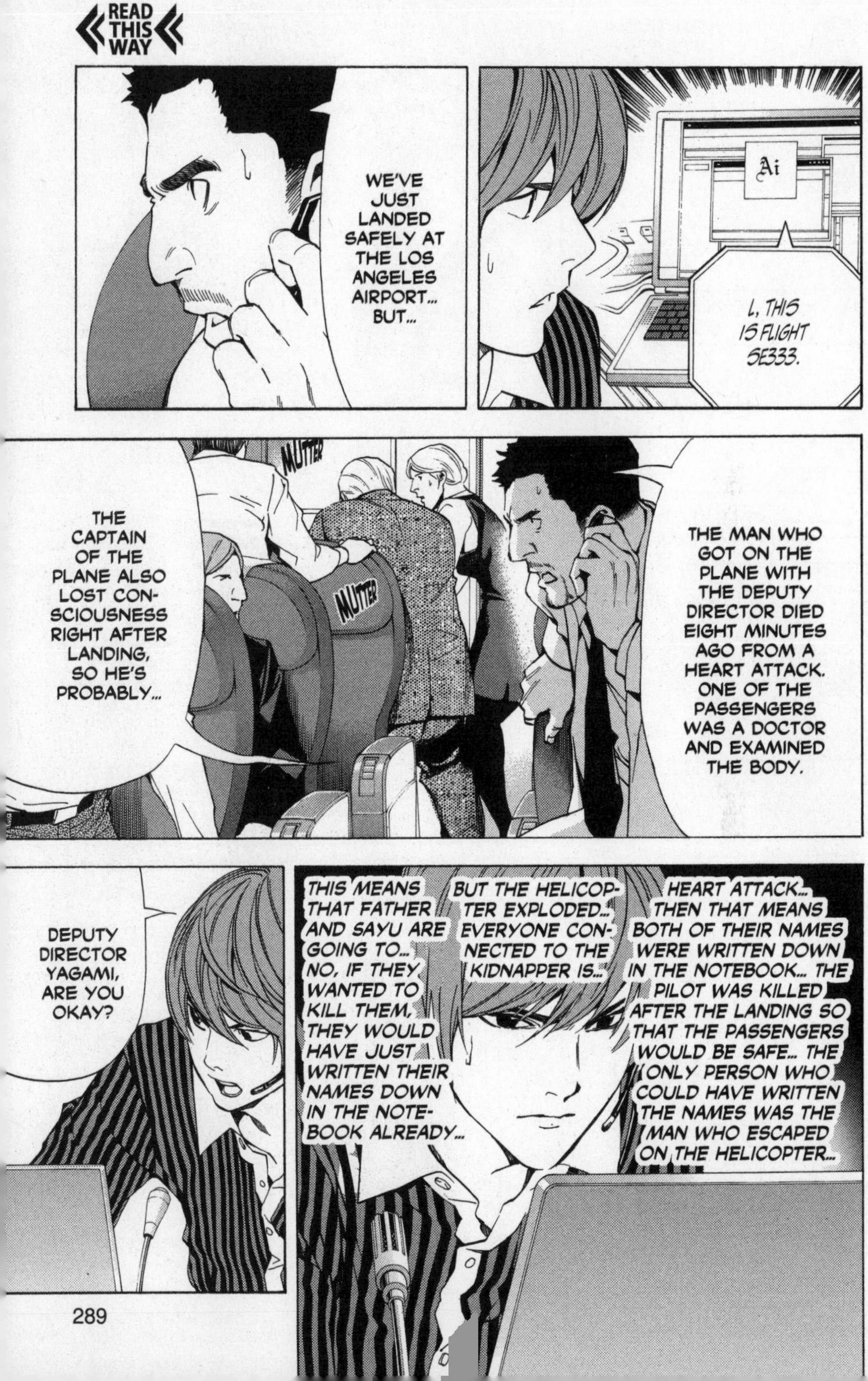
READ THIS WAY
Ai
L, THIS IS FLIGHT SE333.
WE'VE JUST LANDED SAFELY AT THE LOS ANGELES AIRPORT... BUT...
THE MAN WHO GOT ON THE PLANE WITH THE DEPUTY DIRECTOR DIED EIGHT MINUTES AGO FROM A HEART ATTACK. ONE OF THE PASSENGERS WAS A DOCTOR AND EXAMINED THE BODY.
MUTTER
MUTTER
THE CAPTAIN OF THE PLANE ALSO LOST CONSCIOUSNESS RIGHT AFTER LANDING, SO HE'S PROBABLY...
HEART ATTACK... THEN THAT MEANS BOTH OF THEIR NAMES WERE WRITTEN DOWN IN THE NOTEBOOK... THE PILOT WAS KILLED AFTER THE LANDING SO THAT THE PASSENGERS WOULD BE SAFE... THE ONLY PERSON WHO COULD HAVE WRITTEN THE NAMES WAS THE MAN WHO ESCAPED ON THE HELICOPTER...
BUT THE HELICOPTER EXPLODED... EVERYONE CONNECTED TO THE KIDNAPPER IS...
THIS MEANS THAT FATHER AND SAYU ARE GOING TO... NO, IF THEY WANTED TO KILL THEM, THEY WOULD HAVE JUST WRITTEN THEIR NAMES DOWN IN THE NOTEBOOK ALREADY...
DEPUTY DIRECTOR YAGAMI, ARE YOU OKAY?

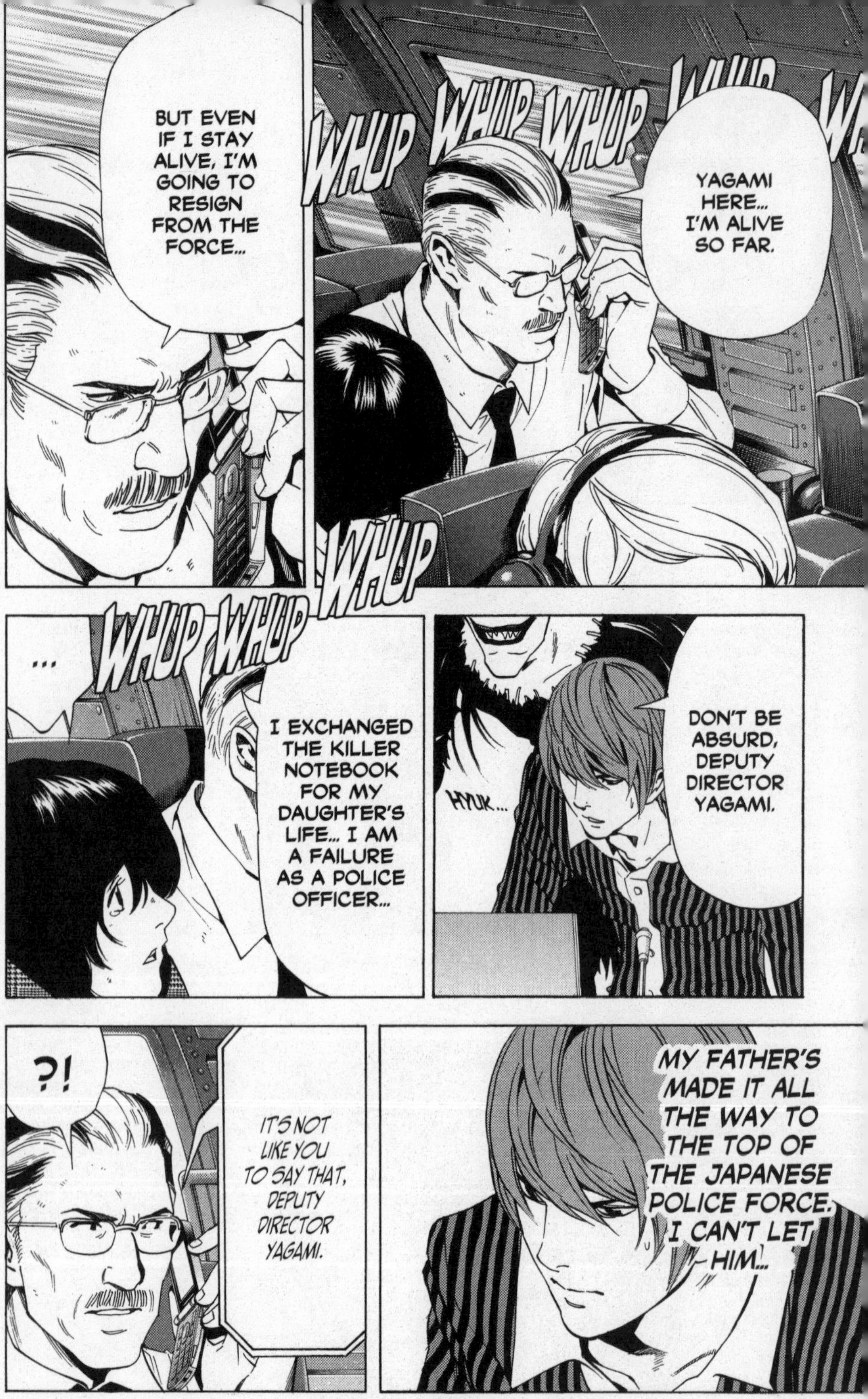
WHUP WHUP WHUP WHUP WH
YAGAMI HERE... I'M ALIVE SO FAR.
WHUP
BUT EVEN IF I STAY ALIVE, I'M GOING TO RESIGN FROM THE FORCE...
DON'T BE ABSURD, DEPUTY DIRECTOR YAGAMI.
HYUK...
WHUP WHUP
I EXCHANGED THE KILLER NOTEBOOK FOR MY DAUGHTER'S LIFE... I AM A FAILURE AS A POLICE OFFICER...
...
MY FATHER'S MADE IT ALL THE WAY TO THE TOP OF THE JAPANESE POLICE FORCE. I CAN'T LET HIM...
IT'S NOT LIKE YOU TO SAY THAT, DEPUTY DIRECTOR YAGAMI.
?!

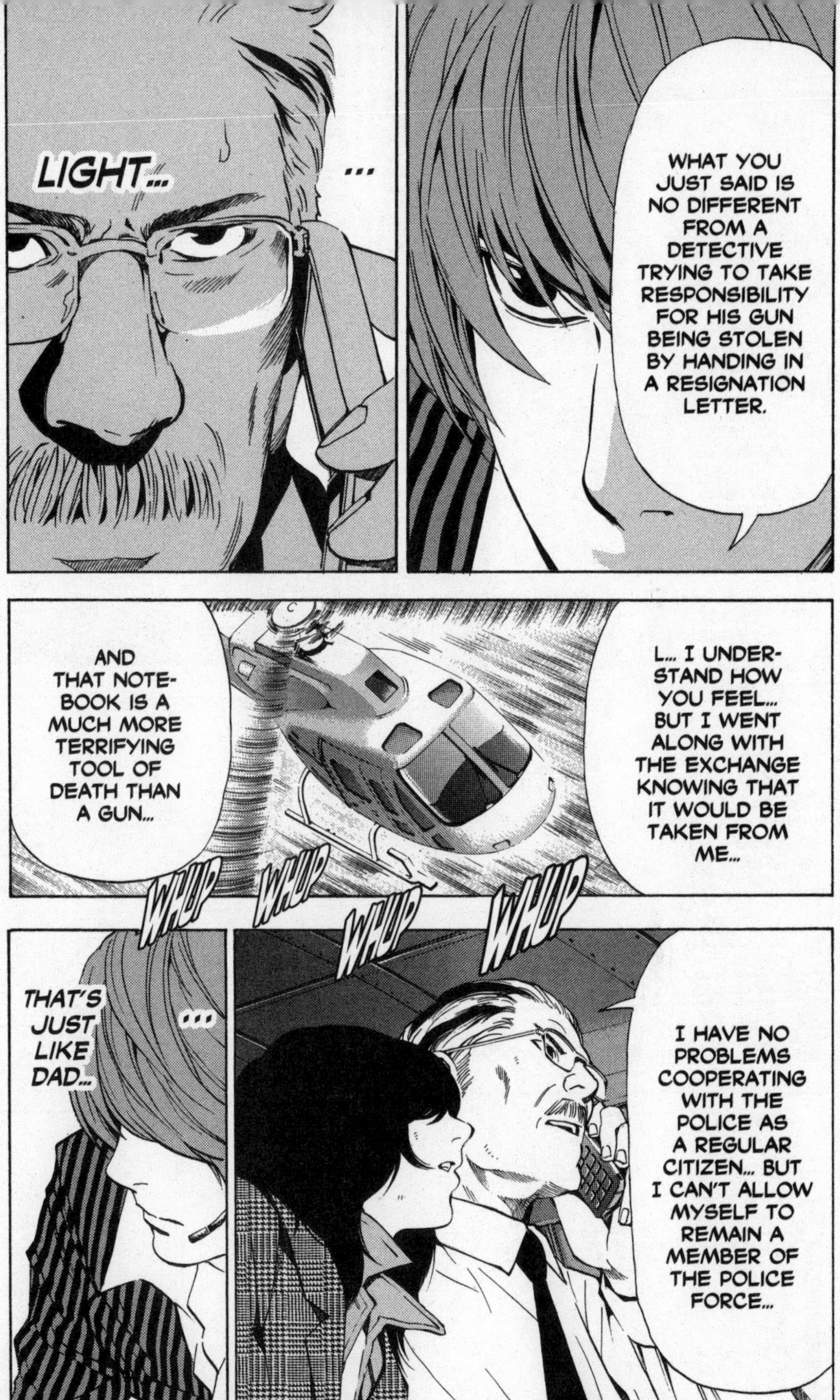
WHAT YOU JUST SAID IS NO DIFFERENT FROM A DETECTIVE TRYING TO TAKE RESPONSIBILITY FOR HIS GUN BEING STOLEN BY HANDING IN A RESIGNATION LETTER.
...
LIGHT...
L... I UNDER-STAND HOW YOU FEEL... BUT I WENT ALONG WITH THE EXCHANGE KNOWING THAT IT WOULD BE TAKEN FROM ME...
AND THAT NOTE-BOOK IS A MUCH MORE TERRIFYING TOOL OF DEATH THAN A GUN...
WHUP
WHUP
WHUP
WHUP
I HAVE NO PROBLEMS COOPERATING WITH THE POLICE AS A REGULAR CITIZEN... BUT I CAN'T ALLOW MYSELF TO REMAIN A MEMBER OF THE POLICE FORCE...
...
THAT'S JUST LIKE DAD...

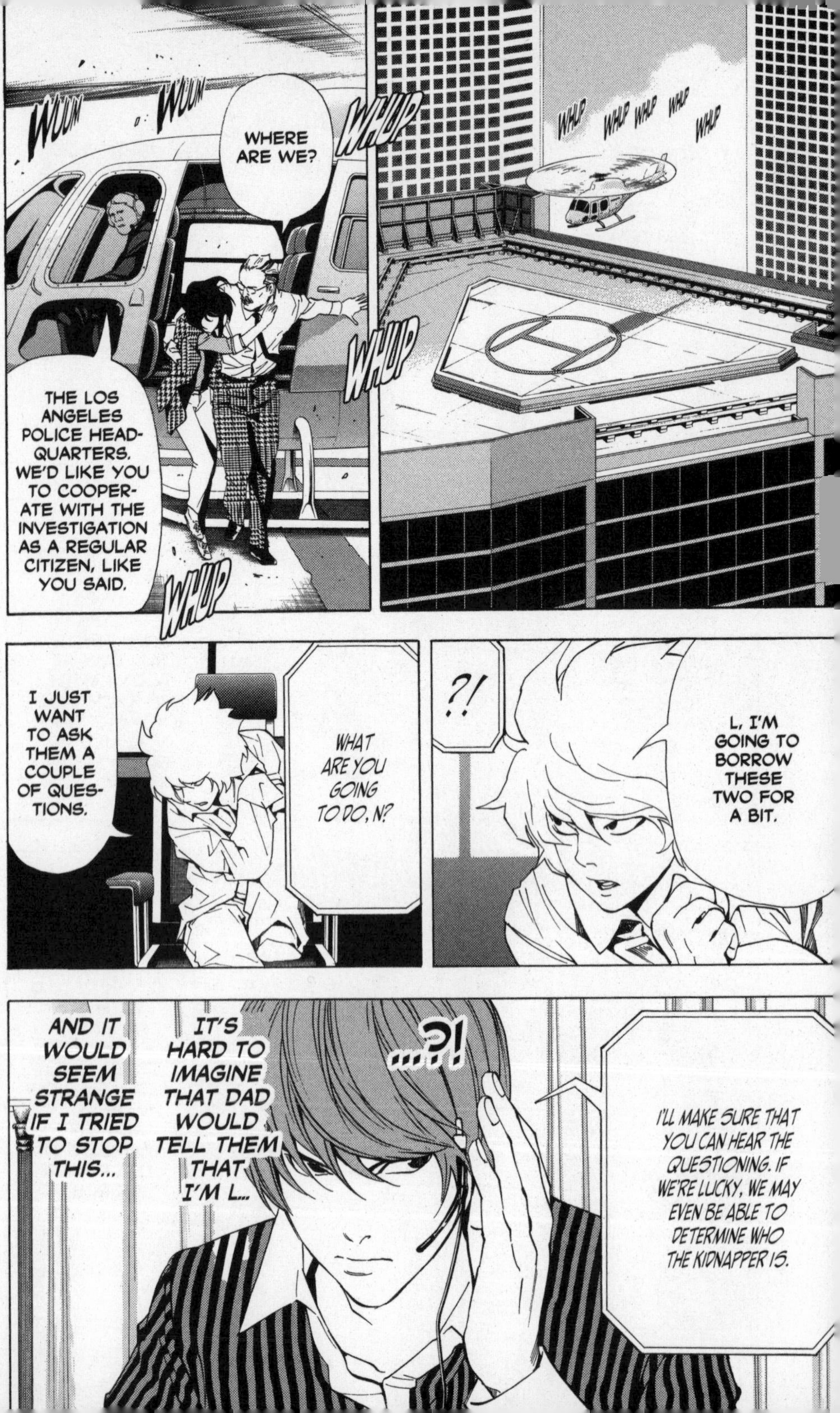
WHUP WHUP WHUP WHUP WHUP
WUUN
WUUN
WHUP
WHERE ARE WE?
THE LOS ANGELES POLICE HEAD-QUARTERS. WE'D LIKE YOU TO COOPER-ATE WITH THE INVESTIGATION AS A REGULAR CITIZEN, LIKE YOU SAID.
WHUP
WHUP
?!
L, I'M GOING TO BORROW THESE TWO FOR A BIT.
WHAT ARE YOU GOING TO DO, N?
I JUST WANT TO ASK THEM A COUPLE OF QUES-TIONS.
I'LL MAKE SURE THAT YOU CAN HEAR THE QUESTIONING. IF WE'RE LUCKY, WE MAY EVEN BE ABLE TO DETERMINE WHO THE KIDNAPPER IS.
...?!
IT'S HARD TO IMAGINE THAT DAD WOULD TELL THEM THAT I'M L...
AND IT WOULD SEEM STRANGE IF I TRIED TO STOP THIS...

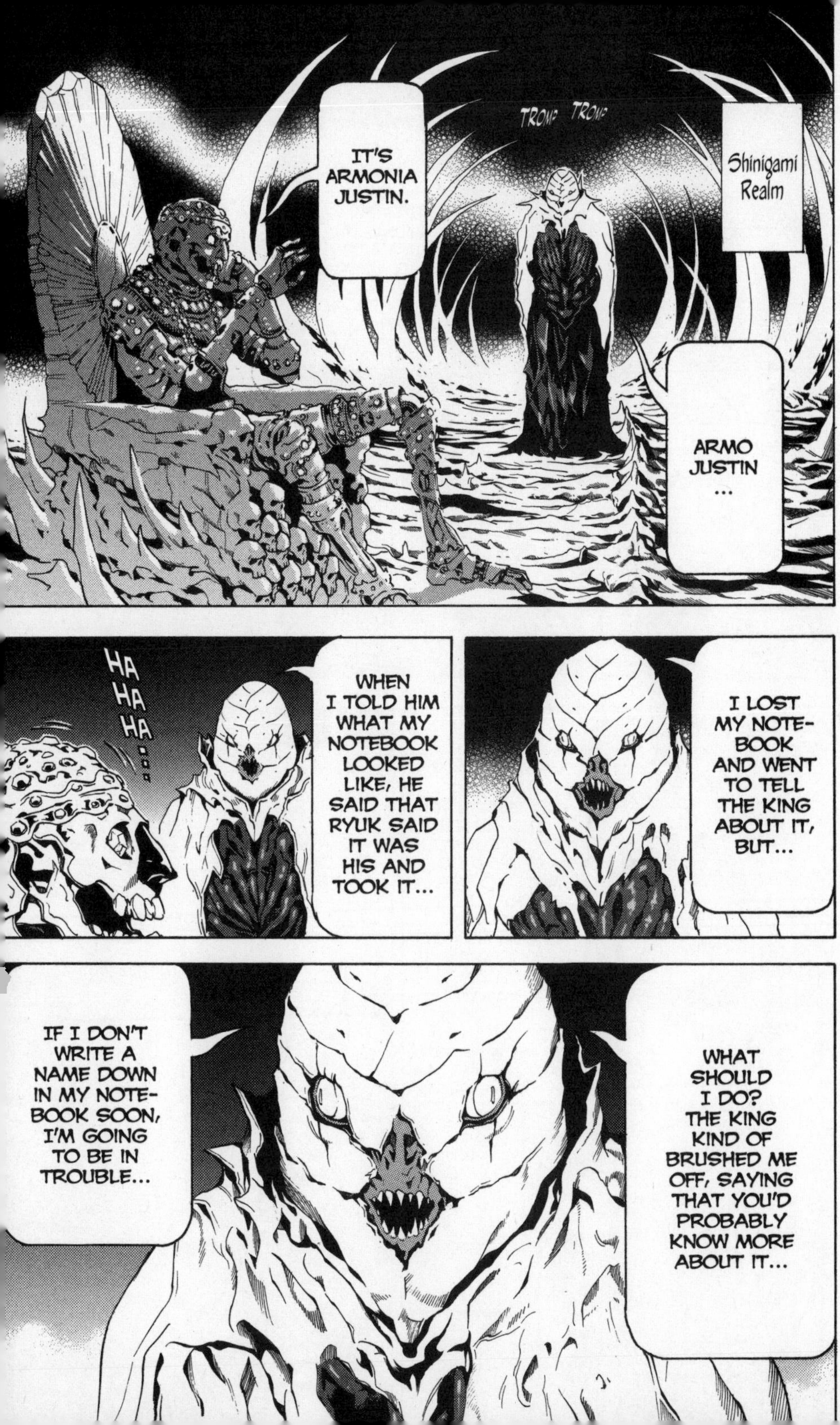
Shinigami Realm
TROMP TROMP
ARMO JUSTIN ...
IT'S ARMONIA JUSTIN.
I LOST MY NOTE-BOOK AND WENT TO TELL THE KING ABOUT IT, BUT...
WHEN I TOLD HIM WHAT MY NOTEBOOK LOOKED LIKE, HE SAID THAT RYUK SAID IT WAS HIS AND TOOK IT...
HA HA HA...
WHAT SHOULD I DO? THE KING KIND OF BRUSHED ME OFF, SAYING THAT YOU'D PROBABLY KNOW MORE ABOUT IT...
IF I DON'T WRITE A NAME DOWN IN MY NOTE-BOOK SOON, I'M GOING TO BE IN TROUBLE...

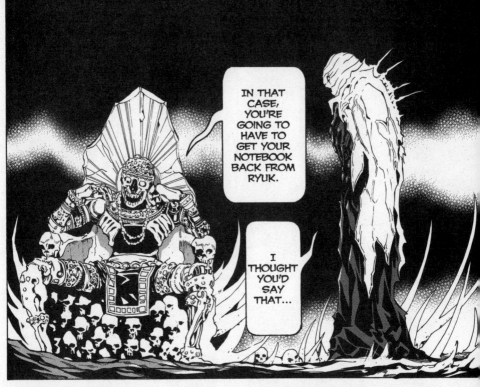

IN THAT CASE, YOU'RE GOING TO HAVE TO GET YOUR NOTEBOOK BACK FROM RYUK.
I THOUGHT YOU'D SAY THAT...
WHAT HAPPENS IF MY NOTEBOOK IS THE ONE THAT RYUK IS LETTING THE HUMAN USE?
THAT'D BE QUITE A DRAG.
BUT EVEN IF YOU DIDN'T HAND THE NOTEBOOK TO THE HUMAN YOURSELF, YOU SHOULD BE ABLE TO STAY IN THE HUMAN WORLD IN ORDER TO GET YOUR NOTE-BOOK BACK FROM RYUK.
SO, I'VE GOT TO GO TO THE HUMAN WORLD...

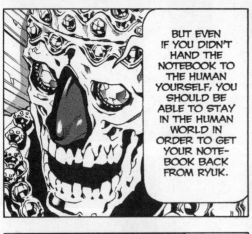

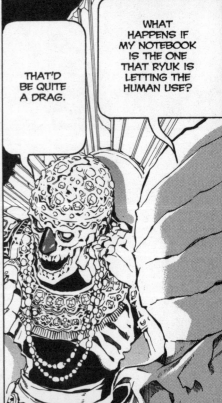

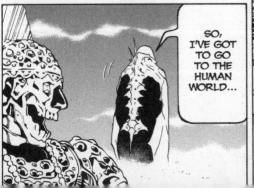

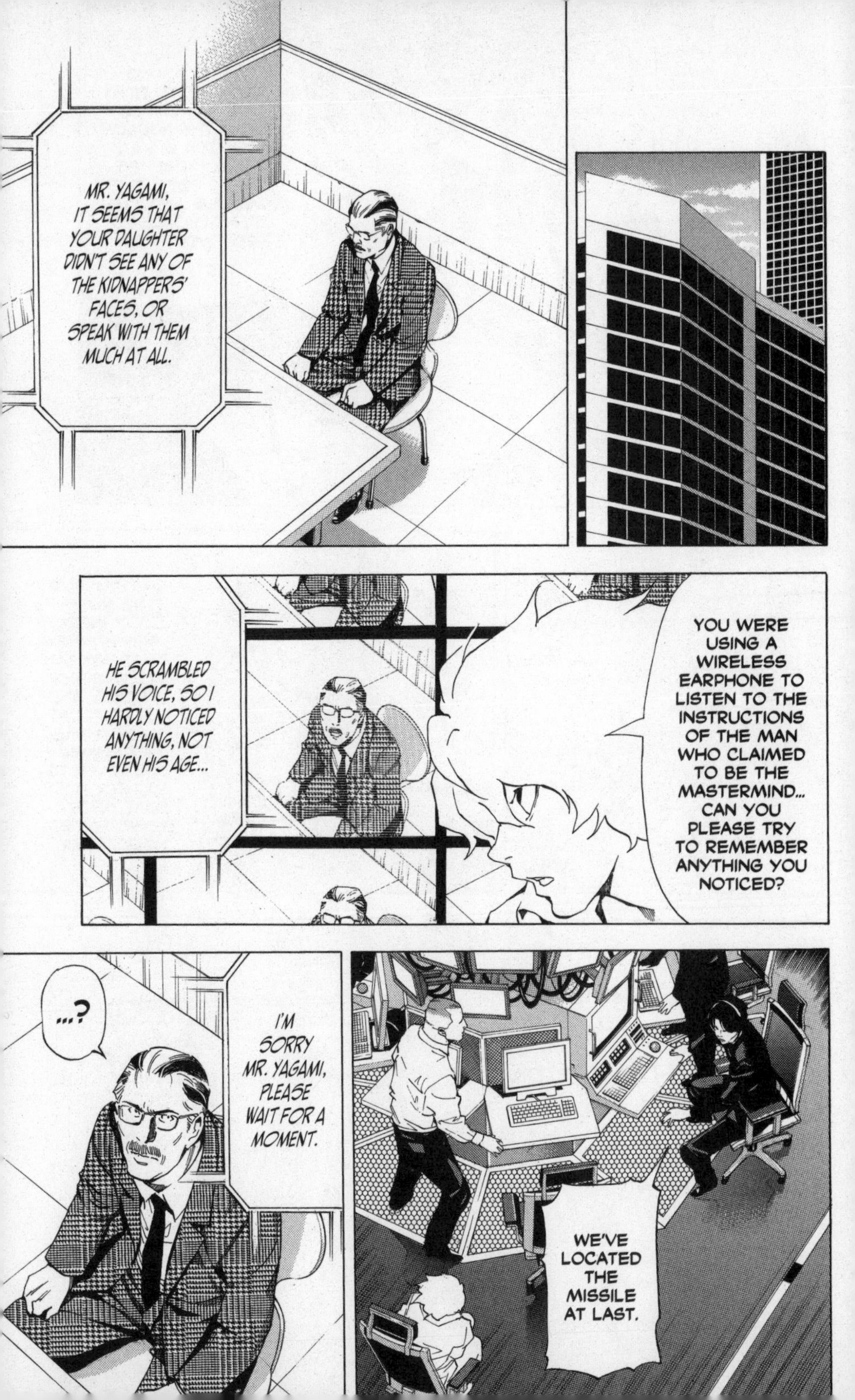
MR. YAGAMI, IT SEEMS THAT YOUR DAUGHTER DIDN'T SEE ANY OF THE KIDNAPPERS' FACES, OR SPEAK WITH THEM MUCH AT ALL.
YOU WERE USING A WIRELESS EARPHONE TO LISTEN TO THE INSTRUCTIONS OF THE MAN WHO CLAIMED TO BE THE MASTERMIND... CAN YOU PLEASE TRY TO REMEMBER ANYTHING YOU NOTICED?
HE SCRAMBLED HIS VOICE, SO I HARDLY NOTICED ANYTHING, NOT EVEN HIS AGE...
WE'VE LOCATED THE MISSILE AT LAST.
I'M SORRY MR. YAGAMI, PLEASE WAIT FOR A MOMENT.
...?

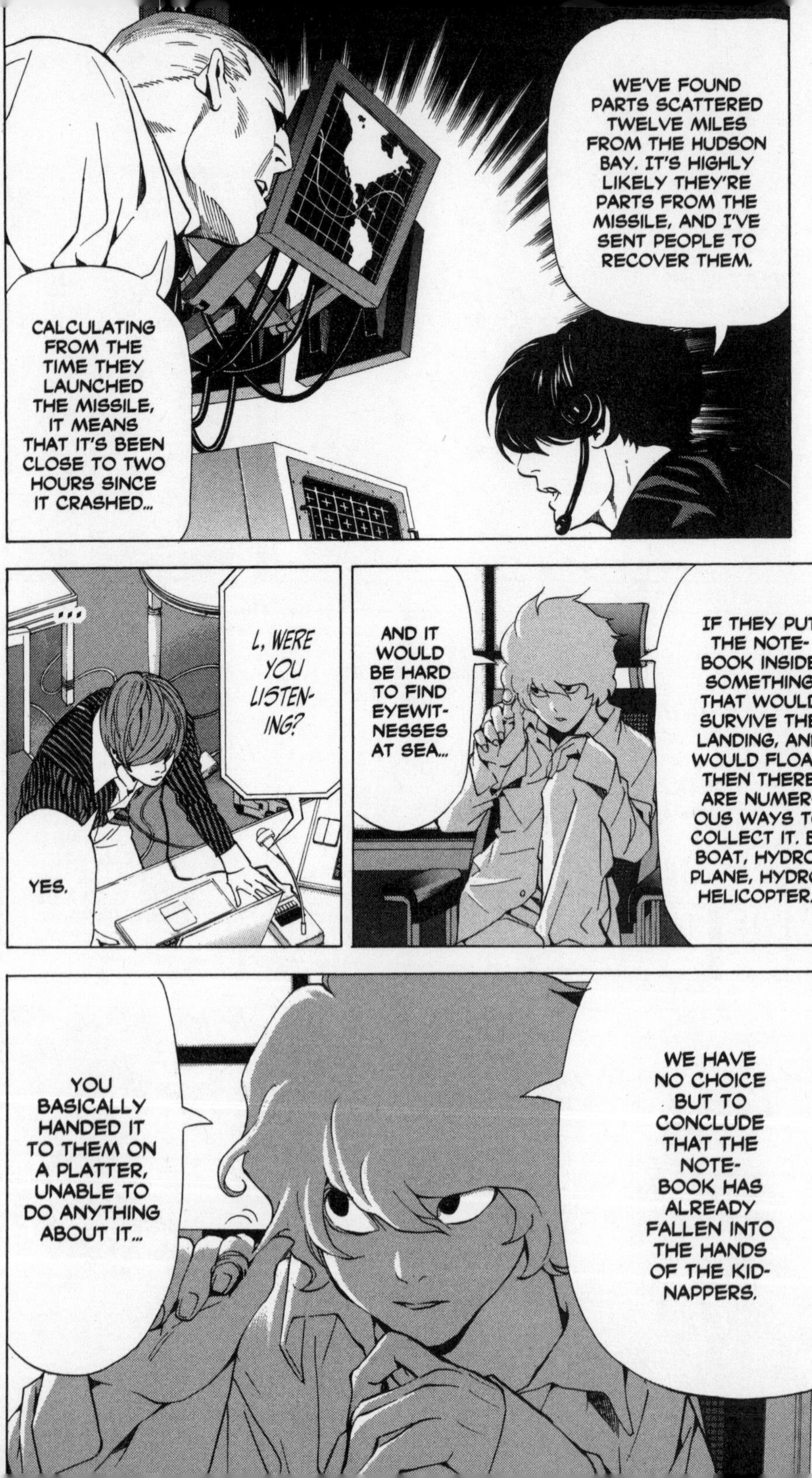
WE'VE FOUND PARTS SCATTERED TWELVE MILES FROM THE HUDSON BAY. IT'S HIGHLY LIKELY THEY'RE PARTS FROM THE MISSILE, AND I'VE SENT PEOPLE TO RECOVER THEM.
CALCULATING FROM THE TIME THEY LAUNCHED THE MISSILE, IT MEANS THAT IT'S BEEN CLOSE TO TWO HOURS SINCE IT CRASHED...
IF THEY PUT THE NOTEBOOK INSIDE SOMETHING THAT WOULD SURVIVE THE LANDING, AND WOULD FLOAT, THEN THERE ARE NUMEROUS WAYS TO COLLECT IT. BY BOAT, HYDROPLANE, HYDROHELICOPTER...
AND IT WOULD BE HARD TO FIND EYEWITNESSES AT SEA...
L, WERE YOU LISTENING?
...
YES.
WE HAVE NO CHOICE BUT TO CONCLUDE THAT THE NOTEBOOK HAS ALREADY FALLEN INTO THE HANDS OF THE KIDNAPPERS.
YOU BASICALLY HANDED IT TO THEM ON A PLATTER, UNABLE TO DO ANYTHING ABOUT IT...

READ THIS WAY

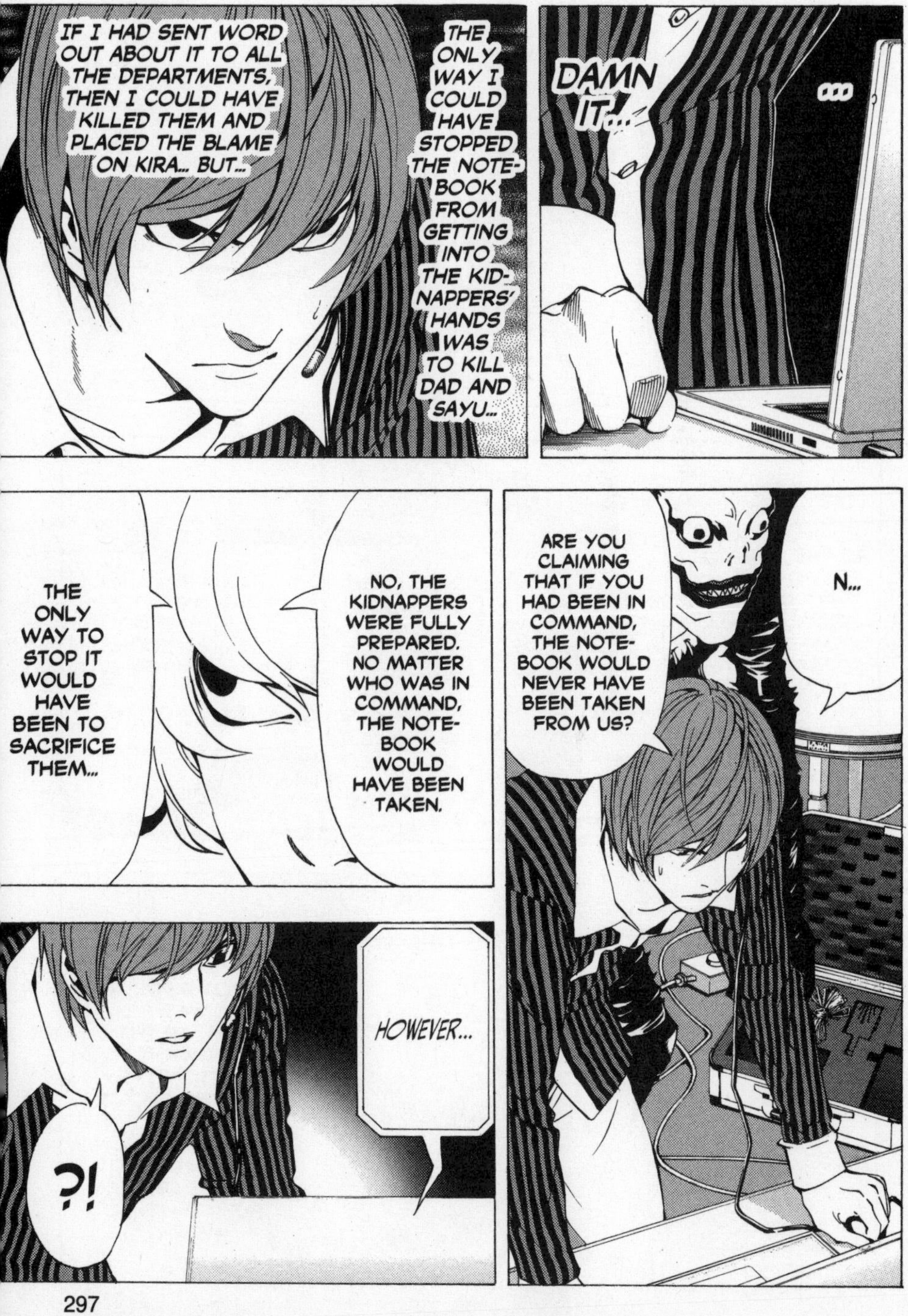
DAMN IT...
...
IF I HAD SENT WORD OUT ABOUT IT TO ALL THE DEPARTMENTS, THEN I COULD HAVE KILLED THEM AND PLACED THE BLAME ON KIRA... BUT...
THE ONLY WAY I COULD HAVE STOPPED THE NOTE-BOOK FROM GETTING INTO THE KID-NAPPERS' HANDS WAS TO KILL DAD AND SAYU...
N...
ARE YOU CLAIMING THAT IF YOU HAD BEEN IN COMMAND, THE NOTE-BOOK WOULD NEVER HAVE BEEN TAKEN FROM US?
NO, THE KIDNAPPERS WERE FULLY PREPARED. NO MATTER WHO WAS IN COMMAND, THE NOTE-BOOK WOULD HAVE BEEN TAKEN.
THE ONLY WAY TO STOP IT WOULD HAVE BEEN TO SACRIFICE THEM...
HOWEVER...
?!

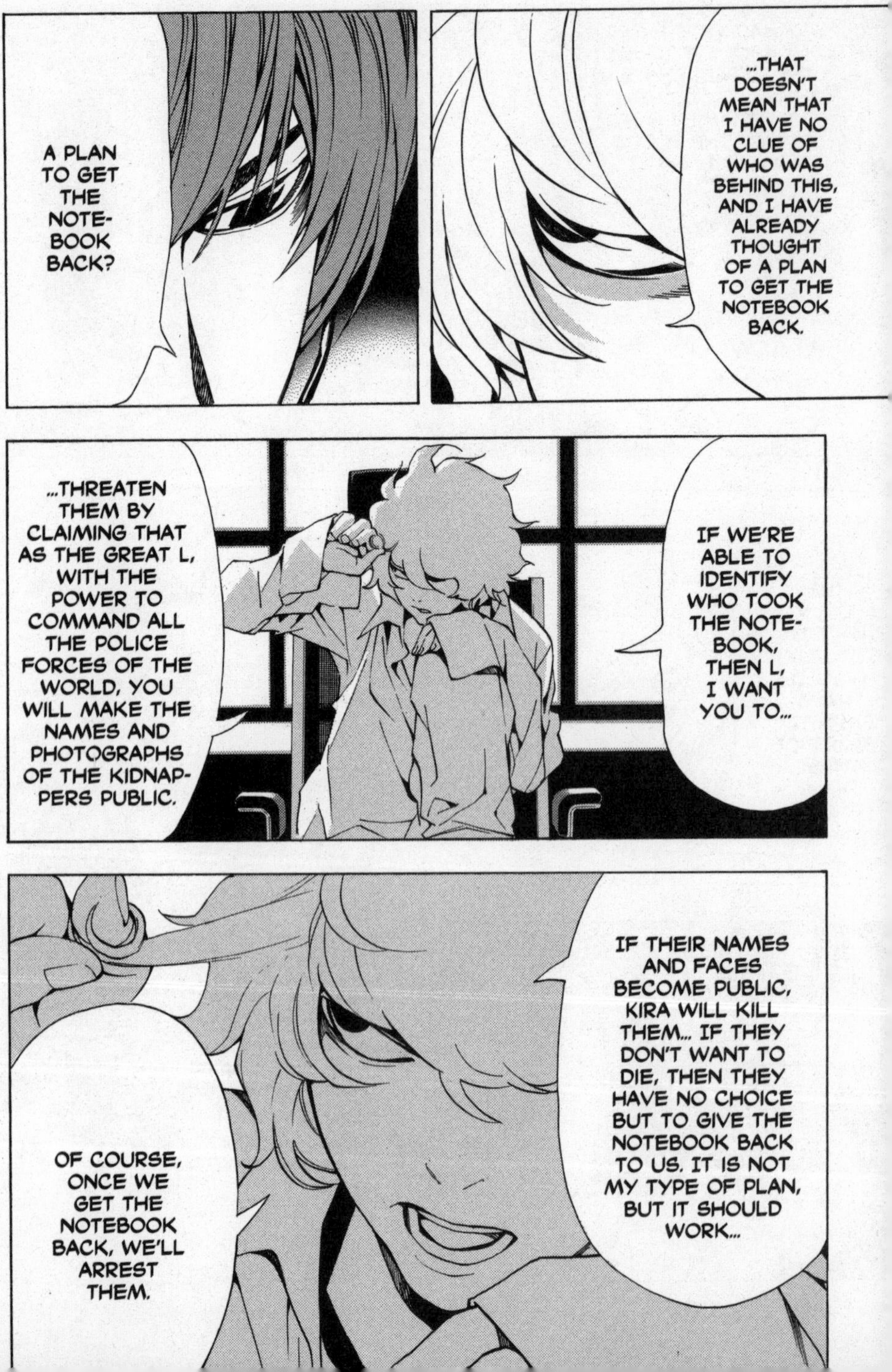
...THAT DOESN'T MEAN THAT I HAVE NO CLUE OF WHO WAS BEHIND THIS, AND I HAVE ALREADY THOUGHT OF A PLAN TO GET THE NOTEBOOK BACK.
A PLAN TO GET THE NOTE-BOOK BACK?
IF WE'RE ABLE TO IDENTIFY WHO TOOK THE NOTE-BOOK, THEN L, I WANT YOU TO...
...THREATEN THEM BY CLAIMING THAT AS THE GREAT L, WITH THE POWER TO COMMAND ALL THE POLICE FORCES OF THE WORLD, YOU WILL MAKE THE NAMES AND PHOTOGRAPHS OF THE KIDNAP-PERS PUBLIC.
IF THEIR NAMES AND FACES BECOME PUBLIC, KIRA WILL KILL THEM... IF THEY DON'T WANT TO DIE, THEN THEY HAVE NO CHOICE BUT TO GIVE THE NOTEBOOK BACK TO US. IT IS NOT MY TYPE OF PLAN, BUT IT SHOULD WORK...
OF COURSE, ONCE WE GET THE NOTEBOOK BACK, WE'LL ARREST THEM.

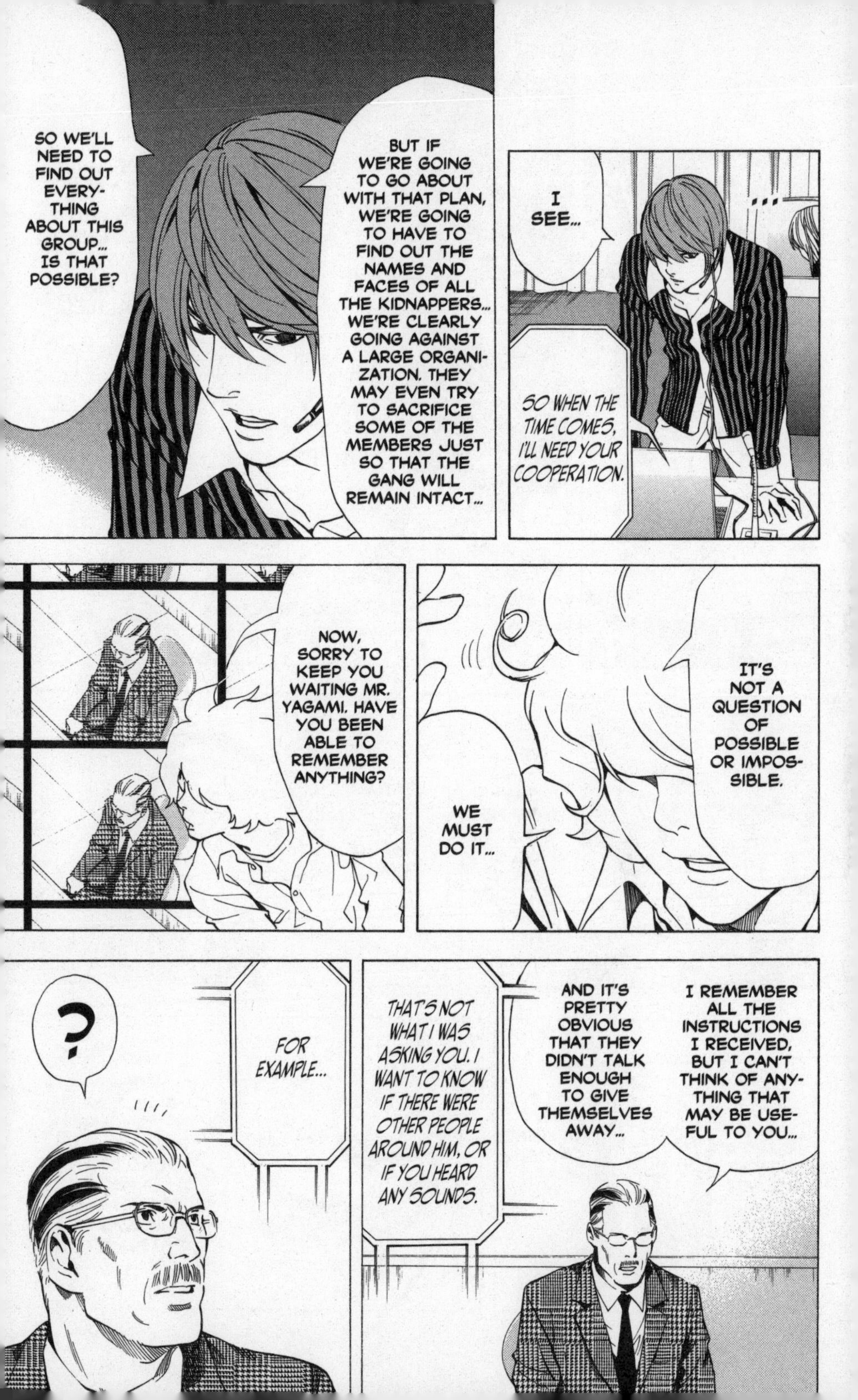

I SEE...
...
SO WHEN THE TIME COMES, I'LL NEED YOUR COOPERATION.
BUT IF WE'RE GOING TO GO ABOUT WITH THAT PLAN, WE'RE GOING TO HAVE TO FIND OUT THE NAMES AND FACES OF ALL THE KIDNAPPERS... WE'RE CLEARLY GOING AGAINST A LARGE ORGANI-ZATION. THEY MAY EVEN TRY TO SACRIFICE SOME OF THE MEMBERS JUST SO THAT THE GANG WILL REMAIN INTACT...
SO WE'LL NEED TO FIND OUT EVERY-THING ABOUT THIS GROUP... IS THAT POSSIBLE?
IT'S NOT A QUESTION OF POSSIBLE OR IMPOS-SIBLE.
WE MUST DO IT...
NOW, SORRY TO KEEP YOU WAITING MR. YAGAMI. HAVE YOU BEEN ABLE TO REMEMBER ANYTHING?
I REMEMBER ALL THE INSTRUCTIONS I RECEIVED, BUT I CAN'T THINK OF ANY-THING THAT MAY BE USE-FUL TO YOU...
AND IT'S PRETTY OBVIOUS THAT THEY DIDN'T TALK ENOUGH TO GIVE THEMSELVES AWAY...
THAT'S NOT WHAT I WAS ASKING YOU. I WANT TO KNOW IF THERE WERE OTHER PEOPLE AROUND HIM, OR IF YOU HEARD ANY SOUNDS.
FOR EXAMPLE...
?

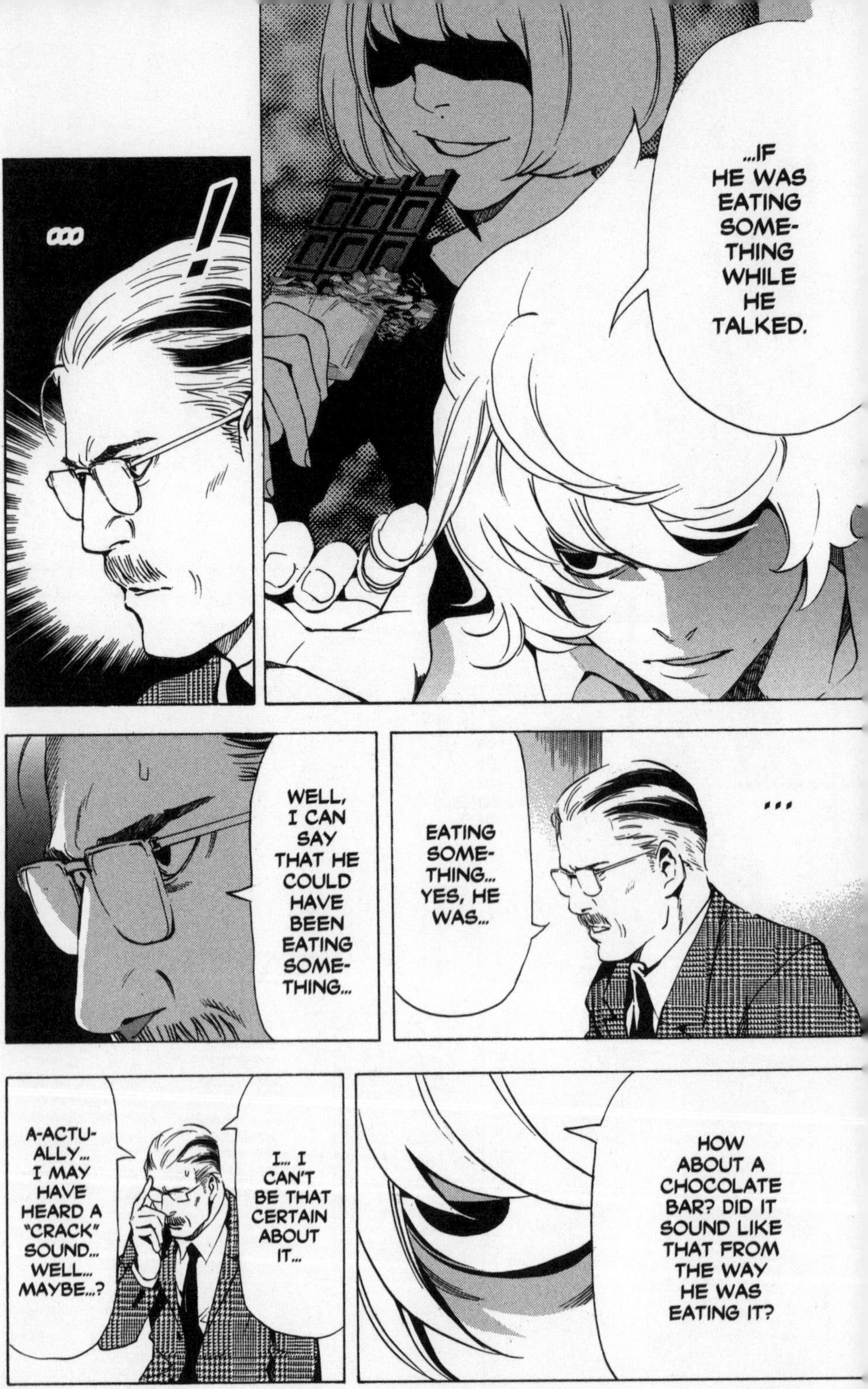
...IF HE WAS EATING SOME-THING WHILE HE TALKED.
!
...
EATING SOME-THING... YES, HE WAS...
WELL, I CAN SAY THAT HE COULD HAVE BEEN EATING SOME-THING...
HOW ABOUT A CHOCOLATE BAR? DID IT SOUND LIKE THAT FROM THE WAY HE WAS EATING IT?
I... I CAN'T BE THAT CERTAIN ABOUT IT...
A-ACTU-ALLY... I MAY HAVE HEARD A "CRACK" SOUND... WELL... MAYBE...?

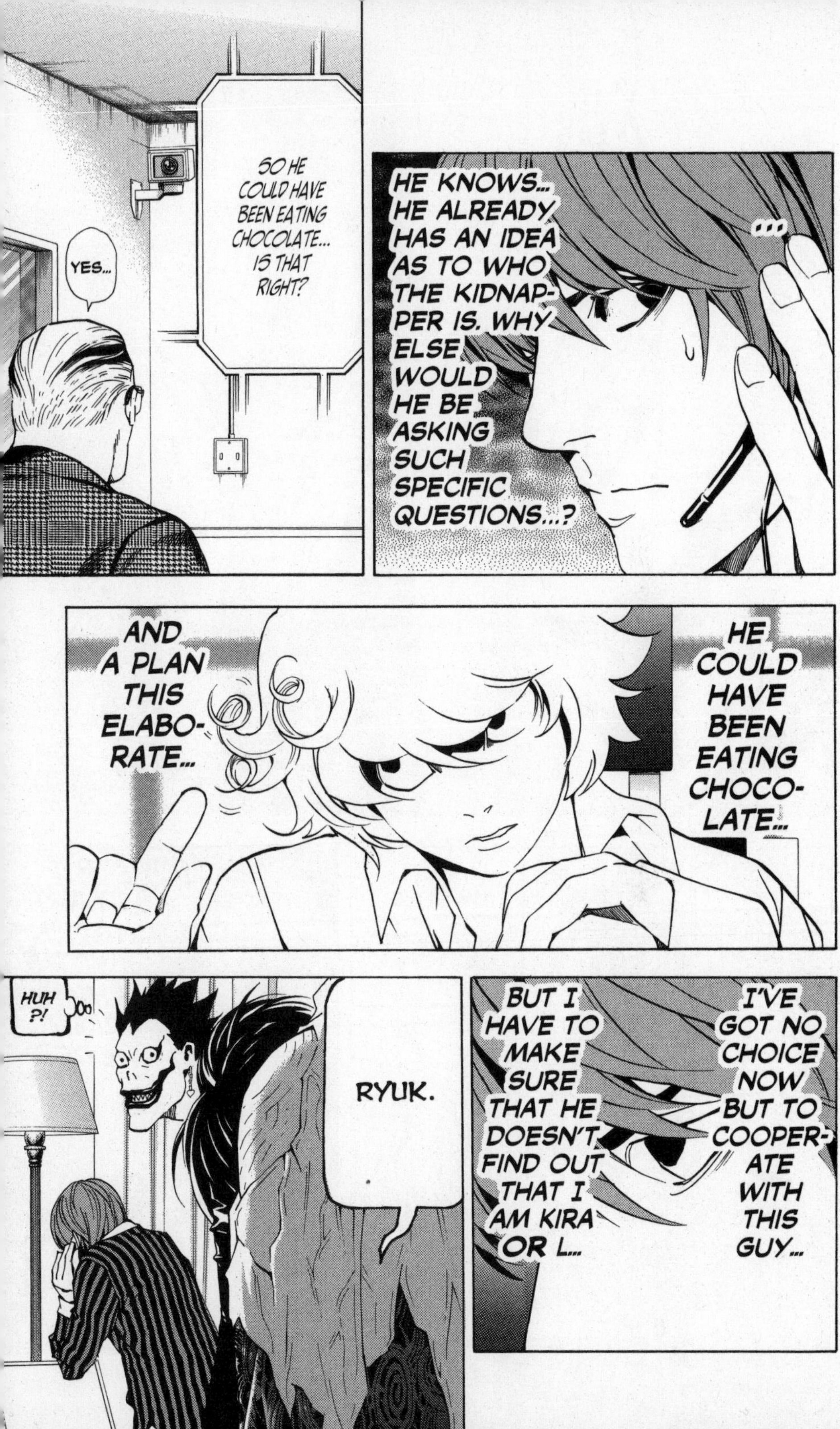
...
HE KNOWS... HE ALREADY HAS AN IDEA AS TO WHO THE KIDNAP-PER IS. WHY ELSE WOULD HE BE ASKING SUCH SPECIFIC QUESTIONS...?
SO HE COULD HAVE BEEN EATING CHOCOLATE... IS THAT RIGHT?
YES...
HE COULD HAVE BEEN EATING CHOCO-LATE...
AND A PLAN THIS ELABO-RATE...
I'VE GOT NO CHOICE NOW BUT TO COOPER-ATE WITH THIS GUY...
BUT I HAVE TO MAKE SURE THAT HE DOESN'T FIND OUT THAT I AM KIRA OR L...
RYUK.
HUH ?!

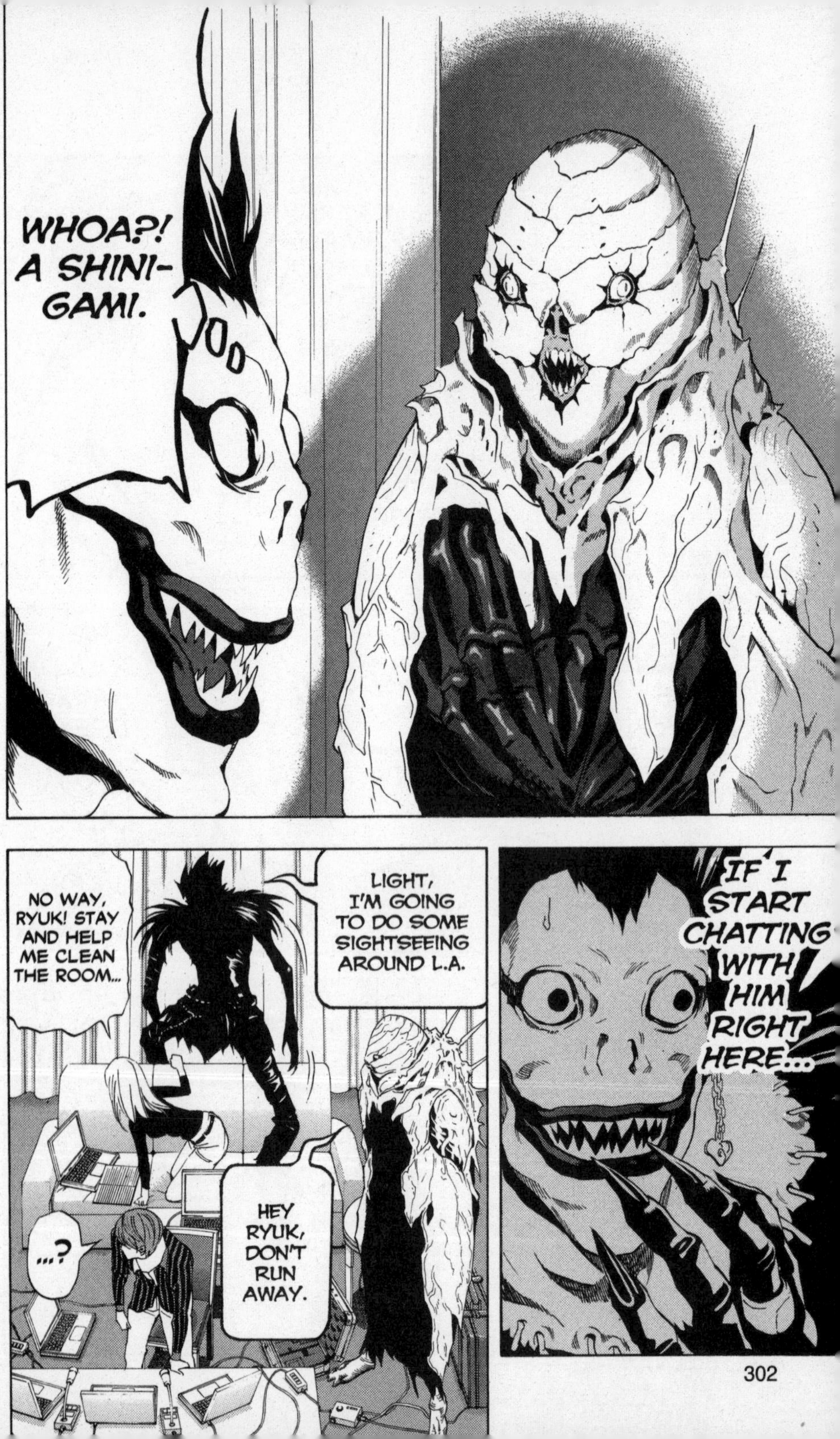
WHOA?! A SHINI-GAMI.
IF I START CHATTING WITH HIM RIGHT HERE...
LIGHT, I'M GOING TO DO SOME SIGHTSEEING AROUND L.A.
NO WAY, RYUK! STAY AND HELP ME CLEAN THE ROOM...
HEY RYUK, DON'T RUN AWAY.
...?

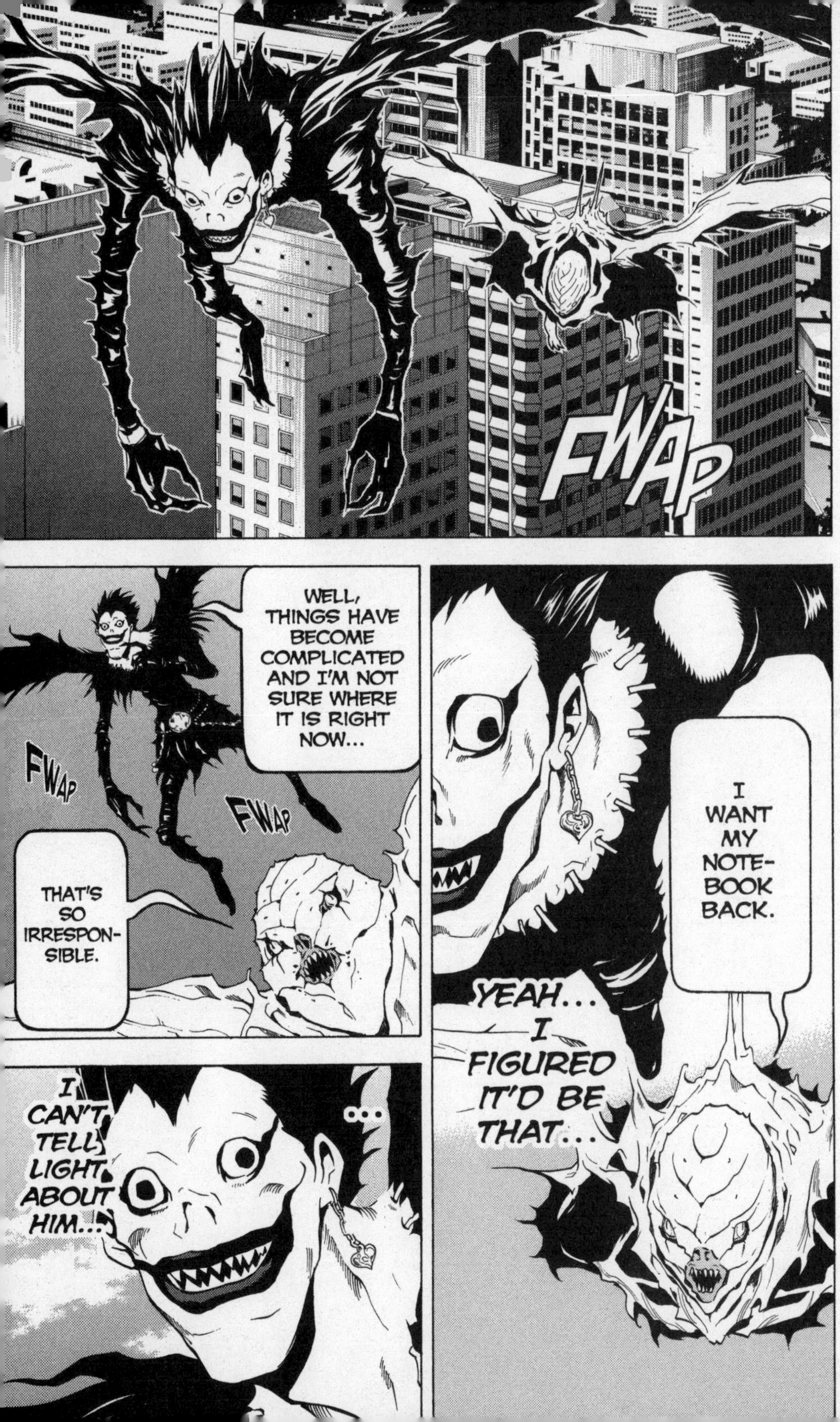
FWAP
I WANT MY NOTE-BOOK BACK.
YEAH... I FIGURED IT'D BE THAT...
WELL, THINGS HAVE BECOME COMPLICATED AND I'M NOT SURE WHERE IT IS RIGHT NOW...
FWAP
FWAP
THAT'S SO IRRESPON-SIBLE.
...
I CAN'T TELL LIGHT ABOUT HIM...

# DEATH NOTE
## How to use it
## XLIII

- If a DEATH NOTE is owned in the human world against the god of death's will, that god of death is permitted to stay in the human world in order to retrieve it.

死神が自分の所有すべきデスノートを
不本意に人間界のものにされている場合、
そのノートを取り戻す目的で人間界に居る事は許される。

- In that case, if there are other DEATH NOTES in the human world, the gods of death are not allowed to reveal to humans that DEATH NOTE'S owner or its location.

その時、人間界に他にもノートが存在していた場合、
人間にそのノートのある場所や所有者を教えてはならない。

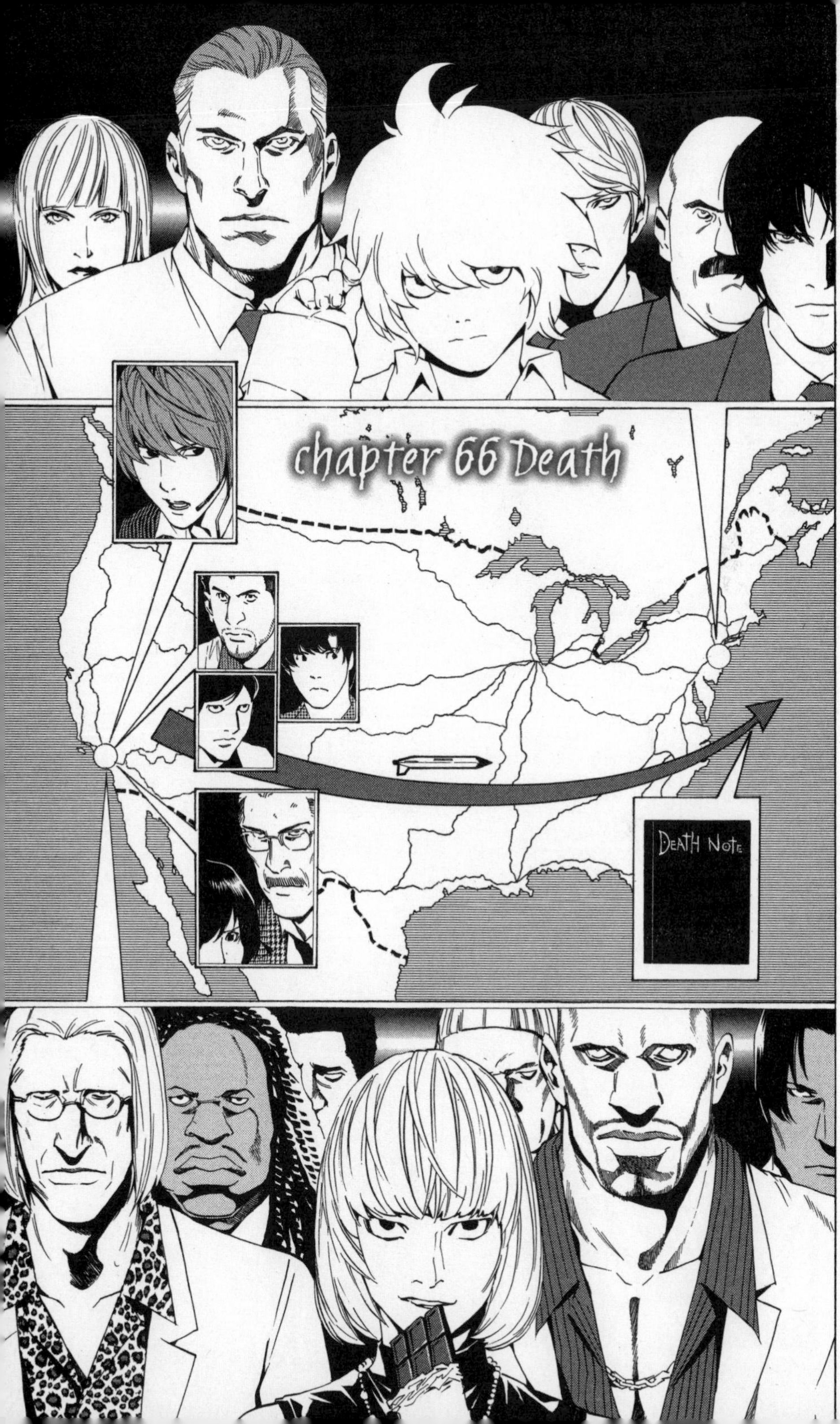
chapter 66 Death
DEATH NOTE

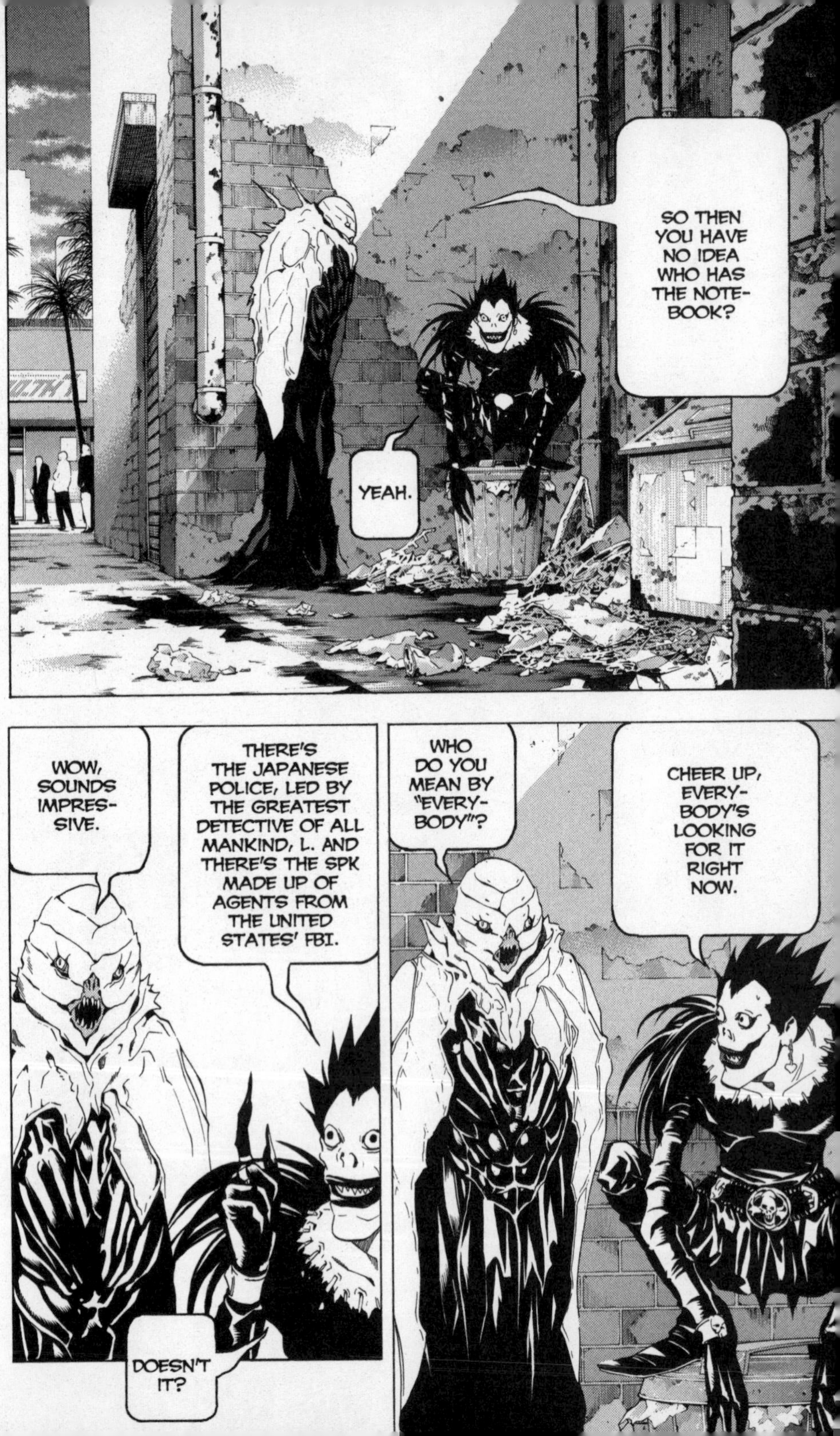
SO THEN YOU HAVE NO IDEA WHO HAS THE NOTE-BOOK?
YEAH.
CHEER UP, EVERY-BODY'S LOOKING FOR IT RIGHT NOW.
WHO DO YOU MEAN BY "EVERY-BODY"?
THERE'S THE JAPANESE POLICE, LED BY THE GREATEST DETECTIVE OF ALL MANKIND, L. AND THERE'S THE SPK MADE UP OF AGENTS FROM THE UNITED STATES' FBI.
WOW, SOUNDS IMPRES-SIVE.
DOESN'T IT?

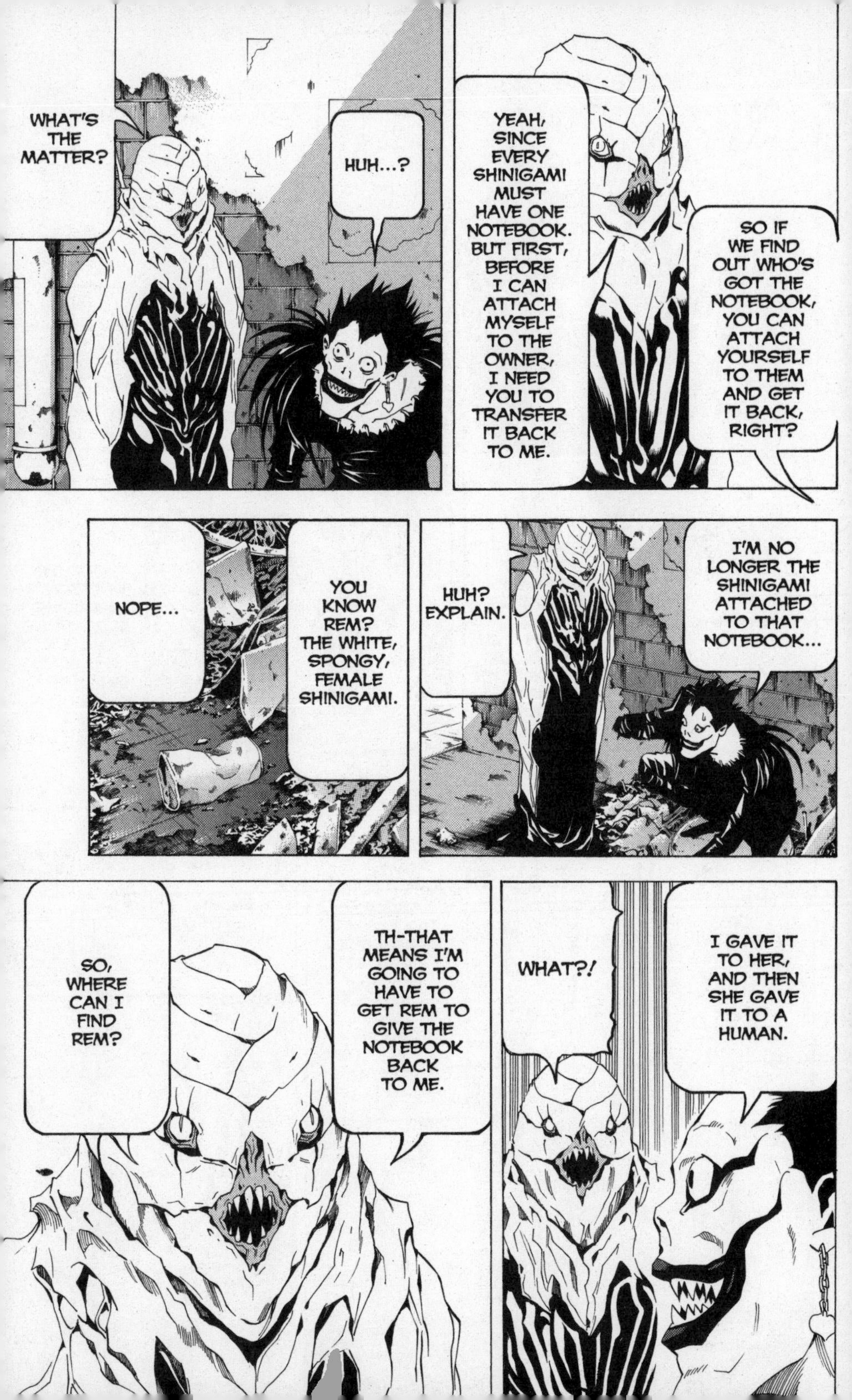
SO IF WE FIND OUT WHO'S GOT THE NOTEBOOK, YOU CAN ATTACH YOURSELF TO THEM AND GET IT BACK, RIGHT?
YEAH, SINCE EVERY SHINIGAMI MUST HAVE ONE NOTEBOOK. BUT FIRST, BEFORE I CAN ATTACH MYSELF TO THE OWNER, I NEED YOU TO TRANSFER IT BACK TO ME.
HUH...?
WHAT'S THE MATTER?
I'M NO LONGER THE SHINIGAMI ATTACHED TO THAT NOTEBOOK...
HUH? EXPLAIN.
YOU KNOW REM? THE WHITE, SPONGY, FEMALE SHINIGAMI.
NOPE...
I GAVE IT TO HER, AND THEN SHE GAVE IT TO A HUMAN.
WHAT?!
TH-THAT MEANS I'M GOING TO HAVE TO GET REM TO GIVE THE NOTEBOOK BACK TO ME.
SO, WHERE CAN I FIND REM?

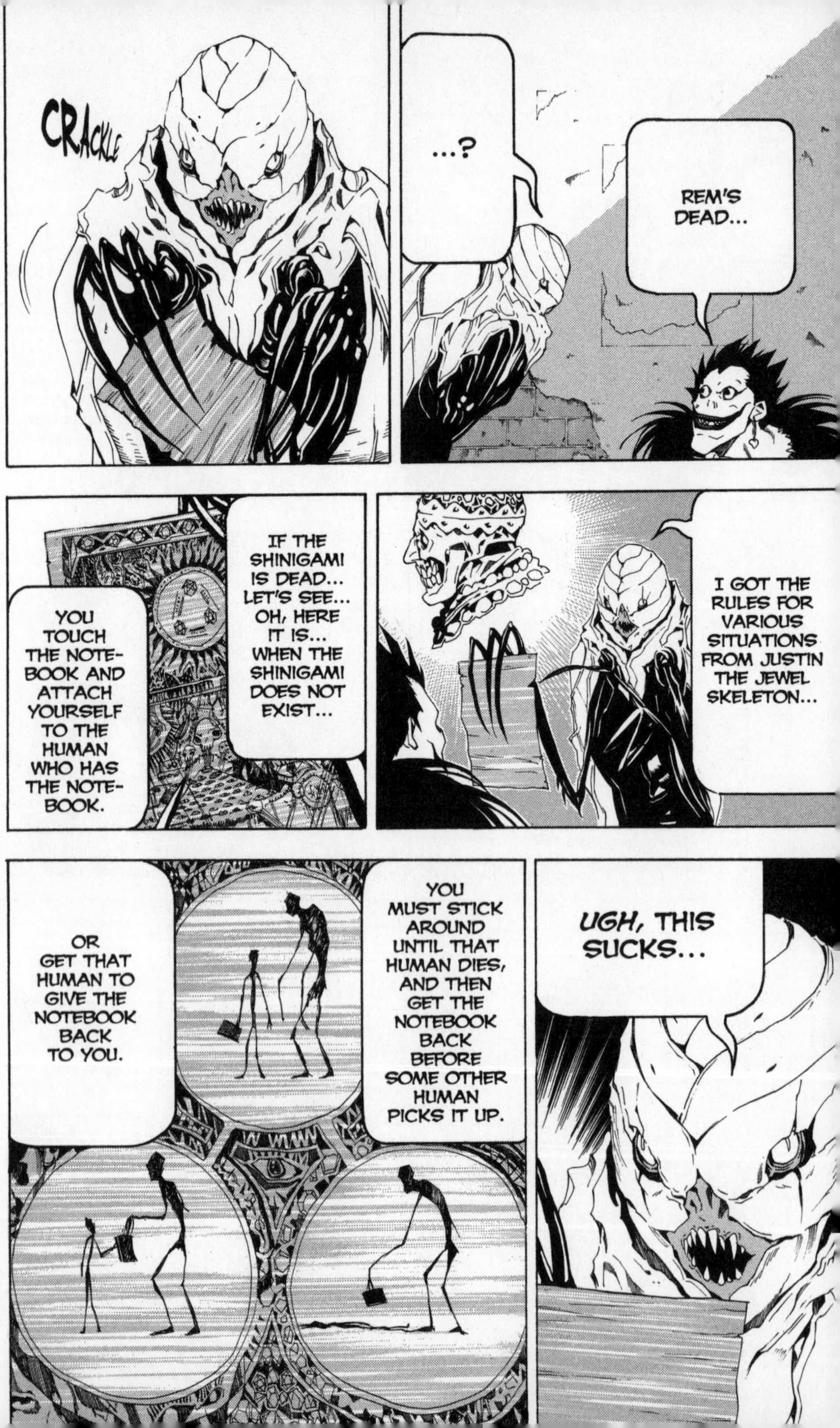
REM'S DEAD...
...?
CRACKLE
I GOT THE RULES FOR VARIOUS SITUATIONS FROM JUSTIN THE JEWEL SKELETON...
IF THE SHINIGAMI IS DEAD... LET'S SEE... OH, HERE IT IS... WHEN THE SHINIGAMI DOES NOT EXIST...
YOU TOUCH THE NOTE-BOOK AND ATTACH YOURSELF TO THE HUMAN WHO HAS THE NOTE-BOOK.
UGH, THIS SUCKS...
YOU MUST STICK AROUND UNTIL THAT HUMAN DIES, AND THEN GET THE NOTEBOOK BACK BEFORE SOME OTHER HUMAN PICKS IT UP.
OR GET THAT HUMAN TO GIVE THE NOTEBOOK BACK TO YOU.

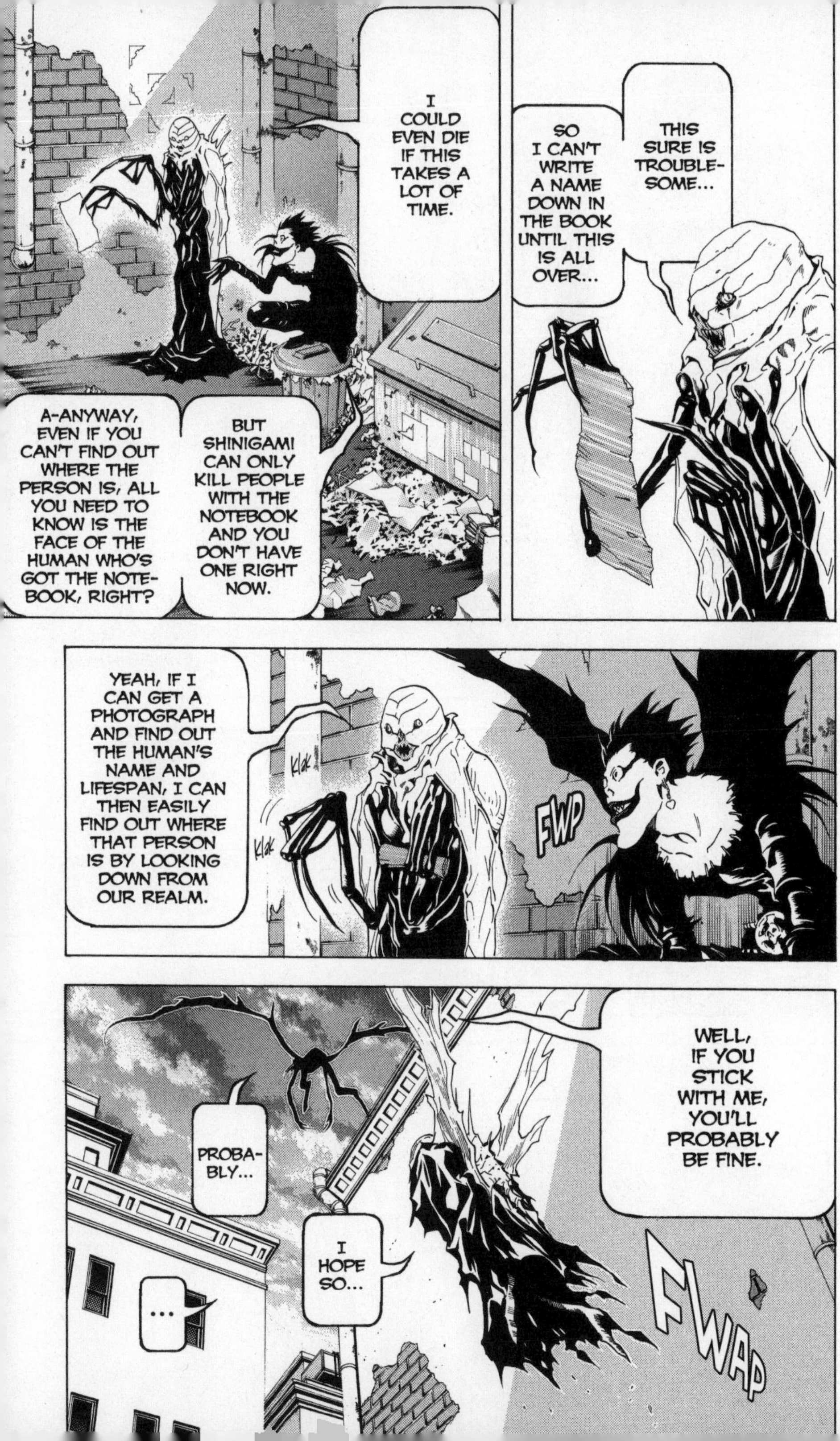
THIS SURE IS TROUBLE-SOME...
SO I CAN'T WRITE A NAME DOWN IN THE BOOK UNTIL THIS IS ALL OVER...
I COULD EVEN DIE IF THIS TAKES A LOT OF TIME.
BUT SHINIGAMI CAN ONLY KILL PEOPLE WITH THE NOTEBOOK AND YOU DON'T HAVE ONE RIGHT NOW.
A-ANYWAY, EVEN IF YOU CAN'T FIND OUT WHERE THE PERSON IS, ALL YOU NEED TO KNOW IS THE FACE OF THE HUMAN WHO'S GOT THE NOTE-BOOK, RIGHT?
FWP
YEAH, IF I CAN GET A PHOTOGRAPH AND FIND OUT THE HUMAN'S NAME AND LIFESPAN, I CAN THEN EASILY FIND OUT WHERE THAT PERSON IS BY LOOKING DOWN FROM OUR REALM.
klak
klak
WELL, IF YOU STICK WITH ME, YOU'LL PROBABLY BE FINE.
PROBA-BLY...
FWAP
I HOPE SO...
...

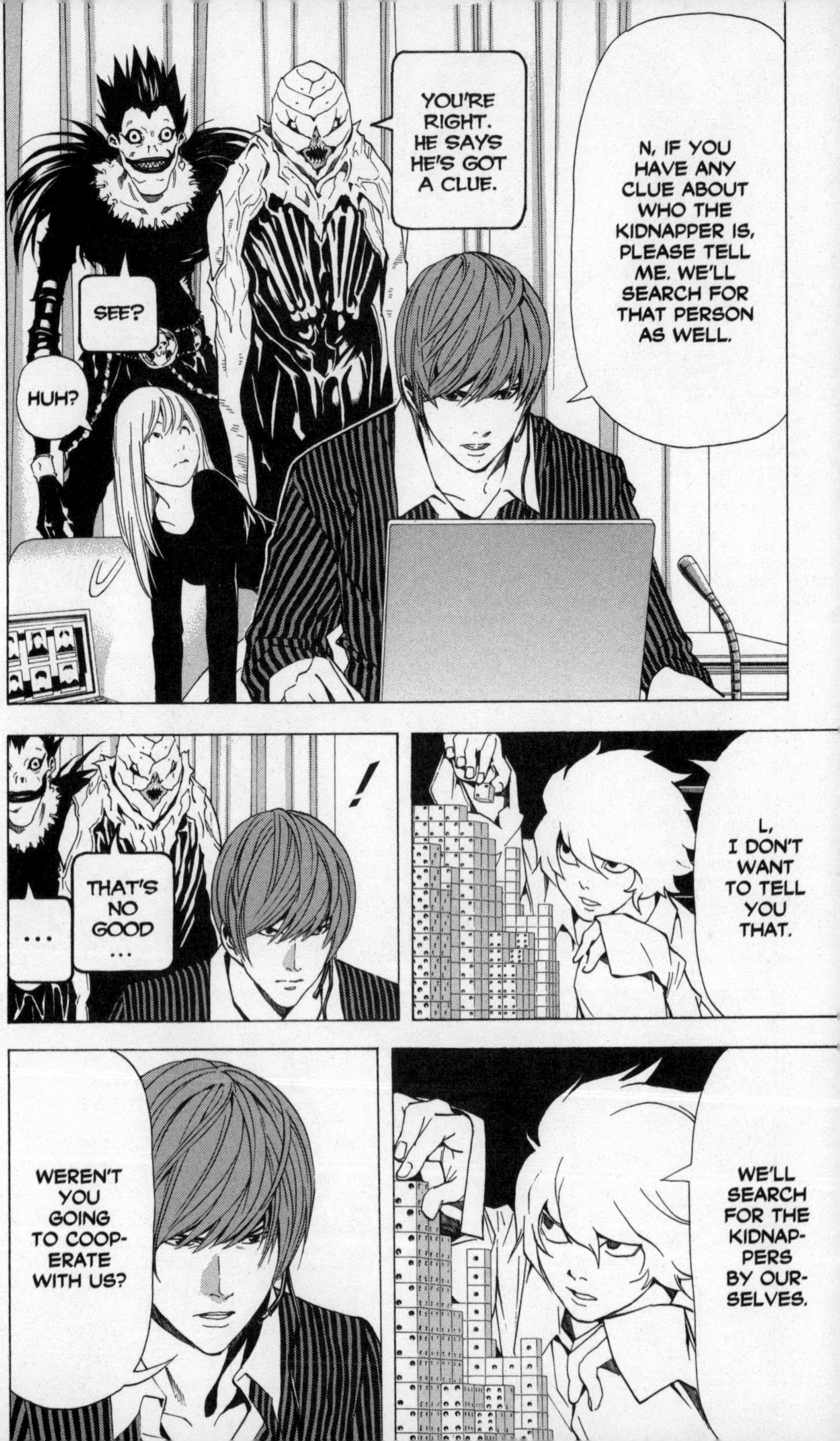
N, IF YOU HAVE ANY CLUE ABOUT WHO THE KIDNAPPER IS, PLEASE TELL ME. WE'LL SEARCH FOR THAT PERSON AS WELL.
YOU'RE RIGHT. HE SAYS HE'S GOT A CLUE.
SEE?
HUH?
L, I DON'T WANT TO TELL YOU THAT.
!
THAT'S NO GOOD ...
...
WE'LL SEARCH FOR THE KIDNAP-PERS BY OUR-SELVES.
WEREN'T YOU GOING TO COOP-ERATE WITH US?

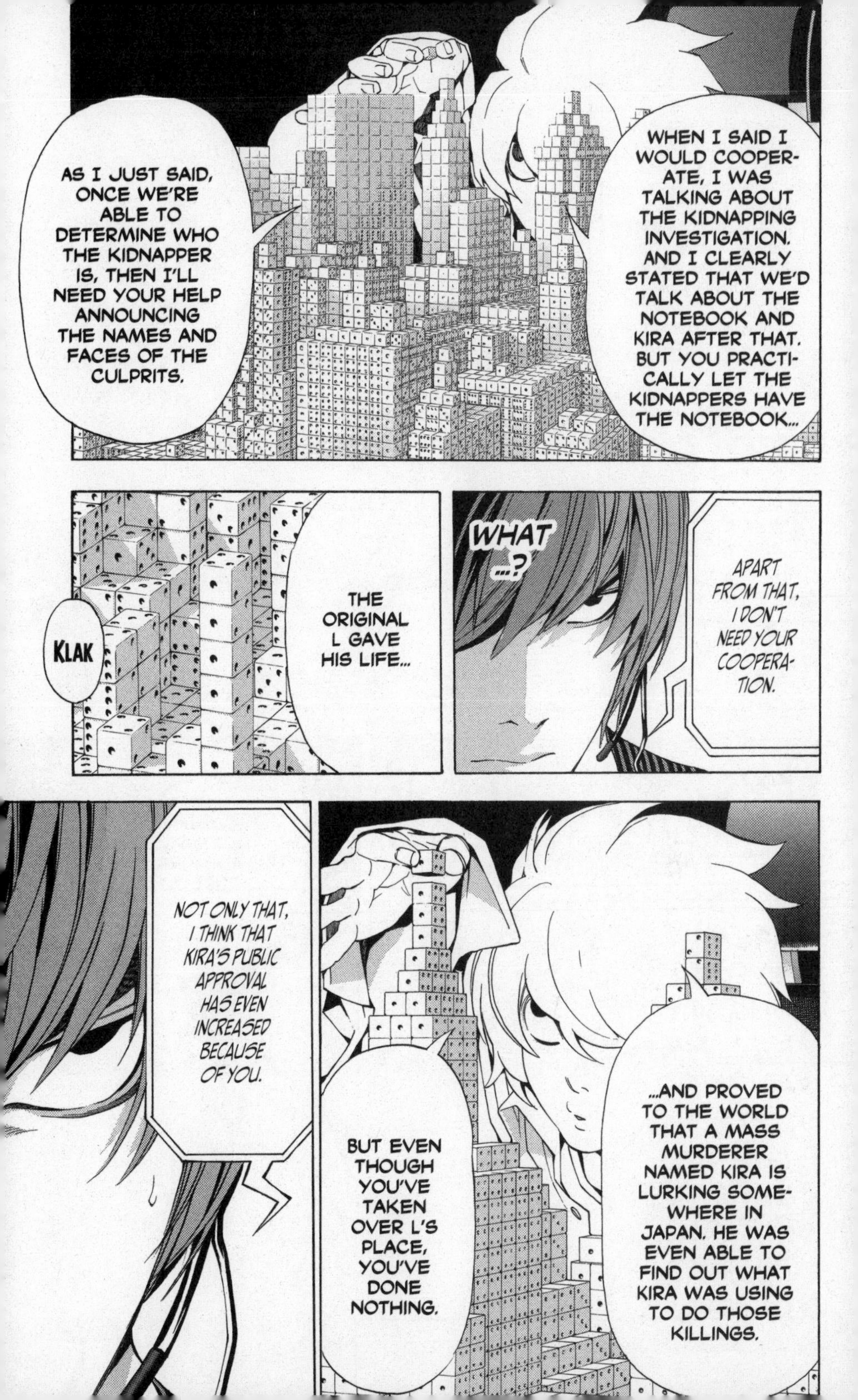
WHEN I SAID I WOULD COOPERATE, I WAS TALKING ABOUT THE KIDNAPPING INVESTIGATION. AND I CLEARLY STATED THAT WE'D TALK ABOUT THE NOTEBOOK AND KIRA AFTER THAT. BUT YOU PRACTICALLY LET THE KIDNAPPERS HAVE THE NOTEBOOK...
AS I JUST SAID, ONCE WE'RE ABLE TO DETERMINE WHO THE KIDNAPPER IS, THEN I'LL NEED YOUR HELP ANNOUNCING THE NAMES AND FACES OF THE CULPRITS.
APART FROM THAT, I DON'T NEED YOUR COOPERATION.
WHAT ...?
THE ORIGINAL L GAVE HIS LIFE...
KLAK
...AND PROVED TO THE WORLD THAT A MASS MURDERER NAMED KIRA IS LURKING SOMEWHERE IN JAPAN. HE WAS EVEN ABLE TO FIND OUT WHAT KIRA WAS USING TO DO THOSE KILLINGS.
BUT EVEN THOUGH YOU'VE TAKEN OVER L'S PLACE, YOU'VE DONE NOTHING.
NOT ONLY THAT, I THINK THAT KIRA'S PUBLIC APPROVAL HAS EVEN INCREASED BECAUSE OF YOU.

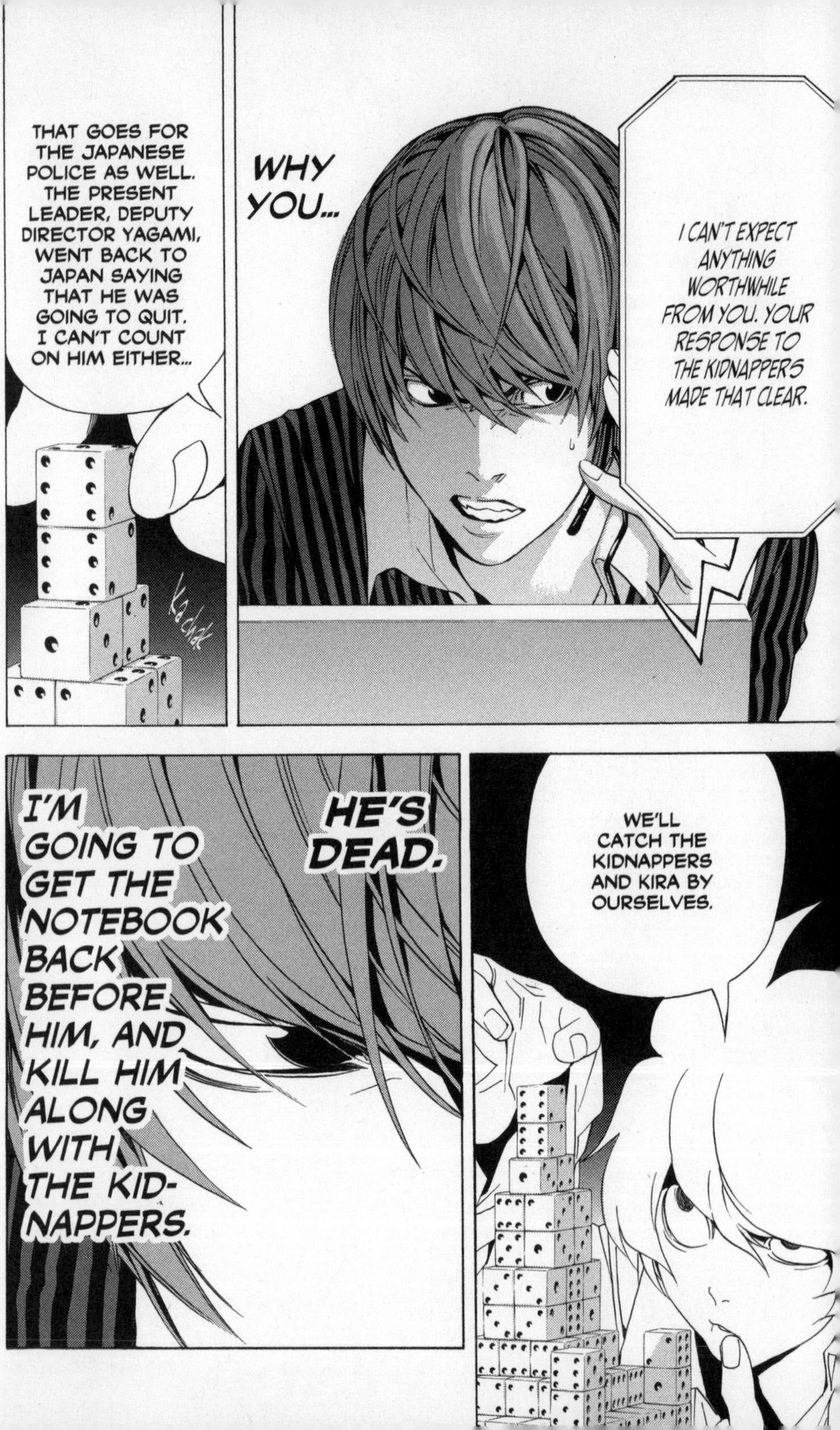
I CAN'T EXPECT ANYTHING WORTHWHILE FROM YOU. YOUR RESPONSE TO THE KIDNAPPERS MADE THAT CLEAR.
WHY YOU...
THAT GOES FOR THE JAPANESE POLICE AS WELL. THE PRESENT LEADER, DEPUTY DIRECTOR YAGAMI, WENT BACK TO JAPAN SAYING THAT HE WAS GOING TO QUIT. I CAN'T COUNT ON HIM EITHER...
ka chak
WE'LL CATCH THE KIDNAPPERS AND KIRA BY OURSELVES.
HE'S DEAD.
I'M GOING TO GET THE NOTEBOOK BACK BEFORE HIM, AND KILL HIM ALONG WITH THE KID-NAPPERS.

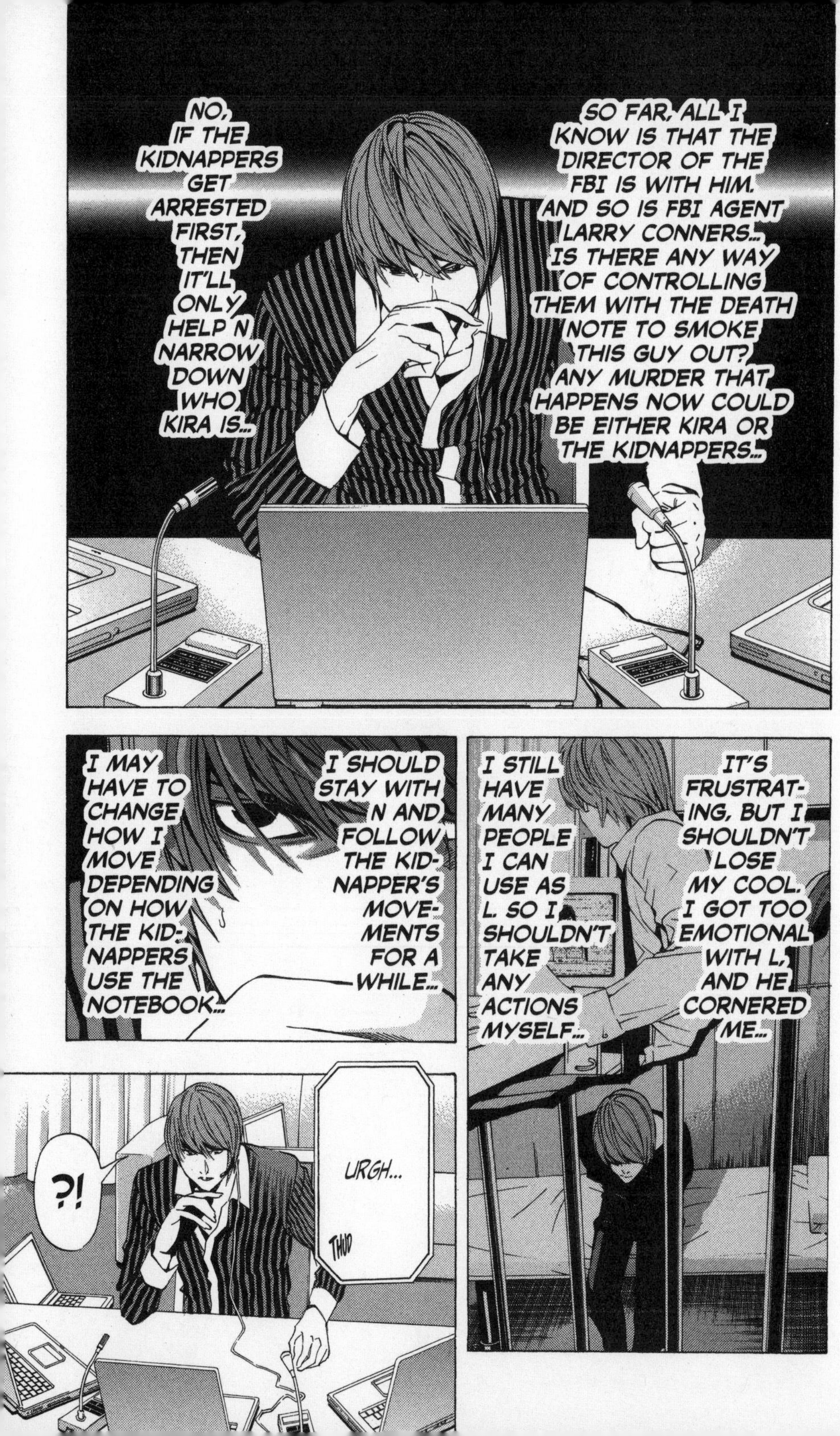
SO FAR, ALL I KNOW IS THAT THE DIRECTOR OF THE FBI IS WITH HIM. AND SO IS FBI AGENT LARRY CONNERS... IS THERE ANY WAY OF CONTROLLING THEM WITH THE DEATH NOTE TO SMOKE THIS GUY OUT? ANY MURDER THAT HAPPENS NOW COULD BE EITHER KIRA OR THE KIDNAPPERS...
NO, IF THE KIDNAPPERS GET ARRESTED FIRST, THEN IT'LL ONLY HELP N NARROW DOWN WHO KIRA IS...
IT'S FRUSTRATING, BUT I SHOULDN'T LOSE MY COOL. I GOT TOO EMOTIONAL WITH L, AND HE CORNERED ME...
I STILL HAVE MANY PEOPLE I CAN USE AS L. SO I SHOULDN'T TAKE ANY ACTIONS MYSELF...
I SHOULD STAY WITH N AND FOLLOW THE KIDNAPPER'S MOVEMENTS FOR A WHILE...
I MAY HAVE TO CHANGE HOW I MOVE DEPENDING ON HOW THE KIDNAPPERS USE THE NOTEBOOK...
URGH...
THUD
?!

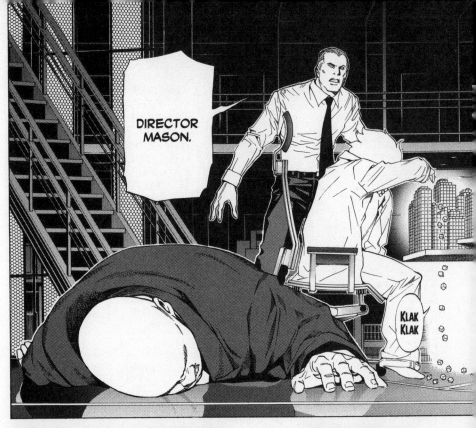

DIRECTOR
MASON.

KLAK
KLAK

chak

RATT?!

GARDNER.

AHH...

CLICK

BANG

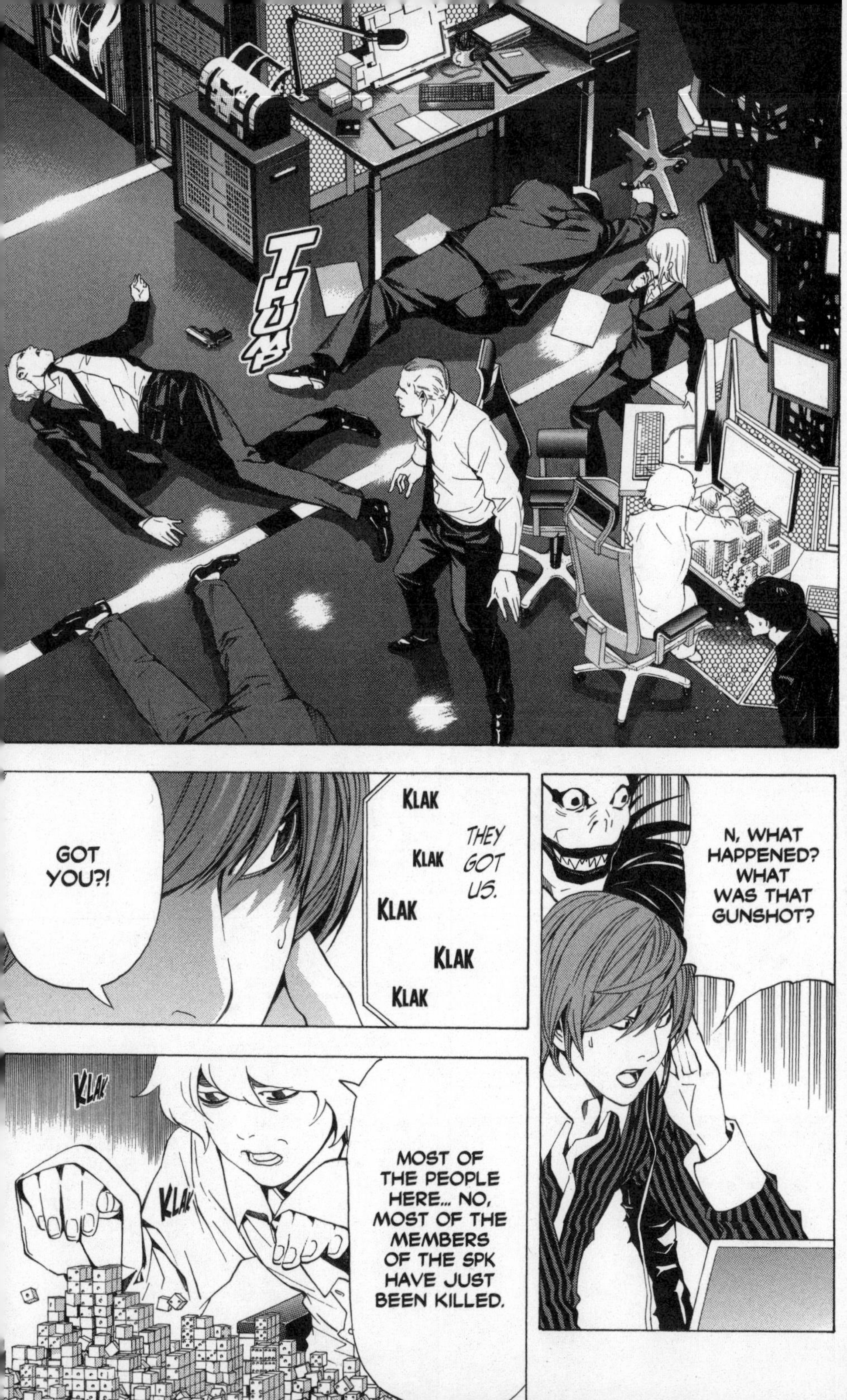
THUMP
N, WHAT HAPPENED? WHAT WAS THAT GUNSHOT?
KLAK
THEY GOT US.
KLAK
KLAK
KLAK
KLAK
GOT YOU?!
KLAK
KLAK
MOST OF THE PEOPLE HERE... NO, MOST OF THE MEMBERS OF THE SPK HAVE JUST BEEN KILLED.

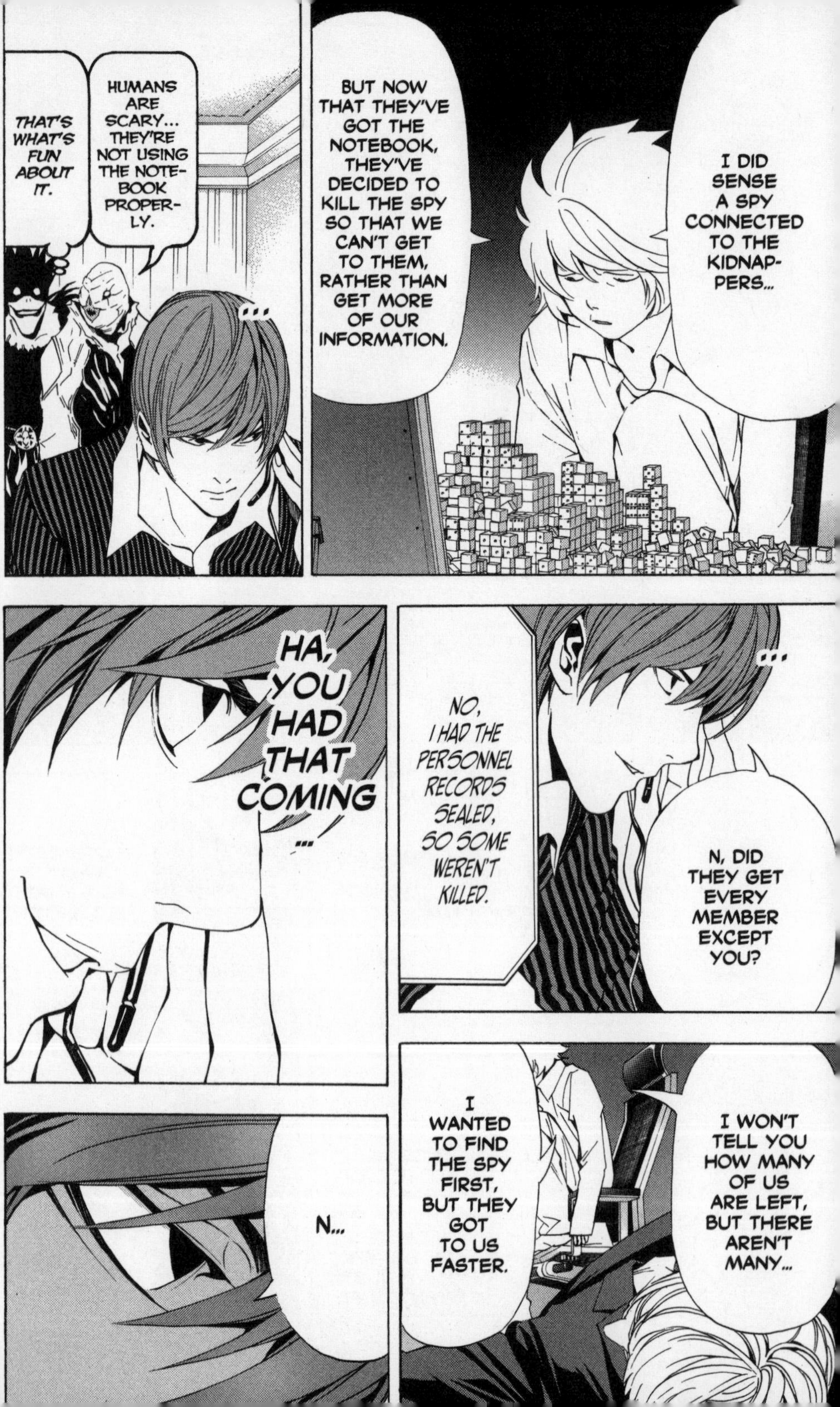
I DID SENSE A SPY CONNECTED TO THE KIDNAPPERS...
BUT NOW THAT THEY'VE GOT THE NOTEBOOK, THEY'VE DECIDED TO KILL THE SPY SO THAT WE CAN'T GET TO THEM, RATHER THAN GET MORE OF OUR INFORMATION.
HUMANS ARE SCARY... THEY'RE NOT USING THE NOTE-BOOK PROPER-LY.
THAT'S WHAT'S FUN ABOUT IT.
...
...
N, DID THEY GET EVERY MEMBER EXCEPT YOU?
NO, I HAD THE PERSONNEL RECORDS SEALED, SO SOME WEREN'T KILLED.
HA, YOU HAD THAT COMING...
I WON'T TELL YOU HOW MANY OF US ARE LEFT, BUT THERE AREN'T MANY...
I WANTED TO FIND THE SPY FIRST, BUT THEY GOT TO US FASTER.
N...

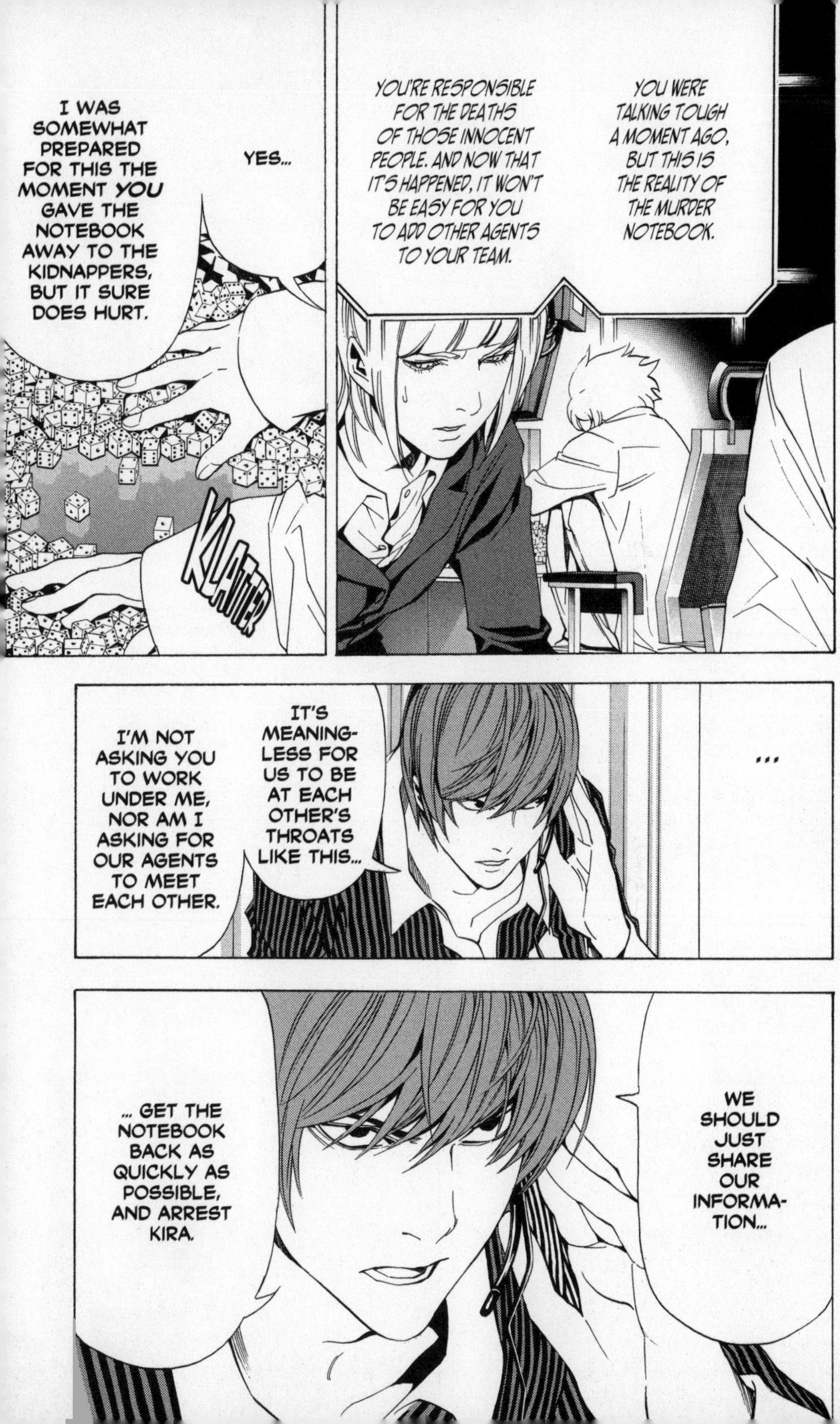
YOU WERE TALKING TOUGH A MOMENT AGO, BUT THIS IS THE REALITY OF THE MURDER NOTEBOOK.
YOU'RE RESPONSIBLE FOR THE DEATHS OF THOSE INNOCENT PEOPLE. AND NOW THAT IT'S HAPPENED, IT WON'T BE EASY FOR YOU TO ADD OTHER AGENTS TO YOUR TEAM.
YES...
I WAS SOMEWHAT PREPARED FOR THIS THE MOMENT *YOU* GAVE THE NOTEBOOK AWAY TO THE KIDNAPPERS, BUT IT SURE DOES HURT.
KLATTER
...
IT'S MEANING-LESS FOR US TO BE AT EACH OTHER'S THROATS LIKE THIS...
I'M NOT ASKING YOU TO WORK UNDER ME, NOR AM I ASKING FOR OUR AGENTS TO MEET EACH OTHER.
WE SHOULD JUST SHARE OUR INFORMA-TION...
... GET THE NOTEBOOK BACK AS QUICKLY AS POSSIBLE, AND ARREST KIRA.

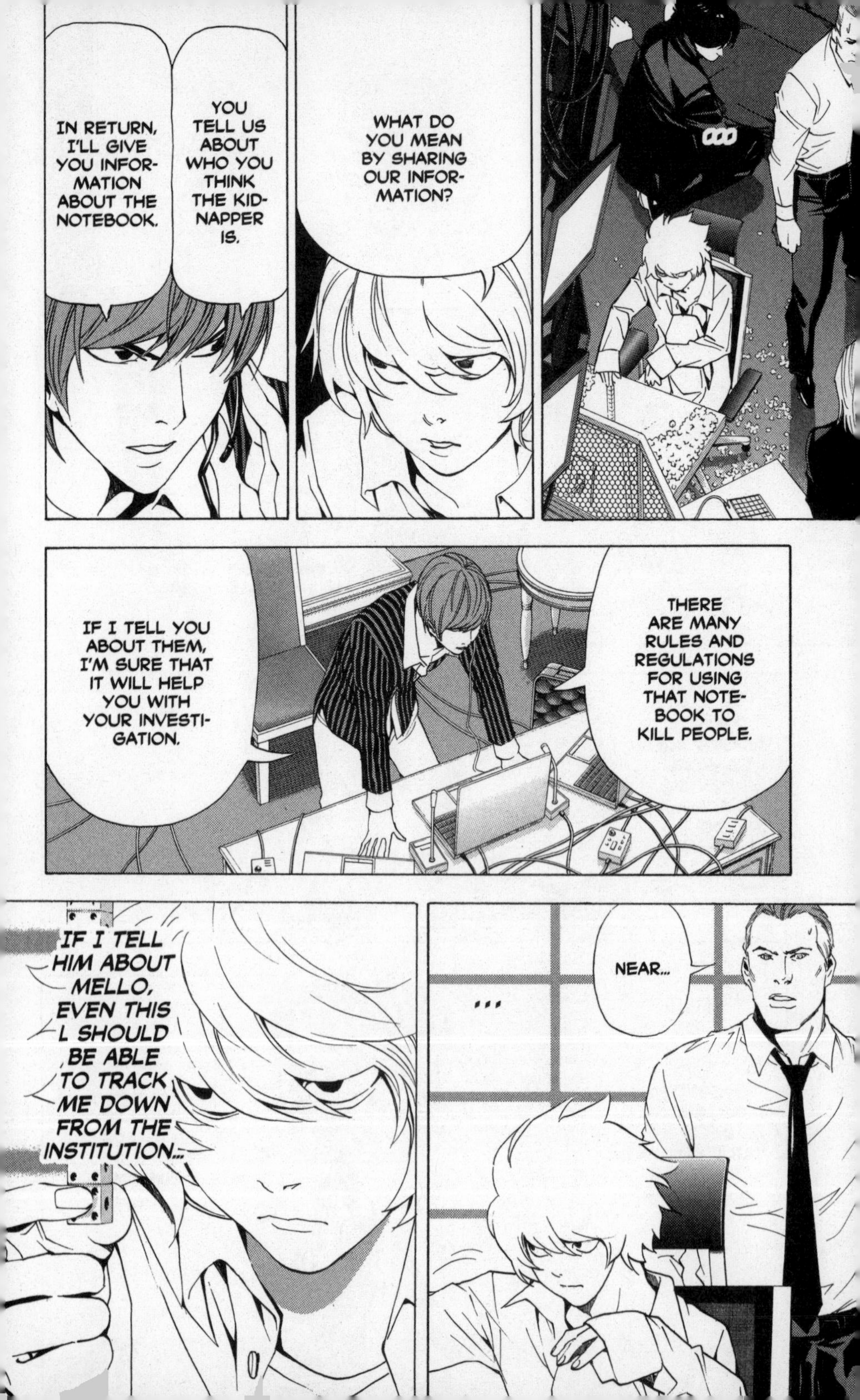
WHAT DO YOU MEAN BY SHARING OUR INFORMATION?
YOU TELL US ABOUT WHO YOU THINK THE KIDNAPPER IS.
IN RETURN, I'LL GIVE YOU INFORMATION ABOUT THE NOTEBOOK.
THERE ARE MANY RULES AND REGULATIONS FOR USING THAT NOTEBOOK TO KILL PEOPLE.
IF I TELL YOU ABOUT THEM, I'M SURE THAT IT WILL HELP YOU WITH YOUR INVESTIGATION.
NEAR...
...
IF I TELL HIM ABOUT MELLO, EVEN THIS L SHOULD BE ABLE TO TRACK ME DOWN FROM THE INSTITUTION...

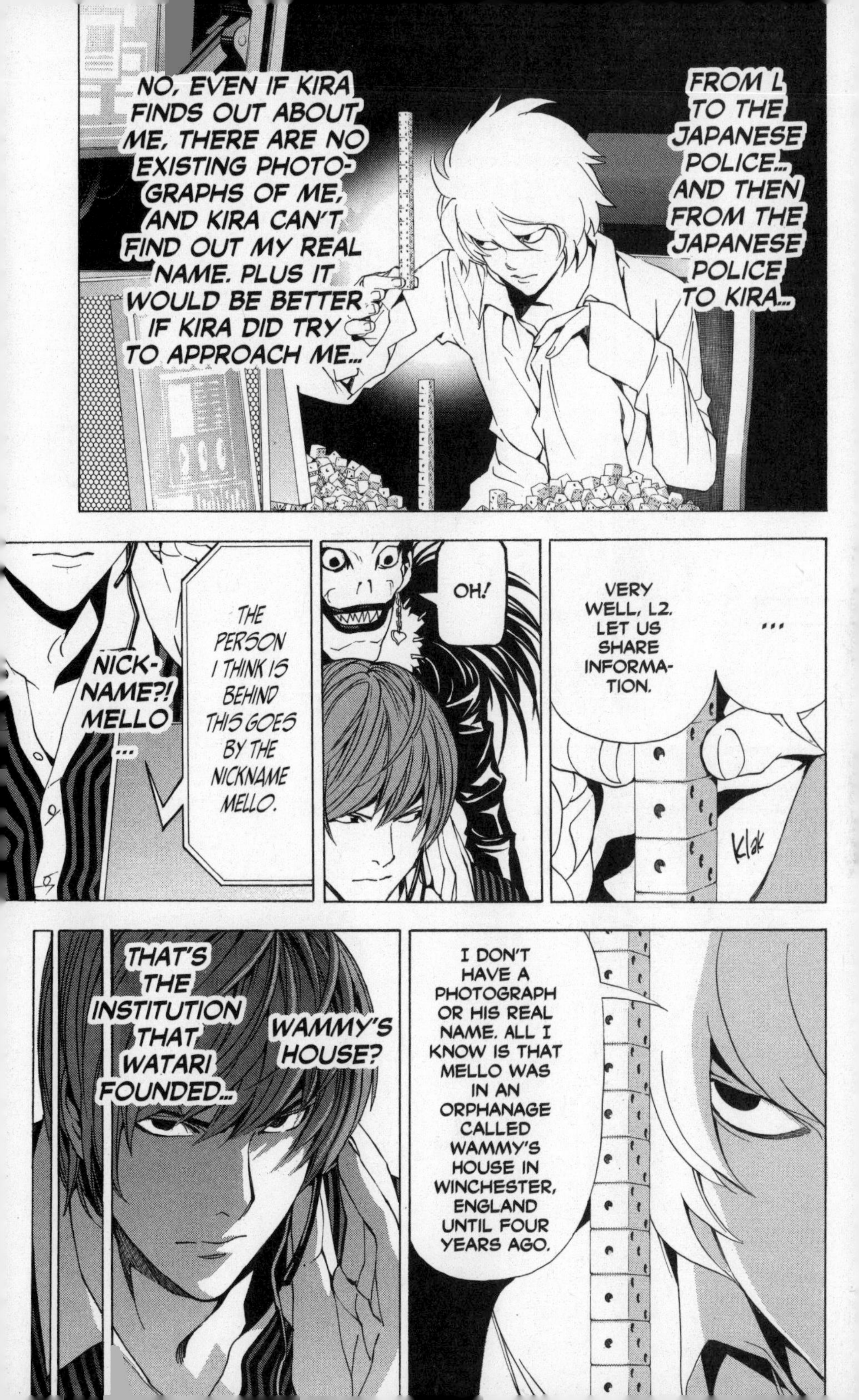
FROM L TO THE JAPANESE POLICE... AND THEN FROM THE JAPANESE POLICE TO KIRA...
NO, EVEN IF KIRA FINDS OUT ABOUT ME, THERE ARE NO EXISTING PHOTOGRAPHS OF ME, AND KIRA CAN'T FIND OUT MY REAL NAME. PLUS IT WOULD BE BETTER IF KIRA DID TRY TO APPROACH ME...
...
VERY WELL, L2. LET US SHARE INFORMATION.
Klak
OH!
THE PERSON I THINK IS BEHIND THIS GOES BY THE NICKNAME MELLO.
NICKNAME?! MELLO ...
I DON'T HAVE A PHOTOGRAPH OR HIS REAL NAME. ALL I KNOW IS THAT MELLO WAS IN AN ORPHANAGE CALLED WAMMY'S HOUSE IN WINCHESTER, ENGLAND UNTIL FOUR YEARS AGO.
WAMMY'S HOUSE?
THAT'S THE INSTITUTION THAT WATARI FOUNDED...

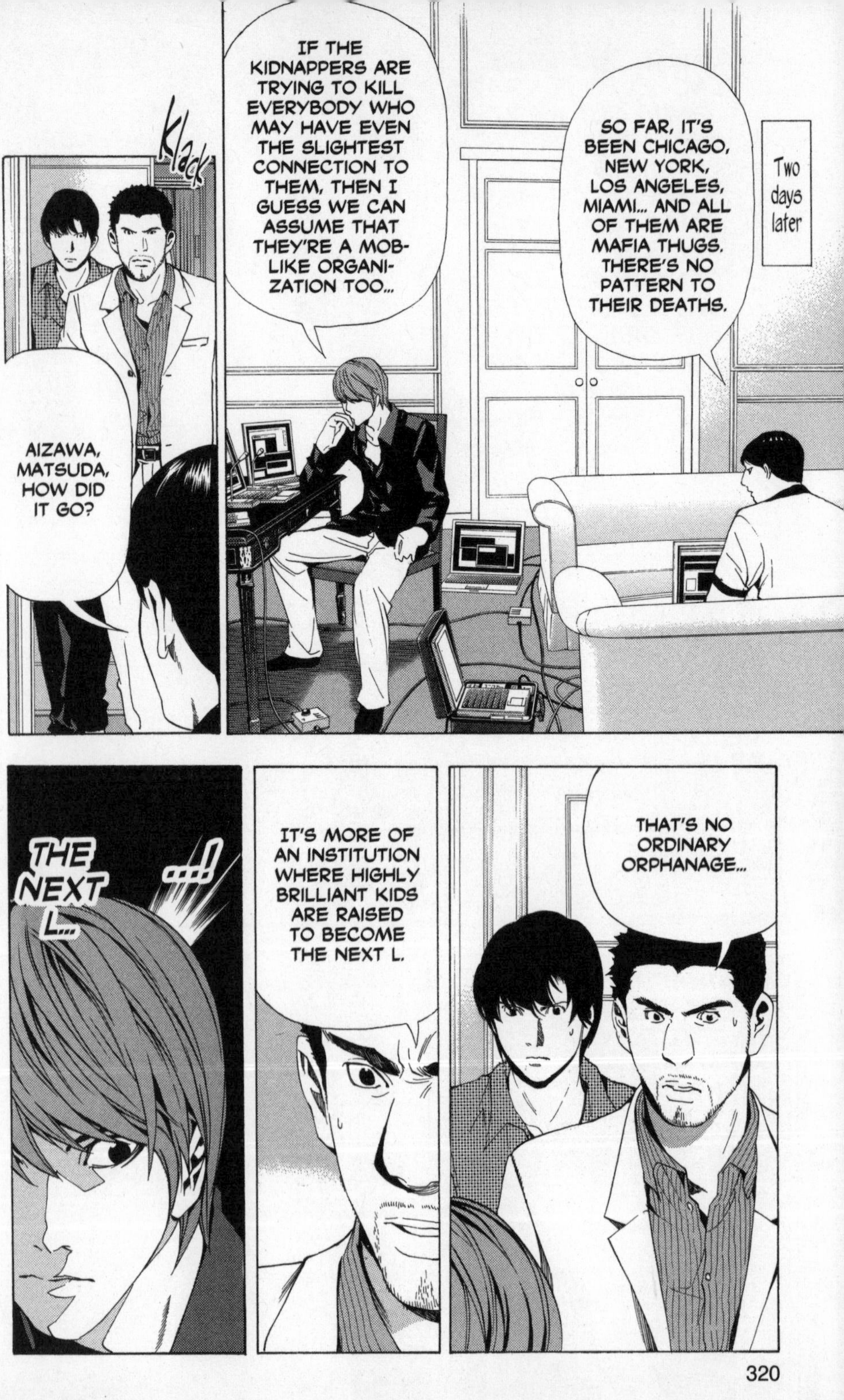
Two days later
SO FAR, IT'S BEEN CHICAGO, NEW YORK, LOS ANGELES, MIAMI... AND ALL OF THEM ARE MAFIA THUGS. THERE'S NO PATTERN TO THEIR DEATHS.
IF THE KIDNAPPERS ARE TRYING TO KILL EVERYBODY WHO MAY HAVE EVEN THE SLIGHTEST CONNECTION TO THEM, THEN I GUESS WE CAN ASSUME THAT THEY'RE A MOB-LIKE ORGANIZATION TOO...
Klack
AIZAWA, MATSUDA, HOW DID IT GO?
THAT'S NO ORDINARY ORPHANAGE...
IT'S MORE OF AN INSTITUTION WHERE HIGHLY BRILLIANT KIDS ARE RAISED TO BECOME THE NEXT L.
...!
THE NEXT L...

READ THIS WAY

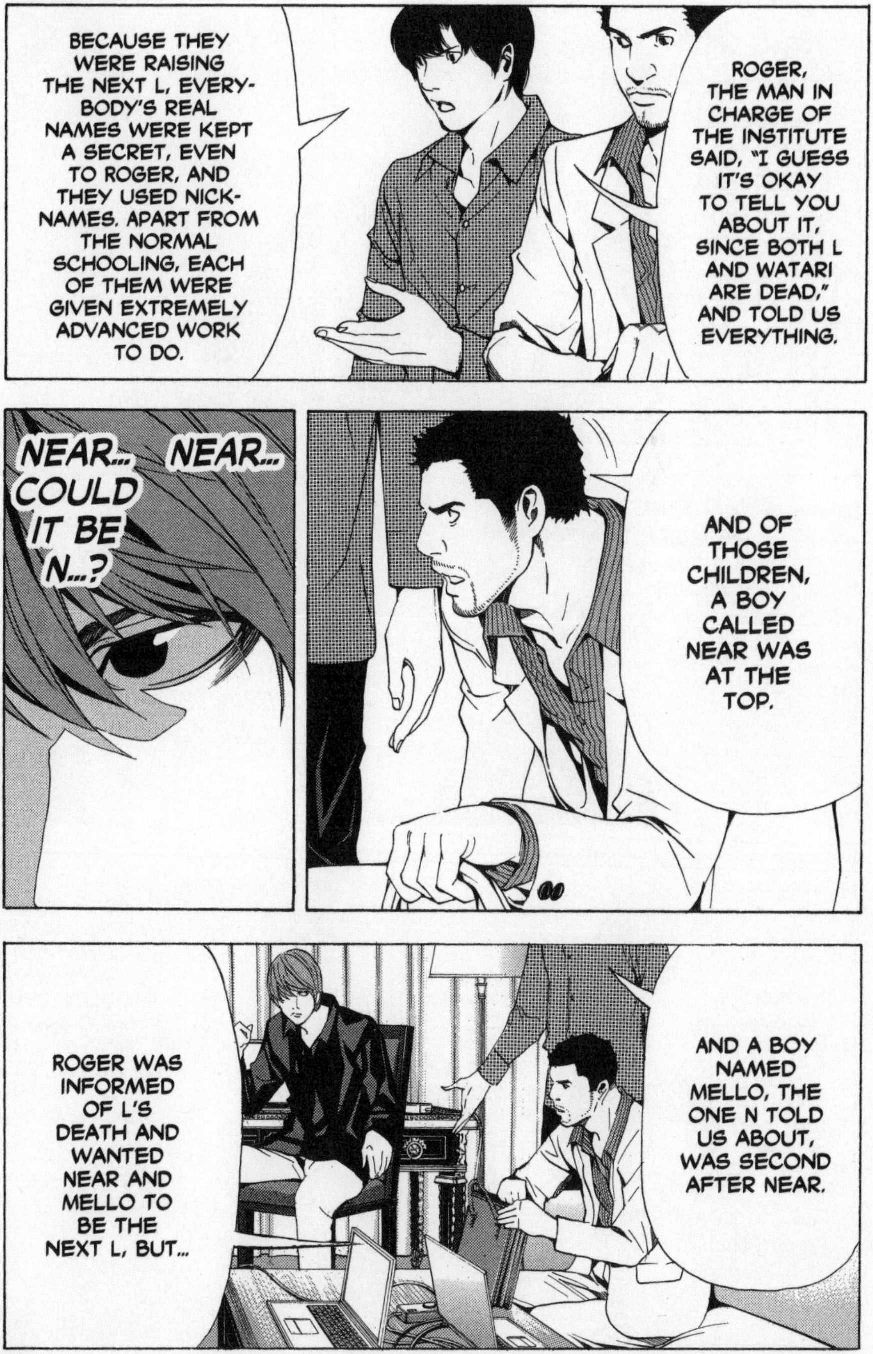
ROGER, THE MAN IN CHARGE OF THE INSTITUTE SAID, "I GUESS IT'S OKAY TO TELL YOU ABOUT IT, SINCE BOTH L AND WATARI ARE DEAD," AND TOLD US EVERYTHING.
BECAUSE THEY WERE RAISING THE NEXT L, EVERY-BODY'S REAL NAMES WERE KEPT A SECRET, EVEN TO ROGER, AND THEY USED NICK-NAMES. APART FROM THE NORMAL SCHOOLING, EACH OF THEM WERE GIVEN EXTREMELY ADVANCED WORK TO DO.
AND OF THOSE CHILDREN, A BOY CALLED NEAR WAS AT THE TOP.
NEAR... NEAR... COULD IT BE N...?
AND A BOY NAMED MELLO, THE ONE N TOLD US ABOUT, WAS SECOND AFTER NEAR.
ROGER WAS INFORMED OF L'S DEATH AND WANTED NEAR AND MELLO TO BE THE NEXT L, BUT...

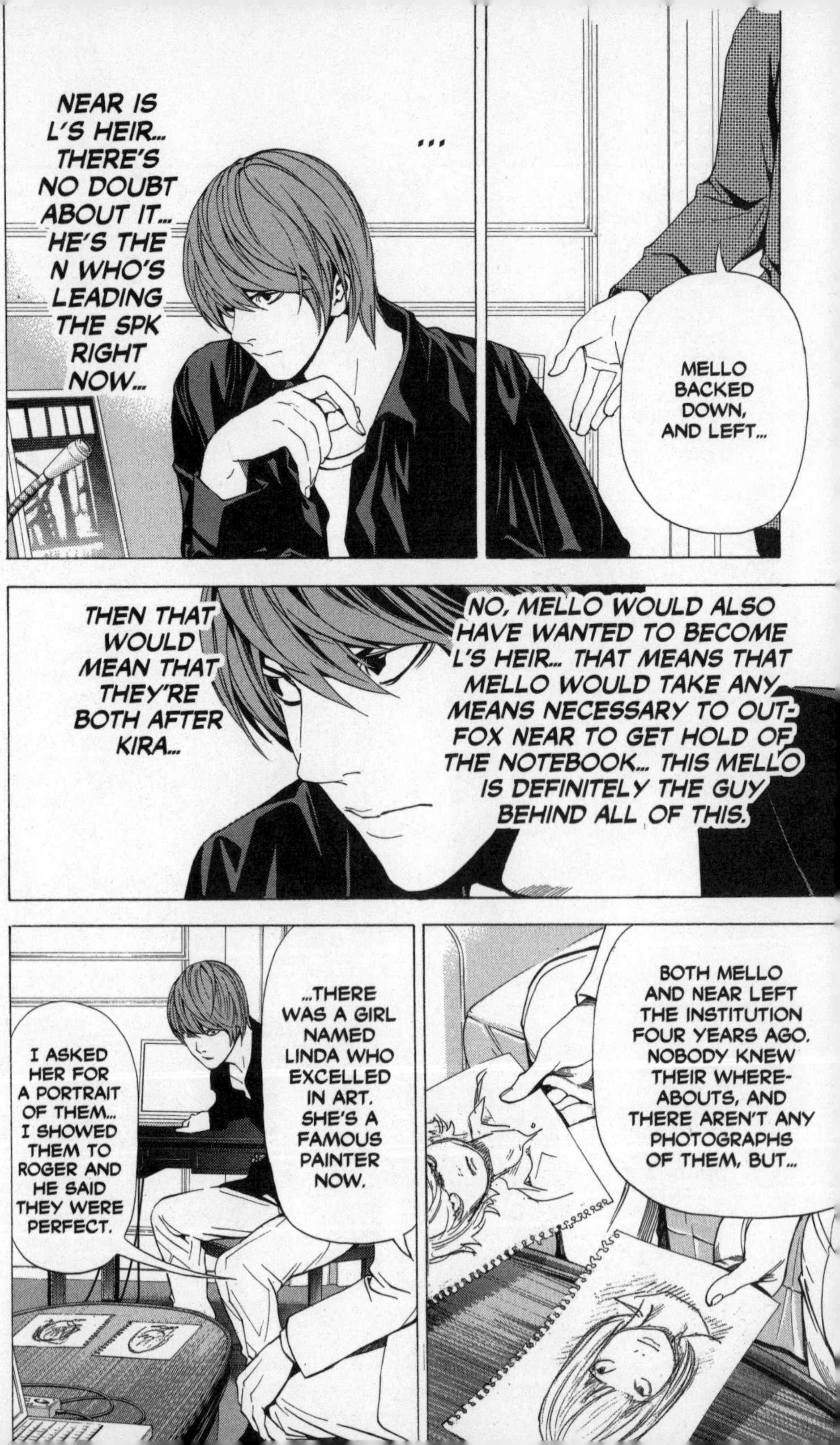
MELLO BACKED DOWN, AND LEFT...
...
NEAR IS L'S HEIR... THERE'S NO DOUBT ABOUT IT... HE'S THE N WHO'S LEADING THE SPK RIGHT NOW...
NO, MELLO WOULD ALSO HAVE WANTED TO BECOME L'S HEIR... THAT MEANS THAT MELLO WOULD TAKE ANY MEANS NECESSARY TO OUT-FOX NEAR TO GET HOLD OF THE NOTEBOOK... THIS MELLO IS DEFINITELY THE GUY BEHIND ALL OF THIS.
THEN THAT WOULD MEAN THAT THEY'RE BOTH AFTER KIRA...
BOTH MELLO AND NEAR LEFT THE INSTITUTION FOUR YEARS AGO. NOBODY KNEW THEIR WHERE-ABOUTS, AND THERE AREN'T ANY PHOTOGRAPHS OF THEM, BUT...
...THERE WAS A GIRL NAMED LINDA WHO EXCELLED IN ART. SHE'S A FAMOUS PAINTER NOW.
I ASKED HER FOR A PORTRAIT OF THEM... I SHOWED THEM TO ROGER AND HE SAID THEY WERE PERFECT.

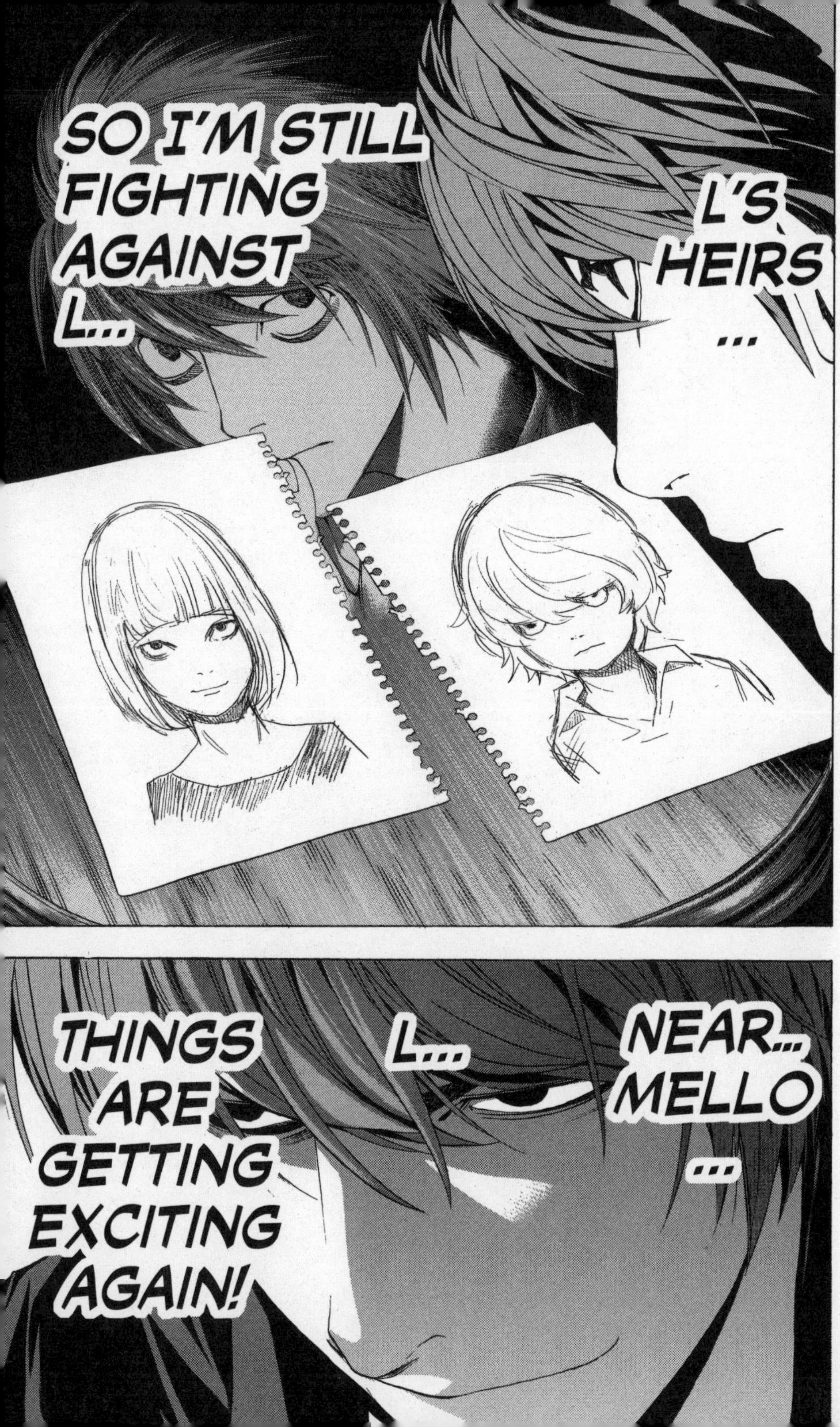
L'S HEIRS ...
SO I'M STILL FIGHTING AGAINST L...
NEAR... MELLO ...
L...
THINGS ARE GETTING EXCITING AGAIN!

# DEATH NOTE
## How to use it
## XLIV

- If the DEATH NOTE that the god of death owns is taken away; by being cheated by other gods of death and so forth, it can only be retrieved from the god of death who is possessing it at the time. If there is no god of death, but a human possessing it, the only way that the god of death can retrieve it will be to first touch the DEATH NOTE and become the god of death that haunts that human. Then wait until that human dies to take it away before any other human touches it or whenever the human shows a will to let go of it.

死神が自分の所有すべきデスノートを
他の死神に騙し取られた等で失った場合、
その時ノートに憑く死神から返してもらうしかない。
憑く死神がいない状態で人間が持っている場合は、
一度ノートに触りその人間に憑く死神となり、
その人間の最期を見届け他の人間が触る前に取り上げるか、
その人間に返してもらわなければならない。

# chapter 67 Button

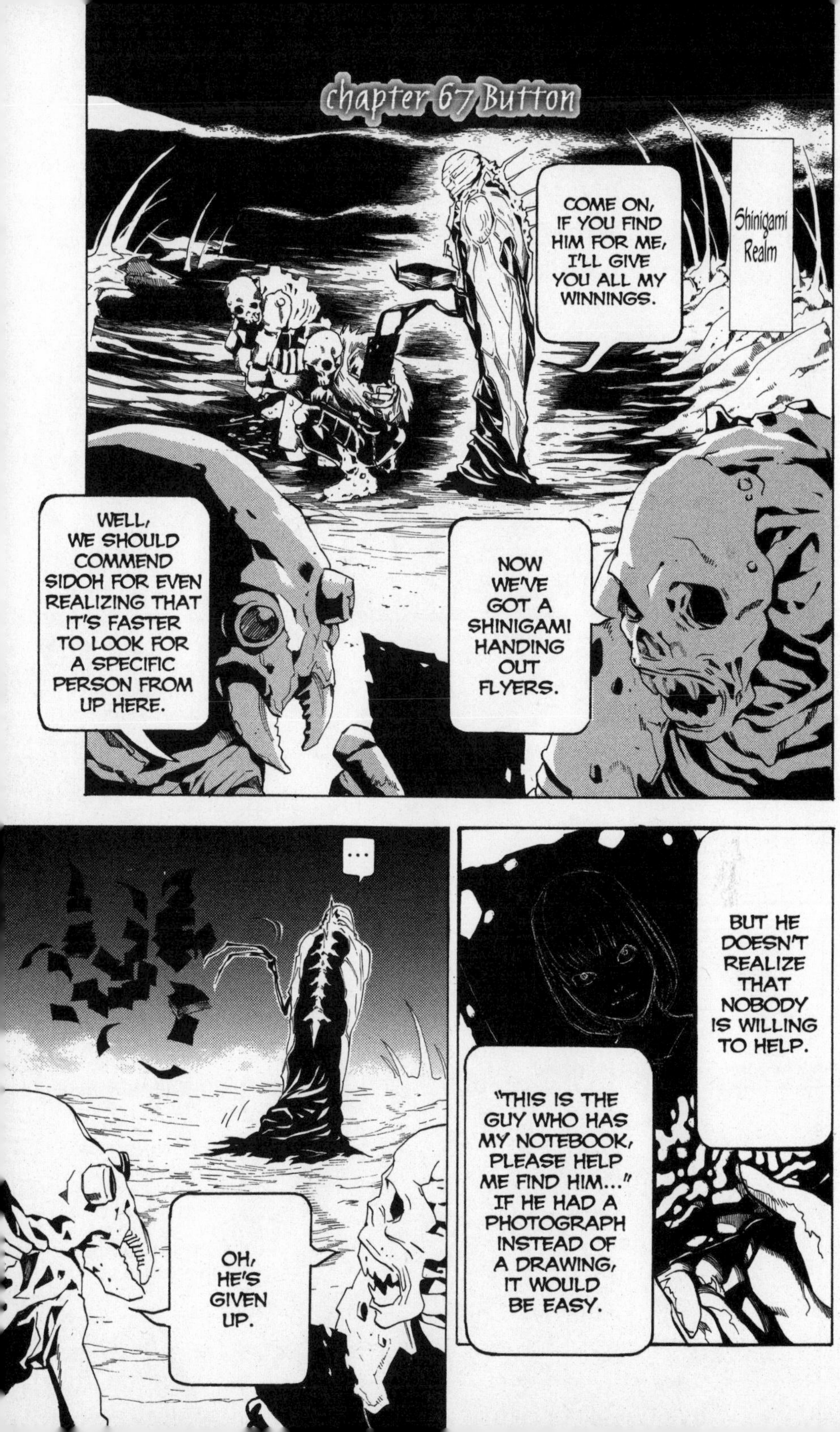
Shinigami Realm
COME ON, IF YOU FIND HIM FOR ME, I'LL GIVE YOU ALL MY WINNINGS.
NOW WE'VE GOT A SHINIGAMI HANDING OUT FLYERS.
WELL, WE SHOULD COMMEND SIDOH FOR EVEN REALIZING THAT IT'S FASTER TO LOOK FOR A SPECIFIC PERSON FROM UP HERE.
BUT HE DOESN'T REALIZE THAT NOBODY IS WILLING TO HELP.
"THIS IS THE GUY WHO HAS MY NOTEBOOK, PLEASE HELP ME FIND HIM..." IF HE HAD A PHOTOGRAPH INSTEAD OF A DRAWING, IT WOULD BE EASY.
...
OH, HE'S GIVEN UP.

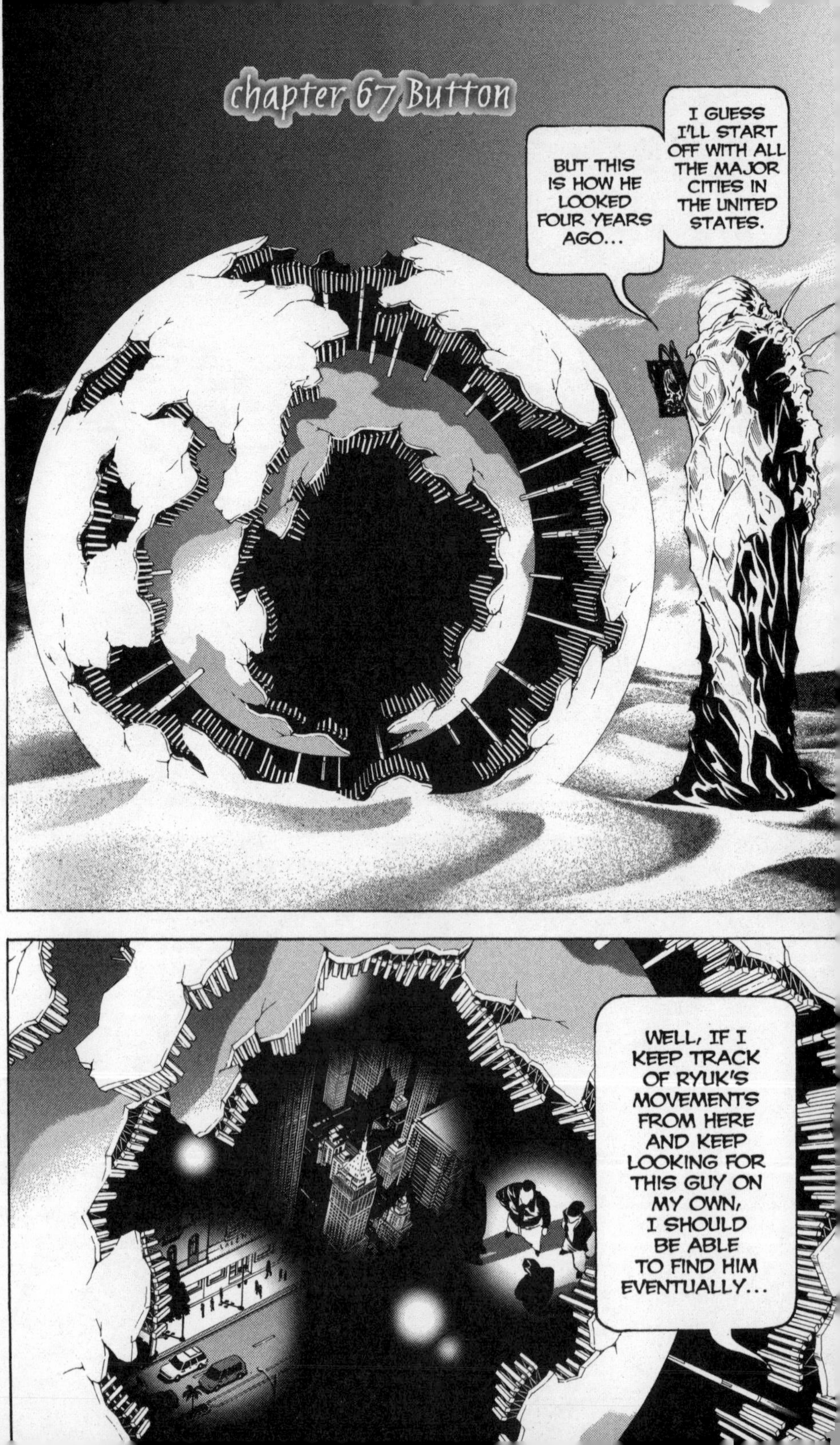
chapter 67 Button
I GUESS I'LL START OFF WITH ALL THE MAJOR CITIES IN THE UNITED STATES.
BUT THIS IS HOW HE LOOKED FOUR YEARS AGO...
WELL, IF I KEEP TRACK OF RYUK'S MOVEMENTS FROM HERE AND KEEP LOOKING FOR THIS GUY ON MY OWN, I SHOULD BE ABLE TO FIND HIM EVENTUALLY...

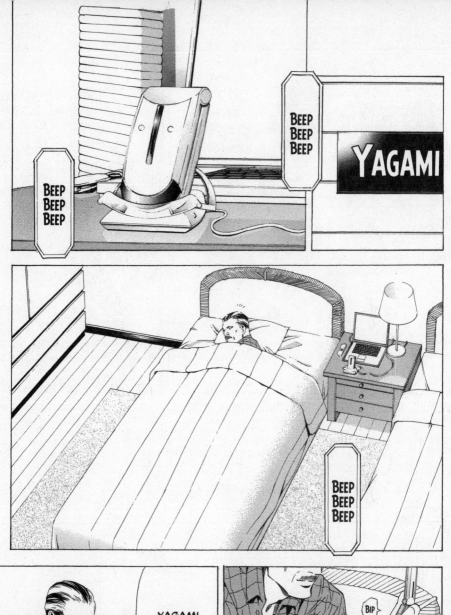

BEEP
BEEP
BEEP

BEEP
BEEP
BEEP

YAGAMI

BEEP
BEEP
BEEP

YAGAMI
HERE.

BIP

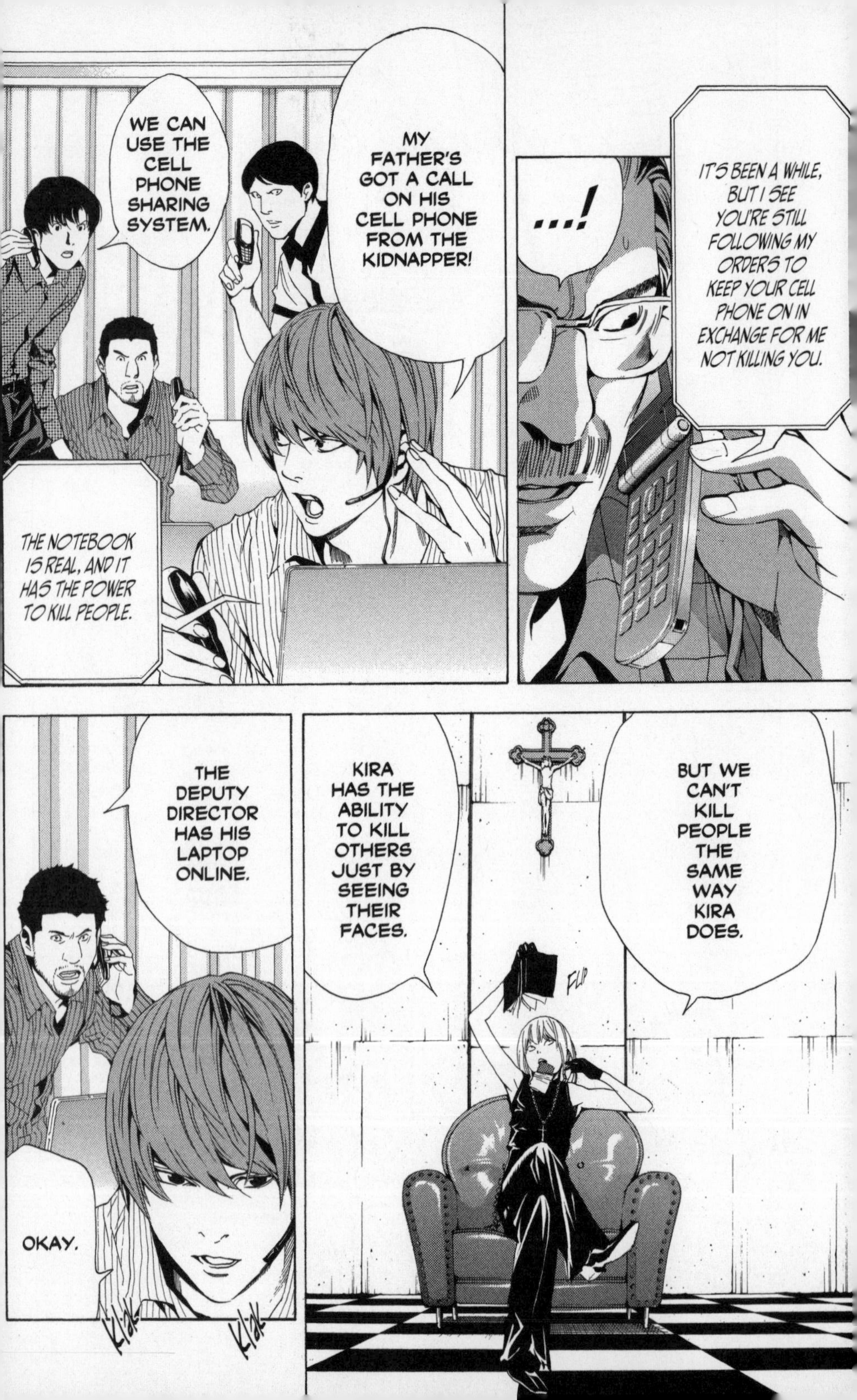
IT'S BEEN A WHILE, BUT I SEE YOU'RE STILL FOLLOWING MY ORDERS TO KEEP YOUR CELL PHONE ON IN EXCHANGE FOR ME NOT KILLING YOU.
...!
MY FATHER'S GOT A CALL ON HIS CELL PHONE FROM THE KIDNAPPER!
WE CAN USE THE CELL PHONE SHARING SYSTEM.
THE NOTEBOOK IS REAL, AND IT HAS THE POWER TO KILL PEOPLE.
KIRA HAS THE ABILITY TO KILL OTHERS JUST BY SEEING THEIR FACES.
BUT WE CAN'T KILL PEOPLE THE SAME WAY KIRA DOES.
FLIP
THE DEPUTY DIRECTOR HAS HIS LAPTOP ONLINE.
OKAY.
KLAK
KLAK

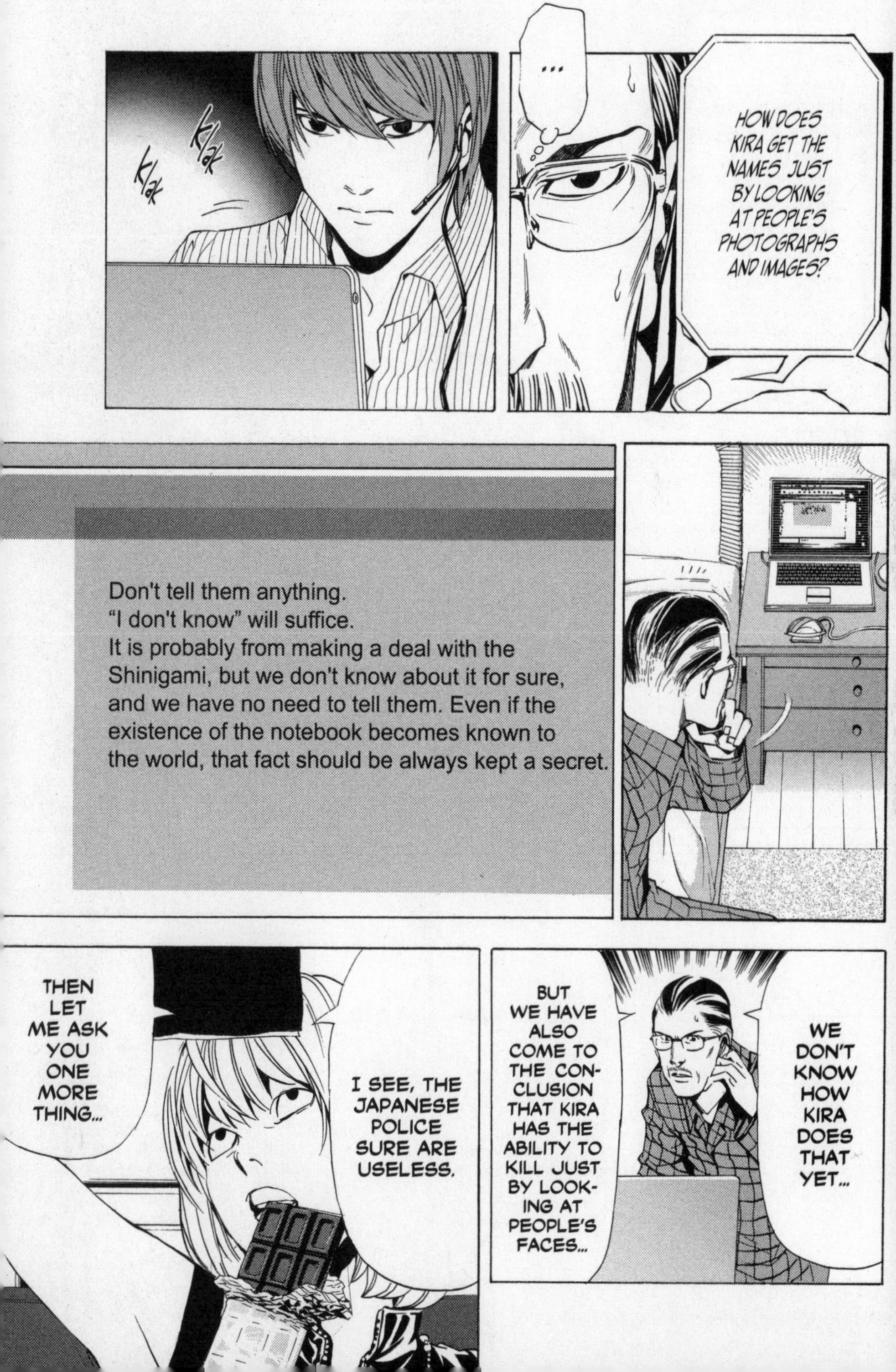
HOW DOES KIRA GET THE NAMES JUST BY LOOKING AT PEOPLE'S PHOTOGRAPHS AND IMAGES?
...
klak
klak
Don't tell them anything.
"I don't know" will suffice.
It is probably from making a deal with the Shinigami, but we don't know about it for sure, and we have no need to tell them. Even if the existence of the notebook becomes known to the world, that fact should be always kept a secret.
WE DON'T KNOW HOW KIRA DOES THAT YET...
BUT WE HAVE ALSO COME TO THE CONCLUSION THAT KIRA HAS THE ABILITY TO KILL JUST BY LOOKING AT PEOPLE'S FACES...
I SEE, THE JAPANESE POLICE SURE ARE USELESS.
THEN LET ME ASK YOU ONE MORE THING...

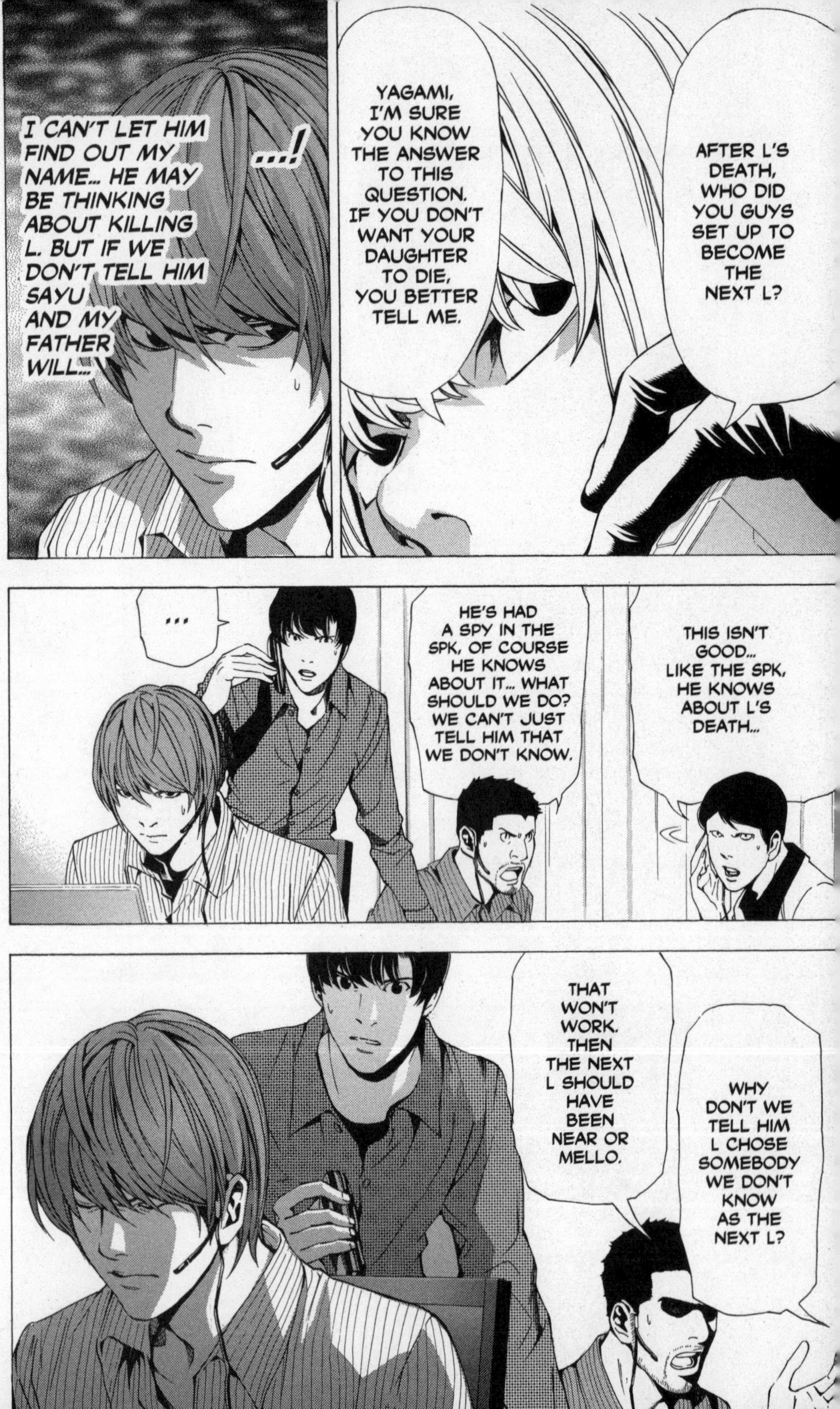
AFTER L'S DEATH, WHO DID YOU GUYS SET UP TO BECOME THE NEXT L?
YAGAMI, I'M SURE YOU KNOW THE ANSWER TO THIS QUESTION. IF YOU DON'T WANT YOUR DAUGHTER TO DIE, YOU BETTER TELL ME.
...!
I CAN'T LET HIM FIND OUT MY NAME... HE MAY BE THINKING ABOUT KILLING L. BUT IF WE DON'T TELL HIM SAYU AND MY FATHER WILL...
THIS ISN'T GOOD... LIKE THE SPK, HE KNOWS ABOUT L'S DEATH...
HE'S HAD A SPY IN THE SPK, OF COURSE HE KNOWS ABOUT IT... WHAT SHOULD WE DO? WE CAN'T JUST TELL HIM THAT WE DON'T KNOW.
...
WHY DON'T WE TELL HIM L CHOSE SOMEBODY WE DON'T KNOW AS THE NEXT L?
THAT WON'T WORK. THEN THE NEXT L SHOULD HAVE BEEN NEAR OR MELLO.

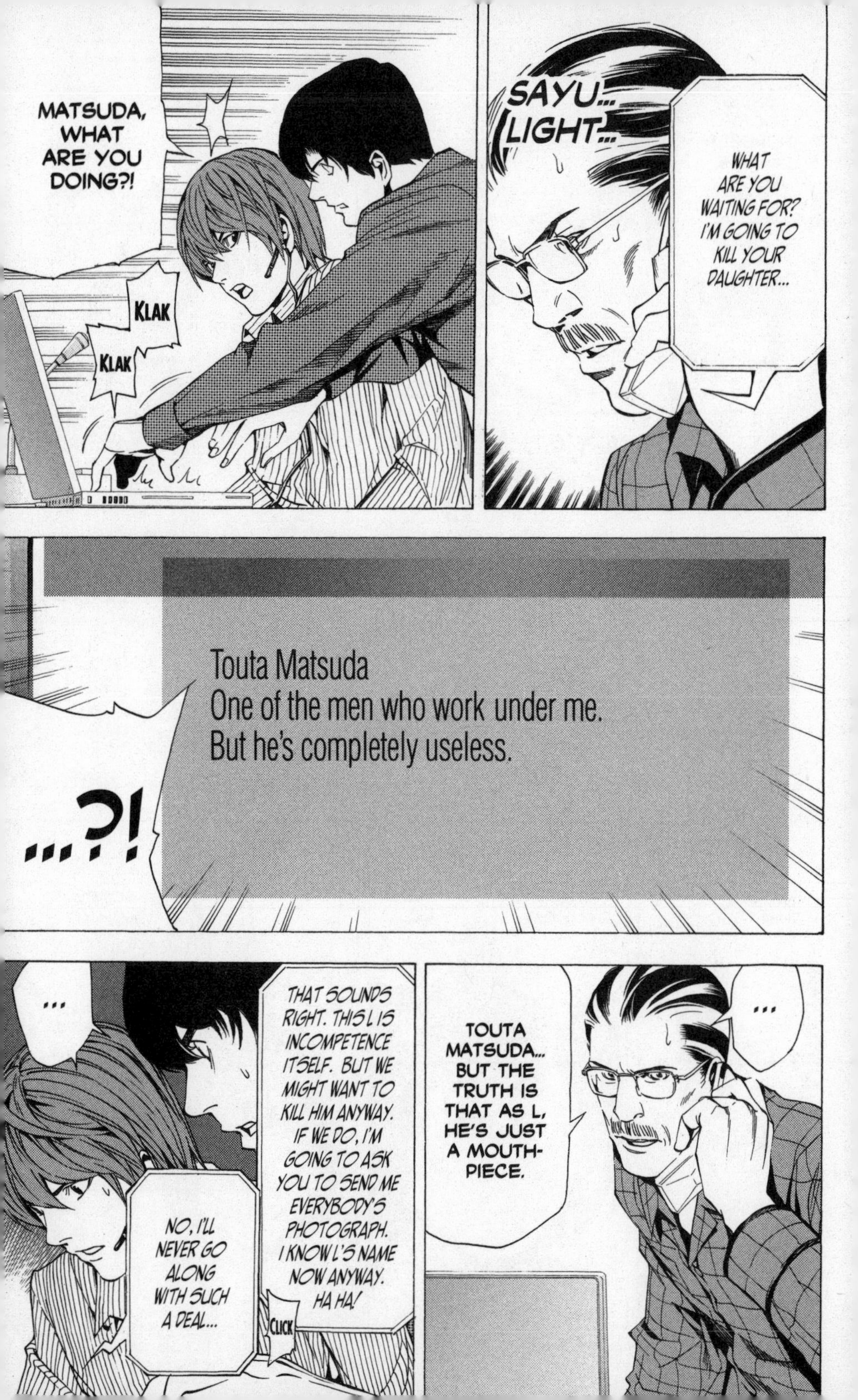
SAYU... LIGHT...
WHAT ARE YOU WAITING FOR? I'M GOING TO KILL YOUR DAUGHTER...
MATSUDA, WHAT ARE YOU DOING?!
KLAK
KLAK
Touta Matsuda
One of the men who work under me.
But he's completely useless.
...?!
...
TOUTA MATSUDA... BUT THE TRUTH IS THAT AS L, HE'S JUST A MOUTH-PIECE.
THAT SOUNDS RIGHT. THIS L IS INCOMPETENCE ITSELF. BUT WE MIGHT WANT TO KILL HIM ANYWAY. IF WE DO, I'M GOING TO ASK YOU TO SEND ME EVERYBODY'S PHOTOGRAPH. I KNOW L'S NAME NOW ANYWAY. HA HA!
...
NO, I'LL NEVER GO ALONG WITH SUCH A DEAL...
CLICK

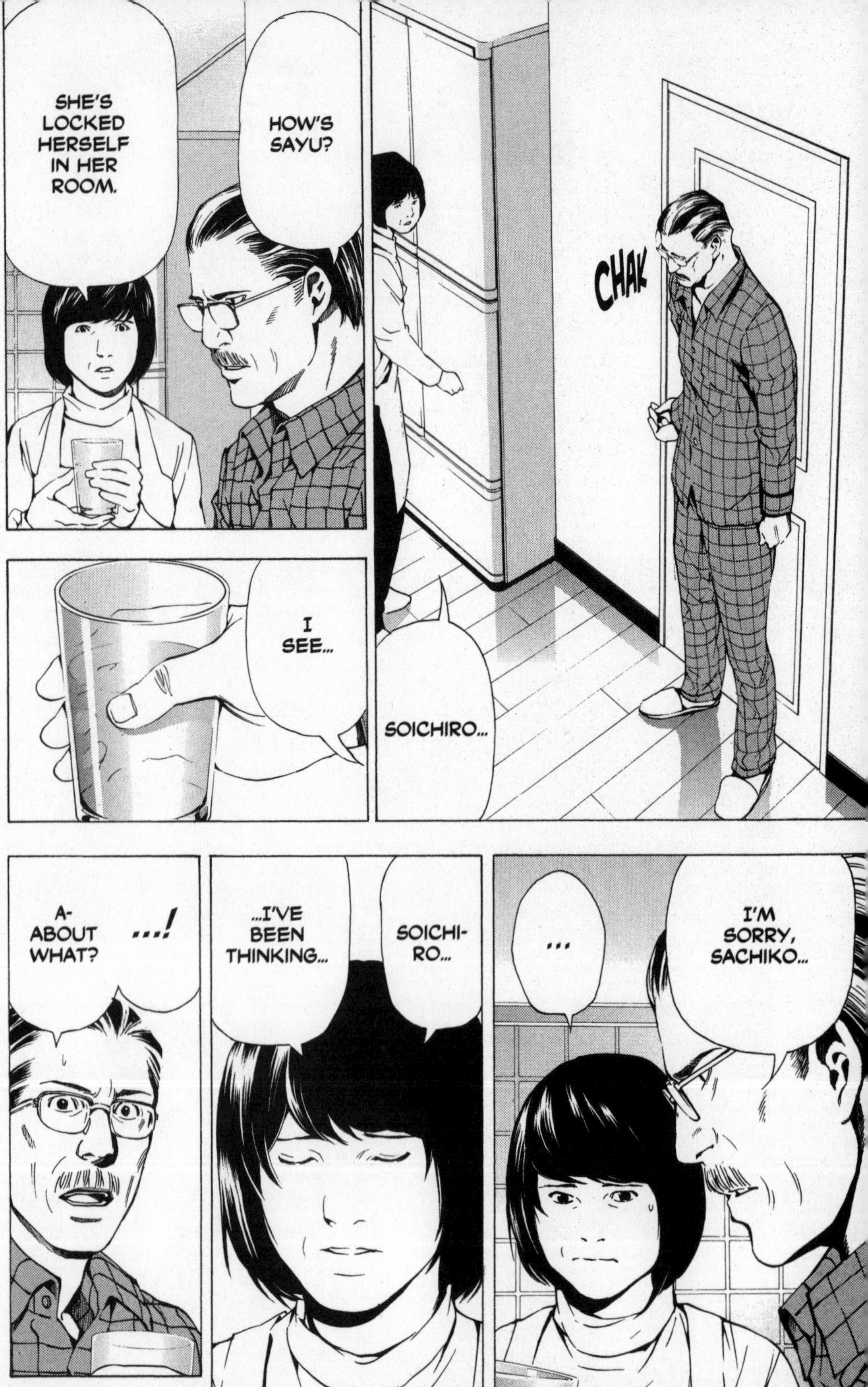

CHAK
SOICHIRO...
HOW'S SAYU?
SHE'S LOCKED HERSELF IN HER ROOM.
I SEE...
I'M SORRY, SACHIKO...
...
SOICHI-RO...
...I'VE BEEN THINKING...
...!
A- ABOUT WHAT?

READ THIS WAY

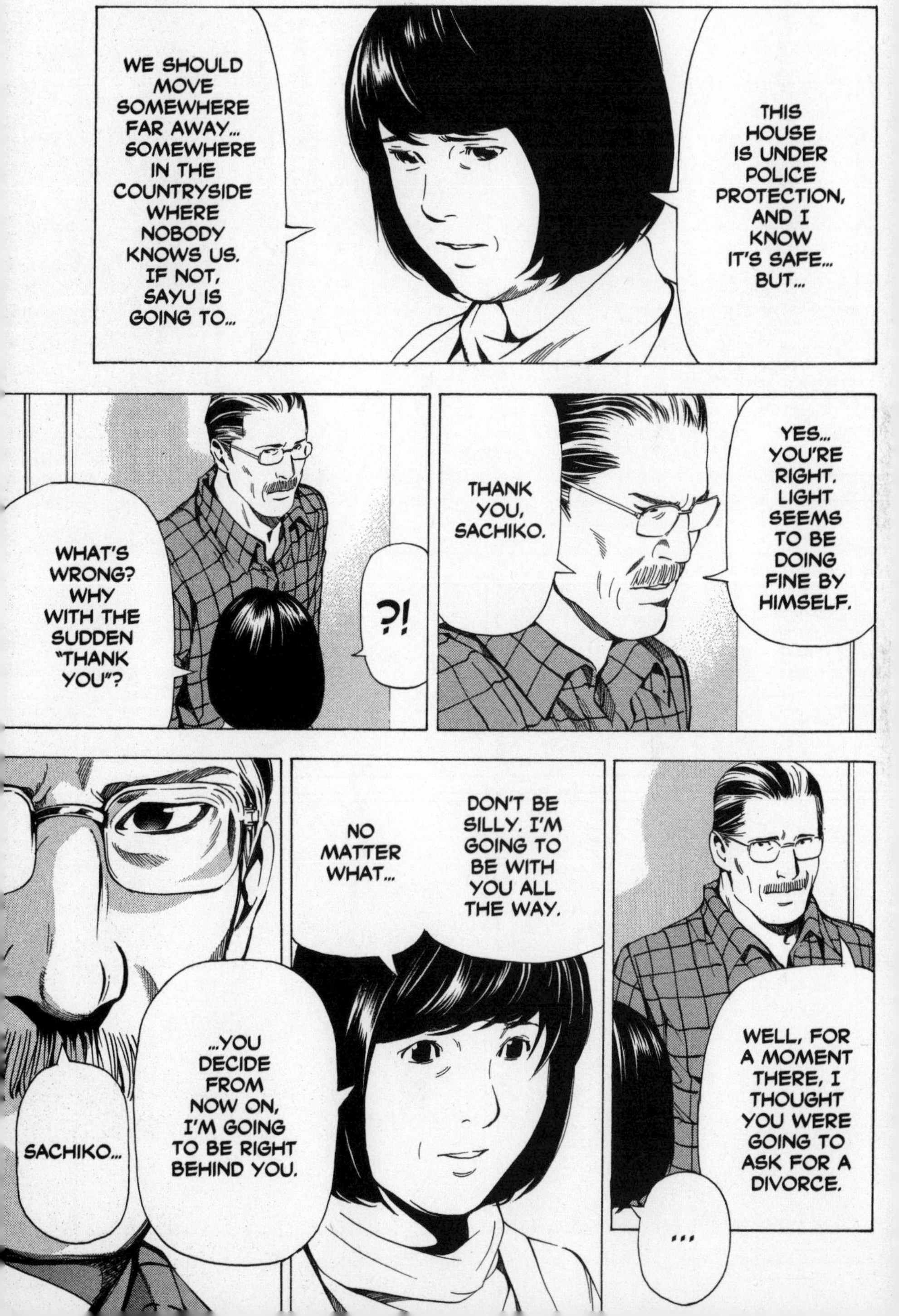
THIS HOUSE IS UNDER POLICE PROTECTION, AND I KNOW IT'S SAFE... BUT...
WE SHOULD MOVE SOMEWHERE FAR AWAY... SOMEWHERE IN THE COUNTRYSIDE WHERE NOBODY KNOWS US. IF NOT, SAYU IS GOING TO...
YES... YOU'RE RIGHT. LIGHT SEEMS TO BE DOING FINE BY HIMSELF.
THANK YOU, SACHIKO.
?!
WHAT'S WRONG? WHY WITH THE SUDDEN "THANK YOU"?
WELL, FOR A MOMENT THERE, I THOUGHT YOU WERE GOING TO ASK FOR A DIVORCE.
...
DON'T BE SILLY. I'M GOING TO BE WITH YOU ALL THE WAY.
NO MATTER WHAT...
...YOU DECIDE FROM NOW ON, I'M GOING TO BE RIGHT BEHIND YOU.
SACHIKO...

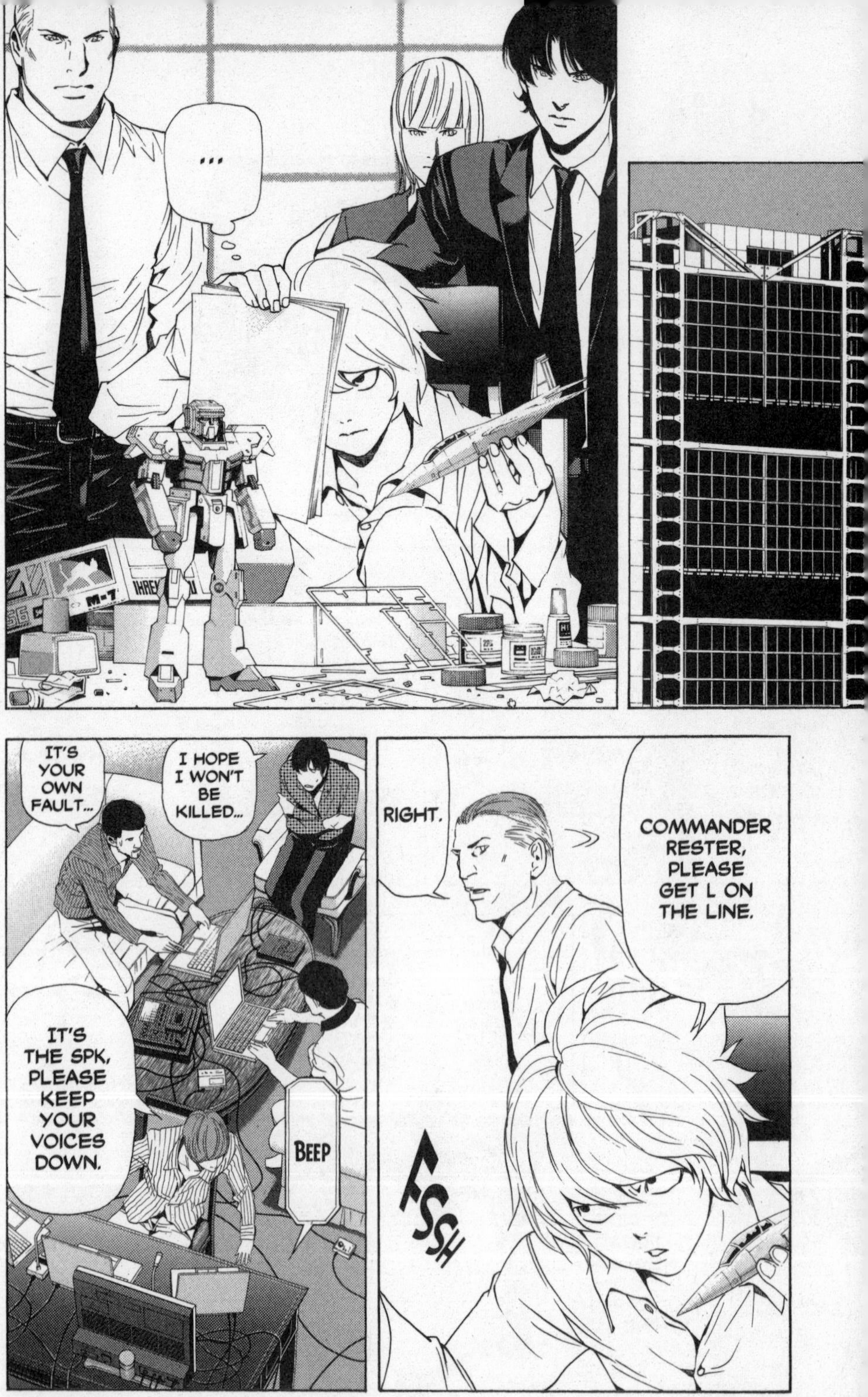
...
COMMANDER RESTER, PLEASE GET L ON THE LINE.
RIGHT.
FSSH
I HOPE I WON'T BE KILLED...
IT'S YOUR OWN FAULT...
BEEP
IT'S THE SPK, PLEASE KEEP YOUR VOICES DOWN.

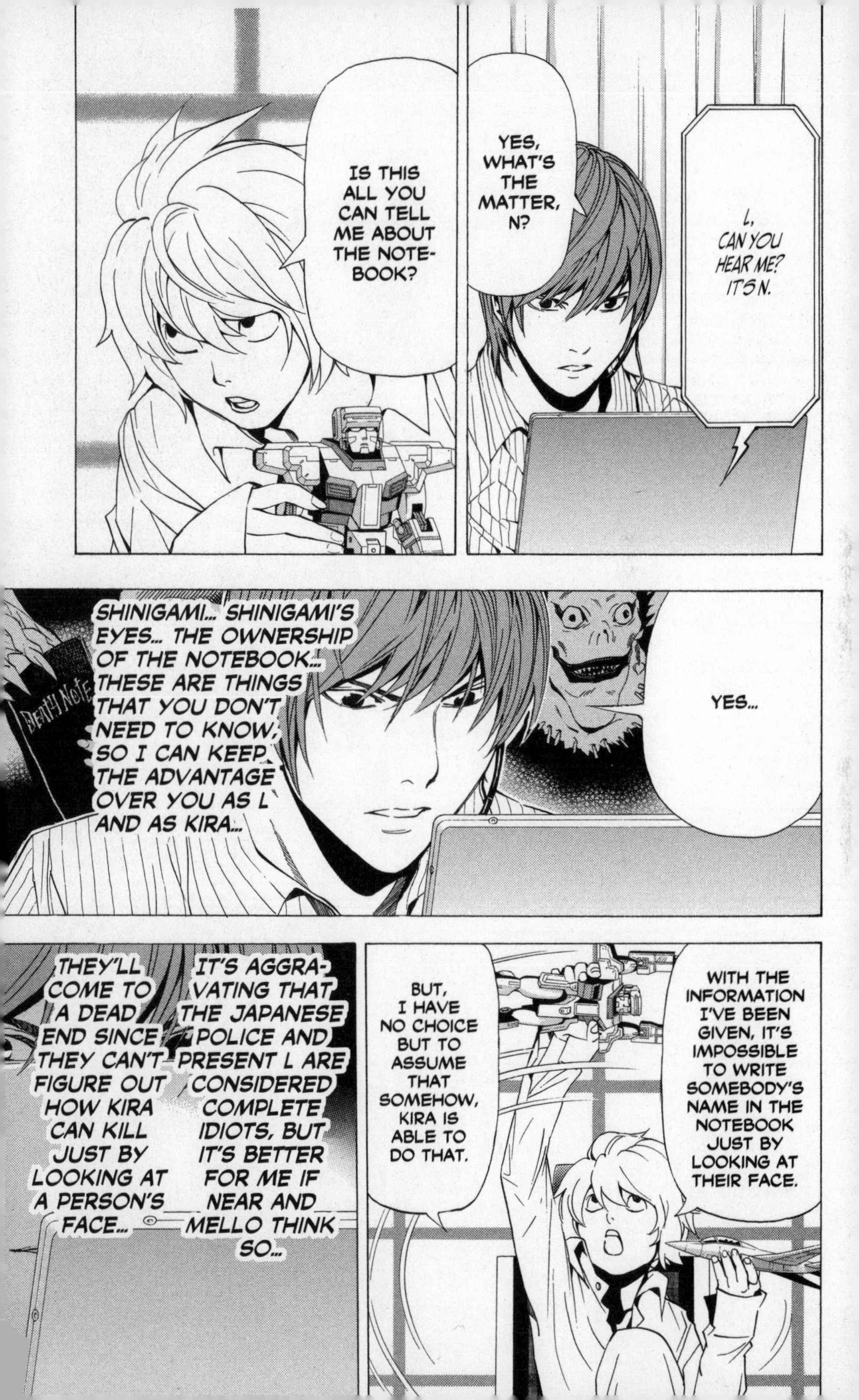
L, CAN YOU HEAR ME? IT'S N.
YES, WHAT'S THE MATTER, N?
IS THIS ALL YOU CAN TELL ME ABOUT THE NOTE-BOOK?
YES...
SHINIGAMI... SHINIGAMI'S EYES... THE OWNERSHIP OF THE NOTEBOOK... THESE ARE THINGS THAT YOU DON'T NEED TO KNOW, SO I CAN KEEP THE ADVANTAGE OVER YOU AS L AND AS KIRA...
DEATH NOTE
WITH THE INFORMATION I'VE BEEN GIVEN, IT'S IMPOSSIBLE TO WRITE SOMEBODY'S NAME IN THE NOTEBOOK JUST BY LOOKING AT THEIR FACE.
BUT, I HAVE NO CHOICE BUT TO ASSUME THAT SOMEHOW, KIRA IS ABLE TO DO THAT.
IT'S AGGRA-VATING THAT THE JAPANESE POLICE AND PRESENT L ARE CONSIDERED COMPLETE IDIOTS, BUT IT'S BETTER FOR ME IF NEAR AND MELLO THINK SO...
THEY'LL COME TO A DEAD END SINCE THEY CAN'T FIGURE OUT HOW KIRA CAN KILL JUST BY LOOKING AT A PERSON'S FACE...

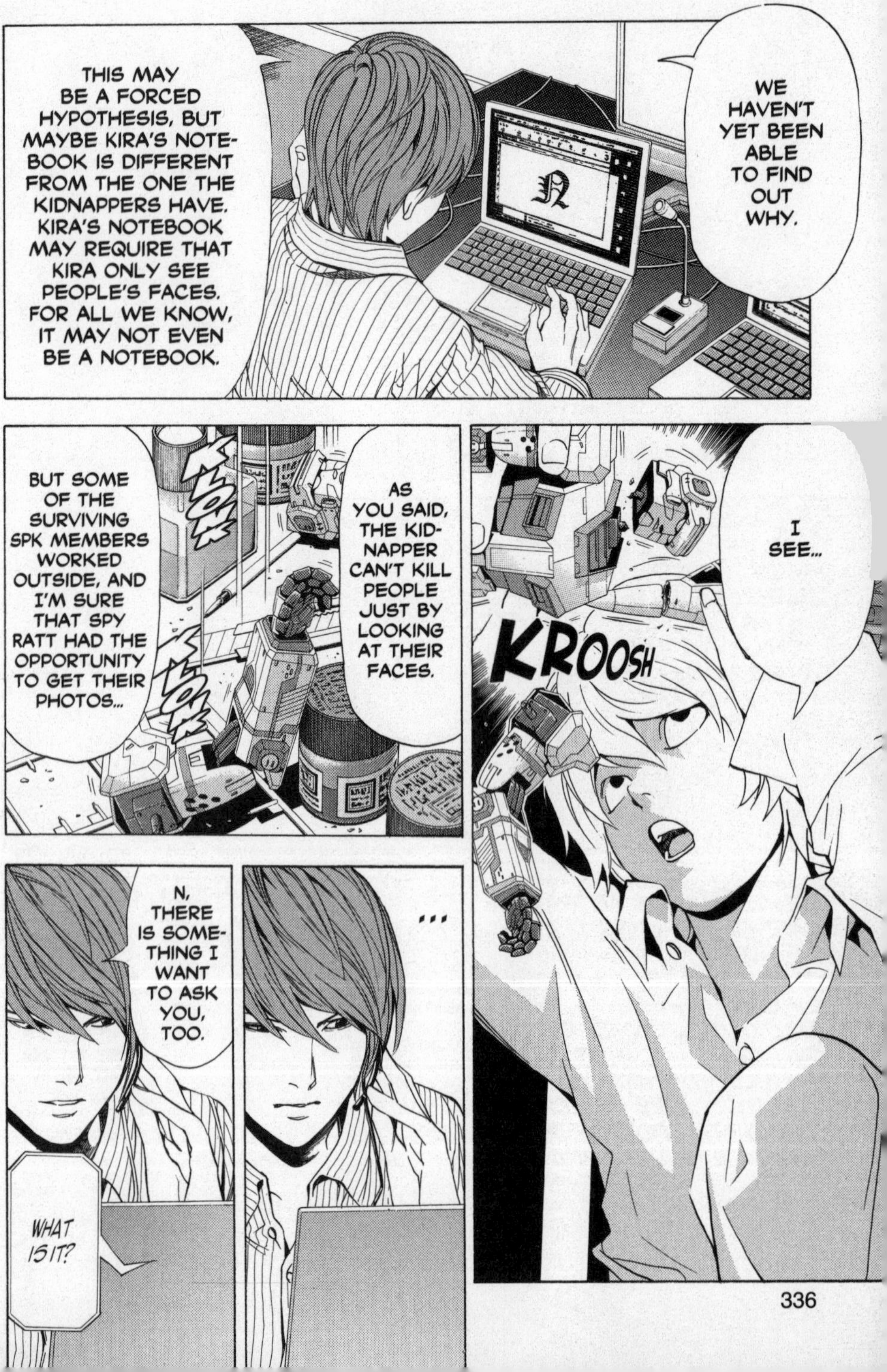

WE HAVEN'T YET BEEN ABLE TO FIND OUT WHY.
THIS MAY BE A FORCED HYPOTHESIS, BUT MAYBE KIRA'S NOTEBOOK IS DIFFERENT FROM THE ONE THE KIDNAPPERS HAVE. KIRA'S NOTEBOOK MAY REQUIRE THAT KIRA ONLY SEE PEOPLE'S FACES. FOR ALL WE KNOW, IT MAY NOT EVEN BE A NOTEBOOK.
I SEE...
KROOSH
AS YOU SAID, THE KIDNAPPER CAN'T KILL PEOPLE JUST BY LOOKING AT THEIR FACES.
KLOMP
KLOMP
BUT SOME OF THE SURVIVING SPK MEMBERS WORKED OUTSIDE, AND I'M SURE THAT SPY RATT HAD THE OPPORTUNITY TO GET THEIR PHOTOS...
...
N, THERE IS SOMETHING I WANT TO ASK YOU, TOO.
WHAT IS IT?

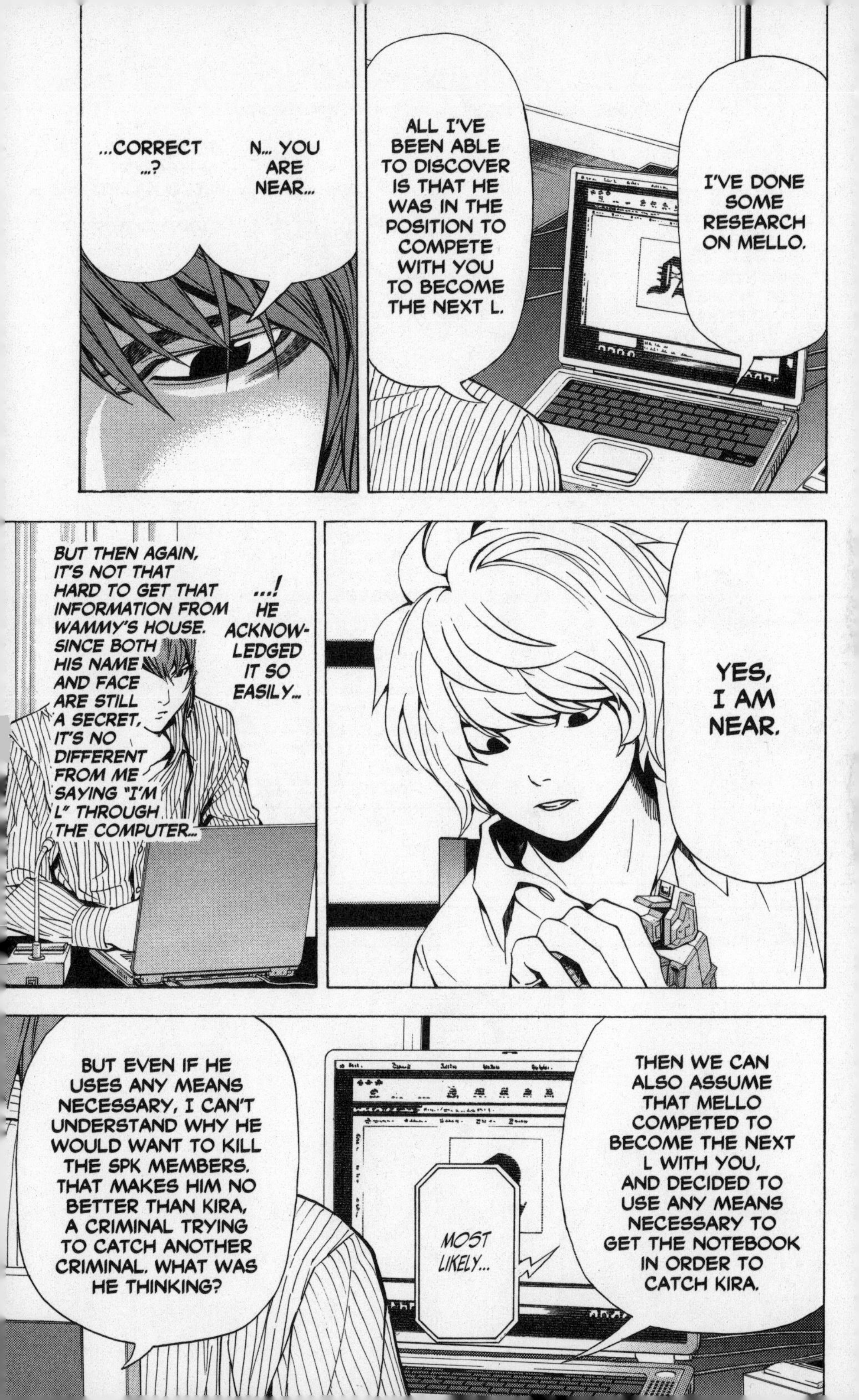
I'VE DONE SOME RESEARCH ON MELLO.
ALL I'VE BEEN ABLE TO DISCOVER IS THAT HE WAS IN THE POSITION TO COMPETE WITH YOU TO BECOME THE NEXT L.
N... YOU ARE NEAR...
...CORRECT ...?
YES, I AM NEAR.
...! HE ACKNOWLEDGED IT SO EASILY...
BUT THEN AGAIN, IT'S NOT THAT HARD TO GET THAT INFORMATION FROM WAMMY'S HOUSE. SINCE BOTH HIS NAME AND FACE ARE STILL A SECRET, IT'S NO DIFFERENT FROM ME SAYING "I'M L" THROUGH THE COMPUTER...
THEN WE CAN ALSO ASSUME THAT MELLO COMPETED TO BECOME THE NEXT L WITH YOU, AND DECIDED TO USE ANY MEANS NECESSARY TO GET THE NOTEBOOK IN ORDER TO CATCH KIRA.
MOST LIKELY...
BUT EVEN IF HE USES ANY MEANS NECESSARY, I CAN'T UNDERSTAND WHY HE WOULD WANT TO KILL THE SPK MEMBERS. THAT MAKES HIM NO BETTER THAN KIRA, A CRIMINAL TRYING TO CATCH ANOTHER CRIMINAL. WHAT WAS HE THINKING?

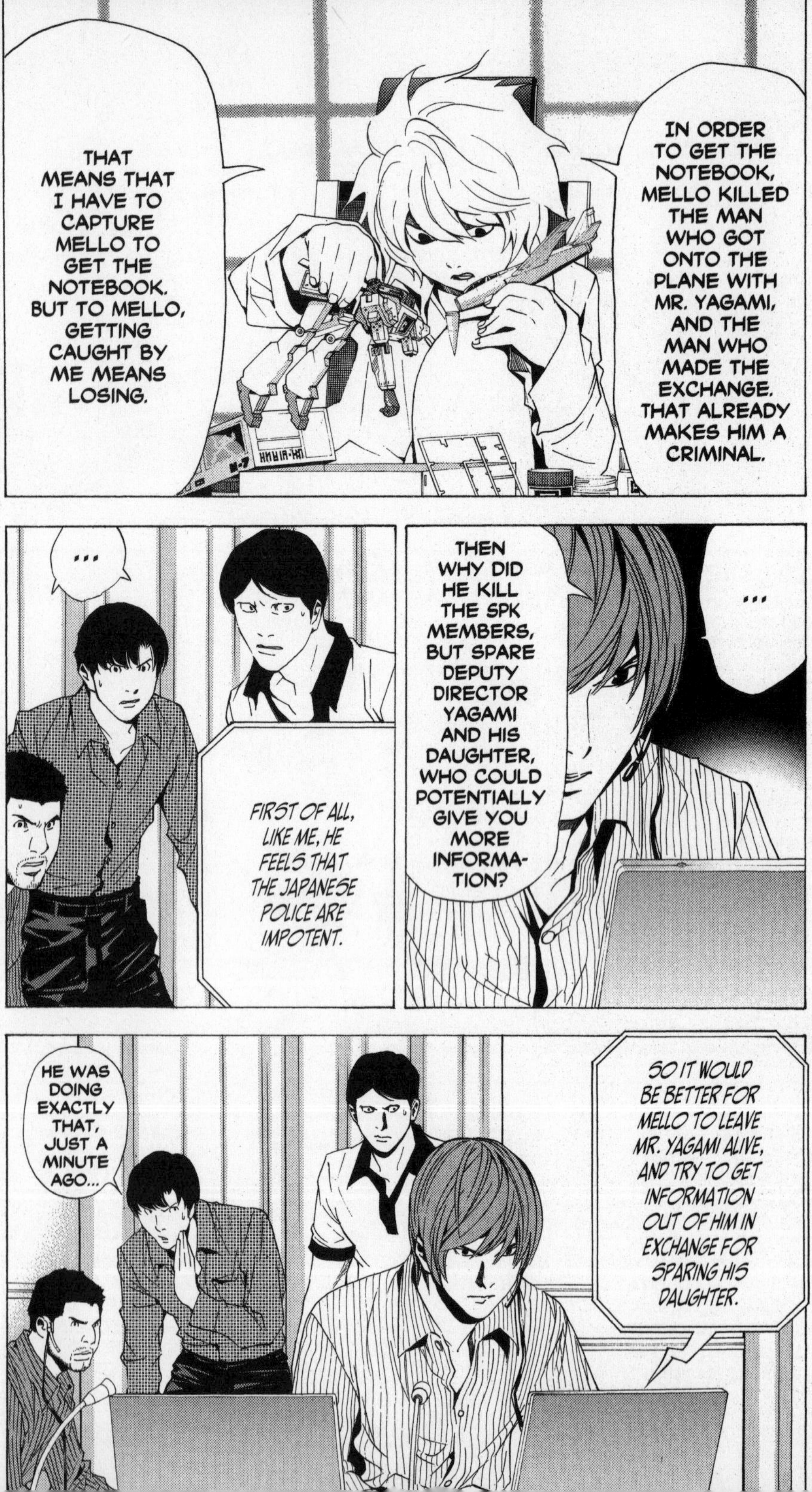
IN ORDER TO GET THE NOTEBOOK, MELLO KILLED THE MAN WHO GOT ONTO THE PLANE WITH MR. YAGAMI, AND THE MAN WHO MADE THE EXCHANGE. THAT ALREADY MAKES HIM A CRIMINAL.
THAT MEANS THAT I HAVE TO CAPTURE MELLO TO GET THE NOTEBOOK. BUT TO MELLO, GETTING CAUGHT BY ME MEANS LOSING.
THEN WHY DID HE KILL THE SPK MEMBERS, BUT SPARE DEPUTY DIRECTOR YAGAMI AND HIS DAUGHTER, WHO COULD POTENTIALLY GIVE YOU MORE INFORMATION?
...
...
FIRST OF ALL, LIKE ME, HE FEELS THAT THE JAPANESE POLICE ARE IMPOTENT.
SO IT WOULD BE BETTER FOR MELLO TO LEAVE MR. YAGAMI ALIVE, AND TRY TO GET INFORMATION OUT OF HIM IN EXCHANGE FOR SPARING HIS DAUGHTER.
HE WAS DOING EXACTLY THAT, JUST A MINUTE AGO...

READ THIS WAY

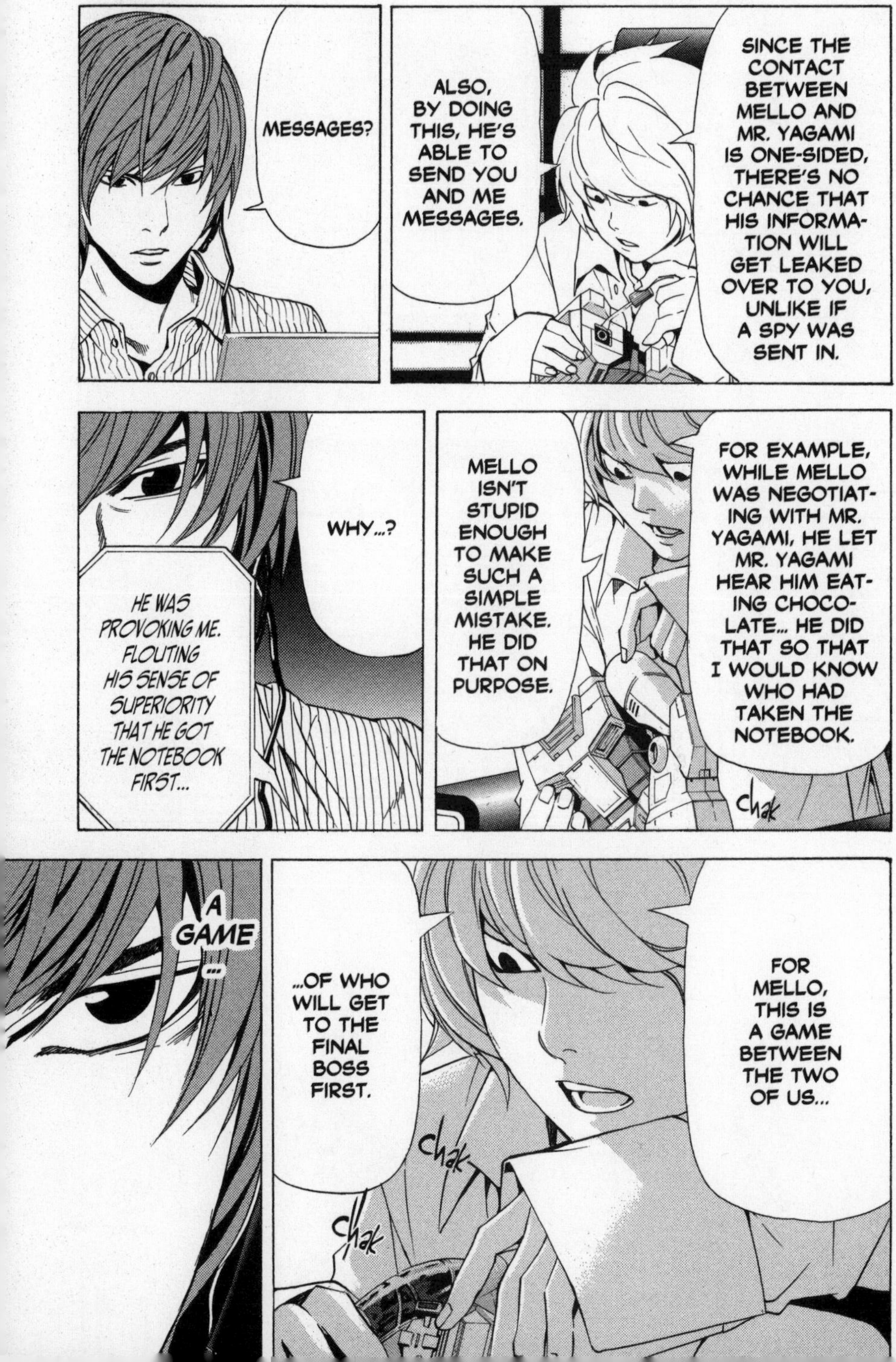

SINCE THE CONTACT BETWEEN MELLO AND MR. YAGAMI IS ONE-SIDED, THERE'S NO CHANCE THAT HIS INFORMATION WILL GET LEAKED OVER TO YOU, UNLIKE IF A SPY WAS SENT IN.
ALSO, BY DOING THIS, HE'S ABLE TO SEND YOU AND ME MESSAGES.
MESSAGES?
FOR EXAMPLE, WHILE MELLO WAS NEGOTIATING WITH MR. YAGAMI, HE LET MR. YAGAMI HEAR HIM EATING CHOCOLATE... HE DID THAT SO THAT I WOULD KNOW WHO HAD TAKEN THE NOTEBOOK.
MELLO ISN'T STUPID ENOUGH TO MAKE SUCH A SIMPLE MISTAKE. HE DID THAT ON PURPOSE.
chak
WHY...?
HE WAS PROVOKING ME. FLOUTING HIS SENSE OF SUPERIORITY THAT HE GOT THE NOTEBOOK FIRST...
FOR MELLO, THIS IS A GAME BETWEEN THE TWO OF US...
...OF WHO WILL GET TO THE FINAL BOSS FIRST.
chak
chak
A GAME...

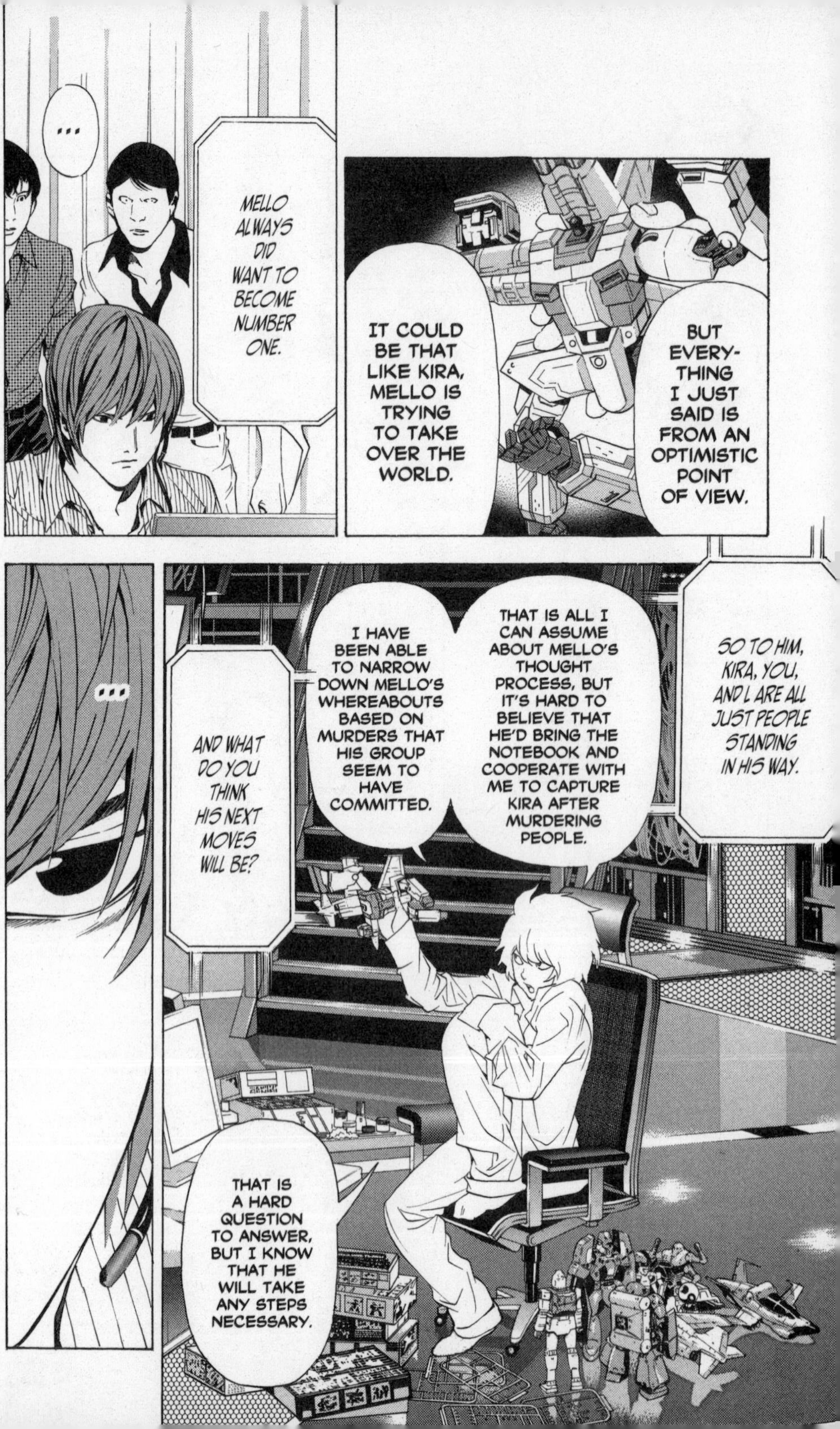
BUT EVERYTHING I JUST SAID IS FROM AN OPTIMISTIC POINT OF VIEW.
IT COULD BE THAT LIKE KIRA, MELLO IS TRYING TO TAKE OVER THE WORLD.
MELLO ALWAYS DID WANT TO BECOME NUMBER ONE.
...
SO TO HIM, KIRA, YOU, AND L ARE ALL JUST PEOPLE STANDING IN HIS WAY.
THAT IS ALL I CAN ASSUME ABOUT MELLO'S THOUGHT PROCESS, BUT IT'S HARD TO BELIEVE THAT HE'D BRING THE NOTEBOOK AND COOPERATE WITH ME TO CAPTURE KIRA AFTER MURDERING PEOPLE.
I HAVE BEEN ABLE TO NARROW DOWN MELLO'S WHEREABOUTS BASED ON MURDERS THAT HIS GROUP SEEM TO HAVE COMMITTED.
AND WHAT DO YOU THINK HIS NEXT MOVES WILL BE?
THAT IS A HARD QUESTION TO ANSWER, BUT I KNOW THAT HE WILL TAKE ANY STEPS NECESSARY.
...

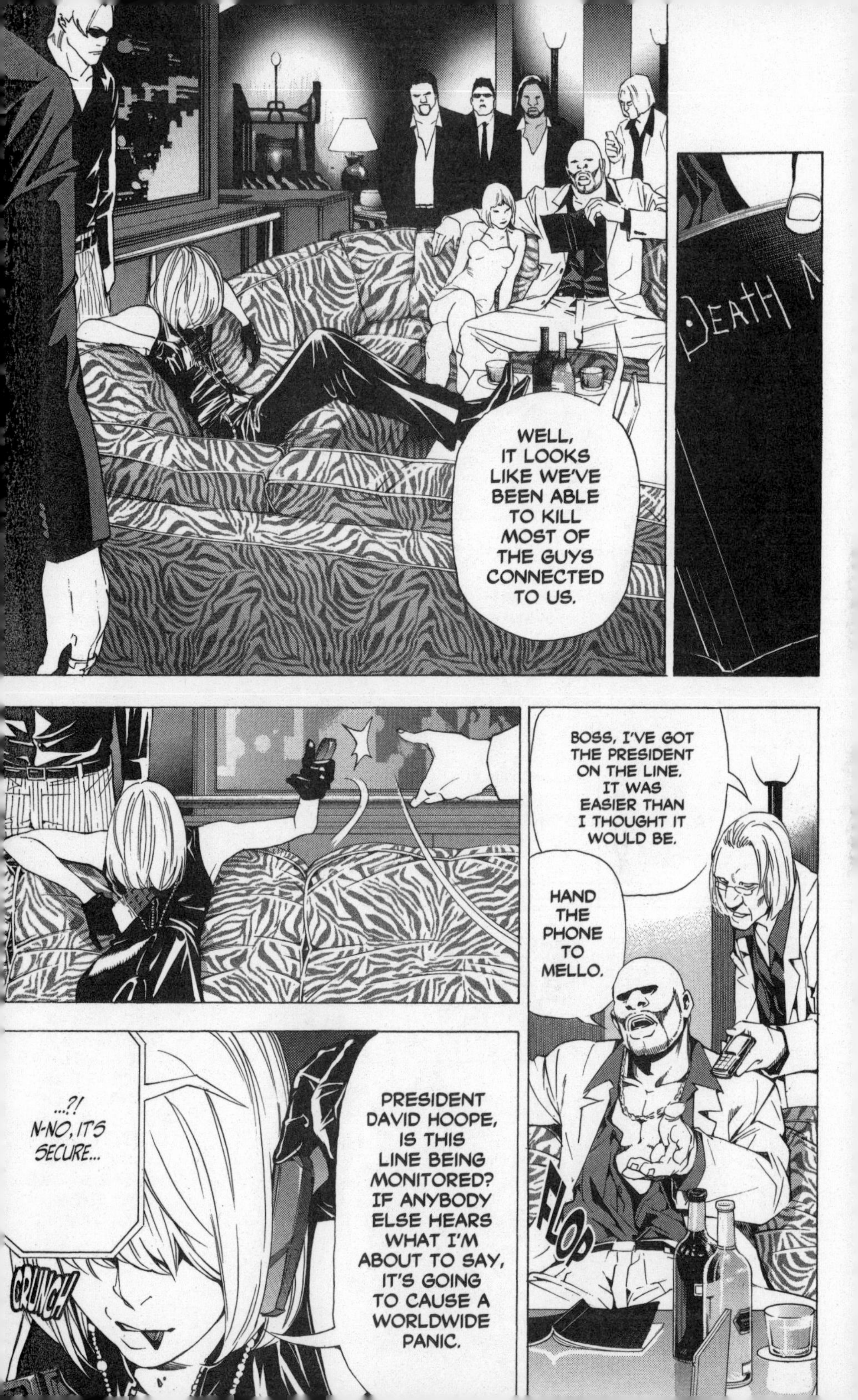
DEATH
WELL, IT LOOKS LIKE WE'VE BEEN ABLE TO KILL MOST OF THE GUYS CONNECTED TO US.
BOSS, I'VE GOT THE PRESIDENT ON THE LINE. IT WAS EASIER THAN I THOUGHT IT WOULD BE.
HAND THE PHONE TO MELLO.
FLOP
PRESIDENT DAVID HOOPE, IS THIS LINE BEING MONITORED? IF ANYBODY ELSE HEARS WHAT I'M ABOUT TO SAY, IT'S GOING TO CAUSE A WORLDWIDE PANIC.
...?! N-NO, IT'S SECURE...
CRUNCH

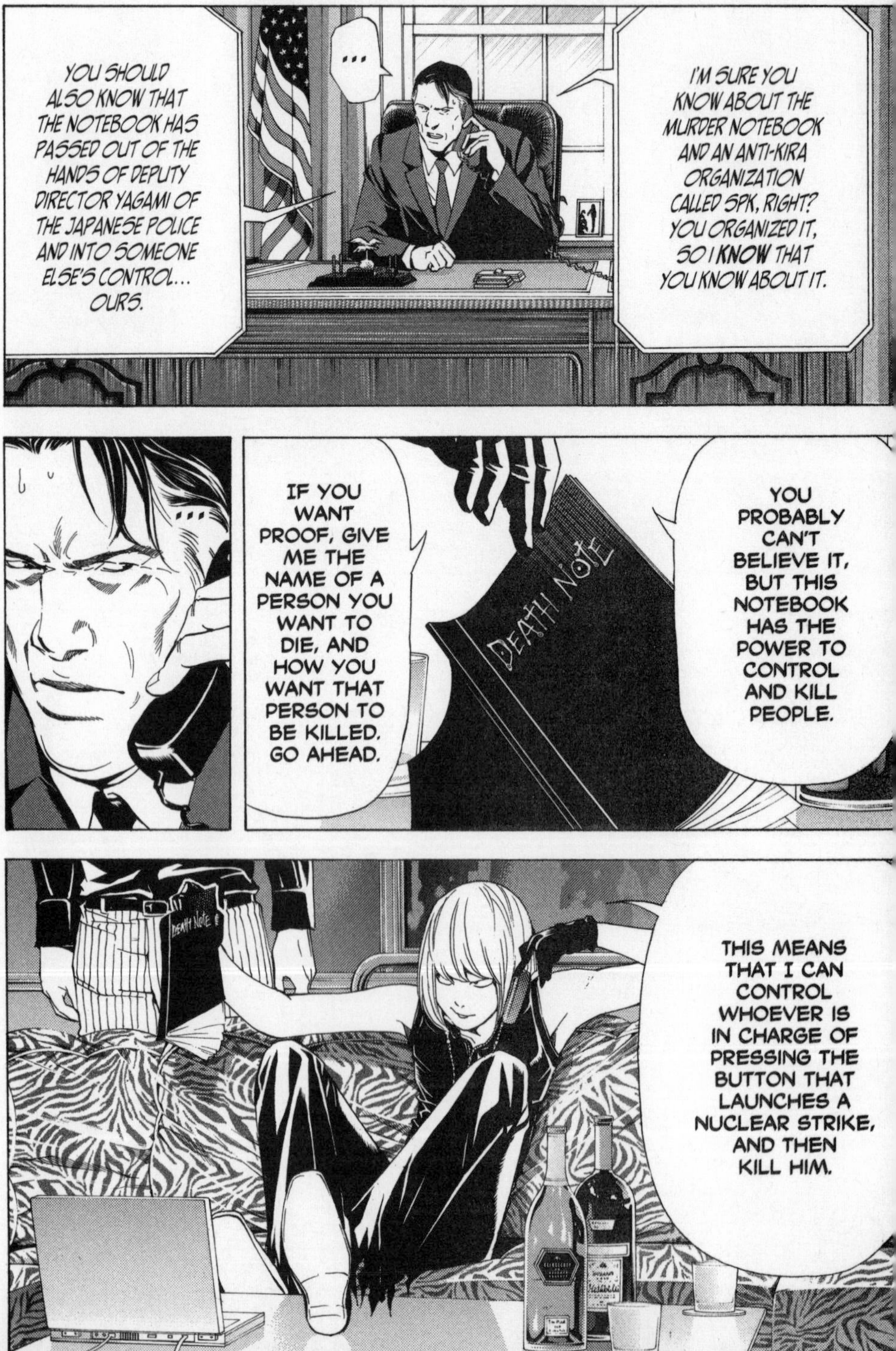
I'M SURE YOU KNOW ABOUT THE MURDER NOTEBOOK AND AN ANTI-KIRA ORGANIZATION CALLED SPK, RIGHT? YOU ORGANIZED IT, SO I **KNOW** THAT YOU KNOW ABOUT IT.
...
YOU SHOULD ALSO KNOW THAT THE NOTEBOOK HAS PASSED OUT OF THE HANDS OF DEPUTY DIRECTOR YAGAMI OF THE JAPANESE POLICE AND INTO SOMEONE ELSE'S CONTROL... OURS.
YOU PROBABLY CAN'T BELIEVE IT, BUT THIS NOTEBOOK HAS THE POWER TO CONTROL AND KILL PEOPLE.
DEATH NOTE
IF YOU WANT PROOF, GIVE ME THE NAME OF A PERSON YOU WANT TO DIE, AND HOW YOU WANT THAT PERSON TO BE KILLED. GO AHEAD.
...
THIS MEANS THAT I CAN CONTROL WHOEVER IS IN CHARGE OF PRESSING THE BUTTON THAT LAUNCHES A NUCLEAR STRIKE, AND THEN KILL HIM.
DEATH NOTE

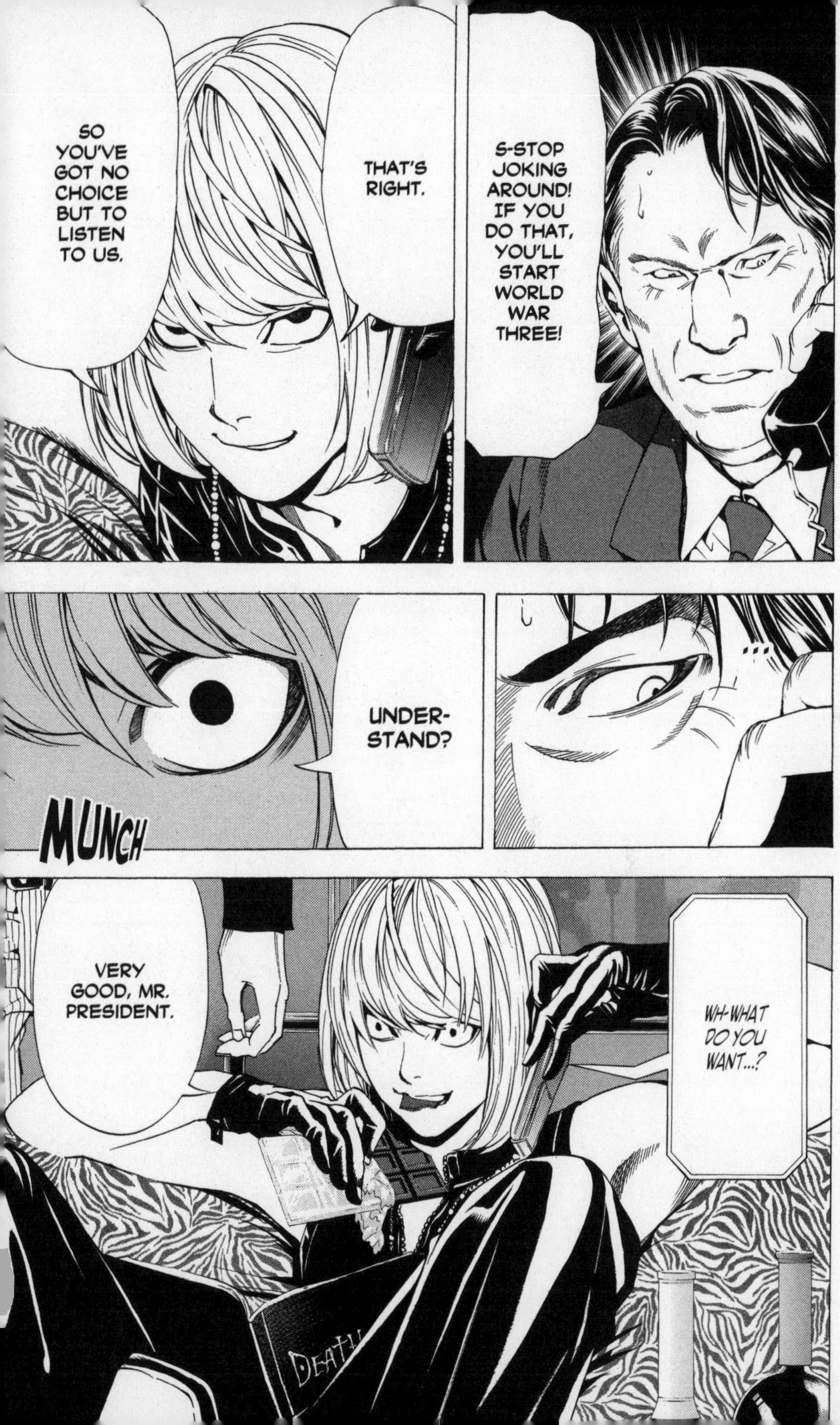
S-STOP JOKING AROUND! IF YOU DO THAT, YOU'LL START WORLD WAR THREE!
THAT'S RIGHT.
SO YOU'VE GOT NO CHOICE BUT TO LISTEN TO US.
...
UNDER-STAND?
MUNCH
WH-WHAT DO YOU WANT...?
VERY GOOD, MR. PRESIDENT.
DEATH

# DEATH NOTE
## How to use it
## XLV

- As long as the god of death has at least once seen a human and knows his/her name and life-span, the god of death is capable of finding that human from a hole in the world of the gods of death.

死神は、一度でも顔を見て名前と寿命がわかっている人間ならば、
死神界の穴からその人間の居場所を知る事ができる。

# chapter 68 Discovery

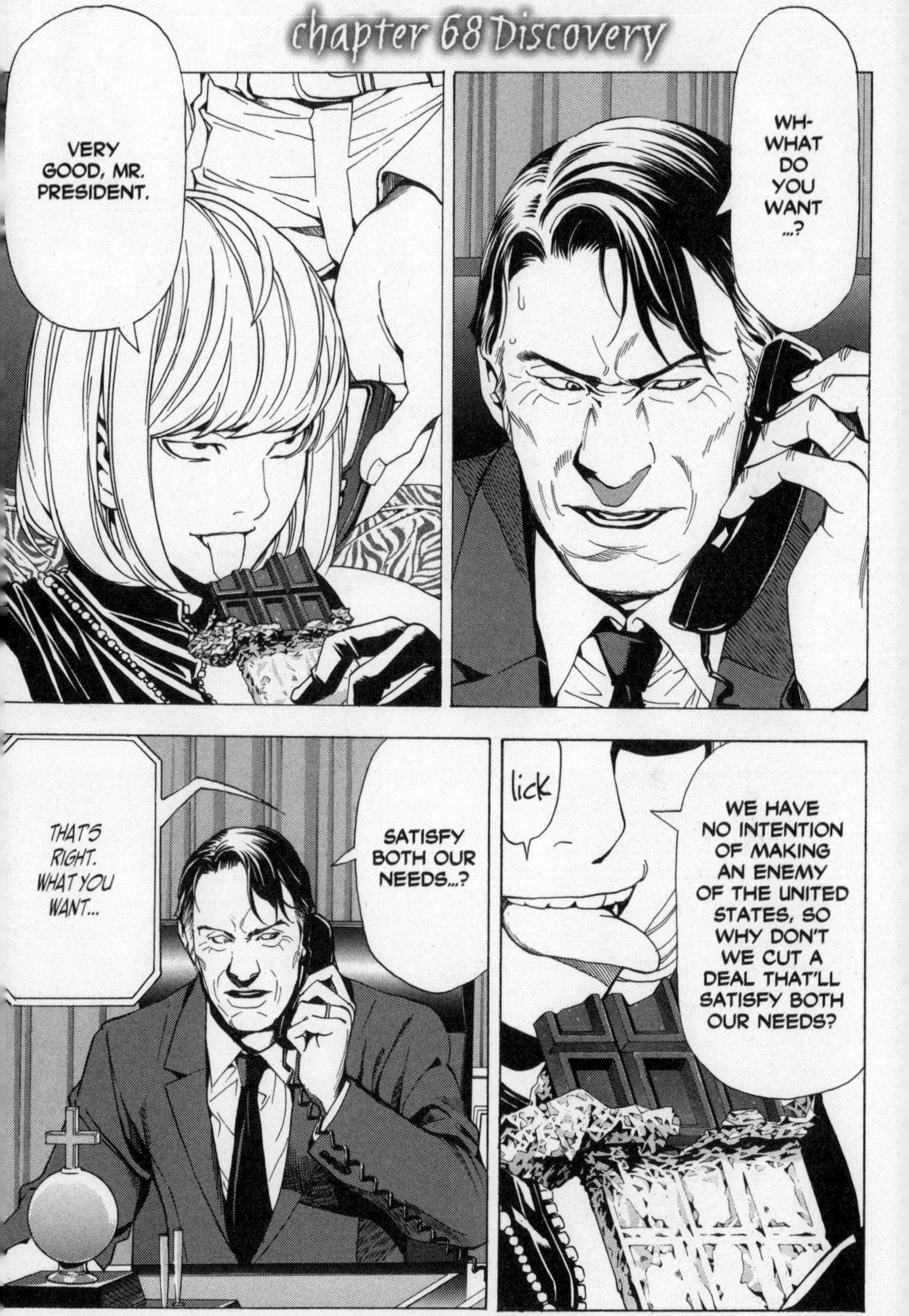
WH-WHAT DO YOU WANT ...?
VERY GOOD, MR. PRESIDENT.
WE HAVE NO INTENTION OF MAKING AN ENEMY OF THE UNITED STATES, SO WHY DON'T WE CUT A DEAL THAT'LL SATISFY BOTH OUR NEEDS?
lick
SATISFY BOTH OUR NEEDS...?
THAT'S RIGHT. WHAT YOU WANT...

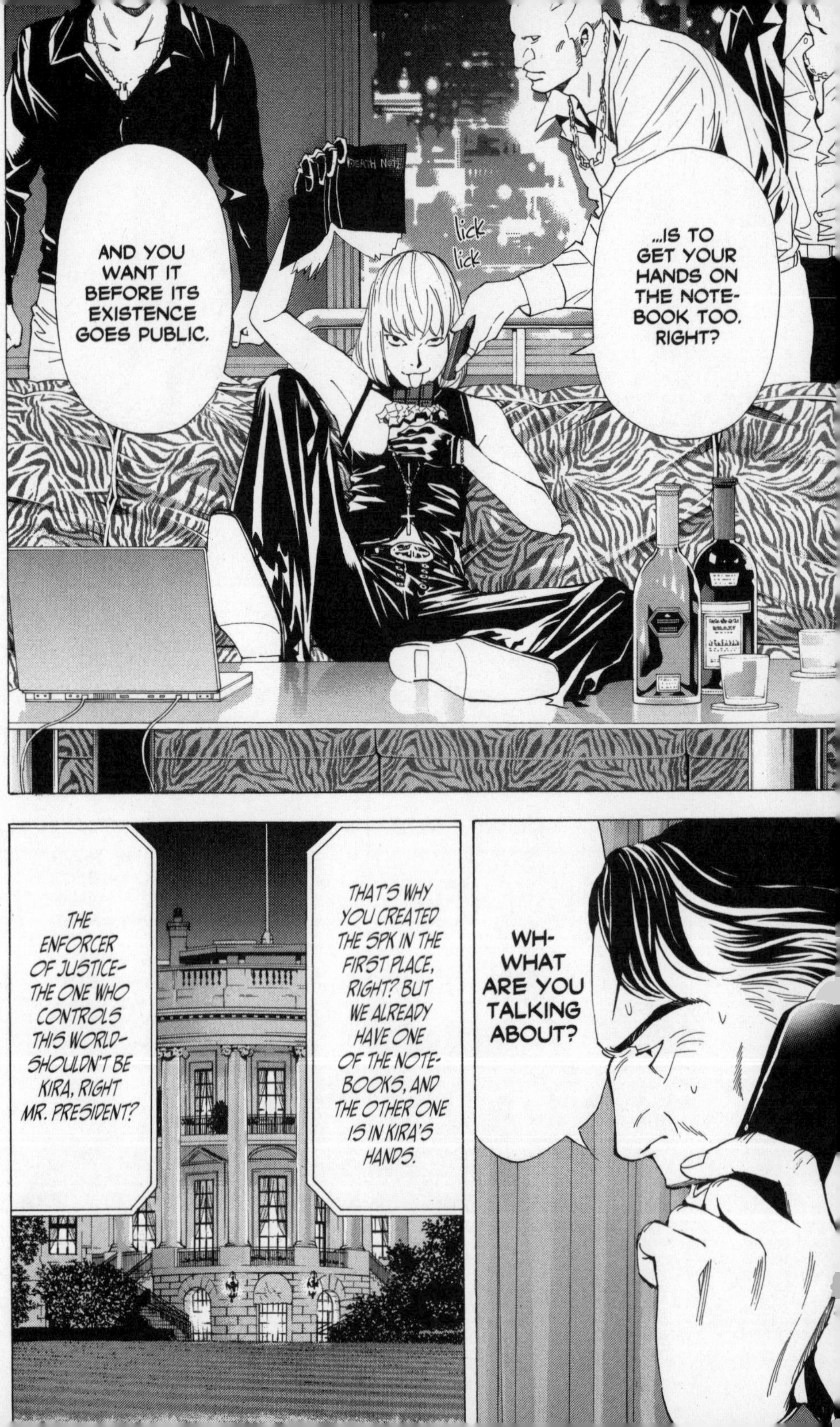
...IS TO GET YOUR HANDS ON THE NOTE-BOOK TOO. RIGHT?
DEATH NOTE
lick lick
AND YOU WANT IT BEFORE ITS EXISTENCE GOES PUBLIC.
WH- WHAT ARE YOU TALKING ABOUT?
THAT'S WHY YOU CREATED THE SPK IN THE FIRST PLACE, RIGHT? BUT WE ALREADY HAVE ONE OF THE NOTE-BOOKS, AND THE OTHER ONE IS IN KIRA'S HANDS.
THE ENFORCER OF JUSTICE- THE ONE WHO CONTROLS THIS WORLD- SHOULDN'T BE KIRA, RIGHT MR. PRESIDENT?

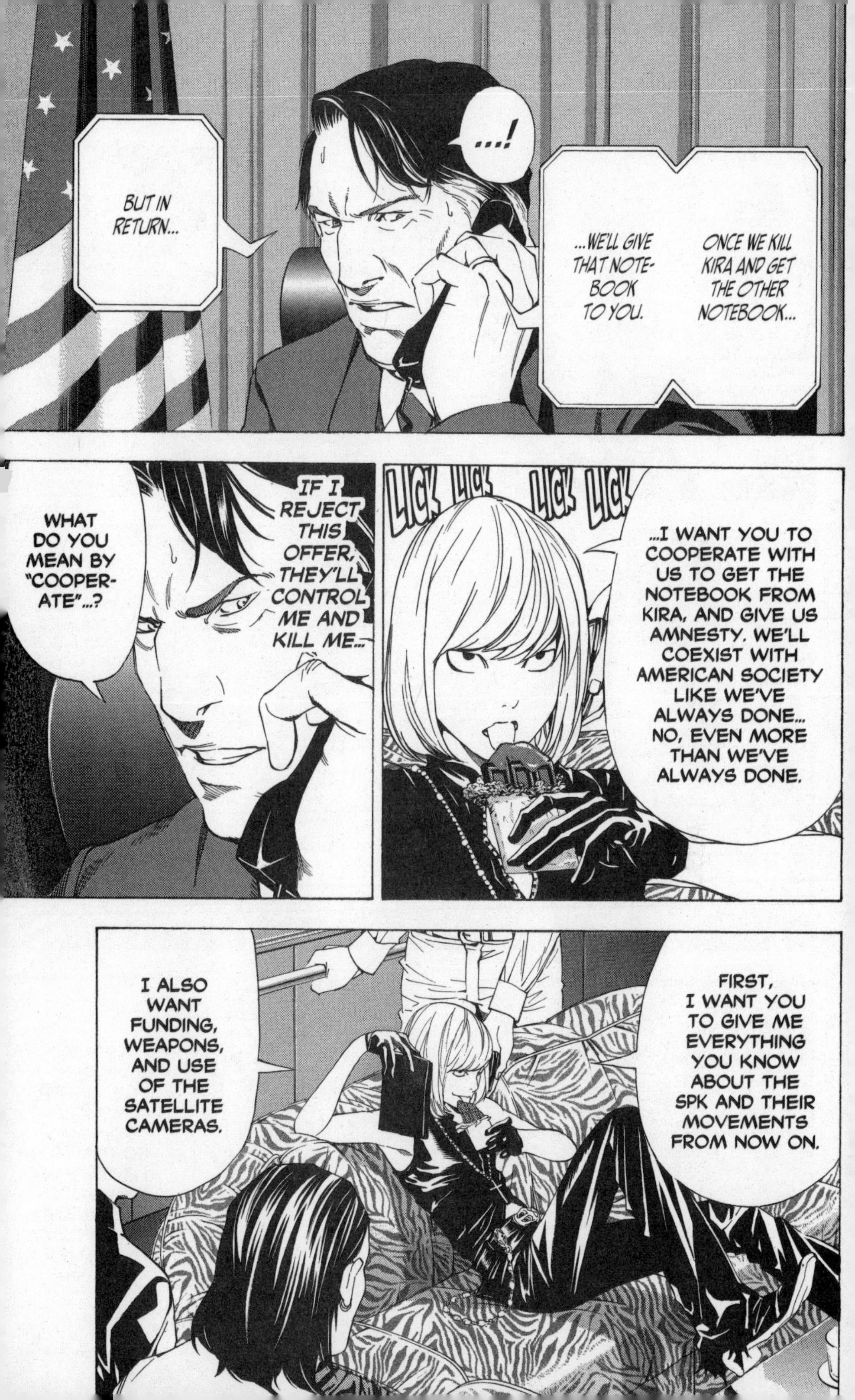
ONCE WE KILL KIRA AND GET THE OTHER NOTEBOOK...
...WE'LL GIVE THAT NOTE-BOOK TO YOU.
BUT IN RETURN...
...!
LICK LICK LICK LICK
...I WANT YOU TO COOPERATE WITH US TO GET THE NOTEBOOK FROM KIRA, AND GIVE US AMNESTY. WE'LL COEXIST WITH AMERICAN SOCIETY LIKE WE'VE ALWAYS DONE... NO, EVEN MORE THAN WE'VE ALWAYS DONE.
IF I REJECT THIS OFFER, THEY'LL CONTROL ME AND KILL ME...
WHAT DO YOU MEAN BY "COOPER-ATE"...?
FIRST, I WANT YOU TO GIVE ME EVERYTHING YOU KNOW ABOUT THE SPK AND THEIR MOVEMENTS FROM NOW ON.
I ALSO WANT FUNDING, WEAPONS, AND USE OF THE SATELLITE CAMERAS.

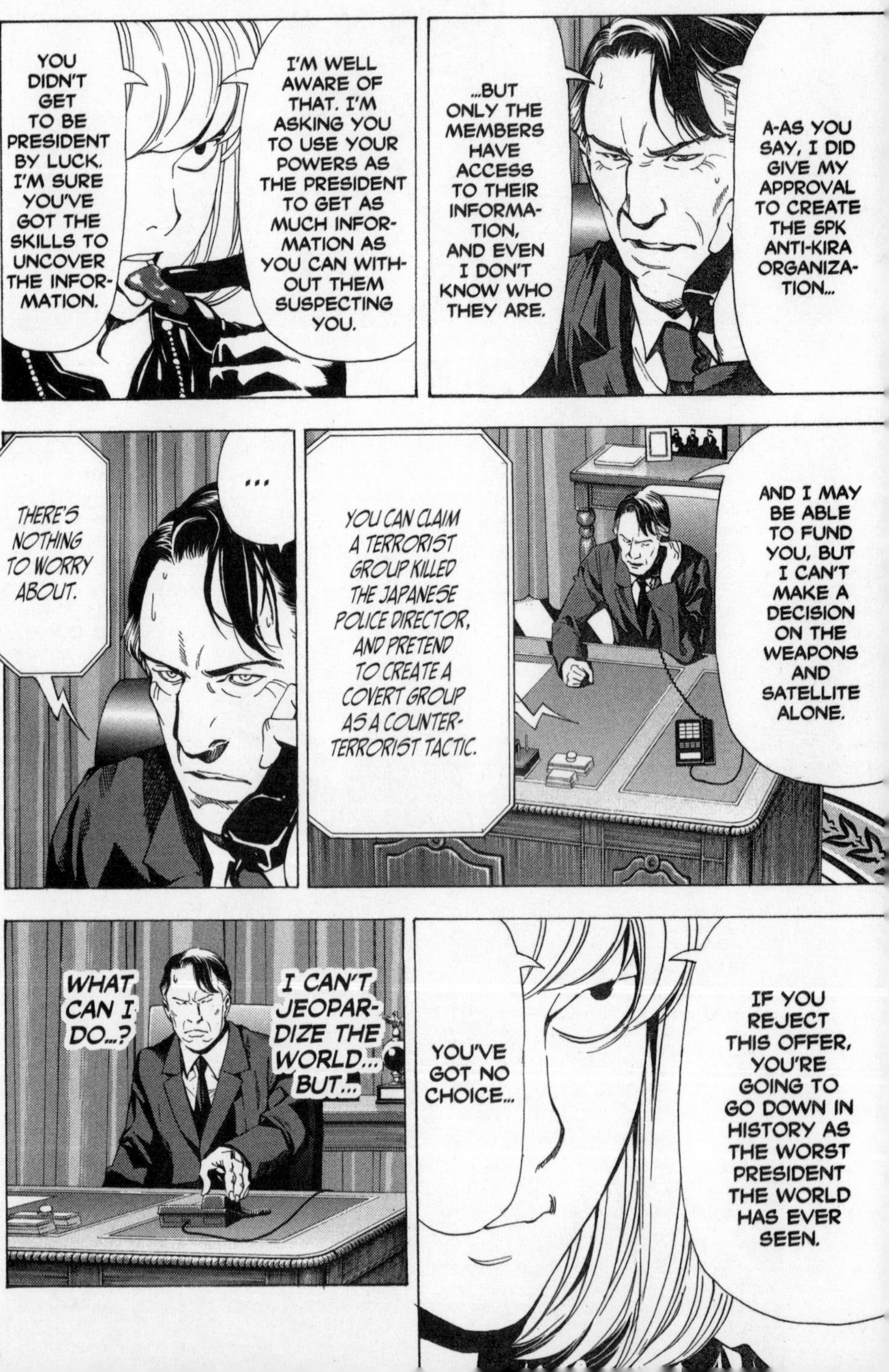
A-AS YOU SAY, I DID GIVE MY APPROVAL TO CREATE THE SPK ANTI-KIRA ORGANIZATION...
...BUT ONLY THE MEMBERS HAVE ACCESS TO THEIR INFORMATION, AND EVEN I DON'T KNOW WHO THEY ARE.
I'M WELL AWARE OF THAT. I'M ASKING YOU TO USE YOUR POWERS AS THE PRESIDENT TO GET AS MUCH INFORMATION AS YOU CAN WITHOUT THEM SUSPECTING YOU.
YOU DIDN'T GET TO BE PRESIDENT BY LUCK. I'M SURE YOU'VE GOT THE SKILLS TO UNCOVER THE INFORMATION.
AND I MAY BE ABLE TO FUND YOU, BUT I CAN'T MAKE A DECISION ON THE WEAPONS AND SATELLITE ALONE.
YOU CAN CLAIM A TERRORIST GROUP KILLED THE JAPANESE POLICE DIRECTOR, AND PRETEND TO CREATE A COVERT GROUP AS A COUNTER-TERRORIST TACTIC.
...
THERE'S NOTHING TO WORRY ABOUT.
IF YOU REJECT THIS OFFER, YOU'RE GOING TO GO DOWN IN HISTORY AS THE WORST PRESIDENT THE WORLD HAS EVER SEEN.
YOU'VE GOT NO CHOICE...
I CAN'T JEOPARDIZE THE WORLD... BUT...
WHAT CAN I DO...?

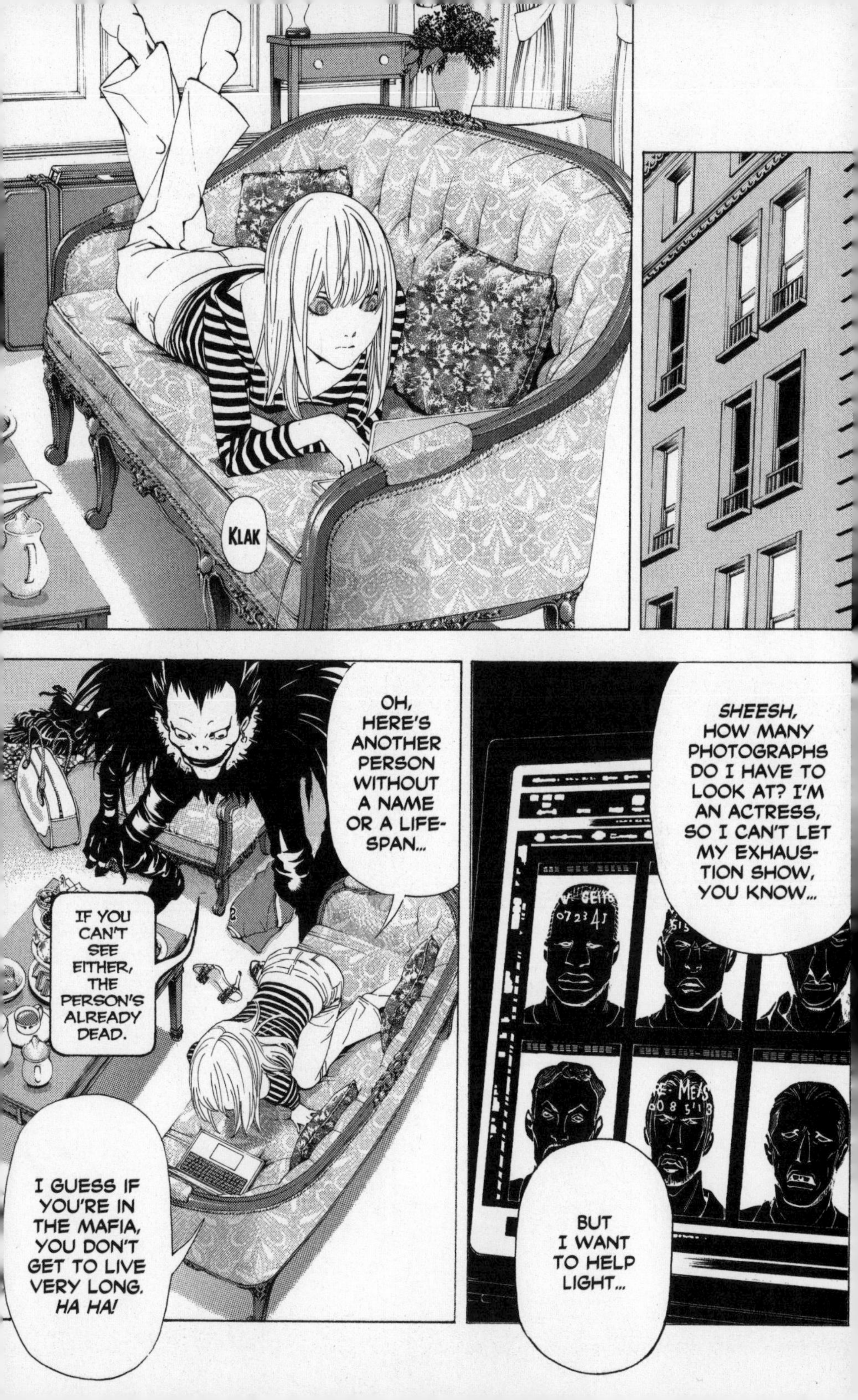
KLAK
SHEESH, HOW MANY PHOTOGRAPHS DO I HAVE TO LOOK AT? I'M AN ACTRESS, SO I CAN'T LET MY EXHAUSTION SHOW, YOU KNOW...
BUT I WANT TO HELP LIGHT...
OH, HERE'S ANOTHER PERSON WITHOUT A NAME OR A LIFE-SPAN...
IF YOU CAN'T SEE EITHER, THE PERSON'S ALREADY DEAD.
I GUESS IF YOU'RE IN THE MAFIA, YOU DON'T GET TO LIVE VERY LONG. *HA HA!*

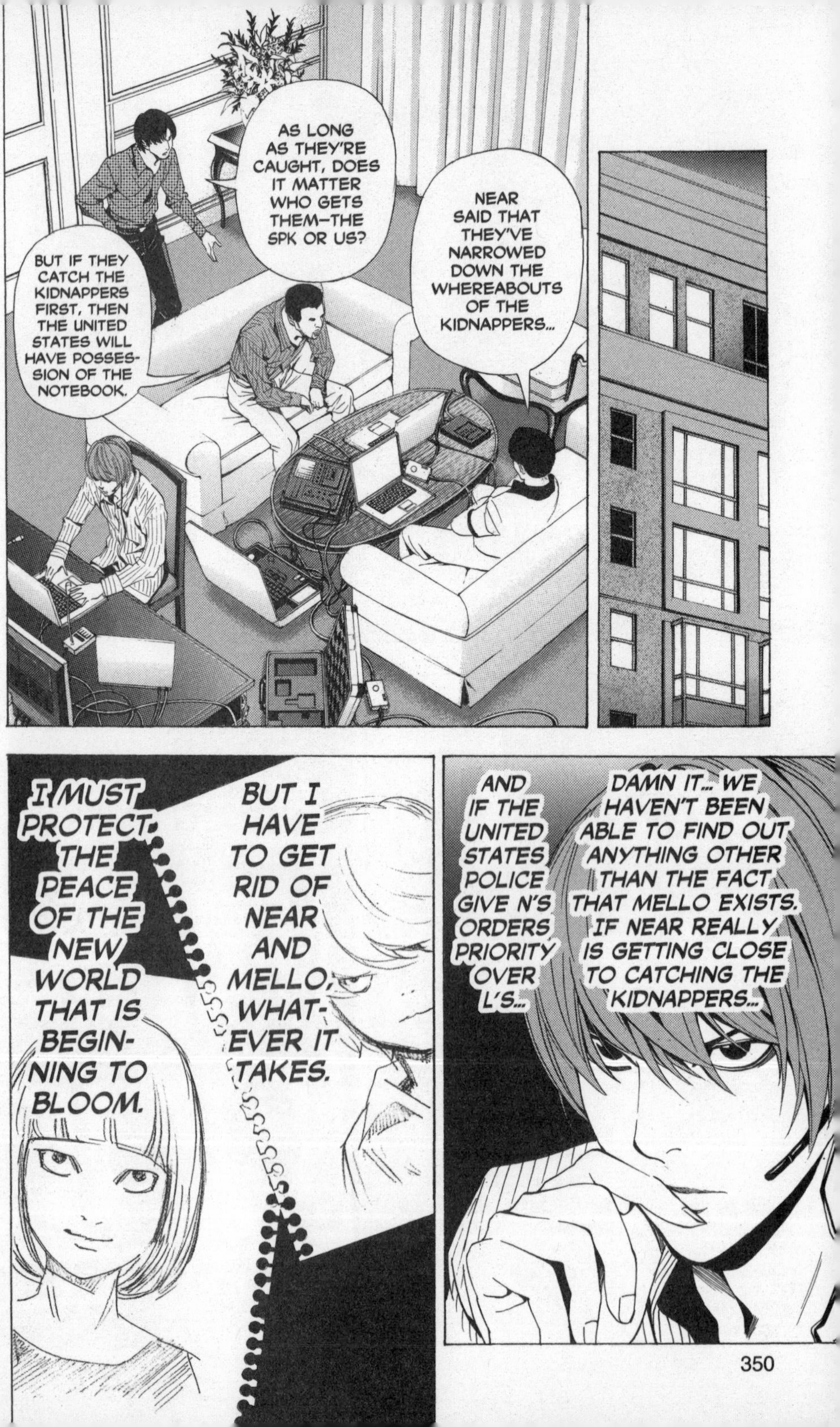
NEAR SAID THAT THEY'VE NARROWED DOWN THE WHEREABOUTS OF THE KIDNAPPERS...
AS LONG AS THEY'RE CAUGHT, DOES IT MATTER WHO GETS THEM—THE SPK OR US?
BUT IF THEY CATCH THE KIDNAPPERS FIRST, THEN THE UNITED STATES WILL HAVE POSSES-SION OF THE NOTEBOOK.
DAMN IT... WE HAVEN'T BEEN ABLE TO FIND OUT ANYTHING OTHER THAN THE FACT THAT MELLO EXISTS. IF NEAR REALLY IS GETTING CLOSE TO CATCHING THE KIDNAPPERS...
AND IF THE UNITED STATES POLICE GIVE N'S ORDERS PRIORITY OVER L'S...
BUT I HAVE TO GET RID OF NEAR AND MELLO, WHAT-EVER IT TAKES.
I MUST PROTECT THE PEACE OF THE NEW WORLD THAT IS BEGIN-NING TO BLOOM.

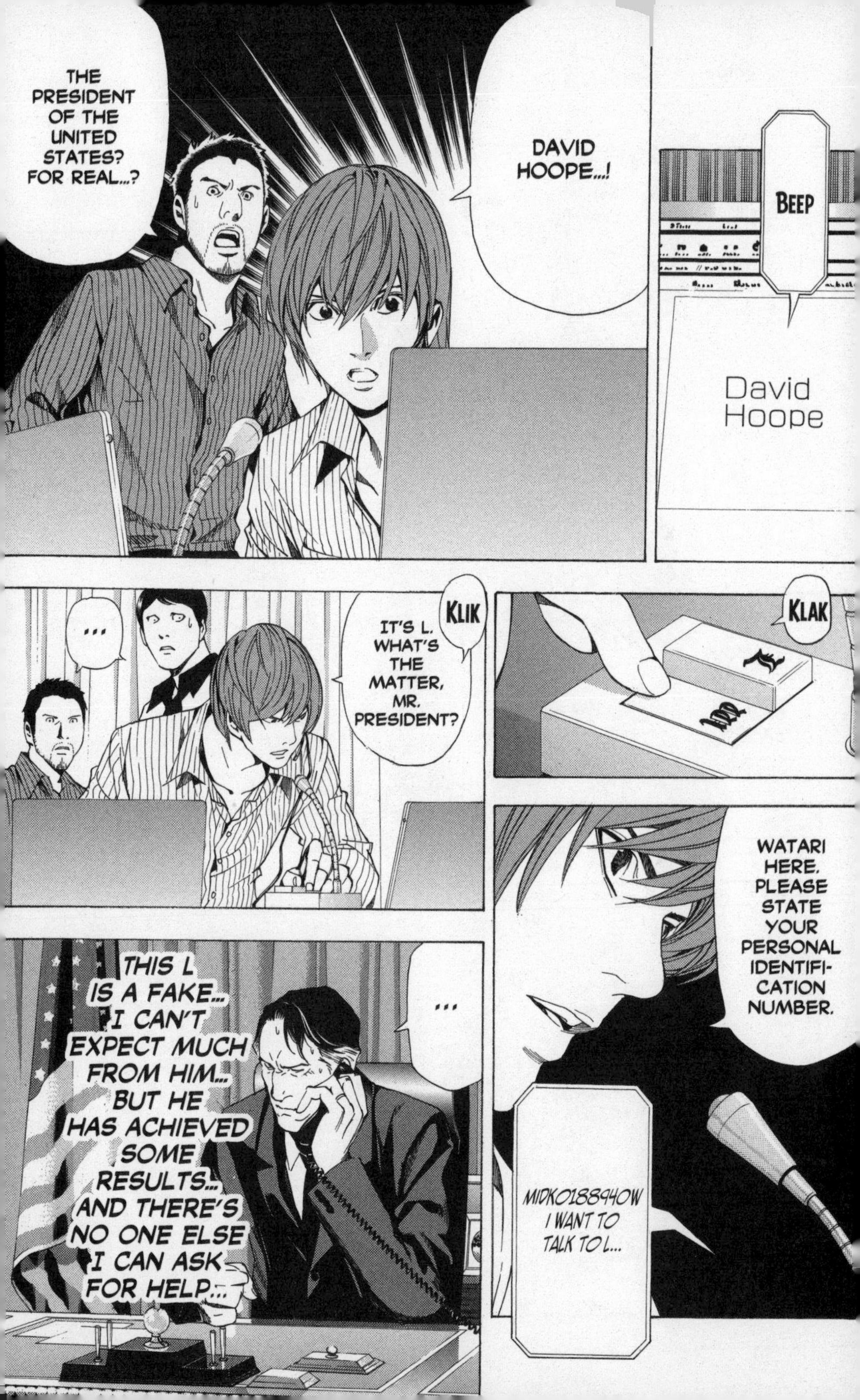
BEEP
David Hoope
DAVID HOOPE...!
THE PRESIDENT OF THE UNITED STATES? FOR REAL...?
KLAK
KLIK
IT'S L. WHAT'S THE MATTER, MR. PRESIDENT?
...
WATARI HERE. PLEASE STATE YOUR PERSONAL IDENTIFI-CATION NUMBER.
MIDKO188940W I WANT TO TALK TO L...
...
THIS L IS A FAKE... I CAN'T EXPECT MUCH FROM HIM... BUT HE HAS ACHIEVED SOME RESULTS... AND THERE'S NO ONE ELSE I CAN ASK FOR HELP...

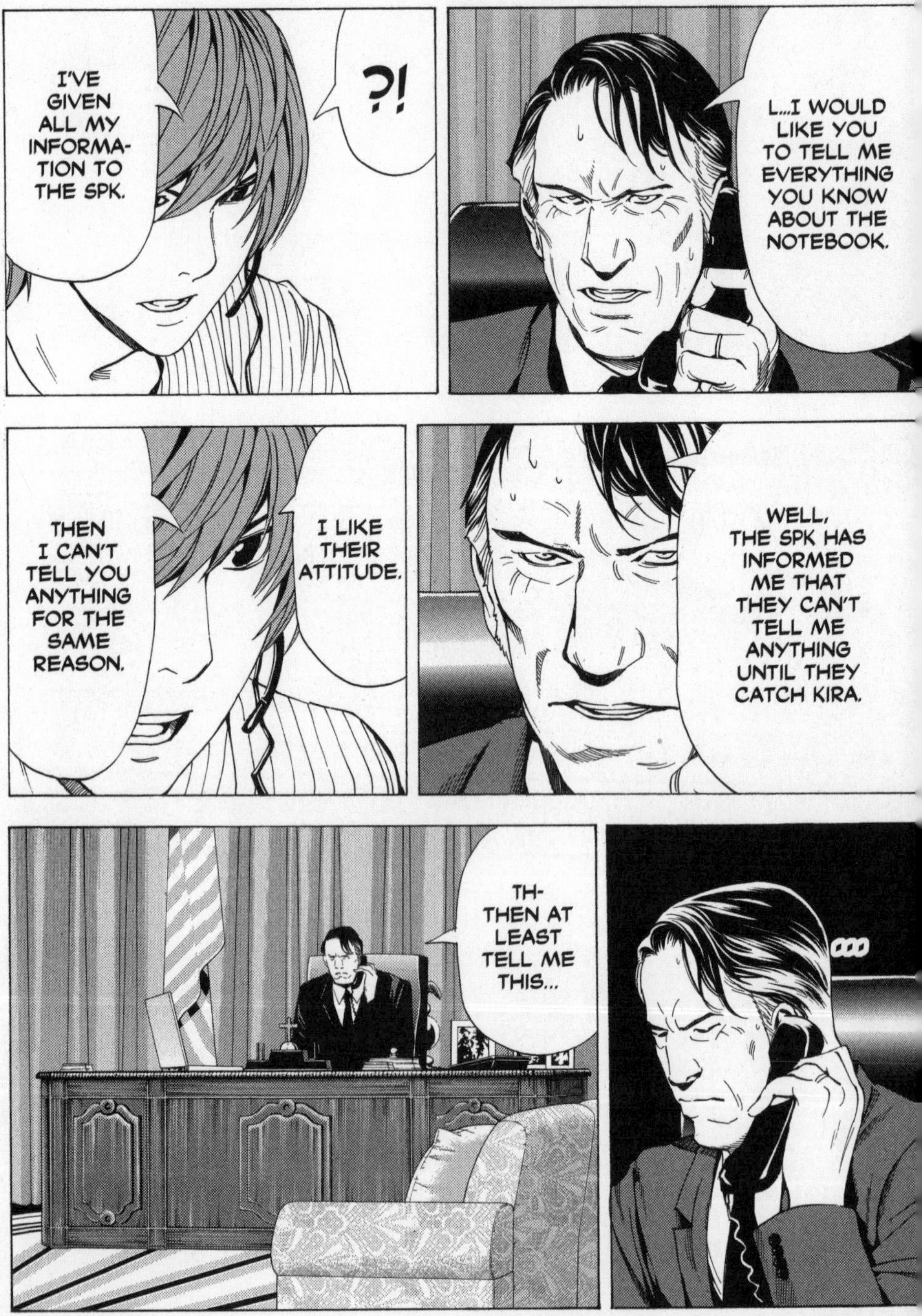
L...I WOULD LIKE YOU TO TELL ME EVERYTHING YOU KNOW ABOUT THE NOTEBOOK.
?!
I'VE GIVEN ALL MY INFORMATION TO THE SPK.
WELL, THE SPK HAS INFORMED ME THAT THEY CAN'T TELL ME ANYTHING UNTIL THEY CATCH KIRA.
I LIKE THEIR ATTITUDE.
THEN I CAN'T TELL YOU ANYTHING FOR THE SAME REASON.
TH- THEN AT LEAST TELL ME THIS...

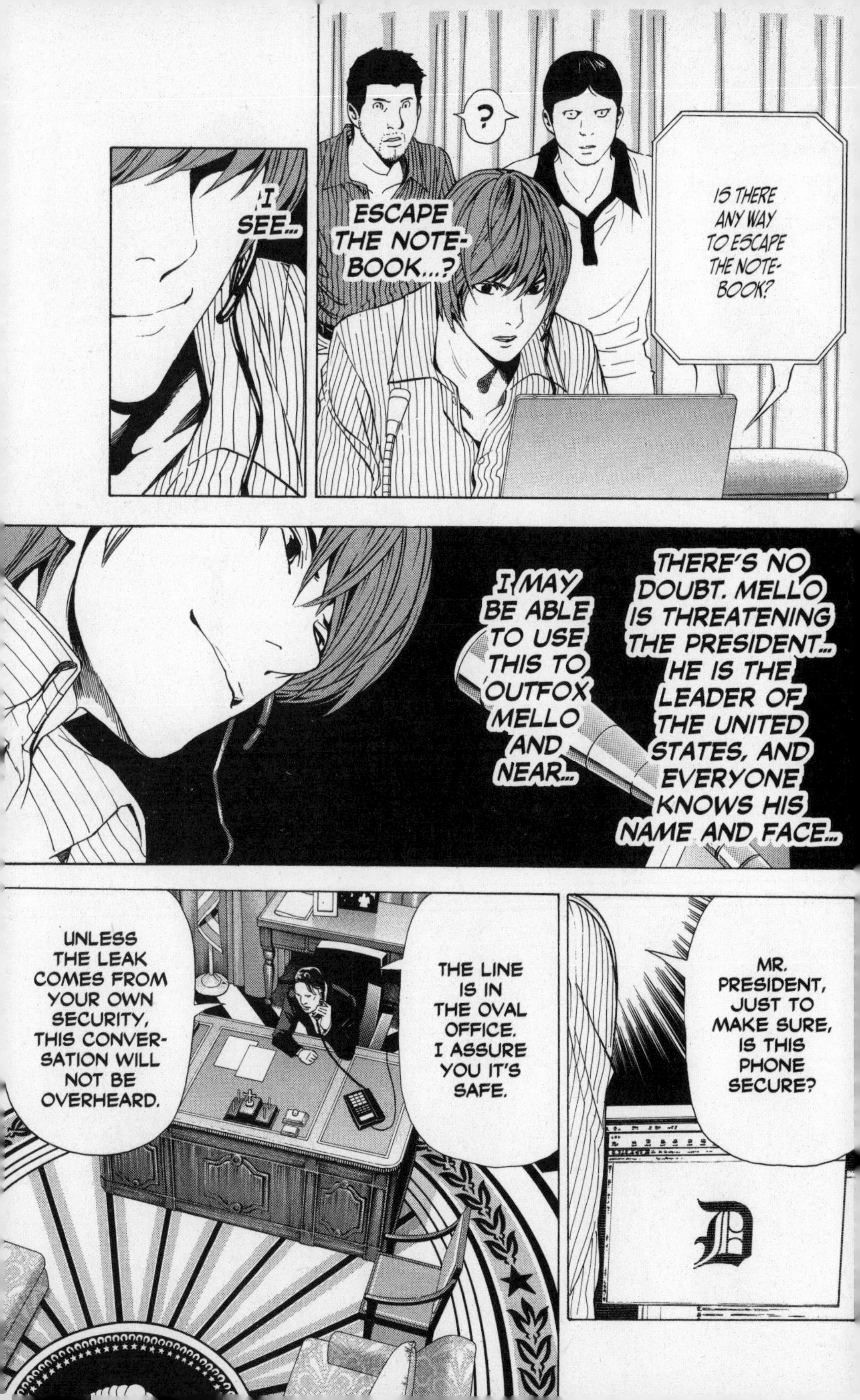
IS THERE ANY WAY TO ESCAPE THE NOTE-BOOK?
?
ESCAPE THE NOTE-BOOK...?
I SEE...
THERE'S NO DOUBT. MELLO IS THREATENING THE PRESIDENT... HE IS THE LEADER OF THE UNITED STATES, AND EVERYONE KNOWS HIS NAME AND FACE...
I MAY BE ABLE TO USE THIS TO OUTFOX MELLO AND NEAR...
MR. PRESIDENT, JUST TO MAKE SURE, IS THIS PHONE SECURE?
THE LINE IS IN THE OVAL OFFICE. I ASSURE YOU IT'S SAFE.
UNLESS THE LEAK COMES FROM YOUR OWN SECURITY, THIS CONVERSATION WILL NOT BE OVERHEARD.

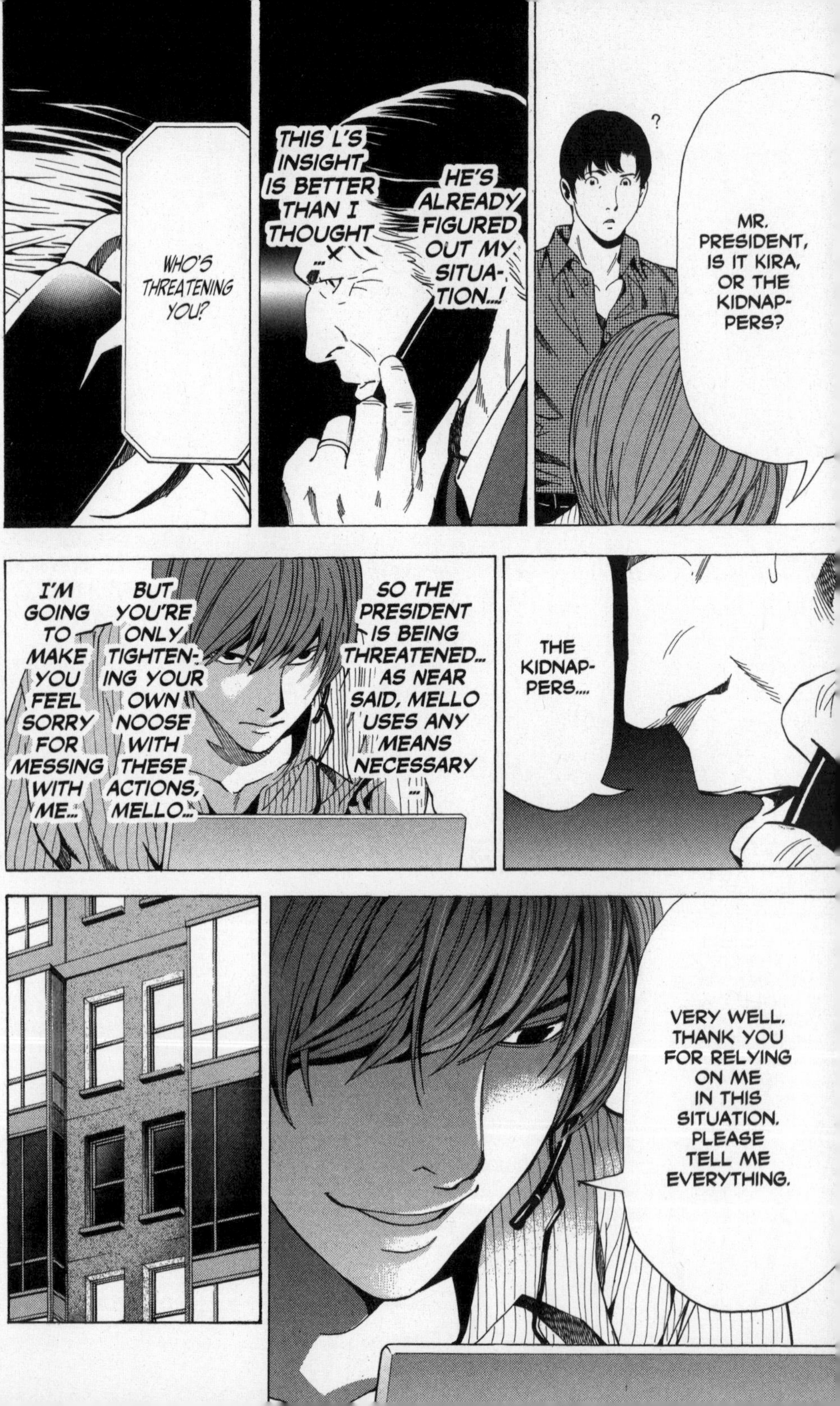
?
MR. PRESIDENT, IS IT KIRA, OR THE KIDNAPPERS?
THIS L'S INSIGHT IS BETTER THAN I THOUGHT...
HE'S ALREADY FIGURED OUT MY SITUATION...!
WHO'S THREATENING YOU?
THE KIDNAPPERS....
SO THE PRESIDENT IS BEING THREATENED... AS NEAR SAID, MELLO USES ANY MEANS NECESSARY...
BUT YOU'RE ONLY TIGHTENING YOUR OWN NOOSE WITH THESE ACTIONS, MELLO...
I'M GOING TO MAKE YOU FEEL SORRY FOR MESSING WITH ME...
VERY WELL. THANK YOU FOR RELYING ON ME IN THIS SITUATION. PLEASE TELL ME EVERYTHING.

READ THIS WAY

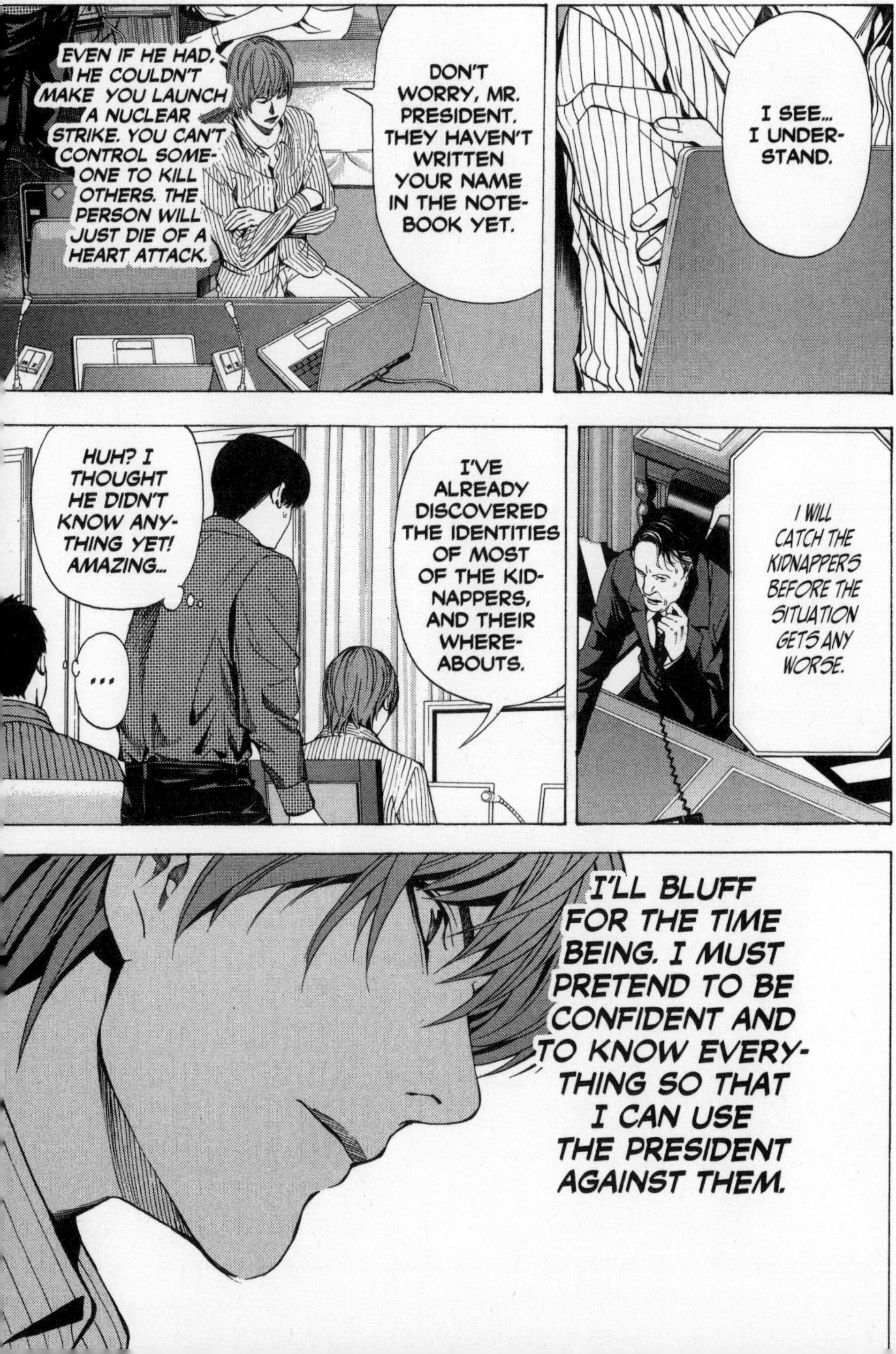
I SEE... I UNDERSTAND.
DON'T WORRY, MR. PRESIDENT. THEY HAVEN'T WRITTEN YOUR NAME IN THE NOTEBOOK YET.
EVEN IF HE HAD, HE COULDN'T MAKE YOU LAUNCH A NUCLEAR STRIKE. YOU CAN'T CONTROL SOMEONE TO KILL OTHERS. THE PERSON WILL JUST DIE OF A HEART ATTACK.
I WILL CATCH THE KIDNAPPERS BEFORE THE SITUATION GETS ANY WORSE.
I'VE ALREADY DISCOVERED THE IDENTITIES OF MOST OF THE KIDNAPPERS, AND THEIR WHEREABOUTS.
HUH? I THOUGHT HE DIDN'T KNOW ANYTHING YET! AMAZING...
...
I'LL BLUFF FOR THE TIME BEING. I MUST PRETEND TO BE CONFIDENT AND TO KNOW EVERYTHING SO THAT I CAN USE THE PRESIDENT AGAINST THEM.

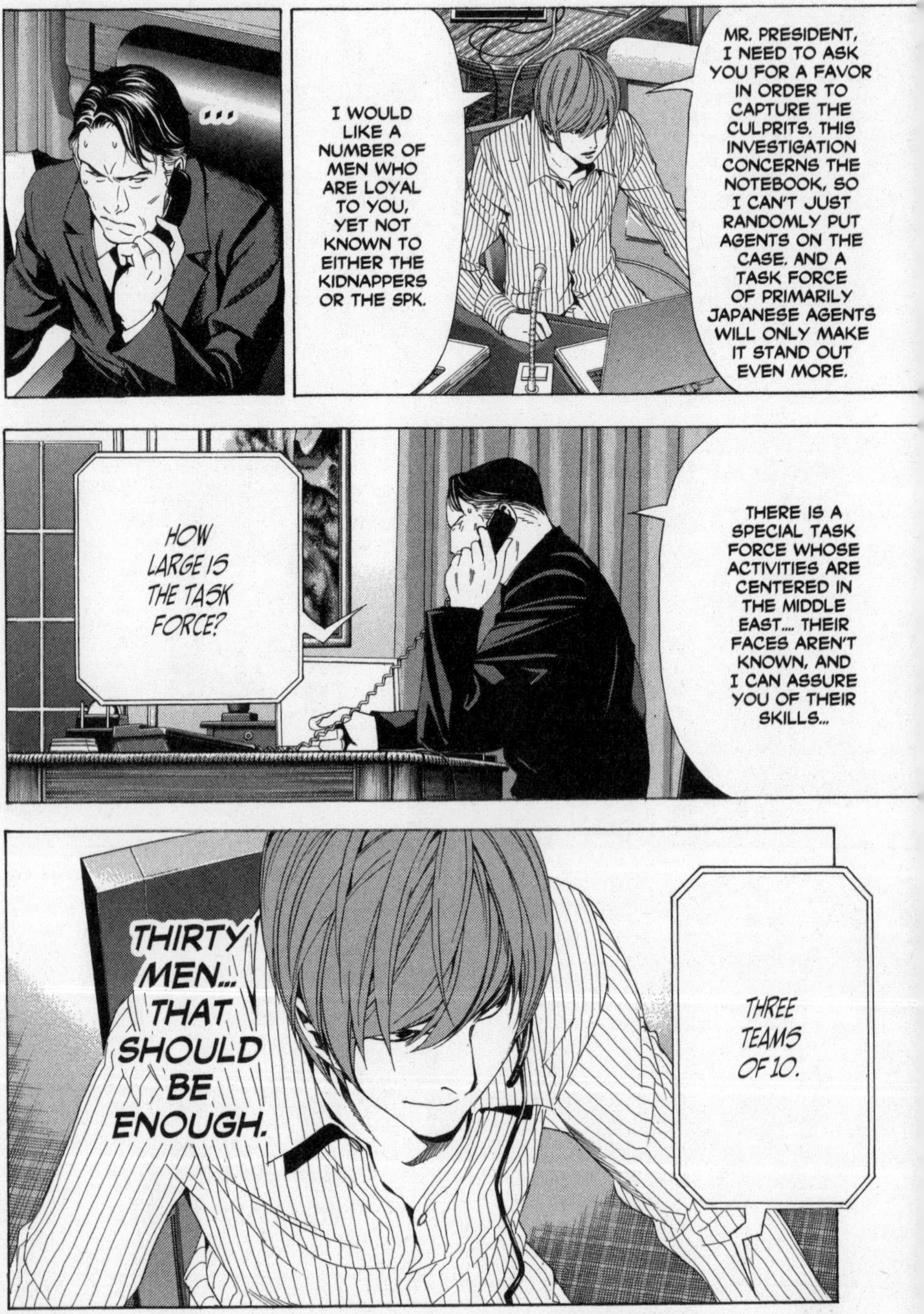
MR. PRESIDENT, I NEED TO ASK YOU FOR A FAVOR IN ORDER TO CAPTURE THE CULPRITS. THIS INVESTIGATION CONCERNS THE NOTEBOOK, SO I CAN'T JUST RANDOMLY PUT AGENTS ON THE CASE. AND A TASK FORCE OF PRIMARILY JAPANESE AGENTS WILL ONLY MAKE IT STAND OUT EVEN MORE.
I WOULD LIKE A NUMBER OF MEN WHO ARE LOYAL TO YOU, YET NOT KNOWN TO EITHER THE KIDNAPPERS OR THE SPK.
...
THERE IS A SPECIAL TASK FORCE WHOSE ACTIVITIES ARE CENTERED IN THE MIDDLE EAST.... THEIR FACES AREN'T KNOWN, AND I CAN ASSURE YOU OF THEIR SKILLS...
HOW LARGE IS THE TASK FORCE?
THREE TEAMS OF 10.
THIRTY MEN... THAT SHOULD BE ENOUGH.

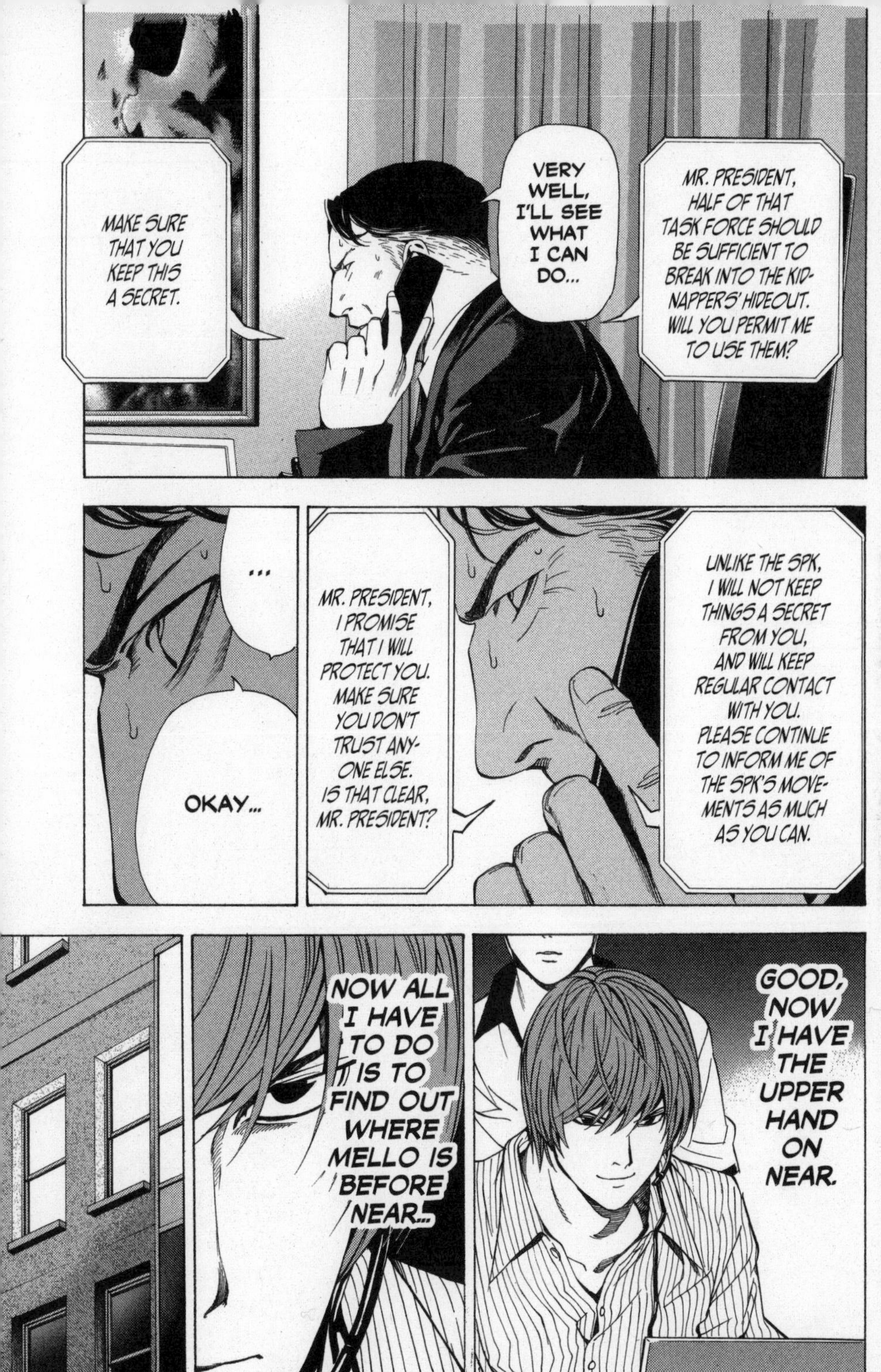
MR. PRESIDENT, HALF OF THAT TASK FORCE SHOULD BE SUFFICIENT TO BREAK INTO THE KID-NAPPERS' HIDEOUT. WILL YOU PERMIT ME TO USE THEM?
VERY WELL, I'LL SEE WHAT I CAN DO...
MAKE SURE THAT YOU KEEP THIS A SECRET.
UNLIKE THE SPK, I WILL NOT KEEP THINGS A SECRET FROM YOU, AND WILL KEEP REGULAR CONTACT WITH YOU. PLEASE CONTINUE TO INFORM ME OF THE SPK'S MOVE-MENTS AS MUCH AS YOU CAN.
MR. PRESIDENT, I PROMISE THAT I WILL PROTECT YOU. MAKE SURE YOU DON'T TRUST ANY-ONE ELSE. IS THAT CLEAR, MR. PRESIDENT?
...
OKAY...
GOOD, NOW I HAVE THE UPPER HAND ON NEAR.
NOW ALL I HAVE TO DO IS TO FIND OUT WHERE MELLO IS BEFORE NEAR...

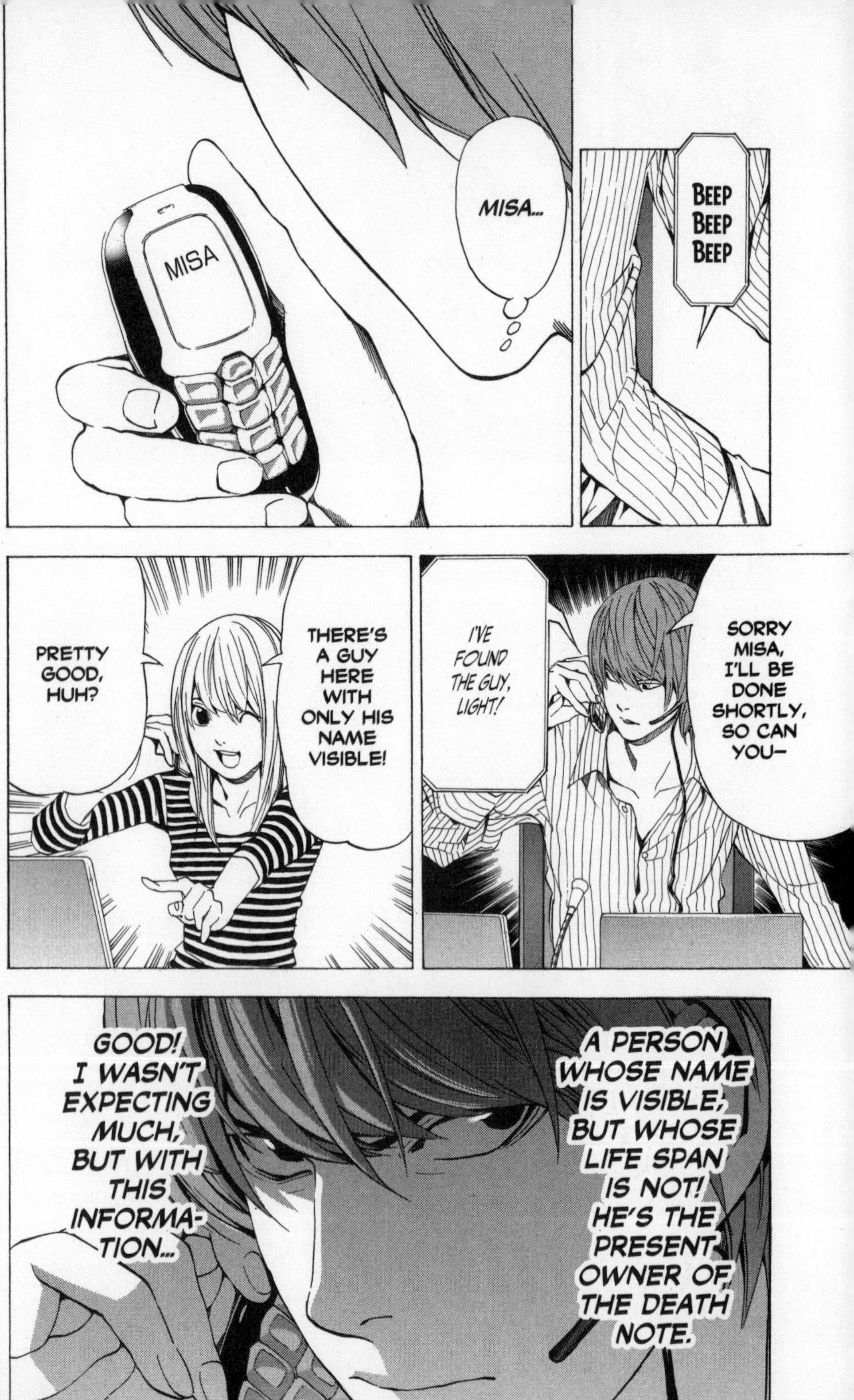
BEEP BEEP BEEP
MISA...
MISA
SORRY MISA, I'LL BE DONE SHORTLY, SO CAN YOU—
I'VE FOUND THE GUY, LIGHT!
THERE'S A GUY HERE WITH ONLY HIS NAME VISIBLE!
PRETTY GOOD, HUH?
A PERSON WHOSE NAME IS VISIBLE, BUT WHOSE LIFE SPAN IS NOT! HE'S THE PRESENT OWNER OF THE DEATH NOTE.
GOOD! I WASN'T EXPECTING MUCH, BUT WITH THIS INFORMA-TION...

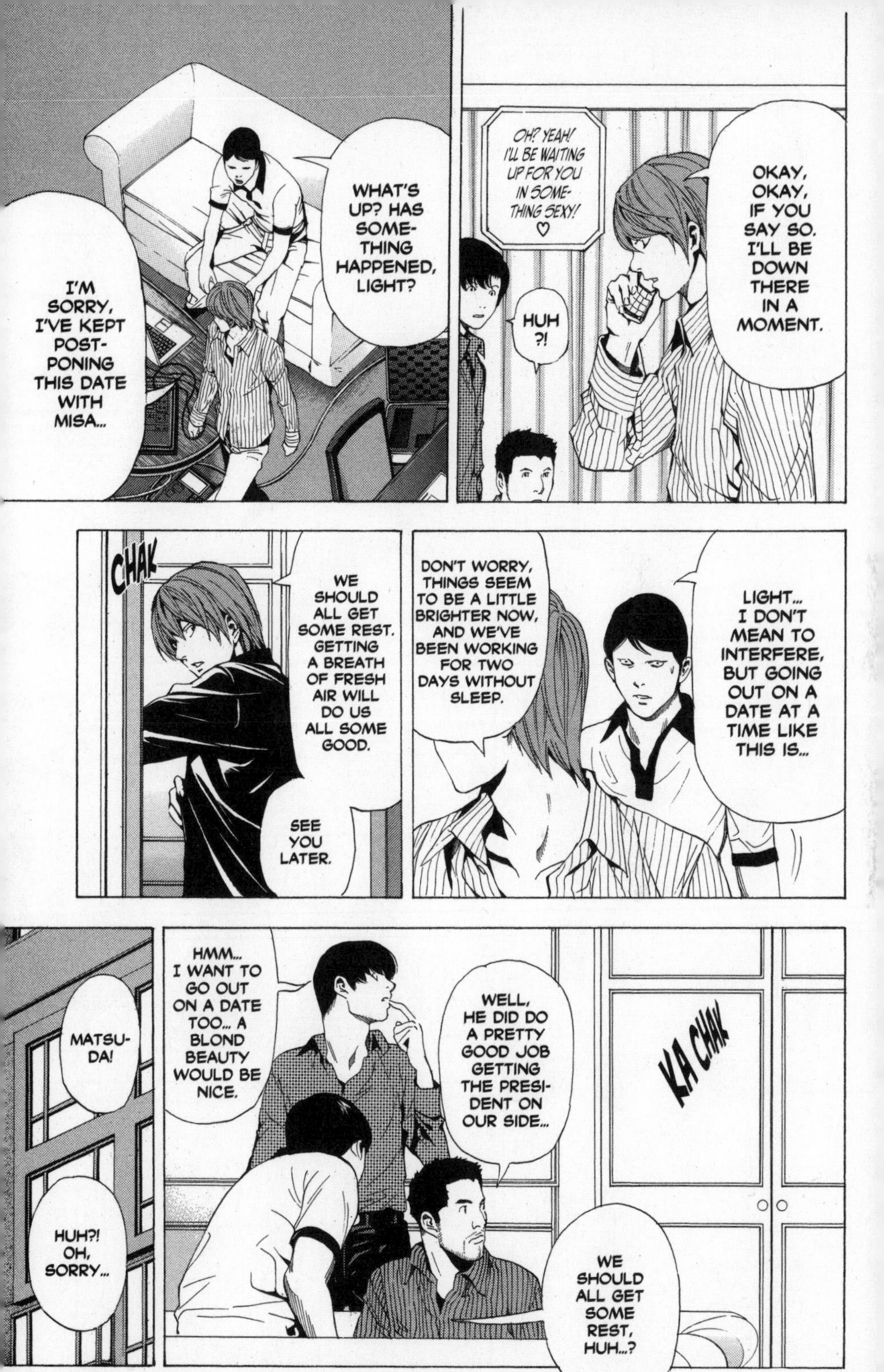
OKAY, OKAY, IF YOU SAY SO. I'LL BE DOWN THERE IN A MOMENT.
OH? YEAH! I'LL BE WAITING UP FOR YOU IN SOME-THING SEXY! ♡
HUH ?!
WHAT'S UP? HAS SOME-THING HAPPENED, LIGHT?
I'M SORRY, I'VE KEPT POST-PONING THIS DATE WITH MISA...
LIGHT... I DON'T MEAN TO INTERFERE, BUT GOING OUT ON A DATE AT A TIME LIKE THIS IS...
DON'T WORRY, THINGS SEEM TO BE A LITTLE BRIGHTER NOW, AND WE'VE BEEN WORKING FOR TWO DAYS WITHOUT SLEEP.
CHAK
WE SHOULD ALL GET SOME REST. GETTING A BREATH OF FRESH AIR WILL DO US ALL SOME GOOD.
SEE YOU LATER.
KA CHAK
WELL, HE DID DO A PRETTY GOOD JOB GETTING THE PRESI-DENT ON OUR SIDE...
WE SHOULD ALL GET SOME REST, HUH...?
HMM... I WANT TO GO OUT ON A DATE TOO... A BLOND BEAUTY WOULD BE NICE.
MATSU-DA!
HUH?! OH, SORRY...

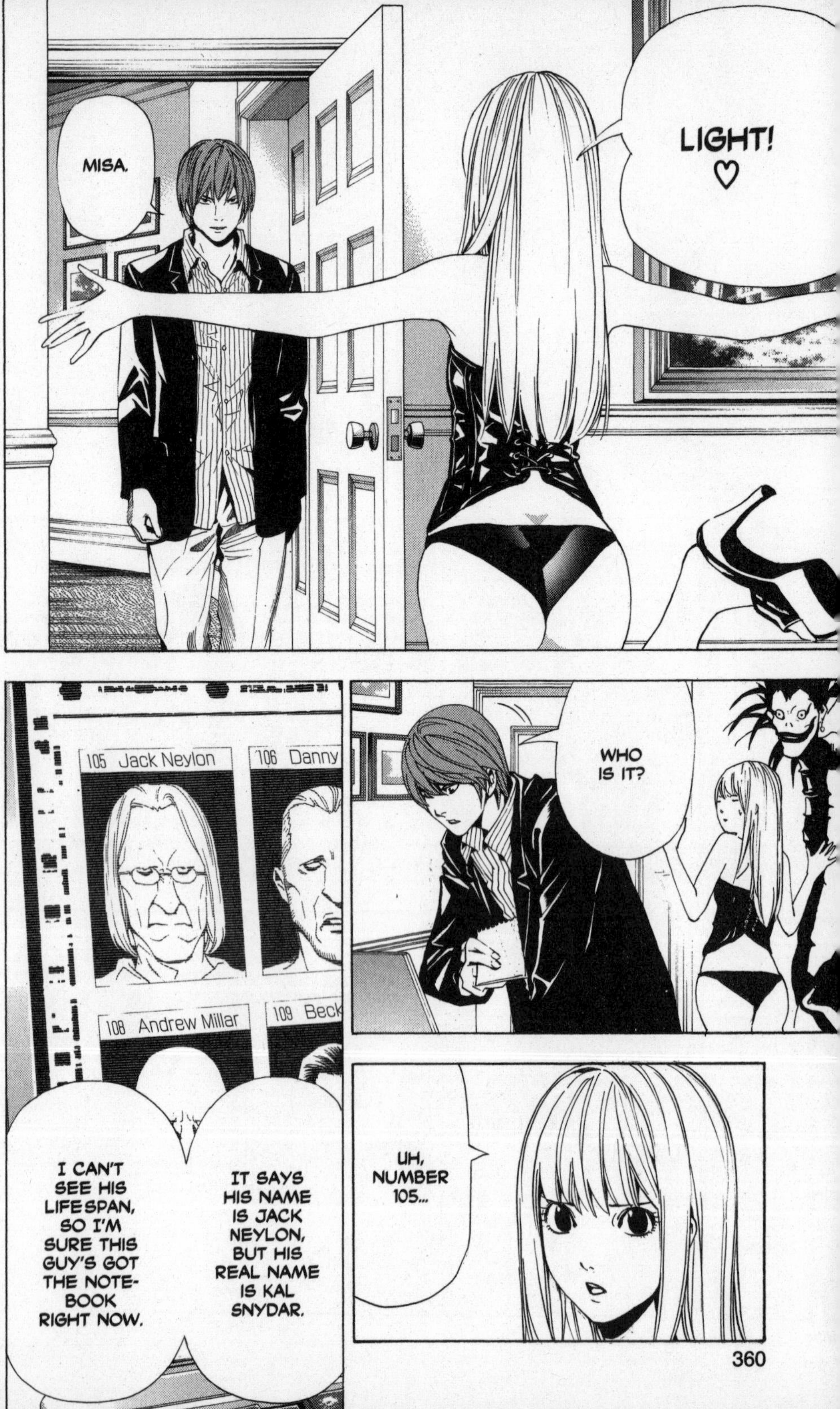
LIGHT! ♡
MISA.
WHO IS IT?
UH, NUMBER 105...
105 Jack Neylon
106 Danny
108 Andrew Millar
109 Beck
IT SAYS HIS NAME IS JACK NEYLON, BUT HIS REAL NAME IS KAL SNYDAR.
I CAN'T SEE HIS LIFESPAN, SO I'M SURE THIS GUY'S GOT THE NOTE-BOOK RIGHT NOW.

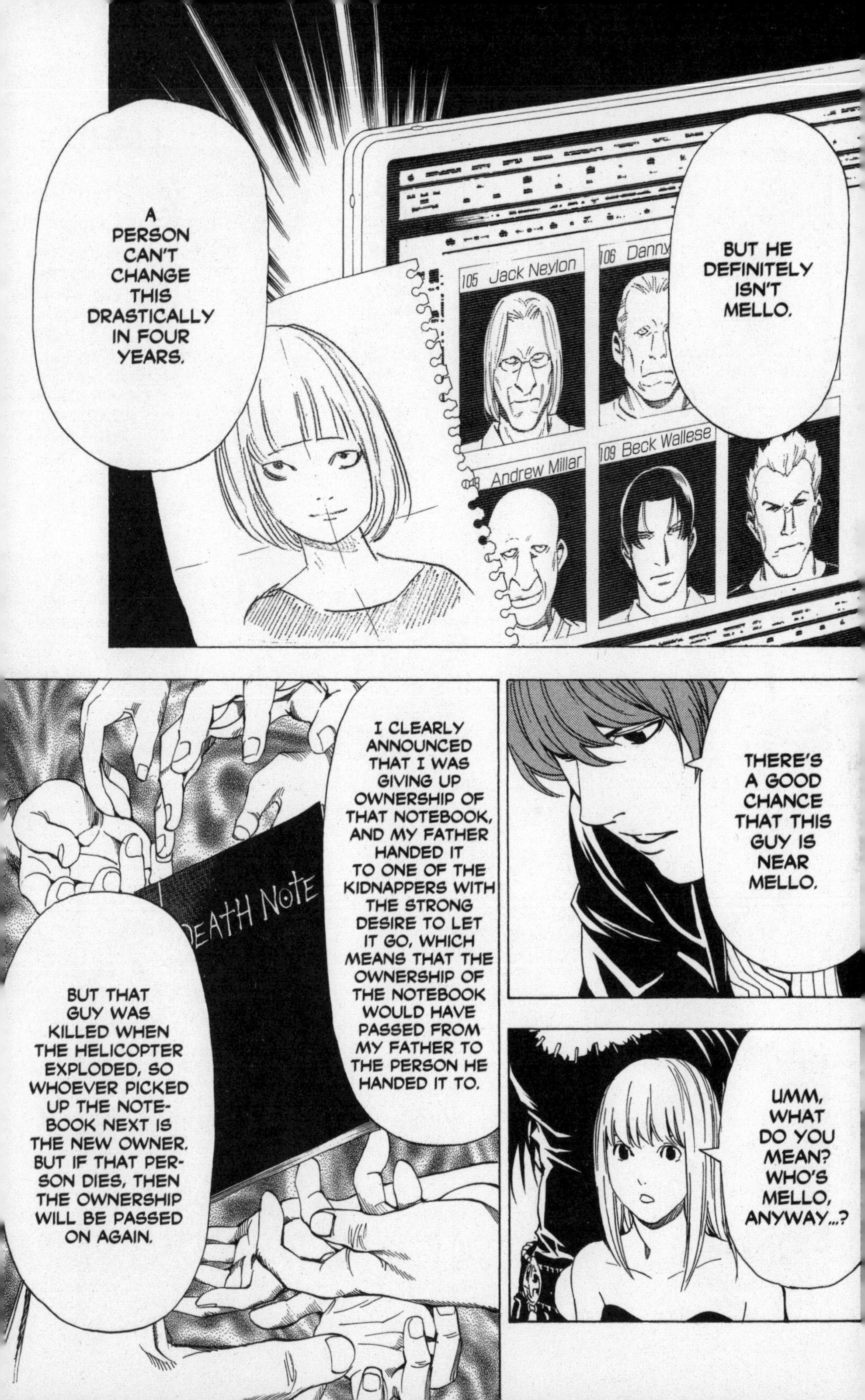
BUT HE DEFINITELY ISN'T MELLO.
105 Jack Neylon
106 Danny
Andrew Millar
109 Beck Wallese
A PERSON CAN'T CHANGE THIS DRASTICALLY IN FOUR YEARS.
THERE'S A GOOD CHANCE THAT THIS GUY IS NEAR MELLO.
UMM, WHAT DO YOU MEAN? WHO'S MELLO, ANYWAY...?
I CLEARLY ANNOUNCED THAT I WAS GIVING UP OWNERSHIP OF THAT NOTEBOOK, AND MY FATHER HANDED IT TO ONE OF THE KIDNAPPERS WITH THE STRONG DESIRE TO LET IT GO, WHICH MEANS THAT THE OWNERSHIP OF THE NOTEBOOK WOULD HAVE PASSED FROM MY FATHER TO THE PERSON HE HANDED IT TO.
DEATH NOTE
BUT THAT GUY WAS KILLED WHEN THE HELICOPTER EXPLODED, SO WHOEVER PICKED UP THE NOTE-BOOK NEXT IS THE NEW OWNER. BUT IF THAT PER-SON DIES, THEN THE OWNERSHIP WILL BE PASSED ON AGAIN.

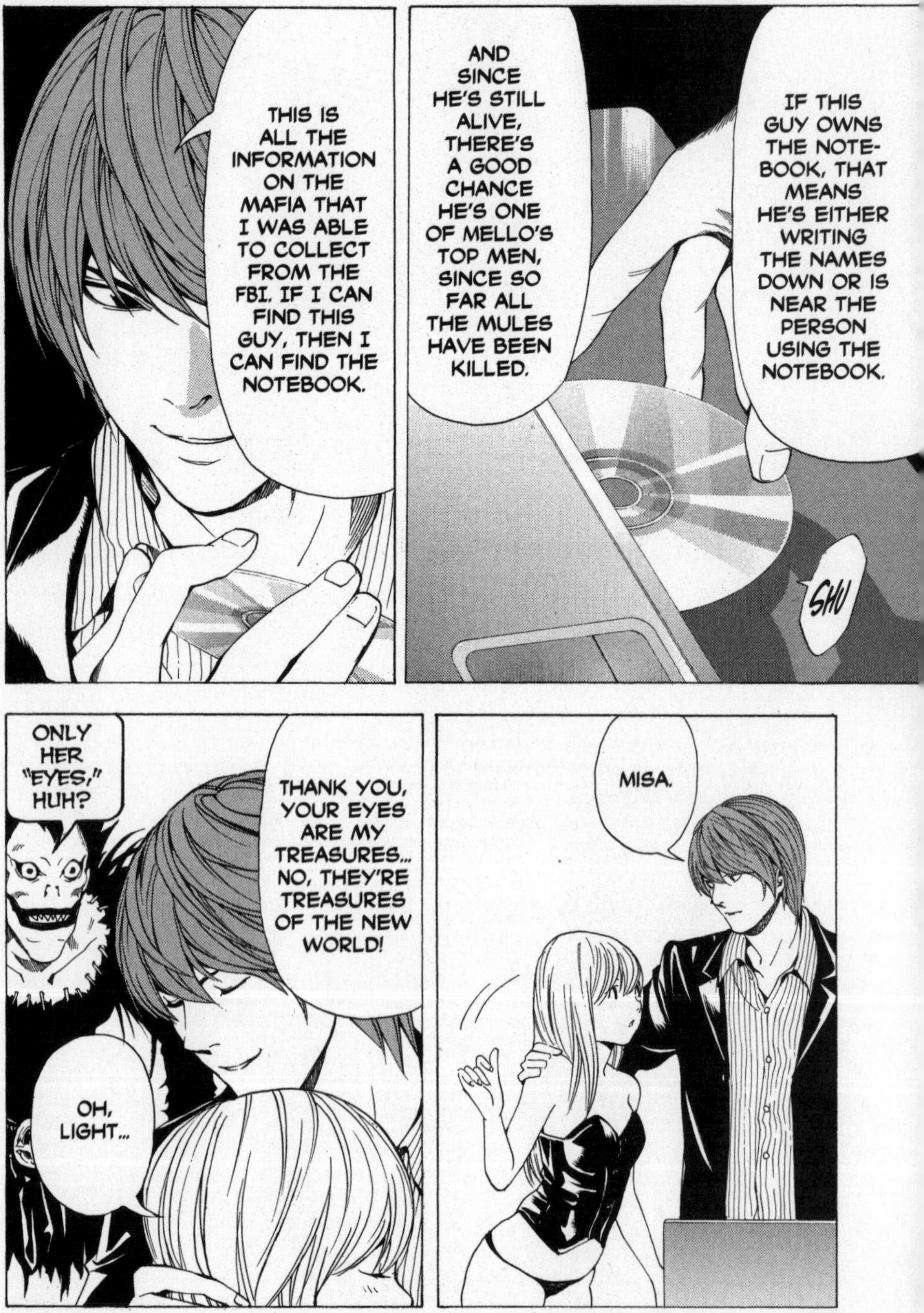
IF THIS GUY OWNS THE NOTE-BOOK, THAT MEANS HE'S EITHER WRITING THE NAMES DOWN OR IS NEAR THE PERSON USING THE NOTEBOOK.
AND SINCE HE'S STILL ALIVE, THERE'S A GOOD CHANCE HE'S ONE OF MELLO'S TOP MEN, SINCE SO FAR ALL THE MULES HAVE BEEN KILLED.
SHU
THIS IS ALL THE INFORMATION ON THE MAFIA THAT I WAS ABLE TO COLLECT FROM THE FBI. IF I CAN FIND THIS GUY, THEN I CAN FIND THE NOTEBOOK.
MISA.
THANK YOU, YOUR EYES ARE MY TREASURES... NO, THEY'RE TREASURES OF THE NEW WORLD!
ONLY HER "EYES," HUH?
OH, LIGHT...

READ THIS WAY

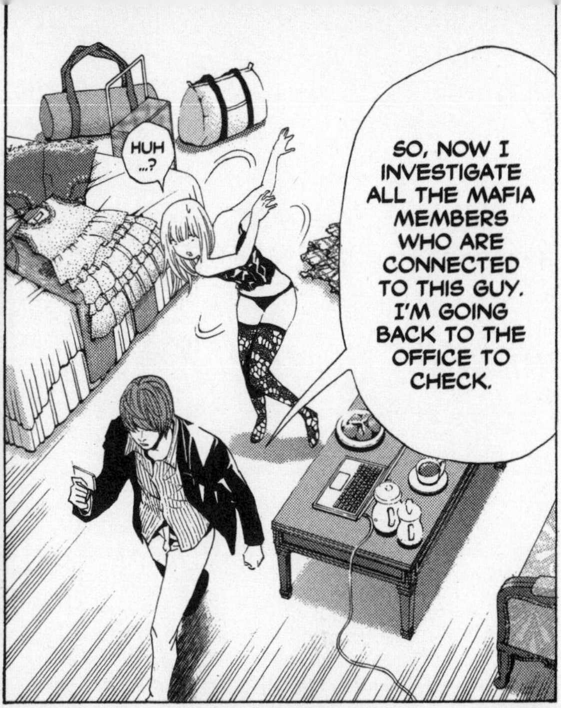
SO, NOW I INVESTIGATE ALL THE MAFIA MEMBERS WHO ARE CONNECTED TO THIS GUY. I'M GOING BACK TO THE OFFICE TO CHECK.
HUH ...?

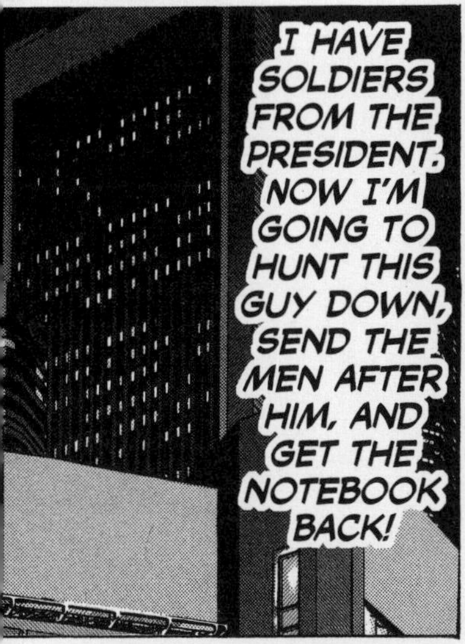
I HAVE SOLDIERS FROM THE PRESIDENT. NOW I'M GOING TO HUNT THIS GUY DOWN, SEND THE MEN AFTER HIM, AND GET THE NOTEBOOK BACK!

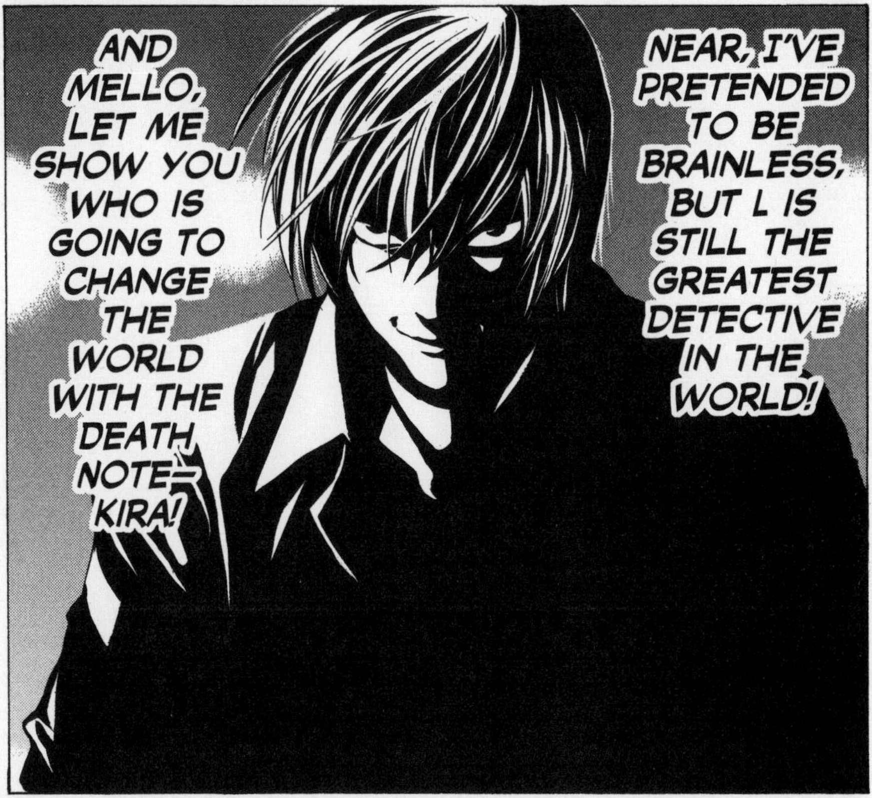
NEAR, I'VE PRETENDED TO BE BRAINLESS, BUT L IS STILL THE GREATEST DETECTIVE IN THE WORLD!
AND MELLO, LET ME SHOW YOU WHO IS GOING TO CHANGE THE WORLD WITH THE DEATH NOTE— KIRA!

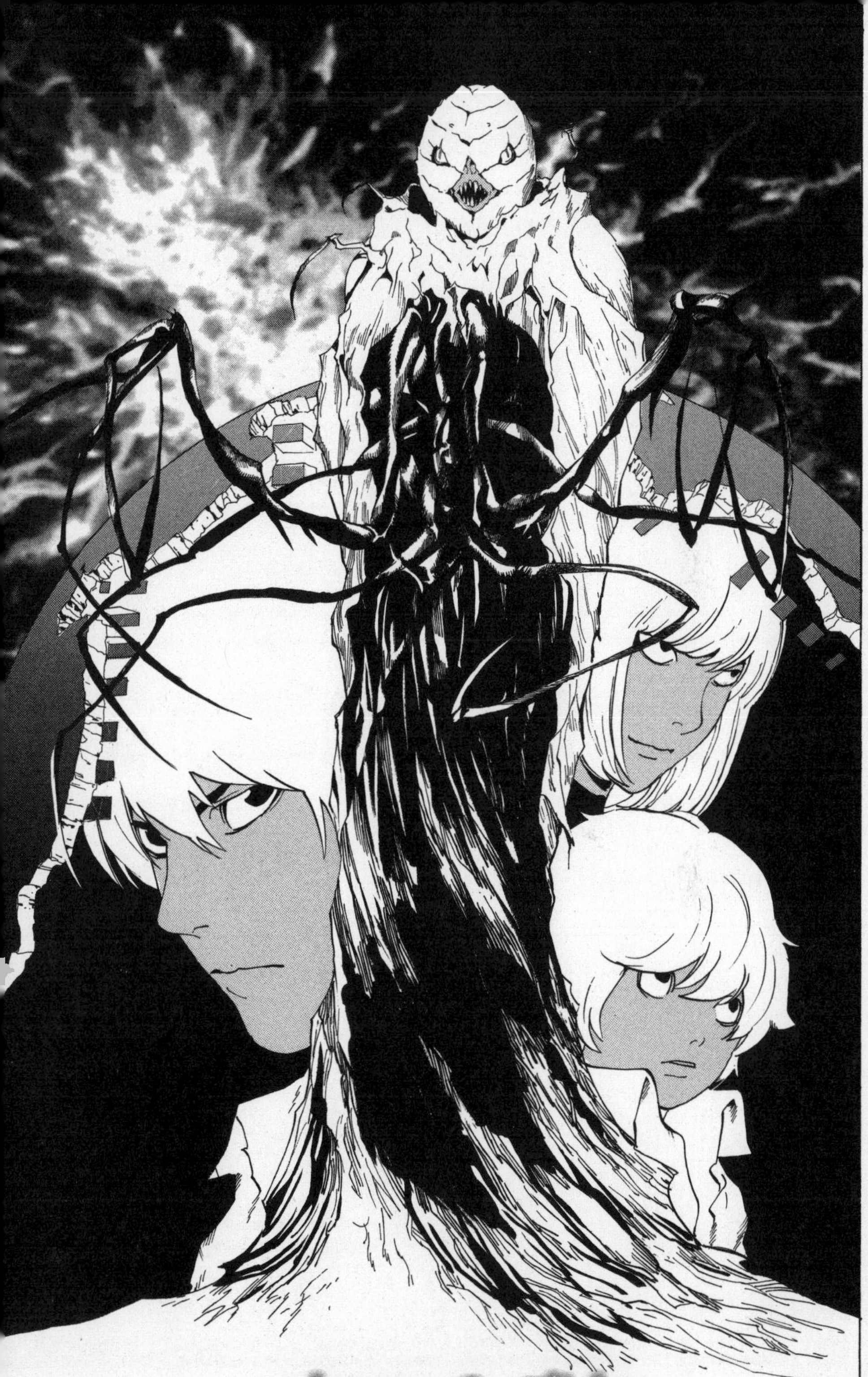

# chapter 69 Flight

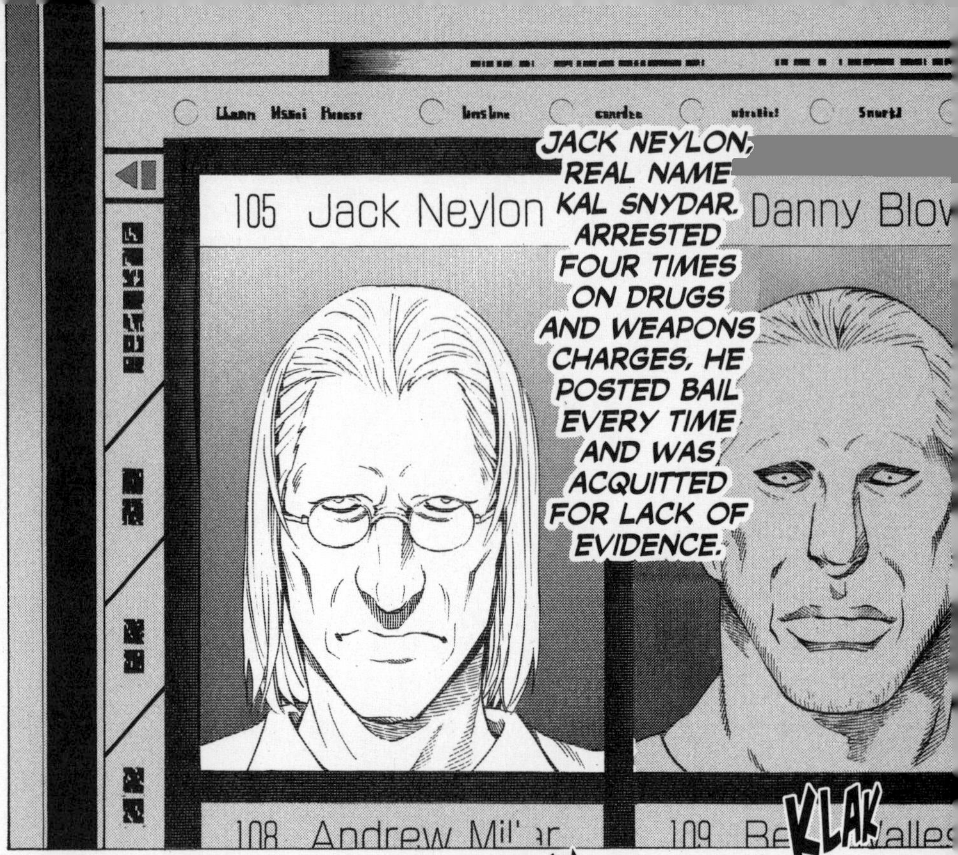
105 Jack Neylon
JACK NEYLON, REAL NAME KAL SNYDAR. ARRESTED FOUR TIMES ON DRUGS AND WEAPONS CHARGES, HE POSTED BAIL EVERY TIME AND WAS ACQUITTED FOR LACK OF EVIDENCE.
KLAK
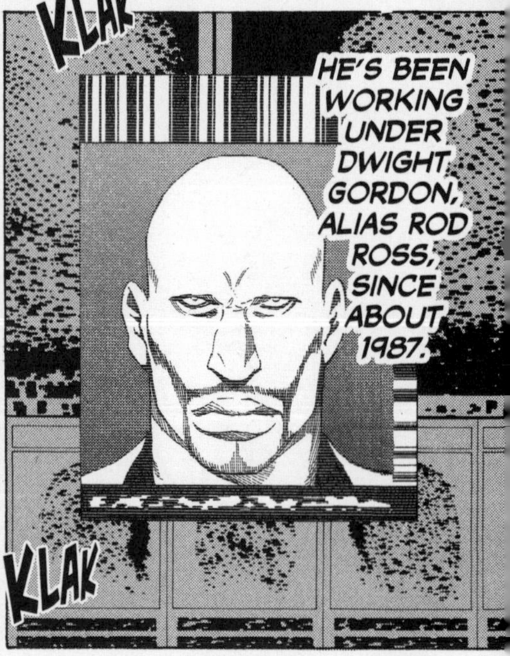
KLAK
HE'S BEEN WORKING UNDER DWIGHT GORDON, ALIAS ROD ROSS, SINCE ABOUT 1987.
KLAK
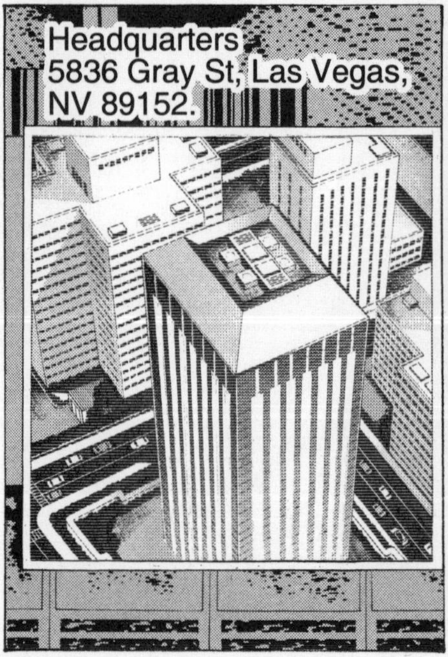
Headquarters
5836 Gray St, Las Vegas, NV 89152.

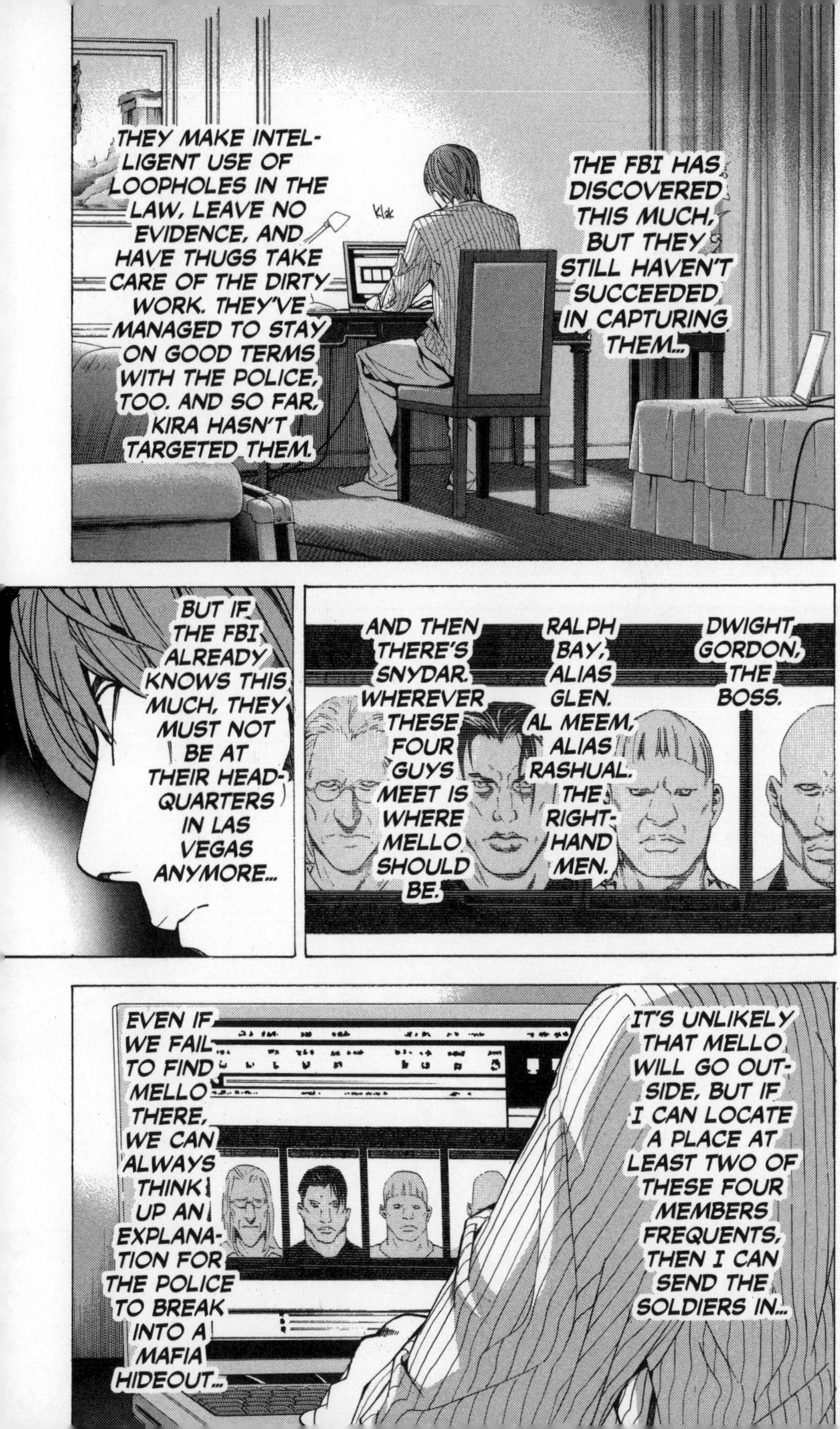
THE FBI HAS DISCOVERED THIS MUCH, BUT THEY STILL HAVEN'T SUCCEEDED IN CAPTURING THEM...
klak
THEY MAKE INTELLIGENT USE OF LOOPHOLES IN THE LAW, LEAVE NO EVIDENCE, AND HAVE THUGS TAKE CARE OF THE DIRTY WORK. THEY'VE MANAGED TO STAY ON GOOD TERMS WITH THE POLICE, TOO. AND SO FAR, KIRA HASN'T TARGETED THEM.
DWIGHT GORDON, THE BOSS.
RALPH BAY, ALIAS GLEN. AL MEEM, ALIAS RASHUAL. THE RIGHT-HAND MEN.
AND THEN THERE'S SNYDAR. WHEREVER THESE FOUR GUYS MEET IS WHERE MELLO SHOULD BE.
BUT IF THE FBI ALREADY KNOWS THIS MUCH, THEY MUST NOT BE AT THEIR HEADQUARTERS IN LAS VEGAS ANYMORE...
IT'S UNLIKELY THAT MELLO WILL GO OUTSIDE, BUT IF I CAN LOCATE A PLACE AT LEAST TWO OF THESE FOUR MEMBERS FREQUENTS, THEN I CAN SEND THE SOLDIERS IN...
EVEN IF WE FAIL TO FIND MELLO THERE, WE CAN ALWAYS THINK UP AN EXPLANATION FOR THE POLICE TO BREAK INTO A MAFIA HIDEOUT...

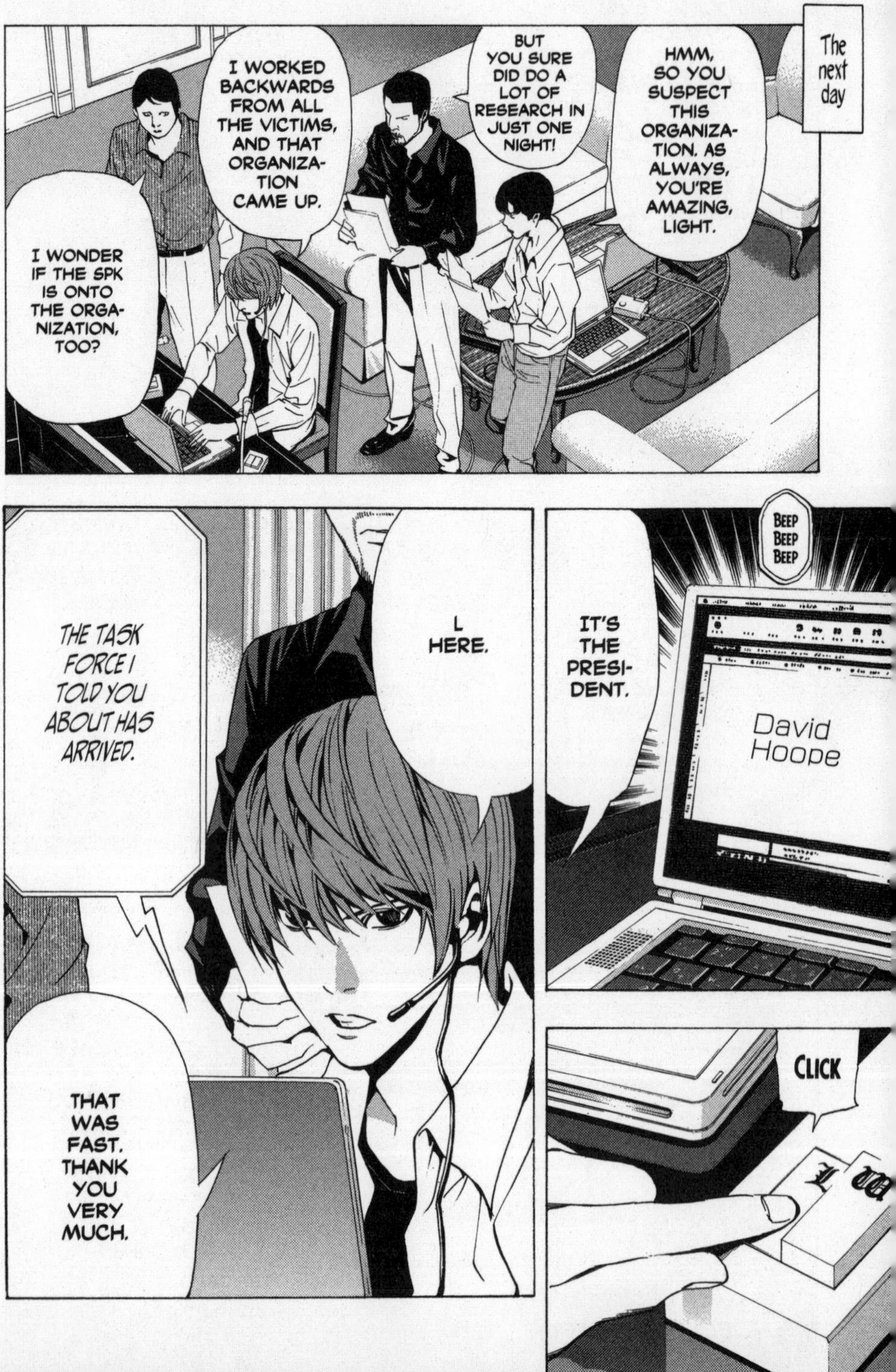
The next day
HMM, SO YOU SUSPECT THIS ORGANIZATION. AS ALWAYS, YOU'RE AMAZING, LIGHT.
BUT YOU SURE DID DO A LOT OF RESEARCH IN JUST ONE NIGHT!
I WORKED BACKWARDS FROM ALL THE VICTIMS, AND THAT ORGANIZATION CAME UP.
I WONDER IF THE SPK IS ONTO THE ORGANIZATION, TOO?
BEEP BEEP BEEP
IT'S THE PRESIDENT.
David Hoope
CLICK
L HERE.
THE TASK FORCE I TOLD YOU ABOUT HAS ARRIVED.
THAT WAS FAST. THANK YOU VERY MUCH.

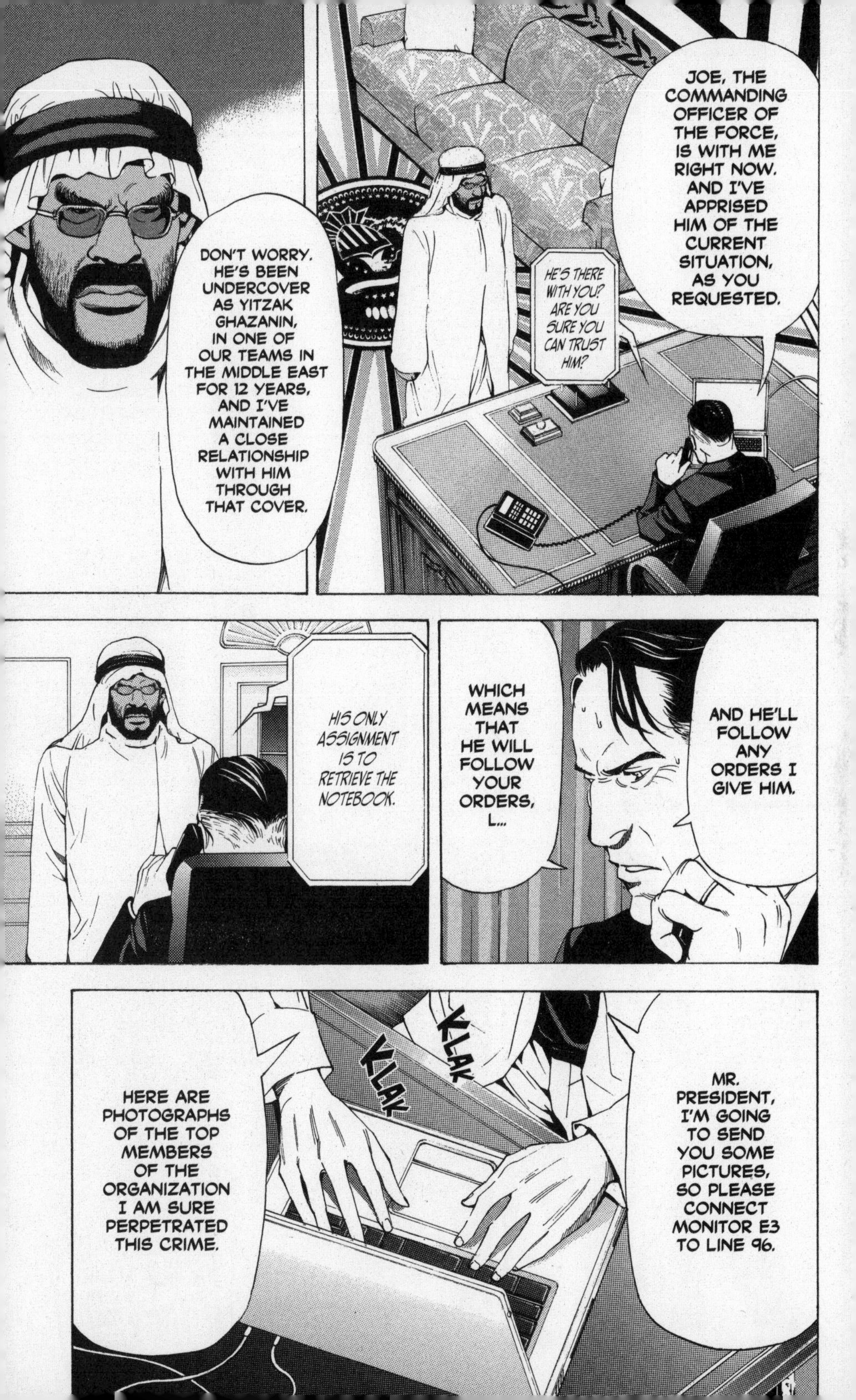
JOE, THE COMMANDING OFFICER OF THE FORCE, IS WITH ME RIGHT NOW. AND I'VE APPRISED HIM OF THE CURRENT SITUATION, AS YOU REQUESTED.
HE'S THERE WITH YOU? ARE YOU SURE YOU CAN TRUST HIM?
DON'T WORRY. HE'S BEEN UNDERCOVER AS YITZAK GHAZANIN, IN ONE OF OUR TEAMS IN THE MIDDLE EAST FOR 12 YEARS, AND I'VE MAINTAINED A CLOSE RELATIONSHIP WITH HIM THROUGH THAT COVER.
AND HE'LL FOLLOW ANY ORDERS I GIVE HIM.
WHICH MEANS THAT HE WILL FOLLOW YOUR ORDERS, L...
HIS ONLY ASSIGNMENT IS TO RETRIEVE THE NOTEBOOK.
MR. PRESIDENT, I'M GOING TO SEND YOU SOME PICTURES, SO PLEASE CONNECT MONITOR E3 TO LINE 96.
KLAK
KLAK
HERE ARE PHOTOGRAPHS OF THE TOP MEMBERS OF THE ORGANIZATION I AM SURE PERPETRATED THIS CRIME.

THE MAN ON THE TOP RIGHT IS ROD ROSS, SAID TO BE THE BOSS. RIGHT UNDER HIM IS GLEN HUMPHREYS. THE TOP LEFT IS RASHUAL BIDD. THESE THREE ARE THE TOP MEMBERS OF THE ORGANIZATION.
AND AT THE BOTTOM LEFT IS MELLO, WHO IS CONSIDERED TO BE THE MASTERMIND BEHIND ALL OF THIS, BUT I DON'T HAVE A PHOTOGRAPH OF HIM.
I'VE COME TO THE CONCLUSION THAT THE NOTEBOOK SHOULD BE AT A PLACE WHERE ALL FOUR OF THOSE MEMBERS ARE, AND THAT IS WHERE YOU'LL STRIKE.
CAN I KILL THEM?
...
YES, WE HAVE NO CHOICE.
...
IF WE HESITATE TO KILL THEM, THE PRESIDENT— NO, THE WHOLE WORLD— COULD BE IN DANGER.

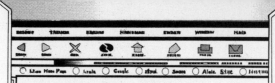

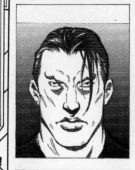

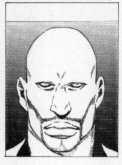

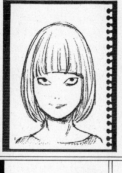

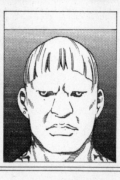

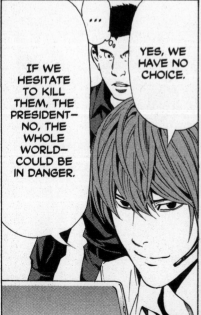

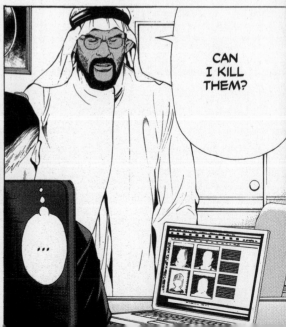

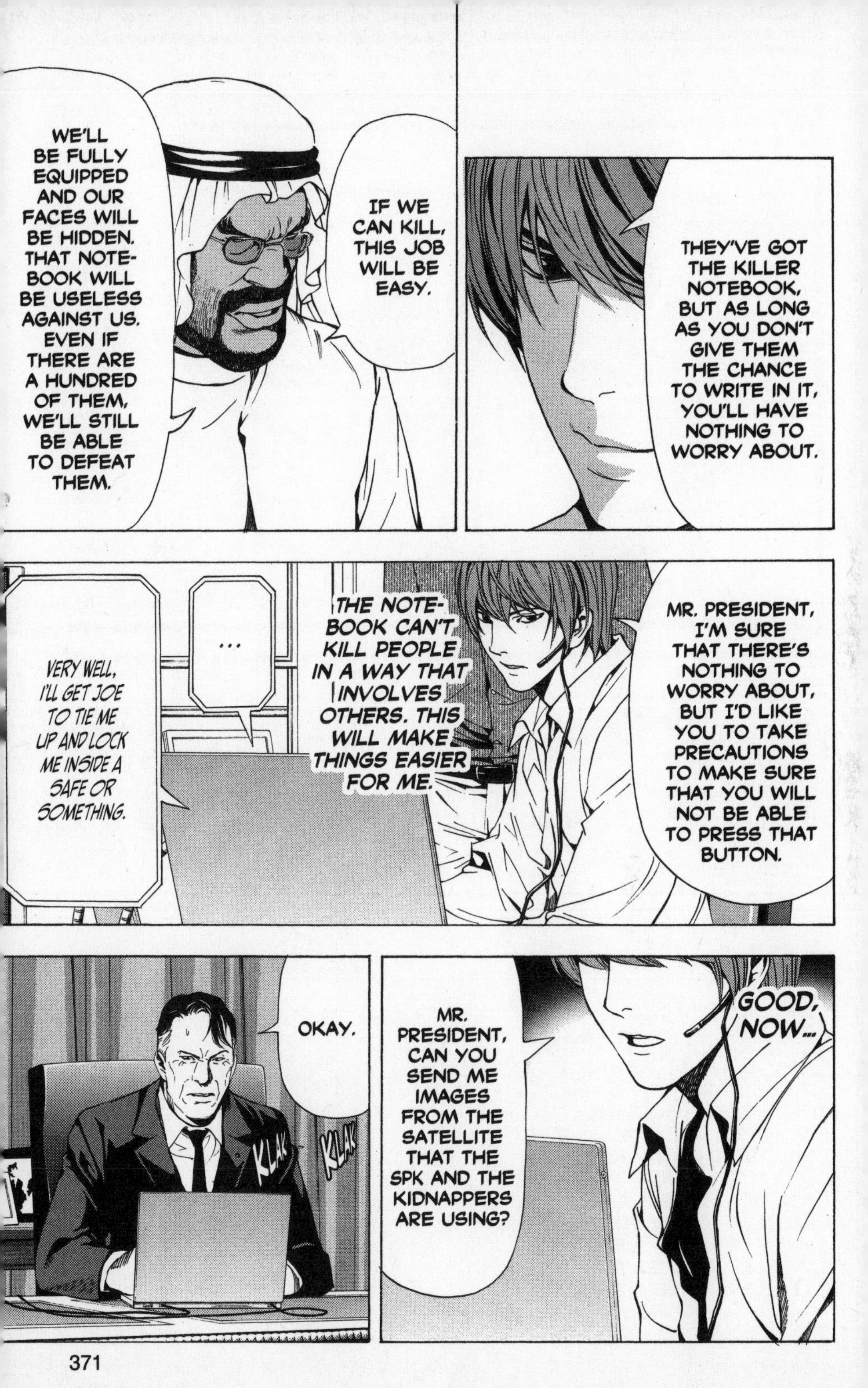
THEY'VE GOT THE KILLER NOTEBOOK, BUT AS LONG AS YOU DON'T GIVE THEM THE CHANCE TO WRITE IN IT, YOU'LL HAVE NOTHING TO WORRY ABOUT.
IF WE CAN KILL, THIS JOB WILL BE EASY.
WE'LL BE FULLY EQUIPPED AND OUR FACES WILL BE HIDDEN. THAT NOTE-BOOK WILL BE USELESS AGAINST US. EVEN IF THERE ARE A HUNDRED OF THEM, WE'LL STILL BE ABLE TO DEFEAT THEM.
MR. PRESIDENT, I'M SURE THAT THERE'S NOTHING TO WORRY ABOUT, BUT I'D LIKE YOU TO TAKE PRECAUTIONS TO MAKE SURE THAT YOU WILL NOT BE ABLE TO PRESS THAT BUTTON.
THE NOTE-BOOK CAN'T KILL PEOPLE IN A WAY THAT INVOLVES OTHERS. THIS WILL MAKE THINGS EASIER FOR ME.
...
VERY WELL, I'LL GET JOE TO TIE ME UP AND LOCK ME INSIDE A SAFE OR SOMETHING.
GOOD, NOW...
MR. PRESIDENT, CAN YOU SEND ME IMAGES FROM THE SATELLITE THAT THE SPK AND THE KIDNAPPERS ARE USING?
OKAY.
KLAK
KLAK

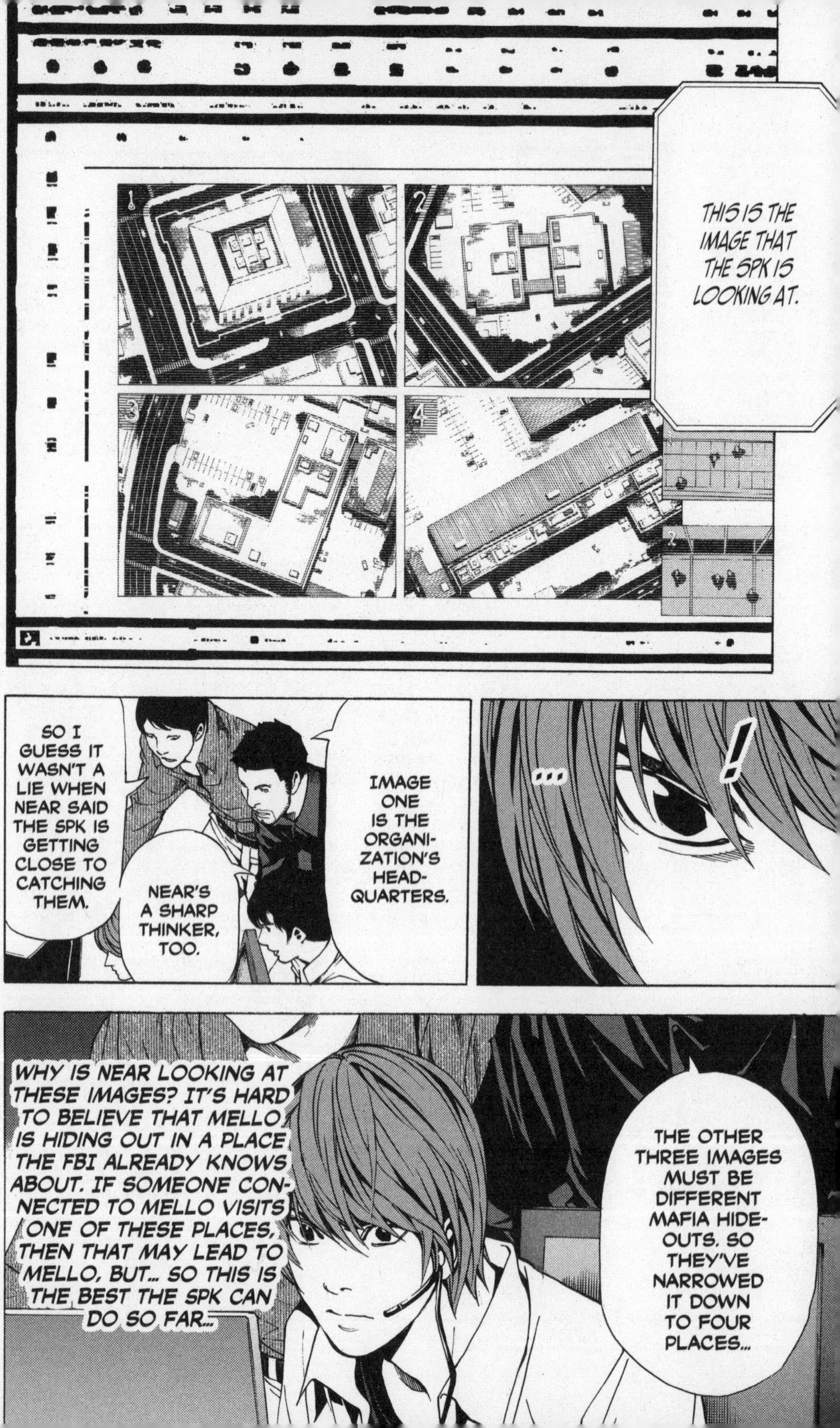
THIS IS THE IMAGE THAT THE SPK IS LOOKING AT.
...
!
IMAGE ONE IS THE ORGANIZATION'S HEADQUARTERS.
SO I GUESS IT WASN'T A LIE WHEN NEAR SAID THE SPK IS GETTING CLOSE TO CATCHING THEM.
NEAR'S A SHARP THINKER, TOO.
THE OTHER THREE IMAGES MUST BE DIFFERENT MAFIA HIDE-OUTS. SO THEY'VE NARROWED IT DOWN TO FOUR PLACES...
WHY IS NEAR LOOKING AT THESE IMAGES? IT'S HARD TO BELIEVE THAT MELLO IS HIDING OUT IN A PLACE THE FBI ALREADY KNOWS ABOUT. IF SOMEONE CON-NECTED TO MELLO VISITS ONE OF THESE PLACES, THEN THAT MAY LEAD TO MELLO, BUT... SO THIS IS THE BEST THE SPK CAN DO SO FAR...

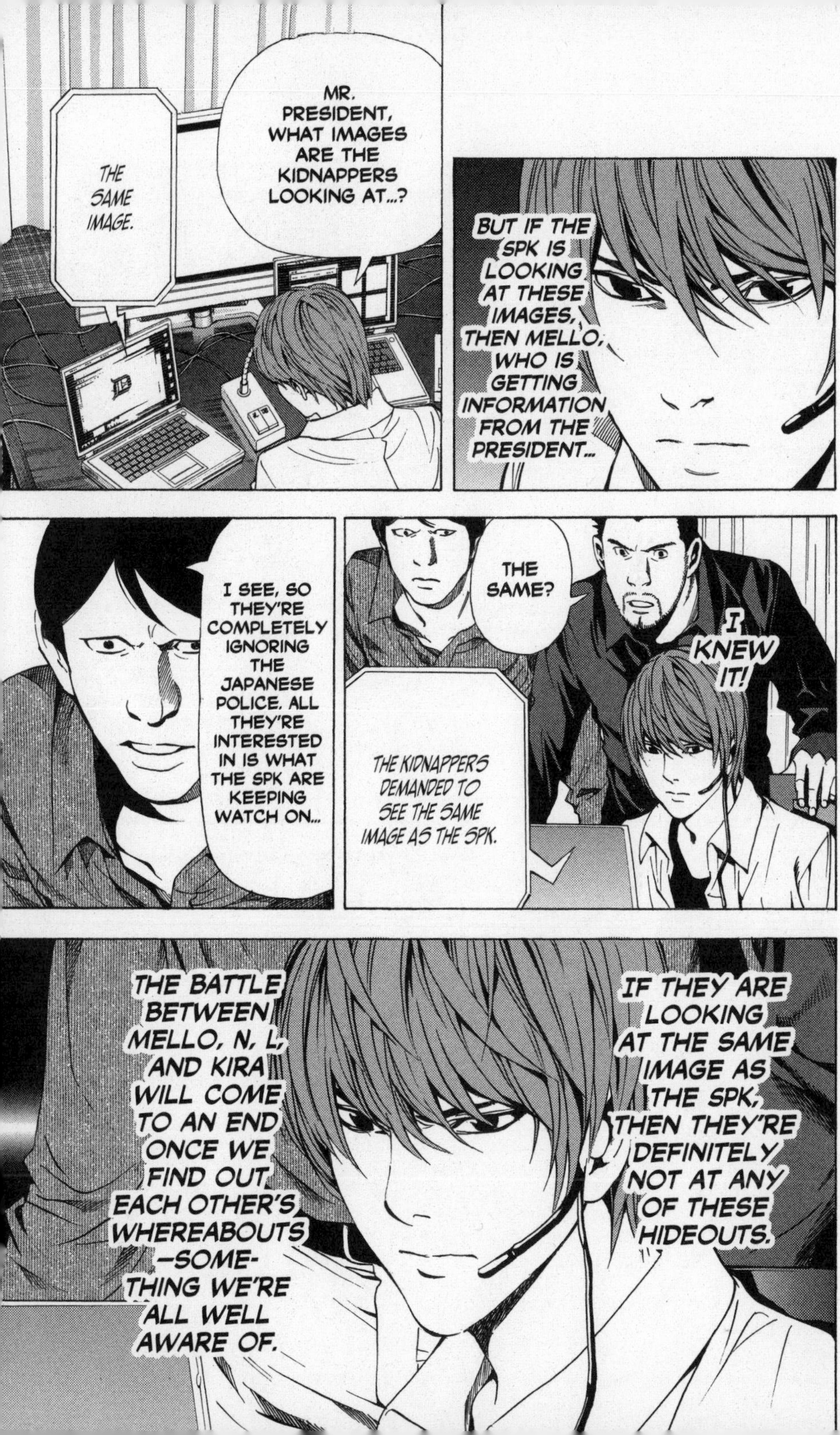
BUT IF THE SPK IS LOOKING AT THESE IMAGES, THEN MELLO, WHO IS GETTING INFORMATION FROM THE PRESIDENT...
MR. PRESIDENT, WHAT IMAGES ARE THE KIDNAPPERS LOOKING AT...?
THE SAME IMAGE.
THE SAME?
I KNEW IT!
THE KIDNAPPERS DEMANDED TO SEE THE SAME IMAGE AS THE SPK.
I SEE, SO THEY'RE COMPLETELY IGNORING THE JAPANESE POLICE. ALL THEY'RE INTERESTED IN IS WHAT THE SPK ARE KEEPING WATCH ON...
IF THEY ARE LOOKING AT THE SAME IMAGE AS THE SPK, THEN THEY'RE DEFINITELY NOT AT ANY OF THESE HIDEOUTS.
THE BATTLE BETWEEN MELLO, N, L, AND KIRA WILL COME TO AN END ONCE WE FIND OUT EACH OTHER'S WHEREABOUTS —SOMETHING WE'RE ALL WELL AWARE OF.

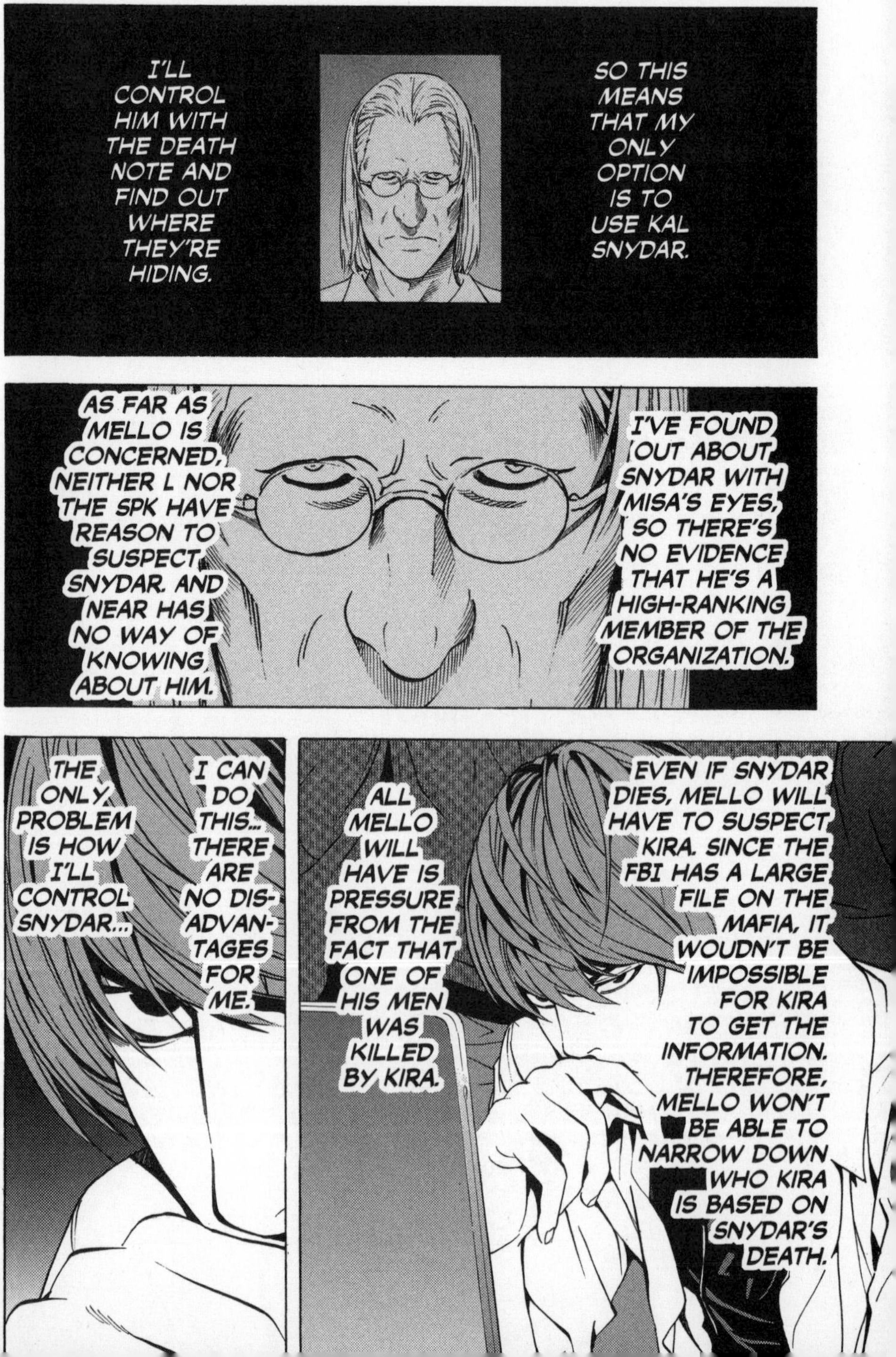
SO THIS MEANS THAT MY ONLY OPTION IS TO USE KAL SNYDAR.
I'LL CONTROL HIM WITH THE DEATH NOTE AND FIND OUT WHERE THEY'RE HIDING.
I'VE FOUND OUT ABOUT SNYDAR WITH MISA'S EYES, SO THERE'S NO EVIDENCE THAT HE'S A HIGH-RANKING MEMBER OF THE ORGANIZATION.
AS FAR AS MELLO IS CONCERNED, NEITHER L NOR THE SPK HAVE REASON TO SUSPECT SNYDAR. AND NEAR HAS NO WAY OF KNOWING ABOUT HIM.
EVEN IF SNYDAR DIES, MELLO WILL HAVE TO SUSPECT KIRA. SINCE THE FBI HAS A LARGE FILE ON THE MAFIA, IT WOUDN'T BE IMPOSSIBLE FOR KIRA TO GET THE INFORMATION. THEREFORE, MELLO WON'T BE ABLE TO NARROW DOWN WHO KIRA IS BASED ON SNYDAR'S DEATH.
ALL MELLO WILL HAVE IS PRESSURE FROM THE FACT THAT ONE OF HIS MEN WAS KILLED BY KIRA.
I CAN DO THIS... THERE ARE NO DIS-ADVAN-TAGES FOR ME.
THE ONLY PROBLEM IS HOW I'LL CONTROL SNYDAR...

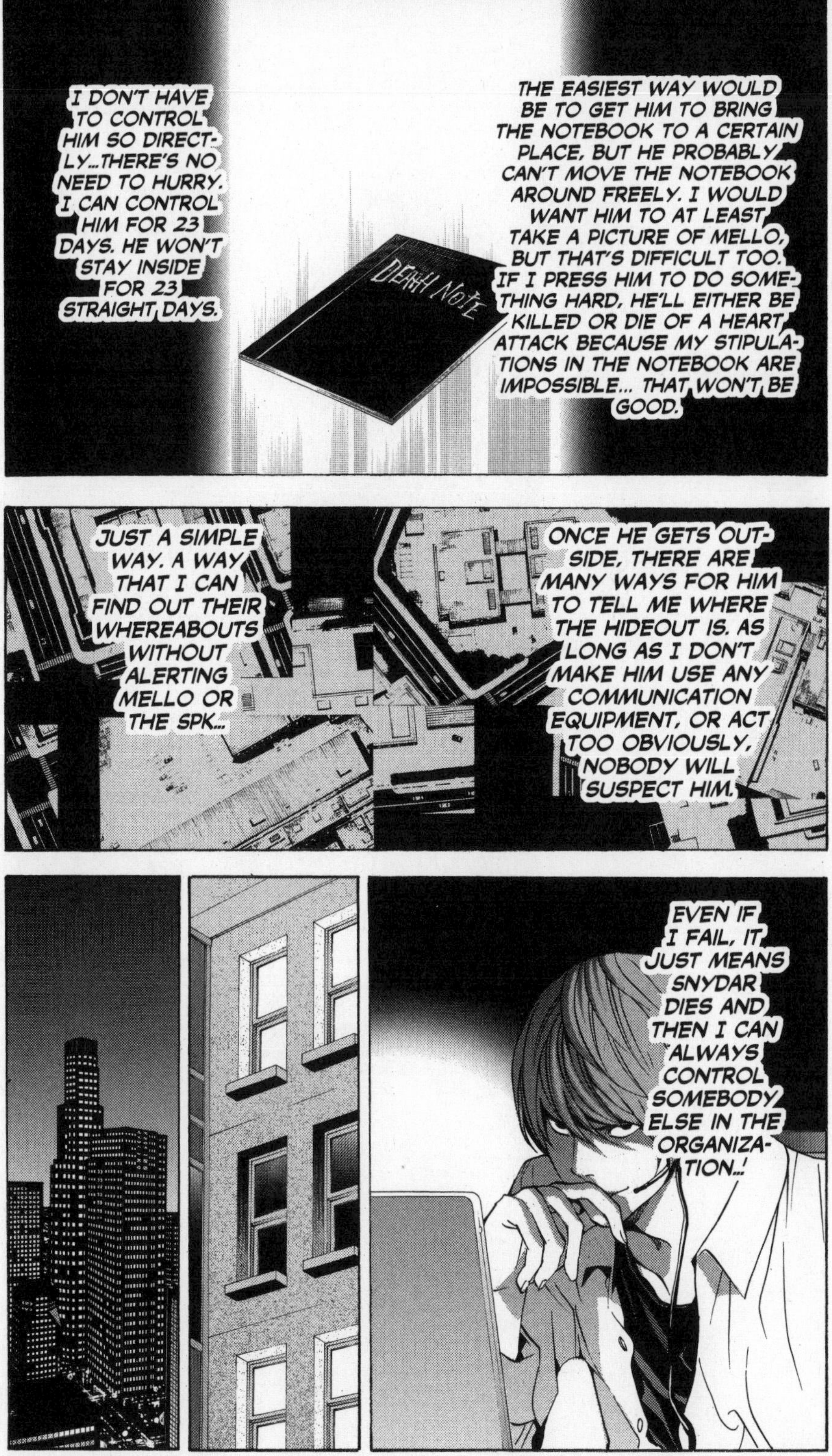
THE EASIEST WAY WOULD BE TO GET HIM TO BRING THE NOTEBOOK TO A CERTAIN PLACE, BUT HE PROBABLY CAN'T MOVE THE NOTEBOOK AROUND FREELY. I WOULD WANT HIM TO AT LEAST TAKE A PICTURE OF MELLO, BUT THAT'S DIFFICULT TOO. IF I PRESS HIM TO DO SOMETHING HARD, HE'LL EITHER BE KILLED OR DIE OF A HEART ATTACK BECAUSE MY STIPULATIONS IN THE NOTEBOOK ARE IMPOSSIBLE... THAT WON'T BE GOOD.
DEATH NOTE
I DON'T HAVE TO CONTROL HIM SO DIRECTLY...THERE'S NO NEED TO HURRY. I CAN CONTROL HIM FOR 23 DAYS. HE WON'T STAY INSIDE FOR 23 STRAIGHT DAYS.
ONCE HE GETS OUTSIDE, THERE ARE MANY WAYS FOR HIM TO TELL ME WHERE THE HIDEOUT IS. AS LONG AS I DON'T MAKE HIM USE ANY COMMUNICATION EQUIPMENT, OR ACT TOO OBVIOUSLY, NOBODY WILL SUSPECT HIM.
JUST A SIMPLE WAY. A WAY THAT I CAN FIND OUT THEIR WHEREABOUTS WITHOUT ALERTING MELLO OR THE SPK...
EVEN IF I FAIL, IT JUST MEANS SNYDAR DIES AND THEN I CAN ALWAYS CONTROL SOMEBODY ELSE IN THE ORGANIZATION...!

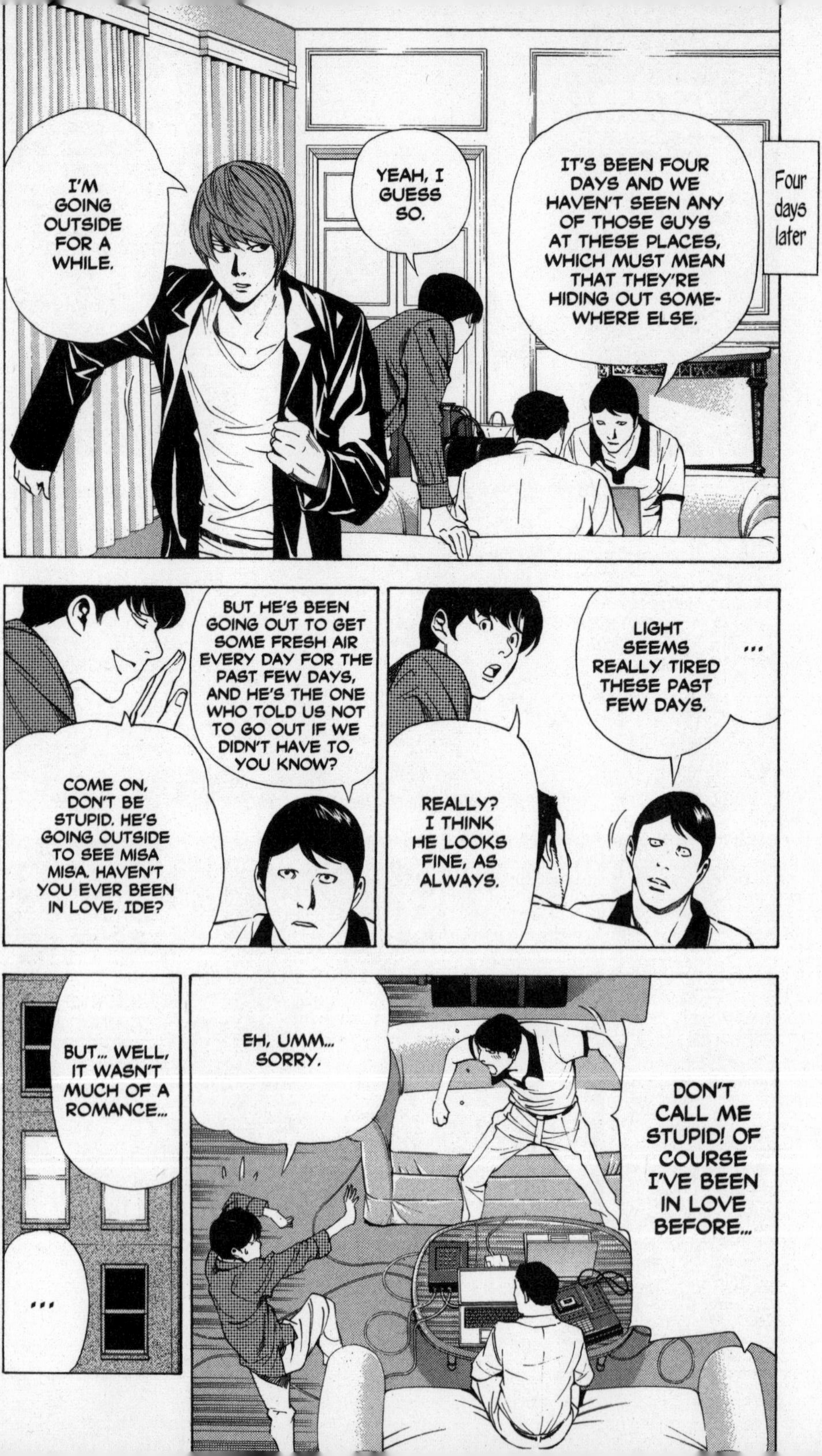

Four days later
IT'S BEEN FOUR DAYS AND WE HAVEN'T SEEN ANY OF THOSE GUYS AT THESE PLACES, WHICH MUST MEAN THAT THEY'RE HIDING OUT SOME-WHERE ELSE.
YEAH, I GUESS SO.
I'M GOING OUTSIDE FOR A WHILE.
LIGHT SEEMS REALLY TIRED THESE PAST FEW DAYS.
...
REALLY? I THINK HE LOOKS FINE, AS ALWAYS.
BUT HE'S BEEN GOING OUT TO GET SOME FRESH AIR EVERY DAY FOR THE PAST FEW DAYS, AND HE'S THE ONE WHO TOLD US NOT TO GO OUT IF WE DIDN'T HAVE TO, YOU KNOW?
COME ON, DON'T BE STUPID. HE'S GOING OUTSIDE TO SEE MISA MISA. HAVEN'T YOU EVER BEEN IN LOVE, IDE?
DON'T CALL ME STUPID! OF COURSE I'VE BEEN IN LOVE BEFORE...
EH, UMM... SORRY.
BUT... WELL, IT WASN'T MUCH OF A ROMANCE...
...

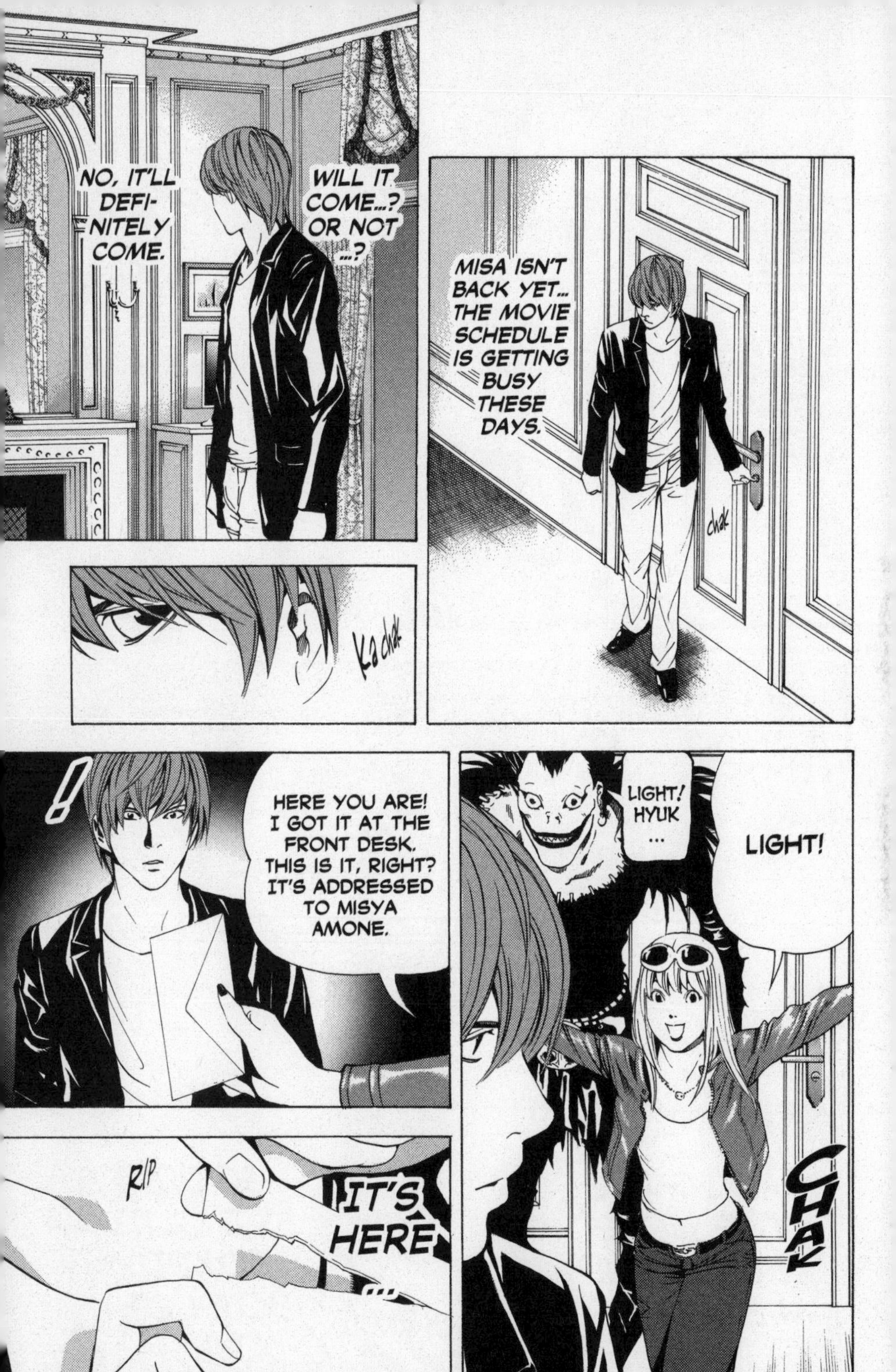
MISA ISN'T BACK YET... THE MOVIE SCHEDULE IS GETTING BUSY THESE DAYS.
chak
WILL IT COME...? OR NOT ...?
NO, IT'LL DEFI-NITELY COME.
Ka chak
CHAK
LIGHT!
LIGHT! HYUK ...
!
HERE YOU ARE! I GOT IT AT THE FRONT DESK. THIS IS IT, RIGHT? IT'S ADDRESSED TO MISYA AMONE.
RIP
IT'S HERE ...

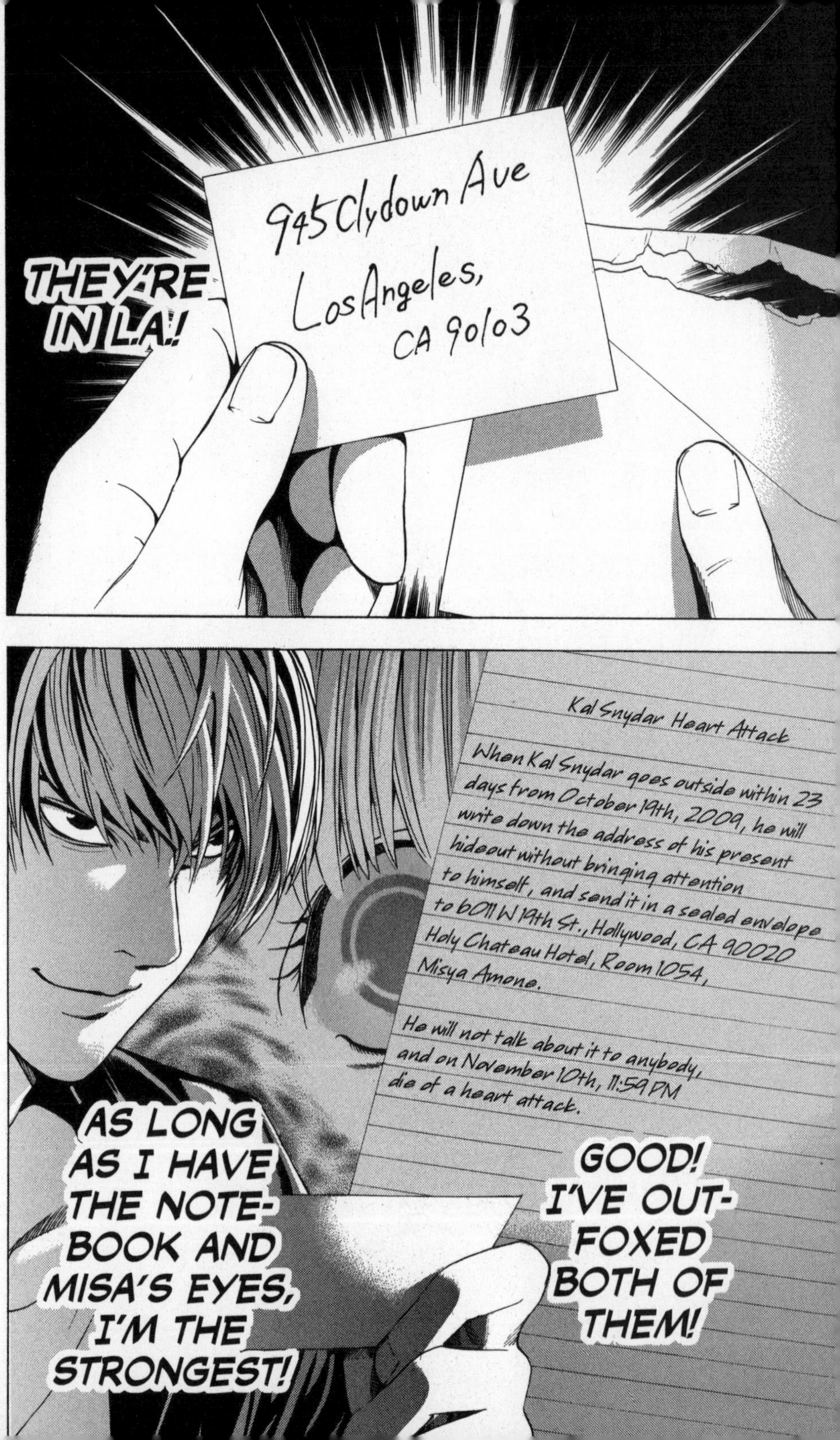
945 Clydown Ave
Los Angeles,
CA 90103
THEY'RE IN L.A.!
Kal Snydar Heart Attack
When Kal Snydar goes outside within 23 days from October 19th, 2009, he will write down the address of his present hideout without bringing attention to himself, and send it in a sealed envelope to 6011 W 19th St., Hollywood, CA 90020 Holy Chateau Hotel, Room 1054, Misya Amone.
He will not talk about it to anybody, and on November 10th, 11:59 PM die of a heart attack.
GOOD! I'VE OUT-FOXED BOTH OF THEM!
AS LONG AS I HAVE THE NOTE-BOOK AND MISA'S EYES, I'M THE STRONGEST!

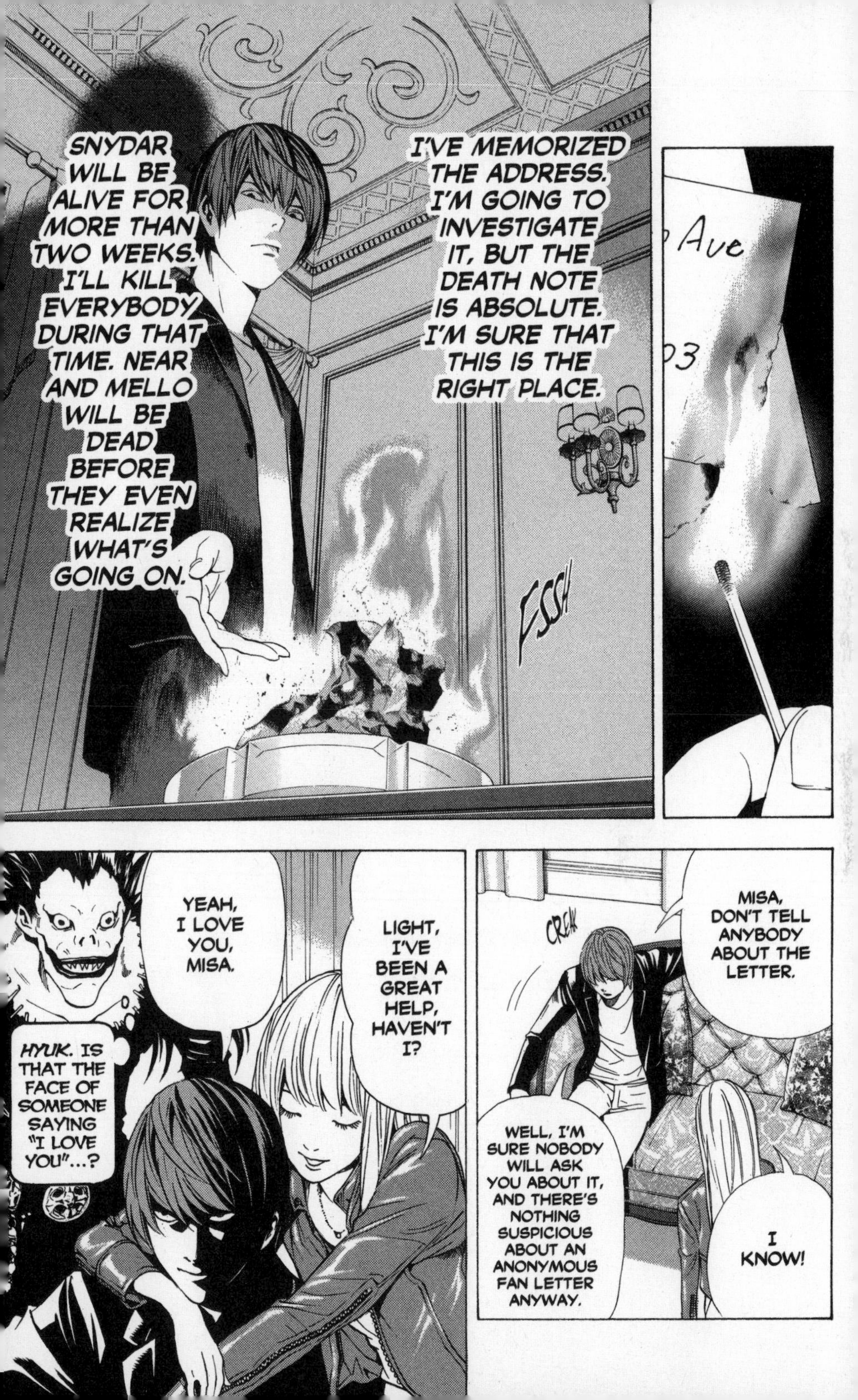
Ave
03
I'VE MEMORIZED THE ADDRESS. I'M GOING TO INVESTIGATE IT, BUT THE DEATH NOTE IS ABSOLUTE. I'M SURE THAT THIS IS THE RIGHT PLACE.
SNYDAR WILL BE ALIVE FOR MORE THAN TWO WEEKS. I'LL KILL EVERYBODY DURING THAT TIME. NEAR AND MELLO WILL BE DEAD BEFORE THEY EVEN REALIZE WHAT'S GOING ON.
FSSH
MISA, DON'T TELL ANYBODY ABOUT THE LETTER.
CREAK
I KNOW!
WELL, I'M SURE NOBODY WILL ASK YOU ABOUT IT, AND THERE'S NOTHING SUSPICIOUS ABOUT AN ANONYMOUS FAN LETTER ANYWAY.
LIGHT, I'VE BEEN A GREAT HELP, HAVEN'T I?
YEAH, I LOVE YOU, MISA.
HYUK. IS THAT THE FACE OF SOMEONE SAYING "I LOVE YOU"...?

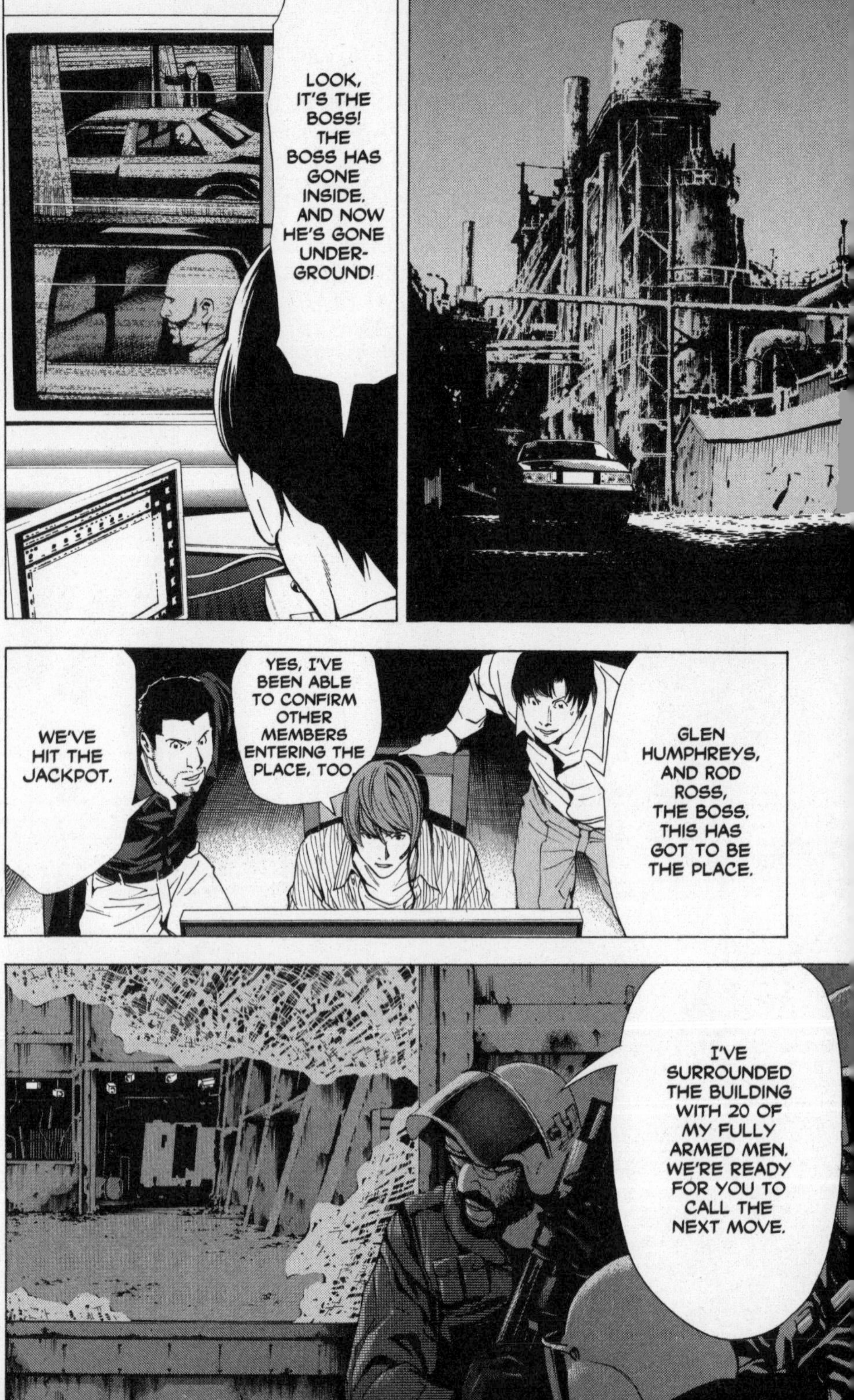
LOOK, IT'S THE BOSS! THE BOSS HAS GONE INSIDE. AND NOW HE'S GONE UNDER-GROUND!
GLEN HUMPHREYS, AND ROD ROSS, THE BOSS. THIS HAS GOT TO BE THE PLACE.
YES, I'VE BEEN ABLE TO CONFIRM OTHER MEMBERS ENTERING THE PLACE, TOO.
WE'VE HIT THE JACKPOT.
I'VE SURROUNDED THE BUILDING WITH 20 OF MY FULLY ARMED MEN. WE'RE READY FOR YOU TO CALL THE NEXT MOVE.

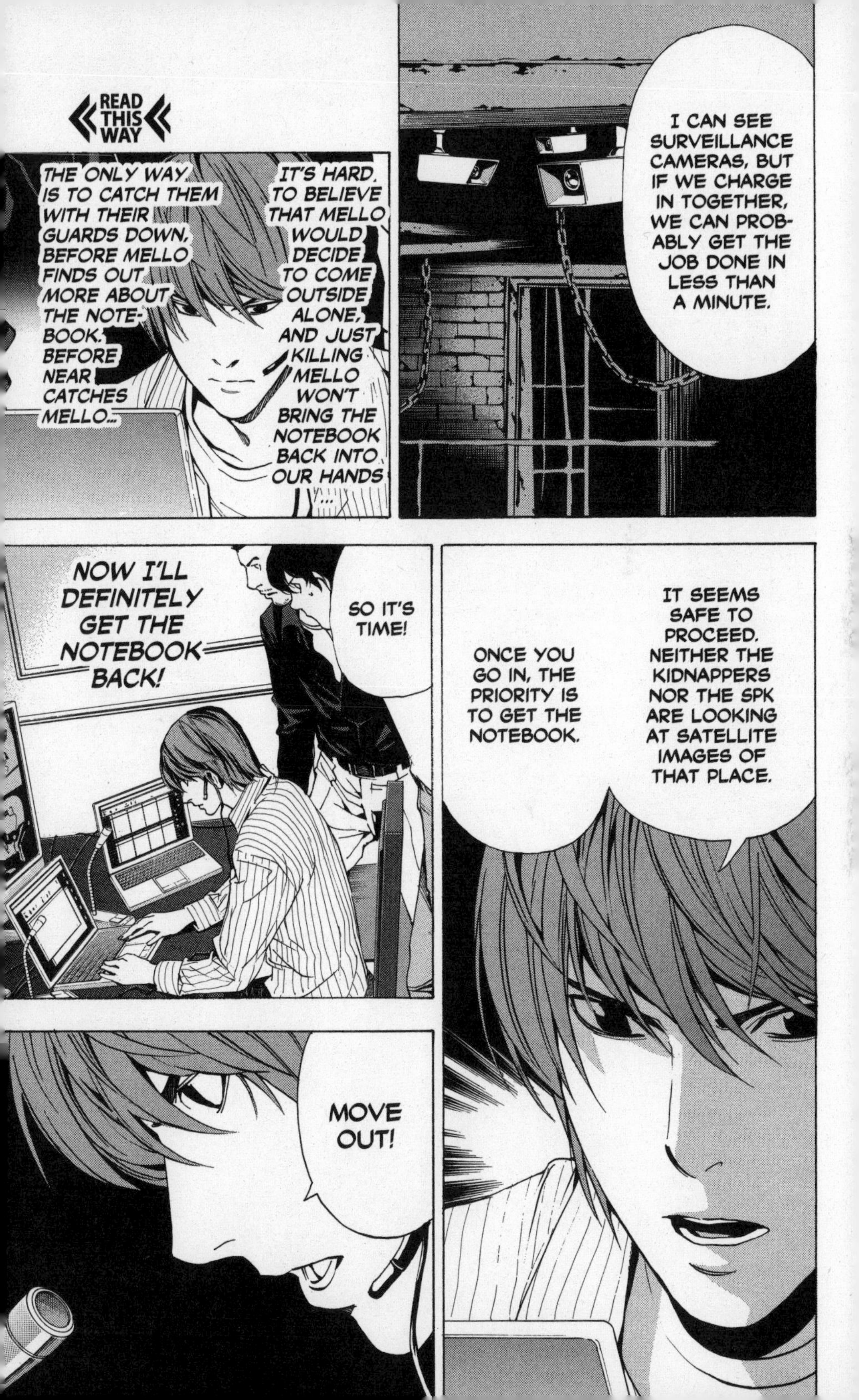
READ THIS WAY
I CAN SEE SURVEILLANCE CAMERAS, BUT IF WE CHARGE IN TOGETHER, WE CAN PROBABLY GET THE JOB DONE IN LESS THAN A MINUTE.
IT'S HARD TO BELIEVE THAT MELLO WOULD DECIDE TO COME OUTSIDE ALONE, AND JUST KILLING MELLO WON'T BRING THE NOTEBOOK BACK INTO OUR HANDS...
THE ONLY WAY IS TO CATCH THEM WITH THEIR GUARDS DOWN, BEFORE MELLO FINDS OUT MORE ABOUT THE NOTEBOOK. BEFORE NEAR CATCHES MELLO...
IT SEEMS SAFE TO PROCEED. NEITHER THE KIDNAPPERS NOR THE SPK ARE LOOKING AT SATELLITE IMAGES OF THAT PLACE.
ONCE YOU GO IN, THE PRIORITY IS TO GET THE NOTEBOOK.
SO IT'S TIME!
NOW I'LL DEFINITELY GET THE NOTEBOOK BACK!
MOVE OUT!

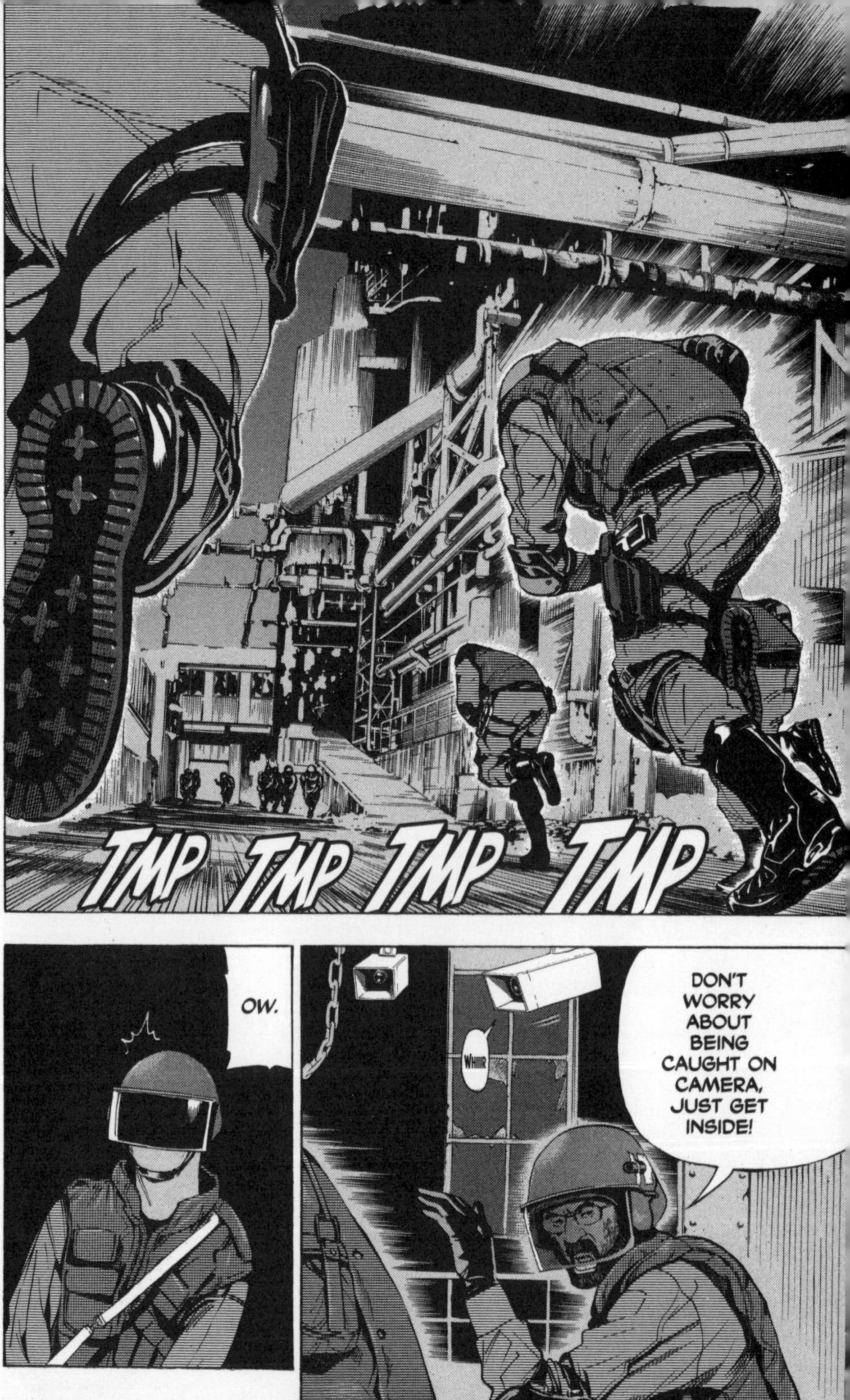
TMP TMP TMP TMP
DON'T WORRY ABOUT BEING CAUGHT ON CAMERA, JUST GET INSIDE!
WHIIR
OW.

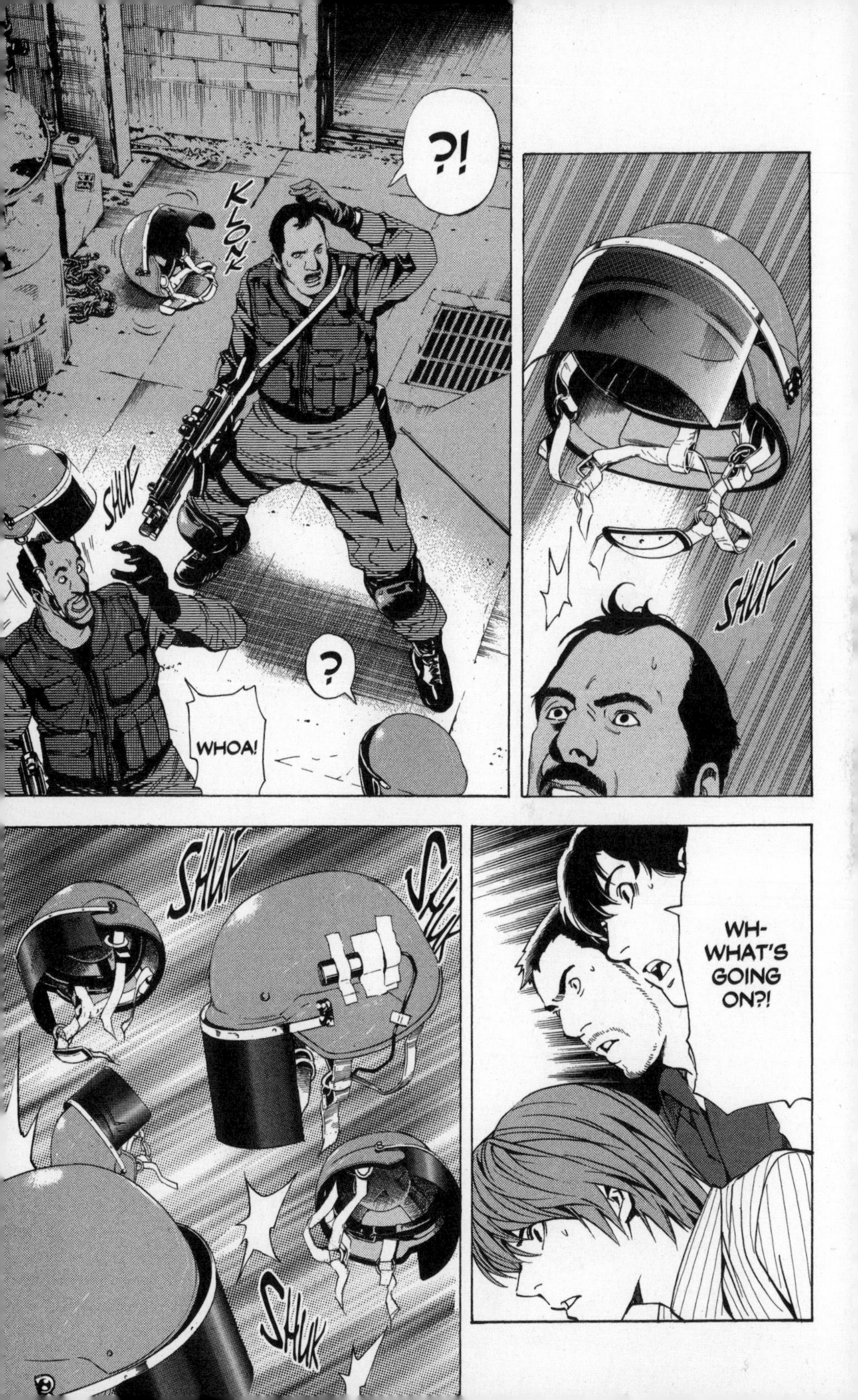
SHUF
?!
KLONK
SHUF
?
WHOA!
WH- WHAT'S GOING ON?!
SHUK
SHUF
SHUK

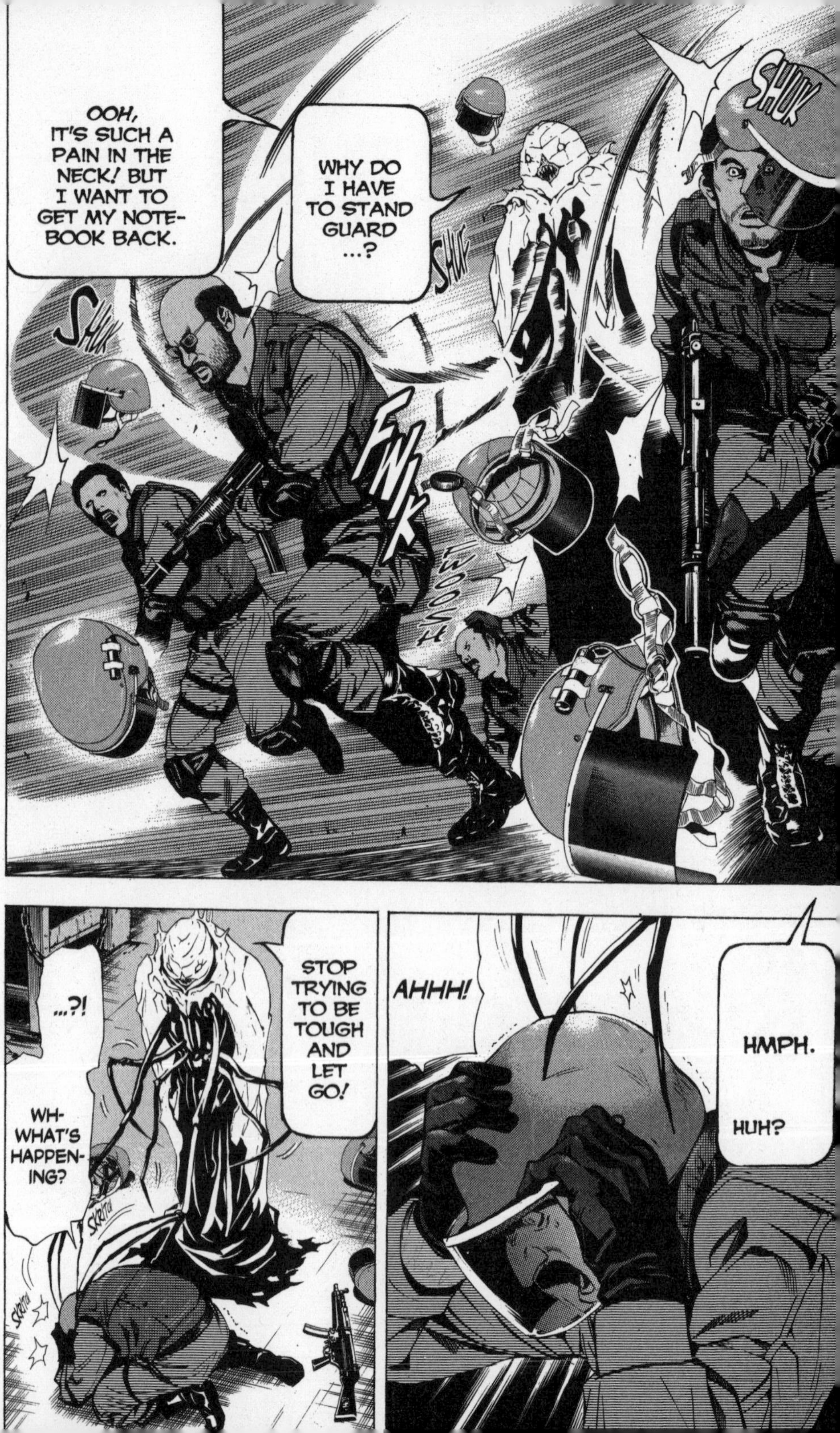
SHUK
WHY DO I HAVE TO STAND GUARD ...?
OOH, IT'S SUCH A PAIN IN THE NECK! BUT I WANT TO GET MY NOTE-BOOK BACK.
SHUK
SHUK
FWIK
FWOOSH
HMPH.
AHHH!
HUH?
STOP TRYING TO BE TOUGH AND LET GO!
...?!
WH-WHAT'S HAPPEN-ING?
SKRITCH

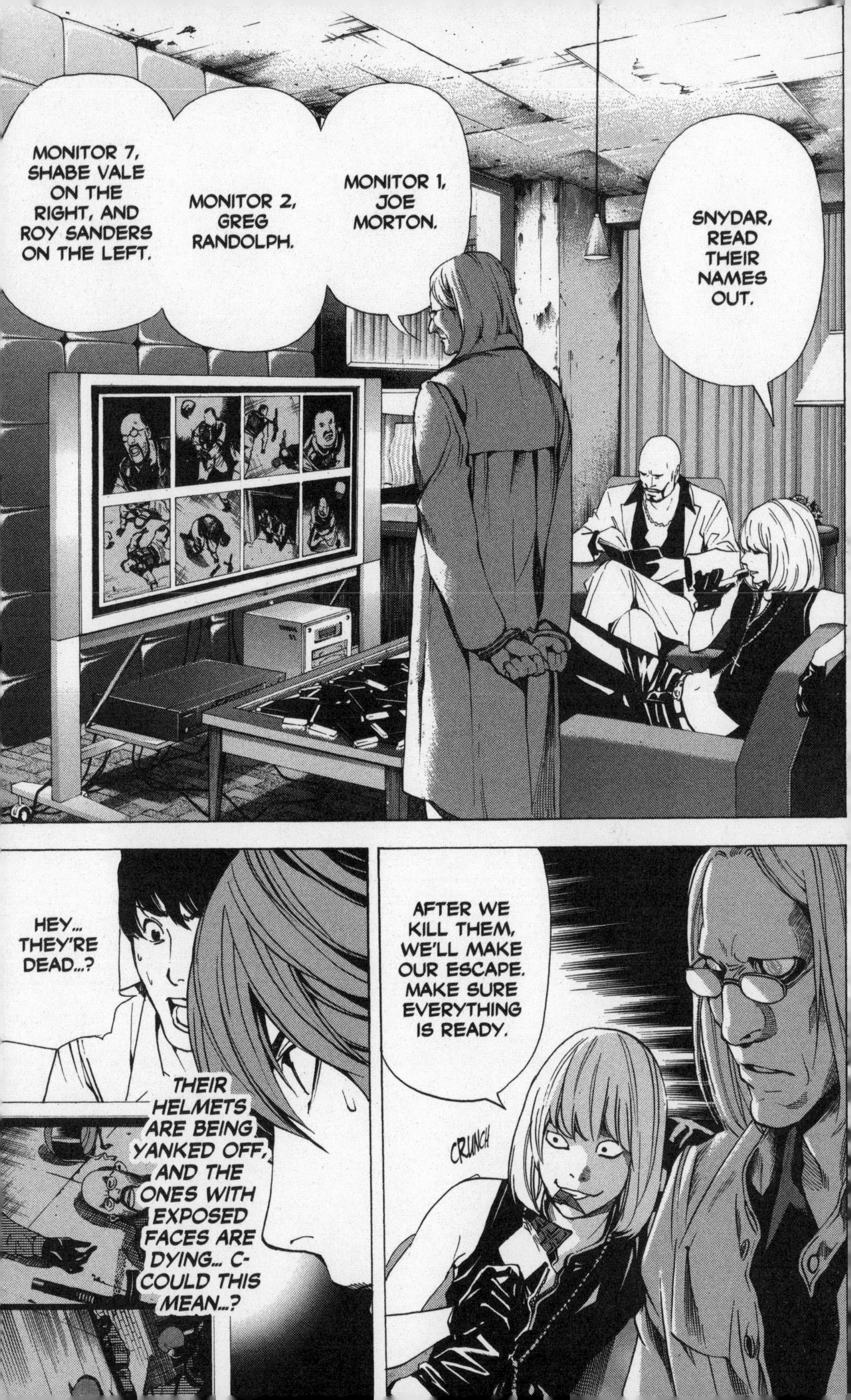
SNYDAR, READ THEIR NAMES OUT.
MONITOR 1, JOE MORTON.
MONITOR 2, GREG RANDOLPH.
MONITOR 7, SHABE VALE ON THE RIGHT, AND ROY SANDERS ON THE LEFT.
AFTER WE KILL THEM, WE'LL MAKE OUR ESCAPE. MAKE SURE EVERYTHING IS READY.
CRUNCH
HEY... THEY'RE DEAD...?
THEIR HELMETS ARE BEING YANKED OFF, AND THE ONES WITH EXPOSED FACES ARE DYING... C-COULD THIS MEAN...?

# chapter 70 Tremble

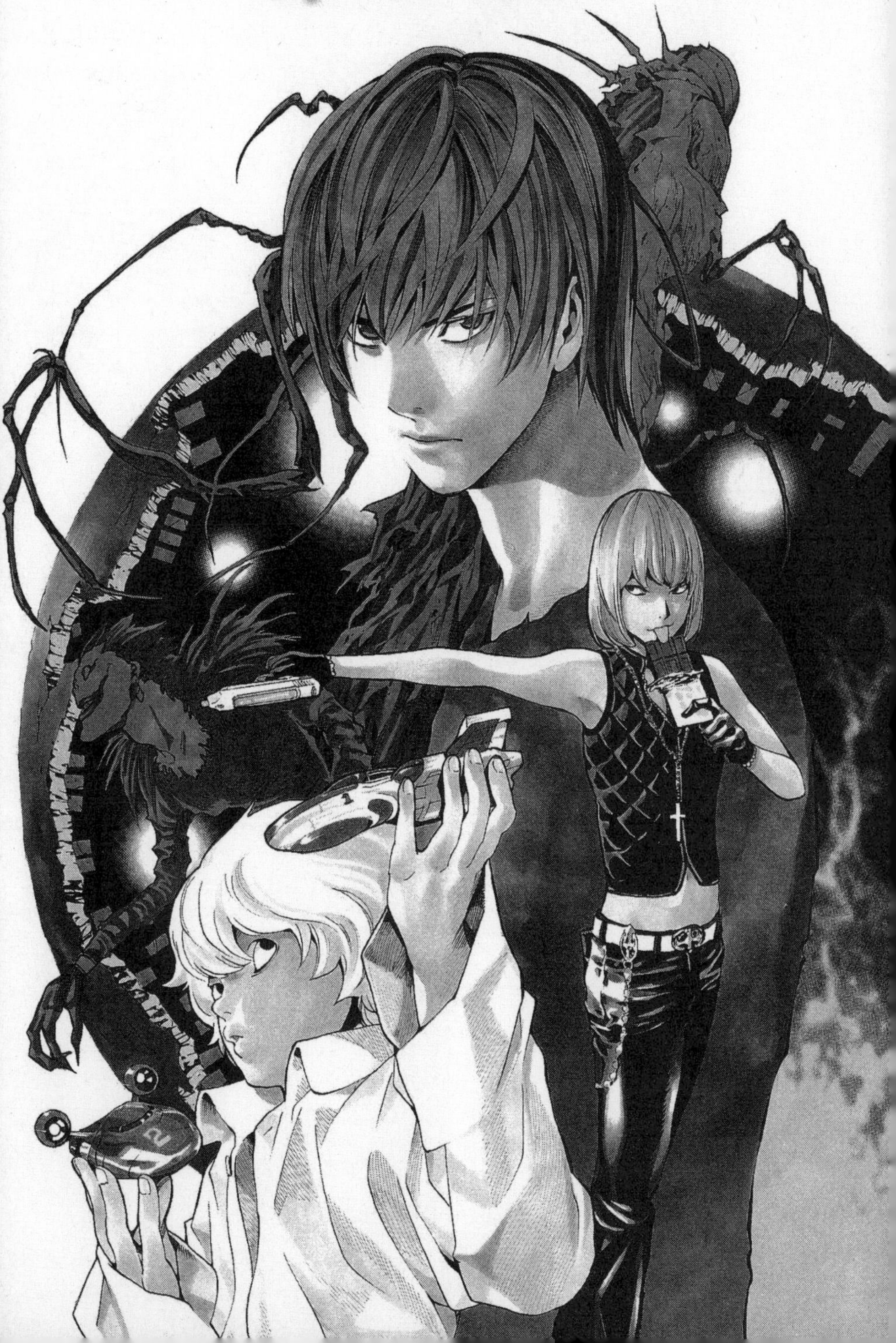

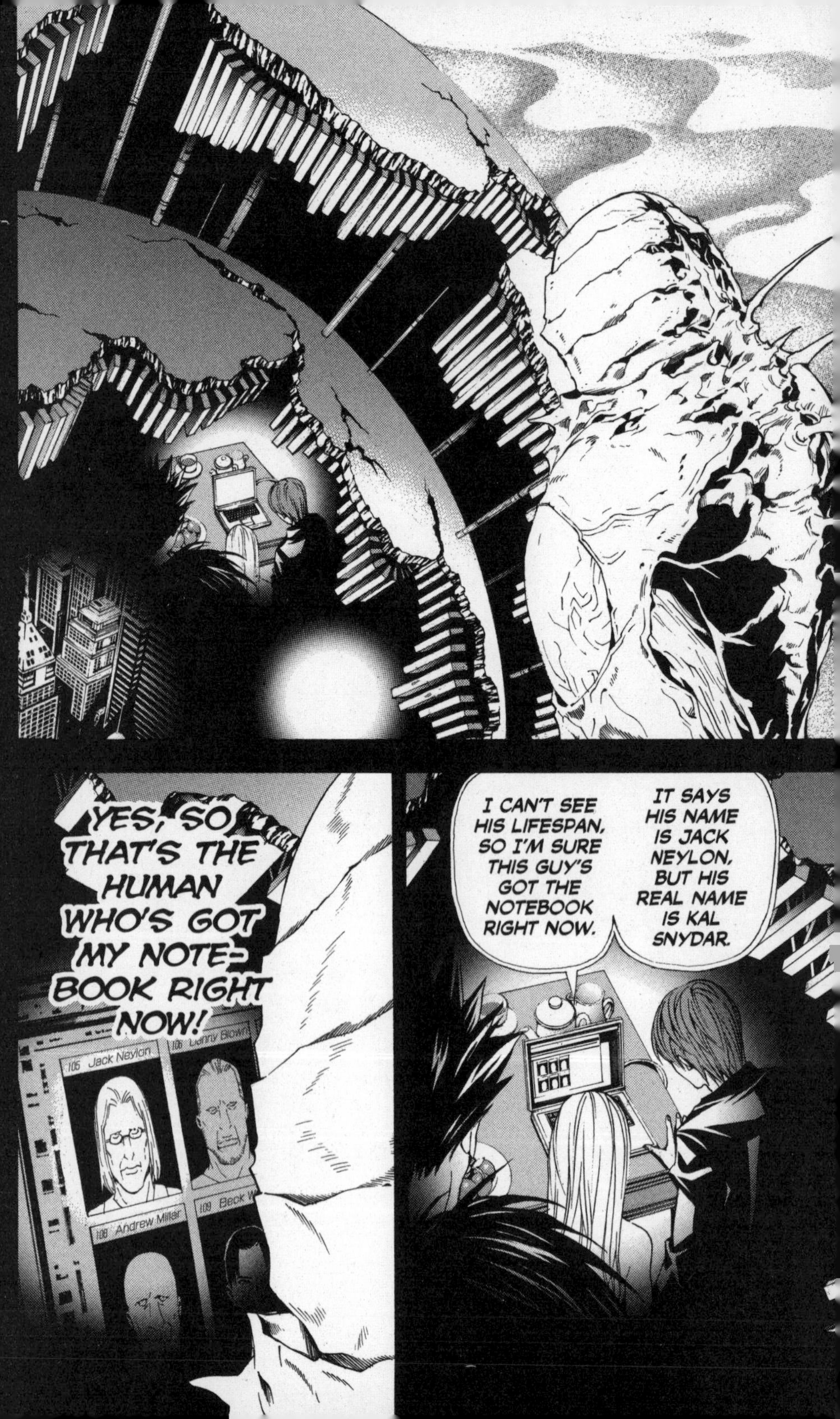
I CAN'T SEE HIS LIFESPAN, SO I'M SURE THIS GUY'S GOT THE NOTEBOOK RIGHT NOW.
IT SAYS HIS NAME IS JACK NEYLON, BUT HIS REAL NAME IS KAL SNYDAR.
YES, SO THAT'S THE HUMAN WHO'S GOT MY NOTE-BOOK RIGHT NOW!
105 Jack Neylon
106 Danny Blown
108 Andrew Millar
109 Beck W

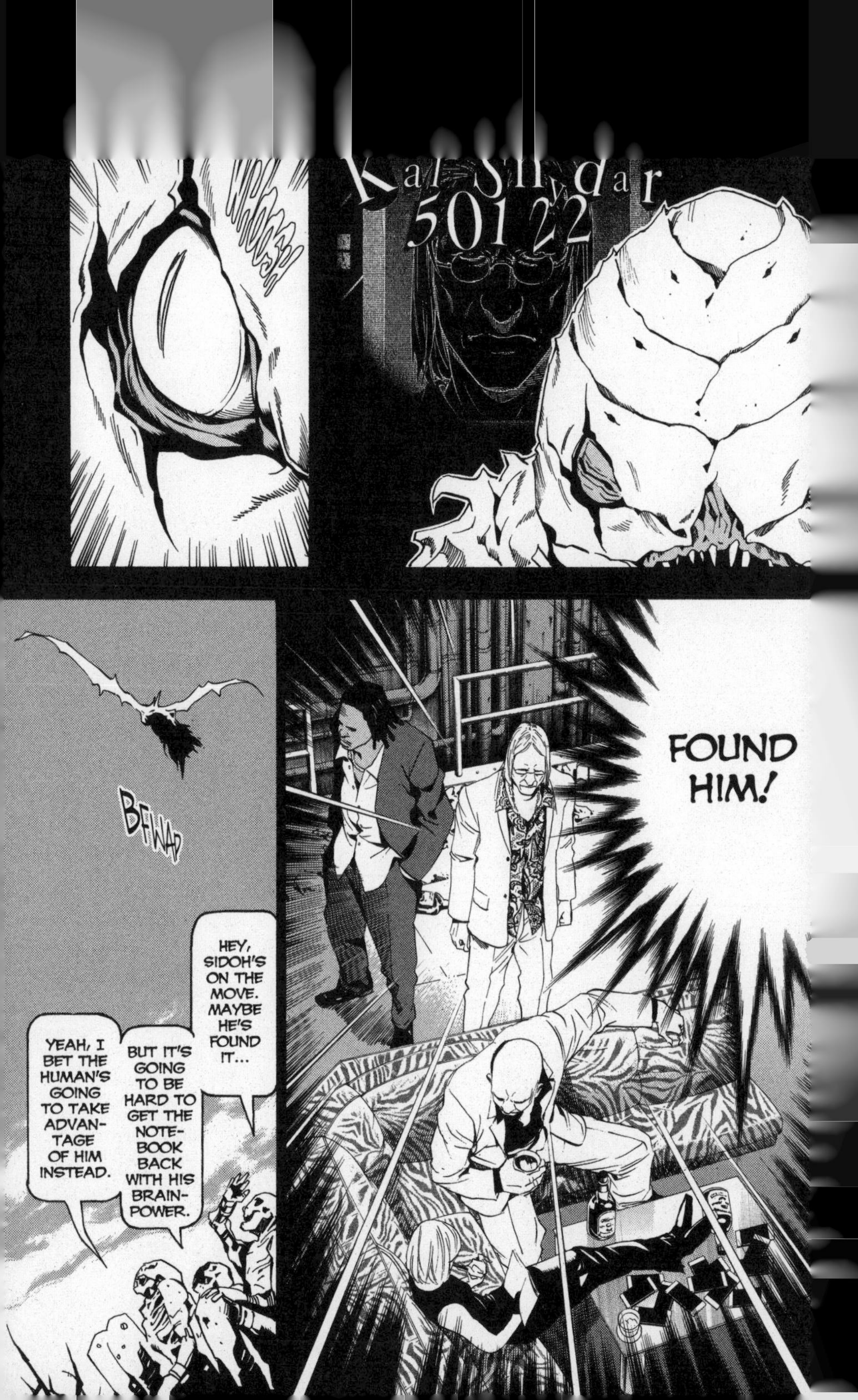
Kal Snydar
50122
FOUND HIM!
BFWAP
HEY, SIDOH'S ON THE MOVE. MAYBE HE'S FOUND IT...
BUT IT'S GOING TO BE HARD TO GET THE NOTEBOOK BACK WITH HIS BRAINPOWER.
YEAH, I BET THE HUMAN'S GOING TO TAKE ADVANTAGE OF HIM INSTEAD.

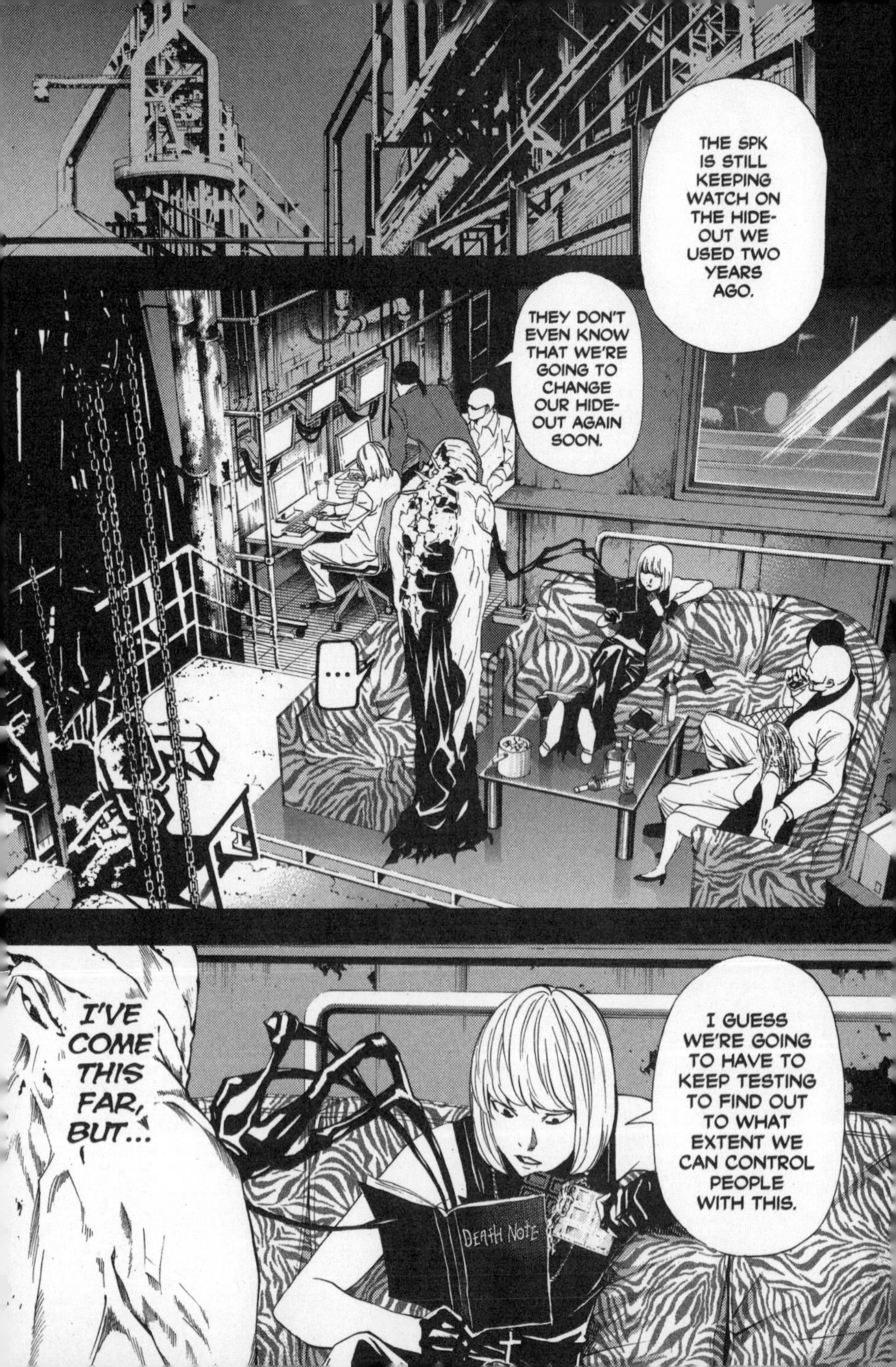
THE SPK IS STILL KEEPING WATCH ON THE HIDE-OUT WE USED TWO YEARS AGO.
THEY DON'T EVEN KNOW THAT WE'RE GOING TO CHANGE OUR HIDE-OUT AGAIN SOON.
....
I GUESS WE'RE GOING TO HAVE TO KEEP TESTING TO FIND OUT TO WHAT EXTENT WE CAN CONTROL PEOPLE WITH THIS.
DEATH NOTE
I'VE COME THIS FAR, BUT...

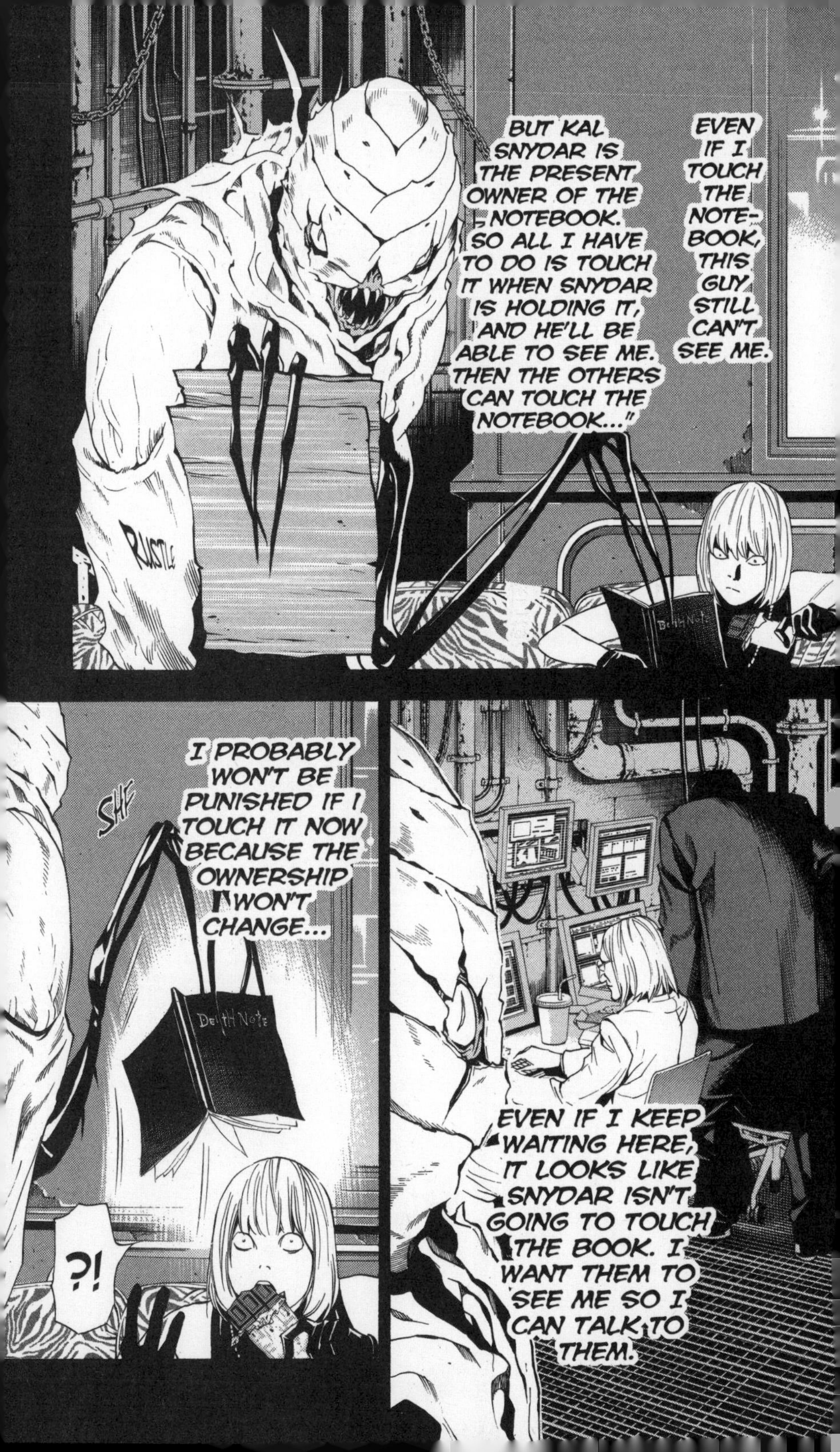
EVEN IF I TOUCH THE NOTE-BOOK, THIS GUY STILL CAN'T SEE ME.
BUT KAL SNYDAR IS THE PRESENT OWNER OF THE NOTEBOOK. SO ALL I HAVE TO DO IS TOUCH IT WHEN SNYDAR IS HOLDING IT, AND HE'LL BE ABLE TO SEE ME. THEN THE OTHERS CAN TOUCH THE NOTEBOOK..."
RUSTLE
EVEN IF I KEEP WAITING HERE, IT LOOKS LIKE SNYDAR ISN'T GOING TO TOUCH THE BOOK. I WANT THEM TO SEE ME SO I CAN TALK TO THEM.
SHF
I PROBABLY WON'T BE PUNISHED IF I TOUCH IT NOW BECAUSE THE OWNERSHIP WON'T CHANGE...
?!

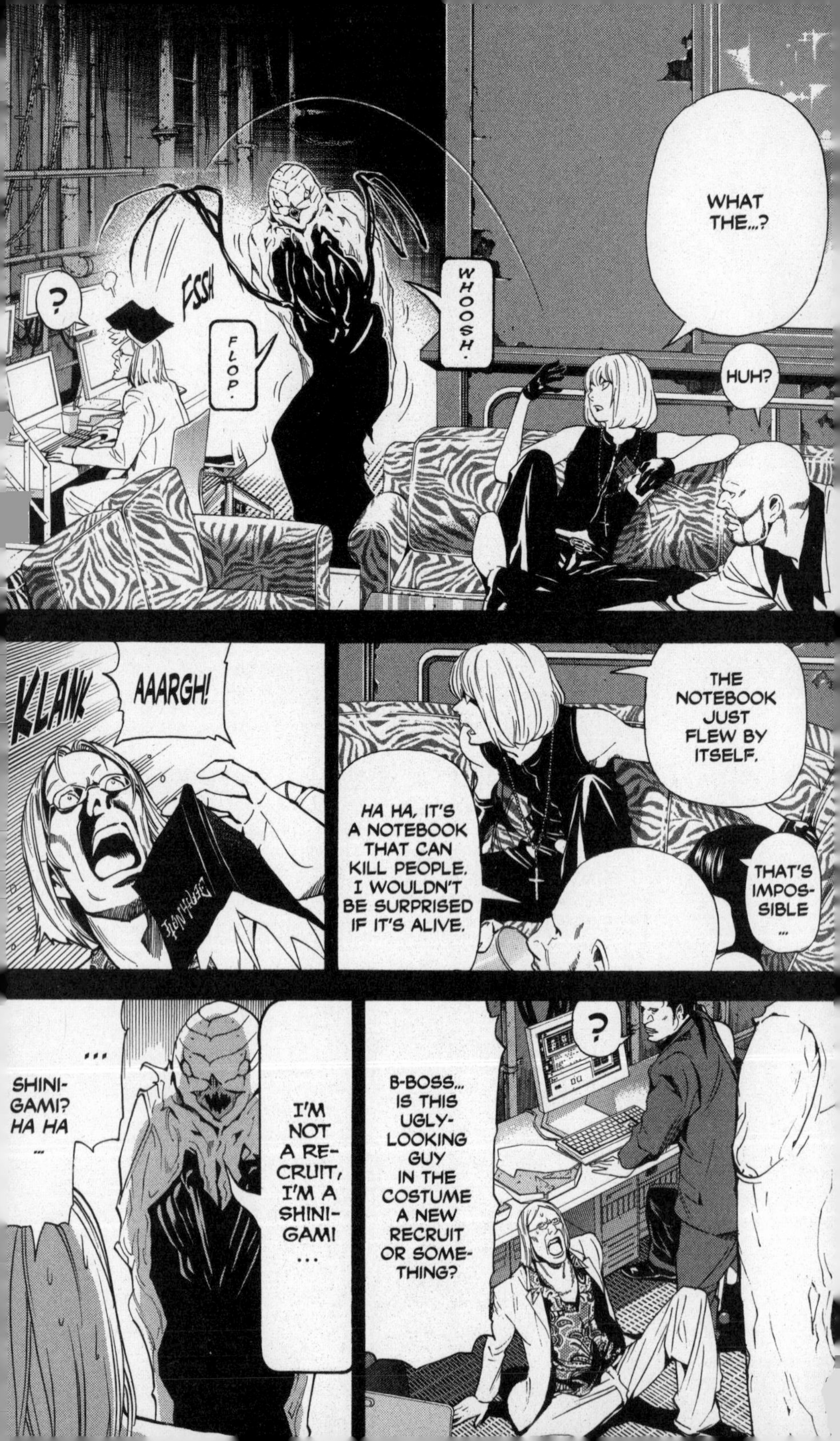
WHAT THE...?
HUH?
WHOOSH.
FLOP.
FSSH
?
THE NOTEBOOK JUST FLEW BY ITSELF.
THAT'S IMPOSSIBLE...
HA HA, IT'S A NOTEBOOK THAT CAN KILL PEOPLE. I WOULDN'T BE SURPRISED IF IT'S ALIVE.
AAARGH!
KLANK
?
B-BOSS... IS THIS UGLY-LOOKING GUY IN THE COSTUME A NEW RECRUIT OR SOMETHING?
I'M NOT A RECRUIT, I'M A SHINIGAMI...
...
SHINIGAMI? HA HA ...

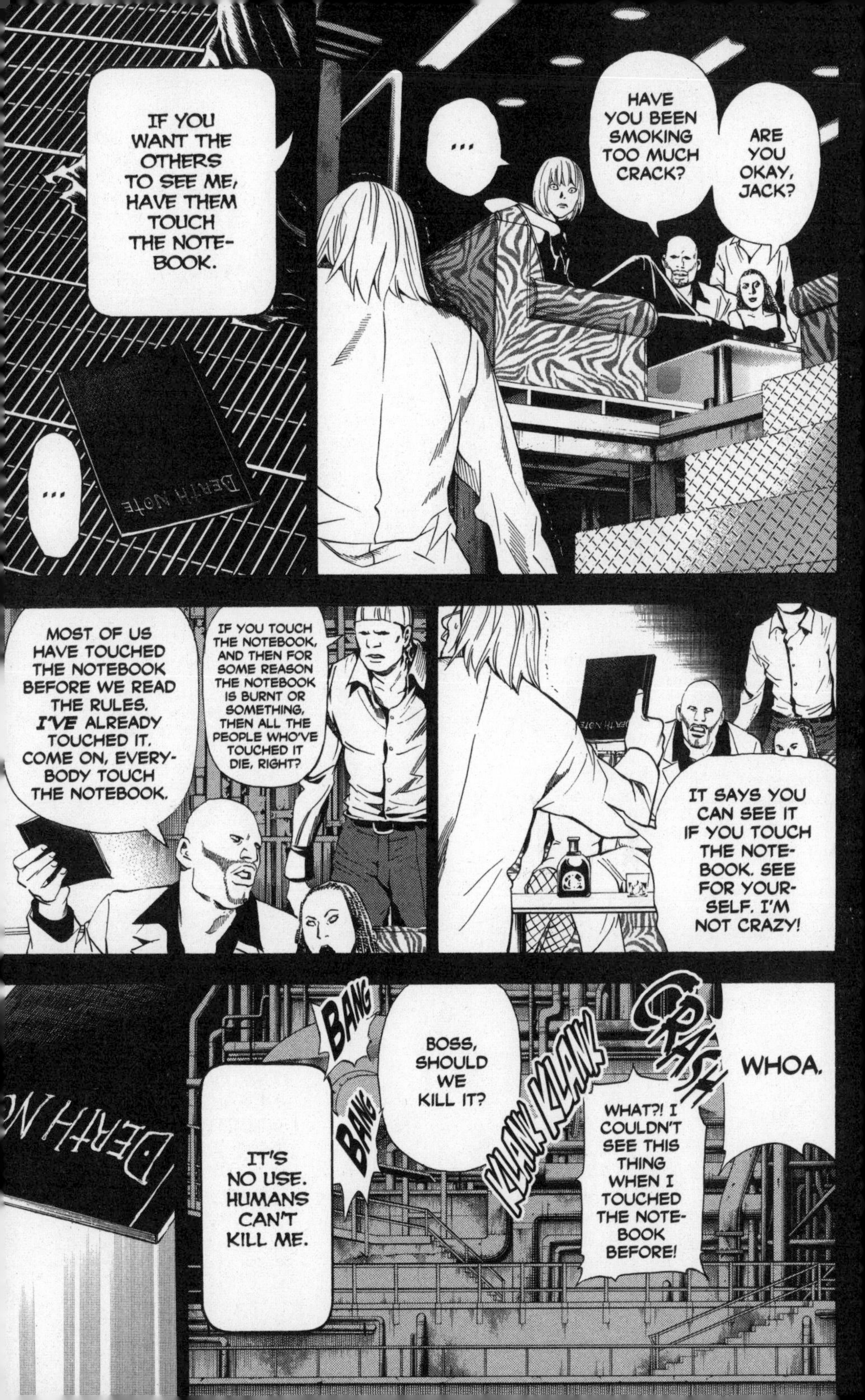
ARE YOU OKAY, JACK?
HAVE YOU BEEN SMOKING TOO MUCH CRACK?
...
IF YOU WANT THE OTHERS TO SEE ME, HAVE THEM TOUCH THE NOTE-BOOK.
...
IT SAYS YOU CAN SEE IT IF YOU TOUCH THE NOTE-BOOK. SEE FOR YOUR-SELF. I'M NOT CRAZY!
IF YOU TOUCH THE NOTEBOOK, AND THEN FOR SOME REASON THE NOTEBOOK IS BURNT OR SOMETHING, THEN ALL THE PEOPLE WHO'VE TOUCHED IT DIE, RIGHT?
MOST OF US HAVE TOUCHED THE NOTEBOOK BEFORE WE READ THE RULES. *I'VE* ALREADY TOUCHED IT. COME ON, EVERY-BODY TOUCH THE NOTEBOOK.
WHOA.
CRASH
KLANK KLANK
WHAT?! I COULDN'T SEE THIS THING WHEN I TOUCHED THE NOTE-BOOK BEFORE!
BANG
BOSS, SHOULD WE KILL IT?
BANG
IT'S NO USE. HUMANS CAN'T KILL ME.

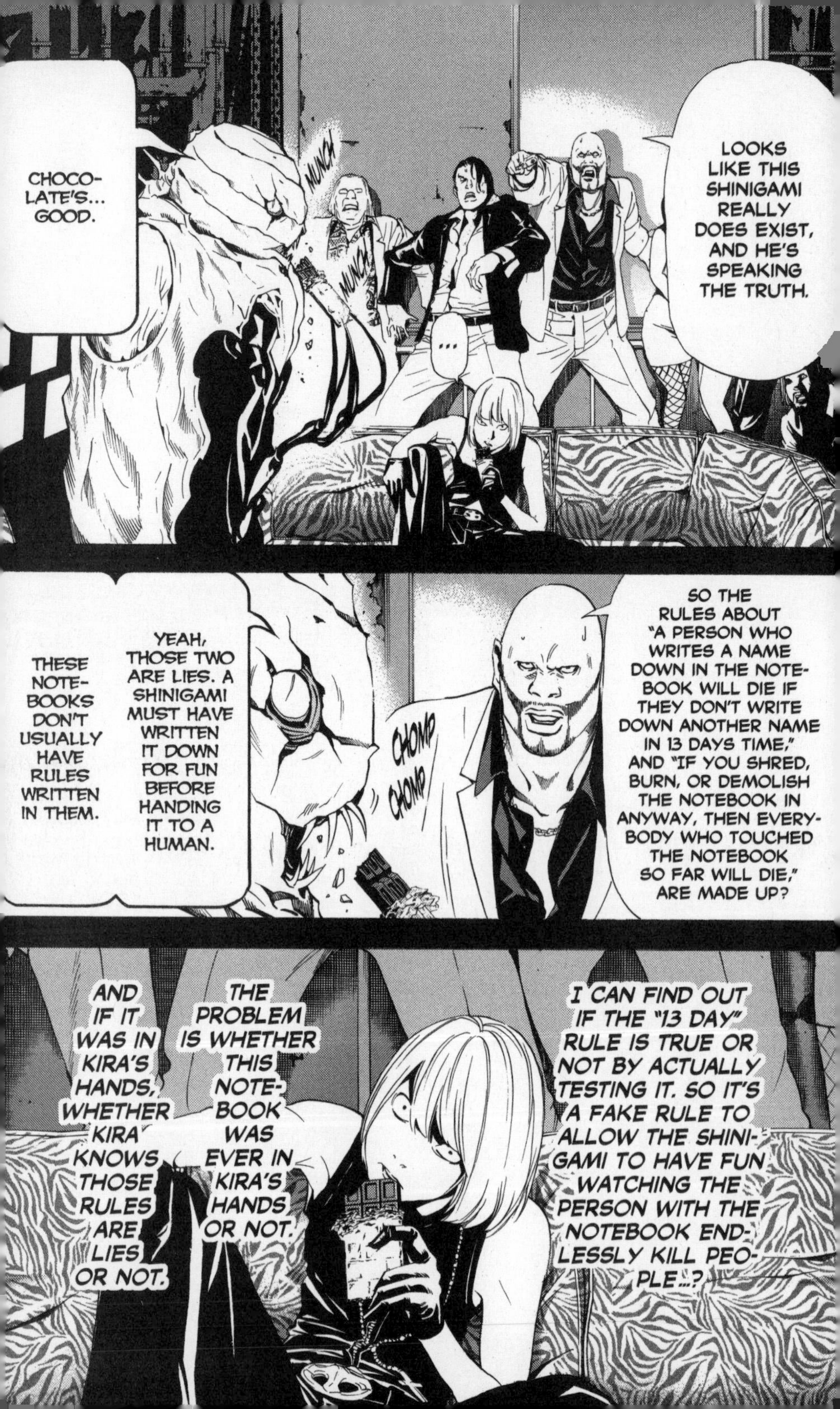
LOOKS LIKE THIS SHINIGAMI REALLY DOES EXIST, AND HE'S SPEAKING THE TRUTH.
MUNCH
MUNCH
...
CHOCO-LATE'S... GOOD.
SO THE RULES ABOUT "A PERSON WHO WRITES A NAME DOWN IN THE NOTE-BOOK WILL DIE IF THEY DON'T WRITE DOWN ANOTHER NAME IN 13 DAYS TIME," AND "IF YOU SHRED, BURN, OR DEMOLISH THE NOTEBOOK IN ANYWAY, THEN EVERY-BODY WHO TOUCHED THE NOTEBOOK SO FAR WILL DIE," ARE MADE UP?
CHOMP
CHOMP
YEAH, THOSE TWO ARE LIES. A SHINIGAMI MUST HAVE WRITTEN IT DOWN FOR FUN BEFORE HANDING IT TO A HUMAN.
THESE NOTE-BOOKS DON'T USUALLY HAVE RULES WRITTEN IN THEM.
I CAN FIND OUT IF THE "13 DAY" RULE IS TRUE OR NOT BY ACTUALLY TESTING IT. SO IT'S A FAKE RULE TO ALLOW THE SHINI-GAMI TO HAVE FUN WATCHING THE PERSON WITH THE NOTEBOOK END-LESSLY KILL PEO-PLE...?
THE PROBLEM IS WHETHER THIS NOTE-BOOK WAS EVER IN KIRA'S HANDS OR NOT.
AND IF IT WAS IN KIRA'S HANDS, WHETHER KIRA KNOWS THOSE RULES ARE LIES OR NOT.

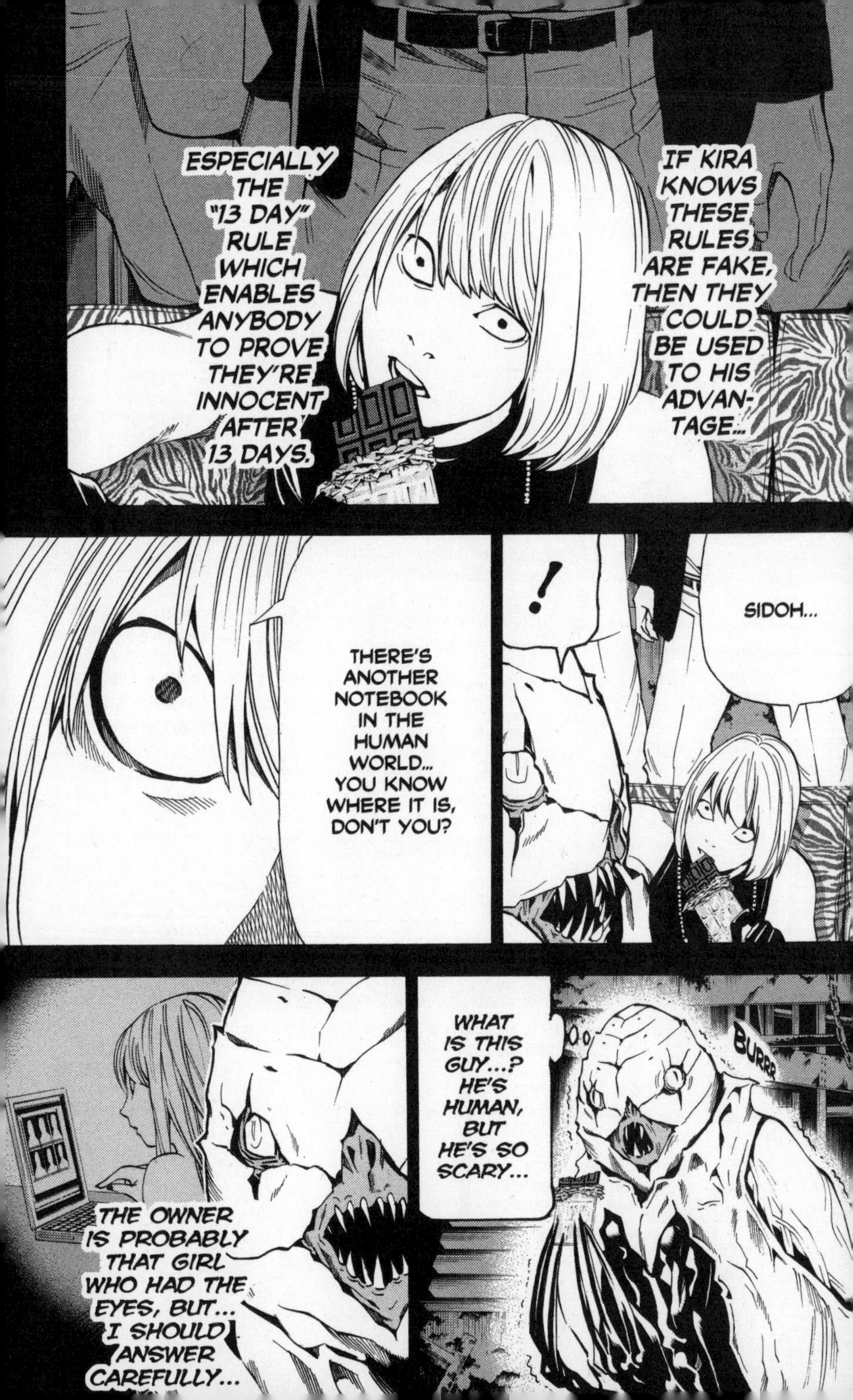
IF KIRA KNOWS THESE RULES ARE FAKE, THEN THEY COULD BE USED TO HIS ADVANTAGE...
ESPECIALLY THE "13 DAY" RULE WHICH ENABLES ANYBODY TO PROVE THEY'RE INNOCENT AFTER 13 DAYS.
!
SIDOH...
THERE'S ANOTHER NOTEBOOK IN THE HUMAN WORLD... YOU KNOW WHERE IT IS, DON'T YOU?
BURRR
WHAT IS THIS GUY...? HE'S HUMAN, BUT HE'S SO SCARY...
THE OWNER IS PROBABLY THAT GIRL WHO HAD THE EYES, BUT... I SHOULD ANSWER CAREFULLY...

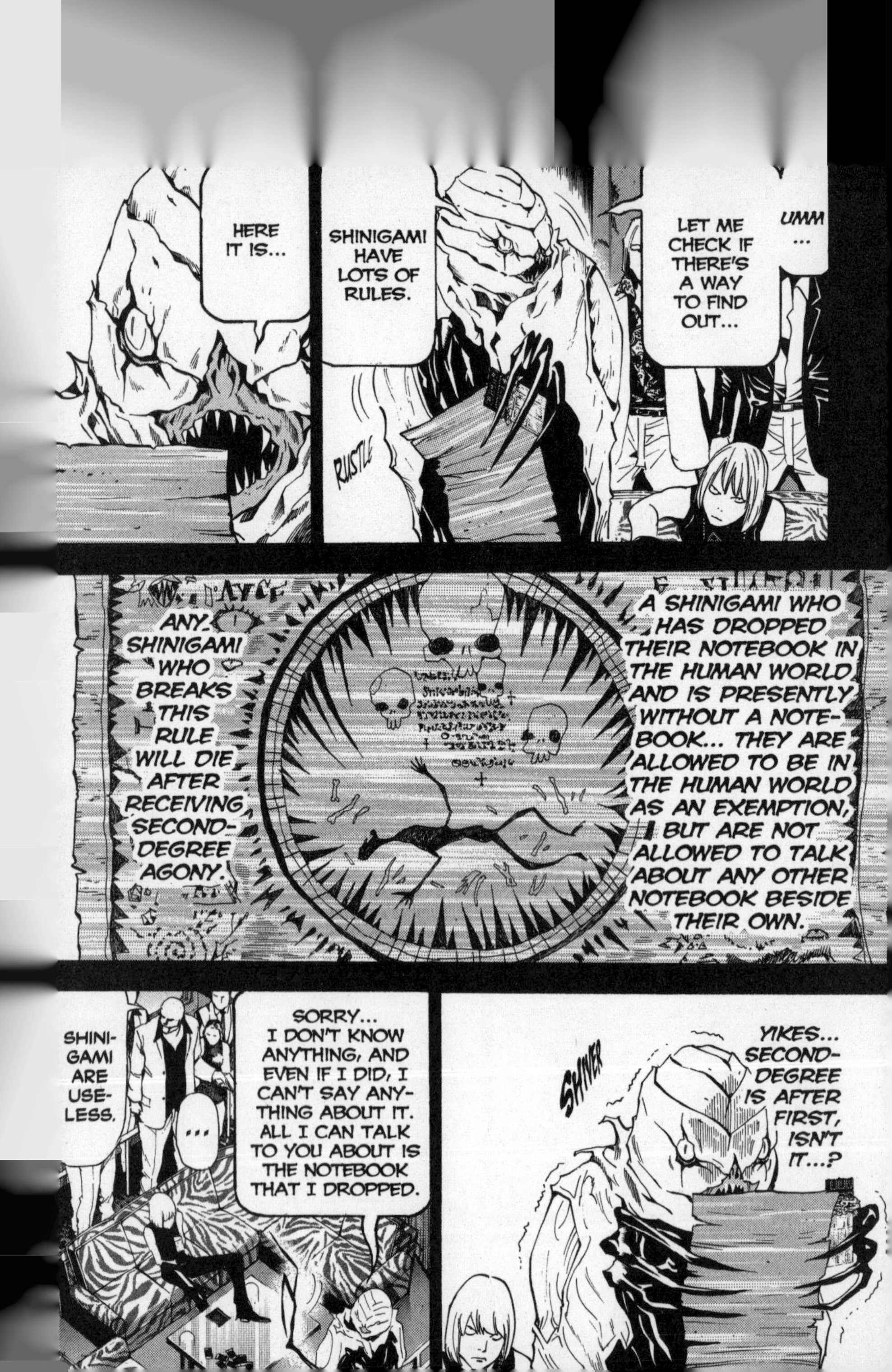
UMM ...
LET ME CHECK IF THERE'S A WAY TO FIND OUT...
SHINIGAMI HAVE LOTS OF RULES.
RUSTLE
HERE IT IS...
A SHINIGAMI WHO HAS DROPPED THEIR NOTEBOOK IN THE HUMAN WORLD AND IS PRESENTLY WITHOUT A NOTE-BOOK... THEY ARE ALLOWED TO BE IN THE HUMAN WORLD AS AN EXEMPTION, BUT ARE NOT ALLOWED TO TALK ABOUT ANY OTHER NOTEBOOK BESIDE THEIR OWN.
ANY SHINIGAMI WHO BREAKS THIS RULE WILL DIE AFTER RECEIVING SECOND-DEGREE AGONY.
SHIVER
YIKES... SECOND-DEGREE IS AFTER FIRST, ISN'T IT...?
SORRY... I DON'T KNOW ANYTHING, AND EVEN IF I DID, I CAN'T SAY ANY-THING ABOUT IT. ALL I CAN TALK TO YOU ABOUT IS THE NOTEBOOK THAT I DROPPED.
SHINI-GAMI ARE USE-LESS.
...

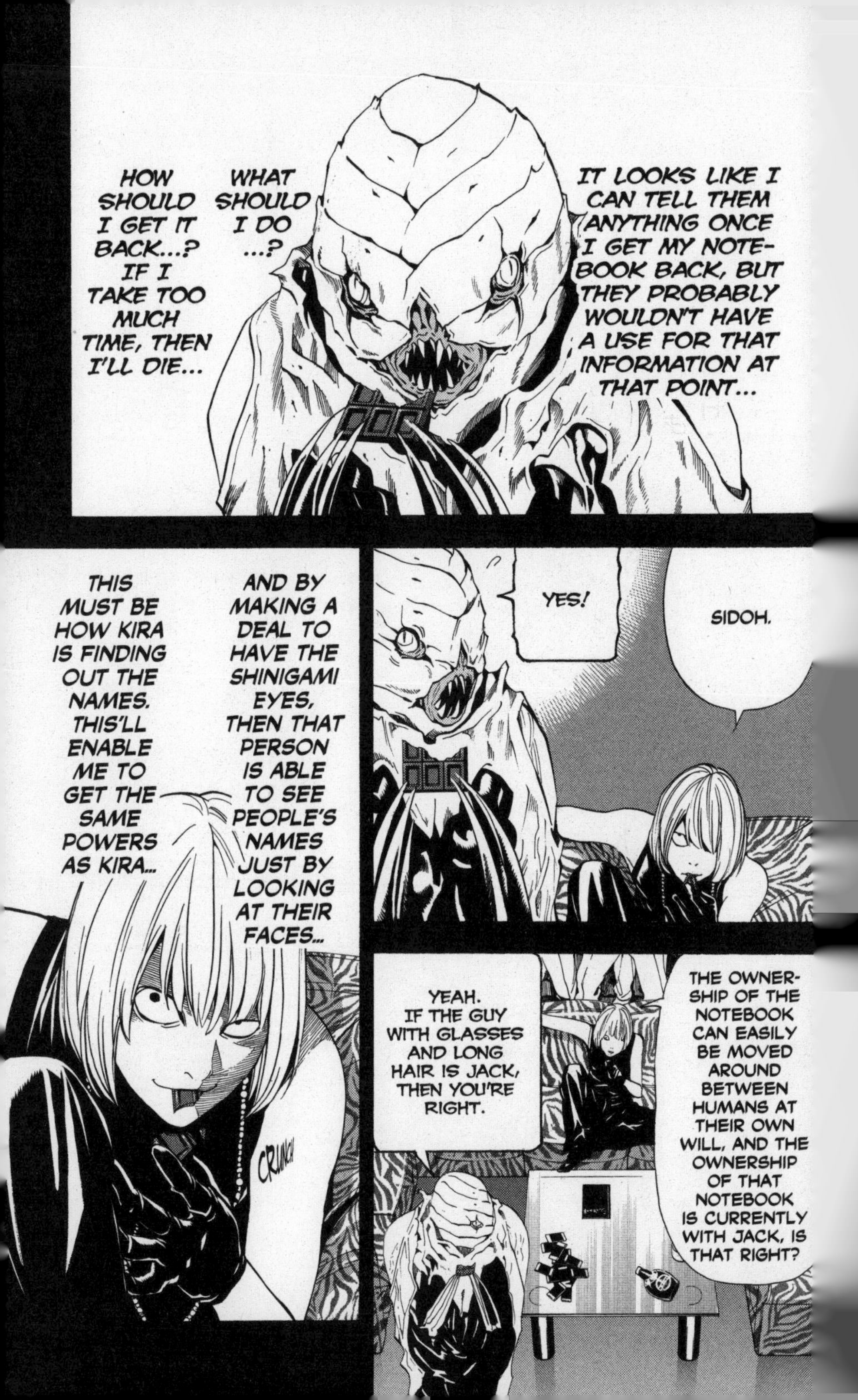
IT LOOKS LIKE I CAN TELL THEM ANYTHING ONCE I GET MY NOTE-BOOK BACK, BUT THEY PROBABLY WOULDN'T HAVE A USE FOR THAT INFORMATION AT THAT POINT...
WHAT SHOULD I DO ...?
HOW SHOULD I GET IT BACK...? IF I TAKE TOO MUCH TIME, THEN I'LL DIE...
SIDOH.
YES!
THE OWNERSHIP OF THE NOTEBOOK CAN EASILY BE MOVED AROUND BETWEEN HUMANS AT THEIR OWN WILL, AND THE OWNERSHIP OF THAT NOTEBOOK IS CURRENTLY WITH JACK, IS THAT RIGHT?
YEAH. IF THE GUY WITH GLASSES AND LONG HAIR IS JACK, THEN YOU'RE RIGHT.
AND BY MAKING A DEAL TO HAVE THE SHINIGAMI EYES, THEN THAT PERSON IS ABLE TO SEE PEOPLE'S NAMES JUST BY LOOKING AT THEIR FACES...
THIS MUST BE HOW KIRA IS FINDING OUT THE NAMES. THIS'LL ENABLE ME TO GET THE SAME POWERS AS KIRA...
CRUNCH

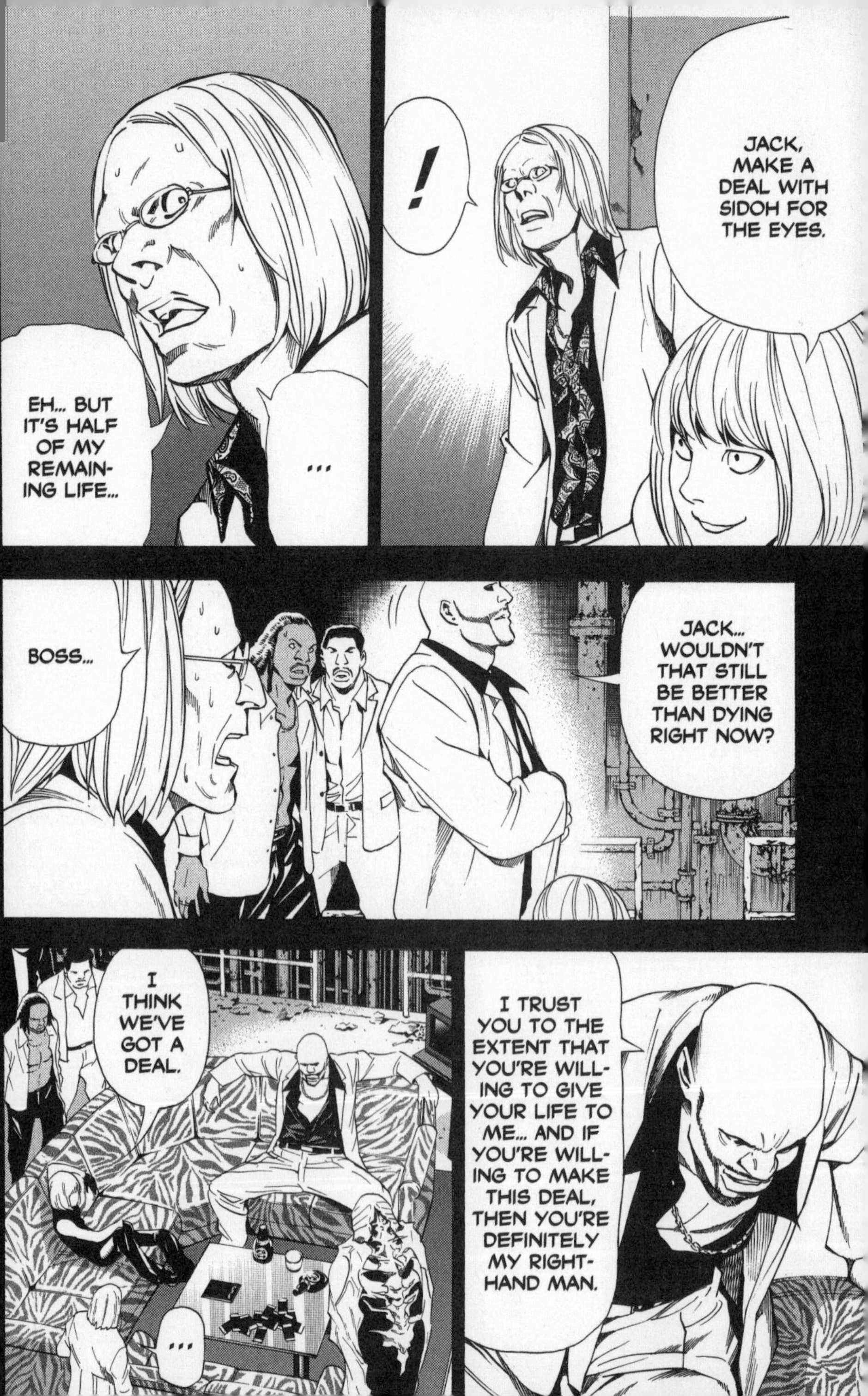
JACK, MAKE A DEAL WITH SIDOH FOR THE EYES.
!
EH... BUT IT'S HALF OF MY REMAINING LIFE...
...
JACK... WOULDN'T THAT STILL BE BETTER THAN DYING RIGHT NOW?
BOSS...
I TRUST YOU TO THE EXTENT THAT YOU'RE WILLING TO GIVE YOUR LIFE TO ME... AND IF YOU'RE WILLING TO MAKE THIS DEAL, THEN YOU'RE DEFINITELY MY RIGHT-HAND MAN.
I THINK WE'VE GOT A DEAL.
...

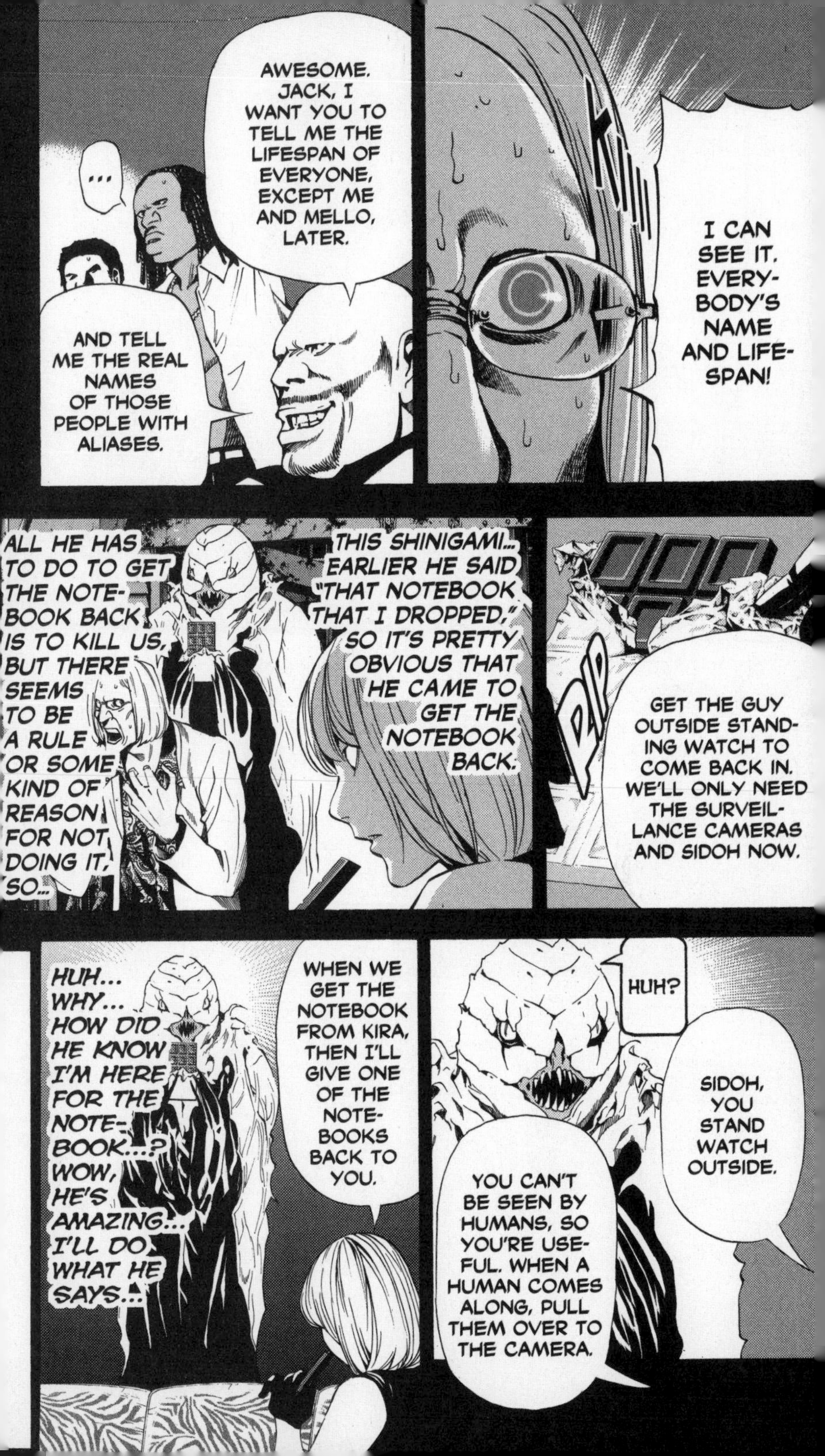

KII
I CAN SEE IT. EVERYBODY'S NAME AND LIFESPAN!
AWESOME. JACK, I WANT YOU TO TELL ME THE LIFESPAN OF EVERYONE, EXCEPT ME AND MELLO, LATER.
...
AND TELL ME THE REAL NAMES OF THOSE PEOPLE WITH ALIASES.
RIP
GET THE GUY OUTSIDE STANDING WATCH TO COME BACK IN. WE'LL ONLY NEED THE SURVEILLANCE CAMERAS AND SIDOH NOW.
THIS SHINIGAMI... EARLIER HE SAID "THAT NOTEBOOK THAT I DROPPED," SO IT'S PRETTY OBVIOUS THAT HE CAME TO GET THE NOTEBOOK BACK.
ALL HE HAS TO DO TO GET THE NOTEBOOK BACK IS TO KILL US, BUT THERE SEEMS TO BE A RULE OR SOME KIND OF REASON FOR NOT DOING IT, SO...
HUH?
SIDOH, YOU STAND WATCH OUTSIDE.
YOU CAN'T BE SEEN BY HUMANS, SO YOU'RE USEFUL. WHEN A HUMAN COMES ALONG, PULL THEM OVER TO THE CAMERA.
WHEN WE GET THE NOTEBOOK FROM KIRA, THEN I'LL GIVE ONE OF THE NOTEBOOKS BACK TO YOU.
HUH... WHY... HOW DID HE KNOW I'M HERE FOR THE NOTEBOOK...? WOW, HE'S AMAZING... I'LL DO WHAT HE SAYS...

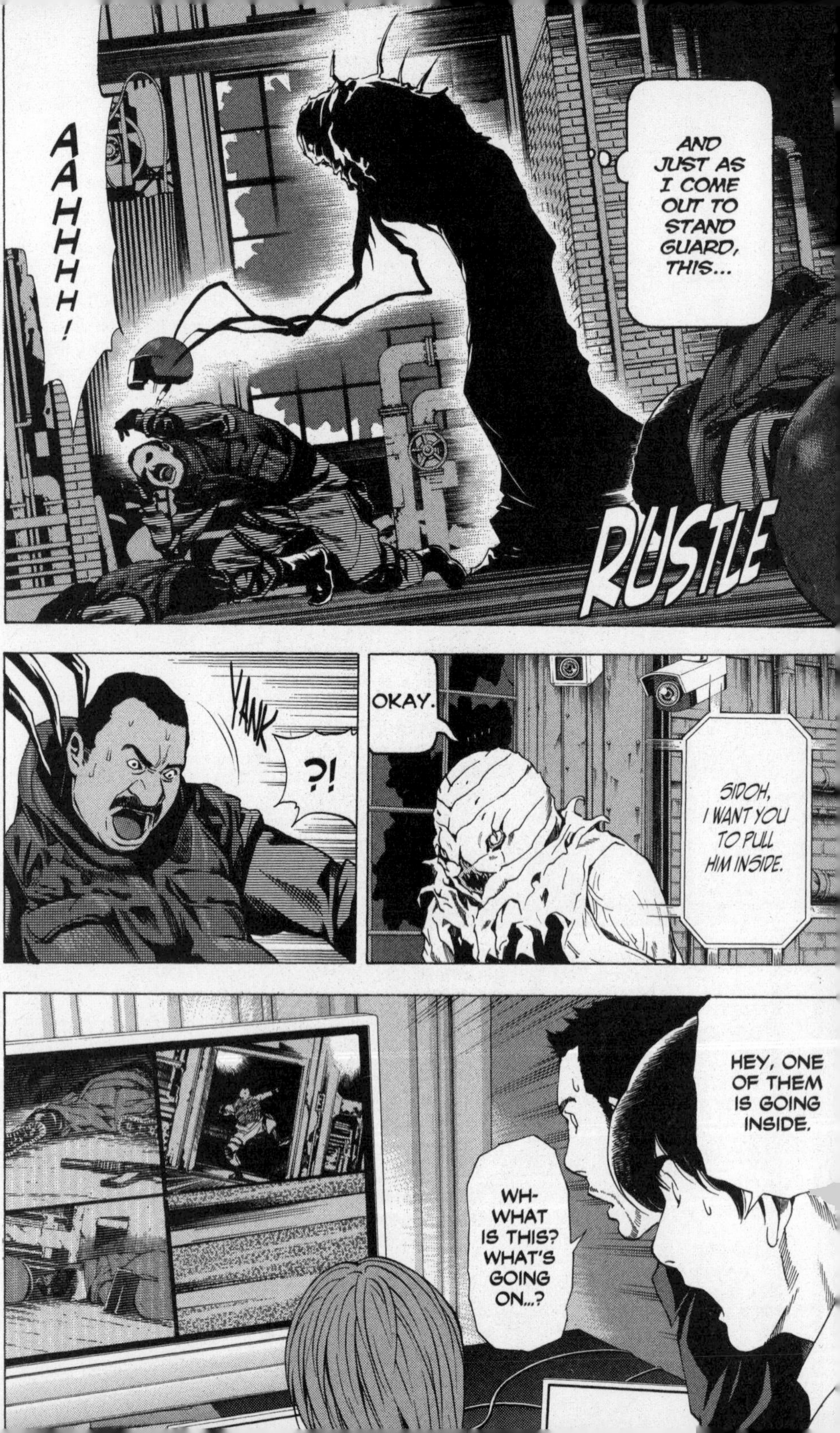
AND JUST AS I COME OUT TO STAND GUARD, THIS...
AAHHHHH!
RUSTLE
SIDOH, I WANT YOU TO PULL HIM INSIDE.
OKAY.
YANK
?!
HEY, ONE OF THEM IS GOING INSIDE.
WH- WHAT IS THIS? WHAT'S GOING ON...?

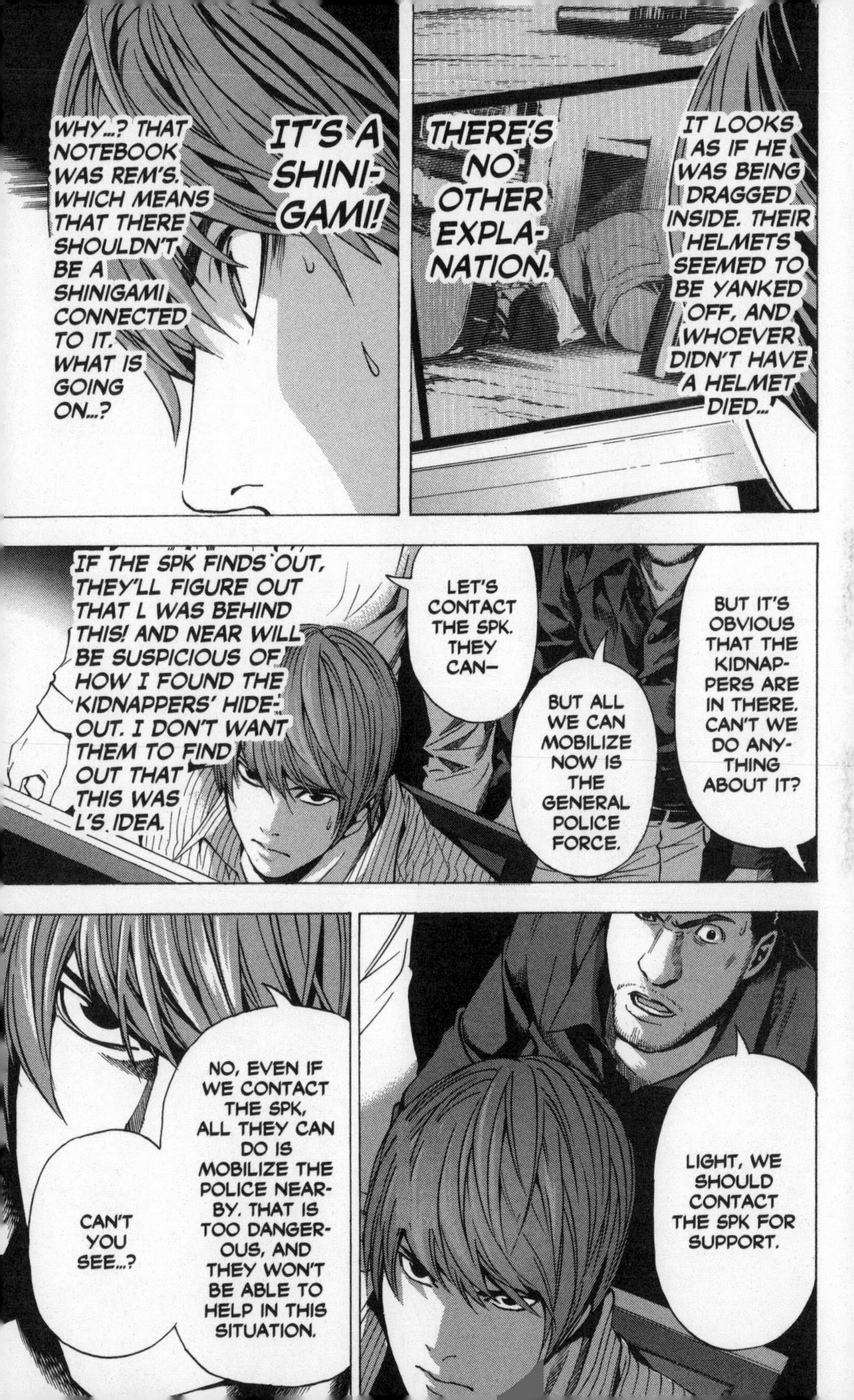
IT LOOKS AS IF HE WAS BEING DRAGGED INSIDE. THEIR HELMETS SEEMED TO BE YANKED OFF, AND WHOEVER DIDN'T HAVE A HELMET DIED...
THERE'S NO OTHER EXPLANATION.
IT'S A SHINIGAMI!
WHY...? THAT NOTEBOOK WAS REM'S. WHICH MEANS THAT THERE SHOULDN'T BE A SHINIGAMI CONNECTED TO IT. WHAT IS GOING ON...?
BUT IT'S OBVIOUS THAT THE KIDNAPPERS ARE IN THERE. CAN'T WE DO ANYTHING ABOUT IT?
BUT ALL WE CAN MOBILIZE NOW IS THE GENERAL POLICE FORCE.
LET'S CONTACT THE SPK. THEY CAN—
IF THE SPK FINDS OUT, THEY'LL FIGURE OUT THAT L WAS BEHIND THIS! AND NEAR WILL BE SUSPICIOUS OF HOW I FOUND THE KIDNAPPERS' HIDE-OUT. I DON'T WANT THEM TO FIND OUT THAT THIS WAS L'S IDEA.
LIGHT, WE SHOULD CONTACT THE SPK FOR SUPPORT.
NO, EVEN IF WE CONTACT THE SPK, ALL THEY CAN DO IS MOBILIZE THE POLICE NEARBY. THAT IS TOO DANGEROUS, AND THEY WON'T BE ABLE TO HELP IN THIS SITUATION.
CAN'T YOU SEE...?

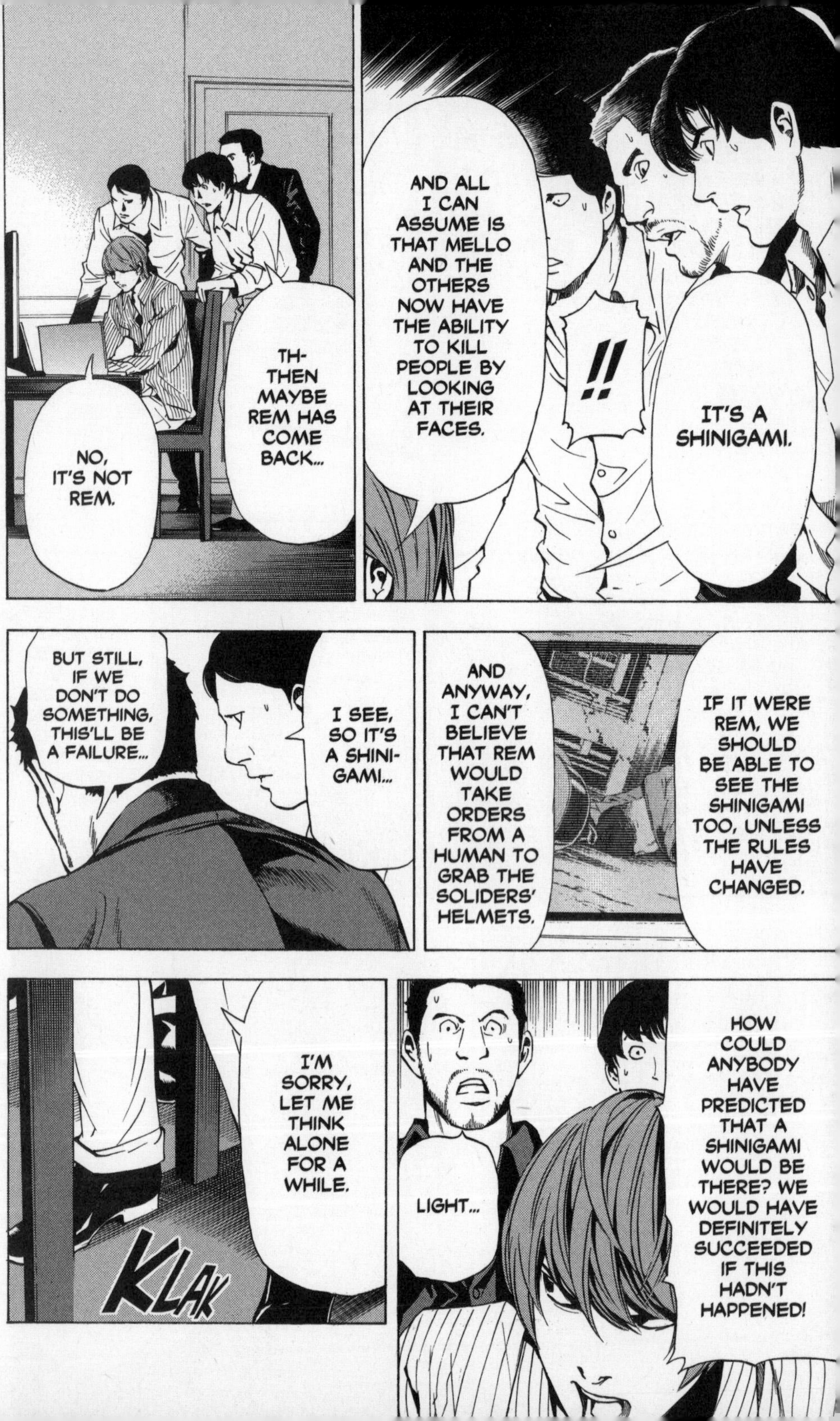
IT'S A SHINIGAMI.
!!
AND ALL I CAN ASSUME IS THAT MELLO AND THE OTHERS NOW HAVE THE ABILITY TO KILL PEOPLE BY LOOKING AT THEIR FACES.
TH-THEN MAYBE REM HAS COME BACK...
NO, IT'S NOT REM.
IF IT WERE REM, WE SHOULD BE ABLE TO SEE THE SHINIGAMI TOO, UNLESS THE RULES HAVE CHANGED.
AND ANYWAY, I CAN'T BELIEVE THAT REM WOULD TAKE ORDERS FROM A HUMAN TO GRAB THE SOLIDERS' HELMETS.
I SEE, SO IT'S A SHINI-GAMI...
BUT STILL, IF WE DON'T DO SOMETHING, THIS'LL BE A FAILURE...
HOW COULD ANYBODY HAVE PREDICTED THAT A SHINIGAMI WOULD BE THERE? WE WOULD HAVE DEFINITELY SUCCEEDED IF THIS HADN'T HAPPENED!
LIGHT...
I'M SORRY, LET ME THINK ALONE FOR A WHILE.
KLAK

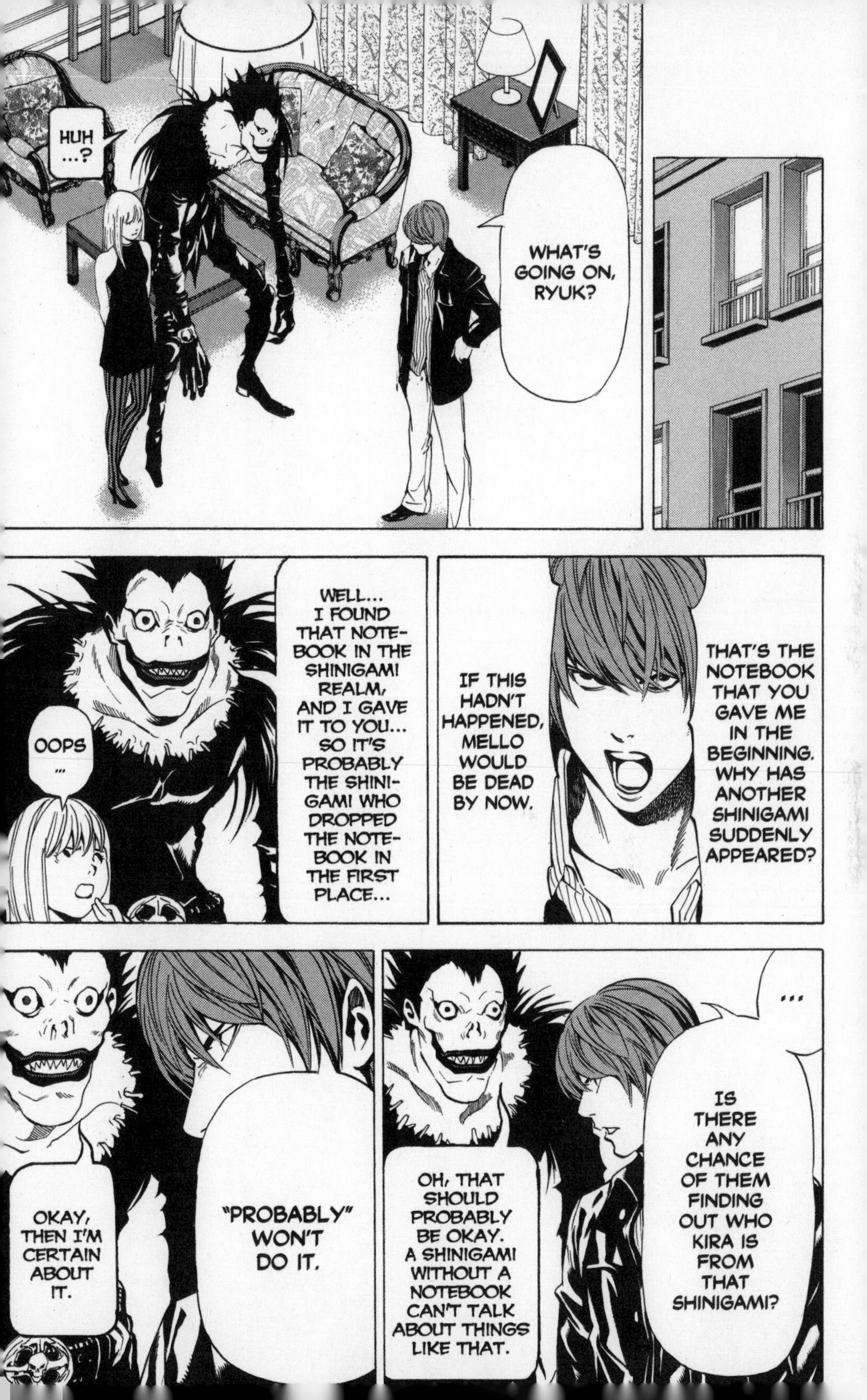
HUH ...?
WHAT'S GOING ON, RYUK?
THAT'S THE NOTEBOOK THAT YOU GAVE ME IN THE BEGINNING. WHY HAS ANOTHER SHINIGAMI SUDDENLY APPEARED?
IF THIS HADN'T HAPPENED, MELLO WOULD BE DEAD BY NOW.
WELL... I FOUND THAT NOTE-BOOK IN THE SHINIGAMI REALM, AND I GAVE IT TO YOU... SO IT'S PROBABLY THE SHINI-GAMI WHO DROPPED THE NOTE-BOOK IN THE FIRST PLACE...
OOPS ...
...
IS THERE ANY CHANCE OF THEM FINDING OUT WHO KIRA IS FROM THAT SHINIGAMI?
OH, THAT SHOULD PROBABLY BE OKAY. A SHINIGAMI WITHOUT A NOTEBOOK CAN'T TALK ABOUT THINGS LIKE THAT.
"PROBABLY" WON'T DO IT.
OKAY, THEN I'M CERTAIN ABOUT IT.

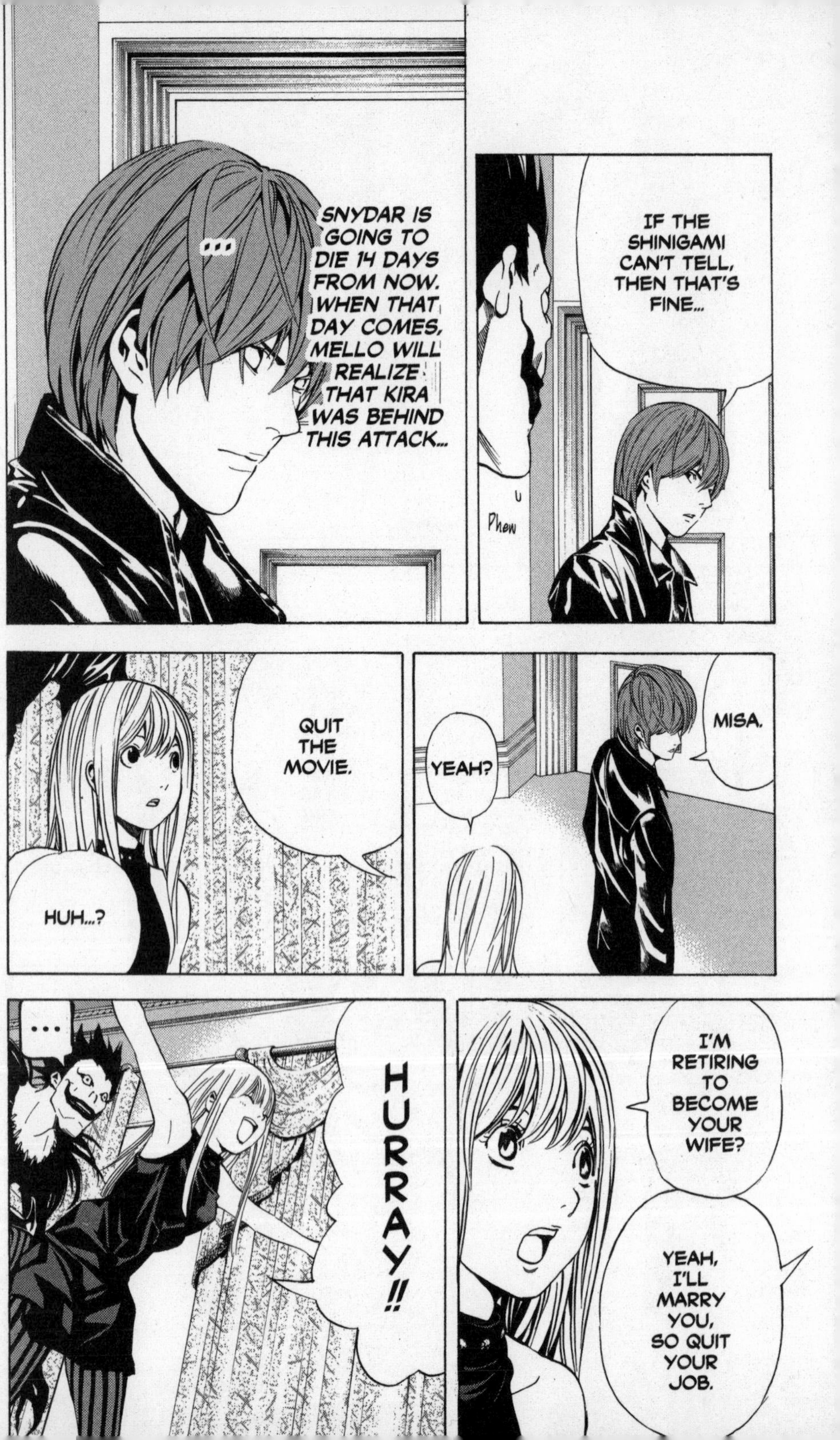
IF THE SHINIGAMI CAN'T TELL, THEN THAT'S FINE...
Phew
...
SNYDAR IS GOING TO DIE 14 DAYS FROM NOW. WHEN THAT DAY COMES, MELLO WILL REALIZE THAT KIRA WAS BEHIND THIS ATTACK...
MISA.
YEAH?
QUIT THE MOVIE.
HUH...?
I'M RETIRING TO BECOME YOUR WIFE?
YEAH, I'LL MARRY YOU, SO QUIT YOUR JOB.
HURRAY!!
...

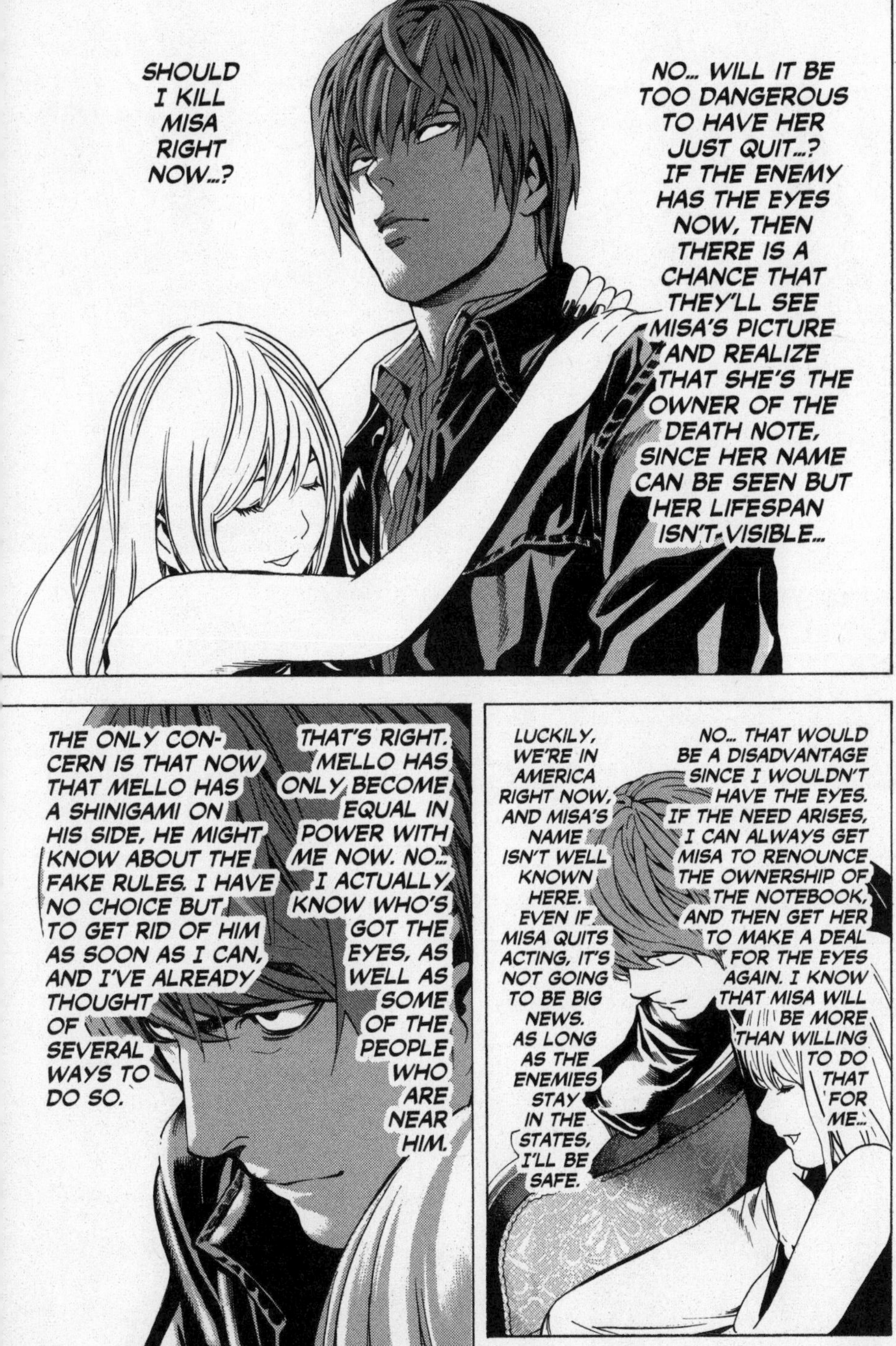
NO... WILL IT BE TOO DANGEROUS TO HAVE HER JUST QUIT...? IF THE ENEMY HAS THE EYES NOW, THEN THERE IS A CHANCE THAT THEY'LL SEE MISA'S PICTURE AND REALIZE THAT SHE'S THE OWNER OF THE DEATH NOTE, SINCE HER NAME CAN BE SEEN BUT HER LIFESPAN ISN'T VISIBLE...
SHOULD I KILL MISA RIGHT NOW...?
NO... THAT WOULD BE A DISADVANTAGE SINCE I WOULDN'T HAVE THE EYES. IF THE NEED ARISES, I CAN ALWAYS GET MISA TO RENOUNCE THE OWNERSHIP OF THE NOTEBOOK, AND THEN GET HER TO MAKE A DEAL FOR THE EYES AGAIN. I KNOW THAT MISA WILL BE MORE THAN WILLING TO DO THAT FOR ME...
LUCKILY, WE'RE IN AMERICA RIGHT NOW, AND MISA'S NAME ISN'T WELL KNOWN HERE. EVEN IF MISA QUITS ACTING, IT'S NOT GOING TO BE BIG NEWS. AS LONG AS THE ENEMIES STAY IN THE STATES, I'LL BE SAFE.
THAT'S RIGHT. MELLO HAS ONLY BECOME EQUAL IN POWER WITH ME NOW. NO... I ACTUALLY KNOW WHO'S GOT THE EYES, AS WELL AS SOME OF THE PEOPLE WHO ARE NEAR HIM.
THE ONLY CONCERN IS THAT NOW THAT MELLO HAS A SHINIGAMI ON HIS SIDE, HE MIGHT KNOW ABOUT THE FAKE RULES. I HAVE NO CHOICE BUT TO GET RID OF HIM AS SOON AS I CAN, AND I'VE ALREADY THOUGHT OF SEVERAL WAYS TO DO SO.

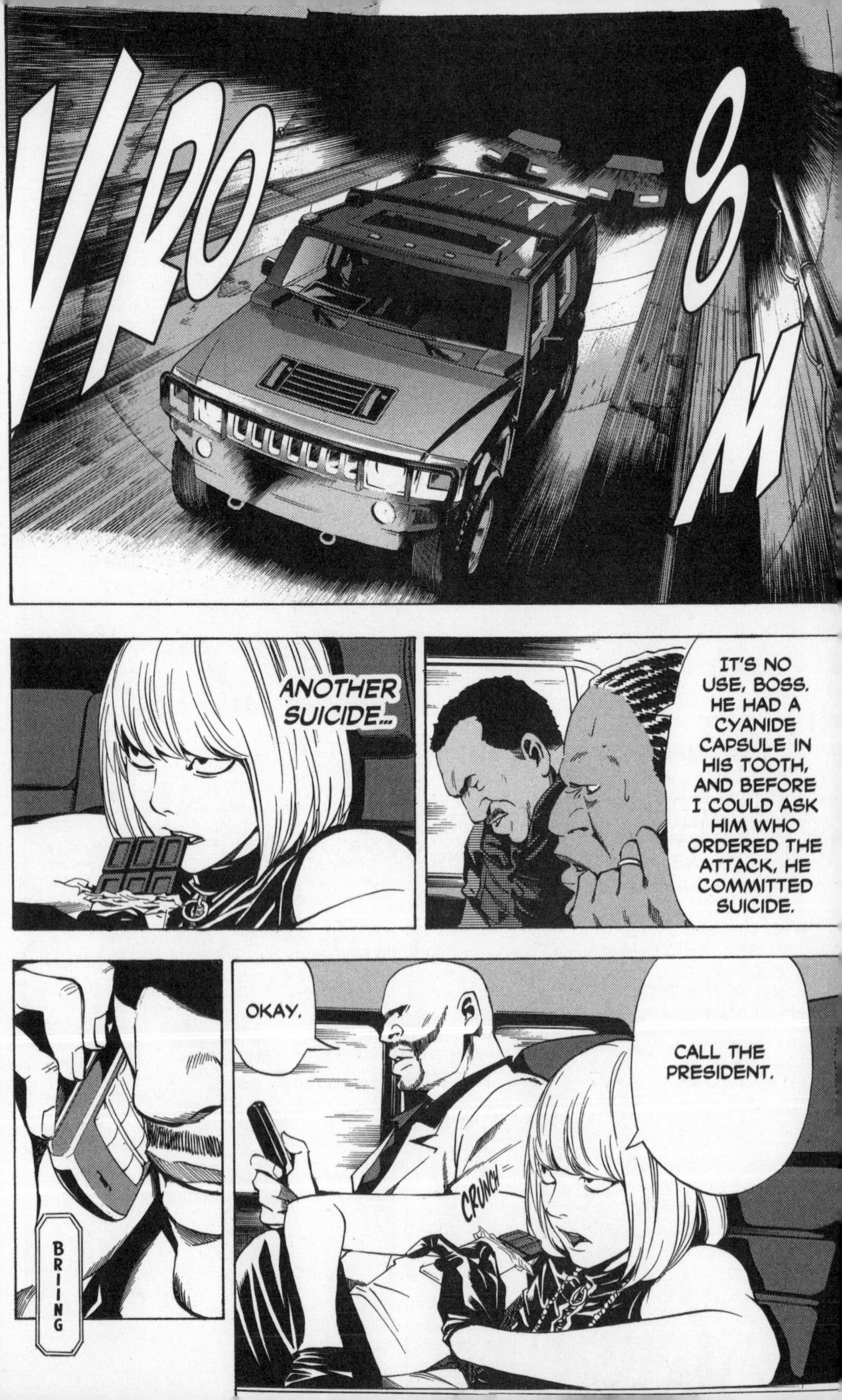
VROOOM
IT'S NO USE, BOSS. HE HAD A CYANIDE CAPSULE IN HIS TOOTH, AND BEFORE I COULD ASK HIM WHO ORDERED THE ATTACK, HE COMMITTED SUICIDE.
ANOTHER SUICIDE...
CALL THE PRESIDENT.
OKAY.
CRUNCH
BRIING

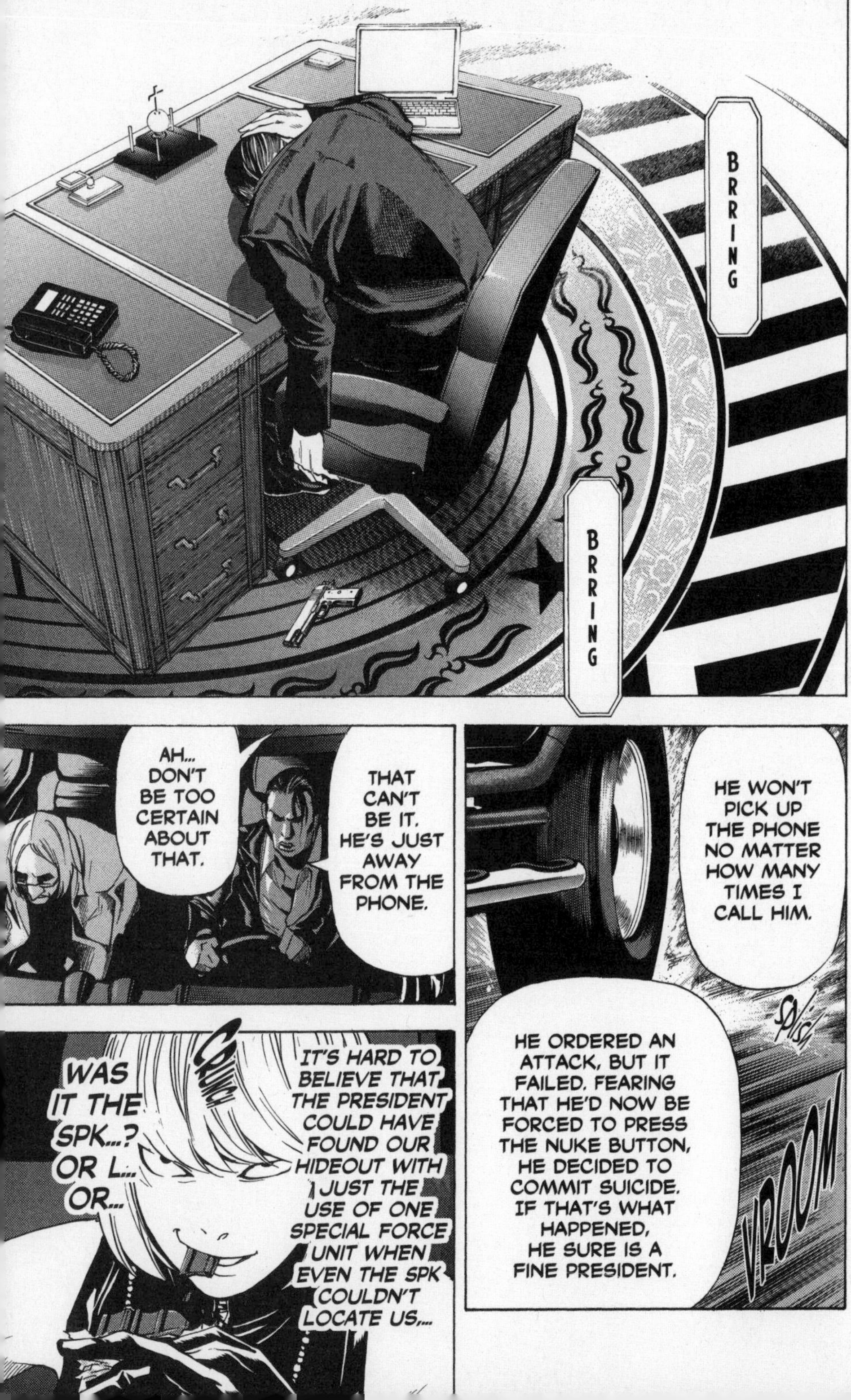
BRRRING
BRRRING
HE WON'T PICK UP THE PHONE NO MATTER HOW MANY TIMES I CALL HIM.
SPLISH
HE ORDERED AN ATTACK, BUT IT FAILED. FEARING THAT HE'D NOW BE FORCED TO PRESS THE NUKE BUTTON, HE DECIDED TO COMMIT SUICIDE. IF THAT'S WHAT HAPPENED, HE SURE IS A FINE PRESIDENT.
VROOM
THAT CAN'T BE IT. HE'S JUST AWAY FROM THE PHONE.
AH... DON'T BE TOO CERTAIN ABOUT THAT.
CRUNCH
IT'S HARD TO BELIEVE THAT THE PRESIDENT COULD HAVE FOUND OUR HIDEOUT WITH JUST THE USE OF ONE SPECIAL FORCE UNIT WHEN EVEN THE SPK COULDN'T LOCATE US,...
WAS IT THE SPK...? OR L... OR...

# DEATH NOTE
## How to use it
## XLVI

• There are laws in the world of gods of death. If a god of death should break the law, there are 9 levels of severity starting at Level 8 and going up to Level 1 plus the Extreme Level. For severity levels above 3 the god of death will be killed after being punished.

死神には死神界で定められた掟があり、それを破ると、
特級・一級から八級まで九段階の罪があり、
三級以上はその罪を課せられた後、死ぬ。

• For example, killing a human without using the DEATH NOTE is considered as the Extreme Level.

たとえば、死神がデスノート以外で人間を殺す事は特級である。

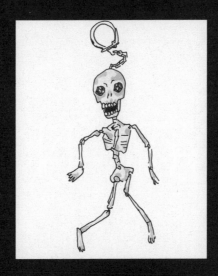

A while ago, we could often find this type of key
chain in souvenir stores at tourist spots. But why is
it that they always have jeweled eyes...?

-Takeshi Obata

# DEATH NOTE

## Cover Gallery

Original Japanese Covers Volumes 5-8

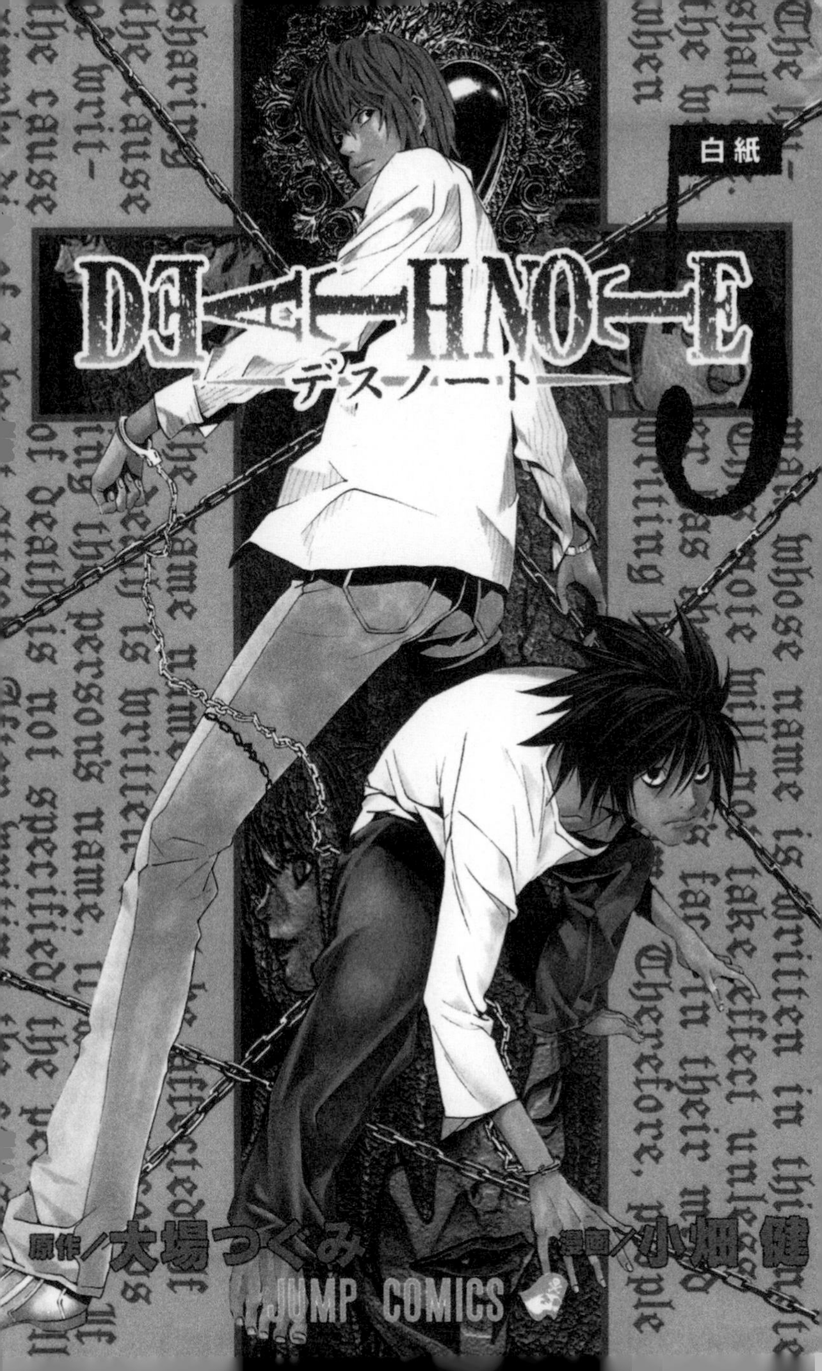

白紙
DEATH NOTE
デスノート
5
原作/大場つぐみ
漫画/小畑健
JUMP COMICS

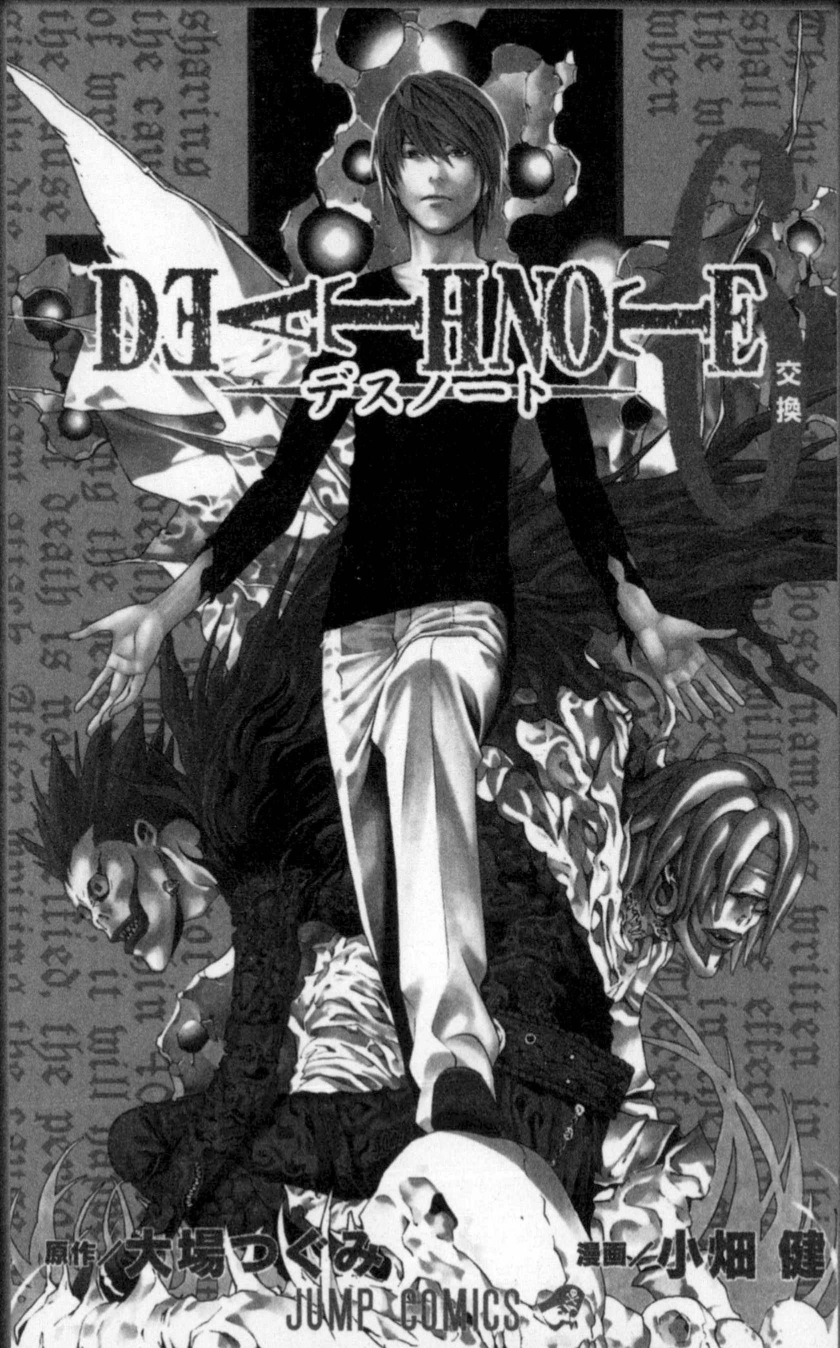
DEATH NOTE
デスノート
交換
原作／大場つぐみ
漫画／小畑 健
JUMP COMICS

Original Japanese Cover Volume 6

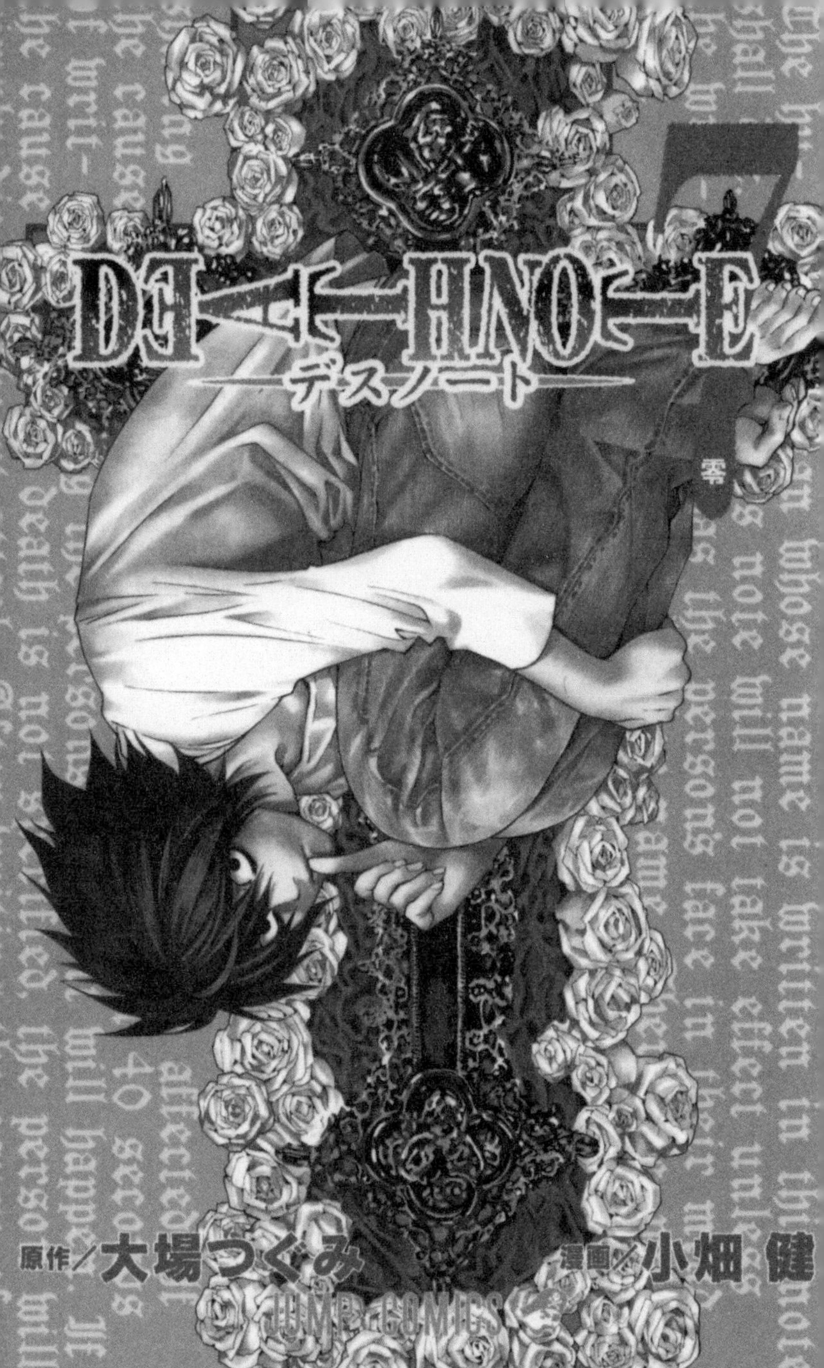
DEATH NOTE
デスノート
7
零
原作/大場つぐみ
漫画/小畑 健
JUMP COMICS

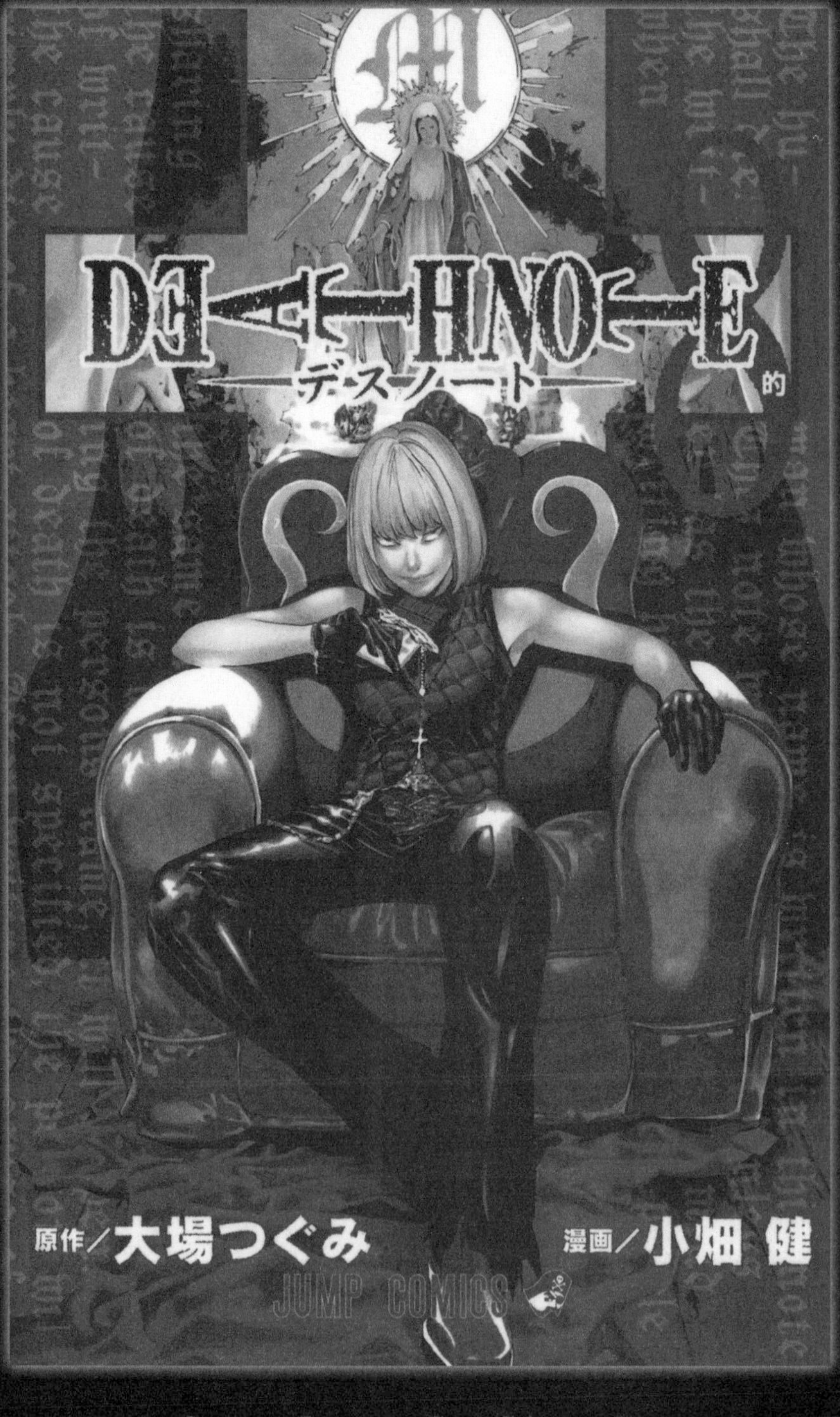
DEATH NOTE
デスノート
原作／大場つぐみ
漫画／小畑 健
JUMP COMICS

Original Japanese Cover Volume 8

# DEATH NOTE

## Black Edition
## IV

SHONEN JUMP ADVANCED Manga Omnibus Edition
A compilation of the graphic novel volumes 7 and 8

Story by Tsugumi Ohba
Art by Takeshi Obata

Translation & Adaptation Volume 7/Alexis Kirsch
Translation & Adaptation Volume 8/Tetsuichiro Miyaki
Touch-up Art & Lettering/Gia Cam Luc
Design/Sam Elzway
Editor – Manga Edition/Pancha Diaz
Editor – Omnibus Edition/Elizabeth Kawasaki

Printed in the U.S.A.

Published by VIZ Media, LLC
P.O. Box 77010
San Francisco, CA 94107

10 9 8 7 6 5 4 3
First printing, July 2011
Third printing, October 2013

PARENTAL ADVISORY
DEATH NOTE is rated T+ for Older Teen and is recommended
for ages 16 and up. It contains scenes of violence.
ratings.viz.com

www.viz.com

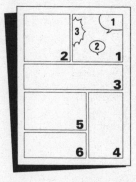

In keeping with the original Japanese format, *Death Note* is meant to be read from right to left, starting in the upper right corner. Turn to the other side of the book and begin reading.

Born in Tokyo, Tsugumi Ohba is the author of the hit series *Death Note*. His current series *Bakuman.* is serialized in *Weekly Shonen Jump*.

Takeshi Obata was born in 1969 in Niigata, Japan, and is the artist of the wildly popular SHONEN JUMP title *Hikaru no Go*, which won the 2003 Tezuka Shinsei "New Hope" award and the Shogakukan Manga award. Obata is also the artist of *Arabian Majin Bokentan Lamp Lamp*, *Ayatsuri Sakon*, and *Cyborg Jichan G*, and the smash hit manga *Death Note*. His current series *Bakuman.* is serialized in *Weekly Shonen Jump*.